# Contemporary High Performance Computing

## From Petascale toward Exascale

# Chapman & Hall/CRC
# Computational Science Series

## SERIES EDITOR

### Horst Simon
Deputy Director
Lawrence Berkeley National Laboratory
Berkeley, California, U.S.A.

## AIMS AND SCOPE

This series aims to capture new developments and applications in the field of computational science through the publication of a broad range of textbooks, reference works, and handbooks. Books in this series will provide introductory as well as advanced material on mathematical, statistical, and computational methods and techniques, and will present researchers with the latest theories and experimentation. The scope of the series includes, but is not limited to, titles in the areas of scientific computing, parallel and distributed computing, high performance computing, grid computing, cluster computing, heterogeneous computing, quantum computing, and their applications in scientific disciplines such as astrophysics, aeronautics, biology, chemistry, climate modeling, combustion, cosmology, earthquake prediction, imaging, materials, neuroscience, oil exploration, and weather forecasting.

## PUBLISHED TITLES

PETASCALE COMPUTING: ALGORITHMS AND APPLICATIONS
Edited by David A. Bader

PROCESS ALGEBRA FOR PARALLEL AND DISTRIBUTED PROCESSING
Edited by Michael Alexander and William Gardner

GRID COMPUTING: TECHNIQUES AND APPLICATIONS
Barry Wilkinson

INTRODUCTION TO CONCURRENCY IN PROGRAMMING LANGUAGES
Matthew J. Sottile, Timothy G. Mattson, and Craig E Rasmussen

INTRODUCTION TO SCHEDULING
Yves Robert and Frédéric Vivien

SCIENTIFIC DATA MANAGEMENT: CHALLENGES, TECHNOLOGY, AND DEPLOYMENT
Edited by Arie Shoshani and Doron Rotem

INTRODUCTION TO THE SIMULATION OF DYNAMICS USING SIMULINK®
Michael A. Gray

INTRODUCTION TO HIGH PERFORMANCE COMPUTING FOR SCIENTISTS AND ENGINEERS
Georg Hager and Gerhard Wellein

PERFORMANCE TUNING OF SCIENTIFIC APPLICATIONS
Edited by David Bailey, Robert Lucas, and Samuel Williams

HIGH PERFORMANCE COMPUTING: PROGRAMMING AND APPLICATIONS
John Levesque with Gene Wagenbreth

PEER-TO-PEER COMPUTING: APPLICATIONS, ARCHITECTURE, PROTOCOLS, AND CHALLENGES
Yu-Kwong Ricky Kwok

FUNDAMENTALS OF MULTICORE SOFTWARE DEVELOPMENT
Edited by Victor Pankratius, Ali-Reza Adl-Tabatabai, and Walter Tichy

INTRODUCTION TO ELEMENTARY COMPUTATIONAL MODELING: ESSENTIAL CONCEPTS, PRINCIPLES, AND PROBLEM SOLVING
José M. Garrido

COMBINATORIAL SCIENTIFIC COMPUTING
Edited by Uwe Naumann and Olaf Schenk

HIGH PERFORMANCE VISUALIZATION: ENABLING EXTREME-SCALE SCIENTIFIC INSIGHT
Edited by E. Wes Bethel, Hank Childs, and Charles Hansen

CONTEMPORARY HIGH PERFORMANCE COMPUTING: FROM PETASCALE TOWARD EXASCALE
Edited by Jeffrey S. Vetter

# Contemporary High Performance Computing

## From Petascale toward Exascale

Edited by
Jeffrey S. Vetter

CRC Press
Taylor & Francis Group
Boca Raton London New York

CRC Press is an imprint of the
Taylor & Francis Group, an **informa** business

A CHAPMAN & HALL BOOK

CRC Press
Taylor & Francis Group
6000 Broken Sound Parkway NW, Suite 300
Boca Raton, FL 33487-2742

© 2013 by Taylor & Francis Group, LLC
CRC Press is an imprint of Taylor & Francis Group, an Informa business

No claim to original U.S. Government works

Printed on acid-free paper
Version Date: 20121214

International Standard Book Number: 978-1-4665-6834-1 (Hardback)

**Library of Congress Cataloging-in-Publication Data**

Contemporary high performance computing : from petascale toward exascale / editor, Jeffrey S. Vetter.
   pages cm. -- (Chapman & Hall/CRC computational science series)
   Includes bibliographical references and index.
   ISBN 978-1-4665-6834-1 (hardback)
   1. High performance computing. I. Vetter, Jeffrey S.

   QA76.88.C68 2013
   004'.35--dc23
   2012039608

**Visit the Taylor & Francis Web site at**
**http://www.taylorandfrancis.com**

**and the CRC Press Web site at**
**http://www.crcpress.com**

# Dedication

To my parents, Sam and Judy
To my wife, Jana
To my son, Alex

# Contents

# List of Figures

# List of Tables

# Preface

We are pleased to present you with this collection of material that captures a snapshot of the rich history of practice in Contemporary High Performance Computing. As evidenced in the chapters of this book, High Performance Computing continues to flourish, both in industry and research, both domestically and internationally. While much of the focus of HPC is on the hardware architectures, a significant ecosystem is responsible for this success.

## Why I Edited This Book

My goal with this book has been to highlight significant systems and facilities in high performance computing. Early on, my main focus was proposed to be on the architectural design of important and successful HPC systems. However, I realized that HPC is about more than just hardware: it is an ecosystem that includes software, applications, facilities, educators, software developers, scientists, administrators, sponsors, and many other factors. This book is a snapshot of these contemporary HPC ecosystems, which are typically punctuated with a site's flagship system. Broadly speaking, HPC is growing internationally, so I invited contributions from a broad base of organizations including the USA, China, Japan, Russia, Germany, and Switzerland.

My excitement about this book grew as I started inviting authors to contribute: everyone said "yes!" In fact, due to the limitations on hardback publishing, we had to limit the number of chapters that we could include in this edition.

As I explain in the introduction, the rate of change in HPC is accelerating. After 15 years of relative stability, scientists and facilities are looking to new architectures and programming models in order to achieve specific objectives in HPC while satisfying other constraints, like facility power and cooling.

## Topic Selection and Organization

This book is organized into two parts. In Part I, the contributors provide perspective on contemporary HPC by examining significant trends in applications, performance, software, and hardware. Next, in Part II, the contributors provide snapshots of contemporary HPC ecosystems by site. While chapters in Part I do not follow a strict structure, I requested authors for chapters in Part II to include the following content:

1. Program background and motivation

2. Applications and workloads

3. Flagship system overview

4. Hardware architecture

5. System software

6. Programming system

7. Storage, visualization, and analytics

8. Data center/facility

9. System statistics

Some of the authors followed this outline precisely while others found creative ways to include this content in a different structure. Once you read the book, I think that you will agree with me that most of the chapters have exceeded these expectations, and have provided a detailed snapshot of their HPC ecosystem, science, and organization.

---

## Helping Improve This Book

HPC and computing, in general, is a rapidly changing, large, diverse field. If you have comments, corrections, or questions, please send a note to me at vetter@computer.org.

# *Editor*

**Jeffrey S. Vetter**, Ph.D., holds a joint appointment between Oak Ridge National Laboratory (ORNL) and the Georgia Institute of Technology (GT). At ORNL, Vetter is a Distinguished R& D Staff Member, and the founding group leader of the Future Technologies Group in the Computer Science and Mathematics Division. At GT, Vetter is a joint professor in the Computational Science and Engineering School of the College of Computing, the principal investigator for the NSF Track 2D Experimental Computing Facility, named Keeneland, for large-scale heterogeneous computing using graphics processors, and the director of the NVIDIA CUDA Center of Excellence. Vetter earned his Ph.D. in computer science from the Georgia Institute of Technology. He joined ORNL in 2003, after stints as a computer scientist and project leader at Lawrence Livermore National Laboratory, and postdoctoral researcher at the University of Illinois at Urbana-Champaign. The coherent thread through his research is developing rich architectures and software systems that solve important, real-world high performance computing problems. Currently, Vetter's research addresses problems in analyzing new architectures for HPC using measurement, modeling, and simulation. In particular, he has been investigating the effectiveness of next-generation architectures, such as graphics processors, massively multithreaded processors, non-volatile memory systems, heterogeneous multicore processors, and field-programmable gate arrays (FPGAs), for important applications. Professionally, Vetter has published over 110 peer-reviewed papers, served on over 50 program committees, as the SC12 Technical Papers Co-chair, and as an associate editor of *IEEE Transactions on Computers*. His papers have won awards at the International Parallel and Distributed Processing Symposium and EuroPar, and as part of a team from Georgia Tech, NYU, and ORNL, he was awarded the Gordon Bell Prize in 2010. Vetter is a Senior Member of the IEEE and a Distinguished Scientist Member of the ACM.

# Part I

# Trends in HPC

# Chapter 1

# Contemporary High Performance Computing

**Jeffrey S. Vetter**

*Oak Ridge National Laboratory and Georgia Institute of Technology*

## 1.1 High Performance Computing

High Performance Computing (HPC) is used to solve a number of complex questions in computational and data-intensive sciences. These questions include the simulation and modeling of physical phenomena, such as climate change, energy production, drug design, global security, and materials design; the analysis of large data sets, such as those in genome sequencing, astronomical observation, and cybersecurity; and the intricate design of engineered products, such as airplanes.

It is clear and well-documented that HPC can be used to generate insight that would not otherwise be possible. Simulations can augment or replace expensive, hazardous, or impossible experiments. Furthermore, in the realm of simulation, HPC has the potential to suggest new experiments that escape the parameters of the observable.

Although much of the excitement about HPC focuses on the largest architectures and on specific benchmarks, such as TOP500, there is a much deeper and broader commitment from the international scientific and engineering community than is first apparent. In fact, it is easy to lose track of history in terms of the broad uses of HPC and the communities that design, deploy, and operate HPC systems and facilities. Many of these sponsors and organizations have spent decades developing scientific simulation methods and software, which serves as the foundation of HPC today. During this time, this community has worked closely with countless vendors to foster the sustained development and deployment of HPC systems internationally.

## 1.2    Terascale to Petascale: The Past 15 Years in HPC

By any measure, the past 15 years have witnessed dramatic increases in both the use and scale of HPC. Thinking back, it was 1997, only 15 years ago, when the ASCI Red system at Sandia National Laboratories in Albuquerque, New Mexico, broke the 1 TFlop/s barrier on TOP500 Linpack using 7264 Pentium P6 processors over a proprietary interconnection network. In 2012, the Sequoia system, a Blue Gene/Q with its system-on-a-chip (SoC) architecture at Lawrence Livermore surpassed 16 PFlop/s on the same benchmark: an increase of 16,000 times in 15 years! It is impressive, indeed, when considering the well-known fact that the performance of commodity microprocessors has slowed due to power and thermal constraints [KBB+08, FPT+07, HTD11].

Although much of the focus is on the #1 system on TOP500, and its architecture, it is important to promote the fact that there are dozens, in fact, hundreds of systems around the world in daily use for solving HPC problems. As shown in Table 1.1, the architectures of these systems span the range from a fully customized processor and interconnection network to a complete commodity solution. In contrast, many of these systems share a tremendous amount of software on their software stack, as listed in Table 1.3. In fact, much of this software is open source software that organizations can download, port, and install on any system.

Aside from the popular TOP500 Linpack benchmark, this period has also witnessed a dramatic performance increase in the Gordon Bell Prizes. As illustrated in Table 1.2, since 1993 (the year that TOP500 started), the increase in the Gordon Bell performance prize winners has been almost 5 orders of magnitude (from 60 GFlop/s to 3,080,000 GFlop/s).

In this book, we have selected contributions from a combination of sites, systems, applications, and sponsors. Rather than focus simply on the architecture or the application, we focus on *HPC ecosystems* that have made this dramatic progress possible. Though the very word ecosystem can be a broad, all-encompassing term, it aptly describes high performance computing. That is, HPC is far more than one sponsor, one site, one application, one software system, or one architecture. Indeed, it is a community of interacting entities in this environment that sustains the community over time. As Table 1.1 illustrates, we have 21 chapters from authors around the world describing their ecosystem, and often focused on their existing flagship system. We not only included the largest systems in the world, but also innovative systems that advance a particular idea, such as the Gordon system at San Diego Supercomputer Center with its focus on data-intensive computing. Likewise, with a growing use of HPC internationally, we have included sites from Europe, China, and Japan. Ultimately, we would have liked to include many more chapters, but we simply ran out of room in the book.

Chapter authors were asked to address the following topics in their chapters:

1. Sponsor and site history

2. Highlights of applications, workloads, and benchmarks

3. Systems overview

4. Hardware architecture

5. System software

6. Programming systems

7. Storage, visualization, and analytics

**TABLE 1.1:** Significant systems in HPC.

| System | Type | Organization | Location | Country |
|---|---|---|---|---|
| Blacklight | SGI UV | Pittsburgh Supercomputing Center | Pittsburgh | USA |
| Blue Waters | Cray XE6, XK6 | National Center for Supercomputing Applications | Urbana | USA |
| JUGENE | Blue Gene/P | Jülich Research Centre, Forschungszentrum Jülich | Jülich | Germany |
| Gordon | x86/IB Cluster | San Diego Supercomputing Center | San Diego | USA |
| HA-PACS | x86/IB/GPU cluster | University of Tsukuba | Tsukuba | Japan |
| Keeneland | x86/IB/GPU cluster | Georgia Institute of Technology | Atlanta | USA |
| Kraken | Cray XT5 | National Institute for Computational Science | Knoxville | USA |
| Lomonosov | T-Platforms | Moscow State University | Moscow | Russia |
| Mole-8.5 | x86/IB/GPU cluster | Chinese Academy of Sciences, Institute of Process Engineering | Beijing | China |
| Monte Rosa | Cray XE6 | Swiss National Supercomputing Centre | Lugano | Switzerland |
| *Numerous* | Cray XE6 | DOD High Performance Modernization Project | Numerous | USA |
| Pleiades | x86/IB Cluster | NASA Ames | Mountain View | USA |
| Roadrunner | x86/Cell/IB cluster | Los Alamos National Laboratory | Los Alamos | USA |
| Sequoia, Mira | Blue Gene/Q | Lawrence Livermore National Laboratory and Argonne National Laboratory | Livermore and Argonne | USA |
| TERA 100 | x86/IB Cluster | CEA | Arpajon | France |
| Tianhe-1A | x86/IB/GPU cluster | National University of Defense Technology | Tianjin | China |
| Titan | Cray XK6 | Oak Ridge National Laboratory | Oak Ridge | USA |
| Tsubame 2.0 | x86/IB/GPU cluster | Tokyo Institute of Technology | Tokyo | Japan |
| Future Grid | Grid/Cloud | Indiana University | Bloomington | USA |
| Magellan | Grid/Cloud | Argonne National Laboratory and Lawrence Berkeley National Laboratory | Argonne and Berkeley | USA |
| LLGrid | Grid/Cloud | MIT Lincoln Laboratory | Boston | USA |

8. Data center/facility

9. Site HPC statistics

---

## 1.3 Performance

The most prominent HPC benchmark is the TOP500 Linpack benchmark. TOP500 has qualities that make it valuable and successful: easily scaled problem size, straightforward validation, an open source implementation, almost 20 years of historical data, a large audience familiar with the software, and well managed guidelines and submission procedures. As shown in Table 1.2, the TOP500 prize for the #1 system has been awarded since 1993. In that time, performance for this prize has grown from 124 GFlops to 17,590,000 GFlops. This increase is 5 orders of magnitude!

Although TOP500 Linpack is a formidable and long-lived benchmark, it does not fully capture the spectrum of applications across HPC as is often pointed out. TOP500 Linpack aside, the HPC community has created many metrics and benchmarks for tracking the success of different HPC solutions. These alternatives include the Gordon Bell Prize, the HPC Challenge benchmark (cf. Ch. 2.1), the NAS Parallel Benchmarks, the Green500 benchmark (cf. Ch. 3.1), the SHOC benchmarks (cf. Ch. 7.8), along with a large number of procurement benchmarks from DoE, DoD, NASA, and many other organizations.

### 1.3.1 Gordon Bell Prize

Aside from standard benchmarks, another indicator of growth in HPC is their performance on real scientific problems. The most well-known scientific accomplishment for these types of problems is the annual ACM Gordon Bell Prize, which is presented at the ACM/IEEE SC Conference. The prize requires authors to submit descriptions, scientific results, and performance results for real-world applications. These submissions are then judged by a group of peers, and one submission is awarded a prize for sustained performance. In one year, the committee can also award other prizes for exemplary submissions in price-performance, or other special categories. In general, the award is meant to reward innovation in applying high performance computing to applications in science. As illustrated in Table 1.2, over the years, these prizes have been awarded to teams with applications ranging from computational fluid dynamics to nanoparticle design to climate modeling to seismic modeling.

Since 1987, the year that this prize started, the sustained performance category has shown an increase of nearly seven orders of magnitude on systems ranging from 8 cores to 663,552 cores. Meanwhile, the price-performance prize has increased 5.5 orders of magnitude from 1989 to 2009. Note that until recently the Gordon Bell submission procedure has not had strict guidelines for submitting performance results, so some of the performance results are not completely documented. For example, it is known that the floating point rate listed in the table is a mix of single precision, double precision, and mixed precision. Nevertheless, in each year of the award, the committee recognized a winning application with exemplary performance and science.

More surprisingly, since 1993 (the same year that TOP500 started), the increase in the performance of Gordon Bell awards, from 60 Gflop/s to 4.45 Pflop/s, is nearly identical to the increase in performance of the TOP500 #1 system of 5 orders of magnitude: 4.87 to 5.15, respectively.

**TABLE 1.2:** Gordon Bell Prize winners for sustained performance compared with the #1 system on the TOP500 ranking since their inception.

| Year | Type | Application | System | Cores | Increase Log10 | GB Prize Gflop/s | Increase Log10 | TOP500 #1 Gflop/s | Increase Log10 |
|---|---|---|---|---|---|---|---|---|---|
| 1987 | PDE | Structures | N-CUBE | 1,024 | | 0.45 | | | |
| 1988 | PDE | Structures | Cray Y-MP | 8 | | 1 | | | |
| 1989 | PDE | Seismic | CM-2 | 2,048 | | 5.6 | | | |
| 1990 | PDE | Seismic | CM-2 | 2,048 | | 14 | | | |
| 1991 | | *NO PRIZE AWARDED* | | | | | | | |
| 1992 | NB | Gravitation | Delta | 512 | | 5.4 | | 124 | - |
| 1993 | MC | Boltzmann | CM-5 | 1,024 | - | 60 | - | 170 | 0.14 |
| 1994 | IE | Structures | Paragon | 1,904 | 0.27 | 143 | 0.38 | 170 | 0.14 |
| 1995 | MC | QCD | NWT | 128 | -0.90 | 179 | 0.47 | 368 | 0.47 |
| 1996 | PDE | CFD | NWT | 160 | -0.81 | 111 | 0.27 | 1,338 | 1.03 |
| 1997 | NB | Gravitation | ASCI Red | 4,096 | 0.60 | 170 | 0.45 | 1,338 | 1.03 |
| 1998 | DFT | Magnetism | T3E-1200 | 1,536 | 0.18 | 1,020 | 1.23 | 2,379 | 1.28 |
| 1999 | PDE | CFD | ASCI Blue Pacific | 5,832 | 0.76 | 627 | 1.02 | 4,938 | 1.60 |
| 2000 | NB | Gravitation | Grape-6 | 96 | -1.03 | 1,349 | 1.35 | 7,226 | 1.77 |
| 2001 | NB | Gravitation | Grape-6 | 1,024 | 0.00 | 11,550 | 2.28 | 35,860 | 2.46 |
| 2002 | PDE | Climate | Earth Simulator | 5,120 | 0.70 | 26,500 | 2.65 | 35,860 | 2.46 |
| 2003 | PDE | Seismic | Earth Simulator | 1,944 | 0.28 | 5,000 | 1.92 | 70,720 | 2.76 |
| 2004 | PDE | CFD | Earth Simulator | 4,096 | 0.60 | 15,200 | 2.40 | 280,600 | 3.35 |
| 2005 | MD | Solidification | BG/L | 131,072 | 2.11 | 101,700 | 3.23 | 280,600 | 3.35 |
| 2006 | DFT | Electronic structures | BG/L | 131,072 | 2.11 | 207,000 | 3.54 | 478,200 | 3.59 |
| 2007 | MD | Kelvin-Helmholtz | BG/L | 131,072 | 2.11 | 115,000 | 3.28 | 1,105,000 | 3.95 |
| 2008 | DFT | Crystal structures | Jaguar/XT-5 | 150,000 | 2.17 | 1,352,000 | 4.35 | 1,759,000 | 4.15 |
| 2009 | DFT | Nanoscale systems | Jaguar/XT-5 | 147,464 | 2.16 | 1,030,000 | 4.23 | 2,566,000 | 4.32 |
| 2010 | FMM | Blood flow | Jaguar/XT-5 | 196,608 | 2.28 | 780,000 | 4.11 | 10,510,000 | 4.93 |
| 2011 | RSDFT | Nanowires | K/Fujitsu | 442,368 | 2.64 | 3,080,000 | 4.71 | 17,590,000 | 5.15 |
| 2012 | NB | Astrophysics | K/Fujitsu | 663,552 | 2.81 | 4,450,000 | 4.87 | | |

*Note:* For a specific year, the system occupying the TOP500 #1 rank may be different from the system listed as the Gordon Bell Prize winner.

*Source:* This table was compiled from a number of sources including ACM and IEEE documents and including conversations with the following scientists: Jack Dongarra, David Keyes, Alan Karp, John Gustafson, and Bill Gropp.

### 1.3.2   HPC Challenge

The HPC Challenge benchmark (cf. Ch. 2.1) was initially designed in 2005 to provide a more diverse set of kernels than those provided by TOP500 HPL [PWDC08]. In addition to kernels with high locality, such as matrix multiply or STREAM TRIAD, the HPC Challenge benchmark suite added several benchmarks to emphasize data movement in the memory subsystem and in the interconnection network: Random Access, FFT, and a global transpose operation. In addition, HPCC was created to enable comparisons of different programming approaches beyond MPI and FORTRAN or C. Since the HPCC kernels are relatively small when compared to real applications, it is easier for scientists to recode and optimize these kernels on new architectures. In fact, for the past six years, the HPCC organizing group has sponsored an annual competition at the ACM/IEEE SC conference to evaluate HPCC results in terms of productivity and performance. Judging the performance prizes is relatively straightforward as long as the submitters stay within the benchmark guidelines. On the other hand, a committee judges the *productivity* of the submitted approaches for the most "elegant" implementation. Given that productivity is subjective and often impractical to measure, the committee often must rely on brief descriptions of the proposed approaches and results to determine the winners. Nevertheless, HPCC has received a substantial number of submissions over the years that provides for an interesting debate in the community. These submissions have included Chapel, Cilk, Co-array FORTRAN, Parallel MATLAB®, Star-P, UPC, X10, XcalableMP, and others.

### 1.3.3   Green500

In 2007, the Green500 benchmark and list (cf. Ch. 3.1) were created in order to recognize the growing importance of energy efficiency in HPC. The list requires submitters to submit both the performance of their system on the TOP500 HPL benchmark *and* the empirically measured power consumption during the benchmark test. Using this information, Green500 calculates and ranks each system by their megaFLOPS/Watt metric. All recent HPC reports predict that energy efficiency will continue to drive the design of HPC systems in the foreseeable future [KBB+08, FPT+07, HTD11], so the Green500 list will allow the community to continue to track progress on this important topic.

### 1.3.4   SHOC

Most recently, heterogeneous systems have become a viable commodity option for providing high performance in this new era of limited power and facility budgets. During this time, several new programming models (e.g., CUDA, OpenCL, OpenACC) and architectural features, such as accelerators attached via PCIe, have emerged that have made it difficult to use existing benchmarks effectively. The Scalable Heterogeneous Computing benchmark suite (cf. Ch. 7.8) was created to facilitate benchmarking of scalable heterogeneous clusters for computational and data-intensive computing. In contrast to most existing GPU and consumer benchmarks, SHOC focuses on scalability so that it can run on 1 or 1000s of nodes, and it focuses on scientific kernels prioritized by their importance in existing applications.

---

## 1.4   Trends

Looking at the contributions in this book and at industry more broadly, it is clear that dominant trends have emerged over the past 15 years that have directly impacted contemporary HPC. These trends span hardware, software, and business models.

For example, Linux was used only as a research operating system in HPC in the 1990s, while now it is the operating system running on nearly all HPC systems. In another example, in the late 1990s, MPI (Message Passing Interface) was just emerging as a new de facto standard that is now ubiquitous. Meanwhile, other trends including multicore processors and graphics processors were not even imagined outside of a few scientists in research communities. Finally, perhaps most important of all, open-source software has grown to be a very strong component of HPC, even resulting in international planning exercises for the path toward Exascale [KBB+08, FPT+07, HTD11]. In the following sections, we examine these trends in more detail.

### 1.4.1 Architectures

Recent architectures for HPC can be categorized into a few classes. First, commodity-based clusters dominate the TOP500 list. These clusters typically have an x86 commodity processor from Intel or AMD, and a commodity-based interconnect, which today is Infini-Band. These clusters offer significant capability at a very competitive price because they are high volume products for vendors. Standard HPC software stacks, much of it open-source, make these clusters easy to install, run, and maintain.

Second, GPU-accelerated commodity-based clusters have quickly emerged over the past three years as viable solutions for HPC applications [OLG+05b]. Two important aspects of these systems often go understated. First, because the GPU leverages multiple markets such as gaming and professional graphics, these GPGPU architectures are *commodity* solutions. Second, the very quick adoption of CUDA and OpenCL for programming these architectures lowered the switching costs for users to port their applications. Recently, the move toward directive-based compilation, with tools like PGI Accelerate, CAPS HMPP, and OpenACC, demonstrates even more support and interest for easing this transition.

Third, customized architectures represent a significant fraction of the top systems. Take, for example, the K Computer [ASS09] and the Blue Gene Q systems [bgp]. These systems have customized logic for both their compute nodes and interconnection networks. They have demonstrated excellent scalability, performance, and energy efficiency.

Finally, even more specialized systems, such as DE Shaw's Anton [SDD+07], have been designed that show excellent performance on specialized problems like protein folding but are likewise inflexible such that they cannot run any of the aforementioned benchmarks like TOP500 or HPCC.

### 1.4.2 Software

Although HPC systems share many hardware components with servers in enterprise and data centers, the HPC software stack is dramatically different from an enterprise or cloud software stack and is unique to HPC. Generally speaking, an HPC software stack has multiple levels: system software, development environments, system management software, and scientific data management and visualization systems. Nearest to the hardware, system software typically includes operating systems, runtime systems, and low level I/O software, like filesystems. Next, development environment is a broad area that facilitates application design and development. In our framework, it includes programming models, compilers, scientific frameworks and libraries, and correctness and performance tools. Then, system management software coordinates, schedules, and monitors the system and the applications running on that system. Finally, scientific data management and visualization software provides users with domain specific tools for generating, managing, and exploring data for their science. This data may include empirically measured data from sensors in the real world that is used to calibrate and validate simulation models, or output from simulations

**TABLE 1.3**: HPC software summary.

| Category | Item |
|---|---|
| Operating Systems | Linux (Multiple versions), CNK |
| Languages | C, C++, FORTRAN |
| Compilers | CAPS, Cray, GNU, IBM, Intel, Pathscale, PGI |
| Scripting Languages | Java, Perl Python, Ruby, Tcl/Tk |
| Distributed Memory Programming Models | Charm++, Co-Array Fortran, Global Arrays, Hadoop/MapReduce MPC, MPI (OpenMPI, MVAIPICH, Intel MPI, Cray MPI, MPICH), MPT, SHMEM, Unified Parallel C, XMP |
| Shared Memory Programming Models | OpenMP, Pthreads, TBB |
| Heterogeneous Programming Models | CAPS HMPP, CUDA, OpenACC, OpenCL, PGI Accelerate, |
| Performance Tools | BPMON, Cray CPMAT, Extrae/Paraver, HPCToolkit, HWLOC, IH-PCT, IPM, Intel Trace Analyzer, MPIP, MPInside, NVIDIA Visual Profiler, Ocelot, oprofile, PAPI, PDToolkit, PerfSuite, SCALASCA, TAU, VampirTrace/Vampir, Vtune |
| Correctness Tools | DDT, GNU GDB, STAT, Threadchecker, Threadspotter, Totalview, Valgrind |
| Scientific Libraries | ACML, ARPACK, BLAS, Boost, CASE, CRAFFT, cuBLAS, cuFFT, cuLA, cuRAND, cuSP, cuSPARSE, ESSL, FFTW, GNU GSL, Gridgen, hypre, LAPACK, MAGMA, MASS, MKL, MUMPS, PARPACK, ParMetis, SPRNG, SUNDIALS, ScaLAPACK, Scotch, SuperLU, Thrust |
| Scientific Frameworks | Arcane, GraphLab, JASMIN, PETSc, Trilinos |
| Parallel Filesystems and Storage | GPFS, GridFtp, HPSS, Lustre, Panasas, StorNext |
| Job Schedulers and Resource Managers | ALPS, GangliaMole, LoadLeveler, Moab, PBSPro, SLURM, Sun Grid Engine, Torque |
| System Management | ACE, ClusterShell, Ganglia, Inca, NFS-Ganesh, NHC, Netlogger, NodeKARE, Robinhood, Rocks, SEC, Shine, TEAL, THRMS, xCAT |
| I/O Libraries and Software | HDF5, Hercule, pnetCDF |
| Visualization | AVS/Express, EnSight, FieldView, Grace, IDL, POV-Ray, ParaView, Tecplot360, VTK, VisIt |
| Integrated Development Environments | Eclipse+PTP |
| Integrated Problem Solving Environnments | MATLAB, Octave, R |
| Virtualization | Eucalyptus, HPUC, Shadowfax, vSMP, Xen |

per se. As Table 1.3 shows, the systems described in this book have a tremendous amount of common software, even though some of the systems are very diverse in terms of hardware. Moreover, a considerable amount of this software is open-source, and is funded by a wide array of sponsors.

Over the past 15 years, HPC software has had to adapt and respond to several challenges. First, the concurrency in applications and systems has grown over three orders of magnitude. The primary programming model, MPI, has had to grow and change to allow this scale. Second, the increase in concurrency has on a per core basis driven lower the memory and I/O capacity, and the memory, I/O, and interconnect bandwidth. Third, in the last five years, heterogeneity and architectural diversity have placed a new emphasis on application and software portability.

### 1.4.3    Clouds and Grids in HPC

Outside of HPC, in the data center and enterprise markets, Clouds and Grids continue to be increasingly popular and important. Both externally visible clouds, like Amazon's

EC2, and internal corporate clouds continue to grow dramatically. IDC indicates that total worldwide revenue from public IT cloud services exceeded $21.5 billion in 2010 (http://www.idc.com/prodserv/idc_cloud.jsp), and they predict that it will reach $72.9 billion in 2015. With this tremendous growth rate – (CAGR) of 27.6% – Clouds and Grids will most likely influence the HPC marketplace, even if indirectly, so we include three chapters on Cloud and Grid systems being used and tested for scientific computing markets. These chapters highlight both the strengths and weaknesses of existing cloud and grid systems.

# Chapter 2

## HPC Challenge: Design, History, and Implementation Highlights

**Jack Dongarra**

*University of Tennessee Knoxville, University of Manchester, Oak Ridge National Laboratory*

**Piotr Luszczek**

*University of Tennessee Knoxville*

## 2.1   Introduction

The HPC Challenge (HPCC)[1] benchmark suite was initially developed for the DARPA's HPCS program [Kep04] to provide a set of standardized hardware probes based on commonly occurring computational software kernels. The HPCS program has initiated a fundamental reassessment of how we define and measure performance, programmability, portability, robustness, and ultimately, productivity in the high-end domain. Consequently, the suite was aimed to both provide conceptual expression of the underlying computation as well as be applicable to a broad spectrum of computational science fields. Clearly, a number of compromises must have led to the current form of the suite given such a broad scope of design requirements. HPCC was designed to approximately bound computations of high and low spatial and temporal locality (see Figure 2.1 which gives the conceptual design space for the HPCC component tests). In addition, because the HPCC tests consist of simple mathematical operations, this provides a unique opportunity to look at language and parallel programming model issues. As such, the benchmark is to serve both the system user and designer communities [Kah97].

Finally, Figure 2.2 shows a generic memory subsystem and how each level of the hierarchy is tested by the HPCC software and what the design goals of the future HPCS system are – these are the projected target performance numbers that are to come out of the winning HPCS vendor designs.

## 2.2   The TOP500 Influence

Most commonly known ranking of supercomputer installations around the world is the TOP500 list [MSDS06]. It uses the equally famous LINPACK Benchmark [DLP03] as a single figure of merit to rank 500 of the world's most powerful supercomputers. The often raised issue of the relation between TOP500 and HPCC can simply be addressed by recognizing all the positive aspects of the former. In particular, the longevity of TOP500 gives an unprecedented view of the high-end arena across the turbulent times of Moore's law [Moo65] and the process of the emerging of today's prevalent computing paradigms. The predictive power of TOP500 will have a lasting influence in the future as it did in the

[1]This work was supported in part by the DARPA, NSF, and DOE through the DARPA HPCS program under grant FA8750-04-1-0219 and SCI-0527260.

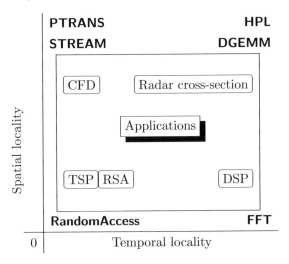

**FIGURE 2.1**: The application areas targeted by the HPCS program are bound by the HPCC tests in the memory access locality space.

past. While building on the legacy information, HPCC extends the context of the HPCS goals and can already serve as a valuable tool for performance analysis. Table 2.1 shows an example of how the data from the HPCC database can augment the TOP500 results.

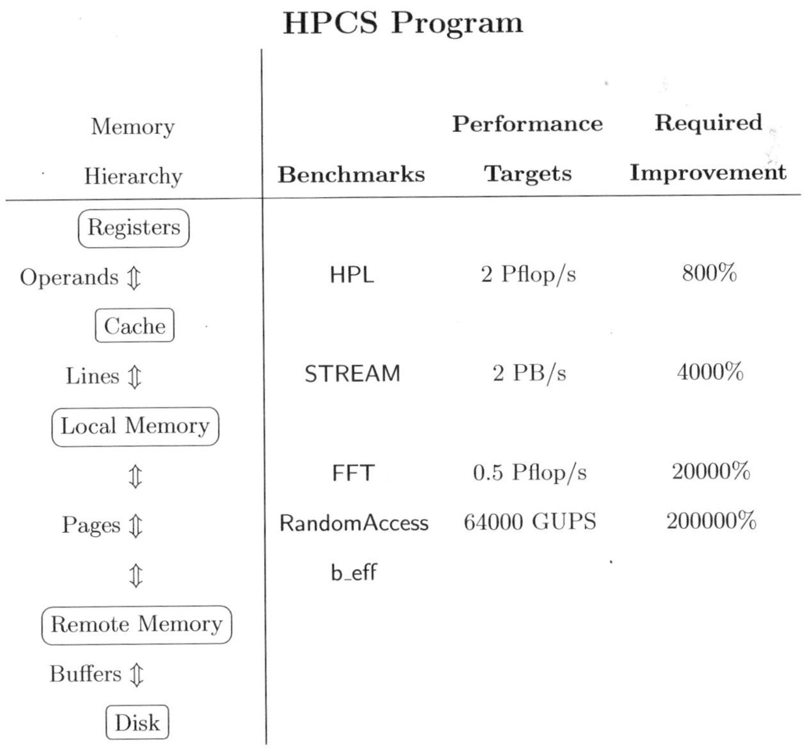

## HPCS Program

| Memory Hierarchy | Benchmarks | Performance Targets | Required Improvement |
|---|---|---|---|
| Registers | | | |
| Operands ⇕ | HPL | 2 Pflop/s | 800% |
| Cache | | | |
| Lines ⇕ | STREAM | 2 PB/s | 4000% |
| Local Memory | | | |
| ⇕ | FFT | 0.5 Pflop/s | 20000% |
| Pages ⇕ | RandomAccess | 64000 GUPS | 200000% |
| ⇕ | b_eff | | |
| Remote Memory | | | |
| Buffers ⇕ | | | |
| Disk | | | |

**FIGURE 2.2**: HPCS program benchmarks and performance targets.

**TABLE 2.1**: All of the top-10 entries of the 27$^{th}$ TOP500 list that have results in the HPCC database.

| Rank | Name | $Rmax$ | HPL | PTRANS | STREAM | FFT | RandomAccess | Latency | Bandwidth |
|------|------|--------|-----|--------|--------|-----|--------------|---------|-----------|
| 1 | Blue Gene/L | 280.6 | 259.2 | 4665.9 | 160 | 2311 | 35.47 | 5.92 | 0.16 |
| 2 | Blue Gene W | 91.3 | 83.9 | 171.5 | 50 | 1235 | 21.61 | 4.70 | 0.16 |
| 3 | ASC Purple | 75.8 | 57.9 | 553.0 | 44 | 842 | 1.03 | 5.11 | 3.22 |
| 4 | Columbia | 51.9 | 46.8 | 91.3 | 21 | 230 | 0.25 | 4.23 | 1.39 |
| 9 | Red Storm | 36.2 | 33.0 | 1813.1 | 44 | 1118 | 1.02 | 7.97 | 1.15 |

## 2.3    Short History of the Benchmark

The first reference implementation of the code was released to the public in 2003. Year 2004 marked two important milestones for the benchmark: 1 Tflop/s was exceeded on HPCC's HPL test and the first submission with over 1,000 processors was recorded in the public submission database. The first optimized submission came in April 2004 from Cray using then recent X1 installation at the Oak Ridge National Laboratory. Ever since then Cray has championed the list of optimized submissions. By the time of the first HPCC birds-of-feather at the Supercomputing conference in 2004 in Pittsburgh, the public database of results already featured major supercomputer makers – a sign that vendors noticed the benchmark. At the same time, a bit behind the scenes, the code was also tried by government and private institutions for procurement and marketing purposes.

At the time, Jack Dongarra described the goals of the HPC Challenge Benchmarks: "The HPC Challenge Benchmarks will examine the performance of HPC architectures using kernels with more challenging memory access patterns than just the High Performance LINPACK (HPL) benchmark used in the TOP500 list. The HPC Challenge Benchmarks are being designed to augment the TOP500 list, provide benchmarks that bound the performance of many real applications as a function of memory access characteristics — e.g., spatial and temporal locality, and provide a framework for including additional benchmarks." HPCC is already up to par with the TOP500 in terms of HPL performance and it also offers a far richer view of today's High End Computing (HEC) landscape as well as giving an unprecedented array of performance metrics for various analyses and comparison studies.

The FFT test was introduced in version 0.6 in May 2004 and the first submission with the new test was recorded in July the same year. As of early October 2005, the fastest system in the database obtained nearly 1 Tflop/s in the Global FFT test (three orders of magnitude increase over time). At the same time, the fastest (in terms of HPL) system was listed at position 11 on June's edition of the TOP500 list, but the result recorded in the HPCC database was four percentage points higher in terms of efficiency. Today all of these achievements have been superseded by submissions from TOP500's highest ranking machines including the number one entry.

Another highlight of 2005 was announcement of a contest: the HPCC Awards. The two complementary categories of the competition emphasized performance and productivity –

the very goals of the sponsoring HPCS program. The performance-emphasizing Class 1 award drew the attention of the biggest players in the supercomputing industry which resulted in populating the HPCC database with most of the top-10 entries of TOP500 (some of which even exceeding performance reported on TOP500 – a tribute to HPCC's continuous results' update policy). The contestants competed to achieve highest raw performance in one of the four tests: HPL, STREAM, RandomAccess, and FFT. The Class 2 award, by solely focusing on productivity, introduced subjectivity factor to the judging but also to the submitter criteria of what is appropriate for the contest. As a result, a wide range of solutions were submitted spanning various programming languages (interpreted and compiled) and paradigms (with explicit and implicit parallelism). It featured openly available as well as proprietary technologies some of which were arguably confined to niche markets and some that are widely used. The financial incentives for entering turned out to be all but needed as the HPCC seemed to have enjoyed enough recognition among the high-end community. Nevertheless, HPCwire kindly provided both: press coverage as well as cash rewards for four winning contestants of Class 1 and the winner of Class 2. At the HPCC's second birds-of-feather session during the SC|05 conference in Seattle, the former class was dominated by IBM's Blue Gene/L from Lawrence Livermore National Lab, while the latter was split among MTA pragma-decorated C and UPC codes from Cray and IBM, respectively.

Over the years, HPCC has received exposure in numerous news outlets including Business Wire, Cnet, eWeek, HPCwire, and Yahoo!. The website often receives over 100,000 hits per month and the source code download rates exceed 1,000 downloads per year. A different kind of publicity comes from the acquisition procedures as supercomputer centers around the world choose HPCC for their required performance testing from bidding vendors.

June 2010 marked the release of version 1.4.1 of the benchmark code. And in 2011, the HPCC Awards competition continued with two classes of submissions; Class 1: Best Performance and Class 2: Most Productivity. While the former still invites submissions from large HPC installations around the globe and awards four winners in four categories (HPL, STREAM, FFT, RandomAccess), the latter evolved over time to invite source code submissions of tests not included in HPCC and implemented in various languages. It stressed the productivity aspect of programming languages and HEC architectures. Usually more than one winner is awarded. The competition results are customarily announced during a BOF session at SC conference series. Additional information about the awards competition can be found on the HPCC Awards website: http://www.hpcchallenge.org/.

Development of the HPC Challenge Benchmarks is being funded by the Defense Advanced Research Projects Agency (DARPA) High Productivity Computing Systems (HPCS) Program. Dr. Charles Holland is the current HPCS program manager. According to him: "The HPCS program is interested in both improved performance and ease of programming. Combining these two will give us the productivity that the national security community needs. For performance, the HPC Challenge benchmarks augment LINPACK with benchmarks that use more challenging memory access patterns, providing a more accurate evaluation of HPC systems."

## 2.4   The Benchmark Tests' Details

Extensive discussion and various implementations of the HPCC tests were given elsewhere [DL05, LD07, TK06, PBV$^+$06, GS06]. However, for the sake of completeness, this section lists the most important facts pertaining to the HPCC tests' definitions.

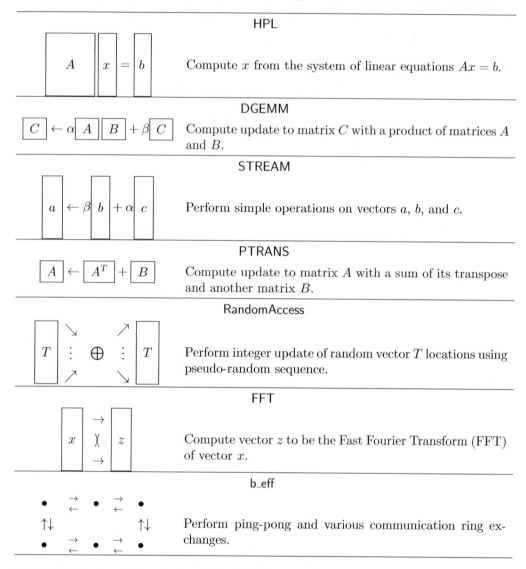

**FIGURE 2.3**: Detail description of the HPCC component tests ($A$, $B$, $C$ – matrices, $a$, $b$, $c$, $x$, $z$ – vectors, $\alpha$, $\beta$ – scalars, $T$ – array of 64-bit integers).

All calculations use *double precision* floating-point numbers as described by the IEEE 754 standard [75485] and no mixed precision calculations [LLL+06] are allowed. All the tests are designed so that they will run on an arbitrary number of processors (usually denoted as $p$). Figure 2.3 shows a more detailed definition of each of the seven tests included in HPCC. In addition, it is possible to run the tests in one of three testing scenarios to stress various hardware components of the system. The scenarios are shown in Figure 2.4.

## 2.4.1   General Guidelines

1. The use of high level languages is encouraged.

2. Calls to tuned library routines could be used in the submission but explicit and "elegant" coding of all aspects of the benchmark is preferred.

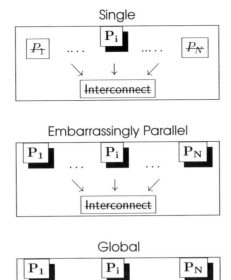

**FIGURE 2.4**: Testing scenarios of the HPCC components.

3. The entire benchmark could be expressed by using a few built-in operators of a hypothetical programming language. However, such submissions are strongly discouraged as they only show operator overloading and function call syntax and say nothing about the language—in particular, how it deals with issues critical to HPC like expressing parallelism and hiding latency.

### 2.4.2   HPL

HPL (High Performance Linpack) is an implementation of the Linpack TPP (Toward Peak Performance) variant of the original Linpack benchmark which measures the floating point rate of execution for solving a linear system of equations.

#### 2.4.2.1   Description

HPL solves a linear system of equations of order $n$:

$$Ax = b; \quad A \in \mathbf{R}^{n \times n}; \ x, b \in \mathbf{R}^n \tag{2.1}$$

by first computing LU factorization with row partial pivoting of the $n$ by $n + 1$ coefficient matrix:

$$P[A, b] = [[L, U], y]. \tag{2.2}$$

Since the row pivoting (represented by the permutation matrix $P$) and the lower triangular factor $L$ are applied to $b$ as the factorization progresses, the solution $x$ is obtained in one step by solving the upper triangular system:

$$Ux = y. \tag{2.3}$$

The lower triangular matrix $L$ is left unpivoted and the array of pivots is not returned.

#### 2.4.2.2    Data Size

$A$ is $n$ by $n$ double precision (in IEEE 754 sense) matrix, $b$ is $n$-element vector. The size of the $A$ matrix ($8n^2$ bytes) should be at least half of the system memory.

#### 2.4.2.3    Initialization

Both $A$ and $b$ should contain values produced by a reasonable pseudo-random generator with an expected mean of zero. "Reasonable" in this context means compact, fast, and producing independent and identically distributed elements.

#### 2.4.2.4    Timed Region

The timed portion of the code performs steps given by Equations (2.2) and (2.3) and does not include time to generate $A$ and $b$.

#### 2.4.2.5    Duration

Until solution to (2.1) is obtained.

#### 2.4.2.6    Verification

Correctness of the solution is ascertained by calculating the following scaled residual:

$$r = \frac{\|Ax - b\|_\infty}{\epsilon(\|A\|_\infty \|x\|_\infty + \|b\|_\infty)n} \tag{2.4}$$

where $\epsilon$ is machine precision for 64-bit floating-point values and $n$ is the size of the problem. The solution is valid if the following holds:

$$r < 16 \tag{2.5}$$

#### 2.4.2.7    Performance

The operation count for the factorization phase is $\frac{2}{3}n^3 - \frac{1}{2}n^2$ and $2n^2$ for the solve phase; thus if the time to solution is $t_S$ the formula for performance (in Gflop/s) is:

$$p_{\mathsf{HPL}} = \frac{\frac{2}{3}n^3 + \frac{3}{2}n^2}{t_S} 10^{-9}. \tag{2.6}$$

#### 2.4.2.8    Alternative Implementations

If an alternative algorithm is chosen it should be able to deal with zeros on the diagonal (some sort of pivoting needs to be used) and the precision of the calculations needs to be preserved.

### 2.4.3    RandomAccess

#### 2.4.3.1    Description

Let $T[\cdot]$ be a table of size $2^n$.
Let $\{a_i\}$ be a stream of 64-bit integers of length $N_U = 2^{n+2}$ generated by the primitive polynomial over $GF(2)^2$:

---

[2]Galois Field of order 2 – The elements of GF(2) can be represented using the integers 0 and 1, i.e., binary operands.

$x^2 + x + 1$.

For each $a_i$, set

$$T[a_i\langle 63, 64 - n\rangle] \leftarrow T[a_i\langle 63, 64 - n\rangle] \oplus a_i \tag{2.7}$$

where:

- $\oplus$ denotes addition in $GF(2)$ i.e., "exclusive or" (XOR)

- $a_i\langle l, k\rangle$ denotes the sequence of bits within $a_i$, e.g., $\langle 63, 64 - n\rangle$ are the highest $n$ bits.

### 2.4.3.2  Data Size

The parameter $m(= 2^n)$ is defined such that:
$m$ is the largest power of 2 that is less than or equal to half of the system memory. Since the elements of the main table are 64-bit quantities, the table occupies $8m$ bytes of memory.

### 2.4.3.3  Initialization

Table elements are set such that:

$$\forall_{0 \leq i < 2^n} T[i] \equiv i \tag{2.8}$$

### 2.4.3.4  Timed Region

The timed region consists of computation (2.7). The initialization (2.8) is not timed.

### 2.4.3.5  Duration

Ideally, $2^{n+2}$ updates should be performed to the main table ($N_U = 2^{n+2}$). However, the computation can be prematurely stopped after 25% of the time of the HPL run (but not shorter than 1 minute). Thus:

$$N_U \leq 2^{n+2} \tag{2.9}$$

### 2.4.3.6  Verification

The update defined by (2.7) should be repeated by an alternative method that is safe (does not generate errors resulting from, for example, race conditions in memory updates). If the benchmarked update was correct, the table should return to its initial state defined by (2.8). However, 1% of entries may have incorrect values, i.e., given a function:

$$f(i) = \begin{cases} 0 & \text{if } T[i] = i \\ 1 & \text{otherwise} \end{cases} \tag{2.10}$$

the following should hold:

$$\sum_{i=0}^{N_U} f(i) \leq 10^{-2} N_U \tag{2.11}$$

### 2.4.3.7  Performance

Let $t_{\text{RandomAccess}}$ be the time it took to finish the timed portion of the test (including $N_U$ updates) then performance (in GUPS: Giga Updates Per Second) is defined as:

$$p_{\text{RandomAccess}} = \frac{N_U}{t_{\text{RandomAccess}}} 10^{-9}. \tag{2.12}$$

### 2.4.3.8    Alternative Implementations

Constraints on the look-ahead and storage before processing on distributed memory multi-processor systems is limited to 1,024 per process (or processing element). The pseudo-random number generator that generates sequence $\{a_i\}$ has to be used.

## 2.4.4    Global EP-STREAM-Triad

### 2.4.4.1    Description

EP-STREAM-Triad is a simple benchmark program that measures sustainable memory bandwidth (in Gbyte/s) and the corresponding computation rate for a simple vector kernel operation that scales and adds two vectors:

$$a \leftarrow b + \alpha\, c \tag{2.13}$$

where:

$$a, b, c \in \mathbf{R}^m; \quad \alpha \in \mathbf{R}.$$

The computation is performed simultaneously on each computing element on its local data set.

### 2.4.4.2    Data Size

$a$, $b$, and $c$ are $m$-element double precision vectors. The combined size of the vectors ($24m$ bytes) should be at least a quarter of the system memory.

### 2.4.4.3    Initialization

Vectors $b$ and $c$ should contain values produced by a reasonable pseudo-random number generator.

### 2.4.4.4    Timed Region

The timed portion of the code should perform operation given by (2.13) at least 10 times.

### 2.4.4.5    Duration

The kernel operation should be repeated at least 10 times.

### 2.4.4.6    Verification

The norm of the difference between reference and computed vectors is used to verify the result: $\|a - \hat{a}\|$. The reference vector $\hat{a}$ is obtained by an alternative implementation.

### 2.4.4.7    Performance

The benchmark measures Gbyte/s and the number of items transferred is $3m$. The minimum time $t_{\min}$ is taken of all the repetitions of the kernel operation. Performance is thus defined as:

$$p_{\text{EP-STREAM-Triad}} = 24 \frac{m}{t_{\min}} 10^{-9} \tag{2.14}$$

## 2.4.5 Global **FFT**

### 2.4.5.1 Description

FFT measures the floating point rate of execution of double precision complex one-dimensional Discrete Fourier Transform (DFT) of size $m$:

$$Z_k \leftarrow \sum_{j}^{m} z_j e^{-2\pi i \frac{jk}{m}}; \quad 1 \le k \le m \tag{2.15}$$

where:

$$z, Z \in \mathbf{C}^m.$$

### 2.4.5.2 Data Size

$Z$ and $z$ are $m$-element double precision complex vectors. The combined size of the vectors ($32m$ bytes) should be at least a quarter of the system memory. The size $m$ of the vectors can be implementation-specific, e.g., be an integral power of 2.

### 2.4.5.3 Initialization

Vector $z$ should contain values produced by a reasonable pseudo-random number generator. The real and imaginary parts of $z$ should be generated independently. The layout of vectors $z$ and $Z$ should not be scrambled either before or after the computation.

### 2.4.5.4 Timed Region

The computation implied by (2.15) is timed together with the portion of code that unscrambles (if necessary) the resulting vector data. Timing for computation and unscrambling can be given separately for informational purposes but the combined time is used for calculating performance.

### 2.4.5.5 Duration

Until the transform defined by (2.15) is obtained.

### 2.4.5.6 Verification

Verification is done by ascertaining the following bound on the residual:

$$\frac{\|z - \hat{z}\|_\infty}{\epsilon \ln m} < 16 \tag{2.16}$$

where $\hat{z}$ is the result of applying a reference implementation of the inverse transform to the outcome of the benchmarked code (in infinite-precision arithmetic the residual should be zero):

$$\hat{z}_k \leftarrow \sum_{j}^{m} Z_j e^{2\pi i \frac{jk}{m}}; \quad 1 \le k \le m \tag{2.17}$$

### 2.4.5.7 Performance

The operation count is taken to be $5m \log_2 m$ for the calculation of the computational rate (in Gflop/s) in time $t$:

$$p_{\mathsf{FFT}} = 5 \frac{m \log_2 m}{t} 10^{-9} \tag{2.18}$$

### 2.4.5.8    Alternative Implementations

The reference implementation splits the algorithm into computational and communication portions which do not overlap. Valid submissions may choose other methods that take advantage of language and architectural features.

The number of processors may be implementation-specific, e.g., be an integral power of 2.

## 2.5    Benchmark Submission Procedures and Results

The reference implementation of the benchmark may be obtained free of charge at the benchmark's web site.[3] The reference implementation should be used for the base run: it is written in portable subset of ANSI C [KR78] using hybrid programming model that mixes OpenMP [Opec, CDK$^+$01] threading with MPI [For94, For95, For97] messaging. The installation of the software requires creating a script file for Unix's `make(1)` utility. The distribution archive comes with script files for many common computer architectures. Usually, few changes to one of these files will produce the script file for a given platform. The HPCC rules allow only standard system compilers and libraries to be used through their supported and documented interface and the build procedure should be described at submission time. This ensures repeatability of the results and serves as educational tool for end users that wish to use the similar build process for their applications.

After, a successful compilation the benchmark is ready to run. However, it is recommended that changes be made to the benchmark's input file that describes the sizes of data to use during the run. The sizes should reflect the available memory on the system and number of processors available for computations.

There must be one baseline run submitted for each computer system entered in the archive. There may also exist an optimized run for each computer system. The baseline run should use the reference implementation of HPCC and in a sense it represents the scenario when an application requires use of legacy code – a code that cannot be changed. The optimized run allows to perform more aggressive optimizations and use system-specific programming techniques (languages, messaging libraries, etc.) but at the same time still gives the verification process enjoyed by the base run.

All of the submitted results are publicly available after they have been confirmed by email. In addition to the various displays of results and raw data export the HPCC web site also offers a kiviat chart display to visually compare systems using multiple performance numbers at once. A sample chart that uses actual HPCC results' data is shown in Figure 2.5.

Figure 2.6 shows performance results of currently operating clusters and supercomputer installations. Most of the results come from the HPCC public database.

## 2.6    Performance Trends

HPCC Awards ever since their introduction in 2005 sparked interest in the HPCC Suite and contributed many new submissions, most importantly, from the largest supercomputer installations in the world. Figures 2.7, 2.8, 2.9, and 2.10 show performance trends for the

---

[3]http://icl.cs.utk.edu/hpcc/

## 64 processors: AMD Opteron 2.2 GHz

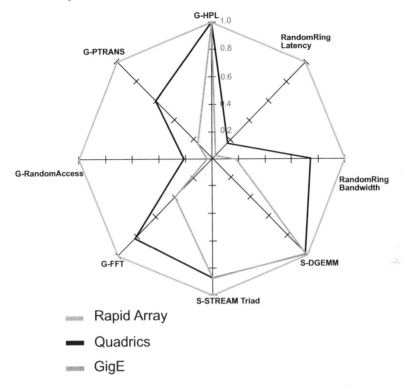

**FIGURE 2.5**: Sample kiviat diagram of results for three different interconnects that connect the same processors.

first, second, and third places in the competition over the 7-year period. In 2011, the K computer from Japan has become an undisputed winner for all four tests tracked by the Performance Category of HPCC Awards. This had not been the case in the prior years. In 2009 and 2010, Jaguar supercomputer from Oak Ridge National Laboratory (ORNL) did not dominate all four tests.

One of the important observations in Figure 2.7 is the fact that the HPL performance from the HPCC Suite is usually lower than the number recorded by TOP500. This is no accident as the code used for HPCC submission usually does not match exactly what was used for TOP500. The former has to satisfy the HPCC submission rules including data layout software interfaces. On the contrary, the TOP500 code is only to fulfill "paper-and-pencil" description of the High Performance LINPACK. But importantly, optimization of HPCC has to focus on all components of the suite which might not necessarily benefit the HPL component. Finally, the competitive pressure from all the TOP500 submissions is a much greater incentive to maximize the HPL score. This may be most visible for the K computer and its 2011 HPCC result of 2118 Tflop/s. This is nearly 80% lower result than the 10510 Tflop/s reported on the TOP500 list. The easiest explanation is the lack of competition – the second fastest system is ORNL's Jaguar at 1534 Tflop/s and so the result reported by the K computer is sufficient to put it as the winner for the HPL test. Clearly, if K computer reported only 1600 Tflop/s it still would have been a winner. The reason for going all the way to over 2000 Tflop/s was the RandomAccess test. The second place contender for

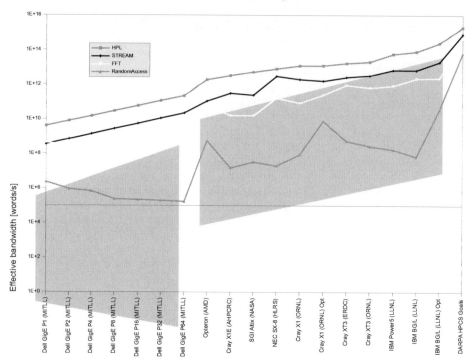

**FIGURE 2.6**: Sample interpretation of the HPCC results.

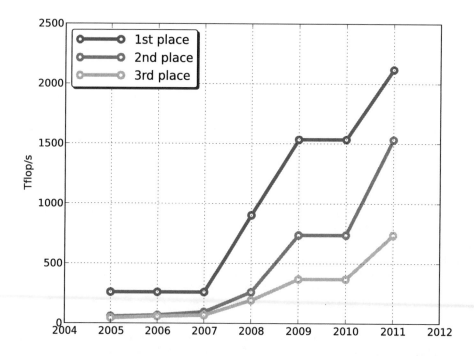

**FIGURE 2.7**: Historical trends for winners of the performance category of the HPCC Awards for Global HPL.

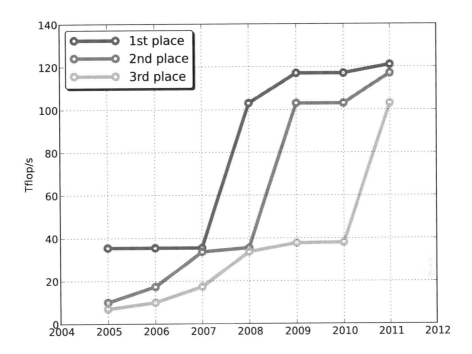

**FIGURE 2.8**: Historical trends for winners of the performance category of the HPCC Awards for Global RandomAccess.

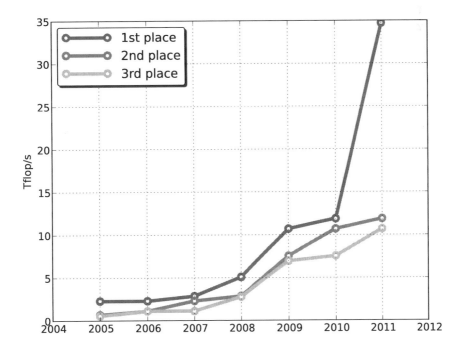

**FIGURE 2.9**: Historical trends for winners of the performance category of the HPCC Awards for Global FFT.

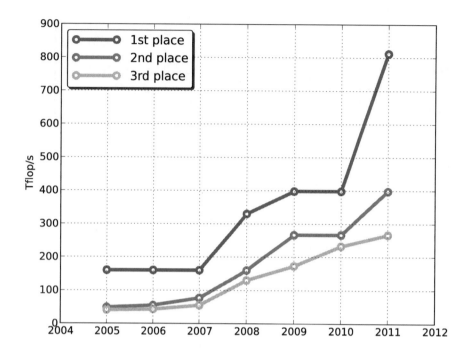

**FIGURE 2.10**: Historical trends for winners of the performance category of the HPCC Awards for Global EP-STREAM-Triad.

RandomAccess is a Blue Gene/P system at Lawrence Livermore National Laboratory at 117 GUPS. For the K computer the reported value was 121 GUPS, only about 3% better result but a sufficient one to win. From our analysis we conclude that large enough partition of the K computer was used to give it a winning score in all four tests tracked by the HPCC Awards in the Performance Category. The partition used for the winning submission consisted of 18432 nodes with 8 cores per node and 147456 cores total. This is far less (almost 80% less) than the 705024 cores used for the TOP500 submission.

## 2.7    Scalability Considerations

There are a number of issues to be considered for benchmarks such as HPCC that have scalable input data to allow for arbitrary sized system to be properly stressed by the benchmark run. Time to run the entire suite is a major concern for institutions with limited resource allocation budgets. Each component of HPCC has been analyzed from the scalability standpoint and Table 2.2 shows the major time complexity results. In the following, it is assumed that:

- $M$ is the total size of memory
- $m$ is the size of the test vector

**TABLE 2.2**: Time complexity formulas for various phases of the HPCC tests.

| Name | Generation | Computation | Communication | Verification | Per-processor data |
|------|:---:|:---:|:---:|:---:|:---:|
| HPL | $n^2$ | $n^3$ | $n^2$ | $n^2$ | $p^{-1}$ |
| DGEMM | $n^2$ | $n^3$ | $n^2$ | $1$ | $p^{-1}$ |
| STREAM | $m$ | $m$ | $1$ | $m$ | $p^{-1}$ |
| PTRANS | $n^2$ | $n^2$ | $n^2$ | $n^2$ | $p^{-1}$ |
| RandomAccess | $m$ | $m$ | $m$ | $m$ | $p^{-1}$ |
| FFT | $m$ | $m \log_2 m$ | $m$ | $m \log_2 m$ | $p^{-1}$ |
| b_eff | $1$ | $1$ | $p^2$ | $1$ | $1$ |

*Note:* $m$ and $n$ correspond to the appropriate vector and matrix sizes; $p$ is the number of processors.

- $n$ is the size of the test matrix

- $p$ is the number of processors

- $t$ is the time to run the test

Clearly any complexity formula that grows faster than linearly with respect to any of the system sizes is a cause of a potential problem time scalability issue. Consequently, the following tests have to be addressed:

- HPL because it has computational complexity $\mathcal{O}(n^3)$

- DGEMM because it has computational complexity $\mathcal{O}(n^3)$

- b_eff because it has communication complexity $\mathcal{O}(p^2)$

The computational complexity of HPL of order $\mathcal{O}(n^3)$ may cause excessive running time because the time will grow proportionately to a high power of total memory size:

$$t_{\mathsf{HPL}} \sim n^3 = \left(n^2\right)^{3/2} \sim M^{3/2} = \sqrt{M^3} \tag{2.19}$$

To resolve this problem we have turned to the past TOP500 data and analyzed the ratio of *Rpeak* to the number of bytes for the factorized matrix for the first entry on all the lists. It turns out that there are on average $6 \pm 3$ Gflop/s for each matrix byte. We can thus conclude that performance rate of HPL remains constant over time ($r_{\mathsf{HPL}} \sim M$) which leads to:

$$t_{\mathsf{HPL}} \sim \frac{n^3}{r_{\mathsf{HPL}}} \sim \frac{\sqrt{M^3}}{M} = \sqrt{M} \tag{2.20}$$

which is much better than (2.19).

There seems to be a similar problem with the DGEMM as it has the same computational complexity as HPL but fortunately, the $n$ in the formula related to a single process memory size rather than the global one and thus there is no scaling problem.

Lastly, the b_eff test has a different type of problem: its communication complexity is $\mathcal{O}(p^2)$ which is already prohibitive today as the number of processes of the largest system in the HPCC database is almost 150 thousand. This complexity comes from the ping-pong component of b_eff that attempts to find the weakest link between all nodes and thus, theoretically, needs to look at the possible process pairs. The problem was remedied in the reference implementation by adapting the runtime of the test to the size of the system tested.

## 2.8    Conclusions and Future Directions

No single test can accurately compare the performance of any of today's high-end systems let alone any of those envisioned by the HPCS program in the future. Thusly, the HPCC suite stresses not only the processors, but the memory system and the interconnect. It is a better indicator of how a supercomputing system will perform across a spectrum of real-world applications. Now that the more comprehensive HPCC suite is available, it could be used in preference to comparisons and rankings based on single tests. The real utility of the HPCC benchmarks are that architectures can be described with a wider range of metrics than just flop/s from HPL. When looking only at HPL performance and the TOP500 list, inexpensive build-your-own clusters appear to be much more cost effective than more sophisticated parallel architectures. But the tests indicate that even a small percentage of random memory accesses in real applications can significantly affect the overall performance of that application on architectures not designed to minimize or hide memory latency. The HPCC tests provide users with additional information to justify policy and purchasing decisions. We expect to expand and perhaps remove some existing benchmark components as we continue learning about the collection.

Looking forward into the High End Computing hardware trends, HPCC has a role to play in testing supercomputer installations that draw the majority of their performance from hardware accelerators. The trend started with TOP500's first Peta-FLOP computer: Roadrunner based on IBM Cell processors. Currently, GPU-based computers have noticeable presence at the prestigious spots of TOP500. HPCC is well positioned to offer a rich view of such systems and their increased complexity. Hence, we are actively looking into extending HPCC availability for hardware-accelerated machines.

# Chapter 3

# The Green500 List: A Look Back to Look Forward

**Wu-chun Feng, Kirk Cameron, and Thomas Scogland**

*Virginia Tech*

## 3.1 Traditional Supercomputing: Performance, Performance, Performance

From the birth of supercomputing, the metric of importance has been *performance* relative to operations per second, or more specifically, floating-point operations per second (FLOPS). From 1992 to 2007, for example, the performance of supercomputers running embarrassingly parallel codes, such as n-body simulations, improved nearly 10,000-fold. In that same time frame, the performance achieved for each watt of power supplied to the machine improved only 300-fold. While the latter is no small feat, it pales in comparison to the former and implies that the power supplied to supercomputers increased more than 30-fold in that same time frame. Based on this look back to the past, we identified the trend of performance at any cost, where space and power were middling concerns in the face of pure speed.

However, the continual increases in power and cooling demand, along with the need for more space, began to require special-purpose machine rooms, and in some cases, special-purpose buildings, to be constructed. Figure 3.1 points to the cause of the lack of increase in efficiency — the exponentially increasing power density within a compute node. As a consequence, machines on the Top500 List in 2007 reached as high as 7.5 megawatts (MW) in power consumption. With the then-market-value of one megawatt of power being on the

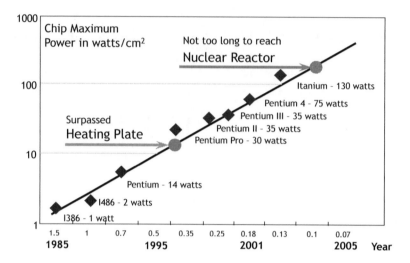

**FIGURE 3.1**: Tracking power density with Moore's law over time.

order of $1 million, this translates to an annual power and cooling budget of $7.5 million. Something had to change.

## 3.2    The Energy Crisis in Supercomputing

With the cost of power, cooling, and facilities all rising rapidly, a departure from the "performance at any cost" mantra came into the public eye in 2002 with the announcement of the "Green Destiny" cluster supercomputer [FWW02, WWF02, Fen03] at Los Alamos National Laboratory (LANL). The cluster used low-power server blades with Transmeta processors and 100-Mb/s networking interfaces, both unheard of in high-performance computing (HPC) at the time, to produce a telephone booth-sized system with significant processing capability, low power, no external cooling, and no special machine room. At the same time and also at LANL, ASCI Q debuted with highly capable compute nodes that consumed significant power and that required a new building to be constructed to meet the power and cooling requirements [Joh02]. In addition, in its two-year lifetime in office space rather than a machine room, Green Destiny experienced no unexpected downtime at all whereas Q suffered failures once every 6.5 hours [FH04].

The juxtaposition between these two radically different approaches to the supercomputing problem created a media firestorm, generally painting a "David vs. Goliath" story for the public [Joh02]. On the other hand, in the supercomputing community, Green Destiny, the first major low-power instantiation of the *Supercomputing in Small Spaces* project, received significant criticism and ridicule. Furthermore, the main takeaway of Green Destiny by the supercomputing community was arguably the wrong one. That is, the supercomputing community embraced the increased computational density achieved by using blades but chose to ignore the decreased power density gained by using low-power processors in that environment. The result, then and now, has been a slew of blade-based supercomputing solutions with exceptionally high and increasing power density, as shown in Figure 3.2.

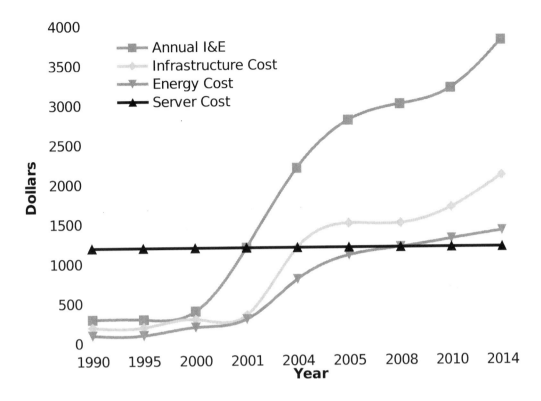

**FIGURE 3.2**: ASHRAE heat-density projection.

For a time, increases in fan speed, quality, or quantity or the addition of heat pipes sufficiently dissipated the increased heat. With increased power density, however, this approach has effectively reached its limit. New architectures are now using liquid cooling, immersion in inert gas, or various other strategies to keep the trend progressing but at a significant material cost.

As a consequence, major players in the datacenter and HPC markets often negotiate favorable energy deals with electrical utility providers to build or upgrade power substations near their computing facilities. With respect to commercial datacenters, examples include Google, Microsoft, and Yahoo! [MH06], while in HPC research, examples include Los Alamos National Laboratory [CCN03], Oak Ridge National Laboratory [ORN07], National Center for Supercomputing Applications [Mei08], and National Security Agency [Gor06, NSA08]. And when not enough power infrastructure can be built at or near such computing facilities, many institutions *move* their computing facilities to the power source, e.g., Google [MH06, Ahm08] and Microsoft [Van06].

However, the above is not a sustainable solution at scale. Instead, as we have seen in recent years, the power and energy efficiency of these systems need to be improved to make more effective use of electricity, particularly for those datacenter or HPC centers that are constrained by the physical power entering a computing facility. As a consequence, power- and energy-efficient computing consortiums and projects have garnered interest from the general populace and supercomputer vendors. Examples of such initiatives include Energy Star [Ene08], SPECPower [spe08], Green Data Centres [gre08], ClimateSavers [cli08], 80-Plus [80p08], and of course, the Green500 [gre], which we discuss next.

## 3.3    The Green500 List

From the turn of the millennium through the first decade of the millennium, the awareness and necessity of green supercomputing continued to increase and build momentum in the HPC community [Fen05, ShHcF06, Fen06]. The Green500 worked with academics, vendors and government agencies to raise awareness of the dire state of energy efficiency in supercomputing throughout this time, and through these interactions, it became evident that while the community was reasonably backing FLOPS as the metric of speed, there was no accepted metric to evaluate large systems running scientific codes [hHcFA05].

The first step in improving anything is measuring it, so a fair metric had to be found, but just measuring performance is not enough. To truly inspire improvement, there must be a mark to beat, a prize to compete for, and in the supercomputing world, the Top500 list provided this for speed. The Top500 serves as a highly visible venue in which labs, companies, and countries of the world compete to be the fastest in the world. What the community needed was a venue in which to compete with respect to energy efficiency, in view of the public eye, with standardized methods and comparable results. Thus was born the Green500.

The Green500 sought to create a common metric for evaluating large-scale computers running scientific codes and to analyze and display the results found by that metric to the world. Two main questions had to be answered before the first list could be created. First, what will the metric be? Second, what machines will be ranked? These questions were much debated between a keynote talk by Feng [Fen05], which first generated interest in the idea in 2005 and the initial release for the first Green500 list two years later in 2007.

### 3.3.1    Measuring Efficiency

For the Green500, both speed and power consumption are first-order constraints. Ranking computers by power consumption, in absence of performance, would certainly yield a different ranking than by speed, but would it be useful? Such a ranking would make no distinction between a computer which draws a megawatt of power over an hour to run a job as one that draws the same to complete the job in 1 minute. Clearly that is not sufficient for our purposes. As such, an aggregate metric is required, which factors in both the speed and the power draw of a given machine while running at that speed.

For the first half of the metric, the speed, the TOP500 already provides a well-accepted solution, the FLOPS metric as measured by the Linpack benchmark. While we, and the principals of the TOP500 as well, acknowledge that Linpack is not a perfect metric for all branches of High Performance Computing (HPC), it is a well-known, consistent benchmark that has persisted through the release of many alternative benchmarks over the years. For these reasons Linpack was chosen as the initial benchmark, with the caveat that it might one day change, and it continues to be the primary benchmark used for the Green500 today.

As to the power or energy measurement itself, and the method to be used for combining them, the decision was less clear-cut. Two primary options were considered: $ED^n$ and FLOPS per watt.

#### 3.3.1.1    Energy Delay Product ($ED^n$)

Commonly applied to circuit design, $ED^n$ combines energy and performance by a simple product, with the abbreviation actually referring to the equation used to compute the metric. The equation in full is $ED^n$, with $E$ representing the energy consumed during an operation, $D$ for the time to complete that same benchmark, and finally $n$ representing a weighting factor for the delay term. This equation effectively accentuates the relationship between performance and efficiency, as running a machine of the same power for less time will result in lower energy use in the end, but biases the results heavily toward faster computers. As $n$ increases, so does the weight given to performance, to the point that small changes in performance so outweigh the contribution of the energy component as to render it insignificant.

### 3.3.1.2 FLOPS per Watt

FLOPS per watt is slightly different. Rather than weighting a component of energy, it measures the amount of performance gained for every watt of power drawn. This avoids the issue of skewing results in the favor of machines with higher performance, but actually has the effect of skewing results toward smaller supercomputers. While the metric itself is not inherently skewed, supercomputers are made up of sets of discrete components, usually nodes in the common cluster design. As you scale the number of nodes, power scales at least linearly with each node added, while performance scales at most linearly. The discrepancy between these means that smaller computers generally produce more FLOPS per node even when composed of the same node hardware as a larger counterpart.

Nonetheless, FLOPS per watt is relatively simple to measure with a minimum of equipment, and already had some traction in the scientific community. As such, FLOPS per watt was chosen to be the official metric of the Green500. We further reduce this bias by requiring a minimum performance threshold to be considered for any Green500 list, more on the alternative lists later on in Section 3.4, such that one cannot submit a single node low power embedded machine to compete with a multi-petaflop supercomputer. The other effect of this is that if a large supercomputer wishes to, they may submit a Linpack run and power measurement taken using a fraction of the machine which still meets that performance requirement, thus allowing for fair efficiency comparisons between machines of varied scales.

### 3.3.2 The First List

The first Green500 list was released at Supercomputing 2007 in Reno, Nevada, and it ranked the 500 fastest supercomputers in the world by their energy efficiency. It is important to note that while the goal of the Green500 list is increasing the awareness of efficiency in computing, and driving a general increase in computer energy efficiency, it does not rank the most energy efficient computers in the world. This was a carefully thought out choice, driven by the desire to focus on large, data-center scale, machines and the large scientific workloads which run on them. In this fashion the Green500 list rewards machines which achieve high performance with high efficiency, and punishes those which achieve high performance at the cost of efficiency.

This first list was almost entirely peak power numbers, power numbers derived from system information, data-sheets and design documents rather than actual measurements, except for those from IBM and some at larger labs which already had power measurement infrastructure in place. IBM's interest in power measurement becomes clear when you look at the distribution of the top of the first Green500, as depicted in Table 3.1, where IBM's Blue Gene architecture dominated the top 26 ranks of the list. An important feature to notice in that same table is that both the number 1 and number 2 machines from the TOP500 made it into the top of the Green500 list. The rest of the top 10 from the TOP500, as depicted in Table 3.2, did not all fare so well, falling as far down as rank 325 on the Green500. Even so, notice that none of them fell below 350. This was a promising sign,

**TABLE 3.1**: The top 10 unique efficiency entries in the November 2007 Green500.

| Rank | Computer | Mflops/Watt | TOP500 | how |
|---|---|---|---|---|
| 1 | Blue Gene/P Solution | 357.23 | 121 | submission |
| 2 | Blue Gene/P Solution | 352.25 | 40 | submission |
| 3 | Blue Gene/P Solution | 346.95 | 24 | submission |
| 4 | Blue Gene/P Solution | 336.21 | 2 | submission |
| 5 | Blue Gene/P Solution | 310.93 | 41 | submission |
| 6-12 | eServer Blue Gene Solution | 210.56 | . . . | submission |
| 13-20 | eServer Blue Gene Solution | 208.31 | . . . | submission |
| 21 | eServer Blue Gene Solution | 205.27.56 | 1 | submission |
| 22 | eServer Blue Gene Solution | 205.06 | 93 | submission |
| 23 | eServer Blue Gene Solution | 204.24 | 37 | submission |

**TABLE 3.2**: The top 10 Top500 ranks in November 2007.

| Rank | Computer | Mflops/Watt | Green500 | how |
|---|---|---|---|---|
| 21 | eServer Blue Gene Solution | 205.27 | 1 | submission |
| 4 | Blue Gene/P Solution | 336.21 | 2 | submission |
| 34 | SGI Altix ICE 8200 | 148.11 | 3 | submission |
| 90 | Cluster Platform 3000 BL460c | 83.94 | 4 | peak |
| 96 | Cluster Platform 3000 BL460c | 75.92 | 5 | peak |
| 273 | Sandia/ Cray Red Storm | 45.63 | 6 | peak |
| 270 | Cray XT4/XT3 | 47.52 | 7 | submission |
| 26 | eServer Blue Gene Solution | 203.77 | 8 | submission |
| 325 | Cray XT4 | 37.2 | 9 | peak |
| 24 | eServer Blue Gene Solution | 203.77 | 10 | submission |

signaling even at the beginning that new machines being built for maximum performance were also being built for efficiency.

On the opposite end of the spectrum, the bottom of the first Green500 list also saw some interesting entries. Both the Japanese Earth Simulator and ASCI Q remained on the TOP500 at that point, and ranked at 497 and 500, respectively, on the Green500 with Mflops/watt scores of 5.6 and 3.65, fully 2 *orders of magnitude* less efficient than the number one machine at 357.23. At that point both machines were still in the top 100 on the TOP500 list.

### 3.3.3    Community Response and List Evolution

Over the course of a year after the release of the first list, the Green500 was fortunate enough to hold two birds-of-a-feather (BoF) sessions, one at the International Supercomputing Conference in June 2008 and the other at SC08 in November of 2008. The release had brought many questions, issues, and ideas to the fore in the community and these sessions, along with those held annually since, gave us a chance to discuss these issues openly. Through these discussions, several recommendations and issues came to the surface that drove the evolution of the list.

1. *What machines should the list rank?* The Green500 List should be more than just a re-ordering of the TOP500 List, open the floor to smaller supercomputers to compete on efficiency, rather than competing on performance then ranking by efficiency.

2. *What benchmark(s) should be used?* The initial reaction to the Linpack benchmark was not highly positive, as it fails to stress many components of the system which contribute to energy efficiency of real codes. Specifically the HPCC benchmark suite was suggested as a replacement.

3. *How much of the infrastructure should be included?* There was no agreement on whether infrastructure, cooling, etc., should be included or not in the overall measurement. Beyond that there were issues with what could be allowed and disallowed, is cooling integrated into a blade chassis not counted for example, and if it's not how can it be factored out of the total power?

### 3.3.3.1 What Is the Requirement to Qualify?

This first bit of feedback was one that hit home immediately. The issue with the initial incarnation of the Green500 is that to qualify to be on it, a machine must make the TOP500 list. While the goal is to rank supercomputers, do they have to be the 500 fastest supercomputers in the world? In order to address this issue the decision was made to produce an experimental list, referred to as the Little Green500, in November of 2009. Rather than ranking the current TOP500 supercomputers, the Little Green500 ranks the 500 most efficient supercomputers which either have been in the TOP500 list in the 18 months prior to the release, or beat the performance of the computer ranked number 500 on the TOP500 18 months before. In that way the list defines a supercomputer as any computer of sufficient performance to have been ranked on the TOP500 18 months before, giving us a moving target that allows smaller machines to submit new numbers without allowing them to be so small as to no longer be reasonably considered supercomputers. Since 2009, the Little list has become a regular part of each Green500 release and occasionally draws in interesting smaller machines that the main list would have missed.

In addition to the little list, there was still the issue of what the procedure for taking measurements would be. What part of the run is measured, how much of the machine is required, and other questions of that nature were left unanswered at first. In November of 2011, the first official run rules for the Green500 were released, specifying many of the minutiae necessary to keep measurements reasonable and consistent across computers. Since then, the Green500 rules have been refined, and the Energy Efficient High Performance Computing Working Group (EEHPCWG) has been established between members of the Green500, TOP500, GreenGrid, and others to create a general standard for the quality of a power measurement which could be used across lists to evaluate a measurement.

### 3.3.3.2 What Benchmark Should Be Run?

Linpack has been a point of contention as long as it has been used in the Green500. Right at the beginning, the community began to clamber for something else, often suggesting a transition to the HPCC benchmark suite to cover more components of a given system. In response, as with the Little list, a new experimental list was created in November of 2009 meant to rank computers by their energy efficiency based on the results of running the HPCC benchmarks. Since the HPCC benchmarks do not result in a single overall score, the list would actually be made up of a variety of rankings based on the subsystem a user was interested in. This became an interesting test case, because the drive in the community for this list appeared to go just far enough to ask for the list, but not far enough to submit to it. In the three years the list was available for submission, one was received. The general consensus from submitters was that the time necessary to get an optimized Linpack run, which is no small feat in and of itself, was enough, whereas attempting to get working optimal runs of all of HPCC was simply not an option for many sites. The Green500 team continues to investigate new benchmarks and metrics, but to the time of this writing, nothing has been found to displace Linpack or FLOPS/watt as the benchmark and metric of choice.

### 3.3.3.3 How Much Gets Counted?

Initially, this discussion focused on major infrastructural elements such as cooling, networking, and datacenter level PDU energy use. While not to the satisfaction of all, the decision was made to include only system energy, eliding networking, cooling, and other costs outside the node or rack. As computer designs have progressed however, gray areas have arisen which complicate this matter significantly. In particular, the issue of cooling which is partially integrated, or internally fan-cooled machines being ranked against machines that are cooled completely by water pumped by an outside device, or issues of network power, as pertains to a NIC in a node. These issues are currently handled by allowing submissions to include a list of what is and what is not included in their power measurement, and this has in fact become part of the measurement quality standard being developed by the EEHPCWG.

---

## 3.4 Emerging Trends and the Greening of Supercomputing

Since the list began in 2007, the energy efficiency of the fastest computers in the world has increased at a steady and rapid pace. In fact, comparing the average efficiency over all 500 to Moore's law shows a strong correlation, while the maximum surges far ahead of that mark increasing much faster than the list as a whole. The vast discrepancy between the highest machines on the list, especially IBM's Blue Gene/Q architecture, and those nearer the average point in the middle of the list raises the average efficiency enough to track Moore's law, though the median actually lags well behind that mark. The results for all lists released to the time of this writing can be seen in Figure 3.3. Each list release the spread between the highest efficiency machines and the average grows wider. Now it has come to the point where all of the machines highest on the list are considered statistical outliers from the rest of the list.

### 3.4.1 The Effect of Accelerators

Accelerator based computers began making serious inroads on the list in November of 2008. While they were by no means common, there were less than 10 Cell accelerator based computers on the list in November of that year, they accounted for the top seven ranks of the Green500. Since then many have begun employing accelerators to increase the energy efficiency of their machines. From 2008-2010 Cell machines were in vogue, and from 2009 to 2011 GPU-based clusters have been making inroads. The efficiency of these accelerator based machines in comparison to the rest of the list can be seen in Figure 3.4. The overall energy efficiency of heterogeneous, or accelerator based, machines has been above that of commodity homogeneous machines from the start, and this is true for both Cell- and GPU-based computers. The differentiation comes when one looks at the performance efficiency

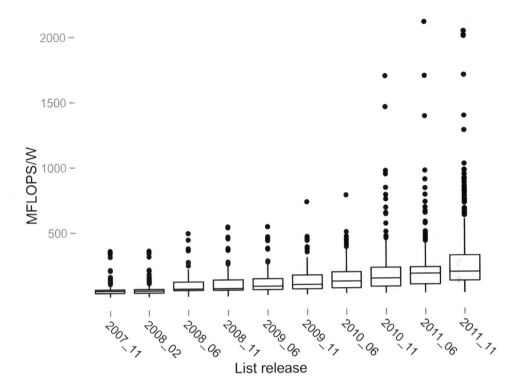

**FIGURE 3.3**: Energy efficiency statistics across Green500 releases.

achieved by machines built using one accelerator or the other. By performance efficiency, we mean the percentage of the theoretical performance of a machine which it actually achieves. The median efficiency of Cell-based machines is consistently over 60%, and in 2009 was just under 80%. GPU machines on the other hand have a median performance efficiency of around 40-50% consistently, implying that while the machines are energy efficient, they are actually wasting 50% or more of their total potential. This can be thought of two ways, it is unfortunate that 50% of the machine's potential is unused, but by the same token, if 100% performance efficiency could be achieved on a GPU-like architecture, it could double the already high energy efficiency of GPU machines. As the list continues, this is a trend we look forward to tracking.

### 3.4.2 Trends for the Future

Every time we reach a new supercomputing high mark, the industry looks toward the next one, usually one representing three orders of magnitude higher FLOPS. With the crossing of the Petaflop barrier in the late aughties, everyone now looks toward Exascale. Planning for that milestone, DARPA's Exascale Computing Study [BBC+08] analyzed the various challenges we are likely to face in attempting to meet it by 2018. Unlike in many studies of its kind in the past, which focused on the necessary bottlenecks in computing performance, this study focuses greatly on power and energy issues. Given predictions that

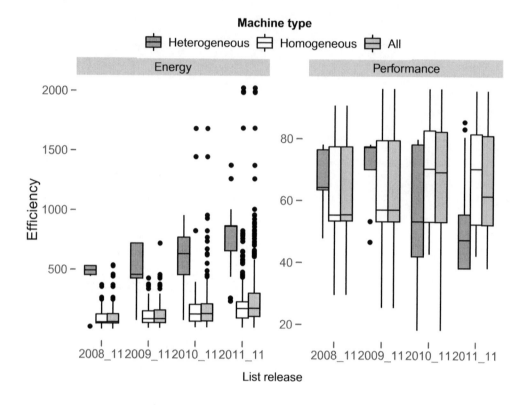

**FIGURE 3.4**: Energy vs. performance efficiency across Green500 releases.

an exascale system may require as much as 100 MW to run, this is entirely understandable, and the goal is a 20-MW exaflop supercomputer in the same time frame. Given that the #1 supercomputer on the TOP500 list in November of 2011 consumes 12MW to produce 10 Petaflops, even the 100 MW mark seems at first a lofty goal. As 2018 approaches, we have begun to focus on using the information gathered as part of the Green500 list to track the advancements made toward the goal of a 20MW exaflop computer, as well as where we would be if we built an exaflop computer today.

One way we track this progress is to draw a projection of the amount of power it would take to run an exaflop computer made entirely out of today's supercomputers. To do this we choose a machine, here the number one ranked machine from the Green500 and Top500 lists, and expand it to exascale by (erroneously) assuming linear scaling of both performance and power. The result of that extrapolation for all top machines since we began the list in 2007 is presented in Figure 3.5. We also include a trend line and 30% confidence interval for each series.

It is important to note that when reading this figure, the Y axis is not, as one would hope, in megawatts, but rather in gigawatts, as that is the more appropriate unit of measure for our current state. We have come a very long way from that first list in 2007. If we had tried to build an exaflop computer then out of the Top500's number 1 rank, even with perfect linear scaling, it would have required almost 5 GW to run. Doing the same with the most energy efficient machine of the time would have required 3 GW. Better, but certainly not

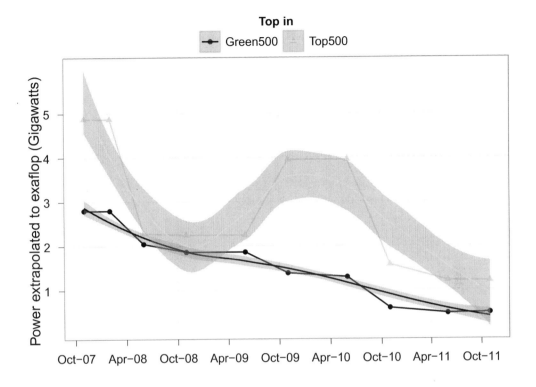

**FIGURE 3.5**: Power projections for exascale systems.

feasible. Over the last four years however, we have come to a point where it could be done for as low as 500 MW. Still a far cry from the goal of 20, but a monumental achievement of engineering. We eagerly anticipate the progress of the coming years, and await the coming shift in the trend. You see, the trend lines, that are sweeping down so quickly in nice lines toward zero, are doing so at a rate which would have our exaflop supercomputers generating power.

# Part II

# Contemporary HPC

# Chapter 4

# Tera 100

**Mickaël Amiet, Patrick Carribault, Elisabeth Charon, Guillaume Colin de Verdière, Philippe Deniel, Gilles Grospellier, Guénolé Harel, François Jollet, Jacques-Charles Lafoucrière, Jacques-Bernard Lekien, Stéphane Mathieu, Marc Pérache, Jean-Christophe Weill, and Gilles Wiber**

*CEA, DAM, DIF*

## 4.1    Overview

### 4.1.1    Sponsor/Program Background

The Tera 100 is the third machine of the Tera program implemented by CEA/DAM. CEA/DAM is a division of CEA (Commissariat à l'énergie atomique et aux énergies alternatives, Direction des Applications Militaires) in charge of building the French Deterrence.

Since the late fifties, France has had a research program to develop nuclear warheads. This program has always used numerical simulation. In 1992, French President Francois Mitterrand decided on a moratorium on nuclear testing which increased the use of HPC at CEA/DAM. In 1996, after a last test campaign, President Jacques Chirac decreed the end of French nuclear tests and the start of the simulation program. This program is based on large physics instruments like the "Laser Mégajoule" or the radiography facility "AIRIX" and on numerical simulation. The objective was to increase by a factor of 20,000 the computing power available to CEA/DAM.

The Tera program started as early as 1996, when France decided to end its nuclear tests and design and guarantee its deterrence through simulation. More than 15 years ago, CEA realized that, in order to fulfill our mission, we needed to deliver to our users a petaflop class machine by 2010.

This computing power was achieved in three steps, ×100 in 2001 (Tera 1), ×1,000 in 2005 (Tera 10), ×25,000 in 2010 (Tera 100), to get a petaflop system. The three Tera systems are based on the same architecture: cluster of commodity servers with a high performance interconnect and an increasing use of open source technologies. These three systems are also large data producers and consumers: Tera 1 needed 7.5 GB/s, Tera 10 100 GB/s, and Tera 100 a mere 500 GB/s.

Tera 1 was a major shift from a long tradition of CRAY vector machines which ended with a CRAY T90. To build Tera 1, we changed our design requirements from using highly efficient proprietary components to using COTS.[1] This introduced the CEA developers to

---

[1] Component off the Shelf

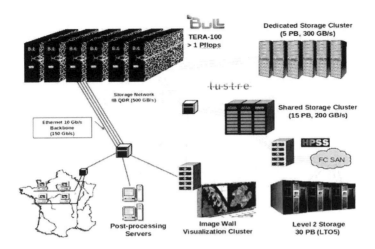

**FIGURE 4.1**: Architecture of the Tera facility.

the world of massive parallelism. Designed by Compaq (then maintained by HP), Tera 1 used the famous Alpha processor with a special Quadrics Elan 3 interconnect.

Designed by BULL, Tera 10 capitalized on Tera 1 lessons and kept the same architecture (a cluster of SMP using the Quadrics Elan 4 interconnect) while moving to Intel's Itanium processor. It was a very stable machine with a high level of productivity. At this step we started using the Lustre filesystem (Figure 4.1).

Tera 100, also designed by BULL, pushed the design even further in relying on the ubiquitous x86_64 architecture, thus providing a seamless environment to our users from the desktop to the supercomputer. We also shifted from the Quadrics interconnect to InfiniBand, which will be described in a later section. A comparison of the Tera machines can be found in Figure 4.5.

Tera 100 is an exceptional general purpose computer, designed for classified workloads coming from various CEA/DAM laboratories. This machine demonstrates unique capabilities as we will show.

### 4.1.2 Timeline

The third step of the simulation program, Tera 100 (Figure 4.2) could not be achieved by the natural evolution of HPC (Moore's law). In particular the new system had to use the same computer room as the Tera 1 system, so it had to be much more dense than what we could expect from the HPC market. The density, the I/O needs, and the efficiency required by CEA/DAM simulation chain brought us to start in 2008 a new way of procurement for this system. For Tera 1 and Tera 10, we made classical RFP for a system; for Tera 100 the project team made an RFP for a shared research program and the machine was an option of this contract which would be exercised if and only if the research program was successful.

The research program started in 2008 and ran for two years. It covered all the aspects of an HPC system used for large production. The main results are:

- a cooling rack based on cold water able to cool up to 40 KW;

- a high density 4 socket Xeon Nehalem server (8 sockets in 3 U);

- a high density 2 socket Xeon Nehalem blade server and a flexible chassis;

**FIGURE 4.2**: Tera 100. (©P. Stroppa/CEA.)

- a new server power distribution based on a capacitor allowing up to 500 ms of electrical power loss;

- a petaflop cluster software stack;

- an InfiniBand topology based on fat-tree islands.

After 18 months of research a prototype system was delivered at CEA. This prototype allowed CEA teams to validate the computer room integration, the software stack, and the hardware technologies. The prototype had a computing power close to the Tera 10 system and was stable enough to allow a successful port of main CEA/DAM codes on the new platform. This success prompted CEA to order the final configuration.

The new cooling system based on cold water injected in the rack door (see Figure 4.17) introduced major changes in the computer room:

- many large pipes had to be installed under the raised floor to bring a water loop to each rack;

- all the power distribution had to be removed from the raised floor and be redone from the ceiling;

- an increase of 6 MW in power distribution was needed.

Tera 100 was installed from March 2010 to September 2010. The best Linpack run happened on October $12^{th}$ (see the benchmark section). The machine was ranked as the first machine in Europe in 2010 and the $6^{th}$ machine of the TOP500 list. After a few weeks of grand challenge computations, the system moved to production in early 2011. The Tera 10 machine was decommissioned on July 2011.

---

## 4.2    Applications and Workloads

As previously stated, Tera 100 is a general purpose computer which handles both production runs for the designers as well as more research-oriented ones conducted by our physicists. This means that the machine, by design, is able to run a wealth of different codes. The spectrum ranges from multimillion lines of $C++$/FORTRAN multi-physics hydro codes to small $C++$ programs intended to investigate some highly specialized aspects of physics or chemistry.

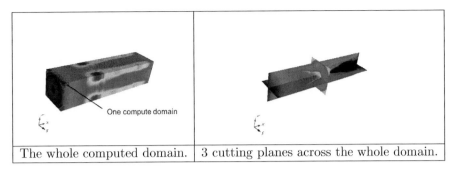

| The whole computed domain. | 3 cutting planes across the whole domain. |

**FIGURE 4.3**: Example of a 4-billion cell computation done on 4096 cores of Tera 100, visualized using our LOVE package.

All the codes are able to run in parallel yet some are less scalable than others. A simulation can span on for multiple weeks if not months. Therefore, it is allowed to run typically by slots of 10 hours monitored by an in-house meta scheduler (called KMS).

The numerous codes cover a variety of fields. The following list is only part of them:

- Nuclear Physics: With our codes, we fully simulate a nuclear weapon.

- Laser Physics: These codes are essential tools to predict and do the interpretation of the experiments we will conduct in our facility called the "Laser Mégajoule" located near Bordeaux. This unique installation requires the most advanced simulation codes to understand the extreme conditions taking place during the experiments.

- Material Sciences: For its mission, CEA uses various materials which have strange physical properties in the long run. To understand the behavior of matter, we have developed codes to peek at the lowest level of matter (at the atom level and beyond). Some of the codes are developed in collaboration with universities, as in the case of ABINIT, which we will describe in the next section.

- Engineering: FLUENT, ABAQUS, and other commercial packages are used to study the properties of the objects manufactured by CEA/DAM.

- Earth Science: Through knowledge gained from underground tests, CEA/DAM has harvested a unique expertise in geosciences which is now used in homeland security projects such as CENALT (CENtre d'Alerte aux Tsunamis). For this mission, highly efficient and predictive codes are needed.

- Post-processing and Visualization: Such a large machine as Tera 100 allows for the largest simulations. We had to develop a visualization system able to cope with the multi-terabyte data set produced by our record-breaking I/O subsystem. This is the LOVE[2] environment built on top of ParaView and VTK. Figure 4.3 illustrates a "Grand Challenge" computation impossible to visualize without LOVE.

None of the aforementioned applications are used as benchmarks for our procurements. For that, we rely on a set of specially tailored kernels or programs as described in Section 4.22.

---

[2]Large Object Visualization Environment

### 4.2.1    Highlights of Main Applications

Two examples illustrate the contribution of HPC to condensed matter physics.

The first one deals with the quantum level: some thermodynamical properties of solids can be computed taking into account the complex interactions between the electrons. It is indeed possible, from first principles, to derive the total energy, charge density, electronic structure, and miscellaneous properties of systems made of electrons and nuclei (molecules and periodic solids), using for instance, a plane wave basis for the wavefunctions of the electrons. This is done in the framework of the Density Functional Theory (DFT) in the electronic structure code ABINIT [Gon08]. This code is a package, delivered under the GNU General Public Licence (GPL) in which multiple levels of parallelization have been developed using the MPI library for the current stable version. According to the kind of system, it is now possible to use it on several thousands of processors. The ABINIT code has been used to compute the low-temperature and high-pressure properties of solid hydrogen [Lou12] and deuterium. A discrete implementation of the Feynmann path-integral formulation of quantum statistical physics has been employed, within a four-level parallelization (on k-points, bands, FFT grids, and imaginary time slices), allowing very efficient computations on several thousands of CPU cores (typically 2048 or 4096 according to the system size), and production of very long trajectories up to 100,000 steps. Such massively parallel calculations allowed us to identify the structure of phase II of solid deuterium and hydrogen, and evidence a strong isotope effect in this phase. The phase II of solid hydrogen, characterized by very large and asymmetric nuclear quantum fluctuations, can be qualified as "quantum fluxional solid," i.e., it is not possible to associate an underlying classical structure to this solid.

The atomic scale is the subject of the second one. Knowing the interaction potential between atoms, it is possible to follow the evolution of a system under Newton's laws applied to a great number of atoms. This has been applied to the numerical study of the Tantalum single crystal spallation using X-micro tomography and non-equilibrium classical molecular dynamics. Experimentally, a single crystal is illuminated by a laser pulse which induces the propagation of a strong unsustained shock. The analyzed data are mainly the number and the shape of pores resulting from the tensile inside the material when the incident shock reflects on the opposite face. Experimental pore size distribution exhibits two power laws attributed to the growth and the coalescence stages. Large-scale molecular dynamics simulations mimic at reduced scale (1/200) the real experiment (Figure 4.4). It is possible to extract from the simulation similar data to that in the experiment. The pore size distribution shows three power laws identified as the nucleation, the growth, and the

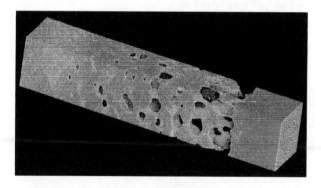

**FIGURE 4.4**: Molecular dynamics simulation of the production of a shock induced tantalum scale.

coalescence stages. The slopes of the last two stages are very similar to the experimental one, confirming the scale invariance of this data as suggested by their analytical form. Such simulations have been made possible thanks to the molecular dynamics STAMP code, which has been especially designed to use the MPI library. The scalability of the code is excellent up to 15,000 processors. A typical spallation [LS12] calculation requires 100 million atoms on 5,000 processors for 50h.

### 4.2.2  Benchmark Results

The acceptance of a new machine relies on the successful run of a set of well-known benchmarks. We use basic benchmarks such as the "Stream" to verify the specifications of the machine. We also have a set of small kernels to check that the codes will run on the new platform. Naturally, we also have larger benchmarks to demonstrate the real potential of the new supercomputer such as the Linpack and TeraTF.[3]

From all the benchmarks we ran for the cluster acceptance, two of them were really big challenges:

- The Linpack: we reached 1.05 Pflops out of 1.25 PFlops peak (efficiency: 83.42%) with a 22-hour run on 4,324 nodes (138,624 cores).

- ES4, a CEA checkpoint restart application benchmark, has demonstrated 300GB/s of the internal Lustre filesystem and 200GB/s for the external one.

TeraTF, a specific CEA benchmark (similar to our codes) reached a performance of 13.18 TFlops sustained on 8,000 cores. This run was to assert the nonregression of Tera 100 compared to the former production machine Tera 10.

## 4.3  System Overview

The Tera 100 system is more than a petaflop computing machine; it is a full computing center with all the services requested by CEA users. The global architecture is data centric (see Figure 4.1) and based on two main networks: a storage network dedicated to data transfers and an access network for all other protocols. Tera systems connected to these networks are:

- The compute cluster named Tera 100

- Tera 100 global shared high performance parallel filesystem cluster, based on Lustre, named GL100

- Tera 100 archival cluster, based on HPSS,[4] named ST100

- Tera 100 high performance NFS service, based on BlueArc servers, named NFS100

- Tera 100 visualization cluster, which drives an image wall, named VIZ100

As shown in Figure 4.5, Tera 100 is a cluster of 4,370 quadri sockets nodes connected by an InfiniBand QDR network. The nodes are connected by a pruned Fat Tree made of 324

---

[3]TeraTF is part of the Spec MPI benchmark suite, see http://www.spec.org/mpi2007
[4]http://www.hpss-collaboration.org/

|  | Tera 1 | Tera 10 | Tera 100 |
|---|---|---|---|
| Number of nodes | 640 | 544 | 4370 |
| Number of racks | 180 | 260 | 220 |
| Number of cores | 2560 | 17408 | 138000 |
| Peak performance | 5TF | 60TF | 1.25PF |
| Processor | Alpha EV68 | Intel Montecito | Intel X7560 @ 2.27GHz |
| Interconnect | Quadrics Elan 3 | Quadrics Elan 4 | IB QDR |
| Memory size | 2.5TB | 30TB | 307TB |
| Disk size | 50TB | 1PB | 20PB |
| Electrical power | 600kW | 1.7MW | 5MW |

**FIGURE 4.5**: Overview of the different Tera supercomputers.

node islands (full fat tree) with a pruning ratio of 1:6. The global memory is 300 TB; the local Lustre filesystem runs at 300 GB/s for a size of 5PBytes. Tera 100 consumes around 5 MW.

The storage network is based on InfiniBand QDR technology, for a usable bandwidth of 200 GB/s from compute cluster to storage cluster.

The storage cluster, GL100, serves a 15 PBytes filesystem at 200 GB/s.

The archival cluster, ST100, manages 20 PBytes of tapes.

All these items will be discussed in the next sections.

## 4.4   Hardware Architecture

CEA-DAM Ile-de-France (in short CEA/DIF) computing center has just integrated a petaflopic cluster and is preparing a second one which will be connected to the European supercomputers network. Installing and bringing to production such machines, we face major challenges.

Everything began with the evaluation of users' needs which is not a trivial thing to do. Afterwards, translating those into computing power is another challenge. The only answer to this need is a cluster architecture.

The Tera 100 cluster is built with different types of compute nodes:

- 4370 standard nodes (bullx S6010) composed of 4 Intel Nehalem-EX processors 2.27GHz (8 cores each), 64GB of DDR3 memory (2GB /core), SATA or SSD local disk, and one ConnectX QDR card

- 298 hybrid nodes: each blade has 2 processors with 24GB of memory and 2 NVIDIA GPU M2090 T20A (Figure 4.6).

- 55 "fat memory" nodes: each node has 16 Nehalem-EX processors 2.27GHz (8 cores each) and 512GB of memory (4GB/core). It is four standard compute nodes which are connected with a Bull Coherency Switch (BCS).

Each kind of node has its own specificity especially the hybrid nodes which are used for computing power, future architecture codes design, and also local and remote visualization.

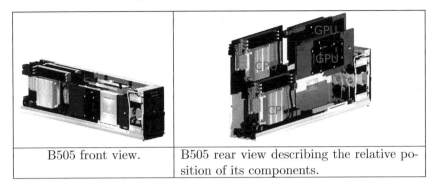

| B505 front view. | B505 rear view describing the relative position of its components. |

**FIGURE 4.6**: The bullx B505 hybrid blade architecture. (©BULL.)

CEA and Bull designed this cluster with a lot of optimizations. For example, to increase compute capability per rack, the shape of each node has been designed: it has an "L" shape so we can put 2 nodes of 4 sockets in 3 U (Figure 4.18) instead of a classical 4 U.

A cluster is not only characterized by the compute power but also by its I/O capability: 5PB internal parallel filesystem at 300GB/s (16 I/O cells made of 4 I/O nodes and 1 SFA10KT DDN storage controller) and a capability to export data with a bandwidth of 200GB/s (through 42 Lustre router nodes).

To connect all these components, a pruned fat tree QDR interconnect was built in which full fat tree islands of 324 nodes were placed (as depicted in Figure 4.7). Each island is about 94 Tflops and all the 13 islands are connected together with 27 switches of 36 ports. The pruning ratio is 1:6.

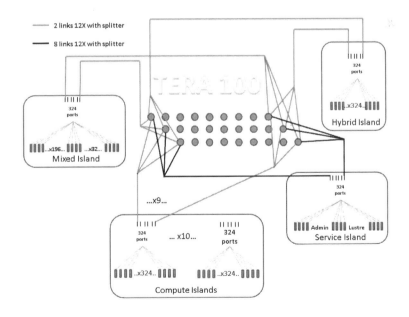

**FIGURE 4.7**: Tera 100 network topology.

| System | |
|---|---|
| OS type | Linux |
| Release Name | Bull AES 2.1, RHEL 6.1 based |
| Compilers | |
| ifort | Intel |
| icc | Intel |
| gcc | OpenSource |
| Debuggers | |
| TotalView | RogueWave |
| DDT | Allinea |
| Profilers | |
| Vtune | Intel |
| valgrind | OpenSource |
| System Management | |
| Robinhood | OpenSource |
| NFS-Ganesha | OpenSource |
| ClusterShell | OpenSource |
| Shine | OpenSource |
| Job Management | |
| Slurm | OpenSource |
| Parallel Filesytem | |
| Lustre | OpenSource |

**FIGURE 4.8**: The software stack of the Tera 100 supercomputer.

CEA and Bull experts managed to install, put in production, and stabilize such a large cluster within a few months. Today the cluster is loaded at more than 90%, filled by users' requests, and demonstrates more than 98% of availability.

## 4.5    System Software

The operating system of the cluster is based on a modified RedHat 6.1 with Lustre 2.1 and the resources manager SLURM integrated by Bull. The whole cluster is managed and monitored by 2 nodes for failover sake. The whole stack is described in Figure 4.8. As one can note, most of it is part of a regular Linux environment.

The remainder of this section will cast some light on a number of Open Source projects CEA developed in order to "drive" the machine.

### 4.5.1    Open Source Software: A New Way of Conducting Industrial Collaboration

Since its early times in the mid-90s, the Tera compute center has known three different generations. Each of them had its own hardware and software architecture, reflecting the evolution of HPC technologies.

Focusing on the software stack, the feedback from various operating systems and products that have been used over the last 15 years shows one thing: HPC is a niche and it is not in any vendor's interest to put all of their resources into it. They will often prefer to invest in a less prestigious yet more profitable area like enterprise IT. This has an immediate consequence: vendor provided HPC tools often look like variations of products dedicated to smaller architectures, which quickly leads to scalability issues. So, if you do not find anything fitting your needs, then do it yourself and develop your own solution.

This may sound like a silly conclusion, but it makes more sense with the advent of the Open Source paradigm. The Free Software and Open Source community are a big chance for HPC and definitely a wise path to be followed in building and designing software. HPC sites have very similar needs, and it is easy for them to gather and cooperate inside a spontaneous community, sharing everyone's experience and knowledge. The bounds between sites and with their respective hardware/software providers is not a burden anymore and can even become an advantage: vendors can join the community as well and participate in the Open Source experience. This can lead to a win-win situation in which HPC sites and leaders of the industry become partners. The HPC folks will get exactly what they want by becoming the designers and actively participating in the development of the tools they use every day. The industry benefits from the knowledge of the community. It is able to drive its technical choice in the same direction as its customer's need and it offers in return all of its industrial knowledge in testing and hardening the solution.

This section will show four examples of such a collaboration made at CEA.

#### 4.5.1.1 RobinHood Policy Engine

Managing a filesystem is a task that can become very difficult as the size of the filesystem increases. While searching files with given properties inside terabytes of local storage takes a few minutes, the same operation can last for hours on a parallel filesystem with a capacity of several petabytes and billions of i-nodes.

At the same time, it is a requirement to be able to perform audits on the contents of a large HPC filesystem. Files have various usages and various profiles based on their access type and frequency, their expected lifetime, and the confidentiality of their contents.

RobinHood[5] is born of this contradictory need. The basic idea is to maintain a database reflecting the state of the files stored in the filesystem at any given time. This image is to be trusted as much as possible and must remain as synchronous as possible to the always-evolving filesystem. RobinHood achieves this by performing permanent background audits and/or using callbacks from the filesystem (like filesystem change logs in Lustre) to update its database.

RobinHood is the first tool of its kind and now has a worldwide community of users across all five continents. Experience and feedback from storage administrators, all using different configurations, helped to add new features and to improve the RobinHood Policy Engine.

#### 4.5.1.2 NFS-Ganesha

Tera's long-term data storage is based on HPSS, a HSM sold by IBM. When the support of a NFS gateway disappeared from HPSS, it was critical for Tera to maintain a NFS front-end to access HPSS's namespace. This is one of the core reasons that led to the development of NFS-Ganesha ([Den07a] and [Den07b]).

---

[5]http://robinhood.sourceforge.net/

NFS-Ganesha[6] is a NFS server running in user space with a strong orientation to aggressively cache metadata. NFS-Ganesha was originally designed to be used with HPSS, but it can now manage several other back-ends, including XFS, ZFS, GPFS, Lustre, and Ceph. It also has a back-end using the "open by handle" feature of recent kernels ($> 2.6.29$) that allows us to export any filesystem relying on the VFS. The Proxy back-end is designed to behave as a basic NFSv4 client [Den09], which turns NFS-Ganesha into a NFS proxy. The FUSE back-end allows any FUSE-ready product to bind with Ganesha to export the data accessible via the FUSE interface.

NFS-Ganesha [PD11] implements all NFS versions (NFSv2, NFSv3, NFSv4, NFSv4.1) and their ancillary protocols. In particular, it implements pNFS, a "sub-protocol" in NFSv4.1 that allows parallel accesses to data using NFS. This last feature is of major interest to vendors involved in the storage market. NFS-Ganesha is a very flexible solution and the user space is a place where you meet fewer constraints than the ones inside the kernel. This is why several of them joined the NFS-Ganesha community. The product is currently developed jointly by CEA, IBM, Panasas, and the Linux Box company. It remains fully Open Source and benefits from the task force and competence of these companies. NFS-Ganesha is currently a core component in products from these vendors and is actively used in production on the CEA's computers.

### 4.5.2    ClusterShell and Shine

#### 4.5.2.1    ClusterShell

Administrating a massive cluster (made of hundreds or thousands of nodes) is quite a big challenge. When some tasks are to be done, it is clearly impossible to log on every host and run the same operation. Administrative tasks are to be executed on all related nodes from a centralized place where unitary tasks are dispatched and outputs are gathered. This is what ClusterShell[7] is made for.

ClusterShell is basically a Python framework based on an event-driven library. The systems administrator will define a command and a set of nodes to run it on. ClusterShell will connect to the selected machines, execute the operation and send back the status and the output to the sysadmin's console. It also has advanced features to aggregate all of these results, providing the end-user with a consolidated output. ClusterShell works by using an asynchronous message based model, which prevents deadlocks from occurring and provides high scalability. Its recent features, like the arborescent propagation of tasks, will follow the same path, making the tool capable of dealing with tomorrow's huge HPC architectures.

#### 4.5.2.2    Shine

The administration of a parallel filesystem like Lustre is, by essence, a set of parallel tasks: starting the distributed components (MDS, OSS...), mounting the filesystem on every client, un-mounting it. The need behind this clearly fits what ClusterShell can do. This is how Shine[8] came to life.

Roughly, Shine is a framework based on the library provided by ClusterShell with a focus on Lustre administration. Fully available as a Free Software, Shine (and its correlated ClusterShell library) is integrated into Bull's Petaflopic Linux distribution, along with other Open Source products like Slurm, Nagios, or the Linux operating system itself.

---

[6]http://nfs-ganesha.sourceforge.net/
[7]http://cea-hpc.github.com/clustershell/
[8]http://sourceforge.net/projects/lustre-shine/

With these four examples, we have seen how Open Source has become a chance for system software developers and researchers. Experience showed that HPC sites as well as the industry will easily enter active Open Source collaborations. Another aspect has to be seriously taken into account too: the scientific visibility of those products. System software oriented conferences are rare and it's difficult to publish articles because of the small number of accepted publications per year. Free Software is now part of computer science's "pop culture" and has a very positive image. Pushing a homemade product (even a small project like a benchmark) and adapting it to make it Open Source is clearly a safe choice. It would not only attract skilled contributors, but will as well give a very accessible scientific showcase.

## 4.6 Programming System

This section lists the parallel programming models, the languages, the frameworks, and the tools defining the programming system on Tera 100. This ecosystem is based on standard tools either open-source or commercial from Bull or other third-party vendors. It also relies on original software developed at CEA.

### 4.6.1 Tera 100 Parallel Programming Models

The parallel programming models are in many ways directed by the Tera 100 architecture: to exploit multiple nodes, the applications have to use the underlying network interconnect, either through the MPI [MPI12] library or by direct calls to the NIC driver (e.g., low-level InfiniBand API). For intra-node communications, it is still possible to use the MPI model but threads are more suitable (through OpenMP [BOA08] for example). Thus the programming models currently used are going from the Pure-MPI model (or MPI-Everywhere approach) to hybrid MPI/OpenMP. But expressing parallelism with such a hybrid model is difficult and error-prone. Nevertheless, this approach is necessary to exploit current and future generations of supercomputers. To tackle the issue of hybrid programming in the context of HPC, CEA started in 2003 to develop an open-source framework called MPC (Multi-Processor Computing [MP08]). MPC[9] is a unified parallel framework for clusters of NUMA nodes. Its goals are twofold: (i) unify various parallel programming models for an efficient exploitation of current petaflop/s architectures and (ii) inter operate with other components of the whole supercomputer software stack.

First of all, MPC provides a thread-based MPI implementation [MP09]. With the help of process virtualization, MPC is a full 1.3-compliant MPI runtime exposing MPI tasks as threads instead of OS processes. This virtualization offers a lighter cost of switching and communicating between tasks located inside the same memory space. Indeed, one of the key advantages of such an approach is the ability to optimize the user-level thread scheduler and thus to create and schedule a large number of threads (including MPI tasks) with a reduced overhead. Furthermore, this scheduler provides a polling method to avoid busy-waiting and to keep a high level of reactivity for communications even when the number of tasks is larger than the number of available cores. Finally, the scheduler integrates the semantics of collective communications to enable efficient barrier, reduction, and broadcast operations. The second programming model available inside MPC is OpenMP [PC10]. MPC is a full OpenMP 2.5 implementation integrated with the MPI runtime to smooth the

---

[9]http://mpc.sourceforge.net

interaction between these two parallel programming models. This integration leads to higher performance when mixing MPI and OpenMP inside the same scientific application. Finally, MPC exposes the PTHREAD API to create regular user-level threads.

But to reach high performance on a petascale supercomputer, MPC has to be fully integrated to the other HPC components belonging to the software stack shipped with the cluster. For this purpose, MPC embeds multiple components: (i) a patched compiler, (ii) a parallel memory allocator, (iii) a topology module, and (iv) a dedicated debugger.

MPC includes a patched version of the GNU compiler GCC [GNU11] mainly to lower the OpenMP directives in applications programmed with C, C++, or FORTRAN. With a total of 5,000 lines of patch, MPC extends the set of static analysis by adding a pass to detect and move global variables [PC11]. Because MPC provides a thread-based implementation of the MPI model, a set of MPI tasks located on the same node now shares global variables. But this behavior is not expected. One way to ensure the thread-safety of MPI applications is to remove global variables. Therefore, this new static compiler pass packs the global variables together and duplicates them for each MPI task. This automatic privatization allows supporting any MPI application and even hybrid MPI/OpenMP programs using global variables and threadprivate variables. Finally, the compiler proposes a new directive to enable automatic hybrid MPI/OpenMP checkpoint/restart. By adding a simple directive to the source code (#pragma omp checkpoint), the runtime automatically dumps the application and runtime memory. This mechanism allows the possibility to restart from this point on. The directive is compatible with MPI, OpenMP, or hybrid MPI/OpenMP programs. This last extension is possible with the help of the parallel memory allocation. MPC is shipped with its own parallel memory allocator optimized for NUMA architecture and multithreaded applications. Article [MP09] exposes experimental results about memory gains obtained with this new allocator inside simple MPI applications. With a realistic MPI hydrodynamics code called HERA [Jou05], MPC is able to gain up to 47% of memory (saving more than 1.3GB out of 2.8GB) with memory-page recycling among MPI tasks located on the same node.

To help the memory allocation, MPC relies on a topology module based on the HWLOC library to learn the organization of the underlying architecture. This helps the runtime to map threads to cores according to the cache hierarchy and the NUMA nodes. Finally, MPC includes a patch to GDB and its own implementation of the LibthreadDB (designed by Sun) to allow user-level thread debugging [Jou10] . With these modifications, users are able to see and follow the threads created by MPC with GDB-based debugger front-ends or with DBX (from Sun).

Since 2010, MPC has also been partly developed within the Exascale Computing Research Center (ECR Lab[10]), a collaboration between CEA, GENCI, the University of Versailles, and Intel.

## 4.6.2    Tera 100's Programming Languages

Tera 100 runs a large variety of legacy numerical codes. They are mainly written using the Fortran 90, the C, or C++ languages. The software stacks being built on a standard RedHat system, it is possible to use a large variety of languages and it is not uncommon to see part of the codes written on Python or even on the C# computer language. As of 2012 no PGAS language is used either for research purposes or for production.

---

[10]http://www.exascale-computing.eu

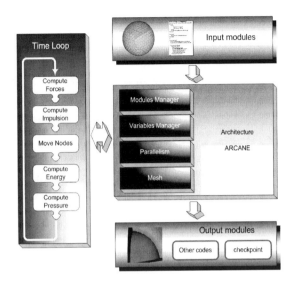

**FIGURE 4.9**: Architectural overview of Arcane.

### 4.6.3 Tera 100's Frameworks

To ease the conception and the making of new numerical codes, CEA started in 2000 to develop its own numerical code framework named Arcane [BL09]. Since 2007, Arcane is now co-developed with IFP Energies Nouvelles (Figure 4.9).

Arcane's goal is to free numerical codes of the burden of some technical parts such as low level parallelism, memory management, I/O, and basic mesh management. All its parts are highly optimized to provide good performance for the numerical codes running on several thousands of cores. Arcane is written in C++ and its size is about 250k lines of code.

Arcane is divided into two parts. The first one encompasses the basic classes while the second one is a library which provides implementation for core services like mesh reading, post processing, load balancing, etc.

A numerical code written for the Arcane Framework is a combination of a collection of independent components, called a module in Arcane terminology, that are sharing variables defined on a mesh, or on a mesh subset (a variable is assigned to a mesh type, that can be either vertex, edge, face, cell, ...). Each module describes its variable, entry points, and configuration options in an XML file. From this file, Arcane generates the C++ parent class of the module which defines class attributes representing the variables, declares the entry points as abstract methods, and provides access to technical services (e.g., mesh access, trace utilities, user data file access).

For some high level functionality that can be used by modules, Arcane permits the definition of some other kind of component, called a service in Arcane terminology. Services can be technical, like a dedicated data persistence, or domain specific, like numerical schemes or algebraic solvers. It provides a contract represented by a set of operations gathered into an interface. Several classes can implement the services; the modules choose the desired implementation of the service via the module XML file. The service itself has it own XML file, in order to provide user data options.

When a code based on the Arcane Framework is executed, Arcane first reads the user data file to create the mesh and to select the desired time loop. The time loop is defined in a XML file and defines a set of call sequences of module entry points for a simulation time step. Then Arcane creates all referenced modules and associates the user data to the modules. For each time step, Arcane plays the entry points sequence by calling each method associated with an entry point.

Arcane provides several parallel execution strategies. The first strategy is based on message passing, using a partitioned mesh from which Arcane computes the ghost elements that are going to be used to exchange data between parts. Arcane provides calls that enable synchronization of mesh variables between parts and also compute associative reductions. The second parallel execution strategy is based on concurrent tasks. Message passing can be implemented using a MPI runtime or a Hybrid MPI/Threads runtime while concurrent tasks are typically implemented using threads.

During the simulation, Arcane also provides a load balancing strategy that dynamically computes a new partition for the mesh based on the run time of previous iterations. Arcane migrates the mesh items and the data associated with the mesh.

Arcane also includes a code steering tool that helps to follow the execution steps of the numerical simulations and to follow the data changes in Arcane variables. This provides a high level debugging tool for numerical modules.

Arcane by defining basic data types and numerical simulation concepts strongly structures a simulation code. This structure, in turn, permits us to offer a graphical representation based on UML of numerical codes based on Arcane. The UML models embedded in the graphical representation are used by tools to generate parts of the code. Those tools speed up the development process by providing a bridge between an abstract representation of the complexity and the concrete C++ code.

### 4.6.4    Tera 100's Libraries

CEA builds its legacy simulation code on top of numerous different libraries. Those libraries are dedicated either to I/O parts, like Hercule described below, or some numerical aspects, physical databases that are shared by simulation codes.

#### 4.6.4.1    Hercule

The Hercule project aims to develop services in reading, writing, and formatting complex and voluminous scientific data produced by numerical simulation codes on massively parallel computers. These services are grouped within a single library that is mainly connected to the numerical simulation codes.

Three different sorts of usages are addressed by Hercule: inter-codes exchanges, post-processing actions, and checkpoint/restart. Because our goal is to maximize the efficiency in volume storage and fast access, the very early analysis in Hercule development departed from the objective of an optimal unique solution.

Nevertheless these three usages rely on the same principles Hercule established. They differ in specific considerations which separately better match their own goals: from pure speed consideration for checkpoint/restart to complete description for inter-codes exchanges. The post-processing, and in particular the interactive visualization, exacerbates this duality.

The best methods have been used at each stage of the middleware realization. In particular, an essential characteristic of Hercule is to offer a language using a dictionary (which can be enriched by the codes) and a grammar. The data written through this language keep a strong semantics all along the chain of codes and tools.

Another of Hercule's characteristics is in asynchronous I/O focusing on effective writes on the "filesystems" of the computing center. This second feature allows for a better and

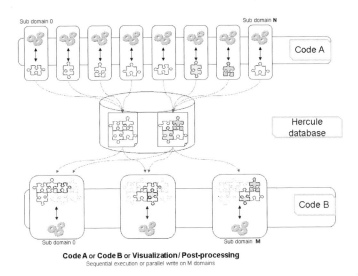

Code A

Hercule database

Code B

**Code A or Code B or Visualization / Post-processing**
Sequential execution or parallel write on M domains

**FIGURE 4.10**: Hercule automatically handles the computational domains of the different codes through its dictionary-based mechanism.

transparent adaptation of the codes to the available resources. Hence codes can easily evolve along with the facility without massive recoding.

By using semantics included in its database, Hercule manages and reorganizes data for future intended purposes (sequential or massively parallel) as depicted in Figure 4.10. So, for interactive data visualization or inter-codes exchanges, data regrouping and/or data decomposition in multi-domains are automatically handled by Hercule.

As a result, Hercule offers a common and simplified management of our three common different types of databases while answering specifics governed by the needs of adaptability and efficiency, as expressed by the code teams and physicists.

### 4.6.5 Tools

Tera 100 software includes the BullX DE tools and libraries that can be used during the entire life cycle of parallel codes. This includes debugging tools such as padb that can help to give a first diagnostic on a parallel problem, and a large collection of profiling tools such as MPI Analyzer, Scalasca, PAPI-C (an extended PAPI which takes into account counters from Tera 100 specific hardware), HPCToolkit, Bpmon, ptools. All these tools give insight into where the codes are spending their time and a complete description of the communication process (latencies, bandwith, waiting time).

BullX DE tools are completed with standard debugging tools such as Totalview and DDT. If Totalview is provided for users who are "too used to it to change," DDT is our favorite debugger and CEA has been sucessfully collaborating with Allinea for years. The items of this collaboration cover scalability (how to debug a program running in more than 10,000 cores), hybrid computing (namely to debug CUDA or OpenCL in a friendly and known environment), or more advanced topics such as debugging MPC programs.

Eclipse and especially the PTP plugin[11] also has been parameterized for the Tera 100 computer. This allows the use of gdb for debugging BullxMPI runs or using open source performance tools like the Tuning and Analysis Utilities (TAU).

## 4.7    Storage, Visualization, and Analytics

### 4.7.1    ST100 and GL100, Two Sides of Tera 100's Storage

Storing data produced by a supercomputer is a challenge that requires specific hardware and software architectures. Specific problems include the large amount of produced data, the wide variety of file types and the management of different file access profiles.

The first point to be considered is the kind of media to use and the access frequency of data. Today's technologies offer various possibilities, from media with large capacity and high latency (tapes) to high-speed to very low-latency but small capacity devices (flash memory arrays, SSDs). On the other hand, a fistful of files will be used very often while many others will be written and almost never read. This gap in both technologies and filesystem usage leads to a similar gap in the storage system architecture, leading to a situation with two interconnected systems: a HSM with large capacity but rather high latency, and a parallel filesystem with high bandwidth but more limited capacity. These systems work in an aggressively collaborative way, managing migration and staging of data across the two systems.

#### 4.7.1.1    ST100: Hierarchical Storage Management to Mix Disks and Tapes inside a Very Capacitive Storage System

The ST100 system runs HPSS, a HSM (Hierarchical Storage Manager) sold by the IBM Company. The principles behind a HSM are really simple and imply a strong separation between the metadata of files (owner, size, access modes, ACLs, etc.) and their content. As metadata are stored in dedicated database tables, data are split into segments that can be stored on various sorts of media.

Usually a HSM like HPSS manages resources into hierarchies: rotational disks (fast storage) are at the top, while tapes (slower but very capacitive) are at the lower levels. The core design idea of a HSM is promotion and demotion applied to the data segments. Incoming data are stored on disk, and would remain on it if frequently accessed. Less used data are demoted to tapes, but may be promoted back to disk if accessed again. The promotion/demotion mechanism is driven by rules defined by the system administrator and managed by dedicated daemons. Since tapes are much less expensive than disks, a HSM is an efficient and affordable way of designing a storage system. Today, the ST100 system stores 21 petabytes of data, and provides a capacity of 90 petabytes. This last limit is not an absolute one, and could be easily increased by extending the tape robotics and by adding tapes to it. ST100 uses about 30 different servers to run its components, manages 1 PB of disks, 46 IBM LTO5 drives, and 15000 LTO5 tapes.

---

[11]http://eclipse.org/ptp

| GL100 ©CEA. | ST100 ©CEA. |

**FIGURE 4.11**: Photos illustrating the density of our storage systems.

#### 4.7.1.2 GL100: Using a High-Performances Storage System as a Front-End to Storage System

GL100 is a 15 PB single parallel filesystem, running Lustre on 88 servers and 66 disk arrays. With its 200 GB/s bandwidth, it provides the supercomputer with a fast and scalable storage system to store data produced by the simulation codes. GL100 is the core component of Tera 100's data-centric architecture. Simulation results are stored there and become immediately accessible to all of Tera 100's machines, including supercomputers and post-processing machines. For example, a user can render the result of his work on his workstation or even CEA/DIF's visualization wall as fast as the files are written.

#### 4.7.1.3 Making ST100 and GL100 Work in an Aggressively Cooperative Way

GL100 has a large yet limited capacity and works jointly with ST100 (hardware is illustrated in Figure 4.11). Older files are moved to the HSM in order to free space for newer ones, and files stored in ST100 can be staged back to the high performance filesystem if the user requests it. This binding between the Lustre filesystem and the HSM works in way similar to the migration process inside the HSM's own hierarchy, with the same kind of promotion/demotion logic. This approach makes GL100 a sort of "huge cache" (15 PB) in front of ST100. Since 2008, CEA has been very active in the design and implementation of the Lustre/HSM binding. This feature is soon to be part of the official Lustre distribution and is used in production in the IFERC Compute Center (Japan). It will enter production on Tera 100 sometime in 2012-2013.

### 4.7.2 Visualization

Most of our users are located on site. For their common visualization needs, we rely on a fast (1 Gb/s) network between buildings and powerful workstations.

When remote users (off site) or very large visualizations are needed, the default architecture isn't sufficient to allow fluid post-processing activities. For these cases, we use the main computer as a visualization platform.

For heroic simulations, we use the main parallel partition (using software rendering – with MESA OpenGL) to run LOVE.

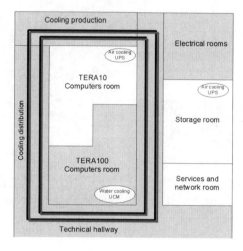

**FIGURE 4.12**: The Tera facility floor plan.

For all other cases, we rely on the hybrid partition using the VisuPortal[12] environment. VisuPortal provides:

- a mechanism to reserve resources (time slot, number of nodes...) through a web browser interface;

- a display showing the 3D graphics and optionally a remote desktop on Tera 100 using HP/RGS.

This environment has been really successful for our users. They can efficiently use it with a wealth of commercial tools as well as in house developments.

---

## 4.8    Data Center and Facility

### 4.8.1    Tera 100: A Large Technical Facility

Hosting petaflops class systems, such as Tera 100, requires building large technical facilities which must be perfectly adapted to the IT equipments' constraints.

The difficulty is to size the building for two generations of supercomputers. Before stopping a former generation of supercomputer, it's imperative to validate the codes running on the new generation of supercomputer.

The CEA's challenge was to install a new supercomputer 20 times more powerful in the same floor space as the previous supercomputers. The power density per computer rack becomes very important and it's mandatory to adapt technical facilities.

#### 4.8.1.1    Tera Building

Tera computing center is located in Bruyères-le-Châtel near Paris, France.

This building (Figure 4.12) is composed of 2000 $m^2$ for IT equipment rooms (computers, storage, network, and services) and 2000 $m^2$ for technical facilities (cooling, electricity, and security systems).

---

[12]http://www.visuportal.com

| | |
|---|---|
| Transformers ©CEA. | Distribution panels ©CEA. |
| Batteries ©CEA. | |

**FIGURE 4.13**: Electricity distribution.

#### 4.8.1.2 Electricity Distribution

The Tera building is supplied by 2 high-voltage loops of 20 kV (including one spare). The power capacity is designed for 10 MW (Figure 4.13).

Only critical IT equipment (disks, network, and storage) and one part of the cooling system (distribution pumps and air conditioners) are secured by UPS and diesel groups:

- 1 UPS APC/MGE of 500 kVA to supply technical facilities;

- 5 UPS (APC/MGE and Chloride) of 800 kVA to supply IT equipment.

All the compute nodes (80% to 90% of the IT configuration) are directly supplied by the power line but are protected by built-in ultra capacitors. This choice of technology was made due to the high quality of the electricity delivered by EDF. Furthermore, all production codes have a mandatory application checkpoint/restart mechanism which allows for an easy restart of production. Therefore a power failure has minimal impact on production.

#### 4.8.1.3 Cooling System

To cool IT equipment and technical facilities such as UPS rooms, Tera cooling capacity has been designed for 7.5 MW with five centrifugal chillers and water cooling tower (including one spare – Figure 4.14):

- 3 chillers (Trane and Carrier) of 2 MW for each;

- 2 chillers (Trane) of 1.5 MW for each.

| Chillers ©CEA. | Towers ©CEA. |

**FIGURE 4.14**: Cooling things down.

The cooling distribution allows connecting air conditioners or water distribution pipes in the computer rooms. Two water loops are installed all around the computer rooms in the technical hallway (one loop of 2 MW for air conditioners and one loop of 5 MW for water distribution pipes).

For Tera 100, the density per rack is between 30 kW to 40 kW for a large part of IT equipment (all compute nodes). These computer racks are cooled with a water distribution in the raised floor (Figure 4.15). This distribution is ready to connect heat exchangers which are integrated just behind the computer rack (BULL cool cabinet door):

- 12 water distribution pipes of 640 kW per pipe;

- 16 connection points per pipe.

The remaining IT equipment (disks, networks, and storage) which are less dense, are cooled with air conditioners.

#### 4.8.1.4   Security System

To protect both IT equipment rooms and technical facilities rooms, important and efficient security systems are installed in the building.

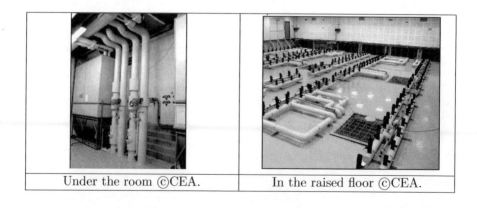

| Under the room ©CEA. | In the raised floor ©CEA. |

**FIGURE 4.15**: Water distribution pipes.

A water security system allows detecting any leakage in the main part of the building:

- Detection in electrical rooms where there are air conditioners;

- Detection in the raised floor of the computer rooms near the water distribution pipes.

These detection systems localize the leakage, alert the security team, and can stop the leakage by automatically closing the involved water distribution pipe.

Because fire is the most important risk in the computing center, the fire security system is very intrusive to get an early detection:

- Fire detection by suction system is installed in the raised floor and false ceiling;

- Rooms are protected by double punctual detection.

The first detection allows compartmentalizing the room to avoid fire propagation. The second detection confirms the fire and triggers servomechanisms (air conditioners and electricity are stopped; extinction by water fog system is switched on).

The water fog diffusion is triggered only in case of a local temperature elevation.

## 4.8.2   Tera 100: Energy Issue

Computers are more and more powerful and the associated electric consumption become very important. They represent a consequent part of the operating budget of a computing center today. For Tera 100, the power supply for IT equipment and technical facilities such as the cooling represents around 5 MW. It becomes mandatory to keep under control and to optimize each electricity consumer.

An indicator commonly used in the HPC world is the PUE (Power Usage Effectiveness). This determines the computing center energy efficiency. The PUE is defined as:

$$PUE = \frac{Total\ building\ power\ consumption}{IT\ power\ consumption}$$

Today, the Tera 100 PUE is 1.35 as explained in Figure 4.16. It means, for 1 MW of IT equipment, it's necessary to bring a power complement of 350 kW to supply associated technical facilities (cooling production and distribution, moisturizing device, transformers, UPS, security systems, etc.).

To obtain this good result, a lot of progress has been made in comparison to the previous generation of computers (Tera 10 PUE=1.6). The energy issue has been taken into account during the project design, two years before the integration of the first IT equipment.

In a R&D common program, the computer vendor and CEA have worked with strong and close collaboration around three optimization axes which have allowed us to obtain energy gains: electricity consumption reduction for IT equipment, use of a more effective cooling system, and the design of a passive device to reduce the UPS use.

### 4.8.2.1   Electricity Consumption Reduction for IT Equipment

Compute nodes have been designed to integrate the last processor generation (Intel Nehalem-EX as of 2010) and very efficient electronic components (power supply, fan). Technical characteristics such as the processor load have been studied to be able to adjust the computer electric consumption according to the compute load. Tera 100 compute power is 20 times greater than Tera 10 for an only 3 times superior electric consumption. A Tera 100 compute job consumes 7 times less electricity than an equivalent compute job on Tera 10.

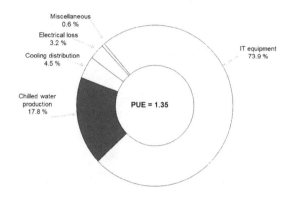

| Building electric capacity | 10MW |
|---|---|
| Cooling capacity | 7.5MW |
| IT equipment | 3.4MW |
| Technical facilities power | 1.2MW |
| Density per rack | between 30kw to 40kw |

**FIGURE 4.16**: The contributions to the PUE.

### 4.8.2.2    A More Effective Cooling System

To be able to install Tera 100 in a limited floor space, the density per rack became very important (30 kW to 40 kW per rack). Air cooling system (with air conditioners, cold aisle, hot aisle) isn't effective enough to dissipate this power. After validation on the CEA prototype platform, BULL has marketed a so-called "cool cabinet door" which answers perfectly the densification constraints.

This cool cabinet door (Figure 4.17) is composed of an air/water heat exchanger, big fans, and a regulation system. It's perfectly integrated just behind the computer rack and it allows a very effective direct cooling of IT components. This solution can cool up to 40 kW per computer rack for a room temperature of 20°C.

### 4.8.2.3    A Passive Device to Reduce UPS Usage

In order to reduce electricity consumption, the CEA operating team has chosen to use UPS only for critical IT equipment and one part of the cooling system. The rest of the IT configuration, all the compute nodes, is directly supplied by the power line and an embedded BULL ultracapacitor module (UCM) is integrated in each server.

The UCM (Figure 4.18) can maintain the power supply during a short power cut (< 300 ms). This solution has been designed by BULL and has the advantage of a very good efficiency in comparison to UPS (in order to 99.8% versus 90% for UPS).

All these energy solutions are operational: operating parameter adjustments for technical facilities (increase room temperature and hygrometry range for example) will be able to allow another optimization. To control and to track energy optimization, the CEA operating team has set up a monitoring system for the entire building (computer rooms and technical facilities).

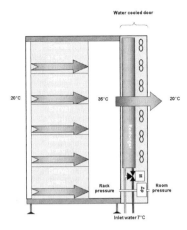

**FIGURE 4.17**: Bull's cool cabinet door principle.

## 4.9 System Statistics

### 4.9.1 Tera Computing Center: Control and Analysis of the Functioning

The Tera computing center is composed of different elements; the health of each element is constantly checked. Thanks to graphics statistics, we can detect potential problems and adapt configurations for best functioning. Moreover, these statistics are essential information for the communication with users and managers.

In the following sections, we will focus on the two main parts of the computing center: the high performance computer Tera 100 and the storage system, because these two parts are the heart of the computing center.

#### 4.9.1.1 Tera 100, the High Performance Computer

The computer is shared by many users. CPU quotas are allocated to the different departments in order to fairly distribute the resources according to the needs of each department. The computer must be reliable and reserve large enough partitions to achieve calculations as quickly as possible. This is done through monitoring of allocations. Furthermore, within the framework of "green IT," the electric consumption is recorded and analyzed in order to check the consumption and develop saving strategies.

Then, reports and statistics are regularly made available: they can be used for internal purposes but they are also reported to users and managers.

#### 4.9.1.2 Control of Availability and Utilization of the Computer

The objective is to verify that the load of the computer is correct: that it is not underused or, on the contrary, not overused (leading to pending jobs). We also have to look after the availability of the computer in order to verify if it is in accordance with the expected availability criteria. Moreover, graphics can bring to light potential dysfunctions. This monitoring is done through the following:

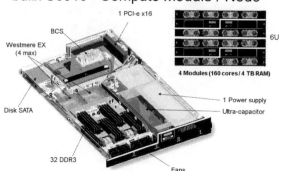

**FIGURE 4.18**: A BullX fat node. The UCM is under the label AC/DC. (©BULL.)

- Monthly, a use and availability graphic is updated. Its purpose is to verify the evolution of the availability and the use of the computer over months.

- A graphic showing the current load is displayed on the operator's control screens to visually check the good functioning of the computer. This graphic is also provided to system administrators and users for information on the machine load.

  In Figure 4.19 (February 2012), the dark gray part represents the allocated cores and the light gray part above the line the amount of cores for pending requests.

- Monthly, a graphic is made showing the average waiting time for requests before being executed. Hence, administrators are able to verify that the computations are achieved within the required time and that the capacity of the computer is adapted to the production.

  Figure 4.20 represents the number of jobs in terms of waiting time (by time slots). The jobs wait when the computer is full: in such cases, the requests are ordered in waiting

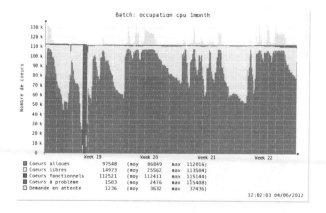

**FIGURE 4.19**: Core usage on Tera 100.

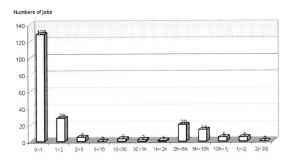

**FIGURE 4.20**: Wait time classes for starting a batch job.

lists following quotas. The execution of large requests could wait until the night or the weekend in order to leave some room for interactive sessions during working days.

### 4.9.1.3 Profiling the Usage

Several kinds of charts are available:

- A graphic is produced monthly to show the repartition of the utilization (compute hours) between the different departments to verify that the quotas are respected.

- A graphic is produced annually to show the repartition of the utilization between the different projects to check the coherence with the projects planning.

- A graphic is provided monthly to show the distribution of jobs following the number of cores they use. The amount of CPU hours and the number of jobs are represented.

- A graphic is provided monthly showing (Figure 4.21), for main local codes, the repartition of the compute hours (productive hours and failure hours).

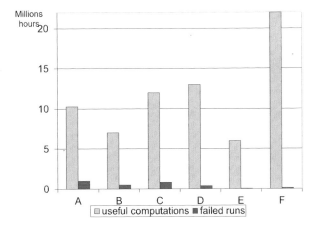

**FIGURE 4.21**: Time spent for useful computations or lost by failed runs for different codes.

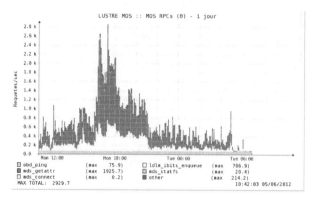

**FIGURE 4.22**: Instantaneous production on the Lustre filesystems.

### 4.9.1.4   Control of the Activity on Parallel Filesystems

The HPC computer is mainly used for simulations calculations which generate a huge amount of data. So, the quality of the IO system is essential for the good operation of the computing center.

On the computer, filesystems are shared through the Lustre software system. Many users access these filesystems simultaneously and we have to keep watch over the activity: actually, if a code has an abnormal behavior, i.e., inopportune and excessive input/output on these shared filesystems, this may slow down other users accessing these filesystems at the same time.

A dynamic graphic is realized to visualize the IO activity on the local Lustre shared filesystems (Figure 4.22). With this graph, it is easy to detect abnormal peaks which could slow-down the access to users' files.

### 4.9.2   Hardware Reports

To estimate the durability of hardware parts and the scope and volume of the maintenance contracts, the number of breakdowns of the different hardware components (cpu, memory, disks, network, etc.) is annually reported.

#### 4.9.2.1   Electrical Consumption Supervision

Two types of data are tracked here:

- A graphic is dynamically displayed to visualize the electric consumption of the Tera 100 computer. With it, we can check the electrical consumption and correlate it with its utilization.

- The electrical consumption is reported at the end of each computation. It offers an opportunity to analyze the electrical consumption linked to the behavior of the code and observe the result of potential optimizations to reduce the consumption (Figure 4.23).

#### 4.9.2.2   The Storage System

In our computing center, a huge amount of data is generated by the computations executed on the Tera 100 computer. The storage system has to be dimensioned consequently (around 100 Po). The storage system is made up of two parts: a very large shared disk

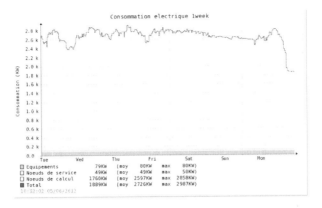

**FIGURE 4.23**: Electrical consumption of different parts of Tera 100.

filesystem (managed via Lustre) and a second level storage system based on robots handling thousands of magnetic tapes stored in libraries. Before being stored on tapes, files transit through and HPSS system. On the Tera 100 computer, the visibility of the HPSS files is possible via NFS (through NFS-Ganesha).

a. A graphic is monthly realized showing the filling of the libraries: number of Gbytes and number of files. Then we can observe the evolution of the amount of data load and verify that the capacity is adapted (enough tapes).

b. Monthly, a graphic is realized showing the amount of data stored during the month by each division (Figure 4.24). Henceforth, the administrators are able to verify the distribution and detect irregularities or overflowing from a division or a user.

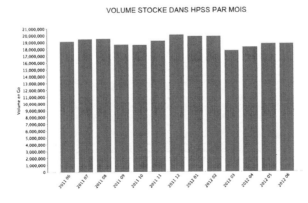

**FIGURE 4.24**: Volume stored in HPSS by a group of users.

## 4.10    Looking Forward

### 4.10.1    The Tera "Family"

The Tera 100 supercomputer is not one of its kind now. Rather, it has been a brilliant demonstration that this technology could be at the core of many projects. It is now a commercial product of BULL.

The first sibling of Tera 100 is the Curie[13] system installed in the TGCC of CEA. This machine is mostly devoted to the European research community.

The second sibling is Helios located in the IFERC[14] computing center. This machine is devoted to nuclear fusion research in strong relation to the ITER[15] project.

Curie and Helios have benefited from advances in processor technology. They are using Intel's Sandy Bridge processors, allowing the machines to exceed 1.5 PFlops, demonstrating the quality of Tera 100 design.

### 4.10.2    En Route to the Future

The Tera project already has two machines on its roadmap, for an Exaflops class machine around 2020. Thus, Tera 100 has also been designed to prepare for the future.

We know that the main challenge for the Exaflop will be electrical power. Only a "many-core" architecture will allow the targeted performance level at a reasonable power budget. Therefore, we introduced a hybrid island in the machine to prepare the mutation of our codes. We chose hybrid blades from BULL[16] based on 396 NVIDIA M2090 GPUs.

Along the same line and since Tera 100 is Nehalem based, we introduced an island of Intel's Sandy Bridge to help our developers to master AVX and to increase the fraction of vectorized sections in their codes.

As a summary, Tera 100 is the demonstration that a strong collaboration with a vendor can lead to the design of a machine well suited to our needs yet open to the future and being a successful line of products. This fact has been acknowledged by HPCWire.[17]

---

[13]http://www-hpc.cea.fr/en/complexe/tgcc.htm

[14]http://www.iferc.org/index.htm

[15]http://www.iter.org/

[16]bullx B505 see http://www.bull.com/catalogue/details.asp?tmp=bxs-blade\&opt=bullx-b0505e00\&cat=bullx\&dt=op

[17]See the "Top supercomputing achievement" section in http://www.hpcwire.com/specialfeatures/2011\_Annual\_HPCwire\_Readers\_Choice\_Awards.html

# Chapter 5

## The Mole-8.5 Supercomputing System

**Xiaowei Wang and Wei Ge**

*Institute of Process Engineering (IPE), Chinese Academy of Sciences (CAS)*

## 5.1 Background

### 5.1.1 Introduction

Process engineering, the focus of all research and development activities at IPE, CAS, is the foundation for the production and transformation of energies, resources, and materials for human society, ranging from chemicals and minerals to foods and cosmetics. In a rough sense, almost all products measured in quantities rather than in numbers are produced by the process industries. The properties and functions of these products are determined by their molecular compositions and structures, which is at the spatio-temporal scales of $10^{-10}$ m to $10^{-6}$ m and $10^{-15}$s to $10^{-9}$s, whereas the equipment and plants producing these products typically operate at the scales of $10^0$ m to $10^3$ m and $10^0$ s to $10^3$ s, and they have to take care of environmental impact which is at global scale [GXX+13]. The huge gap between these two ends proposes a grand challenge to the designing and scaling-up of the production process, and high performance computing (HPC) is playing an increasingly important role in this respect. However, tremendous improvements in the speed, accuracy, and efficiency of the simulation hardware and software are still in demand.

In response to this demand, IPE has been devoted to the multi-scale approach ever since early 1980s. They developed the so-called energy minimization multi-scale (EMMS) model [LTK88, LM94] that describes the meso-scale structures in gas-solid flow, and hence improved the accuracy and reduced the computational cost of continuum-based simulation of gas-solid flow considerably [YWGL03]. The method was later extended to turbulent flow and gas-liquid flow successfully. With the development and extension of the EMMS model to different areas and the expression of the common nature of different discrete methods under the same algorithmic framework, a general multi-scale computing mode [GWY+11, GXX+13] was established for typical complex systems in process engineering. In this mode, the system is discretized on different levels. On the top and middle levels, long range interactions or correlations are treated by imposing stability conditions, which gives the global and local distribution of variables at the statistically steady state with relatively low computational cost. On the middle and bottom levels, local interactions among the discrete elements are treated explicitly based on these distributions, reproducing the dynamic evolution of the system in detail. Taking advantage of the fast distribution process, development of system behavior from the artificial initial condition to the steady state, which is of little interest to engineering practice, can be bypassed almost completely, and hence speed up the simulation considerably.

Integration of these simulation methods gave birth to the so-called EMMS Paradigm [LGK09, GWY+11, LGW+13], which is characterized, on one hand, by the structural consistency among the simulated system, the physical model, the numerical method and algorithm, and finally the computer hardware, and on the other hand, by the strategy of top-down and bottom-up coupling of simulation methods at different scales [LGK09], a high standard of accuracy, capability (speed and scale), and efficiency (ACE) can be achieved [GWY+11], which will bring such simulations to the realm of virtual process engineering (VPE).

## 5.1.2    GPU+CPU Heterogeneous Architecture

The EMMS Paradigm asks for a new type of hardware architecture to efficiently perform the computations based on this scheme. But it is difficult to realize this with only the traditional CPU. In addition, utilizing traditional CPU-based supercomputers, the power of this computing mode cannot be demonstrated fully because the discrete simulation still takes a very long time and the parallelism of discrete simulation is not exploited thoroughly. The appearance of GPU, and especially its application in general purpose computation shed light on the development of the hardware. Although GPUs are formerly associated with graphics rendering, they are also powerful arithmetic engines capable of running thousands of lightweight threads concurrently, which makes them well suited to computations that can support parallel execution well. The advantages of GPU in scientific computing over CPU, such as higher theoretical performance and bandwidth, lower energy consumption, better performance/price ratio, have attracted more and more researchers to begin programming with GPUs. But at an earlier time, people can only interact with GPUs through standard graphic APIs, such as OpenGL, DirectX, and make their applications like graphic rendering, which is difficult to grasp and has some constraints. To facilitate the programming based on GPU and expand its application areas to more general fields besides graphic application, NVIDIA and AMD later released CUDA [Nvi11] and Brook+, respectively, for programming on their GPUs, which boosted general-purpose computation on GPU (GPGPU).

GPUs, facilitated by CUDA, introduced new means to implement the EMMS Paradigm, especially for the computation on the bottom level. As a GPU typically contains hundreds of relatively simple stream processors operated in the SIMD (single-instruction, multiple data) mode, it has good balance, for discrete simulation, between the complexity of the arithmetic and logic operations that can be carried out by a stream processor and the number of parallel threads they issued. The communication among multiple GPUs may present an imperfection, as for the moment it has to resort to the PCIE bus, or even the inter-node network, with limited bandwidth and considerable latency; however, weak scalability is still warranted for most discrete simulations. Therefore, the GPU+CPU heterogeneous architecture is a practical choice for the development of hardware at present.

### 5.1.3 Timeline of Mole-8.5

Based on the GPU+CPU heterogeneous architecture, IPE developed three generations of supercomputer for the EMMS Paradigm from 2008 to 2010. The following description of these systems is partly based on [GWY+11, LGW+13]. Mole-9.7, the first system as pictured in Figure 5.1, was established in February 2008. It consists of 126 HP xw8600 workstations each with 2 NVIDIA Tesla C870 GPU boards (with the addition of 20 GTX9800 GX2 boards afterwards). The workstations were connected by Gigabit Ethernet, through 2D torus meshes of 12x10 and 2x3 for neighborhood communication on two levels, and a switch for nonlocal communications and management. The system was installed in a limited space of about 50 m$^2$ and cooled by home-use air-conditioners. The electrical consumption of the system under typical load (including cooling) was about 70 kW. The system may serve as a traditional PC cluster with a peak performance over 10 Tflops. However, the capability of

**FIGURE 5.1**: Configuration of Mole-9.7 supercomputer. (With kind permission from Springer Science + Business Media: *From Multiscale Modeling to Meso-Science*, 2013, Li, J., Ge, W., Wang, W. et al.)

this system was mainly from its GPUs, which delivered over 100 Tflops peak performance in single precision (SP). Actually, Mole-9.7 is the first Chinese system reaching this level.

In fact, the name of the system also reflects its performance and target applications. That is, Mole bears its original value of the Avogadros number, $6.02214179 \times 10^{23}$, but in addition to the unit for the amount of elementary entities in materials and systems, it is employed as the unit for flops also. In this unit, the peak performance of this system is approximately $10^{-9.7}$ Mole-flops, and hence the name Mole-9.7. Its successors are named accordingly. It provides a convenient measure for the gap between the performance of the named system to that required to simulate macro-scale behavior directly at atomic or molecule level, which will be a major milestone for both HPC and discrete simulation. A Mole+x.x system is required for this purpose.

Mole-9.7 has been successfully applied to the simulation of multi-phase flow, large-scale simulation of a biological macromolecular system after its establishment. This manifests the advantage and potential of the EMMS Paradigm and the availability of GPU+CPU heterogeneous architecture to embody this scheme, which attracted the attention and interest from the Chinese Academy of Sciences (CAS) and Ministry of Finance (MOF). To accelerate further development, MOF and CAS launched the project "High-efficiency and low-cost high performance computing system for multi-scale discrete simulation."

The project gives powerful support to IPE and remarkably accelerated the hardware development. Mole-8.7, the second-generation system, is the first supercomputer with 1.0 Petaflops peak performance in single precision in China, which was formally announced on April 20, 2009. Two major HPC system producers in China, Lenovo and Dawning, helped to build it. Mole-8.7 is composed of four units integrating both NVIDIA and AMD GPUs. Unit A and Unit C use AMD GPUs with peak performance of 200 Tflops and 150 Tflops, respectively, while Unit B and Unit D utilize NVIDIA GPUs with peak performance of 200 Tflops and 450 Tflops, respectively. Unit D is actually based on Mole-9.7 by upgrading the GPUs from C870 to GTX295. The four units are inter-connected with both Gigabit Ethernet and DDR InfiniBand networks. Figure 5.2 shows the configuration of Mole-8.7 system.

Mole-9.7 and Mole-8.7 serve as the predecessors of Mole-8.5, with which IPE accumulated experience on the construction of supercomputers based on the GPU+CPU heterogeneous architecture. Application of such supercomputers also expands to a variety of areas and in

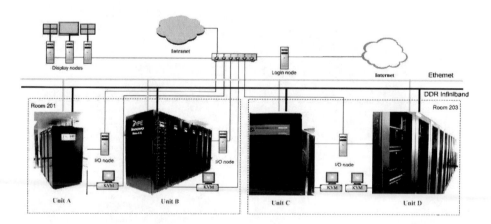

**FIGURE 5.2**: Configuration of Mole-8.7 supercomputer. (With kind permission from Springer Science + Business Media: *From Multiscale Modeling to Meso-Science*, 2013, Li, J., Ge, W., Wang, W. et al.)

**TABLE 5.1**: Development of the computer capacity accessible to IPE in the past 20 years.

| Year | Computer | Peak Performance |
|------|----------|------------------|
| 1987 | VAX-11/780 | 1 Mflops |
| 1991 | AST 386 | 8 Mflops |
| 1993 | Indigo R4400 | 100 Mflops |
| 1995 | Indigo2 R8000 | 250 Mflops |
| 1998 | Indigo2 R10000 | 800 Mflops |
| 2002 | Compaq Cluster | 100 Gflops |
| 2004 | DeepComp 6800 | 4 Tflops |
| 2007 | Dawning 4000A | 11.2 Tflops |
| 2008 | Mole-9.7 | 100 Tflops(SP) |
| 2009 | Mole-8.7 | 1 Pflops(SP) |
| 2010 | Mole-8.5 | 1 Pflops(DP) |

2009, IPE was honored with the CUDA Center of Excellence (CCOE) by NVIDIA. With the support of NVIDIA, IPE become the first batch user of the Fermi GPU and announced Mole-8.5, a petaflops GPGPU supercomputer with Rpeak of 1.1 Pflops in double precision (DP), on April 24, 2010.

In fact, the computing capacity accessible to IPE in the past 20 years has gained an unimaginable increase if traced back to the 1980s when we began performing simulations using computers. The history of the capacity development is summarized in Table 5.1. The increasing capacity reflects the fast development of the supercomputer. The performance of our accessible supercomputer has increased almost $10^9$ times in the past 25 years, doubling every 10 months, which is higher than the Moores law of 18 months for the chip development.

## 5.2 System Overview

Mole-8.5 was established to provide a customized hardware that can take full advantage of the CPU-GPU hybrid architecture to implement the multi-scale computing mode based on EMMS and discrete simulations. As shown in Figure 5.3, it consists of three levels of computing nodes, with an increasing number of GPUs in the nodes. The top level nodes contain only four hexad-core CPUs and it is mainly used for global distribution of the variables in the system. The middle level nodes contain two hexad-core CPUs and two GPUs, which are mainly used for mesh-based continuum methods. Most nodes are for the bottom level, each having two quad-core CPUs and six GPUs, which are designed mainly for the local interactions in discrete simulation. The specifications of the systems can be found in Table 5.2, and a picture of the system in operation is shown in Figure 5.4. The nodes are connected with both Gigabyte Ethernet and QDR InfiniBand. The Ethernet is used mainly for administration, while the InfiniBand is mainly for data transfer during computation with a point to point communication bandwidth of about 3.0 GB/s and a latency of 1.9 $\mu$s, which can meet the requirement of GPU computation.

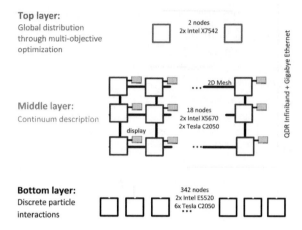

**FIGURE 5.3**: Overview of the Mole-8.5 supercomputing system [GWY$^+$11]. (Reprinted from *Chemical Engineering Science*, Vol 66, Ge, W., Wang, W., Yang, N. et al., Meso-scale oriented simulation towards virtual process engineering (VPE)—the EMMS paradigm, pp. 4426–4458, Copyright 2011, with permission from Elsevier.)

## 5.3    Benchmark Results

### 5.3.1    HPL Linpack

After the establishment of Mole-8.5 in April 2010, IPE carried out a preliminary Linpack test which achieved 207.3 Tflops on 320 nodes (tests on more nodes were not optimized to give better results), ranking Mole-8.5 No. 19 on the 35th Top500 list of June 2010 and No. 3 on the China TOP100 list in October 2010. The power consumption corresponding to this performance (on 320 nodes) is below 480 KW, reaching an average power efficiency of 431 Mflops/Watt, which earns for Mole-8.5 the No. 8 ranking on the Green500 list of July 2010.

The relative efficiency of this Linpack result is fairly poor, reaching only 20.47%, almost half of other GPU+CPU hybrid systems. However, it is both expected and understandable, since the system is not designed as a general purpose one. In late 2011, some optimizations

**TABLE 5.2**: Specifications of the Mole-8.5 system [GWY$^+$11, LGW$^+$13].

| Item | Value(Unit) |
| --- | --- |
| Peak Performance (SP) | 2.206 Petaflop/s |
| Peak Performance (DP) | 1.103 Petaflop/s |
| Number of Nodes/Number of GPUs (Type) | 362/2088 (Tesla C2050) |
| Top Layer | 2/0 |
| Middle Layer | 18/36 (Tesla C2050) |
| Bottom Layer | 342/2052 (Tesla C2050) |
| Total Memory-RAM | 17.8 Terabyte |
| Total Memory-VRAM | 6.5 Terabyte |
| Total Hard Disk Space | 720 Terabyte |
| Management Communication | H3C Gigabit Ethernet |
| Message Passing Communication | Mellanox QDR InfiniBand |
| Occupied Area | 150 M$^2$ |
| Weight | 12.6 Ton |

**FIGURE 5.4**: The Mole-8.5 system at IPE, CAS. (Photo by Xianfeng He.) (With kind permission from Springer Science + Business Media: From Multiscale Modeling to Meso-Science, 2013, Li, J., Ge, W., Wang, W. et al.)

for the Linpack test from NVIDIA, such as reducing the demand for PCIE and memory bandwidth, overlapping GPU computing with that of CPU, and improving the partition of jobs between GPU and CPU, were found effective in this system. Together with the release of CUDA 4.0, the single node (with 6 GPUs) performance was elevated to 1.5 Tflops from 0.9 Tflops previously. And the Linpack tests with different numbers of nodes, as shown in Figure 5.5, have gotten good scalability. The final result on 320 nodes is 496.5 Tflops. In fact, higher performance was reached with more nodes, but not at better efficiency. With these results, Mole-8.5 was ranked No. 21 on the 38th Top500 list of November 2011. Moreover, the power consumption for this performance increased only about 10%, reaching 515.2 KW. Thus the average power efficiency is 963.7 Mflops/Watt, which makes Mole-8.5 No. 9 on the Green500 list of November 2011 (Figure 5.6). In fact, according to that list, we find that Mole-8.5 was, at that time, the most energy efficient supercomputer in the world with peak performance exceeding 1Pflops.

## 5.3.2 Communication Benchmark

The communication between the nodes is important for parallel computation especially for computing nodes with multiple GPUs like Mole-8.5. IPE has tested the communication bandwidth and latency between two random nodes of Mole-8.5 using the OSU_Benchmark with a series of packages of different sizes. The bandwidth and latency test results are shown in Figure 5.7 and Figure 5.8, respectively. The point to point bandwidth between two nodes can approach about 3 GB/s and the latency is about 1.9 $\mu$s, reaching the theoretical performance of QDR InfiniBand. This certainly thanks to the compact architecture of the system, which requires only one InfiniBand switch (Melanox MIS5600) to connect all nodes.

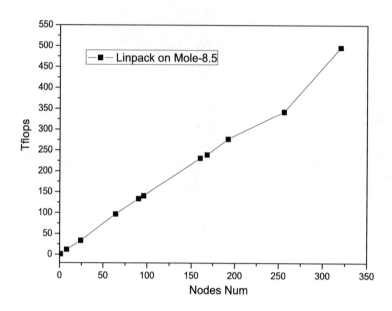

**FIGURE 5.5**: Linpack results of Mole-8.5 with different number of nodes.

**FIGURE 5.6**: Certificate for Mole-8.5 from Green500 in 2011.

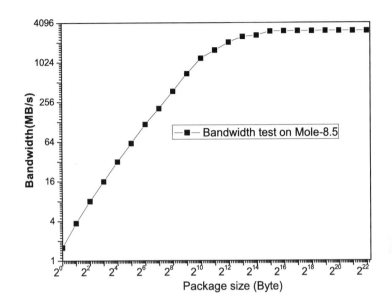

**FIGURE 5.7**: Bandwidth performance between two random nodes.

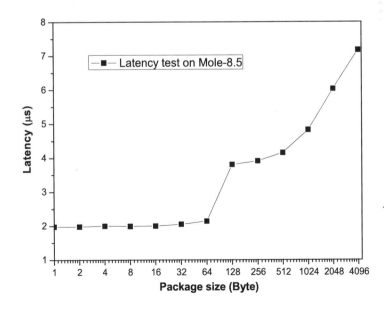

**FIGURE 5.8**: Latency performance between two random nodes.

**TABLE 5.3**: CPU configuration.

| Node type | CPU # | Core # | Model | Frequency | Nodes # |
|-----------|-------|--------|-------|-----------|---------|
| Bottom-nodes | 2 | 4 | Intel E5520 | 2.26 GHz | 342 |
| Middle-nodes | 2 | 6 | Intel X5670 | 2.93 GHz | 18 |
| Top-nodes | 4 | 6 | Intel E7542 | 2.67 GHz | 2 |

## 5.4    Architecture

### 5.4.1    General Information

Figure 5.9 shows the global architecture of Mole-8.5, from which we can see that the whole system includes different kinds of computing nodes, network, visualization system, storage system, and facility infrastructure. In the following subsections, the details of each part will be presented.

### 5.4.2    Hardware Configuration

The Mole-8.5 supercomputer consists of 362 computing nodes. These nodes are divided into three levels, which are already briefly introduced in Section 5.2. The hardware configuration details of these nodes are listed in Table 5.3 through Table 5.7, including CPU, memory, hard disk, network, and GPU.

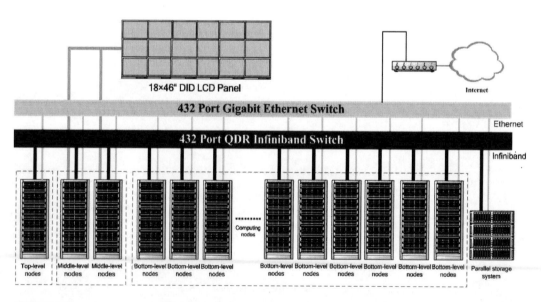

**FIGURE 5.9**: Global architecture of the Mole-8.5 system [XWH+11]. (From Springer and *Chinese Science Bulletin*, volume 56, 2011, pp. 2114–2118, Application of he Mole–8.5 supercomputer: Probing the whole influenza virion at the atomic level, Xu, J., Wang, X.W., He, X.F. et al. with kind permission from Springer Science + Business Media.)

**TABLE 5.4**: Memory configuration.

| Node type | Memory size | Nodes # | Total size |
|---|---|---|---|
| Bottom-nodes | 48 GB | 342 | 16416 GB |
| Middle-nodes | 48 GB | 18 | 864 GB |
| Top-nodes | 256 GB | 2 | 512GB |

**TABLE 5.5**: Hard disk configuration.

| Node type | Capacity | Nodes # | Total capacity |
|---|---|---|---|
| Bottom-nodes | 2000 GB | 342 | 684 TB |
| Middle-nodes | 2000 GB | 18 | 36 TB |
| Top-nodes | 292 GB | 2 | 0.584 TB |

### 5.4.3 System Layout

The Mole-8.5 system is installed in a room with an area of about 180 m$^2$ (the external air cooling unit is not counted here) among which about 145 m$^2$ is occupied by the super-computer itself, while the other space is for the power supply including UPS and cabinet for power distribution). The computing nodes are 4U high, therefore 10 nodes are put into one standard 42U server rack. The aspects of the server rack with computing nodes and single node are shown in Figure 5.10. All these racks are arranged in three rows with 15 racks in each row. Every 15 nodes are allocated one KVM for control in some cases. The Ethernet cables are distributed in the channels underground, while the optical fibers for the QDR InfiniBand are laid in the channels on top of server racks. Figure 5.11 shows the physical layout of the Mole-8.5 system.

### 5.4.4 Computing Node

#### 5.4.4.1 General Information

The typical nodes of Mole-8.5 are based on the GPU+CPU heterogeneous structure with a high density of GPUs, developed jointly by IPE and TYAN. The motherboard used is TYAN S7015, featuring 8 PCI-E X16 slots with double channel distance on the board. Up to 8 NVIDIA Tesla C2050 GPUs can be installed in this type of node, and actually up to 6 GPUs are integrated on each node, which result in a peak performance of 6.18 Tflops in SP and 3.09 Tflops in DP. Two Intel Nehalem E5520 CPUs are configured to supply assistant computation power and also act as the host for GPUs. The total memory in each node is 48 GB using twelve DDR3 1333 MHz 4 GB memory bank. The hard disks of each node are two 3.5 inch enterprise disks with a capacity of 1 TB each. The details of the configuration of each node are list in Table 5.8.

**TABLE 5.6**: Network configuration.

| Network | Network interface | Topology type |
|---|---|---|
| For computation | Intel 82574L GbE | Star |
| For management | QDR InfiniBand | Star |

**TABLE 5.7**: GPU configuration.

| Node type | GPU # | Model | Peak Flops | G Mem | Nodes # |
|---|---|---|---|---|---|
| Bottom-nodes | 6 | Tesla C2050 | 1.03 G | 3 TB | 342 |
| Middle-nodes | 6 | Tesla C2050 | 1.03 G | 3 TB | 18 |
| Top-nodes | / | / | / | / | 2 |

#### 5.4.4.2   Layout of Each Node

The motherboard of the computing node is from TYAN with the model number S7015. It has a two-way server architecture supporting two Intel Nehalem EP series CPUs integrating two Intel Tylersburg IOH followed by two PCIE switch PEX8647. Two PCIE X16 slots are laid behind each PCIE switch and the distance between them is two channels, which make the slot suitable for installing most mainstream GPGPU boards and InfiniBand HCA. 18 DDR3 memory slots are distributed on the board supporting a maximum capacity of 144GB. Four Gigabyte ethernet ports are also integrated on the board.

As there are eight PCIE X16 slots on the motherboard and six GPU boards plus one InfiniBand HCA card are to be installed on these slots, optimization of their distribution and matching is necessary. It is found from the bandwidth test that, if the GPU boards located on the PCIE slots are controlled by the first IOH (IOH0), the unidirectional and bidirectional bandwidth are about 5.2 GB/s and 3.8 GB/s, respectively. While if they are located on the PCIE slots controlled by the second IOH (IOH1), the corresponding values are about 4.3 GB/s and 2.5 GB/s, respectively. This is, according to TYAN, caused by a bug of the two-way server board. Therefore, the GPUs should be located on the PCIE slot controlled by IOH0. But the bandwidth tests of InfiniBand also reflect that the value is lower when located on the PCIE slot controlled by IOH1. Based on the bandwidth test and consideration of enough space for thermal dispersion, three GPUs plus the InfiniBand HCA are distributed on the PCIE X16 slots controlled by IOH0; the other three Tesla C2050 GPUs are laid on the slots controlled by IOH1. Figure 5.12 shows the logical layout in

**FIGURE 5.10**: Aspects of server rack and single node.

**TABLE 5.8**: Detailed configuration of Mole-8.5 computing node.

| Item | Configuration |
|---|---|
| Chipset | 2* Intel Tylersburg chipset +ICH10R |
| CPU | 2* Intel Xeon 5520 2.26G |
| Memory | 12* 4GB DDR3 1333 MHz ECC Reg |
| Hard disk | 2* 1000G SATA |
| GPU | 6* NVIDIA Tesla C2050 |
| Network | 4* Gigabyte Ethernet + QDR InfiniBand |
| Power supply | 2*1200W |
| Other | Integrated IPMI 2.0KVM |
| Dimension | 710x425x176 mm (DxWxH) |

each computing node and Figure 5.13 is the snapshot of the physical layout of a typical computing node.

### 5.4.5 Visualization System

Efficient and convenient comprehension and analysis of the computational results is important to taking full advantage of the computational power of Mole-8.5. As the large-scale simulations run on it will output huge amounts of data, high definition and interactive visualization capabilities are required. For this propose, a parallel visualization system is established based on the middle-layer nodes of Mole-8.5, as shown in Figure 5.14.

The display array consists of 18 DID liquid crystal monitors with narrow margins, aligned in three lines with 6 columns in each line. The size of each liquid crystal screen is 46 inches

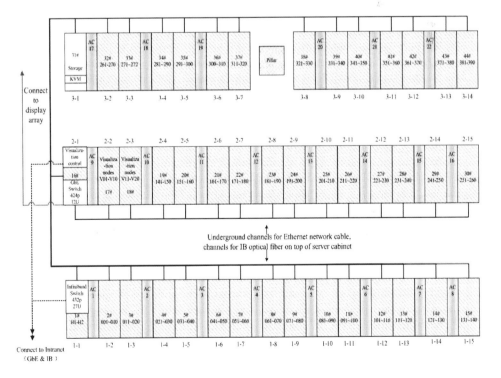

**FIGURE 5.11**: Physical layout of a Mole-8.5 system (network connection is partly shown for clarity).

**TABLE 5.9**: Components of Mole-8.5 storage system.

| Storage type | Capacity (TB) | Model | Max I/O bandwidth GB/s (read) |
|:---:|:---:|:---:|:---:|
| HP | 300 | X9320 | 1 |
| Panasas | 80 | Panasas 8 | 2 |
| DDN | 600 | SFA10000 | 11 |

(1025mm x 578.8mm) with a resolution of 1366x768; thus the combined resolution of the whole display array can reach 8196x2304. Each DID screen is connected to a middle-layer node of Mole-8.5 via a VGA matrix with 18 input ports and 18 output ports. In this way, each screen can be used both individually and jointly, with all different possibilities of combination for specific purposes.

The results of a large-scale direct numerical simulation of a gas-solid system with 1 million solid particles [XLZ+12] running on 512 GPUs is visualized on this display array, as shown in Figure 5.15 [GWY+11]. The details of the velocity field around each solid particle of such a large system is clearly shown, which is unimagined without such a display array. In addition, as each liquid crystal DID is connected to a GPU server, which can carry out numerical and graphical operations simultaneously, real-time interactive simulation is made easy with this visualization system. Figure 5.16 is a quasi real-time simulation of the particle flow in an industrial scale rotating drum, in which each GPU computes one domain of the drum and outputs the visualization results to different screens synchronously [GWY+11, XQF+11].

### 5.4.6   Storage System

The storage system of Mole-8.5 includes three parts as summarized in Table 5.9. The first part is from HP with a capacity of 300 TB. This part is used mainly as backend for data backup or some applications with low IO frequency. The second part is from Panasas with a capacity of 80TB. It has a higher data access speed compared with the first part and is mainly for some applications with a moderate IO frequency but limited data size. The third part is from DDN with a capacity of 600 TB. It mainly works for the production run with high frequency and larger data size.

Figure 5.17 shows the configuration of the DDN storage system of Mole-8.5. It includes five disk enclosures with a total of 300 2TB SATA enterprise hard disk plugged in. Two

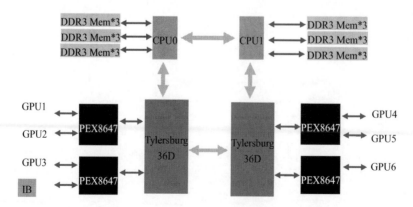

**FIGURE 5.12**: Logical layout of the components in a typical Mole-8.5 node.

**FIGURE 5.13**: Internal structure of a typical computing node in Mole-8.5.

MDS nodes, four OSS nodes, and two controllers are also included. The MDS nodes, the OSS nodes and controllers are configured as fail-over pair to make the system more robust. All the back-end connections are based on QDR InfiniBand. The filesystem for this storage system is Lustre. Figure 5.18 shows the performance of this system with different numbers of clients. As all the clients and the backend system are connected with QDR InfiniBand, the system can delivers max IOPS and massive throughput at the same time. We found that the aggregated peak performance is 8.5 GB/sec for write and 11.5 GB/sec for read; both are 98-100% of the Lustre backend performance of this configuration.

### 5.4.7 Facility Infrastructure

The supercomputer room is on the first floor of the IPE new main building. The floor of the room is designed to support a burden of 500 kg/m$^2$. As mentioned in Section 5.3.1,

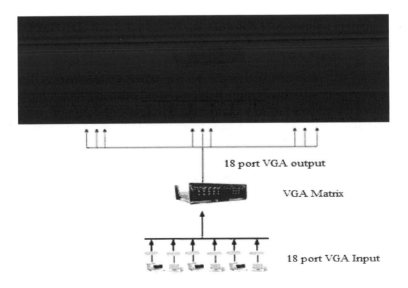

**FIGURE 5.14**: Layout of the Mole-8.5 visualization system.

**FIGURE 5.15**: High-resolution visualization of the velocity field of a DNS simulation of gas-solid system with 1 million solid particles [XLZ$^+$12, GWY$^+$11].

the max power consumption of Mole-8.5 is about 543 kW, plus the power consumption of about 200 kW for air conditioners. The total power consumption may exceed 700 kW. To guarantee the power supply of Mole-8.5, an 800 KVA transformer is set up exclusively for its use. In addition, efficient UPS system is configured to regulate and stabilize the current and serves as temporary power supply in case of a power outage. The air conditioner of this system is configured as a row-based type to cope with the high thermal load of GPU servers. There are, in all, 22 APC ACRC 103 units which are placed in line with the server racks to draw hot air directly from the rear and discharge cool air in the front. Chilled water works as the exchange media flowing through an internal underground pipe from the chiller plant outside the supercomputer room. A monitor system for the operation environment is set up which measures and records power load, temperature, and humidity of the supercomputer room in real-time and sends an alarm message in case of water leakage, smoke, or fire. Some of the infrastructure data of the system is listed in Table 5.10.

## 5.5    Software Environment

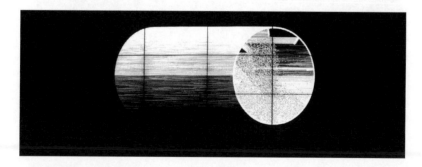

**FIGURE 5.16**: Quasi real-time simulation of the particle flow in a rotating drum on the display array [XQF$^+$11, GWY$^+$11]. (Reprinted from *Chemical Engineering Science*, Vol 66, Ge, W., Wang, W., Yang, N. et al., Meso-scale oriented simulation towards virtual process engineering (VPE)—the EMMS paradigm, pp. 4426–4458, Copyright 2011, with permission from Elsevier.)

### 5.5.1 System Software

The operation system of each node is CentOS 5.4 Linux with the kernel version of 2.6.18-164.el5. On each node, program softwares are configured for parallel CPU-GPU computation, such as CUDA, GCC, G++, MPI. Open source software GANGLIA is installed to monitor the workload and hardware status. Some in-house shell scripts are used for the system administration. Other software including job scheduler, data preprocessing, and postprocessing are also configured. The detailed information of these software programs is listed in Table 5.11.

### 5.5.2 Application Software

The main applications running on Mole-8.5 are based on discrete simulation, which covers a variety of systems and processes, such as granular flow, emulsions, polymers and proteins, foams and micro-/nano- flows, crystals and reaction-diffusion processes. Inspired by their common nature, IPE developed a general purpose algorithmic platform [TGW+04] for discrete methods at different scales. At micro-scale, the elements are fluctuating but con-

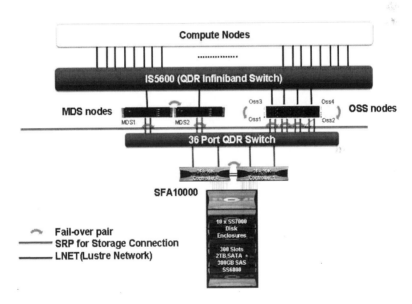

**FIGURE 5.17**: Configuration of the DDN storage of Mole-8.5 (provided by DDN).

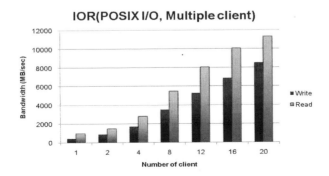

**FIGURE 5.18**: Performance of the DDN storage of Mole-8.5.

**TABLE 5.10**: Infrastructure data of Mole-8.5.

| Item | Value(units) |
|---|---|
| Occupied area | 180 M$^2$ |
| Designed load bearing | 500 Kg/M$^2$ |
| Max power consumption | 515 KW |
| Power consumption of air conditioner | 200 KW |
| Total power consumption | 715 KW |
| Weight | 12600 Kg |
| Cooling power | 520 KW |

**TABLE 5.11**: Mole-8.5 software configuration.

| Item | Configuration |
|---|---|
| Operation system | CentOS 5.4 |
| Kernel version | 2.6.18-164.el5 SMP X86_64 |
| C compiler | GCC-4.1.2 |
| C++ compiler | G++-4.1.2 |
| MPI version | mvapich-1.2.1 mvapich2-1.4.1 openmpi-1.4.2 |
| GPU driver | NVIDIA Linux X86_64 256.35 |
| GPU software | CUDA_Toolkit_4.0_rhel5_x86_64 CUDA_SDK_4.0 |
| Others | GangliaMole-8.5 job scheduler, library for multi-scale computation and communication, interface software for preprocess and postprocess |

serve kinetic energy, with examples of molecular dynamics (MD [RC86]), direct simulation Monte Carlo (DSMC [OC98]), and pseudo-particle modeling (PPM [GL96]). At meso-scale, the elements are both fluctuating and dissipative (that is, transforming mechanical energy into heat); typical examples are dissipative particle dynamics (DPD [HK92]) and lattice Boltzmann method (LBM [MZ88]). At macro-scale, the element motion is smooth and the elements dissipate energy also, such as smoothed particle hydrodynamics (SPH [Mon92]) and discrete element method (DEM [CS79]). With these methods, the full range of phenomena in process engineering, from atoms to apparatus, can be simulated, but computationally the essential differences among these methods are whether the elements are freely moving or pinned, that is, particle-based (such as MD) or lattice-based (such as LBM), and the mathematical formulation for the interactions between these particles. Therefore, as shown in Figure 5.19, with several algorithmic modules developed for particle- and lattice-based discrete methods respectively, all these methods can be implemented in the same framework with the corresponding interaction description module plugged in.

This platform for particle simulation was originally developed for CPU-based massive parallel systems [TGW+04]. With the development of GPGPUs and its programming environments, it is natural to transplant the platform to CPU+GPU hybrid systems. Although other approaches, like the implicit PDE solver for the gas, have been tried with encouraging success, particle simulation in a broader sense is, in general, more suitable for GPU implementation. As described [GWY+11], the cell list and neighbor list schemes are combined in GPU implementation, where cell list is employed to traverse all elements and find their interaction neighbors which are then put into their neighbor list. When putting the particles into cells, one thread is preferably assigned with one particle. Thanks to the atomic functions supported by the new generation NVIDIA GPUs (C2050 and later), one cell can contain several particles, but the write conflict, which occurs when multiple threads write to the global memory, can be avoided. The neighbor list thus generated for each particle is stored in a two-dimensional array (NxM) in the global memory of the GPU, where N is the particle number plus the padded number given by *cudaMallocPitch*, and M is the maximum neighbor number for a particle. In this way, although memory redundancy is unavoidable, coalesced global memory access is achieved. When generating the neighbor list, one block corresponds to one cell with each particle in it assigned to a different thread to speed up the computation. The particle information of the local and neighboring cells is buffered in the shared memory to reduce the global memory access. The data copy between GPU and CPU and communication through network can be overlapped by asynchronous execution. The boundary particles can be computed first and then sent to adjacent process. The data copy and transfer can be done simultaneously with the computation of inner particles. The overall flow chart for the general algorithm is shown in Figure 5.20.

## 5.6    Application

### 5.6.1    Quasi-Realtime Simulation of Industrial-Scale Rotating Drum [XQF⁺11, GWY⁺11]

We start with a simpler case without the presence of gas flow. Rotating drums are widely used in many industries ranging from metallurgy to pharmacy, for mixing, granulation, as well separation. With a simplified DEM overlooking the tangential component of the contact force and particle rotation, our algorithm achieved the highest speed of 8.98e7 particle*step/second (pss) for 0.123 million particles on a single C2050 board, and 7.89e7 pss for a maximum of 0.443 million particles. To simulate the industrial scale rotating

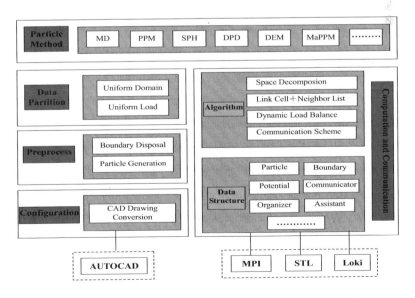

**FIGURE 5.19**: General algorithmic platform for discrete simulation. (From Springer and Science in China Series B Chemistry, volume 47, 2004, pp. 434–442, Parallelizing of macro-scale pseudo-particle modeling for particle-fluid systems, Tang, D., Ge, W., Wang, X. et al. With kind permission from Springer Science + Business Media.)

drum, we use MPI for parallel implementation. A rotary kiln, 13.5 meters in length and 1.5 meters in diameter, is simulated in 1D domain-decomposition along the rotation axis. The main simulation parameters are: particle density 7860 kg/m$^3$, diameter 1cm, elasticity 7.95 GN/m, restitution coefficient 0.78, time step 0.1 ms, rotating speed 5 rpm. A total of 9,606,450 particles are simulated using up to 270 GPUs. Each hosts 35,000 particles on average. The corresponding performance is about 1.64e7 pss, reaching only 18.3% of the optimal performance on a single board due to the high communication cost incurred by fine-grain partition in parallelization. However, the system evolves at about 1/10th of the real process, which is the highest overall performance of this series of simulations. Figure 5.21 shows some snapshots from the simulation. A more comprehensive tangential interaction model was later added to the simulations, and the performance was 50% lower in general. However, no major setback in the relative efficiency of the algorithm was seen, as many more operations are needed for particle interactions as compared to additional operations for particle searching, indexing, and data communications. This method can also be used in other simulations which have similar properties or as a base to develop codes simulating more complex systems.

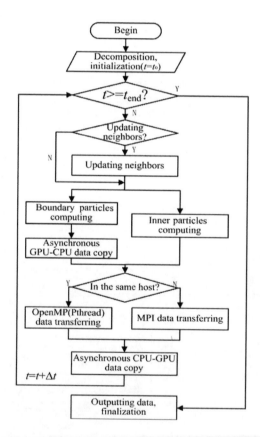

**FIGURE 5.20**: General purpose particle simulation algorithm on multiple GPUs [GWY$^+$11]. (Reprinted from *Chemical Engineering Science*, Vol 66, Ge, W., Wang, W., Yang, N. et al., Meso-scale oriented simulation towards virtual process engineering (VPE)— the EMMS paradigm, pp. 4426–4458, Copyright 2011, with permission from Elsevier.)

### 5.6.2 Direct Numerical Simulation of Gas-Solid Suspension [XLZ$^+$12, GWY$^+$11, LGW$^+$13]

With multi-GPU computing in LBM, a two-dimensional gas-solid suspension in a domain of 11.5 cm x 46 cm with 15,360 x 61,440 lattices, and a three-dimensional suspension in a domain of 0.384 cm x 1.512 cm x 0.384 cm with 512 x 2016 x 512 lattices are simulated at sub-particle level, that is, direct numerical simulation (DNS). The particle numbers involved are 1,166,400 and 129,024, respectively. The evolution of the solid particles was computed by the CPUs while that of the gas flow was carried out by the GPUs simultaneously. These domain sizes and particle numbers are large enough for the suspensions to display continuum properties which can be sampled reasonably and give very useful information to higher level simulation methods. At the same time, about 20-60X speedup is obtained compared to one core of an Intel E5520 CPU core with icc -fast compiling.

A snapshot of the two-dimensional suspension at four instants and the three-dimensional suspension are shown in Figure 5.22 and Figure 5.23, respectively, where distinct particle clusters can be observed. In such a large domain, they are fully developed, with a statistically stabilized size distribution and display kaleidoscopic morphology due to their interactions with the surrounding gas flow. The clusters may contain only several particles, but some may have tens of thousands of particles, which has not been seen in DNS previously.

### 5.6.3 Atomistic Simulation of a Virus in Vivo [XWH$^+$11, GWY$^+$11, LGW$^+$13]

The influenza virion, with a diameter of approximately 100 to 150 nm, is a major cause of global infection and mortality. However, the dynamic structure of the virion in solution is not clear due to finite resolving power of current experimental facilities. MD simulations can be used as a "computational microscope" to provide atomic details of the virion. Based on

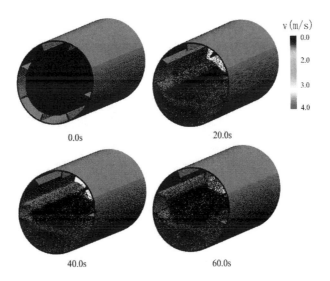

**FIGURE 5.21**: Snapshots from the simulation of the industrial scale rotary drum [XQF$^+$11]. (Reprinted from *Particuology*, Vol 9, J. Xu, H. Qi, X. Fang et al., Quasi-real-time simulation of rotating drum using discrete element method with parallel GPU computing, pp. 446–450, Copyright 2011, with permission from Elsevier.)

the crystal structures of component macromolecules and the general structure of influenza virions, an atomic but stationary picture of the 3D structure of influenza virion can be reconstructed. The simulated virion consists of 2,363 proteins, 63,471 DPPC molecules, and 8 RNA strands, resulting in 300 million atoms in a periodic cube with each side of 148.5 nm long (Figure 5.24 left). A software package, GPU_MD-1.0.5, has been developed for large-scale parallel MD simulations based on the general platform of Mole-8.5. With tremendous computational power of 1,728 C2050 GPUs, the simulation has reached a speed of 770 ps/day with an integration time step of 1fs. Starting from the predefined structure, the virus experiences a significant change to obtain a stable structure. As shown in Figure 5.24 right, the three components of radius of gyration (Rgx, Rgy, and Rgz), calculated for all the atoms in the lipid membrane and transmembrane proteins, show similar behaviors during the 0.5 ns simulation. The simulated structure of influenza virion in solution at atomic level can provide valuable knowledge to understand its biological function and help design anti-influenza drugs to prevent influenza epidemics.

### 5.6.4    Atomistic Simulation of Crystalline Silicon [HXW$^+$12a,b, GWY$^+$11, LGW$^+$13]

We also carried out large-scale MD simulation on crystalline silicon and its surface reconstruction, which is of general significance to the simulation of another prominent chemical and physical phenomena, that is, crystalline silicon. The MD simulation for pure crystalline silicon on GPUs has reached 339 Tflops (SP) using 1500 GPUs, reaching 22% of the corresponding peak performance. The simulation has been extended from the Mole-8.5 system to the Tianhe-1A supercomputer. Using all 7,168 GPUs on Tianhe-1A, The simulation of

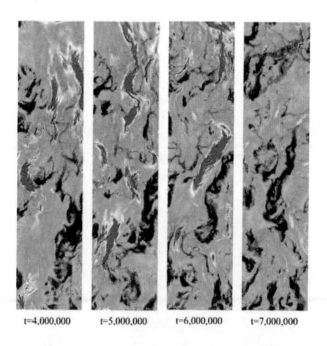

t=4,000,000      t=5,000,000      t=6,000,000      t=7,000,000

**FIGURE 5.22**: Snapshots of the two-dimensional DNS of gas-solid suspension. (Reprinted from *Chemical Engineering Science*, Vol 66, Ge, W., Wang, W., Yang, N. et al., Mesoscale oriented simulation towards virtual process engineering (VPE)—the EMMS paradigm, pp. 4426–4458, Copyright 2011, with permission from Elsevier.)

crystalline silicon using the Tersoff potential reaches 1.87 Pflops in single precision, which is 25.3% of its peak performance. Around 80% of instruction throughput and memory throughput can be employed on a single GPU. The simulation reproduces the microscopic behaviors of about 110 billion atoms. Furthermore, by coupling 86,016 CPU cores on Tianhe1A, we achieved a sustainable performance of 1.17 Pflops in single precision plus 92 Tflops in double precision for the simulation of surface reconstruction involving 111.2 billion atoms and

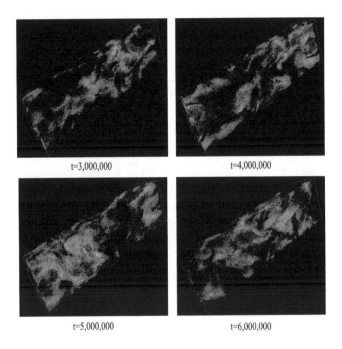

**FIGURE 5.23**: Snapshots of the three-dimensional DNS of gas-solid suspension. (Reprinted from *Chemical Engineering Science*, Vol 66, Ge, W., Wang, W., Yang, N. et al., Meso-scale oriented simulation towards virtual process engineering (VPE)—the EMMS paradigm, pp. 4426–4458, Copyright 2011, with permission from Elsevier.)

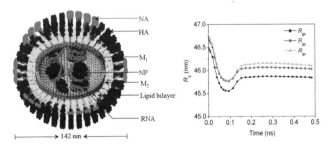

**FIGURE 5.24**: (Left) Structure of the simulated influenza virion with a quarter of the outer sphere moved over to show the interior details. Components are shown in different colors for better visualization. (Right) Radius of gyration of exterior structure of the virion as a function of simulation time [XWH+11]. (From Springer and *Chinese Science Bulletin*, volume 56, 2011, pp. 2114–2118, Application of the Mole-8.5 supercomputer: Probing the whole influenza virion at the atomic level, J. Xu, X.W. Wang, X.F. He et al. With kind permission from Springer Science + Business Media.)

approaching millimeter scale in one dimension. The algorithms developed in the simulations can potentially be used to investigate solid covalent material, nano-/micro-fluidics devices, silane pyrolysis, and the silicon deposition process, and so on. Also, the simulation provides an opportunity to be coupled with the larger scale directly to achieve trans-scale simulation from atoms to reactors, which will be of high significance to a wide range of industries and disciplines.

It is expected that the performance of the simulations can be further improved slightly by combining statistical or control operations to the updating kernel. But the major performance elevation of the coupling algorithm may come from the optimization of the communication among CPUs and the load balancing among the threads on the CPUs in one node. 2D and 3D partitions are also promising, so that problems with more complicated geometries can be simulated with higher flexibility and efficiency. Defects, impurities, and irregular grain boundaries can be taken into account also.

---

## 5.7   Conclusion and Prospect

Starting from application requirements, IPE proposed and developed a multi-scale supercomputing mode with high efficiency and low cost. It embodies the consistency of simulated system, model, software, and hardware structures, providing powerful methods to solve problems in engineering and scientific computation. The application-oriented development mode and the extremely low cost-effect ratio demonstrated by the Mole-8.5 supercomputer, as compared to the current mainstream HPC systems, may set a new paradigm for computation with innovative architecture, which sheds light on the coming of virtual process engineering in the near future.

---

## Acknowledgments

We thank all members of the EMMS group at IPE. The development and application of the Mole series supercomputers introduced in this chapter is a long-term endeavor by the whole group, while we only act here as reporters on this work. Most content in this chapter is based on previous publications of the group as cited. This work is sponsored by the National Natural Science Foundation of China under a series of grants, the Ministry of Finance under grant no. ZDYZ2008-2, and the Chinese Academy of Sciences under grants nos. KGCX2-YW-124 and KGCX2-YW-222. We also thank NVIDIA for sponsoring the CUDA Center of Excellence (CCOE) at IPE.

# Chapter 6

## Supercomputing in the DoD High Performance Computing Modernization Program

**John E. West, Roy L. Campbell, and Larry P. Davis**

*Department of Defense High Performance Computing Modernization Program*

## 6.1 Overview

The Department of Defense High Performance Computing Modernization Program (HPCMP) was initiated in 1992 in response to Congressional direction to modernize the Department of Defense (DoD) laboratories' high performance computing capabilities. The HPCMP was assembled out of a collection of two dozen or so smaller high performance computing departments that had independently evolved within the Army, Air Force, and Navy laboratories and test centers.

Today, the HPCMP (http://www.hpc.mil) provides the supercomputer capability, high-speed network communications, and computational science expertise that enables the Defense laboratories and test centers to conduct a wide range of focused research, development, and test activities. This partnership puts advanced technology in the hands of U.S. forces more quickly, less expensively, and with greater certainty of success. By providing advanced computational resources to the DoD, the HPCMP advances department's fundamental understanding of materials, aerodynamics, chemistry, fuels, acoustics, signal image recognition, electromagnetics, and other areas of research; as well as enabling advanced test and evaluation environments such as synthetic scene generation, automatic control systems, and virtual test environments.

In its most recent technology insertion, the HPCMP acquired eight systems totaling 5PF of peak capability and 316K compute cores. Of these systems, only one contains a non-InfiniBand interconnect – the Cray XE6, which is located at the U.S. Army Corps of Engineers, Engineer Research and Development Center (ERDC) in Vicksburg, MS. This system provides 1.5PF of peak capability using 151K compute cores, and is the feature of the discussion below.

### 6.1.1    Program Background

Broadly speaking, the mission of the HPCMP is to accelerate the development and transition of new technologies into superior defense capabilities through the strategic application of high performance computing, networking, and computational expertise. HPC is particularly important to the execution of the department's mission in three critical areas: in research, where HPC enables DoD to explore new theories and evaluate them well beyond what is practical using experiment alone; in acquisition, through the use of validated applications in design and testing which significantly reduces the time and cost of developing weapon systems and improves the quality of their designs; and in operations, where real-time calculations produce just-in-time information for decision makers on the battlefield.

Within DoD, high performance computing amplifies the creativity, productivity, and impact of the DoD research, development, test, and evaluation (RDT&E) communities by giving them access to insight about the physical world and human actions within it that would otherwise be too costly, too dangerous, or too time-intensive to obtain through observation and experiment alone.

The development and use of high performance computing has been an important contributor to the U.S. leadership in military technology. It has an impressive legacy going back to the early days of electronic computing and the ENIAC in 1946 (Electronic Numerical Integrator And Calculator, shown in Figure 6.1). The need for ENIAC was born, as with many new discoveries, from DoD requirements for the timely production of artillery firing tables. The original ENIAC patent, filed in 1947, provides a statement of need that is as relevant today as it was 65 years ago: "The most advanced machines have greatly reduced the time required for arriving at solutions to problems which might have required months or days by older procedures. This advance, however, is not adequate for many problems encountered in modern scientific work and the present invention is intended to reduce to seconds such lengthy computations" [EM].

Today, the HPCMP serves as the central resource for expertise in the application of high-end computing within the DoD, providing the people, expertise, and technologies that increase the productivity of the DoD's RDT&E community. As of this writing this community includes several thousand HPC users to whom the HPCMP provides supercomputers, software application development expertise, and high-bandwidth wide area network capabilities.

The HPCMP deploys the most advanced computing technologies available for routine use in the DoD through an architecturally diverse, annually refreshed base of supercomputers and storage systems deployed at five supercomputing centers located across the nation. The five centers provide a complete computational environment to the user community which includes a central customer assistance center, a consolidated data analysis and visualization capability, application support personnel, domain scientists, system and system software support personnel, and the management needed to make it all operate effectively.

**FIGURE 6.1**: Programming the ENIAC at the Ballistics Research Laboratory (U.S. Army Photo).

In addition to providing a common source of supercomputers to run critical defense applications, the HPCMP is responsible for modernizing the base of DoD science and engineering applications by providing the vision, funding, and expertise to develop advanced physics-based computational analysis capabilities through the Department's network of laboratories and warfare centers. The HPCMP also executes software projects that develop a specific product while at the same time demonstrating and maturing large-scale scientific software development practices within the Department. Finally, the HPCMP maintains a conduit for the DoD through which the latest university and industrial research can be injected into the computational practices of the RDT&E community, and through which the DoD computational workforce can be trained in modern computational practice.

A critical piece of enabling infrastructure for research, development, and testing in general within the DoD, and for supercomputing in specific, is the Defense Research and Engineering Network (DREN). The HPCMP provisions and manages the DREN on behalf of the DoD as a component of the Global Information Grid (GIG). The DREN provides rich connectivity among DoD science and technology, test and evaluation, and computational research communities and DoD supercomputing centers, and also serves as a proving ground for next-generation technologies in networking and cybersecurity. Figure 6.2 provides a graphical overview of the program today.

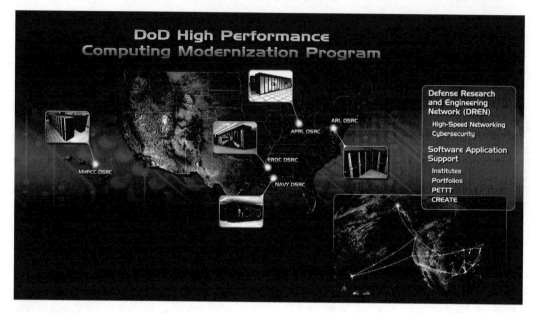

**FIGURE 6.2**: The major components of the DoD High Performance Computing Modernization Program (HPCMP).

## 6.1.2    Timeline

There are perhaps as many approaches to specifying and purchasing supercomputers as there are programs that run them, and each acquisition approach reflects the specific nature of the mission being served as well as the expectations and requirements of each program's users. The HPCMP's approach to system acquisition centers around the routine (generally annual) deployment of new, commercially available, state-of-the-practice HPC systems that interface with a stable, long-term service architecture that includes data archive, analysis and visualization resources, and the other services expected of modern supercomputing centers. These services are updated with new technologies and expanded capabilities regularly as well, but on a different time scale than the HPC systems. This approach is in contrast to another common approach in which a single very large system is acquired once every four or five years along with significant increases in storage and support hardware.

Meeting the expectations of the DoD user community requires that the HPCMP develop, demonstrate, and mature state-of-the-practice supercomputers and related technologies, rather than to directly fund the development of new types of supercomputers or special-purpose system software (although the HPCMP does fund the development of selected large-scale scientific and engineering applications). Stated another way, the HPCMP employs a "fast follower" strategy for its HPC technology that offers a balance between an agile response to the emergence of new technology, and the expectations of its user community of a stable, productive computing environment.

HPCMP hardware acquisitions are generally conducted annually and, as of the time of this writing, result in the addition of two to three new supercomputers in its centers with an aggregate value of $40M-$50M. These systems are planned for a nominal 48-month lifecycle, at which point it is generally no longer cost-effective to continue to operate a machine versus replacing it with more reliable and more capable current-generation technology. Each year a number of systems are retired from the program and new systems are introduced. Because of historical performance and price/performance improvements in microprocessor technologies, the historical trend is for the net effect of HPC system retirements and new installations to roughly double the total installed compute capability of the program each year.

## 6.2 Applications and Workloads

The workload on DoD HPCMP systems is complex and varied. As discussed earlier, it spans activities from basic research to the testing and product improvement of developing and existing DoD systems. The bulk of computational work supported by the program is focused in the early stages of the research and development cycle, primarily basic research through technology development, but the program is also increasing efforts to transform the later stages of this cycle, system development, testing, and improvement, through the judicious use of HPC.

The HPCMP characterizes its computational workload in broad categories of scientific and engineering disciplines called computational technology areas (CTAs). The DoD identifies and categorizes existing and new computational projects on an annual basis through a detailed requirements gathering process targeted at the entire DoD RDT&E community. Each of the approximate 600 computational projects completes an extensive questionnaire covering all aspects of that project's computational needs, including hardware, software, communications, and training. The total computational needs in each CTA, along with the specific software applications that are used in each CTA, are key inputs to selection and weighting of application benchmark codes that are used to acquire new HPC systems.

The program's eleven computational technology areas are shown in Table 6.1. The first five of the CTAs shown in Table 6.1, plus the environmental quality modeling and simulation CTA, reflect traditional supercomputing disciplines that are similar to computational work performed by other federal agencies, such as DOE, NASA, and NSF.

CFD has traditionally been the largest of the CTAs in the HPCMP, both in terms of overall requirements and numbers of users. All three of the Services use CFD to model air flow and performance of air, land, and sea vehicles. CSM includes work in both traditional structural mechanics and dynamics structures under small deformations and shock physics, which models large deformation and breakup of structures under projectile impact or explosion.

The fastest growing CTA over the last decade has been computational chemistry, biology, and materials science (CCM). Much of this work occurs is basic research, and includes traditional quantum chemistry, molecular dynamics, and materials modeling. Primary areas of interest include new energetic materials, new structural materials including additives to existing materials, and non-linear optical materials. A big challenge in this area is coupling disparate length and time scales from the atomistic to bulk materials properties.

Computational electromagnetic and acoustics (CEA) includes the interaction of electromagnetic waves with objects (as when calculating the radar cross section of an aircraft) and magnetohydrodynamics modeling of microwave and laser devices. Recent developments in microwave devices have shown significant promise in the limitation of the electronics capability of an opposing force and in non-lethal control of personnel in a hostile environment.

The climate/weather/ocean modeling and simulation (CWO) CTA includes modeling of both atmospheric and oceanic conditions that are of importance to the DoD system operating environment. The weather and ocean predictions produced by these simulations, using applied CFD techniques, is made available to DoD operational forces on a near-real-time basis. Finally, environmental quality modeling and simulation helps the DoD to

**TABLE 6.1:** HPCMP Computational Technology Areas.

| Technology Area | Description |
|---|---|
| Computational Structural Mechanics (CSM) | Covers the high-resolution multidimensional modeling of materials and structures subjected to a broad range of loading conditions including quasi-static, dynamic, electromagnetic, shock, penetration, and blast. It also includes the highly inter-disciplinary research area of materials design, where multi-scale modeling of different scales from atomistic to macro is essential. |
| Computational Fluid Dynamics (CFD) | Covers high-performance computations whose goal is the accurate numerical solution of the equations describing fluid and gas motion, and the related use of digital computers in fluid dynamics research. CFD is used for basic studies of fluid-dynamics for engineering design of complex flow configurations, and for predicting the interactions of chemistry with fluid flow for combustion and propulsion. |
| Computational Chemistry, Biology, and Materials Science (CCM) | Covers computational tools used to predict basic properties of chemicals and materials, including nano- and biomaterials. Phenomena such as molecular geometries and energies, spectroscopic parameters, intermolecular forces, reaction potential energy surfaces, and mechanical properties are being studied. |
| Computational Electromagnetics and Acoustics (CEA) | Provides high-resolution multidimensional solutions of electromagnetic and acoustic wave equations in solids, fluids, and gases. |
| Climate/Weather/Ocean Modeling and Simulation (CWO) | Focuses on the accurate numerical simulation of the earth's atmosphere and oceans on space and time scales important for both scientific understanding and DoD operational use. |
| Signal/Image Processing (SIP) | Covers the extraction of useful information from sensor outputs in real-time. DoD applications include surveillance, reconnaissance, intelligence, communications, avionics, smart munitions, and electronic warfare. |
| Forces Modeling and Simulation (FMS) | Focuses on the research and development of HPC-based physical, logical, and behavioral models and simulations of battlespace phenomenology in the correlation of forces. |
| Environmental Quality Modeling and Simulation (EQM) | Supports the investigation of DoD impacts on the environment and the impacts of this environment upon DoD activities. Technical activities involve the high-resolution modeling of hydrodynamics, geophysics, and multi-constituent fate/transport through the coupled atmospheric/land surface/subsurface environment, and their interconnections with numerous biological species and anthropogenic activities. |
| Electronics, Networking, and Systems/ C4I (ENS) | Focuses on the use of computational science in support of analysis, design, modeling, and simulation of electronics from the most basic fundamental, first-principles physical level to its use for communications, sensing, and information systems engineering; activity ranges from the analysis and design of nano-devices to C4ISR systems-of-systems. |
| Integrated Modeling and Test Environments (IMT) | Addresses the application of integrated modeling and simulation tools and techniques with live tests and hardware-in-the-loop simulations for the testing and evaluation of DoD weapon components, subsystems, and systems in virtual and composite virtual-real environments. |
| Space and Astrophysical Sciences (SAS) | Embodies the use of mathematics, computational science, and engineering in the analysis, design, identification, modeling, and simulation of the space and near-space environment, and of all objects therein, whether artificial or natural. |

understand both its impact on the environment, and also the effect of the environment on DoD systems. Specific problems that are studied include atmospheric and water transport, including both subsurface and surface water.

In addition to these six "traditional" supercomputing disciplines, Table 6.1 shows another five CTAs that include work that is more real-time in nature, unique to DoD, or both. Much of this work requires access to HPCMP systems based on delivery modes different from the traditional batch-oriented job scheduling systems that work well for the traditional disciplines. The HPCMP provides these alternative delivery modes through several mechanisms, including: dedicated HPC project investments, which provide modest-sized dedicated HPC systems for projects that cannot use the shared resources at centers; dedicated support partitions, which create a virtual machine within one of the large, shared HPC systems at HPCMP centers for projects that require dedicated nodes for extended periods of time; and an advanced reservation service for projects with jobs that require very predictable access to HPCMP systems. Typical requirements that dictate one or more of these alternative delivery mechanisms include real-time requirements driven by attached experimental or test equipment or human-in-the-loop computational work, classified computational work at levels higher than Secret, evaluation of new architectures not available at HPCMP centers, and use of operating systems or unique computational environments not generally present on HPCMP systems.

Signal/image processing, or SIP, is among this set of five non-traditional CTAs. The majority of work in this CTA involves real-time processing of an experimental or test instrument data stream, and much of it can be done in single-precision computation. The processed data is then used for analysis of the progress of the test or experiment and thus can be used to alter experimental or test conditions as the experiment or test is in progress. Clearly this computational work cannot be batch-scheduled on a shared HPC resource.

One CTA with computational work unique to DoD is forces modeling and simulation, or FMS. In this CTA discrete-event engines simulate the interactions among many entities on two or more opposing forces. These entities can be individual soldiers, vehicles, and weapons, or they can be larger aggregates representing entire military units, depending on the nature of the interactions between entities and the required fidelity. Often simulations are carried out in federations of resources in which some entities are simulated on an HPC system and others are real soldiers, equipment, or vehicles. In this case, the real players are networked into the simulation, sometimes from remote locations. This is another clear case for which traditional batch scheduling will not work. When the simulation is based on a detailed interaction among only a few entities at high fidelity, it falls into the integrated modeling and test environments CTA, with many of the same characteristics as a complete conflict simulation exercise.

One type of modeling that has developed more recently is the modeling of networks, included in the electronics, networking, and systems/C4I CTA. This CTA also includes modeling of electronic devices in general. Some of this computational work involves real-time simulations of components, while other work can be done on traditional batch systems. The final non-traditional CTA, space and astrophysical sciences, primarily involves space situational awareness, including image enhancement of objects in space for identification purposes. Much of this work is real-time in nature.

## 6.2.1 Highlights of Main Applications

We will focus on examples of major applications for each of the first five (traditional) CTAs, and provide appreciable details on two of these. Together this set of applications claims a significant share of the total computational requirements of the HPCMP customer community, and of the total computational work done on HPCMP systems.

Much of the work in the computational structural mechanics CTA is done with shock physics codes such as CTH, EPIC, and ALEGRA. Depending on conditions and materials, each of these codes has contributed to the development of new armor and anti-armor materials and techniques by helping to reach a more complete understanding of how materials and structures react when exposed to an energetic event. The DoD has used CSM codes over the past several years to help redesign armor plating on military vehicles deployed to the Mideast that face significant risk from improvised explosive devices. The use of HPCMP systems to rapidly model alternative designs and materials to protect these vehicles has saved many lives.

The computational fluid dynamics CTA uses a wide variety of application codes, including commercial codes such as ANSYS-CFD (formerly FLUENT) and Cobalt, individual project-developed codes, and DoD-developed codes. Of particular note is the fixed-wing air vehicle application being developed by the HPCMP called Kestrel. Kestrel originally used the AVUS computational kernel which, along with Cobalt, developed from the Air Force Research Laboratory code Cobalt-60, but has now moved on to rely upon its own kernel. It is an unstructured grid code with a 2nd order flow solver that can be integrated with a structural mechanics model to solve coupled structure/flow problems. It also has the capability to treat two or more bodies with separate, but interacting, grids. Kestrel has already been used for a wide variety of air vehicle applications, and its capability to model two bodies in relative motion to each other has allowed it to be particularly useful for aircraft-store certification.

Whenever DoD wishes to configure a specific aircraft with a combination of stores (such as weapons and external fuel tanks) different from what has previously been flown, the proposed combination of stores on that particular aircraft must be certified that it is a safe configuration to fly. Historically this has been done by physical testing, which can be expensive and time-consuming. Over the last ten years, increasingly accurate and efficient CFD models have been used to assist in the certification of new aircraft-store configurations, including simulations of store release, and these models have now progressed to the point that some aircraft-store configurations can be certified with limited or no flight testing, although this capability is generally reserved for new configurations fairly close to previously certified configurations. The development of Kestrel over the last two years has enabled DoD to use CFD simulations on HPC systems to play a major role in the aircraft-store certification process. An example of a system for which store certifications are required is the F-16C with tip AIM-9 missiles shown in Figure 6.3. A comparison of the CFD results from both Kestrel and Cobalt to flight test data is illustrated in Figure 6.4 for some of the CFD coefficients. Agreement is very good for both codes.

**FIGURE 6.3**: Pressure contours on an F-16C configured with tip AIM-9 missiles at Mach 0.9, the same as for the data comparisons shown in Figure 6.4.

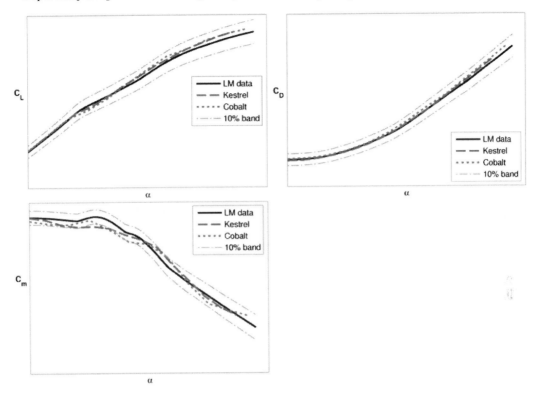

**FIGURE 6.4**: Comparisons among F-16C CFD computations (Kestrel and Cobalt, full-scale) with LEF = 0 degrees vs. performance data with LEF = 0 degrees for CL, CD, and Cm, Mach 0.9.

Applications in the computational chemistry, biology, and materials science CTA include a variety of codes that are used to calculate molecular and materials structure, energy levels, and interactions among them under various conditions. At the atomistic level, basic quantum chemistry codes such as GAMESS or GAUSSIAN can calculate molecular properties using an increasingly complex and accurate set of approximations to the true wave function, but at the price of greatly increasing computational requirements. Once molecular properties are determined at a suitable level of accuracy, these properties can be fed into a molecular dynamics code, such as LAMMPS, to simulate the motions of groups of molecules over a time frame of interest that allows study of properties of the material. LAMMPS has the ability to treat systems of billions of atoms, and can simulate materials composed of sets of much larger particles than molecules, such as ensembles of soil grains, provided the interaction potential of these interacting particles is known to a reasonable degree of accuracy.

The U.S. Army Engineer Research and Development Center (ERDC) has done much computational modeling using LAMMPS on high-strength fibers composed of carbon nanotubes, including the development of a design for a scalable carbon nanotube fiber that has a predicted tensile strength of about 60 GPa (8.6-million psi), one of the world's strongest scalable fiber designs as of this writing [CW11]. In addition, ERDC is using LAMMPS to guide development of a crystalline design for a super ceramic composite of polycrystalline silicon carbide(SiC) reinforced with high-strength tensile members, such as carbon nanotubes or graphene. Technical ceramics, such as SiC and boron carbide, have very good high-temperature, high-compressive strength, and high-stiffness properties, and have relatively low densities (on par with aluminum). Their stiffness-to-weight and compressive strength-to-weight ratios are three times or better those of high-strength aluminum and high-strength steel, making them near-ideal candidates as very lightweight replacements for steel and aluminum in structures and in transportation systems, including cars, ships, and aircraft. Unfortunately technical ceramics also have relatively low tensile strengths, are quite brittle, and fail catastrophically when subjected to critical amounts of stress. The idea behind the carbon nanotube or graphene additives is to cause the ceramic composites to fail much more gracefully, and thus their inherent strength and low density could be taken advantage of for applications where catastrophic failure is not an option.

Molecular dynamics simulation methods for polycrystalline ceramics are complex because of the range of atomic species interactions that must be modeled, and because of the number of crystalline structures, the variety of crystalline sizes and orientations, and the complex boundary regions that must be modeled to predict composite material behavior. The simulation methods for ceramics are being developed, refined, and validated as they are being used. The simulations allow the ceramic parameter space to be explored much more efficiently than can be done by experiment, and provide much greater insight into the causes for material response. The simulations, in fact, allow investigation of material constructs that currently may be impossible to formulate experimentally. Figure 6.5 provides the molecular dynamics simulation results for a columnar volume of a polycrystalline silicon carbide subjected to tensile loads. The SiC volume was composed of 10-nm diameter crystalline grains. Only the atoms along fracture surfaces that are under-coordinated (bonds broken) or are completely dislocated are shown. These simulations employed a total of 1-10 million atoms, and used about 50,000 cpu-hours overall, with typical jobs using hundreds to thousands of processors. Interestingly, the non-intuitive transgranular-type failure that was predicted as part of the failure surface has also been observed experimentally in the laboratory. These types of simulations are revealing underlying causes of a material's response – in this case the crystal grain orientation and shear plane relative to the propagating fracture surface. They are being used to guide design toward a ceramic composite with much improved tensile strength and fracture toughness. Experimental work will then be used to verify the predicted property improvements.

The computational electromagnetics and acoustics CTA also includes a variety of computational techniques and applications, but we focus here on an area that has made much progress recently – modeling of microwave devices. The primary application developed and used by DoD for this purpose is ICEPIC, a particle-in-cell plasma physics code. This class of applications calculates the electromagnetic fields present in a device, the effects of those fields on the charged particles in terms of their motion in each cell of the device, and then feeds back the effects of that motion to the originating electromagnetic fields themselves. The oscillatory motions of the particles produce microwaves that are then focused out of the device and onto a target. The target can be hostile electronics equipment, against which microwaves of the proper frequency and amplitude can be disruptive, or an opposing force, against which these same microwaves can be intensely painful but not harmful. As highlighted on the CBS television program "60 Minutes" recently, these devices might present an effective yet humane mechanism for controlling hostile crowds without causing long-term damage.

The Department has also been developing and delivering an increasingly sophisticated set of ocean and atmospheric models over the last 30 years for use in weather and ocean-state forecasts. The most recent of these ocean models is the hybrid ocean coordinate model (HYCOM). Current atmospheric models include NOGAPS, a global atmospheric model, and COAMPS, a regional atmospheric model. Extensive development and testing of these models is done on HPCMP systems, and the "hindcasts" made by these models are then compared with measured conditions to validate them. All of these models make extensive use of measured atmospheric and ocean conditions as input to "spin up" forecasts that

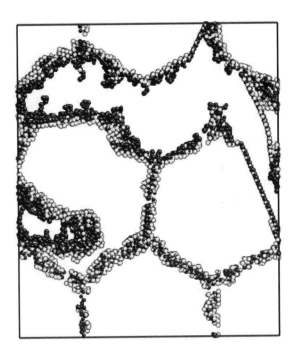

**FIGURE 6.5**: Molecular dynamics simulated response of 10-nm dia. polycrystalline-grained silicon carbide subject to tensile failure. Only atoms along fracture surfaces or grain boundaries are shown, with black and gray atoms denoting under-coordinated or dislocated atoms, respectively.

are made at least several days into the future. As forecasts improve significantly with the increased resolution and sophistication of the physics incorporated, the fleet can better plan its deployments and operational activities.

## 6.3   System Overview

During its 20-year history, the HPCMP has provided 175 HPC systems to the DoD community ranging from the Intel Paragon and Cray Y-MP of the early 1990s to the Cray XE6, IBM iDataPlex, and SGI Carlsbad 3 of today. Over time, DoD Supercomputing Resource Centers (DSRCs) have housed 90 HPCMP systems (as summarized in Figure 6.6), with the remaining 85 systems being placed in the proximity of specific projects or within smaller distributed centers.

As a result of a 2012 technology insertion, the HPCMP acquired eight HPC systems totaling 5PF of peak capability using 316,000 compute cores. Of these systems, only one contains a non-InfiniBand interconnect – the Cray XE6. This XE6 (located at the U.S. Army Corps of Engineers, Engineer Research and Development Center (ERDC) in Vicksburg, MS) provides 1.5PF of peak capability using 151K compute cores, and is the feature of the discussion below.

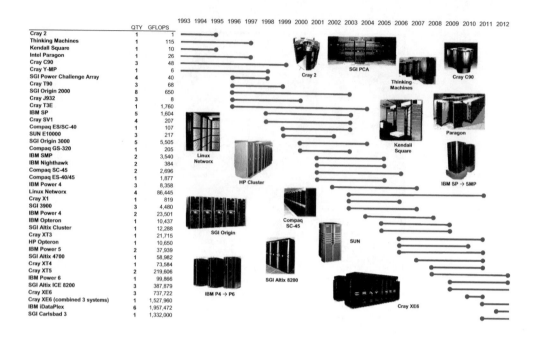

**FIGURE 6.6**: Historical overview of HPCMP supercomputers (1993-2012).

## 6.4    Hardware Architecture

Although the HPCMP's workload is predominantly MPI-based [DCJWJH07], it spans many scientific and engineering disciplines, and therefore requires a flexible architecture that can address a broad array of requirements. The Cray XE6 provides a scalable and reliable solution that can easily be configured to address both general and special-purpose needs. This architecture was a natural progression for the HPCMP, given its successful use of XT3, XT4, and XT5 architectures over the past six years, and demonstrates a strategic leveraging of years of DARPA High Productivity Computing Systems (HPCS) research and development [DGH+08], exhibited most profoundly in the XE6's interconnect – Gemini. The combination of commodity-based nodes (containing AMD Interlagos processors) and a specialized interconnect allows the HPCMP to address capability and capacity jobs with one system, providing broad applicability of petascale computing to the DoD HPC community.

The ERDC XE6 will contain 1,179 compute blades, each containing eight 2.5GHz 16-core AMD Interlagos processors, for a total of 150,912 compute cores. Each core nominally retires four instructions per clock, thereby yielding a system peak of 1.5PF. The Interlagos chip is particularly advantageous to the HPCMP, since it is socket compatible with MagnyCours, which allowed the HPCMP to upgrade and consolidate its production Cray assets to build this powerful monolithic system. Interlagos is manufactured with a feature size of 32nm using a layered silicon-insulator-silicon substrate to reduce parasitic device capacitance commonly observed in traditional silicon substrates. Each processor contains two dies packaged in a multi-chip module (MCM) [AMD12]. Each die contains four modules, and each module contains two processing cores. Each core has a private 16KB L1 data cache. Each pair of cores shares a 2MB L2 cache, for an effective L2 cache of 1MB per core. The eight cores on a die share an 8MB L3 cache, for an effective L3 cache of 1MB per core. A larger effective

L2 cache per core is particularly important for the HPCMP's general purpose workload, given the dramatic difference in access time for L2 versus L3 cache (in clock cycles) and the likelihood that the working set size will be less than 1MB per core for a reasonable portion of the HPCMP workload.

The XE6 has two types of nodes: compute nodes and service nodes [Cra12c]. Services nodes address various system support functions including user login, system administration, queue management, and I/O. Compute nodes, in contrast, address job execution. Each compute node contains one Gemini network interface, two AMD Interlagos processors, and eight 8GB DIMMs for a total of 32 cores and 64GB of memory. Approximately 90% of the HPCMP's workload can be addressed with a memory per core density of 2GB. When necessary, this density can be increased to 4GB or 8GB for a select portion of the system. Each processor has four DDR3-1600 memory controller channels, one per 8GB DIMM, providing 51.2GB/s of peak memory throughput per processor (or 102.4GB/s per node) and providing main memory accesses within less than 100ns. Memory bandwidth is of particular concern for HPCMP jobs with larger working sets sizes using low-stride accesses, and memory latency is important for large-stride or random memory accesses. In total, the system contains 300TB of DDR3 memory distributed across 4,716 nodes.

To improve throughput, processors use AMD's Hyper Transport 3.0 to communicate with the Gemini ASIC (bypassing the PCI bus). Each Gemini ASIC contains two network interfaces (one for each of two nodes). The ASIC communicates with external nodes via the Gemini network, which is configured as a 3-D torus and provides a peak injection bandwidth of 9.6GB/s per node. The interconnection of all compute and services nodes with this tightly-coupled, low-latency, high-bandwidth network provides substantial performance to both capability and capacity jobs. Capability jobs require a large number of nodes which communicate frequently, typically with a diverse set of message sizes. Large messages are impacted mainly by network bandwidth, and small messages are impacted mainly by network latency. Capacity jobs can become fragmented across the system and benefit from Gemini's relatively flat latency profile – below a microsecond for (one-sided) remote puts, typically one to two microseconds for other point-to-point communications, and no more than three microseconds for communications between any two nodes. The Gemini ASIC distinguishes among certain communications types and accelerates each differently.

Over 200 object storage servers provide access to 5PB of spinning disk storage through a Cray-enhanced Lustre filesystem. The storage subsystem is connected by InfiniBand 4x QDR (40Gbps). High-quality disks (i.e., 2.5in. 450GB 10kRPM SAS drives) and RAID6(8+2) are used to ensure reliable I/O transactions for a wide range of HPCMP storage use cases.

All administrative aspects of the system can be monitored and managed through the hardware supervisory system (HSS). A separate 1 Gbps HSS network connects the system management workstation (SMW) to embedded hardware controllers throughout the system. At boot up, a system administrator logs into the system management workstation (SMW) and establishes the HSS and the high speed network (HSN; i.e., the Gemini interconnect). The system administrator then (via the network attached boot node) distributes Compute Node Linux (CNL) to the diskless compute nodes via the HSN.

Ten login nodes are provided for system access, compiling, linking, and job launching. Seven data virtualization service (DVS) nodes are provided to ensure compute nodes can access dynamic, shared libraries during execution. Eighteen PBS Pro machine-oriented mini-servers (MOMs) manage system batch scheduling.

## 6.5    System Software

For the compute nodes, the underlying services of the SUSE Linux kernel are strategically configured to minimize OS jitter and packaged under the moniker "Compute Node Linux (CNL)." OS jitter is of particular concern for tightly-coupled capability jobs, since stray (unsynchronized) OS interrupts can create imbalances in the job execution across nodes and lead to unnecessary wait time as interrupted processes catch up. The XE6 has the ability to dynamically enable additional services inside the kernel (as necessary based on job execution), which has proven useful for various independent software vendor codes within the HPCMP's workload.

Login nodes have standard Linux kernels to facilitate a user's productivity in compiling, linking, preparing input, job launching, and parsing/structuring output. A management node allows the system administrator to build and configure a login node image and push this image to all login nodes. User jobs are launched and managed by Altair's PBS Pro [Cra12d].

Lustre software is used to build and access user home directories and system scratch space. To ensure that dynamic, shared libraries can be accessed by PBS Pro launched jobs, data virtualization service (DVS) nodes project a special directory to the compute and login nodes, thereby providing a path that is invariant across the system [Cra12b].

Administrators control 4,716 compute nodes and nearly 300 services nodes via a hardware supervisory system (HSS). At boot up, a system administrator logs into the system management workstation (SMW) and (via the 1Gbps management network) establishes the HSS and the high speed network (HSN). The system administrator then distributes CNL to the diskless compute nodes via the HSN. A system database records component and system anomalies and failures to aid the system administrator in determining when it is necessary to update software, reconfigure nodes, and/or disable/replace components.

## 6.6    Programming System

Since the XE6 is a distributed memory system, only message passing methods can be used among nodes. Within a node, however, either message passing (e.g., MPI) or shared memory (e.g., SHMEM, OpenMP) methods can be used. Most codes in the HPCMP workload use MPI; a small number of codes use SHMEM or OpenMP, and an even smaller number use partitioned global address space (PGAS) models. PGAS models allow a user to designate variables as private or shared; private variables are kept local to a particular thread, while shared variables are placed in a global space that is allocated across all threads.

The XE6 supports MPI, OpenMP, SHMEM, and PGAS models (such as Unified Parallel C, Co-array Fortran, and Chapel) [Cra12a]. The Gemini interconnect provides hardware support for PGAS models, thereby yielding significant performance improvements over traditional library-based MPI methods when these PGAS models are used. Legacy code often cannot take advantage of PGAS models; therefore, the MPI stack has been optimized to exploit the various features of the Gemini interconnect.

C, C++, Fortran, Unified Parallel C, Co-array Fortran, and Chapel programming languages, and Cray, PGI, PathScale, and GNU compilers are supported. C and Fortran are the most commonly used languages among current DoD supercomputing applications. Re-

**TABLE 6.2**: Basic software provided on HPCMP systems.

| | |
|---|---|
| Math Libraries | ARPACK (eigenvalues/eigenvectors), FFTW (discrete Fourier transforms), PETSc (general), SuperLU (direct sparse linear solver), LAPACK (numerical linear algebra), ScaLAPACK (parallelized LAPACK), BLAS (ATLAS, GotoBLAS) (basic linear algebra), GSL (general) |
| Editors | EMAcs, Vim |
| Scripting Tools and Shells | Bash, Tcsh, Expect, Java, Perl, Ruby, Tcl/Tk |
| Debuggers | Allinea DDT, GNU Debugger (GDB), TotalView |
| Compilers | GNU |
| Performance/Profiling Tools | PAPI, SCALASCA, TAU, Valgrind |
| High Productivity Languages and Libraries | Python, NumPy, PyMPI, SciPy, Octave, Matplotlib |
| MPI Functionality | MPI-2 |
| Commercial Applications | ABAQUS, Accelrys, ANSYS, CFD++, Cobalt, Fluent, GASP, Gaussian, Gaussview, LS-DYNA, MATLAB |

garding compilers, users have a broad array of preferences. High performance libraries such as LAPACK, ScaLAPACK, SuperLU, BLAS, and Cray Scientific Libraries are supported.

TotalView and Allinea are available for debugging parallel programs. Cray Performance Measurement and Analysis Tools (CPMAT) are available for identifying code bottlenecks and load imbalances [Cra11c].

All HPCMP systems are required to provide a basic set of software (as summarized in Table 6.2). Compliance is tracked and summarized at http://www.ccac.hpc.mil/consolidated/bc/policy.php and http://www.afrl.hpc.mil/consolidated/softwareSUPPORT.php.

## 6.7 Storage, Visualization, and Analytics

As discussed earlier, the new supercomputers acquired by the HCPMP each year fit into an established broad service architecture that is itself regularly refreshed, although on a longer cycle. The recent trend in growth of HPCMP high performance computing capability is for each annual purchase to roughly double the existing compute capability in the program. This annual compounding effect has significantly increased the quality of the computational work that the science and technology communities of the Department of Defense are able to pursue.

One of the side effects of these increasingly sophisticated simulations is a growth in size and quantity of simulation data products that need to be transferred, analyzed, and stored. Many scientists and engineers conducting research on behalf of the DoD have mission needs that require they keep their data at least five years for long-term analysis of trends and relationships; however, some science areas in the Department need to keep the data for as long as 30 years. Given this, the amount of data the HPCMP stores and manages in its data archive has increased dramatically in the past seven years, growing from one million gigabytes (1 petabyte) to 32 petabytes – and this does not include data stored in intermediate staging areas or directly attached to individual supercomputers, only data stored in the enterprise data archive itself. The total amount of data in the enterprise archive is currently growing at about 140% per year.

The HPCMP takes a bottoms-up approach to storage, beginning with the local scratch (or work) disks and parallel storage that is procured with each system. Figure 6.7 shows a high level view of the computational architecture of the ERDC DSRC; details are shown

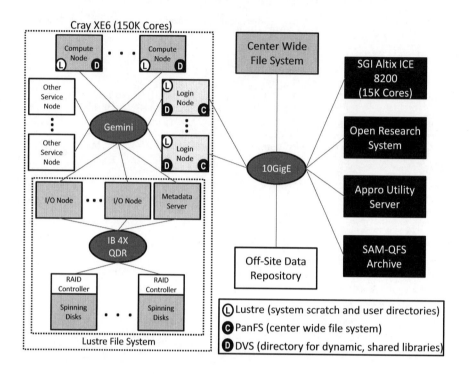

**FIGURE 6.7**: The configuration of the ERDC DSRC is representative of the computation and storage architecture of all HPCMP supercomputing centers. Machines and services in this diagram are depicted as blocks; only the Cray XE6 discussed earlier is shown in detail.

for the Cray XE6 discussed previously. Each HPC system has its own dedicated workspace storage (large, high speed disk) that user jobs access while running. Data on this workspace storage is not long-term storage for user data, and is regularly scrubbed to delete oldest data to facilitate new HPC job runs. The typical user workflow involves a step to move any input data to the HPC workspace before starting their jobs, and a step to move output data from the HPC workspace to managed archive storage.

To facilitate longer-term storage, each HPC center provides its users access to a center-wide shared filesystem which serves as a storage "hub." The user transfers files to and from the center-wide shared filesystem with the equivalent of get, put, copy, and move commands. The center-wide shared filesystem is directly mounted to each HPC login node, enabling users to easily transfer files among HPC systems.

The mass storage archive service located at each HPC center for long-term storage is based around the Oracle Sun Storage Archive Manager and Quick File System (SAM-QFS) hosted on a Fibre Channel infrastructure. Incoming files are cached on a spinning media subsystem when they arrive from an HPC system, and then later released to long-term tape storage depending upon age, access, and file size criteria. Outgoing files are staged from tape to disk prior to transfer to the requesting HPC system. The mass storage archive service is connected to HPC systems in each center via a 10 gigabit Ethernet backbone.

In addition to storing each user file locally, every file written to the mass storage archive at an HPC center is duplicated at a single remote disaster recovery site in a protected location. In the event of a catastrophic loss of an HPC center, the user files stored at that center can be recovered at a surviving HPC center to enable DoD work to continue with minimal interruption. The disaster recovery site is architected very similar to individual HPC centers in order to reduce the complexity of the solution, and to maximize reliability. A side benefit of the disaster recovery architecture is the ability to recover a user file that has become corrupted due to media failure at any local HPC center. In this case, the good copy of the file is simply read from the disaster recovery site on demand when a corrupted file is detected on the local site.

A project is under way in the HPCMP at this writing to deploy robust metadata tagging of mass storage data for users. The project, called Storage Lifecycle Manager (SLM), employs a storage resource broker to track metadata and interface with the existing SAM-QFS architecture. Once operational, HPCMP users will be able to apply tags to data and perform data file transfers using a much improved user interface, with the future possibility of inter-site transfers.

### 6.7.1 The HPCMP Utility Service

Of course, the numerical simulation itself is only part of the computational workflow; users must generate input data and solution grids prior to simulations, and analyze the output data following a run. Although these steps of the workflow were often performed on the user's local workstation a decade ago, today these steps are often supercomputing tasks in their own right.

To address this need, the HPCMP recently architected and deployed a Utility Service for use at each HPC center. The Utility Service is an interactive, heterogeneous HPC cluster, designed to complement (but not replace) the larger HPC systems at each of the HPCMP centers by providing key services and enhancing workflow efficiency for the HPCMP user community. The system includes a robust software stack and is designed to provide a single point of access for pre- and post-processing, data visualization and analysis, software development, and center-wide remote job management.

Three node types are available in the Utility Service: Compute nodes, Graphics nodes, and Large Memory nodes. Graphics nodes include GPUs for hardware accelerated visualization, and Large Memory nodes have twice the memory of Compute nodes for memory-intensive applications.

The Utility Service is "unallocated" – meaning that users of the service do not need to "spend" any of their annual allocation of supercomputer time to take advantage of it – and designed for high availability to support interactive work. All nodes are exclusive, meaning that a user reserving a node (or nodes) on the system will have exclusive use of those nodes. Although small batch processing jobs are supported, batch processing is not the intended use of the system.

As with the larger HPC systems, each cluster in the Utility Service is connected to the center-wide filesystem to enable efficient transfer of files within each HPC center.

### 6.7.2 Data Visualization and Analysis

The visualization tools provided as part of the Utility Service are primarily provided to meet self-service data analysis requirements. This addresses some, but not all, of the needs of the DoD user community. In many situations the data are too large, too complex, or the analysis needs are too sophisticated for a user to productively perform the analysis herself. In these cases the HPCMP provides dedicated hardware, software, and visualization specialists through its Data Analysis and Assessment Center (DAAC). The requirements for data analysis and visualization services vary widely throughout the diverse HPCMP user community, and the DAAC offers a spectrum of resources to help.

DAAC services are divided into three broad categories: community, collaborative, and custom services. The community service is primarily for researchers that are either new to visualization and wish to get started with minimal effort, or for those who want to learn more about how to effectively visualize their own data. The primary entry point for this level of assistance is the DAAC web site, http://visualization.hpc.mil, at which users find "anytime, anywhere" access to information about supported software tools, tutorials, how-to guides, and so on. The web site also offers contact and collaboration services to allow users to easily transition into a more hands-on service model with the DAAC staff.

The collaborative visualization service offering is for users who require assistance from DAAC staff members to analyze their data. In this model, a DAAC staff member will work closely with the HPC user to develop a robust approach to understanding a specific dataset, recommending tools and methods to produce the visualizations, and even generating a work flow so that the researcher can generate subsequent analyses without further support. This service model is targeted at both the day-to-day visualizations that scientists and engineers use as a means of validating their simulations, and at producing images and animations that are suitable for an audience of peer scientists (at technical reviews or conferences, for example).

Finally, the custom visualization service is for users that require high-quality images and animations of their data for which they also need to show the data in context or natural environment. For example, rather than just visualizing flow data in a combustion chamber, a custom visualization product might show a computer animation of a tank, zooming in from an outside view showing the armor off to reveal the tank's engine, before finally moving into the combustion chamber itself to study visualizations of the simulated flow inside the chamber. Often this level of service requires conceptual images or animations to demonstrate an idea or to explain the research problem to an audience that is interested but nontechnical.

## 6.8  Supercomputing Facility

The supercomputing facility of the ERDC DSRC which houses the HPCMP's new Cray XE6 is the result of a facility and infrastructure plan that spans many decades.

As the price per unity of supercomputing capability fell throughout the latter half of the 1990s and beginning of the 2000s, and DoD user requirements continued their robust growth, it became evident that the existing supercomputing facilities would not be adequate to support the growing demand presented by the projected supercomputer acquisition. In 2004 the ERDC made its last addition of 2 MW of uninterruptible power to its existing supercomputing facility (constructed in the early 1990s) as it began construction of a new supercomputing facility to support hardware deployments in 2009 and beyond.

The ERDC DSRC's phased approach began with rapid construction of a 10,000 square foot, 8 MW supercomputing facility. The computing infrastructure was designed for reliability as an N+1 configuration, with 2 MW of power in the initial build out that would then be scaled in 2 MW increments to a total available UPS power of 8 MW. The facility was also designed to make efficient use of power: with a recently measured PUE of approximately 1.3 the facility is considered "best practice" as of the time of this writing.

In the design of the new supercomputing facility several factors were considered. First, the facility needed to harmonize with the architectural features of the existing adjacent campus and fit in with a planned new two-story office structure that would wrap around the new supercomputing facility. Also, given the challenges inherent in new construction, the ERDC wanted to design the facility for maximum length of service. This meant taking early consideration of the likelihood that future computers would use a DC power source, which introduced a need to minimize the distances over which power is distributed to the facility. ERDC needed to be scalable to at least 8 MW on the floor, but also needed to initially support less dense computer solutions. Designing for the future also meant taking into account the increasing trends in supercomputer floor weight requirements and the move back to liquid-cooled supercomputers.

In order to maximize space for supercomputers and to minimize heat load in the computer facility the UPS was placed outdoors in the support yard alongside chillers and other infrastructure equipment (see Figure 6.8, taken during the later stages of construction). To further increase operating efficiency for the supercomputers the facility itself is dedicated only to the support of the machines, with no offices or comfort facilities included in the construction. To ensure effective use of power with minimal conversion loss a line interactive UPS was installed which operates at utility line voltage (13,800 volts); this type of UPS operates at 98-99% efficiency. High efficiency transformers step the incoming voltage down from utility levels to 480V; these transformers are placed outside to continue the practice of locating heat producing devices in the open air, rather than inside the building which would add to the cooling load.

When the facility is operating at its full 8 MW capacity there is a requirement for approximately 2,300 tons of chilled water cooling. This capability is provided via seven 75 horsepower pumps, and a 12" water line to provide enough water flow capacity for the total compute space.

The new facility has a 4-foot-high raised floor that today can support up to 625 pounds per square foot of load. The additional under-floor height provides design and installation flexibility for the infrastructure, management, and network systems that support modern supercomputers. Deployments in the new facility conform to a three layer facilities support policy for under floor utility layout that places water pipes at the lowest level, closest to the facility foundation with electrical at mid-level and communications networks at the top just below the raised floor. Figure 6.9 shows the wet and electrical layers in a typical region under

**FIGURE 6.8**: ERDC DSRC supercomputing facility during the later stages of construction.

**FIGURE 6.9**: A look under the raised floor showing the three-level assignment of infrastructure support systems in the ERDC supercomputing facility.

the facility raised floor; the trays supporting interconnect cables for the supercomputer are just visible at the top of the image.

Even though the facility was initially fitted with only 2 MW of power capacity, the initial construction included a chilled water pipe under the raised floor sized to match up with the maximum power requirements, eliminating the need to re-plumb later. All piping inside the facility is installed with change in mind: there are no welded joints, and piping is intended to be reused as new machines are deployed in the facility. The ERDC DSRC team encourages distribution of 480 volts directly to installed supercomputers when possible to reduce power loss, copper wire consumption, and labor installation costs. The team also distributes voltages as high as the newly installed computers allow, minimizing losses in transmission. The location of equipment on and under the machine room floor is supported by CFD analysis to maximize the effectiveness of equipment cooling and minimize energy consumption.

The first system placed in this facility after construction in 2009 was an SGI Altix Ice with peak electrical draw of 887 kW/h and a cooling load of 253 tons of chilled water. In 2010 two Cray XE6's were added to the facility with a combined electrical and heat load of 1.1 MW and 326 tons of chilled water, respectively. The 151,000 core Cray XE6 that is the subject of this chapter's study has a total electrical requirement of 3.5 MW and 1,000 tons of chilled water demand. This system is being operated in service with the SGI and several other machines in the same facility, presenting a total demand to support the supercomputers of 4.3 MW, and 1,300 tons of chilled water. This is still well within the design point of the facility, which is expected to remain a relevant component of the HPCMP supercomputing support infrastructure for many more years.

## 6.9 Workload-Based Acquisition in the HPCMP

As discussed earlier, to ensure that the supercomputing capabilities of the DoD remain reliable, relevant, and cost effective, the HPCMP adds between \$40M and \$50M of new systems to its deployed suite of supercomputers each year, retiring older systems that have reached the end of a nominal 48-month lifecycle. This annual process is designed to produce fully operational systems within a few months after an acquisition is completed, so the focus is on acquiring state-of-the-practice HPC architectures.

Since its first formal HPC system acquisition in 1994, the HPCMP has used both system performance and usability criteria to choose which systems to purchase, and the process is designed to maximize the overall capability for the DoD user base rather than the capabilities for any one center. Figure 6.10 summarizes the approach to system acquisition current in the HPCMP as of the time of this writing; the following text provides a more detailed discussion of the elements in this workflow.

Usability factors considered during a system evaluation separate into two broad classes: those that impact system users and those that impact a center's ability to operate a system. Among the former are such factors as system reliability, I/O subsystem capability, support software (including development tools such as compilers and debuggers), and balanced system design; among the latter are system management, security, and facilities requirements. The HPCMP also considers each vendor's track record for successfully providing, installing, and operating large HPC systems. Each of these factors is evaluated qualitatively using a color scale. Equal weights are given to performance and price/performance (as a combined factor), usability, and the vendor's past performance (as a combined factor) for the overall system selection.

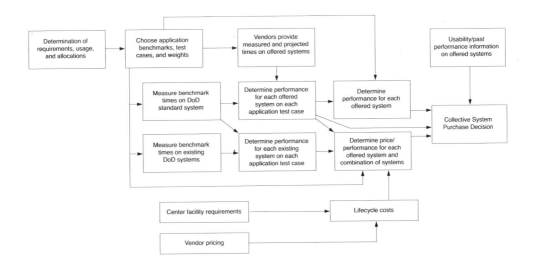

**FIGURE 6.10**: Overview of the HPCMP supercomputer acquisition process.

**TABLE 6.3**: HPCMP application benchmarks, 2011.

| Name | CTA | Language | Lines of Code | Notes |
|------|-----|----------|---------------|-------|
| ADCIRC | CWO | Fortran | 205,000 | Ocean circulation and storm surge model www.adcirc.org |
| ALEGRA | CSM | C | 978,000 | Hydrodynamic and solid dynamics plus magnetic field and thermal transport http://www.cs.sandia.gov/ ALEGRA/Alegra\_Home.html |
| AVUS | CFD | Fortran | 29,000 | Turbulent flow model www.afrl.hpc.mil/software/ description.html?app=avus |
| CTH | CSM | Fortran/C | 900,000 | Shock physics model www.sandia.gov/CTH |
| GAMESS | CCM | Fortran | 330,000 | Ab initio quantum chemistry www.msg.ameslab.gov/gamess |
| HYCOM | CWO | Fortran | 31,000 | Ocean circulation model www.hycom.org |
| ICEPIC | CEA | C | 350,000 | Particle-in-cell magnetohydro-dynamics www.benchmarking.hpc.mil/\# ICEPIC_Magnetron |
| LAMMPS | CCM | C++ | 45,000 | Molecular dynamics model lammps.sandia.gov |

The foundation of the HPCMP's performance assessment is a set of key application codes that have been selected for representativeness of the current and future HPCMP user community workload. These applications are used as time-to-solution benchmarks for realistically assessing HPC system performance.

The selection of applications that comprise the benchmark suite starts with data from an annual survey of the computational needs of the HPCMP's user communities on an individual project basis. This survey considers all aspects of HPC requirements, including CPU hours on individual HPC systems, memory, I/O, numbers of processors, job length, system and applications software, training, and wide-area networking. These requirements are then aggregated over all requested systems using the average system performance determined from application benchmark results. This projected workload is categorized into the computational technology areas (CTAs) discussed above, and those CTAs with a significant proportion of overall requirements are represented in the application benchmark suite by one or more representative applications as determined by requirements and actual use. Because the workload changes over time, the HPCMP annually reviews the codes included in the application benchmark suite and updates them as required. For each application benchmark, two test cases are typically chosen: a standard test case representing typical use of the system by most users, and a large test case representing more robust use as typified by DoD challenge projects. Table 6.3 provides a brief summary of the codes used in 2011.

The HPCMP scores an HPC system's performance for a particular application test case by comparing that system's time to solution over a range of processor counts with the DoD standard system's baseline; the ratio of time at a target processor count is used to provide a relative measure of a system's performance on that application test case compared with a DoD standard system. During the assessment process, the HPCMP first determines the relative performance in terms of DoD-standard equivalents for each individual application test case for the measured system, and then aggregates these into an overall system performance in that same unit by taking a weighted average of all application test cases.

Once a performance score for each application test case on a candidate system is computed, overall performance per system across all test cases can be computed using relative benchmark weights. Relative weights for the benchmark test cases are based upon the percentages of the user workload that each benchmark represents (as calculated by CTA from requirements, usage, and allocation data), the percentage of use for each application within a CTA (when applicable), and the fraction of work in each CTA that falls into the standard and large subcategories. The resulting sets of time-to-solution-based performance measures constitute an aggregate figure of merit across the entire user community's current and projected future workload, and are the primary determinant of overall performance and price/performance scores used in the purchase evaluation process.

In addition to determining overall performance scores for each evaluated HPC system, the HPCMP does an additional analysis that produces compatible solution sets of systems best able to address the overall DoD computational workload from a price/performance perspective. Because of performance differences in proposed systems across individual application test cases, it's quite possible that a combination of systems could produce a better overall total performance for the same price over a single system with the best overall average performance across all application benchmark test cases. The goal of this analysis is to determine the system solution set (i.e., combination of one of more offered systems) that will maximize the total performance for the entire program for a fixed acquisition price.

The optimization process is designed to maximize total system performance with two types of constraints: the first is the fixed acquisition cost (usually a price band) and the second ensures that the combination of systems in any given solution set provides a balanced capability across the entire program workload, as expressed by the application benchmark test case weights. The optimization algorithm is designed to match these weights within a tolerance (usually +/- 10 percent) – for example, given an application test case weight of 5 percent, the portion of the overall workload allocated to this particular application test case must be between 4.5 percent and 5.5 percent, using the standard tolerance.

The methodology requires a separate optimization on each potential solution set of systems (i.e., System 1 from Vendor A plus System 2 from Vendor B, and so on) with a combined acquisition cost that falls within the allowed acquisition price band. Depending on the price band's width and the systems offered, the number of possible solution sets can range from thousands to billions. For each separate optimization, the technique shifts the workload among systems to get an allocation that maximizes total program performance, while still keeping the overall distribution within the previously discussed constraints. The performance evaluator then divides the maximized performance for that solution set into the total lifecycle cost (which includes facilities and power costs as well as system maintenance), yielding a price/performance figure of merit that can be used to rank order the possible solution sets and inform the final purchase decision. In an interesting feedback loop, the predicted optimal workload distribution can be provided to resource allocators after deployment to be used as a guide for assigning projects and application codes to specific machines.

While there are many ways to buy the large-scale supercomputers that are the focus of the present work, we hope it is evident from the preceding that the HPCMP has developed robust, requirements-driven process for HPC system evaluation that combines qualitative usability factors with quantitative performance and price-per-performance factors to determine which HPC systems to acquire in its annual modernization process. The process is somewhat intricate, but not unnecessarily complex, and has resulted in a decade of technology upgrades that in FY2013 will provide over 3 billion hours of computational resources to the Department of Defense for research, development, test, and evaluation.

## Acknowledgments

The authors would like to acknowledge the support of several colleagues whose contributions greatly enriched the content of this chapter: Scott Morton of the DoD High Performance Computing Modernization Program for details and figures for the F-16 application example; Charles Welch of the U.S. Army Corps of Engineers Engineer Research and Development Center for details and the figure for the molecular dynamics applications example; Charles Nietubicz for background on the Army's use of the ENIAC; James Cliburn for details on the technical configuration of a DSRC; and to Greg Rottman for details on the design and construction of the ERDC supercomputing facility.

# Chapter 7

## Keeneland: Computational Science Using Heterogeneous GPU Computing

**Jeffrey S. Vetter**

*Oak Ridge National Laboratory and Georgia Institute of Technology*

**Richard Glassbrook, Karsten Schwan, Sudhakar Yalamanchili, Mitch Horton, Ada Gavrilovska, Magda Slawinska**

*Georgia Institute of Technology*

**Jack Dongarra**

*University of Tennessee and Oak Ridge National Laboratory*

**Jeremy Meredith, Philip C. Roth, Kyle Spafford**

*Oak Ridge National Laboratory*

**Stanimire Tomov**

*University of Tennessee*

**John Wynkoop**

*National Institute for Computational Sciences*

## 7.1    Overview

The Keeneland Project[VGD+11] is a five-year Track 2D grant awarded by the National Science Foundation (NSF) under solicitation NSF 08-573 in August 2009 for the development and deployment of an innovative high performance computing system. The Keeneland project is led by the Georgia Institute of Technology (Georgia Tech) in collaboration with the University of Tennessee at Knoxville, National Institute for Computational Sciences, and Oak Ridge National Laboratory.

---

**NSF 08-573: High Performance Computing System Acquisition - Towards a Petascale Computing Environment for Science and Engineering**

*An experimental high-performance computing system of innovative design.* Proposals are sought for the development and deployment of a system with an architectural design that is outside the mainstream of what is routinely available from computer vendors. Such a project may be for a duration of up to five years and for a total award size of up to $12,000,000. It is not necessary that the system be deployed early in the project; for example, a lengthy development phase might be included. Proposals should explain why such a resource will expand the range of research projects that scientists and engineers can tackle and include some examples of science and engineering questions to which the system will be applied. It is not necessary that the design of the proposed system be useful for all classes of computational science and engineering problems. When finally deployed, the system should be integrated into the TeraGrid. It is anticipated that the system, once deployed, will be an experimental TeraGrid resource, used by a smaller number of researchers than is typical for a large TeraGrid resource. (Up to 5 years' duration. Up to $12,000,000 in total budget to include development and/or acquisition, operations and maintenance, including user support. First-year budget not to exceed $4,000,000.)

---

### 7.1.1    The Case for Graphics Processors (GPUs)

The Keeneland team originally assessed numerous technologies to propose in 2008. The team's conclusion was that heterogeneous architectures using GPUs provided the right balance of performance on scientific applications, productivity, energy-efficiency, and overall system cost.

Recently, heterogeneous architectures have emerged as a response to the limits of performance on traditional commodity processor cores, due to power and thermal constraints. Currently, most commodity multi-core architectures use a small number of replicated, general purpose cores that use aggressive techniques to maximize single thread performance using techniques like out-of-order instruction execution, caching, and a variety of speculative execution techniques. While these approaches continue to sustain performance, they can also carry high costs in terms of energy efficiency.

Simultaneously, other approaches, like graphics processors, have explored architecture strategies that constitute different design points: large numbers of simple cores, latency hiding by switching among a large number of threads quickly in hardware, staging data in very low latency cache or scratchpad memory, and, wider vector (or SIMD) units. For GPUs, in particular, these techniques were originally intended to support a fixed pipeline of graphics operations (e.g., rasterization).

A number of early adopters recognized that these design points offered benefits to their scientific applications, and they began using GPUs for general purpose computation [AAD$^+$, OLG$^+$05a] (so called 'GPGPU'). Shortly thereafter, the GPU ecosystem started to include programming systems, such as Cg [MGAK03], CUDA [NB07], and OpenCL [SGS10], to make GPUs available to an even wider non-graphics audience.

Eventually, GPUs have added critical features that have made them applicable to a wider array of scientific applications and large-scale HPC systems. For example, NVIDIA's Fermi [NVI09a], was the first GPU to add much improved performance on IEEE double precision arithmetic (only 2 times slower than single precision), and error correction and detection, which makes these devices more reliable in a large-scale system. These new capabilities, when combined with the original niche of GPUs, provide a competitive platform for numerous types of computing, such as media processing, gaming, and scientific computing, in terms of raw performance (665 GF/s per Fermi), cost, and energy efficiency.

Accordingly, these trends have garnered the attention of HPC researchers, vendors, and agencies. Beyond the Keeneland project, a significant number of large GPU-based systems have already been deployed. Examples include China's Tianhe-1A (cf. §19.1), Nebulae at the National Supercomputing Centre in Shenzhen (NSCS), Tokyo Tech's TSUBAME2.0 (cf. §20.1), Lawrence Berkeley National Laboratory's Dirac cluster, FORGE at the National Center for Supercomputing Applications, and EDGE at Lawrence Livermore National Laboratory. Notably, the Chinese Tianhe-1A system at the National Supercomputer Center in Tianjin achieved a performance of 2.57 pf/s on the TOP500 LINPACK benchmark (http://www.top500.org), which placed it at #1 on the list in November 2010. All of these examples are scalable heterogeneous architectures that leverage predominantly commodity components: scalable node architectures with a high performance interconnection network, where each node contains memory, network ports, and multiple types of (heterogeneous) processing devices. Most experts expect this trend for heterogeneity to continue into the foreseeable future, given current technology projections and constraints.

### 7.1.2   Timeline

The Keeneland project is a five-year effort, and it is organized into two primary deployment phases. The initial delivery system was deployed in the fall of 2010 and the full-scale system was deployed in the summer of 2012. The first phase provides a moderately-sized, initial delivery system for the development of software for GPU computing, and for preparing and optimizing applications to exploit GPUs. The Keeneland Initial Delivery (KID) system was not available as an official production resource to NSF users, but it was made available to over 200 users across 100 projects.

The second phase of Keeneland was deployed during the summer of 2012 and it provides a full-scale system for production use by computational scientists as allocated by the NSF's XRAC Allocation Committee. The Keeneland Full Scale (KFS) system is similar to the KID system in terms of hardware and software (see Table 7.1). The KFS system is an XSEDE resource available to a broad set of users. Although there now appears to be a large migration of the HPC community to these heterogeneous GPU architectures, a critical component of the Keeneland Project is the development of software to allow users to exploit these architectures, and to reach out to applications teams that have applications that may map well to this architecture, in order to encourage them to port their applications to architectures like Keeneland.

## 7.2    Keeneland Systems

### 7.2.1    Keeneland Initial Delivery System

The KID system has been installed, and operating since November 2010; it is primarily used for the development of software tools and preparation of applications to use this innovative architecture. In addition, KIDS served the scientific community with over 100 projects and 200 users through discretionary accounts in order to allow scientists to evaluate, port, and run on a scalable GPU system.

As of June 2012, the KID system configuration (cf. Table 7.1) is rooted in the scalable node architecture of the HP Proliant SL-390G7, shown in Figure 7.1. Each node has two Intel Westmere host CPUs, three NVIDIA M2090 6GB Fermi GPUs, 24GB of main memory, and a Mellanox Quad Data Rate (QDR) InfiniBand Host Channel Adapter (HCA). Overall, the system has 120 nodes with 240 CPUs and 360 GPUs; the installed system has a peak performance of 255 TFLOPS in 7 racks (or 90 sq ft including the service area).

More specifically, in the SL390, memory is directly attached to the CPU sockets, which are connected to each other and the Tylersburg I/O hubs via Intel's Quick Path Interconnect (QPI). GPUs are attached to the node's two I/O hubs using PCI Express (PCIe). The theoretical peak for unidirectional bandwidth of QPI is 12.8 GB/s and for PCIe x16 is 8.0 GB/s. In particular, with these two I/O hubs, each node can supply a full x16 PCIe link bandwidth to three GPUs, and x8 PCIe link bandwidth to the integrated InfiniBand QDR HCA. This design avoids contention and offers advantages in aggregate node bandwidth when the three GPUs and HCA are used concurrently, as they are in a scalable system. In contrast, previous architectures used a PCIe-switch-based approach, where the switch could quickly become a performance bottleneck. Using this PCIe-switch-based approach, vendors are currently offering systems with up to 8 GPUs per node.

The node architecture exemplifies the architectural trends described earlier, and has one of the highest number of GPUs counts per node in the Top500 list. The SL390 design has significant benefits over the previous generation architecture, but also exhibits multiple levels of non-uniformity [MRSV11]. In addition to traditional NUMA effects across the two

**TABLE 7.1**: Keeneland hardware configurations.

| Feature | KIDS (July 2012) | KFS System |
|---|---|---|
| Node Architecture | HP Proliant SL390 G7 | HP Proliant SL250s G8 |
| CPU | Intel Xeon X5660 | Intel Xeon E5-2670 |
| CPU Microarchitecture | Westmere | Sandy Bridge |
| CPU Frequency (GHz) | 2.8 | 2.6 |
| CPU Count per Node | 2 | 2 |
| Cores per CPU | 6 | 8 |
| Node Memory Capacity (GB) | 24 | 32 |
| Node PCIe | Gen 2 | Gen 3 |
| GPU | NVIDIA Tesla M2090 | NVIDIA Tesla M2090 |
| GPU Count per Node | 3 | 3 |
| GPU Memory Capacity (GB) | 6 | 6 |
| Interconnection Network | InfiniBand QDR | InfiniBand FDR |
| Network Ports per Node | 1 IB QDR HCA | 1 IB FDR HCA |
| Compute Racks | 5 | 11 |
| Total Number of Nodes | 120 | 264 |
| Peak FLOP Rate (TF) | 201 | 615 |

**FIGURE 7.1**: HP Proliant SL390 node.

Westmere's integrated memory controllers, the dual I/O hub design introduces non-uniform characteristics for data transfers between host memory and GPU memory. These transfers will perform better if the data only traverses one QPI link (such as a transfer between data in the memory attached to CPU socket 0 and GPU 0) than if it traverses two QPI links (such as a transfer between data in the memory attached to CPU socket 0 and GPU 1 or GPU 2).

In addition, KIDS's GPUs include other features that can greatly affect performance and contribute to non-uniformity. For instance, each GPU contains Error Correcting Code (ECC) memory. ECC memory is desirable in a system designed for scalable scientific computing. Enabling ECC gives some assurance against these transient errors, but results in a performance penalty and adds yet another complexity to the GPU memory hierarchy.

### 7.2.2 Keeneland Full Scale System

The KFS system has been installed and operating since October 2012; it is an XSEDE production resource, which is allocated quarterly by XSEDE's XRAC allocations committee.

As of July 2012, the KFS system configuration (cf. Table 7.1) is very similar to the KID system architecture, but with upgraded components in most dimensions. In particular, each node is a HP Proliant SL250G8 server with two Intel Sandy Bridge host CPUs, three NVIDIA M2090 6GB Fermi GPUs, 32GB of DDR3 main memory, and a Mellanox Fourteen Data Rate (FDR) InfiniBand HCA. Overall, the system has 264 nodes with 528 CPUs and 792 GPUs; the installed system has a peak performance of 615 TFLOPS in 11 compute racks.

A major difference between the KID and KFS systems is the host processor and node configuration. First, the KFS system uses Intel's new Sandy Bridge architecture. This change has several benefits including an increase from six to eight cores per socket, 40 lanes of integrated PCIe Gen3, and new AVX instructions. This integrated PCIe Gen3 eliminates the need for a separate Tylersburg I/O hub, as was the case for KIDS's Westmere architecture. Second, the Proliant SL250G8 node adapts to the new Sandy Bridge architecture by expanding memory, eliminating I/O chips, while retaining the capacity for 2 CPUs, 3 GPUs, and an FDR IB port, all at full PCIe Gen3 bandwidth.

## 7.3 Keeneland Software

The system software used on the Keeneland systems reflects the perspective that the systems are Linux x86 clusters with GPUs as compute accelerators. Both the KID and KFS systems use CentOS, a clone of Red Hat Enterprise Linux, as the fundamental Linux distribution. This distribution provides the Linux kernel, plus a large collection of user-level programs, libraries, and tools. The KFS system was deployed with CentOS 6.2. KIDS was deployed using CentOS version 5.5, but was upgraded to version 6.2 when the KFS system was deployed. In addition to the stock CentOS distribution, the NVIDIA GPU driver and the NVIDIA Compute Unified Device Architecture (CUDA) Software Development Kit are installed on each compute node to allow programs to use the system's GPUs. Likewise, Mellanox's variant of the OpenFabrics Enterprise Distribution (OFED) is installed on each system node to support the use of the InfiniBand interconnection networks. The InfiniBand network is routed using the Open Subnet Manager (OpenSM) on KIDS and Mellanox's Unified Fabric Manager (UFM) on KFS.

**TABLE 7.2**: Keeneland software configurations.

| Feature | ‖ KIDS | KFS System |
|---|---|---|
| Login Node OS<br>Compute Node OS<br>Parallel Filesystem | CentOS 5.5<br>CentOS 5.5<br>Lustre 1.8 | CentOS 6.2<br>CentOS 6.2 |
| Compilers | Intel 12<br>PGI 12 with support for compiler directives<br>CAPS HMPP 2.4.4<br>GNU 4.1<br>NVIDIA Toolkit 4.1 | <br><br><br>GNU 4.4<br>NVIDIA Toolkit 4.2 |
| MPI | OpenMPI (default)<br>MVAPICH | |
| Notable Libraries | HDF5<br>netcdf/pNetCDF<br>Intel Math Kernel Library<br>Thrust<br>Boost<br>FFTW | |
| Job Scheduler<br>Resource Manager | Moab<br>Torque | |
| Debugging Tools<br><br>Performance Tools | Allinea DDT<br>NVIDIA cuda-gdb<br>TAU<br>HPCToolkit<br>NVIDIA Visual Profiler | |

## 7.3.1 Filesystems

Two primary filesystems are used on the Keeneland systems. The Network File System (NFS) version 3 is used for filesystems that are not expected to need the high I/O performance provided by a parallel filesystem, such as home directories and installations of shared software (i.e., commonly-used numerical libraries and tools). For programs that require high I/O performance, such as parallel climate simulations that write large checkpoint files, a parallel file system is available. These file systems are part of the NICS center-wide storage systems that serve not only the Keeneland systems but also the other systems operated by NICS personnel. Initially, the NICS parallel filesystem accessible to KIDS users was IBM's General Parallel File System (GPFS), but that filesystem was replaced in 2011 by a Lustre parallel file system. In 2012, NICS' center-wide Lustre filesystem was further expanded. This expanded filesystem gives the Keeneland systems access to over 4 Petabytes of scratch space with a maximum throughput of over 70 Gigabytes per second. The shared Lustre filesystem is accessed using a center-wide QDR InfiniBand network. Unlike some high performance computing systems, both the home directories and the parallel file system are accessible to programs running on Keeneland system compute nodes.

## 7.3.2 System Management

The KID system was initially deployed using a combination of Preboot Execution Environment (PXE) to boot the nodes via the network and Kixstart, a scripted installer that is included with CentOS, to perform the OS installation. The open source configuration management tool puppet was used to maintain the configuration of the KID system. The KID system was modified to use a shared NFS root model in Fall 2012 to better mirror the configuration of KFS. The system uses the nfsroot package developed by Lawrence Livermore National Laboratory to provide the shared root implementation. KFS also utilizes a shared root filesystem. However, the management is done via the CMU tool. Job scheduling on both systems is provided via the Moab batch environment with Torque deployed as the resource manager. To facilitate remote power control and remote console access the HP Integrated Lights Out (iLO) controllers and HP Advanced Power Manager (APM) management systems are deployed in both systems. KIDS uses HP's iLO 3, while the KFS system uses the iLO 4.

## 7.4 Programming Environment

The Keeneland programming environment is a blend of standard HPC software, such as MPI, augmented by GPU-enabled programming environments. Keeneland offers a variety of approaches for exploiting GPUs including GPU-enabled libraries, writing CUDA or OpenCL directly, or using directive-based compilation. Keeneland also offers a set of development tools for correctness and performance investigations.

In addition to commercial and research tools available from the community, the Keeneland project team is developing several tools for GPU-enabled systems. These tools include GPU-enabled scientific libraries (MAGMA), productivity tools (Ocelot), and virtualization support.

### 7.4.1    Programming Models

Developing software for the KID and KFS systems involves a process similar to that used when developing for a traditional Linux cluster. However, to make use of the systems' GPUs, the traditional process must be augmented with development tools that can produce and debug code that runs on the GPUs.

**MPI for Scalable Distributed Memory Programming.** As described in Section 7.2, both KID and KFS are distributed memory systems, and a message passing programming model is the primary model programs used for communication and synchronization between processes running on different compute nodes. Several implementations of the Message Passing Interface (MPI) are available on the systems; OpenMPI is the default. These implementatons are built to take advantage of the systems' high performance InfiniBand interconnection networks. Although the KID system is capable of using the NVIDIA GPUDirect inter-node communication optimization across Mellanox InfiniBand networks, it has not yet been enabled due to challenges in deploying it with the CentOS 5.5 kernel used on that system. KFS, which uses a newer CentOS kernel, uses the GPUDirect inter-node optimization.

**CUDA and OpenCL.** In contrast to the near-ubiquity of MPI for inter-node communication and synchronization, we observe much more variety in the approaches used to make use of the systems' GPUs and multi-core processors. With respect to using the GPUs, NVIDIA's Compute Unified Device Architecture (CUDA) is currently the most common approach, but some programs running on the Keeneland systems use OpenCL. On the Keeneland systems, support for developing CUDA and OpenCL programs is provided by development software freely available from NVIDIA. The NVIDIA CUDA compiler, nvcc, is part of the CUDA Toolkit, and the NVIDIA GPU Computing Software Development Kit (SDK) is available for developers that use the utility software from that SDK. The CUDA Toolkit also provides libraries needed to develop OpenCL programs that use NVIDIA GPUs.

**Directive-Based Compilation.** Using CUDA or OpenCL can provide excellent performance on systems like KID and KFS, but some developers feel that these approaches require programming at a level of abstraction that is too low. Developers seeking not only high performance but also high productivity are often drawn to the idea of using *compiler directives*. Such directives are pragmas (in C or C++ programs) or comments (in Fortran programs) embedded in the program's source code that indicate to the compiler the parts of the code that should be executed on a GPU. In most cases, if a program containing compiler directives is processed by a compiler without support for the directives or such support is disabled, the compiler still produces a valid, single-threaded program executable that executes only on the system's CPU.

Several compilers supporting compiler directives are provided on the Keeneland systems. For programs using GPUs, the PGI Fortran, C, and C++ compilers are available with support for both OpenACC and PGI Accelerate directives in the Fortran and C compilers. We also make available the CAPS HMPP compiler supporting the OpenHMPP compiler directives. The GNU and Intel compilers are also available, and although they do not provide any particular support for developing programs that use GPUs, they do support OpenMP compiler directives for producing multi-threaded programs for the CPUs in Keeneland system compute nodes.

**GPU-Enabled Libraries.** Multi-threaded and GPU-enabled libraries provide another high-productivity approach for developers targeting systems like KID and KFS. For instance, NVIDIA's CUDA Toolkit provides several libraries containing GPU-accelerated implementations of common operations such as the Basic Linear Algebra Subroutines (BLAS) and Fast Fourier Transform (FFT). The Intel compilers include the Intel Math Kernel

Library that provides OpenMP-enabled BLAS and FFT implementations for targeting the Keeneland systems' multi-core CPUs.

To make best use of the computational hardware available in KID and KFS compute nodes, a multi-level hybrid programming model is possible that combines MPI tasks, OpenMP, and one of the previously mentioned GPU programming models. In such a model, a program places a small number of MPI tasks on each compute node, each of which uses CUDA function calls to make use of one of the node's GPUs, and is multi-threaded using OpenMP to make use of the node's CPU cores. An interesting question for the application user is whether to use two MPI tasks to match the number of processors in each node, or three MPI tasks to match the number of GPUs.

**Development Tools for Performance and Correctness.** Converting source code into executable code is only part of the software development task. Finding and fixing functional and performance problems in programs are also important software development tasks. For functional problems, the Allinea Distributed Debugging Tool (DDT) is available on the Keeneland systems. DDT is a debugger that implements the traditional breakpoint and single-step debugging models for parallel programs. It has support for programs that use MPI and OpenMP. Most importantly for a scalable heterogeneous computing system like the Keeneland systems, DDT supports setting breakpoints and single-stepping through CUDA kernel code, and observing data held in GPU memory. In addition to DDT, we also provide the NVIDIA debugger cuda-gdb, though this debugger is more suitable for use with single-process programs than the multi-node parallel programs that are the target workload for the Keeneland systems.

With respect to tools for identifying the source of performance problems, we rely on both NVIDIA and third-party tools. As part of the CUDA Toolkit, we make available NVIDIA's Compute Profiler that collects performance data about a program's GPU use, analyzes that data, and then makes recommendations about how to improve the program's use of the system's GPUs. As with cuda-gdb, this tool is targeted mainly at single-process programs. For programs that use processes running on multiple compute nodes, third-party tools are available such as the Tuning and Analysis Utilities [SM06a] (TAU) from the University of Oregon and HPCToolkit [ABF+10] from Rice University. In addition to support for collecting performance data regarding a program's MPI and OpenMP behavior, TAU now supports the collection of performance data about CUDA and OpenCL kernels. HPCToolkit has been highly useful in collecting performance profiles for full applications at scale, though the versions we have used do not have support for collecting profiles of code running on the system's GPUs.

## 7.4.2 Keeneland Developed Productivity Software

**Libraries and Frameworks.** An integral part of the Keeneland project is the development of fundamental linear algebra algorithms and numerical libraries for hybrid GPU-CPU architectures. The goal is to enable the efficient use of the KID and KFS systems, as well as to ease the porting of key applications to them. Existing GPU-only libraries, that implement the most basic algorithms, capturing main patterns of computation and communication, are available on the Keeneland systems. In particular, for dense linear algebra (DLA) this is the NVIDIA CUBLAS library [NVI12a], for sparse linear algebra the NVIDIA CUSPARSE [NVI12c], for spectral methods the NVIDIA CUFFT [NVI12b], etc. The NVIDIA Thrust library [HB10], providing a C++ template GPU functionality with an interface similar to the C++ Standard Template Library (STL), is also available. The CPU equivalents provided from libraries such as MKL from Intel, ACML from AMD, GotoBLAS, and Atlas, are installed as well.

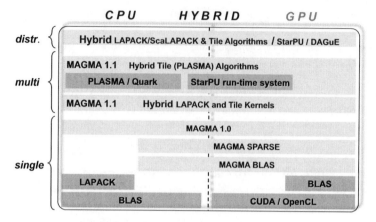

**FIGURE 7.2**: MAGMA software stack.

Developing higher level algorithms, as well as applications in general, for hybrid GPU-CPU systems by simply replacing computational routines with their equivalents from the GPU- or CPU-centric libraries is possible, but will lead to inefficient use of the hardware due for example to all synchronizations of the fork-join parallelism at every parallel routine call, and GPU-CPU communications in preparing the data. The goal of the Keeneland project, as related to libraries, has been to overcome challenges like these and to develop numerical libraries for hybrid GPU-CPU architectures.

To this end, in what follows, we outline the main development challenges to numerical libraries for hybrid GPU-CPU systems and how to overcome them. Illustrations are given using the Matrix Algebra on GPU and Multicore Architectures (MAGMA) library [TDB10] that we develop. Its newest release, MAGMA 1.2 [mag12], targeting DLA algorithms is installed on Keeneland. The Trilinos [HBH+05] and PETSc [MSK12] libraries, targeting specifically sparse linear algebra computations, are also available on the Keeneland systems.

The MAGMA project aims to develop the next generation of LAPACK and ScaLAPACK-compliant linear algebra libraries for hybrid GPU-CPU architectures. MAGMA is built on the GPU- or CPU-centric libraries mentioned above, which is also illustrated in Figure 7.2, giving the software stack for MAGMA. The currently released software is for shared memory multicore CPUs with single GPU or multiple GPUs (see Figure 7.3 for more details). Software for distributed memory systems has also been developed [STD12] and will be added to subsequent releases after further development.

| MAGMA 1.1 ROUTINES & FUNCTIONALITIES | SINGLE GPU | MULTI-GPU STATIC | MULTI-GPU DYNAMIC |
|---|---|---|---|
| One-sided Factorizations (LU, QR, Cholesky) | ✓ | ✓ | ✓ |
| Linear System Solvers | ✓ | | ✓ |
| Linear Least Squares (LLS) Solvers | ✓ | | ✓ |
| Matrix Inversion | ✓ | | ✓ |
| Singular Value Problem (SVP) | ✓ | | |
| Non-symmetric Eigenvalue Problem | ✓ | | |
| Symmetric Eigenvalue Problem | ✓ | | |
| Generalized Symmetric Eigenvalue Problem | ✓ | | |

| | |
|---|---|
| SINGLE GPU | Hybrid LAPACK algorithms with static scheduling and LAPACK data layout |
| MULTI-GPU STATIC | Hybrid LAPACK algorithms with 1D block cyclic static scheduling and LAPACK data layout |
| MULTI-GPU DYNAMIC | Tile algorithms with StarPU scheduling and tile matrix layout |

**FIGURE 7.3**: MAGMA 1.1 supported functionality.

There are a number of challenges in the development of libraries for hybrid GPU-CPU systems, and numerical libraries in general. Most notably, just to mention a few, these are:

- **Synchronization**, as related to parallelism and how to break the fork-join parallel model

- **Communication**, and in particular, the design of algorithms that minimize data transfers to increase the computational intensity of the algorithms

- **Mixed precision methods**, exploiting faster lower precision arithmetic to accelerate higher precision algorithms without loss of accuracy

- **Autotuning**, as related to building "smarts" into software to automatically adapt to the hardware

Synchronization in highly parallel systems is a major bottleneck for performance. Figure 7.4 quantifies this statement for the case of the LU factorization using the fork-join LAPACK implementation (with parallel high-performance BLAS from the MKL library) *vs.* MAGMA 1.1. Note that the systems compared have the same theoretical peaks and the expectation is that the performances will be comparable. Because of the fork-join synchronizations, LAPACK on this 48 core system is about $4X$ slower than MAGMA on a system using a single Fermi GPU (and a four core CPU host).

To overcome this bottleneck MAGMA employs a Directed Acyclic Graph (DAG) approach. The DAG approach is to represent algorithms as DAGs in which nodes represent subtasks and edges represent the dependencies among them, and subsequently schedule the execution on the available hardware components. Whatever the execution order of the subtasks, the result will be correct as long as these dependencies are not violated. Figure 7.5 illustrates a schematic DAG representation for algorithms for multicore on the left and for hybrid systems on the right [ADD+09]. The difference with hybrid systems is that the GPU tasks must be suitable and large enough for efficient data-parallel execution on the GPU.

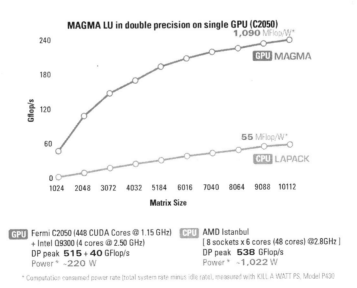

**FIGURE 7.4**: Performance of LU – LAPACK on multicore vs MAGMA on hybrid GPU-CPU system.

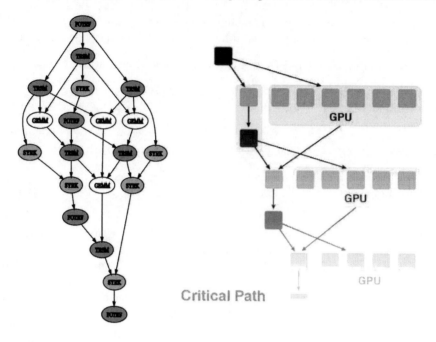

**FIGURE 7.5**: Algorithms as DAGs for multicore (left) and hybrid systems (right).

To account for this we have extended the DAG approach to a hybridization methodology where the critical path of the algorithm is determined and in general scheduled for execution on the multicore CPUs. This approach has been applied to the main DLA algorithms for solving linear systems of equations and eigenvalue problems [TNLD10, TND10], and extended to multiple GPUs in MAGMA 1.1 [YTD12]. Figure 7.6 illustrates the performance obtained for the LU factorizations using all GPUs on a Keeneland node. Performance scales

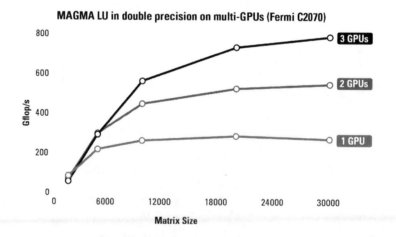

**FIGURE 7.6**: LU factorization on a multiGPU–multicore Keeneland system node.

as we increase the number of GPUs. The algorithms involve static 1-D block cyclic data distribution with look-ahead, where the panels are factored on the CPU [YTD12]. Similarly to the case of one GPU, the algorithm reduces GPU-CPU communications by placing the entire matrix on the GPUs, and communicating only the panels. The cases where the matrix does not fit on the GPU memories is handled as well by implementing left-looking versions that are known to reduce communications [YTD12].

If the execution is statically scheduled, look-ahead techniques have been successfully applied to matrix factorizations [TNLD10, YTD12] to remedy the problem of barrier synchronizations introduced by the non-parallelizable tasks in a fork-join parallelization. Current efforts are concentrated on **dynamic scheduling** where an out-of-order execution order is determined at run-time in a fully dynamic fashion. For further information and examples on hybrid scheduling (using the QUARK scheduler on the multicore host and static on the GPU) see [HTD11], and for fully dynamic scheduling using StarPU see [AAD+].

Finally, to build the DAG approach into efficient frameworks, the scheduling should allow building applications by combining components – available in libraries as DAGs – without synchronization between them. We call this feature **DAG composition**, illustrated in Figure 7.7 with the execution traces on a 48 core system with and without DAG composition. This feature is becoming available in the DAG schedulers that we use such as QUARK [YKD11], StarPU [ATNW10], and DAGuE [BBD+12].

**Productivity Tools: Correctness and Performance Debugging.** The Keeneland system is host to a set of productivity tools developed for CUDA applications and distributed as part of the Ocelot dynamic execution infrastructure [DKYC10]. Ocelot was originally conceived to facilitate and accelerate research in GPGPU computing using CUDA, and has evolved into an infrastructure to support research endeavors across a broad spectrum of hardware and software challenges for GPGPU computing. One of the main challenges has been software productivity faced by the designers of GPGPU architectures and systems with integrated GPGPUs. Major challenges to software productivity are seen to be i) execution portability, ii) performance portability, and iii) introspection, e.g., performance tuning and debugging tools.

At its core, Ocelot is a dynamic compiler that translates compute kernels for execution on NVIDIA GPUs. Ocelot's internal representation is based on NVIDIA's parallel thread

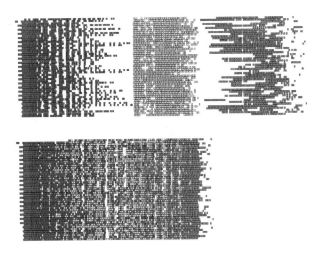

**FIGURE 7.7**: Composition of DAGs – execution traces on a 48 core system with synchronization (top) vs. with DAG composition (bottom).

execution (PTX) low level virtual instruction set architecture (ISA). Ocelot implements a just-in-time (JIT) compiler by translating kernel PTX to the intermediate representation (IR) of the LLVM compiler infrastructure and using LLVM's back-end code generators [LA04]. Back-ends have been built and tested for i) multicore x86, ii) Intel SSE, iii) NVIDA GPUs, iv) AMD GPUs [DSK11], and v) execution on GPUs attached to remote nodes. Ocelot includes a re-implementation of the CUDA runtime to support these back-end devices, and existing CUDA applications can be executed by simply linking with the Ocelot runtime.

Within this infrastructure we have two main additions that support software productivity tools. The first is an additional back-end device that is a functionally accurate emulator for the PTX ISA [AAD+]. The emulator is instrumented for trace generation. Event trace analyzers coupled with the emulator can be used for correctness checks, workload characterization, and performance debugging. The second addition is an interface for the specification and dynamic instrumentation of PTX kernels. This latter capability does not require any modification to the CUDA source. Such dynamic instrumentation can host a number of correctness checks and debugging support substantially several orders of magnitude faster than the emulator. The functionality provided by these two infrastructures is described in the following.

**The Ocelot Emulation Environment.** A key information gathering infrastructure in Ocelot is the trace generation capability coupled with event trace analyzers. These provide for correctness checking functionality such as memory alignment checks as well as performance analysis support such as the assessment of control-flow uniformity and data sharing patterns. These trace generators and event trace analyzers can be selectively attached to the application when executing on the emulator. When executing a PTX kernel, the emulator records detailed state immediately prior to and immediately after the execution of each PTX instruction, e.g., PC, memory addresses referenced, and thread ID, producing a stream of event object containing this state information. These event object streams are analyzed by individual event trace analyzers which are of two types: correctness checking and performance analysis. Correctness checking trace generators check for illegal behavior in the application and throw an exception if one is detected. Performance analysis examines the trace of an application and presents key information on its behavior patterns.

For example, a memory checker trace analyzer can detect alignment and out-of-bounds access errors in memory operations (load, store, and texture sampling instructions). Bounds checking compares every memory access with a list of valid memory allocations created at runtime. Alignment errors occur when a data is accessed at an address not a multiple of its data size. Instructions that result in an error trigger a runtime exception showing the thread ID, address, and PC. For example, listing 7.1, 7.2, and 7.3 demonstrate an unaligned memory access in CUDA form, PTX form, and Ocelot's output. Since memory is byte addressable and an integer data type is four bytes wide, memory references to an integer must be divisible by four. The example introduces an offset of 1 to the parameter pointer to create an unaligned access.

**Listing 7.1**: Example of unaligned memory access.

```
__global__ void badRef(int *A)
{
  char *b = reinterpret_cast<char *>(a);
  b += 1;
  a = reinterpret_cast<int *>(b);
  a[0] = 0;                          // faulting store
}
```

**Listing 7.2**: Same example in PTX form.

```
mov.s32 %r0 , 0
ld.param.u32 %r1 , [__cudaparm__Z12badRefPi___val_parama]
st.global.s32 [%r1 + 1], %r0              //offset of one
exit
```

**Listing 7.3**: Memory checker output.

```
==Ocelot== Ocelot PTX Emulator failed to run kernel "_Z12badRefPi"
with exception:
==Ocelot== [PC 2] [thread 0] [cta 0] st.global.s32 [%r1 + 1], %r0 –
Memory access 0x8151541 is not aligned to the access size ( 4 bytes )
==Ocelot== Near tracegen.cu:19:0
==Ocelot==
terminate called after throwing an instance of 'hydrazine::Exception'
what(): [PC 2] [thread 0] [cta 0] st.global.s32 [%r1 + 1], %r0 –
Memory access 0x8151541 is not aligned to the access size ( 4 bytes )
Near tracegen.cu:19:0
```

Ocelot includes many such event trace analyzers. For example, a branch trace generator and analyzer records each branch event and the number of divergent threads and generates branch statistics and branch divergence behavior such as the percentage of active threads and the number of branches taken. This can be beneficial for finding areas of high divergence and eliminating unnecessary branch divergence to speed up execution by re-factoring or otherwise modifying the application code. Another example is where the analysis of memory references can track inter-thread data flow. For example, Figure 7.8 shows the amount of inter-thread communication in many benchmark applications as a percentage of loads to shared memory, and also as a fraction of the total dynamic instruction count. This requires support within the emulator to track producer and consumer threads. Such insights are useful when tuning the memory behavior and sharing patterns between threads to maximize performance.

**Dynamic Instrumentation.** While the emulator provides significant functional fidelity at the PTX instruction set level, software emulation can be time consuming. A second tool chain developed for Ocelot is *Lynx* — an infrastructure for dynamic editing of PTX kernels to provide real-time introspection into platform behavior for both performance debugging and correctness checks [FKE+12a]. Lynx is a dynamic instrumentation infrastructure for constructing customizable program analysis tools for GPU-based, parallel architectures. It provides an extensible set of C-based language constructs to build program analysis tools that target the data-parallel programming paradigm used in GPUs. Lynx provides the capability to write instrumentation routines that are (1) *selective*, instrumenting only what is needed, (2) *transparent*, without changes to the applications' source code, (3) *customizable*,

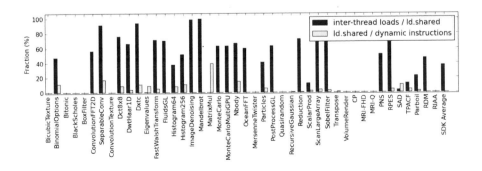

**FIGURE 7.8**: Measuring inter-thread data sharing.

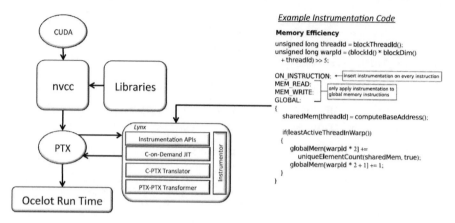

**FIGURE 7.9**: Lynx: a dynamic editing tool for PTX.

and (4) *efficient.* Lynx is embedded into the broader GPU Ocelot system, which provides run-time code generation.

An overview of Lynx is shown in Figure 7.9. Instrumentation code is specified in a C-based instrumentation language that is JIT compiled into PTX. The figure shows an example of instrumentation code that computes memory efficiency at run-time. The compiled PTX instrumentation code is then patched into the kernel using a Ocelot compiler pass over the PTX code. This pass modifies the PTX kernel to correctly place instrumentation code as well as supporting code to manage instrumentation data. Run-time support further enables the transfer of this instrumentation data to the host.

The major utility of Lynx is the ability to create user customizable code that can measure and quantify behaviors that cannot be captured by the vendor supplied tools [NVI11a, NVI11b]. In general, vendors cannot anticipate all of the functionality that their customers will need and that their instrumentation tools should provide. Lynx provides the capability to address such needs. However, it should be kept in mind that dynamic instrumentation perturbs the application code and changes its runtime behavior, e.g., cache behaviors. Lynx is best suited for measurements that are not affected by such perturbations.

In summary, Ocelot provides an open source dynamic compilation infrastructure that includes fully functional PTX emulator as the anchor for an ecosystem of productivity tools to support introspection primarily for the purpose of correctness checking and performance debugging. These open source tools fill a gap left by vendors to permit user customizable behaviors that can augment traditional GPU vendor tools. Research explorations continue to investigate the productivity tools requirements for Keeneland class machines and pursue prototypes that can enhance developer productivity and application performance.

**Virtualization.** The addition of accelerators like GPUs [NVI09b] to general purpose computational machines has considerably boosted their processing capacities. We argue that, with increasingly heterogeneous compute nodes and new usage models, it is important to move beyond current node-based allocations for next generation infrastructure. We base this argument on the following. With node-based allocations, to efficiently use heterogeneous physical nodes, application developers have to laboriously tune their codes so as to best leverage both the CPU and GPU resources present on each node. This means that codes must be re-configured for each hardware platform on which they run. For instance, for the Keeneland machine, where nodes are comprised of two Intel Xeon X5560 processors coupled with three Fermi GPUs, to efficiently use this configuration, an application must not only accelerate a substantial portion of its code, but must do so in ways that utilize each node's twelve CPU and over one thousand GPU cores. If this is not the case, then (1) end users may be charged for node resources they do not use, and (2) machine providers may see low or inadequate levels of utilization. This implies wasted opportunities to service other jobs waiting for machine resources and higher operational costs due to potentially wasted energy in underutilized nodes.

To address these challenges, we provide software that permits applications to acquire and use exactly the cluster resources they need, rather than having to deal with coarse-grained node-based allocations. Specifically, we provide logical—*virtual*—rather than physical sets of CPU/GPU nodes (Figure 7.10), which are constructed using an abstraction termed *GPU assemblies*, where each assembly is comprised of a 'slice' of the machine containing some number of CPUs and GPUs (along with proportional use of memory as well as network resources). One slice can be an assembly consisting mainly of nodes' CPUs for running a CPU-intensive application, but then those nodes' GPUs (since the locally running CPU-intensive programs do not need them) can be made available to other, GPU-intensive

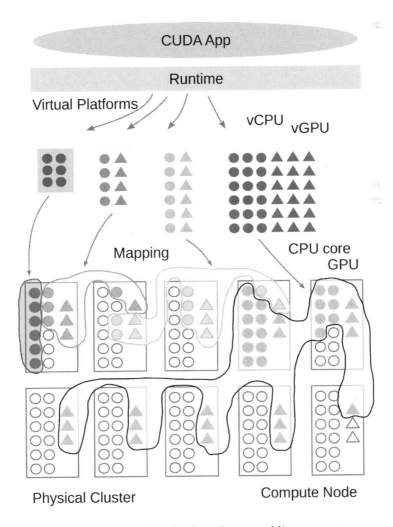

**FIGURE 7.10**: Shadowfax: the assemblies concept.

programs running at the same time (i.e., running on other cluster nodes). Such sharing of GPUs can reduce the need for tuning applications to specific hardware, make it easier to fully exploit the accelerator capabilities determined by processing requirements rather than static machine configurations, and offer levels of flexibility in job scheduling not available on current systems. Furthermore, by allowing applications to specify, and use, virtual cluster configurations, distinct from what the underlying hardware offers, we achieve an additional benefit of improved application *portability*, by obviating the need to extensively tune each code to the physical configuration of underlying hardware.

In order to evaluate the feasibility and utility of creating virtual cluster instances and of enabling fine grain sharing of machine resources, as argued above, we develop a system-level runtime—Shadowfax—which permits assembly construction and management. Shadowfax offers support for characterizing the applications that can benefit from assembly use, and it addresses the challenges in sharing physical hardware (i.e., node and network) resources across multiple assemblies. This creates new opportunities for both end users and machine providers, because when using assemblies, a job scheduler simply maps an application to a "logical" (i.e., virtual) cluster machine, i.e., a GPU assembly, and Shadowfax then tracks the physical resources available, monitors their consequent levels of utilization (and/or other performance metrics), and informs end users about the effectiveness of their choices (Figure 7.11). Specifically, Shadowfax captures and uses monitoring data about both application performance and machine utilization, and it provides such data to end users to better understand the performance of their high-end codes. It also ensures resource availability before sharing node and machine assets, by actively monitoring the use of both the CPU and GPU resources present on cluster nodes. Monitoring at system-level is used to allocate appropriate distributed resources to different assemblies, and monitoring GPU invocations at application-level provides the feedback needed to make appropriate decisions about using local vs. remote accelerators. For instance, for throughput-intensive codes, remote accelerators can be equally effective as local ones, whereas latency-sensitive codes will benefit from or require locally accessible GPUs. An additional benefit of Shadowfax instrumentation is that it can be used to isolate applications from each other, so as to prevent one application from interfering with the execution of another, e.g., by starving it or by causing undue levels of noise [CH11]. As a result, with Shadowfax, capacity computing is assisted by making it possible to map user applications to hardware resources already used by other codes, and is enhanced by providing codes that can use more GPUs than those physically present on each node with the additional resources they require.

The implementation of Shadowfax builds on the (i) interception and (ii) remoting support for GPU access and sharing, described in [MGV+11, GGS+09, GST+11], but extends it in several ways.

The interception of applications' GPU accesses is key for decoupling the application-perceived GPU context from the physical one supported by the underlying hardware. This permits both sharing of GPU resources across multiple applications, and transparent redirection of GPU operations to remote resources. GPU accesses are intercepted via a lightweight interposing library, and are redirected to a designated management process, one per node, as illustrated in Figure 7.11. The management entity communicates via RPC to other management entities, to redirect GPU operations to remote physical GPUs, and to create and maintain the required virtual platform properties. The interposing library in Shadowfax supports (a subset of) the NVIDIA CUDA API, but extensions are easily made and similar solutions can be provided for OpenCL or others. This approach permits application software to remain unchanged to take advantage of the virtual platforms provided by Shadowfax. All that is needed for applications to use Shadowfax, is to run 'runtime main' on a designated node, to run 'runtime minion ip_addr_to_main' on the remote side(s), and on the local side, we preload the interposer library with the app executable: 'LD_PRELOAD=libipser.so·

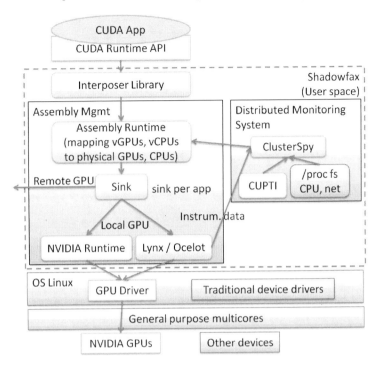

**FIGURE 7.11**: Shadowfax: the components of the system.

matrixMul...' if the code matrixMul is being run. It is a bit more involved to also add instrumentation support for detailed GPU measurement via Lynx, requiring the app to be recompiled and linked with libocelot.so rather than with libcuda.so. We note that such instrumentation support is only per specific user requests, meaning that un-instrumented applications can be run without recompilation.

Additional features of the assembly middleware include (1) efficient implementation of remoting software on InfiniBand-based cluster interconnects, (2) maintainance of per-node and cluster-wide profile information about system, GPU, and assembly resources, including monitoring data about how applications exploit GPUs, and (3) use of performance models derived from profile and runtime data to evaluate a system's capacity to dynamically host workloads, considering both a node's remaining capacity as well as a workload's sensitivity to remoting. Such data includes utilization information on the CPU, in- and out-bound network traffic on the InfiniBand fabric, node memory capacity, and NVIDIA CUDA PTX instrumentation, the latter made possible through Lynx [FKE+12b]. Combined with offline analysis of workloads' runtime characteristics of GPU use (e.g., using CUDA API traces), such information enables the intelligent mapping and the scheduling strategies needed to scale applications, increase cluster utilization, and reduce interference.

In summary, with GPGPU assemblies, by multiplexing multiple virtual platforms and thereby sharing the aggregate cluster resources, we leverage *diversity* in how applications use underlying CPU, GPU, and network hardware, to better schedule the resources of heterogeneous cluster-based systems like Keeneland. Making it easy for applications to use local or remote GPUs helps obtain high application performance and enables scaling beyond physical hardware configurations, while at the same time, improving system utilization. For instance, on a 64-node hardware configuration, multiple instances of two implementations of the LAMMPS molecular simulator—one implemented for CPUs and one for GPUs—were

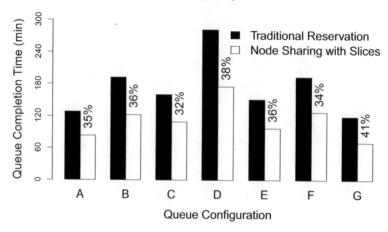

**FIGURE 7.12**: Shadowfax: cluster throughput with various hardware slices using LAMMPS.

placed into a job queue (Queue "G" in Figure 7.12, with Queues "A"-"G" representing 1-64 nodes allocated) with each implementation assigned different assemblies representing individual hardware needs, enabling concurrent execution of each implementation, to achieve an increase in system throughput of 41% as compared to traditional job scheduling, where for a common set of hardware one job maintains exclusive access for the duration of its execution. Additional experimental results demonstrate low overheads for remote GPU use, particularly for applications using asynchronous CUDA calls that can be batched to better utilize the interconnect and offer flexibility in exactly when some CUDA call must be run on a GPU.

Finally, and going beyond the current Keeneland based implementation of the virtual cluster functionality provided by Shadowfax, we are also exploring the utility of leveraging system-level virtualization technology to achieve assembly-like functionality without necessitating any changes at all to applications. To do so, we leverage the fact that virtualization solutions like Xen [BDF+03] can be supported with low overheads on modern hardware. This is also true for I/O virtualization of high performance fabrics such as the InfiniBand interconnect in Keeneland [LHAP06, RKGS08], and our group has made significant progress in providing low-overhead virtualization and sharing of GPU devices [GGS+09]. In fact, the initial prototype of the Shadowfax solution was implemented in a virtualized Xen-based environment [MGV+11], in part in order to directly leverage hypervisor support for isolation and scheduling on heterogeneous nodes such as those present in Keeneland [GST+11]. For the HPC domain addressed by the current realization of Shadowfax, we have chosen to build a lightweight, user-level implementation of these concepts to be able to operate on large-scale cluster machines running standard Linux operating systems and up-to-date device drivers. We are continuing, however, to explore the suitability of leveraging existing virtualization support provided by open-source hypervisors like Xen for use in large-scale systems, and new open source CUDA software available for the latest NVIDIA GPUs [KMMB12].

## 7.5  Applications and Workloads

As the Keeneland Initial Delivery System is primarily intended to help applications scientists prepare their codes for scalable heterogeneous systems, the dominant workloads are heavily represented by applications under active development. System usage is spread among a variety of science domains. For example, in the biology domain we see peptide folding on surfaces using AMBER [she12], simulating blood flow with FMM, protein-DNA docking via a structure-based approach [hon12], and biomolecular simulations with NAMD [PBW⁺05]. Materials science applications include the LAMMPS molecular dynamics simulator, Quantum Monte Carlo for studying correlated electronic systems using QMCPACK [qmc12] and high temperature superconductor studies using DCA++ [ASM⁺08, MAM⁺09], a 2009 Gordon Bell Prize winner. We also see applications in high energy physics (hadron polarizability in lattice QCD) [had12], combustion (turbulence, compressible flow) and some codes with application to national security. We also see pure computer science applications, such as development and testing of numerical linear algebra libraries (MAGMA) [TDB10], new programming models like Sequoia/Legion [seq12, leg12], and improvements to existing programming models like MPI [SOHL⁺98].

The codes occupying the greatest proportion of node hours are as follows:

- AMBER is typically the most heavily used software package, ranging from 34% to 59% of total machine use. AMBER is a package of molecular simulation programs with full GPU support. The CPU version has been in use for more than 30 years.

- LAMMPS usage is consistently around 11% of the system. LAMMPS is 175K+ lines of classical molecular dynamics code that can be run in parallel on distributed processors with GPU support for many code features. LAMMPS can model systems with millions or billions of particles.

- MCSim usage fluctuates from 5% to 32%, depending on the month. MCSim is Monte Carlo Markov chain simulation software. MCSim is versatile; it is not tailored for a specific domain.

- TeraChem usage can be as high as 19%. TeraChem is the first computational chemistry software program written entirely from scratch to benefit from GPUs. It is used for molecular dynamics.

Since the full-scale Keeneland system focuses primarily on production science, less time is allocated to application development and computer science research. The initial allocation requests apportion 50% of the KFS system usage for testing universality in diblock copolymers (driven by materials science); 25% for understanding ion solvation at the air/water interface from adaptive QM/MM molecular dynamics (driven by chemistry); 13% for molecular dynamics of biological and nanoscale systems over microseconds, and salt effect in peptides and nucleic acids (both driven by biology); and 2% for simulation of relativistic astrophysical systems (driven by computational astrophysics).

### 7.5.1  Highlights of Main Applications

**MoBo.** During the early KIDS acceptance testing, we ported and successfully ran the main kernel (Fast Multipole Method) for a blood simulation application; the results were presented at the 2010 International Conference on High Performance Computing, Networking, Storage, and Analysis, where this paper was awarded the SC10 Gordon Bell prize [RLV+10]. The application is a fast, petaflop-scalable algorithm for Stokesian particulate flows. The goal is the direct simulation of blood, a challenging multiscale, multiphysics problem. The method has been implemented in the software library MoBo (for "Moving Boundaries"). MoBo supports parallelism at all levels, inter-node distributed memory parallelism, intra-node shared memory parallelism, data parallelism (vectorization), and fine-grained multithreading for GPUs. MoBo has performed simulations with up to 260 million *deformable* RBCs (90 billion unknowns in space). The previous largest simulation at the same physical fidelity involved O(10,000) RBCs. MoBo achieved 0.7 PF/s of sustained performance on NCCS/Jaguar.

**AMBER**. ("Assisted Model Building with Energy Refinement") refers to two things: a set of molecular mechanical force fields for the simulation of biomolecules (which are in the public domain, and are used in a variety of simulation programs); and a package of molecular simulation programs which includes source code and demos. This package evolved from a program that was constructed in the 1970s, and now contains a group of programs embodying a number of powerful tools of modern computational chemistry, focused on molecular dynamics and free energy calculations of proteins, nucleic acids, and carbohydrates. Molecular dynamics simulations of proteins, which began about 25 years ago, are now widely used as tools to investigate structure and dynamics under a variety of conditions; these range from studies of ligand binding and enzyme reaction mechanisms to problems of denaturation and protein refolding to analysis of experimental data and refinement of structures. AMBER is the collective name for a suite of programs that allows users to carry out and analyze molecular dynamics simulations, particularly for proteins, nucleic acids, and carbohydrates. None of the individual programs carries this name, but the various parts work reasonably well together, providing a powerful framework for many common calculations. It should be recognized, however, that the code and force fields are separate; several other computer packages have implemented the AMBER force fields, and other force fields can be used within the AMBER programs. For the past 16 years, new versions of AMBER have been released on a two-year schedule. Under way are continued improvements in code cleanup, with an eye toward maintainability, portability, and efficiency. Amber is a code that is heavily used by its developers, and reflects their interests, but attempts are being made to lower the learning curve for scientists new to the simulation field. For more information, see http://ambermd.org/.

**LAMMPS**. ("Large-scale Atomic/Molecular Massively Parallel Simulator") is a molecular dynamics application from Sandia National Laboratories. LAMMPS makes use of MPI for parallel communication and is free open source code. LAMMPS is a classical molecular dynamics code that models an ensemble of particles in a liquid, solid, or gaseous state. It can model atomic, polymeric, biological, metallic, granular, and course grained systems using a variety of force fields and boundary conditions. LAMMPS is freely available source code and is designed to be easy to modify or extend with new capabilities, such as force fields, atom types, boundary conditions, or diagnostics. The 1995 reference paper *Fast parallel algorithms for short-range molecular dynamics* [Pli95] has more than 2,500 citations.

Figure 7.13 shows results on Keeneland from a 250k particle simulation of nanodroplet formation using the Gay-Berne potential in LAMMPS. This figure shows the speedup from using all three GPUs in each of up to 32 nodes of KIDS (with varying numbers of processes per node) relative to using all 12 CPU cores on each node.

## 7.5.2    Benchmarks

To understand the usefulness of a system for running a particular workload, it is critical to measure the performance of real-world applications from that workload running on the system. However, because real-world applications can be highly complex and because they

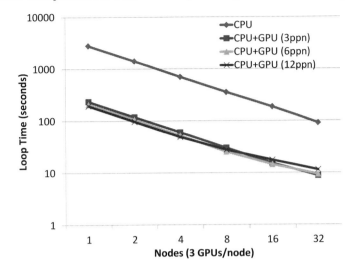

**FIGURE 7.13**: CPU and GPU results from a 250k particle Gay-Berne LAMMPS simulation on KIDS.

tend to exercise many facets of a system, it can be very useful to focus on the performance of each facet individually using benchmark programs. To better understand the strengths of the Keeneland systems, we used the TOP500 High-Performance Linpack (HPL) and the Scalable HeterOgeneous Computing (SHOC) benchmark suites.

**TOP500 HPL.** High-Performance Linpack is a commonly used reference point for supercomputers involving solutions to dense linear systems in double precision. On KIDS, HPL achieved 106.30 TFLOPS, placing Keeneland at position 111 in November 2011's TOP500 list and rating its power efficiency at 901 MFLOPS/W.

Initially, our experiments on HPL only a few days after KIDS was deployed in November of 2011, reached 63.92 TFLOPS; this early version of HPL did not stream data to the GPU, and hence it had a relatively low efficiency for floating-point rate. Even with this inefficiency, KIDS ranked at position 117 on the November 2010 TOP500 list, and given its low power usage of 94.4 kW during the run, placed the system as the 9th most power-efficient supercomputer in the world at 677 MFLOPS/W on the Green500 list.

**SHOC.** Early on, our Keeneland team could not find a set of scalable heterogeneous GPU benchmarks for testing the reliability and performance of these types of systems, so we designed the Scalable Heterogeneous Computing (SHOC) benchmark suite [DMM+10]. SHOC plays an integral part of not only the KIDS and KFS acceptance tests but also health checks on the deployed systems. For more information about SHOC and performance results on KIDS, see Section 7.8.

## 7.6   Data Center and Facility

The Keeneland systems are co-located at Oak Ridge National Laboratory's Leadership Computing Facility (OLCF), along with other HPC systems from DOE, NSF, NOAA, and other customers. Power and cooling are provided as part of the facility co-location fees.

The KID system was originally located in a traditionally designed datacenter that utilizes a raised floor design. Computer Room Air Conditioners (CRACs) located around the perimeter of the room pull air from near the ceiling, chill the air, and then duct it below a 36" floor to provide positive cold air pressure under the raised floor. Perforated tiles are then placed in front of the equipment racks to direct chilled air to the equipment. Hot air is exhausted from the rear of the equipment rack into the datacenter. Power is provided via monitored circuits fed from the facility's line side. Due to the large power draw of such a system, it was not cost effective to connect the KID system to the facility UPS.

In conjunction with the deployment of the KFS system, KIDS was relocated to a new datacenter. Both the KID and KFS systems are installed in a newly remodeled datacenter designed to take advantage of cold isle containment techniques and in-row chilled water air handlers. The new datacenter is designed with an 18" raised floor. The systems are deployed in 20 rack sections, nicknamed pods, with the racks deployed in rows with the fronts of the equipment racks opposing each other. Due to the limited under-floor space, In-Row air handlers were installed between equipment racks to pull hot air from the rear of the equipment racks (the hot aisle), remove the heat from the air, and deposit it in the enclosed area in the front of the racks (the cold aisle). This design makes use of containment techniques, such as blanking panels in the racks and panels over covering the rows, to ensure that the hot air from the exhaust does not infiltrate the cold aisle. By reducing the mixing of hot and cold air at the equipment intake, it is possible to ensure a constant inlet temperature, thus providing more effective cooling. Both systems are powered via dedicated transformers located at the end of the pod. Using dedicated transformers reduces the impact of maintenance performed on other systems to the Keeneland systems.

## 7.7   System Statistics

The KID system has been in operation for almost two years, and during this time, we have monitored its operation closely. The KFS system has only been operational for a few months, and as such, its statistics have been dominated by transients. Hence, we discuss only our KID system statistics here.

KIDS has been used for software and application development activities; for education, outreach, and training; and by many groups to test codes in a GPU-accelerated environment. At a high level, the research areas utilizing KIDS include computer science and computational research, astronomical sciences, atmospheric sciences, behavioral and neural sciences, biological and critical systems, chemistry, design and manufacturing systems, Earth sciences, materials research, mathematical sciences, mechanical and structural systems, molecular biosciences, physics, cross-disciplinary activities, and education/training. Both the number of users and the breadth of science fields is well beyond what was initially envisioned for KIDS. Unlike production resources, the majority of KIDS usage is discretionary, rather than allocated by a review committee. KIDS has an architecture very similar to the KFS system, so it can be used for production workload as necessary, and applications that have been successfully tuned for the KIDS architecture should run well on the KFS system architecture. Although the number of accounts has been reduced as we prepare to go into production, KIDS had 83 project accounts and 244 users in May 2012 with almost half of them active in any given month.

KIDS utilization has fluctuated around 60% during the past year with the peak utilization of 84.5% in September 2011, before we changed our usage policy to encourage more development jobs and larger scale jobs. May 2012 is an example where the utilization was

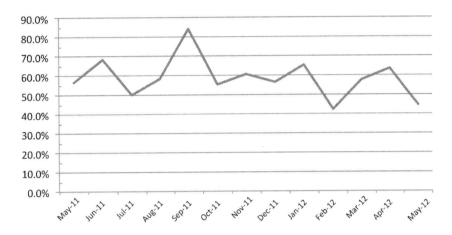

**FIGURE 7.14**: KIDS percent utilization/month.

down by design as we added more capability periods to allow users to run scaling tests for SC12 papers that were due, and we needed blocks of time for Keeneland staff to test the system after the upgrade from NVIDIA M2070 GPUs to M2090 GPU (see Figure 7.14). The draining of KIDS for these jobs resulted in lower utilization, but provided an opportunity for paper authors to complete their work in time for submission and our preparation for XSEDE production. The number of large jobs run in May 2012 was more than the prior two months combined.

As shown by Figure 7.15, there is significant variability of the workload distribution from month to month. There has usually been a large portion of the workload for small node-count jobs, and there has been a general shift toward mid-sized jobs. Workload for the large jobs tends to be smaller because these jobs need to be scheduled once per week and tend to be scaling runs that, unlike production runs, tend to be shorter in duration.

KIDS shows a fairly common usage pattern: the majority of jobs are small single-node

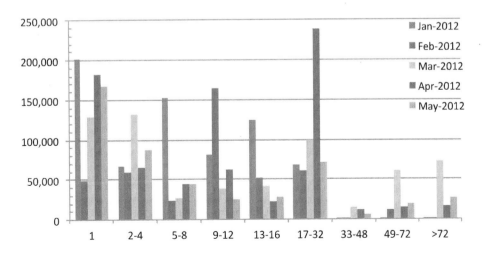

**FIGURE 7.15**: KIDS workload distribution by numbers of nodes/job.

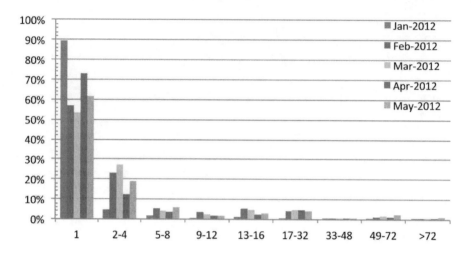

**FIGURE 7.16**: KIDS workload distribution by percentage of jobs at number of nodes.

jobs, but the majority of the workload is comprised of single-node jobs and multimode jobs in the range of 9-32 nodes. KIDS is being used in a hybrid mode, where part of the system is reserved for development work during prime hours of the day while pre-production (capacity) work is also being accomplished. The entire machine is reserved once per week for capability jobs that need more than 72 nodes for a single job. This capability reservation allows users to perform scaling studies and benchmark codes in an environment that is not generally available (see Figures 7.16 and 7.17).

The Keeneland user community represents a wide variety of scientific disciplines. However, the majority of the workload comes from molecular biosciences and physics, followed by chemistry and materials research. Table 7.3 shows the dominance of those areas and the fluctuation in the workload for those research areas over the six-month period from December 2011 through May 2012. The workload is presented as node-hours of usage.

The Keeneland Initial Delivery System is used in a hybrid mode with preference given

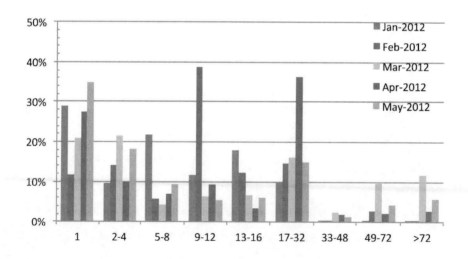

**FIGURE 7.17**: KIDS workload distribution by percentage of machine at number of nodes.

**TABLE 7.3**: KIDS node-hours by scientific discipline.

| Research Area | Dec11 | Jan12 | Feb12 | Mar12 | Apr12 | May12 |
|---|---|---|---|---|---|---|
| Molecular Biosciences | 12,353 | 11,643 | 16,868 | 16,684 | 32,317 | 13,946 |
| Physics | 6,782 | 27,609 | 10,894 | 18,298 | 9,946 | 5,794 |
| Chemistry | 15,957 | 11,926 | 646 | 5,157 | 900 | 3,721 |
| Materials Research | 10,902 | 1,197 | 469 | 3,570 | 2,764 | 1,868 |
| Scientific Computing | 0 | 0 | 86 | 371 | 2,708 | 7,024 |
| Cross-Disciplinary | 1,605 | 17,987 | 195 | 929 | 336 | 523 |
| Computation Research | 1,873 | 741 | 504 | 1,995 | 547 | 3 |
| Bio./Critical Systems | 0 | 1,876 | 2,062 | 0 | 0 | 0 |

to development activities during prime hours but with production workloads allowed after hours or when the system is not fully utilized. Looking at only the aggregate usage masks some of the detail of how the machine is used by various projects. Even within a particular research area, there are differences in how the system is used. Table 7.4 shows that the production workload for the highest usage projects in node-hours/month fluctuates from month to month but remains at high utilization. This represents more of a production workload, while other projects farther down the table demonstrate a start-up/development usage that starts low, peaks, and then drops back down. Each of the projects used enough resources in a given month to be one of the top ten users in at least one month, but over the six-month period, most actually represent a relatively low utilization. A few projects have multiple cycles of peak utilization followed by low utilization.

During the six-month period discussed above, the top five usage projects per month averaged over 80% of the KIDS workload. As Keeneland moves into a stable XSEDE production environment, the workload on the KFS system is expected to come from a limited number of users who either have jobs that require a large scalable system to complete in a reasonable time frame or who have an equivalent aggregate workload. The development workload is expected to continue to run on KIDS with overflow from the KFS system using

**TABLE 7.4**: KIDS workload.

| Research Area | Dec11 | Jan12 | Feb12 | Mar12 | Apr12 | May12 |
|---|---|---|---|---|---|---|
| Molecular Biosciences 1 | 10,427 | 6,577 | 7,397 | 16,683 | 32,317 | 12,738 |
| Physics 1 | 4,887 | 12,937 | 8,676 | 4,851 | 3,925 | 3,791 |
| Chemistry 1 | 14,490 | 11,060 | 642 | 5,157 | 900 | 3,721 |
| Materials Research 1 | 10,853 | 1,197 | 304 | 2,266 | 2,699 | 1,868 |
| Physics 2 | 1,871 | 11,191 | 646 | 946 | 3,016 | 446 |
| Physics 3 | 0 | 712 | 292 | 12,501 | 3,005 | 1,558 |
| Molecular Biosciences 2 | 561 | 5,066 | 9,471 | 1 | 0 | 1,209 |
| Scientific Computing 1 | 0 | 0 | 86 | 255 | 1,872 | 6,285 |
| Molecular Biosciences 3 | 67 | 4 | 54 | 1,555 | 3,254 | 1,993 |
| Cross-Disciplinary 1 | 1,569 | 2,995 | 0 | 0 | 0 | 0 |
| Physics 4 | 24 | 2,769 | 1,280 | 0 | 0 | 0 |
| Bio./Critical Systems 1 | 0 | 1,876 | 2,062 | 0 | 0 | 0 |
| Computation Research 1 | 1,873 | 0 | 460 | 1,238 | 0 | 0 |
| Computation Research 2 | 0 | 741 | 44 | 757 | 547 | 3 |
| Materials Research 2 | 49 | 0 | 164 | 1,304 | 66 | 0 |
| Molecular Biosciences 4 | 1,395 | 0 | 0 | 0 | 0 | 0 |
| Chemistry 2 | 967 | 228 | 4 | 0 | 0 | 0 |
| Cross-Disciplinary 2 | 0 | 0 | 195 | 857 | 67 | 0 |
| Scientific Computing 2 | 0 | 0 | 0 | 116 | 811 | 27 |
| Cross-Disciplinary 3 | 36 | 15 | 0 | 71 | 268 | 523 |
| Scientific Computing 3 | 0 | 0 | 0 | 0 | 25 | 711 |
| Chemistry 3 | 0 | 638 | 0 | 0 | 0 | 0 |

the remaining cycles. As the XSEDE workload transitions to the KFS system, the KFS system is exhibiting longer queue backlogs and a higher utilization, while KIDS continues to exhibit the same or a higher degree of bimodal usage. Considering that a single project requested (but did not receive) half of the available allocation on the KFS system for a year, it is clear that there is a significant demand for this type of system and that system utilization will be high over its lifecycle.

## 7.8    Scalable Heterogeneous Computing (SHOC) Benchmark Suite

As systems like Keeneland become more common, it is important to be able to compare and contrast architectural designs and programming systems in a fair and open forum. To this end, the Keeneland project has supported the development of the Scalable HeterOgeneous Computing benchmark suite (SHOC)[1].

The SHOC benchmark suite was designed to provide a standardized way to measure the performance and stability of non-traditional high performance computing architectures. The SHOC benchmarks are distributed using MPI and effectively scale from a single device (GPU or CPU) to a large cluster.

The SHOC benchmarks are divided into two primary categories: stress tests and performance tests. The stress tests use computationally demanding kernels to identify OpenCL devices with bad memory, insufficient cooling, or other component defects. The other tests measure many aspects of system performance on several synthetic kernels as well as common parallel operations and algorithms. The performance tests are further subdivided according to their complexity and the nature of the device capability they exercise.

In addition to OpenCL-based benchmarks, SHOC also includes a Compute Unified Device Architecture (CUDA) version of its benchmarks for comparison with the OpenCL version. As both languages support similar constructs, kernels have been written with the same optimizations in each language.

**Level Zero: "Speeds and Feeds."** SHOC's level zero tests are designed to measure low-level hardware characteristics (the so-called "feeds and speeds"). All level zero tests use artificial kernels, and results from these benchmarks represent an empirical upper bound on realized performance. As these are designed for consistency, they can be used not just as a comparative performance measure, but can also detect a variety of issues, such as lower than expected peak performance, chipsets with only eight PCI-Express (PCIe) lanes, or systems with large variations in kernel queueing delays.

**Level One: Parallel Algorithms**. Level One benchmarks measure basic parallel algorithms, such as the Fast Fourier Transform (FFT) or the parallel prefix sum (a.k.a. scan). These algorithms represent common tasks in parallel processing and are commonly found in a significant portion of the kernels of real applications.

These algorithms vary significantly in performance characteristics, and stress different components of a device's memory subsystem and functional units. Several of the benchmarks are highly configurable and can span a range of the spectrum based on problem size or other input parameters.

**Level Two: Application Kernels**. Level two kernels are extracted routines from production applications:

**SHOC on Keeneland.** SHOC was a major component in the acceptance test for the

---

[1] http://j.mp/shocmarks

**TABLE 7.5**: SHOC components.

| Component | Description |
|---|---|
| **Level Zero** | |
| Bus Speed Download and Readback | Measures the bandwidth of the interconnection bus between the host processor and the OpenCL device (typically the PCIe bus) by repeatedly transferring data of various sizes to and from the device. |
| Device Memory Bandwidth | Measures bandwidth for all device memory address spaces, including global, local, constant, and image memories. The global address space is benchmarked using both coalesced and uncoalesced memory accesses. |
| Kernel Compilation | OpenCL kernels are compiled at runtime, and this benchmark measures average compilation speed and overheads for kernels of varying complexity. |
| Peak FLOPS | Measures peak floating point (single or double precision) operations per second using a synthetic workload designed to fully exercise device functional units. |
| Queueing Delay | Measures the overhead of launching a kernel in OpenCL's queueing system. |
| Resource Contention | Measures contention on the PCIe bus between OpenCL data transfers and MPI message passing. |
| **Level One** | |
| FFT | Measures the performance of a two-dimensional Fast Fourier Transform. The benchmark computes multiple FFTs of size 512 in parallel. |
| MD | Measures the speed of a simple pairwise calculation of the Lennard-Jones potential from molecular dynamics using neighbor lists. |
| Reduction | Measures the performance of a sum reduction operation using floating point data. |
| Scan | Measures the performance of the parallel prefix sum algorithm (also known as Scan) on a large array of floating point data. |
| GEMM | This benchmark measures device performance on an OpenCL version of the general matrix multiply (GEMM) BLAS routine. |
| Sort | Measures device performance for a very fast radix sort algorithm [SHG09] which sorts key-value pairs of single precision floating point data. |
| Stencil2D | Measures performance for a standard two-dimensional nine point stencil calculation. |
| Triad | An OpenCL version of the STREAM Triad benchmark[DL05]. |
| **Level Two** | |
| S3D | Measures the performance of the S3D's computationally intensive getrates kernel, which calculates the rate of chemical reactions for the 22 species of the ethylene-air chemistry model. |
| QTC | Measures the speed of a complex quality threshold clustering operation. QTC clustering is conceptually similar to the more well-known $k$-means clustering, but requires no prior knowledge of the appropriate value of $k$. |

KID system; indeed, the KIDS acceptance test was a primary motivation for the initial development of SHOC. SHOC was also used in the acceptance test for the KFS system.

Figure 7.18 shows the performance of the SHOC Stencil2D benchmark program on KIDS. Stencil2D implements a nine-point stencil operation over the values in a two-dimensional matrix. In its MPI version, Stencil2D splits the matrix across all the available MPI tasks and a halo exchange is used between tasks that are neighbors with respect to the program's two-dimensional Cartesian task organization. The program uses a weak-scaling model, where the total size of the matrix is proportional to the number of tasks available. The figure shows the program's performance as the number of GPUs used was varied, for both CUDA and OpenCL versions of the program. For this experiment, we used a pre-release version

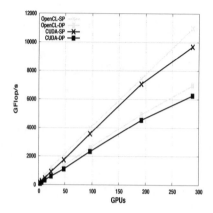

**FIGURE 7.18**: Performance of SHOC Stencil2D benchmark on KIDS, CUDA, and OpenCL versions.

of SHOC version 1.1.4 with CUDA version 4.1. We placed three MPI tasks per compute node so that each task controlled a GPU and no GPUs were left idle. We did not use any process affinity control for this experiment. The algorithms used by the CUDA and OpenCL versions of Stencil2D are the same. Unlike the case with many of the SHOC benchmark programs, the MPI+OpenCL version of this program slightly outperforms the MPI+CUDA version. We hypothesize that this is a result of using GPU work distributions that, by default, are slightly more amenable to the OpenCL version. Also, the GPU Direct software was not enabled on KIDS when these data were collected. Because of the frequent halo exchanges needed in this program, we expect that the GPU Direct optimization would provide a substantial performance boost to the MPI+CUDA version that would allow it to outperform the OpenCL version.

## Acknowledgments

Keeneland is funded by the National Science Foundation's Office of Cyberinfrastructure under award #0910735. The Keeneland team includes Georgia Institute of Technology, Oak Ridge National Laboratory, and the University of Tennessee at Knoxville.

# Chapter 8

## Blue Gene/P: JUGENE

**Norbert Attig, Jutta Docter, Wolfgang Frings, Johannes Grotendorst, Inge Gutheil, Florian Janetzko, Olaf Mextorf, Bernd Mohr, Michael Stephan, Klaus Wolkersdorfer, and Lothar Wollschläger**

*Jülich Supercomputing Centre, Institute for Advanced Simulation, Forschungszentrum Jülich*

**Stefan Krieg, and Thomas Lippert**

*Jülich Supercomputing Centre, Forschungszentrum Jülich, and Universität Wuppertal, Fachbereich C - Physik*

## 8.1   Background

With the IBM Blue Gene/P supercomputer JUGENE, inaugurated in May 2009 at the Jülich Supercomputing Centre (JSC), the Forschungszentrum Jülich has entered the era of petaflop supercomputer performance in Europe.

### 8.1.1   Forschungszentrum Jülich, Jülich Supercomputing Centre

Forschungszentrum Jülich [fzj] is a multi thematic German research center that aims at creating knowledge which benefits society in the fields of health, energy and environment, and information technology, imparting it and putting it to use in applications.

The Jülich Supercomputing Centre (JSC) [jsc], as a part of the Institute for Advanced Simulation [ias] within the Forschungszentrum Jülich, operates supercomputers of the highest performance class in Europe. It enables national and European scientists and engineers to solve challenging problems of high complexity in science and engineering in collaborative infrastructures. JSC also offers various education opportunities and support for top research in the simulation sciences. It cooperates with leading computer manufacturers in developing next generation supercomputers.

The Jülich Blue Gene/P system - called JUGENE - is funded in equal parts by Germany's Federal Ministry of Education and Research and the government of the state of North Rhine-Westphalia, with the objective to be the first leadership-class system providing cycles to the European supercomputing infrastructure "Partnership for Advanced Computing in Europe" (PRACE).

PRACE [prab] is a registered organization of more than 20 European countries to create a Tier-0 supercomputer infrastructure. The four principal partner countries within PRACE (Germany, France, Spain, and Italy) have made binding commitments to contribute Tier-0 resources each with a value of 100 million € within five years. Germany is represented in PRACE by the Gauss Centre for Supercomputing e.V. (GCS) [gcs], an association of the three leading German supercomputing centers in Jülich, Stuttgart, and Garching (Munich).

JUGENE offers computing time to various user communities and is utilized by scientists and engineers all over Germany and Europe. The computer time for national users is distributed through the John von Neumann Institute for Computing (NIC) [nic]. In more than 25 years of its function, the NIC has developed a highly respected peer review scheme that is strictly based on the scientific quality of the proposals. With the start of the PRACE infrastructure, part of the JUGENE capability is distributed through the Europe-wide peer review process by the PRACE Scientific Steering Committee.

In addition to JUGENE, the JSC runs an Intel-based general-purpose supercomputer JuRoPA (Jülich Research on Petaflop Architectures) [jur] for moderately parallel applications. Its twin system HPC-FF (High Performance Computing for Fusion) is dedicated to the European fusion community.

## 8.1.2 From Blue Gene/L to Blue Gene/Q

When IBM Blue Gene technology became available in 2004/2005, Forschungszentrum Jülich recognized the potential of this architecture as a leadership-class system for capability computing applications [Att09].

In early summer 2005, Jülich started testing a single Blue Gene/L rack named JUBL (Jülich Blue Gene/L) with 2,048 IBM PowerPC 440 processors (700 MHz, 2.8 GFlops) and a peak performance of 5.6 TFlop/s, especially for applications from Lattice Quantum Chronodynamics (LQCD). It soon became obvious that many more applications than initially expected were ported and efficiently run on the Blue Gene architecture. Due to the fact that the system is well balanced in terms of processor speed, memory latency, and network performance, many applications could be successfully scaled up to large numbers of processors.

Therefore in January 2006, the system was expanded to 8 racks with 16,384 processors. The 8-rack system has been successfully in operation for over two years. About 30 research projects, which were carefully selected with respect to their scientific quality, ran their applications on the system using between 1,024 and 16,384 processors.

In early 2007, Forschungszentrum Jülich decided to procure a powerful next-generation Blue Gene system. In October 2007, a 16-rack Blue Gene/P system with 65,536 processors was installed. With its peak performance of 222.8 TFlop/s and a measured LINPACK computing power of 167.3 TFlop/s, Jülich's Blue Gene/P — alias JUGENE — was ranked No 2 in the November 2007 edition of the Top500 list.

The principal design of Blue Gene/L remained unchanged. The main differences between Blue Gene/P and Blue Gene/L concern the processor and networks. The key features of Blue Gene/P [bgp] are four PowerPC 450 processors (850 Mhz, 13.6 GFlops) combined in a four-way SMP (node) chip. This allows a hybrid programming model with MPI and OpenMP (up to four threads per node). The network interface is DMA capable (direct memory access), which increases the performance while reducing the processor load during message handling. The available memory per processor has been doubled to 2 GB per node allowing even more applications to be run on Blue Gene/P. The external I/O network has been upgraded from a 1 to a 10 Gigabit Ethernet.

In 2008, the GCS funded the first Petaflop supercomputer in Germany and the Forschungszentrum Jülich signed a contract with IBM for upgrading the JUGENE computer from 16 to 72 racks Blue Gene/P containing 294,912 processors, which can be seen in

**FIGURE 8.1**: JUGENE at Jülich Supercomputing Centre.

Figure 8.1. By then IBM had changed the design of the Blue Gene/P to use water-cooled heat exchangers between the racks to cool the air flowing through the racks. This implied major work on the infrastructure of the machine hall to install water-cooling and the extended power supply for more racks. The installation of the system and the subsequent integration of the already existing 16 racks took about three months.

At the beginning of user operation in June 2009 the machine was the most powerful in Europe and Number 2 on the Top500 list. It stayed among the top 10 systems worldwide for two years. From mid 2009 to mid 2011 it was the most parallel system in the world.

JUGENE [jug] is fully integrated into the Jülich supercomputer infrastructure. Its I/O nodes are connected to the fileserver JUST (Jülich STorage server, see Section 8.11) by FORCE 10 E1200i switches, based on 10 Gigabit Ethernet technology, shown in Figure 8.2.

The lifetime of the largest Blue Gene/P in the world ended in mid 2012 after having been in operation for over three years and being superseded by an IBM Blue Gene/Q system.

## 8.2    System Overview

Blue Gene/P is an MPP type (massively parallel) system with the design goal of achieving an optimal Performance/Watt ratio and extreme scalability. It uses CPUs with low power consumption in a high density packaging, bringing 1,024 compute nodes (4,096 cores) into a single rack. Each rack houses two so-called midplanes with 512 nodes in 16 nodecards, where the nodes may have up to 4 GB of memory and are connected via a proprietary high speed network (Figure 8.3).

The JUGENE system in Jülich consists of 72 Blue Gene/P racks, configured as 9 rows with 8 racks each, which sums up to 73,728 nodes (294,912 cores). Every node has 2 GB of memory, resulting in 144 TB. 600 I/O nodes connect the system to the outside world.

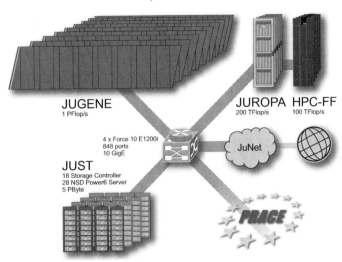

**FIGURE 8.2**: JSC supercomputer network connections.

The Blue Gene/P hardware itself is completely stateless and is controlled by a service node (IBM p6-550, running Linux®). Two front-end nodes (IBM p6-550, running Linux®) are available to users, where login, cross compiling, and job submission are done.

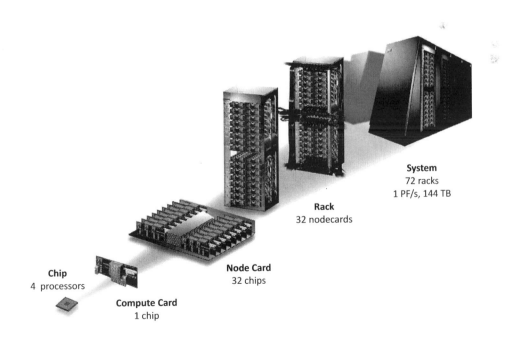

**FIGURE 8.3**: Blue Gene/P hardware packaging.

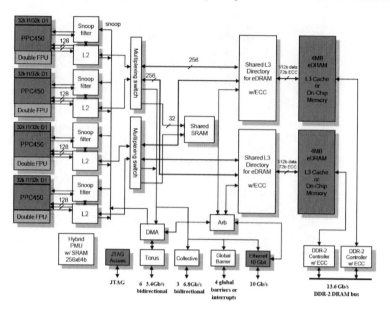

**FIGURE 8.4**: Logical setup of Blue Gene/P compute ASIC.

## 8.2.1    Hardware Architecture

Blue Gene/P uses a PowerPC 450 processor with 4 compute cores. Each core utilizes a "Double Hummer" floating point unit (double data  single instruction) and has its own private L1 cache (32 KB) and private L2 cache (14x stream pre-fetching). The processor has full SMP (symmetric multiprocessing) capability and an 8 MB shared L3 cache. With a clock rate of 850 MHz, the peak performance of the processor is 13.6 GFlop/s with a memory bandwidth of 13.6 GB/s (3.4 GB/s per core), giving a ratio of 1 Byte/Flop. In addition to the compute cores a Blue Gene/P ASIC (Application Specific Integrated Circuit) contains a memory controller and the whole DMA capable network infrastructure (Figure 8.4).

A Blue Gene/P node, see Figure 8.5, consists of a compute ASIC and 2 GB of shared memory (ECC + ChipKill). The interface to the proprietary Blue Gene network is part of the ASIC. A nodecard (see Figure 8.6) contains 32 compute nodes which may be complemented by up to 2 I/O nodes.

**FIGURE 8.5**: Blue Gene/P node.

**FIGURE 8.6**: Blue Gene/P nodecard.

A Blue Gene/P system has three different internal networks. A 3D-torus for point-to-point communication, a tree network for collective operations and a low latency network for global barriers (Table 8.1).

While logically positioned at the root of a compute node tree the I/O nodes interact with the compute nodes via the collective network. Each nodecard is capable of hosting up to 2 I/O nodes with their 10GE optics. The I/O node per compute nodes ratio may be chosen by the BG/P installation site and may vary from as high as 1:16 down to as low as 1:128, depending on the desired I/O rates.

## 8.2.2 I/O Network Design

The deployed I/O ratio of the JUGENE system is one I/O node per 128 compute nodes (four per midplane) which results in 576 10GE-interfaces, plus additional 24 I/O nodes on one rack which is used for applications running on a small number of nodes for testing. 600 I/O nodes solely at the Blue Gene/P side plus the necessary number of GPFS (General Parallel File System) fileservers with sufficient I/O bandwidth for disk access resulted in the need for about 750 10GE connections.

**TABLE 8.1**: Blue Gene/P network specifications.

| Torus Network | Bandwidth | 62425 MB/s = 5.1 GB/s |
| | Hardware Latency (Nearest Neighbor) | 100 ns (32 B packet) |
| | | 800 ns (256 B packet) |
| | Hardware Latency (Worst Case) | 3.2 s (64 hops) |
| | Total Bandwidth | 188 TB/s (73,728 nodes) |
| Tree Network | Bandwidth | 20.85 GB/s = 1.7GB/s |
| | Hardware Latency (Worst Case) | 3.5 s |
| Barrier Network | | 0.65 s (73,728 nodes) |

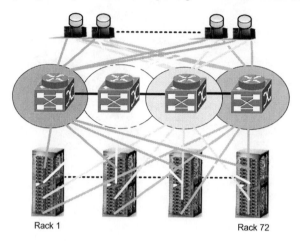

Rack 1                                   Rack 72

**FIGURE 8.7**: JUGENE network structure. Blue Gene/P I/O nodes connected to the GPFS fileservers through four Force10 switches.

At the time of deployment, no 10GE switch was available on the market that was able to aggregate 750 10GE-interfaces (even when accepting a reasonable amount of oversubscription). Therefore, a network was designed that is able to offer sufficient bandwidth for the access to the GPFS filesystems via four separate switch fabrics.

Knowing the GPFS access patterns and the maximum transfer rate per I/O node (by intensive testing), the JUGENE I/O nodes, with 4 GB memory each, were striped over four Force10 E1200i switches in four different IP networks. The switch-side restrictions like a slightly oversubscription at port group level were resolved by distributing the JUST fileserver and the I/O node connections accordingly. In addition it was decided to strip even the four I/O nodes of each single midplane to different switch fabrics, which is shown in Figure 8.7. This way addressing all involved GPFS fileservers is already possible for small jobs, running on less than a midplane, with their maximum network bandwidth (4 x 10GE each).

By this design JUGENE is able to access the GPFS filesystems of the fileserver JUST with a bandwidth of 66 GByte/s while on the other hand utilizing the flexibility and interoperability of the 10 Gigabit Ethernet technology for interconnecting with other local clusters and even European research networks (e.g., DEISA/PRACE).

The two front-end nodes are connected to the public internet and the internal I/O network via 10 GE interfaces. The Blue Gene I/O nodes are connected only to the internal I/O network. For both networks separate switches/routers are used. The internal 10 GE network (Force10 E1200i) is not routed outside the JUGENE/JUST storage complex.

## 8.3 Benchmark Results

To test and demonstrate the capabilities of JUGENE different benchmarks were run on the system.

### 8.3.1 LINPACK

The LINPACK benchmark [PWDC] was used to obtain the peak performance of the system by measuring the floating point rate of execution for solving a linear system of equations. Using a problem size of $N = 4{,}043{,}519$ on the full JUGENE system (72 racks) in Virtual Node mode with the default process mapping XYZT a maximal performance $R_{\max} = 825.5$ TFLOP/s was achieved. This corresponds to 82.3% of the theoretical peak performance of the system.

### 8.3.2 LinkTest

The characteristics of the network of JUGENE were measured with the LinkTest program [Fri] which was developed at the Jülich Supercomputing Centre. The LinkTest program implements a scalable parallel Ping-Pong algorithm to measure all possible MPI connections of a machine. As a result a full communication matrix is obtained showing the bandwidth and message latency between each task pair and a report is provided including the bandwidth and latency profiles. The LinkTest runs for $n$ tasks in $n$ steps where in each step $n/2$ pairs of tasks will perform the MPI Ping-Pong test in parallel. The slowest $n$ connections will be tested again to avoid distortion of results due to network congestions. The selection of the pairs is random but after running all steps all possible pairs are covered. An example of such a communication matrix is shown in Figure 8.8. This matrix was obtained on the full system (72 racks) of JUGENE and revealed a network latency of 2.6 to 9.4 $\mu$s.

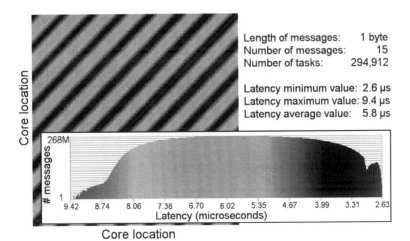

**FIGURE 8.8**: Detail (2048×2048 cores) of the communication matrix and the full latency profile (logarithm of the number of messages versus the latency in $\mu$s) are shown, obtained with the LinkTest benchmark on the full system (72 racks, 294,912 compute cores).

### 8.3.3    Application Benchmark Suites

Application benchmarks were run on JUGENE to provide different scientific communities with information on how their main algorithms and software packages perform on the system. The application benchmark suites of the two European projects DEISA (Distributed European Infrastructure for Supercomputing Applications) [deib] and PRACE (Partnership for Advanced Computing in Europe) [prab] were used, which cover a broad variety of codes and algorithms from various scientific areas: astrophysics, chemistry, climate research, earth science, fluid mechanics, life sciences, informatics, materials science, plasma physics, and quantum chromodynamics. Both benchmark suites use the benchmark environment JuBE (Jülich Benchmarking Environment) [FSM⁺10] developed at JSC. A detailed analysis of the results is beyond the scope of this book chapter. However, JUGENE results of the DEISA benchmark suit can be found on the web [deia] as well as information about the PRACE benchmark suite and its results on JUGENE [praa].

---

## 8.4    Applications and Workloads

JUGENE is used by scientists from different scientific areas using a variety of algorithms and applications. Characteristics of these applications are a very high scalability (up to almost 300,000 compute cores can be used on JUGENE) and the need for a fast network connection between the cores. Furthermore, an efficient parallel I/O strategy is necessary in order to handle the transfer of large amounts of data to and from the compute cores. National and European projects are granted resources on JUGENE in general for one year after they pass a technical and scientific peer-review process. Figure 8.9 shows the combined granted computing time for national projects in the granting periods started in May and November 2011, sorted by scientific area. In total 70 projects were accepted for these two periods. More than a quarter of the computational time granted for national projects is used by projects belonging to elementary particle physics, followed by projects from the area of fluid dynamics and condensed matter chemistry/physics. Similarly, the largest part of the computing time given to European projects is used by projects from the area of fundamental physics, followed by engineering and astrophysics.

The workload of JUGENE is high, on average around 90% as can be seen in Figure 8.10. Idle times occur when the batch system frees a bigger part of the machine in order to allow large jobs to start. The down time of about 10% in July 2010 was caused by a power outage due to a thunder storm.

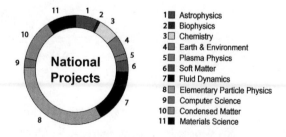

**FIGURE 8.9**: Computational time on JUGENE granted national projects sorted by scientific area.

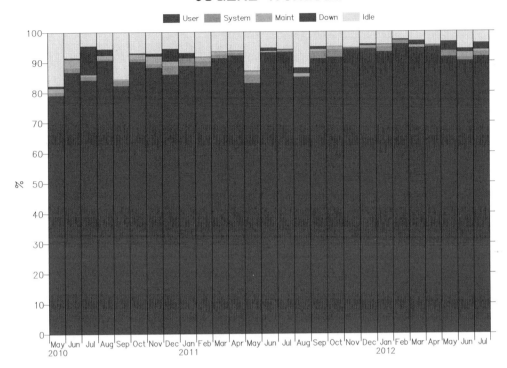

**FIGURE 8.10**: Workload of JUGENE (in %) between May 2010 and July 2012.

## 8.5  Blue Gene Scaling Workshops in Jülich

Before being admitted to the machine, the scalability of a code must be proven. Following this philosophy, the number of accepted projects on JUGENE is limited. A substantial increase of the scalability up to 294,912 cores of JUGENE could be reached for several applications in quite a few workshops between 2006 and 2011, like the "Big Blue Gene Weeks" and the "Blue Gene Scaling Workshops," which have been held in cooperation between JSC/NIC, IBM, and the Blue Gene Consortium [bgc]. They have been offered to the international Blue Gene user community and attracted participants from various countries and scientific fields, who had exclusive usage of JUGENE of up to three days. In most cases, the users were able to scale their program to running on all processors and in this way to enable applications to make efficient use of today's capability computing on higher and higher numbers of cores. For a more detailed description and results of the workshops 2009-2011, see [bgwa],[bgwb],[bgwc].

## 8.6  Highlights of Main Applications

JUGENE has enabled scientists from various scientific fields to gain insight into scientific problems by running simulations which would not have been possible otherwise. As examples we briefly describe three of the cutting-edge simulations which have been performed recently.

Further outstanding scientific results obtained from simulations on JUGENE can be found in the inSiDE magazine [GCfS].

### 8.6.1   Ab Initio Calculation of the Hoyle State — On the Origin of Carbon-Based Life

A breakthrough in research into the creation of elements in the universe was recently made by simulations on JUGENE [EKLM11]. Life on earth is based on carbon-12. Carbon is produced in massive, hot stars by the fusion of three alpha particles (helium-4 nuclei). More than 50 years ago, the astronomer Fred Hoyle predicted an excited state of the carbon nucleus with its energy tuned in such a way that a sufficient amount of carbon is generated. This new state was later called the Hoyle state. It was experimentally verified in 1957, but no one had ever been able to reproduce the Hoyle state from scratch, starting from the known interactions of protons and neutrons.

This has now changed. Earlier at the Forschungszentrum Jülich, Evgeny Epelbaum, Ulf Meißner and collaborators had developed an effective field theory of the nuclear forces that had been successfully tested in few-nucleon systems. In collaboration with Dean Lee from North Carolina State University, they now put six protons and six neutrons on a discretized representation of space-time and calculated the spectrum of carbon-12 using Monte Carlo methods. In order to access the spectrum of carbon-12, they developed a new determinantal projection Monte Carlo scheme. Such an algorithm is ideally suited for JUGENE and the total CPU time used for the Hoyle state calculations was about four million CPU hours. The Hoyle state appeared together with other observed states of carbon-12, proving the theory to be correct from first principles. The total disk storage used for the Hoyle state calculations is about four terabytes. With these stored configurations, it is now possible to analyze in detail the structure of the Hoyle state, such as its spatial extension or electromagnetic transition strengths. The method paves the way for solving other problems relevant to astrophysics, such as a precise calculation of the cross section of the carbon-12 alpha-particle fusion, which is of prime importance for the generation of oxygen-16. See Figure 8.11.

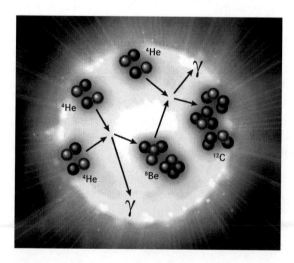

**FIGURE 8.11**: The fusion process of three alpha particles (helium-4 nuclei) in massive, hot stars leads to carbon-12. The Hoyle state of carbon-12 could now be calculated for the first time using the computational power of JUGENE. ©Forschungszentrum Jülich GmbH, ©fotolia.com (Uladzimir Bakunovich).

## 8.6.2 Unravelling Structures in DVD Materials

Although the storage of films and music on a DVD is part of our digital world, the physical basis of the storage mechanism is not understood in detail. Now researchers from Jülich, Finland, and Japan provide insight into the read and write processes in a DVD [MAK+11]. This knowledge should enable improved storage materials to be developed.

Information is stored in a DVD in the form of microscopic bits (each less than 100 nanometers in size) in a thin layer of a polycrystalline alloy containing several elements. The bits can have a disordered, amorphous, or an ordered, crystalline structure. The transition between the two phases lasts only a few nanoseconds and can be triggered by a laser pulse. Common alloys for storage materials such as DVD-RAMs or Blu-ray Discs contain germanium (Ge), antimony (Sb), and tellurium (Te) and are known as GST after the initials of the elements. The most popular alloys for DVD-RW are AIST alloys, which contain small amounts of silver (Ag) and indium (In) as well as antimony (Sb) and tellurium (Te).

In addition to experimental data and x-ray spectra from the Japanese synchrotron SPring-8, the world's most powerful x-ray source, the team of scientists used extensive simulations on the Jülich supercomputer JUGENE. The combination of experiment and simulations has enabled the structures of both phases to be determined for the first time and allowed the development of a model to explain the rapid phase change.

The phase change in AIST alloys proceeds from the outside of the bit, where it adjoins the crystalline surroundings, toward its interior. In *Nature Materials* [MAK+11], the team explains this using a "bond exchange model," where the local environment in the amorphous bit is changed by small movements of an antimony atom as explained in Figure 8.12. The calculation of the structure of amorphous AIST is the largest yet performed in this area of research, with simulations of 640 atoms over the comparatively long time of several hundred

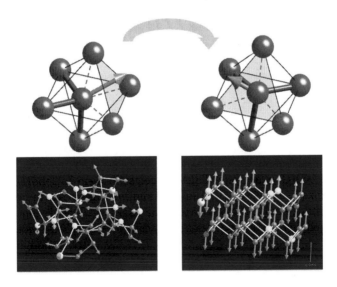

**FIGURE 8.12**: Model of crystallization of AIST alloy in a DVD. Upper left: a laser pulse causes motion of the central antimony atom (left), which then exchanges its bonds to two neighbors. Upper right: The vector sum (arrow) of the three short bonds (thick solid lines) changes. Below: A sequence of such processes leads from the amorphous (left) to the crystalline form (right).

picoseconds. Some 4,000 processors of the Jülich supercomputer JUGENE were used for over four months in order to obtain the necessary precision.

### 8.6.3    Ab Initio Determination of Light Hadron Masses

Under this title the NIC (John von Neumann Institute for Computing) Research Group "Elementary Particle Physics" headed by Zoltan Fodor published a paper in the 21 November 2008 issue of *Science* [DFF+08] that is already regarded as a milestone by many physicists. They report on a breakthrough in computer simulations which allowed them to tackle the numerically challenging fundamental theory of strong interactions.

Experimentalists can only observe composite particles like the nucleons (protons, neutrons) everyday matter is made of. However, the underlying theory known as quantum chromodynamics or QCD is formulated in terms of quarks and gluons and their interactions, the latter giving rise to the actually observed masses (Figure 8.13). The NIC group was able to calculate the masses of the proton and of a few other particles, known as $\Sigma, \Lambda, \Delta, \Sigma^*, \Xi^*, \Omega$. The calculation[1] is ab initio, that is without any uncontrolled approximation. This result further corroborates the correctness of QCD in describing strong interactions. At the same

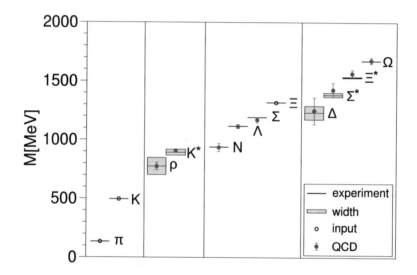

**FIGURE 8.13**: The light hadron spectrum of QCD. Horizontal lines and bands are the experimental values with their decay widths. The calculated results are shown by solid circles. Vertical error bars represent the combined statistical (SEM) and systematic error estimates. $\pi$, K, and $\Xi$ have no error bars, because they are used to set the light quark mass, the strange quark mass, and the overall scale, respectively. [DFF+08].

time, it demonstrates the capability of the JUGENE supercomputer to deliver the performance needed for high-end massively parallel applications. This work has been voted one of the "top 10 scientific breakthroughs of the year 2008" by the editors of *Science*.

---

[1] A detailed description of the implementation is given in Section 8.7.

## 8.7 Tuning Lattice Chromodynamics to Blue Gene/P

### 8.7.1 Introductory Remarks

The IBM Blue Gene/P is, very much like its predecessor, the Blue Gene/L, perfectly suited for simulations of Lattice Quantum Chromodynamics. This comes as no surprise, given that both machines carry the genes of the QCDOC,[2] the ancestor of the Blue Gene line of supercomputers. Therefore, such simulations are and were one of the major users of the Blue Genes all over the world. In this section we describe the details of one particular implementation of a simulation suite for Lattice Quantum Chromodynamics. We will start with a few words on the theory itself and then proceed to discuss the important hardware features used for this particular software. Afterwards, we will discuss the implementation and conclude with performance results.

### 8.7.2 Lattice Quantum Chromodynamics

It is well established that Quantum Chromodynamics [FGML73] is the theory describing the "strong force" which binds protons and neutrons to form the atomic nucleus. Evidence was mainly gathered through accelerator experiments, where the high energy sector of the theory can be accessed and analyzed. Here, due to the large momenta involved, comparison to theory is possible through results derived by analytic methods.

In the low energy sector, however, one has to rely on models or alternatively on simulations of the lattice discretized theory, called Lattice Quantum Chromodynamics (LQCD).

Important quantities such as the hadron spectrum, including the proton and neutron masses, are only accessible through such calculations.[3]

Simulations of LQCD, however, require large amounts of computational resources, which can only be provided by modern supercomputers such as the Blue Gene/P (BGP).

### 8.7.3 Relevant Hardware Features

The Blue Gene/P features a 3-dimensional torus network with low latency and high bandwidth. Most importantly, network and the node's floating point performance are particularly well balanced.

Three freely selectable dimensions of the 4-dimensional space-time lattice of LQCD can be directly mapped to the torus hardware; the remaining 4th dimension can be parallelized using the 4 cores of each Blue Gene/P node[4] (see Figure 8.14).

#### 8.7.3.1 Communication Hardware

One important feature of the Blue Gene/P is the method by which the torus network is used: the Blue Gene/P features a DMA communication controller (subsequently just called DMA), which can be used to move data over the torus network while the CPU is busy

---

[2]QCD on a chip [B+04].

[3]A good example of such a calculation is [DFF+08], which used the Blue Gene/P and the simulation code described here. Compare also Section 8.6.3.

[4]This implementation is using the VN mode of the Blue Gene/P, where only a small window of shared memory is left that is used for global operations (see Section 8.7.5). The main reason is the increased memory bandwidth: memory operations will not require cache coherency related synchronization between the cores (see Section 8.7.3.2).

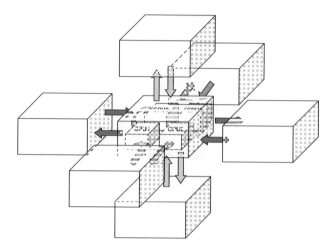

**FIGURE 8.14**: Parallelization scheme: three dimensions are mapped to the torus hardware, here depicted by arrows pointing from and to the neighboring nodes (boxes), and the 4th dimension uses the 4 cores inside a Blue Gene/P node.

doing computations (see Figure 8.15). The CPU is only required to set up and/or start the communication process; it is not involved in moving the data.

To set up the communication process, a so-called "DMA memory injection FIFO" is required (see Figure 8.15). The injection FIFO can be thought of as a chunk of ordinary memory, where "message descriptors" can be stored. Each of these descriptors describes one message, that is one contiguous chunk of data which is to be transferred. It also contains a reference to an injection and a reception counter and a "send" and a "reception" memory offset.

The injection counter counts down the number of bytes to be sent, the reception counter, located on the receiving node, will count down the bytes that have arrived there. These counters have a memory address associated with them which serves as a base address. The descriptor's "send" offset will then be interpreted by the DMA as relative to the base address associated with the injection counter specified in the descriptor. The same applies to the "reception" offset, only this time the DMA of the receiving node will use that node's reception counter and that counter's base address to calculate the memory address where the data is to be stored.

When a descriptor is injected into the FIFO, it will be stored at the so-called FIFO tail and the tail will be incremented. In addition to the tail, there is a FIFO head, pointing to the location of the next descriptor to be serviced by the DMA, and a FIFO starting and ending address (see Figure 8.15). The DMA will stop servicing the FIFO when the FIFO head reaches the FIFO tail. Both FIFO head and tail wrap around to the FIFO starting address when they reach the FIFO ending address. Thus the FIFO size is only an issue when new descriptors are injected more quickly than the DMA can service the existing ones. The FIFO head can be controlled and the FIFO activated and deactivated by the user via the SPI.[5] Persistent[6] send and receive operations can thus be set up by deactivating a FIFO, injecting descriptors into the deactivated FIFO, then moving the FIFO head to the

---

[5]The SPI is a software interface available on any Blue Gene/P. Documentation is available through the files themselves.

[6]By persistent send/receives we refer to those communication operations that communicate the same amount of data between the same nodes and from/to the same addresses in memory.

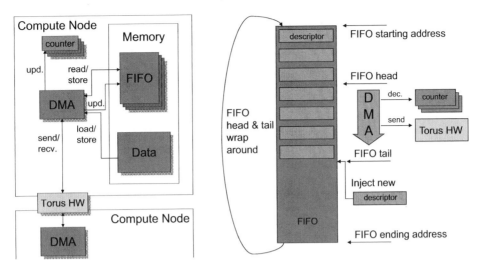

**FIGURE 8.15**: Left: The Blue Gene/P DMA communication controller. It is capable of performing communications independently from the cores. Right: The Blue Gene/P DMA FIFO. It contains message descriptors (one for each contiguous chunk of data) that are read and then executed by the DMA.

tail manually, and afterwards activating the FIFO. The communication process can then be started by setting up the reception and injection counters and by moving the FIFO head back to its original position.

It is also possible to use the DMA to perform communications that are local to a node. These are effectively simple memory copies, but when the DMA is used, they can be hidden behind the computations as well. Also, by carefully rearranging the data within these copies, the memory access pattern of the computations that use the transferred data later on can be optimized.

In addition to the 3D torus network, the Blue Gene architecture features specialized global networks, which are used for collective operations such as an allreduce or a global barrier. The functionality of these networks is fully accessible by the SPI. Operations such as a global unsigned integer sum or unsigned integer max are supported by the hardware. Operations with floating point numbers have to be implemented by software, based on the collective unsigned integer operations.

### 8.7.3.2 The PowerPC 450 Core

Beyond the DMA, another important feature of the Blue Gene/P's nodes is cache coherency for the four PowerPC 450 cores. Cache coherency related synchronization between the cores, however, reduces the effective memory bandwidth. In VN mode, because each node will be working in its own space, the synchronization overhead is reduced (as bandwidth measurements suggest). This implementation therefore uses the VN mode. Communication between the cores is possible via a shared memory window or DMA driven memory copies.

Each core has a double floating point unit (FPU), where the secondary FPU is only accessible via special SIMD instructions. That is, in order to get beyond 50% of theoretical peak, one has to use this special instruction set. Since the core can only issue a limited number of instructions per cycle, for real-world applications it is necessary to use these

SIMD instructions to get acceptable performance. This, however, makes automated code optimization in many cases too difficult for the compiler.

There are two ways to solve this problem by investing time on the programmer's side. The first and most certainly time consuming is to write the most computationally intense parts of the code in assembly language. Secondly, one can write optimized code by using special compiler macros of the IBM XL C compiler ("intrinsics"). Each of these macros corresponds directly to a certain assembler instruction and most often also has the same name. So even in this case the user has to select an assembly instruction for each logical operation; however, the compiler will take over scheduling (and might even choose to use other instructions, if this benefits performance).

### 8.7.4    The Wilson Kernel

Most of the cycles in a Lattice QCD Simulation are spent within a, in terms of lines of code, small fraction of the program, the kernel. This kernel is an implementation of the fermion "Dslash" matrix vector multiplication, e.g., required for the approximation of the fermionic determinant. The details of the kernel depend on the specific discretization used.

Here we discuss the implementation of the Wilson kernel. This kernel is a matrix vector multiplication defined as[7]

$$\Psi_n = \sum_{m=1}^{V} D_{W\,n,m}\Phi_m = \sum_{\mu=1}^{4}(1-\gamma_\mu)\otimes U_\mu(n)\Phi_{n+\hat{\mu}} + (1+\gamma_\mu)\otimes U_\mu^\dagger(n-\hat{\mu})\Phi_{n-\hat{\mu}}$$

Here $n$ is the index of a lattice site of the (4d) lattice, $V$ is the number of lattice sites, and $n+\hat{\mu}$ is the neighboring lattice site of $n$ in positive $\mu$ direction. $\gamma_\mu$ are complex $4\times 4$ and $U_\mu$ are SU(3) ($3\times 3$) matrices in a tensor product. $U^\dagger(n)$ is the hermitian conjugate of $U(n)$.

From its explicit form it is clear, that the Wilson matrix connects only nearest neighboring sites. This is important, because as a consequence all communication is limited to nearest neighboring nodes as well. The parallelization scheme is the same as is used for the whole code (see Figure 8.14).

### 8.7.4.1    Communication Setup

As mentioned in Section 8.7.5, it is desirable to use persistent communications in order to reduce latencies. In the case of the Wilson kernel this can be straightforwardly done. This is because the vectors $\lambda_{\mu,n} = (1-\gamma_\mu)\Phi_{n+\hat{\mu}}$ and $\chi_{\mu,n} = (1+\gamma_\mu)\otimes U_\mu^\dagger(n-\hat{\mu})\Phi_{n-\hat{\mu}}$ can be stored in a temporary buffer which is the same for each call to the kernel. Since this buffer has a fixed address and all relative addresses within the buffer are identical as well, the same set of descriptors can be reused in every call to the kernel. This is also true when even/odd preconditioning is used, if the local lattice volume is restricted to be an even number.

The complete setup therefore requires two reception and two rejection counters, one for communication in positive (forward), one for communication in negative (backward) direction. Additionally one FIFO for each direction is required; that is, 8 FIFOs for the double precision and 8 FIFOS for the single precision kernel. The descriptors are injected into each FIFO at the beginning of the simulation. Scattering of the buffers can then be started by simply setting the counter values to the number of bytes that are to be communicated

---

[7]The precise definition of the Wilson matrix includes a diagonal term which is ignored here since it is implemented outside the kernel.

(different for double and single precision) and by having each FIFO head point to the first descriptor.

### 8.7.4.2 Single vs. Double Precision Arithmetics

The Blue Gene/P FPU is capable of double precision arithmetics, but contrary to the typical FPU it is not capable of performing single precision floating point calculations. It is however possible to load single precision numbers, which are then converted "on the fly" to double precision and stored in a double precision register. Results can be rounded to single precision within these registers and then stored as a single precision number. Since the number of floating point operations per cycle is unchanged, this does not increase the theoretical peak performance.

The kernel is memory bandwidth bound. Thus by using single precision, in principle, twice as many floating point numbers per cycle can be loaded from memory (or be communicated) compared to when using double precision. Latencies remain unchanged or actually increase due to the required extra rounding step. As a consequence the performance of the single precision kernel is significantly better but will not be twice the performance of the double precision variant (if the latter still fits into cache).

However during the simulation, double precision accuracy is required. The linear solvers, which call the kernel, have to calculate solution vectors which are more precise than the full single precision accuracy. This problem can be solved by using "mixed precision" solvers [DFH+09]. The idea is that the solver mainly calls the single precision kernel and uses the double precision variant only to correct for the difference. This way the inverters have the improved performance along with the higher precision.

### 8.7.5 Optimized Communication Layer

As for the Wilson kernel described in the previous section, also in the remainder of the LQCD simulation code, communication mostly takes place between neighboring nodes. For these purposes, additional generic communication routines are required. Another 8 FIFOs are set aside, again one for each direction. The number of injection (and also reception) counters used in this case is typically 8 but is not fixed and can be chosen at runtime. With 8 pairs of reception and injection counters also 8 independent communication operations can proceed at any time. Any further communication operation will have to wait until a set of counters becomes available. The descriptors will be injected into a FIFO dedicated to the direction in which the data will be sent. Again, communication that is local to a node may be implemented as a DMA memory copy.

Moreover, for the linear system solvers collective operations are required as well. Such routines will be most efficient when using the low latency tree network of the Blue Gene/P. Global barriers will use the barrier network, whereas local, that is node wide barriers, will use the so-called "lockbox" to synchronize.

As mentioned in Section 8.7.3, the global allreduce (tree) network is capable of performing unsigned integer operations only. However, what is required by the code is a global double precision floating point sum and a global double precision floating point maximum operation. It is therefore necessary to split the floating point numbers into mantissa and exponent and to perform separate operations on these numbers. If the sign of the original floating point number was negative, the mantissa has to be replaced by the two's complement. To, e.g., calculate the global sum, the first step is to compute the global maximum of the exponent. Since this already is an unsigned integer, the maximum can be computed right away. Afterwards all mantissa have to be shifted according to the global maximum exponent. Typically for a double precision floating point number, the mantissa will be converted to a 128 bit unsigned integer, to make sure the precision of the global unsigned sum on the shifted mantissa is precise enough. Finally mantissa and exponent have to be reassembled into a floating point number.

### 8.7.6    Performance Results

Most of the tuning efforts went into the single precision Wilson kernel, since with mixed precision inverters it is the single precision kernel that dominates the performance of the whole simulation. In Figure 8.16 the performance of both the single and double precision kernel is shown for a strong scaling analysis of a $64^3 \times 144$ lattice. The curve of the single precision kernel is flat, indicating that the scaling is close to perfect. The total performance of the single precision kernel, as can be expected, scales (almost) perfectly. The kernel reaches a performance of 37.5% of machine peak (3.4 GFlops per core).

In order to be able to compare performance figures, we have implemented a version of the single precision Wilson kernel based on the XL C intrinsics and MPI communications. On comparable local volumes, it reaches only up to 20% of machine peak, considerably less than the implementation described in this paper. The scaling is worse as well, because of the larger latencies (and potential cache effects) of the MPI library.

The performance of the routines of the remaining code, which have been optimized by using a set of macros based on compiler intrinsics, can even exceed the performance of the kernel. A simple SU(3) matrix multiply add for instance reaches 50% of machine peak. Since these routines typically also scale rather well, the scaling behavior of the whole simulation code is excellent over a large range of CPUs.

---

## 8.8    System Software

### 8.8.1    Operating Systems

The login (front-end) nodes and service nodes run SLES 10 (SUSE Linux® Enterprise Server version 10 from Novell) allowing cross compilation and job submission of the Blue Gene/P applications as well as Blue Gene/P system management. Access validation for users is done via an LDAP (Lightweight Directory Access Protocol) server, which serves all the supercomputer systems at JSC to enable login and access to user data. User login via SSH (Secure Shell) is restricted to ssh-key authorization only. In addition the gsissh package [gsi] from the Globus Toolkit is installed and allows certificate-based login to the system.

The complete Blue Gene/P hardware is controlled by an IBM proprietary system management software [Lak09], storing the full system status in a DB2 database. This database contains the configuration of the system, the reliability, availability, and serviceability (RAS) information as well as the environmental status of the hardware and the job and job history details.

Blue Gene/P compute nodes can be combined into blocks and booted as partitions of variable size including one or more I/O nodes which act as a gateway for the compute nodes in their respective rack, and connect the block to the service node and the GPFS filesystems.

On the compute nodes a special "Compute Node Kernel" CNK (optimized Linux® Kernel) provides MPI support for hardware implementation, the control system and system diagnostics. Three different modes are supported from Symmetric Multi-Processing (SMP) mode, where one MPI process can start three additional threads, to Dual Mode (DUAL)

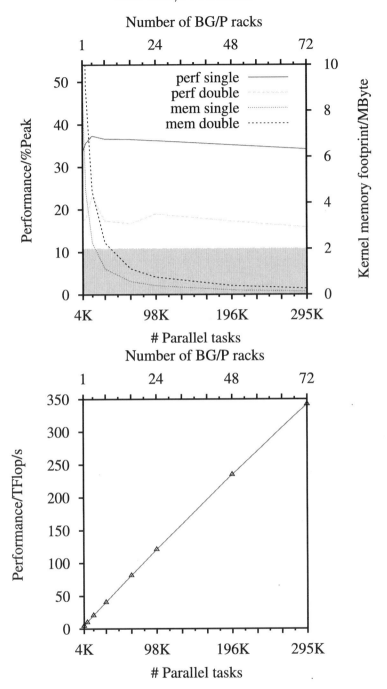

**FIGURE 8.16**: Top: Performance of the Wilson kernel in a strong scaling analysis ($64^3 \times 144$ lattice). The performance of the highly optimized single precision kernel is given by the solid line, the kernel memory footprint per core is given by the dotted line. Since the solid curve is relatively flat, the strong scaling is close to perfect. Also shown is the performance (dashed curve) and the memory footprint (short dashed curve) of the double precision kernel. The gray shaded area gives the L3 cache size per core. Bottom: Shown is the same strong scaling analysis, but this time the total performance of the single precision kernel is given. Close to 350 TFlops are reached when running on 72 racks.

and Virtual Node Mode (VN) where four MPI ranks have to split the available memory. On the I/O nodes a full Linux® kernel and services enable NFS and GPFS filesystem access.

## 8.8.2    Filesystem

The local storage comprises IBM disk storage systems IBM DS4700, which are used by the local GPFS cluster of the front-end and service nodes. Local filesystems are exported via NFS to the I/O nodes providing access to system files for the Blue Gene/P environment and the DB2 database.

All user data resides on the GPFS fileystems, provided by JUST, described in Section 8.11.

## 8.8.3    System Administration

Installation and upgrade of the Blue Gene software is done on the service node and is applied to the compute and I/O nodes by booting the Blue Gene/P partitions. There are two service nodes, one in production mode and one configured as a "backup service node" with identical software status, which can be activated manually in case of a failure. To balance the workload of user logins over the front-end nodes "round robin DNS" (Domain Name System) is implemented. For software and (configuration) file distribution to the front-end and service nodes an additional Linux® system running "CFEngine" (configuration management for system administrators) [cfe] is used.

## 8.8.4    Schedulers

The Tivoli workload scheduler "LoadLeveler" version 3.5 is installed for batch job processing. Job scripts, prepared and running on the front-end nodes, include an "mpirun" call to execute the parallel application. Loadleveler checks for an existing partition to be reused or boots a new one to fit the job's needs and executes the program.

One Blue Gene/P rack can be used for small testing jobs (32–256 nodes, max. 30 minutes); the remaining 71 racks are reserved for production jobs (min. 512 nodes, max. 24 hours). The "Backfill Scheduler" manages the workload with a job priority proportional to the size of the job, where big jobs have a higher priority than small jobs. Above that a locally defined priority mechanism is used to give all users a fair share of the system. It ensures that jobs still within their assigned project quota have a higher priority than jobs out of quota, which will nevertheless get executed if no other fitting requests are in the queue.

To run bigger jobs without wasting too much compute time on nodes waiting to be allocated in a partition of the right size, a mix of shorter-running, small jobs is needed to fill the "holes." To attract such jobs, some users have been assigned extra compute time under the premise that they will split their work into one-midplane jobs of just a few hours. This leads to an overall usage of more than 90% (compare Figure 8.10). Full machine jobs are run and carefully monitored on special days after the nodes have been freed for maintenance or with a reservation.

Job monitoring is done with the standard features of LoadLeveler (e.g., the "llq" command) and self-developed tools like "llqx" which shows an extended, priority ordered list of all jobs.

### 8.8.5 Job Monitoring with LLview

On large-scale systems like JUGENE system-wide monitoring of the batch system usage is not only helpful for system administrators to control the workload of the system, but also for users. A graphical monitoring tool helps to understand where and in which configuration (shape) the user's jobs are running.

Starting in 2004, JSC developed the batch system monitoring tool LLview, which gives a one window look into the batch system usage shown in Figure 8.17.

The key element is the node display which shows the physical or logical representation of the system hardware. The current usage is displayed by color-coding the component of the system (rectangles) according to the job that is running there. Further elements of LLview include the list of running jobs, usage history, usage statistics, and a prediction window. All elements of LLview are mouse-sensitive, e.g., moving over a job element exposes detailed information and clicking on a job element marks the job location in all other elements of LLview.

LLview is a client-server application allowing the visualization client to run on a local computer. In the case of JUGENE the server component is running on the service node, obtaining information from LoadLeveler and the Blue Gene/P system database. Monitoring data is stored in XML format and files are automatically transferred to a web server, from where the LLview client can retrieve the data.

Besides LoadLeveler, LLview supports also PBSpro, Torque, and other batch systems. The configuration of the client is very flexible, e.g., all elements can be arranged or resized within the window. LLview is mainly implemented in the scripting language Perl/Tk.

Recent developments are the definition of a system independent and scalable XML scheme (LML) and a Java implementation of the client, which allows to invoke the monitoring tool within a web browser. In addition, JSC is partner in a US-DOE funded project to improve the scalability of the Eclipse Parallel Tools Platform (PTP) to petascale. Eclipse/PTP is a development environment for parallel codes including remote execution and debugging.

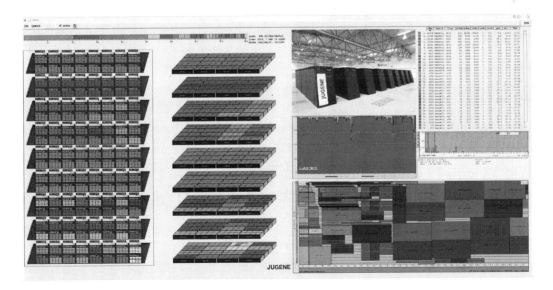

**FIGURE 8.17**: LLview job monitoring shows the allocation of the 72 racks in physical and logical view, as well as a list of running jobs, the overall usage statistics of the last days, and a prediction of the jobs to be processed next.

Most of the Java-based LLview components are meanwhile integrated into the official PTP version and allow users a more detailed insight into the remote systems and will also give feedback about the application execution process [WFK+11].

### 8.8.6    JUGENE Software Overview

**BG/P control system:** Blue Gene/P System Software V1R4M2

**GPFS:** Global Parallel FileSystem

**LoadLeveler:** Tivoli Workload Scheduler

**IBM XL C/C++:** C/C++ Advanced Edition for Blue Gene/P

**IBM XLF:** Fortran Advanced Edition for Blue Gene/P

**MPICH2:** High-performance implementation of Message Passing Interface

**UNICORE:** Uniform Interface to Computing Resources

**ESSL:** Engineering and Scientific Subroutine Library

**LAPACK:** Linear Algebra PACKage (Library of subroutines for solving dense linear algebra problems)

**FFTW:** Fastest Fourier Transform in the West

**GSL:** GNU Scientific Library

**ScaLAPACK:** Scalable Linear Algebra PACKage

**(P)ARPACK:** (Parallel) Fortran77 subroutines to solve large-scale eigenvalue problems

**PETSc:** Portable, Extensible Toolkit for Scientific computation

**MUMPS:** MUltifrontal Massively Parallel Solver

**SPRNG:** Scalable Parallel Random Number Generators Library (SPRNG) for ASCI Monte Carlo Computations

**ParMETIS:** Parallel Graph Partitioning and Fill-reducing Matrix Ordering

**hypre:** high performance preconditioners

**SUNDIALS:** SUite of Nonlinear and DIfferential/ALgebraic equation Solvers

**hdf5:** Management of extremely large and complex data collections

**(Parallel) NetCDF:** Self-describing, machine-independent data formats

**CPMD:** Car-Parrinello Molecular Dynamics

**GPAW:** Grid-based Projector-Augmented Wave method (density functional theory (DFT) code)

**GROMACS:** Groningen Machine for Chemical Simulations (for classical molecular dynamics)

**LAMMPS:** Large-scale Atomic/Molecular Massively Parallel Simulator (molecular dymanics code)

**NAMD:** NAnoscale Molecular Dynamics (molecular dynamics code)

**Tremolo:** Massively parallel software package for numerical simulation in molecular dynamics

**Totalview:** Parallel debugger (Rogue Wave)

**DDT:** Parallel debugger (Allinea)

**Scalasca:** Scalable parallel performance measurement and analysis tool (JSC)

**TAU:** Parallel performance profiling tool (Univ. of Oregon)

**Vampir:** Parallel event trace measurement and visualization tool (TU Dresden)

**Extrae/Paraver:** Parallel event trace measurement and visualization tool (BSC)

**HPCToolkit:** Parallel call-path sampling tool (Rice Univ.)

**mpiP:** MPI profiling library

**IHPCT:** MPI profiling and tracing libraries (IBM)

**PAPI:** Portable hardware event counter access library

**PDToolkit:** Program analysis and instrumentation toolkit (Univ. of Oregon)

## 8.9 Programming System

### 8.9.1 Programming Environment

The Blue Gene/P programming environment is not much different from a usual HPC cluster with a Linux operating system making the porting of applications to the system easy. The main programming models supported are MPI for message passing between the nodes and OpenMP and Pthreads for multi-threading inside a node. The MPI implementation is based on MPICH2 version 1.1 with special adapter components for the Blue Gene/P torus, collective, tree, and barrier synchronisation networks. Compilers for Fortran (IBM xlf 11.1 and GNU gfortran 4.1.2) and C/C++ (IBM xlc/C 9.0 and GNU gcc/g++ 4.1.2) are provided. There is also an unsupported version of the GNU compiler suite (version 4.3.2) available. Many public domain and open source packages are also available due to the similarity of the programming environment to a common Linux cluster. The biggest difficulty for porting software arises if programs and libraries have to be split between the front-end (e.g., for pre- and postprocessing) and the compute nodes (e.g., the actual parallel main program) and the configuration process of the software package is not suitable to handle such a situation.

### 8.9.2    Performance Analysis and Debugging Tools

The usual performance analysis and debugging tools are also available. Both commercially available parallel debuggers, totalview (from Rogue Wave Software) [Rog] and DDT (from Allinea) [All] have been ported to Blue Gene/P. Both are based on a special debugging support layer from IBM residing on the I/O nodes. From there, it is possible to attach to the processes and threads running on the nodes controlled by the individual I/O node. This way, the debugger control is using the separate I/O network and does not interfere with the message passing of the application under debugging. For light-way debugging, LLNL designed and implemented a very scalable tool called STAT [DHAS09] which allows to collect the current call path of each process and thread and displays it in a unified tree. For example, this allows to quickly investigate where a program hangs in case of a deadlock.

### 8.9.3    Open Source Performance Tools

Almost all open source performance tools have been ported to the Blue Gene architecture: e.g., HPCToolkit from Rice University [ABF+10], TAU from the University of Oregon [SM06b], Extrae/Paraver from BSC [JL06], and the VampirTrace/Vampir toolset from the University of Dresden [KBD+08]. The large number of nodes available in systems around the world (32 racks at LLNL, 40 racks at ANL, as well as the 72-rack JUGENE system in Jülich) made them ideal platforms to investigate and solve many issues related to scalability of performance analysis and other tools.

### 8.9.4    Scalasca

At JSC, performance tool research is centered around the Scalasca tool. Scalasca (SCalable Analysis of LArge SCale Applications) is a free software tool that supports the performance optimization of parallel programs by instrumenting, measuring, and analyzing their runtime behavior [GWW+10]. The tool has been specifically designed for use on large-scale systems including IBM Blue Gene and Cray XT, but is also well suited for small- and medium-scale HPC platforms. The analysis identifies potential performance bottlenecks – in particular those concerning communication and synchronization – and offers guidance in exploring their causes. Scalasca mainly targets scientific and engineering applications based on the programming interfaces MPI and OpenMP, including hybrid applications based on a combination of the two. The user of Scalasca can choose between two different analysis modes: (i) performance overview on the call path level via runtime summarization (aka profiling) and (ii) in-depth study of application behavior via event tracing. A distinctive feature of Scalasca is its ability to identify wait states that occur, for example, as a result of load imbalance – even at very large scales. Analysis results of Scalasca can be investigated with the result browser CUBE (see Figure 8.18). The software is installed at numerous sites in several countries and has been successfully used to optimize academic and industrial simulation codes. The software is available for download under the New BSD open source license at http://www.scalasca.org.

## 8.10    Mathematical Libraries and Their Performance

JSC provides a variety of pre-installed mathematical libraries on JUGENE for its user community. Performance data of important solvers, in particular of new solvers, is of

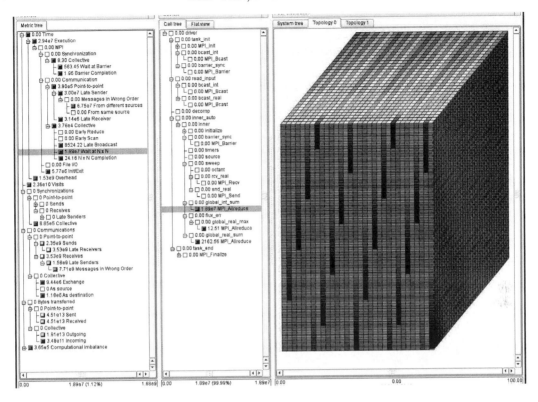

**FIGURE 8.18**: The left panel shows the hierarchy of measured metrics. The middle panel shows the distribution of the selected metric over the call tree of the program. Finally, the right panel shows the distribution of the selected metric at the selected call site over the machine topology. The screen shot shows the result of a trace analysis experiment with the ASC sweep3D benchmark running on all 294,912 cores of JUGENE.

great interest for scientists using JUGENE in simulation projects. In this section we compare eigensolvers of the well-established Scalable Linear Algebra PACKage (ScaLAPACK) [BCC+97] and the new library Elemental [PMH+10]. The eigensolvers in both libraries perform the same three numerical steps for the solution of the dense symmetric (or Hermitian) eigenvalue problem: reduction of the full matrix to a real tridiagonal matrix using Householder transformations, solution of the tridiagonal eigenvalue problem, and back transformation of eigenvectors. The main differences between the two libraries are the way the matrix is distributed to the processors and the programming language. ScaLAPACK is written in FORTRAN 77 and uses a two-dimensional block-cyclic distribution of matrices to processors whereas Elemental is written in C++ and uses a two-dimensional element by element (elemental) distribution of the matrices to the processors. Both libraries use block algorithms for the computations. This allows for a better computation to load/store operation ratio. The block-cyclic distribution needs the same block size $nb$ for distribution and for the block computations whereas the elemental distribution allows selecting the so-called algorithmic block size for the computational blocking independently.

## 8.10.1 ScaLAPACK

ScaLAPACK release 2.0 contains four different driver routines for the solution of the dense symmetric eigenvalue problem. They mainly differ in the way the tridiagonal eigenvalue problem is solved. The oldest routine is PDSYEV which uses the QR algorithm; the second-oldest is PDSYEVX which uses bisection and inverse iteration for step 2; a newer routine PDSYEVD uses Cuppen's divide-and-conquer algorithm [Cup81] for the solution of the tridiagonal eigenvalue problem; and the latest routine PDSYEVR uses the MRRR algorithm [Vi10]. Only the bisection and inverse iteration and the MRRR algorithm allow the computation of a selected part of the eigenvalues and eigenvectors of the matrix; the other two algorithms deliver all eigenvalues and eigenvectors.

### 8.10.2    Elemental

For our tests we used Elemental release 0.66, which is still under development. It contains only one routine for the solution of the symmetric eigenvalue problem using the MRRR algorithm. The user can only choose between two different reduction routines for the first step, one that works on general rectangular processor grids and one that works on quadratic processor grids. The routine investigated allows the computation of a selected part of the eigenvalues and eigenvectors.

### 8.10.3    Data Used for Testing

As bisection and inverse iteration is very sensitive to clustered eigenvalues we choose two types of matrices for the performance tests, those with isolated eigenvalues, and those with clustered eigenvalues. The matrices are constructed by first generating the eigenvalues randomly and then transforming a diagonal matrix with the generated eigenvalues by a random Householder transformation to a full symmetric matrix. The matrix sizes were taken from $N = 1024$ to $N = 12288$ by steps of 512. These sizes are rather small to avoid the costs of running larger problems. Due to the fact that the original matrix had to be stored for testing the results, the memory on JUGENE was not large enough even for these small matrices. Thus we used only one MPI-process per node.

### 8.10.4    Parameters Optimized

As mentioned before the block size $nb$ is important for optimization. Small distribution block sizes lead to better load balance than large blocks. Small algorithmic block sizes do not allow good memory re-use in computations. For ScaLAPACK this means that the block size has to be small for good load balance and large for the computational part. In our investigations we found the best block size for ScaLAPACK at $nb = 32$ but for larger matrices a larger block size might be better. Elemental distribution of matrices is optimal for load balance but at the expense of slightly more communication than blocked distribution. The algorithmic block sizes for Elemental could be chosen larger than for ScaLAPACK. A value of 128 turned out to be optimal in all cases.

For the ScaLAPACK bisection and inverse iteration there is one more parameter that has a large influence on performance; that is the parameter $ORFAC$ which says that eigenvalues lying closer to each other than $ORFAC \cdot \|A\|$ ($\|A\|$ being the 1-norm of matrix $A$) are treated as clustered and thus their corresponding eigenvectors are re-orthogonalized. This has to be done on a single processor because there is no parallel routine for Gram-Schmidt orthogonalization. The default value is $10^{-3}$ but using $10^{-4}$ makes the routine run much faster and allows the computation of eigenvectors of bigger matrices as not so many eigenvectors have to be put into a single processor's memory. In our measurements we took $ORFAC = 10^{-4}$ and the orthogonality of the eigenvectors was still very good.

The user of Elemental can only choose between two different parallelization strategies for the reduction phase, one that can be used on rectangular processor grids, which we shall call TRI_NORMAL, and a newer version which must be implemented on a square processor grid which can be arranged row-first or column-first. We shall call these variants TRI_SQ_ROW and TRI_SQ_COL. The parallelization on the square processor grid is based on an algorithm HJS by Hendrickson, Jessup, and Smith [HJS96] and it is also used in the PDSYNTRD of ScaLAPACK which is the reduction routine for the bisection and inverse iteration and the MRRR version.

### 8.10.5 Results and Discussion

Figure 8.19 shows on the top the execution times of all routines investigated on a square processor grid and with matrices with isolated eigenvalues. It can be seen that the QR algorithm is by far the slowest; thus the routine PDSYEV should only be chosen if all eigenvalues and eigenvectors are needed and the eigenvectors have to be orthogonal to working precision. The fastest algorithms for matrices with isolated eigenvalues are bisection and inverse iteration and the MRRR algorithm from Elemental. In general the routine from Elemental using the square grid for the reduction routine is the fastest. This still holds for non-square processor numbers, even though the matrices are redistributed to the largest square processor grid that fits into the number of processors used. The difference between the row and the column version is negligible; thus we only show the data for the row version.

The ScaLAPACK routine using MRRR has a performance problem for 1024 processors being very slow for small matrices and slowly getting better for large matrices. With a smaller number of processors this problem did not occur. When the eigenvalues are clustered things look different. From Figure 8.19 on the bottom we can see that the bisection and inverse iteration becomes the slowest algorithm, much slower even than the QR algorithm. This is due to the fact that the re-orthogonalization of the eigenvectors belonging to a large cluster of eigenvalues is done by Gram-Schmidt orthogonalization and this is done sequentially on one processor. This not only leads to very long execution times but also to very high memory requirements, and thus we could not even run the larger examples.

As many applications require only a part of the eigenspectrum we also investigated the performance of that case where possible. For isolated eigenvalues bisection and inverse iteration is as in the case of the full eigenspectrum almost as fast as TRI_SQ_ROW from Elemental and the MRRR-algorithm from ScaLAPACK is the slowest in that case. The problem that occurred with small matrices, however, has vanished if only 10% of the eigenspectrum has to be computed. This time the problem seems to occur for large matrices.

## 8.11 Jülich Storage Cluster – JUST

JUGENE is part of a supercomputer complex in Jülich, embedded in a common storage infrastructure. A key part of this infrastructure is the Jülich Storage cluster (JUST), which was expanded in 2009 to an online disk capacity of around 6 PetaByte. It is connected to the supercomputers via the 10 GigE technology (FORCE10 E1200i switch) with a maximum I/O bandwidth of 60 GB/s. The system takes on the fileserver function for GPFS (General Parallel File System) and is accessed apart from JUGENE by different clusters in the Jülich Supercomputing Centre.

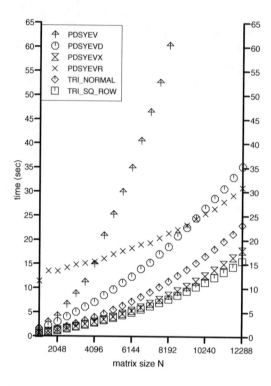

(a) isolated eigenvalues

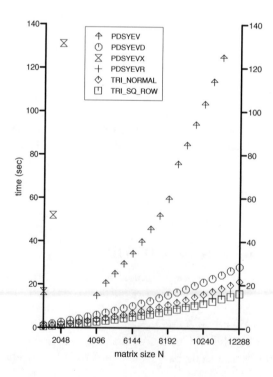

(b) clustered eigenvalues

**FIGURE 8.19**: Execution times of all routines, 1024 processors arranged on a 32x32 grid.

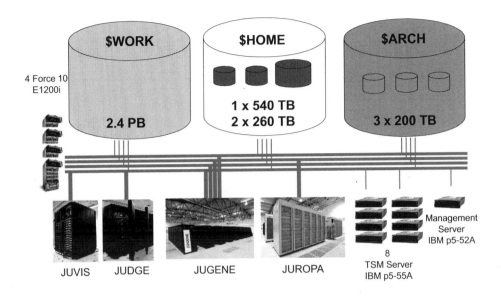

**FIGURE 8.20**: JUST filesystems.

The storage is split into a number of filesystems, used as HOME filesystems, scratch space, and multiple HSM managed filesystems, where users can put data for long-term storage on tape. GPFS data and metadata are stored on 18 IBM DS5300 controllers, 2 for Metadata (RAID 1) and 16 for Data (RAID 6 (8+2)) with 416 enclosures serving more than 6,000 disks, managed by 28 IBM Power 6 servers. For data backup TSM (Tivoli Storage Manager) is used. All (new) data is backed up daily to a dedicated TSM server, that is part of the configuration of the storage subsystem. Two ORACLE SL8500 tape libraries, with a capacity of 80 PB, serve as backend storage, which are exclusively used by TSM.

On JUGENE three different filesystems (see Figure 8.20) are available: WORK (2.4 PB), HOME (1.2 PB), and ARCH (0.6 PB), [bes], the latter one being accessible from the front-end nodes only. In the user environment three corresponding shell environment variables are set to directories (entry points in these filesystems) to which the user has read and write access. $WORK, $HOME, and $ARCH are absolute pointers into a unified namespace that is shared by all nodes.

WORK is the best filesystem to use for large-scale and demanding I/O. There is no backup service in place for this filesystem and files that are older than 90 days will be deleted automatically. If a job's results have to be kept for a longer time, they have to be saved to a HOME or ARCH filesystem. The per-group data limit is set to 20 TB, the per-group file or I-node limit is 4 million.

HOME is intended as a general repository of user resources: source codes, binaries, libraries, and files that are consulted on a regular basis. A daily incremental backup service is in place, creating backups of all new and recently modified files. The per group data limit is 6 TB, the per group file or I-node limit is set to 2 million.

ARCH is intended as an archive facility. Results that have to be kept for the life of the user's project (and potentially longer) may become too large to be kept on the HOME filesystem. Basically all files that will not be actively used for some time can be moved to the archive. Files that have resided on an archive filesystem for a while will be migrated

**TABLE 8.2**: The optimal GPFS file system performance can only be reached by using the specified minimal number of midplanes with their I/O nodes.

| Filesystem | Filesystem bandwidth | GPFS block size | min. # midplanes |
|---|---|---|---|
| WORK | 34.0 GB/s | 4 MB | 16 |
| HOME | 8.5 GB/s | 1 MB | 4 |

to tape. A daily incremental backup service is in place. If a file is migrated to tape, an independent backup copy, residing on another tape is made. The per-group I-node limit is set to 2 million. There is no automatic enforcement of a data limit on archive filesystems. Users are urged to organize their files in (tar) container files to reduce the number of files/I-nodes, compress the container files, and not to exceed 1 TB per file. This improves the overall performance of handling metadata and retrieving data from tape, which takes about two minutes per file plus the data transfer rate of about 250 MB/s back to the disk cache.

## 8.12    Data Center/Facility

The new JSC building in Figures 8.21 and 8.22 where the Blue Gene/P system is hosted, including the machine hall and some offices, was constructed between February 2003 and January 2004 with an initial power and air cooling capacity of 1.5 MW for IT equipment (Figure 8.23).

In preparation for the installation of the 72-rack Blue Gene/P system in 2009 the electrical power capacity was increased to 6 MW for IT equipment with a cooling capacity of 1.2 MW air and 4.8 MW of water-cooled systems. The cooling water is supplied at a temperature level of 6°C (42.8°F) and is mixed with return water to reach the specified incoming temperature level of 16°C (60.8°F). The outcoming water temperature is 24°C (75.2°F). The machine hall has a floor space of 1,000 m$^2$ (10,800 ft$^2$) with a self-supporting roof construction eliminating any pillars in the room (see floorplan in Figure 8.25 and Figure 8.1). The raised floor is 80 cm (2.62 ft) high with a maximum load of 1000 kg/m$^2$ (200 lb/ft$^2$) (see Figure 8.24).

One of the challenging parts of the infrastructure installation was the pipework. While running two systems plus a storage cluster in full production mode all the time, abrasive cutting and welding inside the machine hall was not possible. In Figure 8.24 one can see the pipes that had to be pre-produced in pieces, installed under the raised floor and flange-connected to build the cooling circuit for the Blue Gene/P system.

The room has an early fire detection and an argon gas fire estinguisher system. Uninteruptible electric power supply is only available for disks, servers, and monitoring units, not for the Blue Gene/P racks.

The footprint of the 72 JUGENE racks is 8.4 m (25.6 ft) x 15.6 m (46 ft) resulting in 131 m$^2$. The power consumption of JUGENE sums up to 2.5 MW, including about 20% for cooling.

**FIGURE 8.21**: JSC building at Forschungszentrum Jülich.

## 8.13   System Statistics

In the beginning of 2012, more than 1,000 users of about 220 different groups have been active on the system, executing about 40,000 jobs per month.

### 8.13.1   Accounting

The JUGENE accounting statistics are taken from LoadLeveler accounting records, which report the start and the end of jobs and the number of used nodes. Jobs are accounted for by wall clock time, no matter how compute or I/O intensive the jobs are. Job accounting data is collected once per night and deducted from the user group's quota, refitting quota values to steer the job proccessing, which allows jobs out of quota to run with a lower priority if no other jobs are available. To ensure an equal distribution of usage over time, monthly quotas have been established, allowing use of the quota no more than one month in delay or in advance.

### 8.13.2   Stability

Overall, the downtime of JUGENE has been surprisingly low due to the RAS (Reliability, Availability, Serviceability) features of the Blue Gene/P and the ability to exchange parts

**FIGURE 8.22**: Old (left) and new (right) machine hall of the Jülich Supercomputing Centre.

**FIGURE 8.23**: New machine hall of the Jülich Supercomputing Centre during construction phase in 2003.

while production continues. Monitoring of RAS events and environmental values, which indicate the status of the components, led to preventive exchanges of nodes and nodecards. The rate went down from about 80 to 15 nodes and from about 5 to 1 nodecard per month, in spite of the high number of components (73,623 nodes and 2,304 nodecards). The failure of nodes or other components, which causes an abort of applications went down from about 10 in the beginning to about 8 per month in 2011.

Preventive maintenance slots have also gone down from one per week to one per quarter, which is also an indicator of the stability of the software and the fewer updates which had to be installed.

**FIGURE 8.24**: Raised floor in the new machine hall with power cables and water pipes for the Blue Gene/P installation.

### 8.13.3 Special Challenges

A special challenge for system administrators was the interpretation of the categories of the Blue Gene/P RAS events and finding the right reactions that had to be taken.

The boot time of a full machine partition with 576 I/O nodes (4 per rack) was brought down from 47 minutes to about 30 minutes by different optimizations like serializing initialization of the nodes and decreasing GPFS mount time.

DB2 database software cannot be seen as a black box as it was announced, but the site had to provide some DB2 knowledge to handle install, upgrade, backup, and optimize processes or locally add tables to the DB2 database, e.g., to allow an association between jobs and used midplanes after the jobs are completed.

The provided Blue Gene/P diagnostic runs were improved and matured over time while being used on JUGENE.

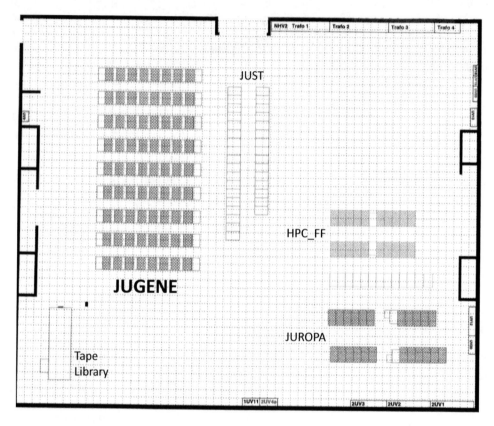

**FIGURE 8.25**: JSC Machineroom floorplan with JUGENE, JUST, and JUROPA/HPC-FF.

# Chapter 9

## Roadrunner: The Dawn of Accelerated Computing

**Sriram Swaminarayan**

*Los Alamos National Laboratory*

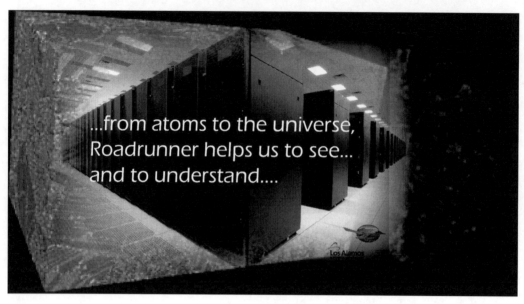

## 9.1    The Path Leading to Roadrunner

Named for the state bird of New Mexico, Roadrunner was conceived by Los Alamos National Laboratory (LANL),[1] and designed and built by IBM. Roadrunner demonstrates the future of high performance computing with its fast, power-efficient hybrid architecture. Over the next decade, supercomputers will be judged as much on their power efficiency as for their speed, and Roadrunner is leading the way.

Roadrunner heralded a new era in supercomputing. It was the world's first petaflop/s supercomputer, first hybrid supercomputer, first accelerated supercomputer, and the first top 5 supercomputer on the TOP500 list to also be in the top 5 of the Green500 list (http://www.green500.org/lists/2008/06/top/list.php). Its hybrid design made it one of the most power-efficient supercomputers in the world when it was released. The two supercomputers that outranked it in power efficiency were identical in design to Roadrunner, but $1/10^{th}$ the size. Roadrunner introduced the world to both heterogeneous and accelerated computing at an unprecedented scale. In fact, at the time Roadrunner was introduced, there were no other accelerated supercomputers in the top 10 (http://top500.org/lists/2008/06).

Roadrunner showed the world that not only could we use accelerators for supercomputing, but that they were extremely power efficient. In the four short years since Roadrunner was introduced, almost half of the supercomputers in the top 10 of the TOP500 list are ac-

---

[1]Los Alamos National Laboratory (LANL), Los Alamos, NM, is one of two U.S. government laboratories that are responsible for the design and maintenance of nuclear weapons. (The other is Lawrence Livermore National Laboratory (LLNL), Livermore, CA.) LANL is a U.S. Department of Energy (DOE) national laboratory, managed and operated by Los Alamos National Security (LANS). The Laboratory is one of the largest science and technology institutions in the world. LANL researchers work in many technical fields, including national security and weapons, space exploration, mathematics, geoscience, chemistry, materials science, renewable energy, medicine, nanotechnology, and supercomputing. Close to one-third of the Laboratory's technical staff members are physicists, one quarter are engineers, and one-sixth are chemists and materials scientists. The Laboratory's annual budget is approximately $2.2 billion. Read more about Los Alamos National Laboratory at http://www.lanl.gov. Additional information on Roadrunner can be found at http://www.lanl.gov/roadrunner. This publication is LA-UR-12-22216.

celerated supercomputers (http://top500.org/lists/2011/11). In essence, Roadrunner paved the way for the large-scale GPU (Graphics Processing Unit) accelerated machines that have made an appearance in the top 10 of this list.

In a lot of ways, Roadrunner could only have originated in LANL, which has an impressive series of firsts in supercomputing. In fact, LANL started the field of scientific computing and has always been an early adopter of transformational high performance computing (HPC) technology. Here are a few pegposts along the way.

### 9.1.1 Computing Begins at Los Alamos

Although LANL is now world-famous for its HPC programs and expertise, it started modestly in the spring of 1943 when the Manhattan Project began secret operations in Los Alamos to develop the first atomic weapon. In those days, the word "computer" meant the people using mechanical adding machines to do calculations. However, by the end of World War II in 1945, LANL scientists were using the ENIAC, the world's first electronic computer. Mathematician John von Neumann created a cooperative arrangement between the Princeton Institute for Advanced Studies, home of the ENIAC, and Los Alamos. Computational work at Los Alamos by Enrico Fermi, John Pasta, and Stanislaw Ulam led to the modern field of nonlinear dynamics. Others at Los Alamos used computers to study microscopic mechanics for the melting of solids using a particular type of Monte Carlo method that is now called the Metropolis algorithm. The magazine, *Computing in Science & Engineering*, named the Metropolis algorithm as one of the 10 most significant numerical methods of the 20th century [DS00]. Because of its simplicity and power, the algorithm is now standard in diverse fields such as psychology, finance, and political science.

### 9.1.2 Los Alamos Builds a Computer

The Laboratory's own first electronic computer, the MANIAC, was built at Los Alamos by a team led by Nicholas Metropolis and completed in 1953. MANIAC ran the first computations modeling the structure of protons, the quantum nature of superfluids, the growth of tumors, and artificial intelligence, to name a few. Soon the Lab built the MANIAC II, and then purchased the IBM 7030 (Stretch) in 1961. It was the fastest computer in the world from 1961 until 1964, until the Control Data Corporation's CDC 6600, which LANL also purchased, and its successor, the CDC 7600.

### 9.1.3 First Use of Supercomputers

The term "supercomputer" was first used to describe Seymour Cray's Cray-1. The very first Cray-1 was installed at LANL in 1976. To increase the speed of this system, the Cray-1 had a unique "C" shape, which enabled integrated circuits to be closer together. The company Thinking Machines delivered its CM-2 computer to the Los Alamos Advanced Computing Lab in 1989. The CM-2 had the first massively parallel architecture, where independent processors in chips could connect with other processors, creating multiple, fast pathways. In 1992, the Lab acquired the first production model of its successor, the CM-5, which was the #1 supercomputer on the very first TOP500 list (http://www.top500.org/lists/1993/06).

### 9.1.4    First HPC Computing Environment

Supercomputers were generating increasingly large data files. LANL experts foresaw the bottlenecks in the connections between supercomputers, file storage, and other devices inside the machine room. Moving the files began to take almost as much time as generating them. LANL created a high performance computing environment, the Integrated Computer Network (ICN), making the computers, networks, data storage, and visualization tools work together. HIPPI, a fast network data transmission method developed for the ICN, became a national standard (ANSI) in 1990.

### 9.1.5    U.S. Weapons Stewardship Using Supercomputing

In 1992, nuclear weapons production stopped and a full test ban was signed in 1996. In response, the U.S. Department of Energy created the Accelerated Strategic Computing Initiative (ASCI) (now the Advanced Simulation and Computing [ASC] program) to transition from test-based certification of the safety of the U.S. nuclear stockpile to science- and simulation-based certification. ASCI funded the acquisition of the LANL Blue Mountain computer in 1998. The Los Alamos Computing Science Institute (LACSI) was also founded in 1998. LACSI collaborates with computer science departments at universities and with companies in support of the ASC program.

### 9.1.6    Los Alamos Supercomputing Today

The Laboratory's Nicholas C. Metropolis Center for Modeling and Simulation was dedicated in May 2002. It has a 43,500 sq ft computer room (nearly the size of a football field), two immersive visualization theaters, two supercomputers–Roadrunner and Cielo–and many computer clusters. Roadrunner was the world's first hybrid supercomputer, the first supercomputer to attain a sustained petaflop/s, and #1 on the TOP500 list in 2008. Its successor, Cielo, with a theoretical peak performance of 1.37 petaflops, was installed in the Metropolis Center in 2010-2011 and is now used for ASC computing campaigns.

### 9.1.7    A Brief History of Roadrunner

Roadrunner began to take shape in 2002. At that time, scaling a supercomputer to 4,000 nodes was manageable. However, even at that scale, a petascale system would require nodes operating at more than 1/4 of a teraflop/s. Achieving this level of performance within a reasonable power envelope required something extraordinary–a modification of the Sony, Toshiba, and IBM-developed Cell chip used in the PlayStation®3.

The original design was to be delivered in two phases. The initial phase was delivered in 2006, an AMD Opteron™–based cluster with empty space in the cabinets to accommodate future Cell chips in 2008. However, in late 2006 and early 2007, IBM and LANL redesigned Roadrunner as a standalone integrated 1.4 petaflop/s system. This redesign had two primary advantages: the initial delivery system provided uninterrupted valuable resources to the weapons program, and the connection speeds on the integrated system were increased by 4x.

In October 2007, the Roadrunner project passed DOE review, thus allowing IBM and LANL to proceed to build, deliver, and accept the full system. This review focused on four important DOE applications codes: Implicit Monte Carlo (radiation transport), VPIC (plasma physics), SPaSM (molecular dynamics), and Sweep3D (neutron transport) that were part of seven open science projects on Roadrunner. In June 2008, Roadrunner became the very first system to achieve a sustained petaflop/s.

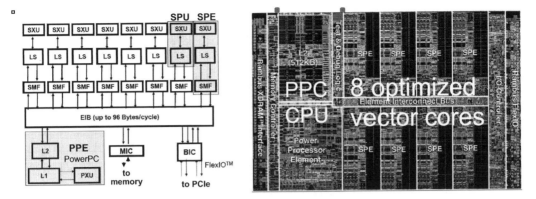

**FIGURE 9.1**: Eight high-performance Synergistic Processing Elements (SPEs) plus one Power Processing Element (PPE) are in a Cell processor. The SPEs are highly tuned SIMD cores containing a processing unit (SXU), a local $256kB$ scratchpad memory/local store (LS), and a Direct Memory Access (DMA memory engine (SMF) to move data into and out of the local store from the large shared off-chip DRAM-based memory. The PowerXCell 8i version of this chip can perform at 102.4 GF/s using all 8 SPEs simultaneously and has an off-chip memory bandwidth of 25.6 GB/s.

At a petascale, Roadrunner is providing critical resources for DOE mission and science applications. However, its most lasting contribution will likely be as a harbinger of the future of high performance computing, a future both challenging and replete with opportunity.

### 9.1.8 The Hybrid Architecture of Roadrunner

Roadrunner consists of a hybrid architecture of commodity server nodes with attached acceleration devices. The secret to Roadrunner's record-breaking performance is the use of 3,060 compute nodes that each consist of two AMD Opteron™ dual-core processors plus four IBM PowerXCell 8i™ processors used as computational accelerators. These node-attached Cell accelerators are what make Roadrunner different than typical clusters. We call Roadrunner a Cell-accelerated hybrid supercomputer.

The PowerXCell 8i chip used in Roadrunner is a slightly modified version of the Cell processor chip used in the Sony PlayStation®3. It is very similar to the original Cell chip except that its floating point units can do double precision arithmetic at much greater speed, and its memory subsystem uses conventional DDR2 DRAM (double data rate synchronous dynamic random access memory). Without these changes, Roadrunner could not have reached its supercomputing goals. The Cell chips are actually hybrid multicore consisting of one Power Processing Element (PPE) and eight special compute cores known as Synergistic Processing Elements, or SPEs, as shown in Figure 9.1. Figure 9.2 shows how the Cell chips fit into the compute nodes. They have a highly optimized and unique way of processing that achieves great performance in a single chip with great power efficiency. New programming techniques are required, and modified codes and algorithms are needed to effectively run on the Cell processors with good efficiency.

Building Roadrunner from Opterons and PowerXCell 8i processors was an engineering feat that leveraged two existing IBM compute server blade products. One LS21 Opteron blade is connected to two QS22 Cell blades using a Roadrunner custom expansion blade to form a Cell-accelerated compute node, called a triblade due to its three active processor blades. The triblade achieves a design goal of having one Cell processor for each Opteron

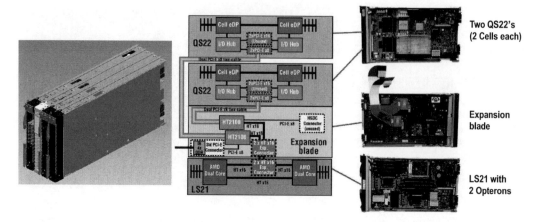

**FIGURE 9.2**: A Roadrunner triblade compute node composed of one LS21 and two QS22 blades with four independent PCIe x8 links to the two Opteron chips on the LS21 blade with two independent HyperTransport links. This was the highest performing and most direct connection possible using the available IBM blade-based building block.

core and also provides 16 GB (4 x 4 GB) of shared memory for the four Opteron cores plus 16 GB (4 x 4 GB) for the Cells. IBM and LANL collaborated to create custom drivers, a data transfer protocol, and the Data Communications and Synchronization (DaCS) runtime library to move data between the Cells and Opterons, and to launch, control, and monitor processes running on the Cells from the Opterons. The DaCS application programming interface (API) was designed and implemented to have both direct memory access (DMA)-like interfaces, similar to those in the Cell's SPEs, and message passing interfaces similar to MPI; data transfers can be initiated from either side. The full Roadrunner configuration uses these Cell-accelerated triblades, organized into 17 subclusters or CUs of 180 triblades each with accompanying I/O gateway nodes, to provide off-machine connectivity to a Panasas parallel filesystem. The full machine is composed of 3,060 triblades containing 12,240 PowerXCell 8i chips and 6,120 dual-core Opterons (see Figure 9.3). The overall performance from just the SPEs in the Cell chips is 1.33 petaflop/s, while there is only 44 teraflop/s (~3%) of performance in the Opterons.

## 9.2    Programming Roadrunner

### 9.2.1    The Three Faces of Roadrunner

Writing a code to run on Roadrunner requires three interoperating programs, typically created by breaking an existing program into an Opteron piece, a Cell PPE piece, and a Cell SPE piece, and then adding the control logic and API calls to exchange data as needed to make them work together. Each Opteron process is part of a typical MPI-based cluster application and, through the DaCS library, spawns a Cell PPE process, which then goes on to spawn SPE processes.

Since almost all of the performance of Roadrunner is in the Cell's SPEs, the most important step is to get the compute-intensive portion(s) of an application running in parallel on the eight SPEs of each Cell chip. This is where the most program restructuring

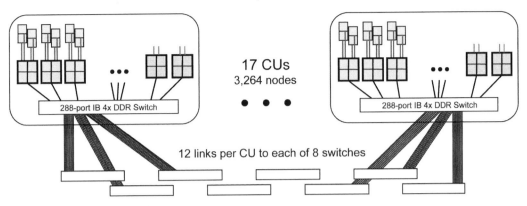

**FIGURE 9.3**: Roadrunner is composed of 17 Connected Unit (CU) groupings, each comprising 180 triblade compute nodes plus 12 I/O gateway nodes. All nodes in a CU are connected to a single 288-port InfiniBand 4x DDR switch, and those 17 switches are uniformly interconnected at a second level using 8 more of the large switches to form a 2:1 oversubscribed fat tree interconnect. A total of 3,060 triblade nodes contain the 12,240 PowerXCell 8i chips in the machine and have 1.33 petaflop/s of double precision performance, while the 6120 Opteron chips contribute only an additional 44 teraflop/s.

is potentially needed to: 1) present threaded parallelism to eight SPEs in 128-bit SIMD form, and 2) tile or block the application into work chunks that fit and can be used within the small 256-KB scratchpad local stores of each SPE. The SPE DMA engines are called via simple APIs in the SPE code to retrieve work chunks and send them back to main Cell memory after computing on them. Optimal performance is achieved by simultaneously having the next work chunk prefetched and the previous one written back while the SPU computes on a current work chunk.

The Cell's PPE process is launched by its Opteron host process via DaCS. It sets up and synchronizes the eight SPEs and works with the Opteron process to exchange data between the Cell and Opteron memories as needed. Typically the PPE code will control the overall advancing of an application's steps or cycles, and in doing so, synchronize the SPEs doing the actual computations. Since the PPE is a stripped-down PowerPC, application and code developers typically target as little work as possible for the PPE.

A standard MPI environment is used to launch and run the first part of the code that is distributed on the Opteron cluster, and is the heart of every Roadrunner run. Typical application functions like setup, cycle monitoring, and checkpoint/restart run on the Opterons with only minimal code changes to send data to or retrieve data from the Cells. The Opteron process uses DaCS to start a coupled Cell PPE code. The PPE and the Opteron coordinate and process data exchanges as needed between Cell and Opteron memories. Applications requiring data exchange with neighboring cluster nodes do so only through the Opterons and usually create an MPI-relay form of messaging to do so via the following four steps: 1) the Cell PPE first sends data to the Opteron process; 2) the Opteron then forwards the data via an MPI send operation to the appropriate neighboring Opteron rank; 3) the Opteron also receives data from other neighboring Opteron ranks using MPI receives; 4) and finally, the Opteron or Cell PPE sends the data up to the Cell.

The codes selected for the Open Science projects represent a variety of types. Several contain particle-based segments, including VPIC (particle-in-cell), SPaSM (molecular dynamics), IMC (Implicit Monte Carlo), and RRU (Roadrunner Universe Project). Only one selected code, CFDNS, is a primarily grid-based code. Another, the Human Immunodeficiency Virus (HIV) phylogenetics code, requires the evaluation of tree structures using a Markov chain-branching model. The good use of the coarse hybrid aspect of the Roadrunner system is an issue that has yielded different engineering approaches, as well as different algorithms. Some codes are feasible and appropriate for centering on Cell processors (termed "Cell-centric"), thereby using the Opterons simply to handle data movement across the cluster. Other developers worked with very complex legacy codes that had to move in a more incremental fashion to Cell acceleration. Nevertheless, the basic considerations involved in successful porting of the codes are those that should apply to the development of any hybrid application, and, to a large extent, to hybrid architectures in the near future.

### 9.2.2    A Developer's View of Roadrunner

From a coding perspective, the Roadrunner hybrid architecture presents some unique challenges. Most obvious is the need to write three separate, but coupled, codes for the Opteron, PPE, and SPE, each with its own programming paradigms and languages (see Section 9.1.8 for an overview of the hardware). Due to the exacting data-alignment requirements on the PPE and SPE, most of the open science codes utilize C or C++ (with appropriate processor-specific extensions) for the Cell portions. Some codes have retained Fortran for the Opteron code, whereas others were originally C/C++.

Less obvious are the limitations imposed by the SPE, most notably poor branching performance. Although the need to explicitly manage data movement between Cell main memory and local store is a significant departure from "normal" programming models, it is, along with the excellent memory performance of the Cell architecture, responsible for the speedup that is observed even in the absence of significant arithmetic intensity within kernels. By and large, the transition to explicit DMA management has been straightforward. In general, the PPE was shown to be a weak performer, so most codes minimized its contribution, except where the PCIe bus speed made it necessary; that is, where the same operations would have been quicker on the Opteron in isolation, there are cases (e.g., RRU, see [PHL+10]) where having the PPE perform computations is faster than moving the data back to the Opteron.

One consequence of the speedup provided by the Cell is the exposure of the effects of data movement and latency, which are inherent in all the non-computation portions of any code. These include not just the usual inter-node communications overhead, but also the time needed to move data between Opteron and Cell main memory (across the PCIe bus), and the overhead associated with kernel invocation on the Cell. The last means that for a small work block, the Cell kernel cannot be viewed as simply calling a subroutine from the main program, since the kernel invocation overhead will dominate the total execution time. Rather, most of the codes invoke a kernel once on the Cell and then use signals among the three levels for managing the progression of the code. This extra level of data movement is also a factor when inter-node communication is present, because it introduces extra latency. Although some users developed programming abstractions to mask the complexity of these data movements (allowing "direct" messaging between Cells), the topology of the machine is such that the extra lag cannot be avoided.

### 9.2.3    Identification of Kernels to Be Ported

Typically, the identification of kernels to be ported involves identifying "hotspots" in the code, where significant computational time is spent during a simulation. Because the PCIe bus is a potential bottleneck, the data movement between kernels is also a factor in the overall computational time.

### 9.2.4 Modification of Data Structures

The Cell is a (short) vector processor that operates on 128-bit words. Experience has shown that the number of DMA requests affects the performance (a few large DMAs execute faster than many small ones for the same total data movement). As such, the underlying data structures must be amenable to large coalesced loads and vectorizing without data reorganization on the fly. While the original CFDNS code used an array-of-structures (AoS) data layout, the Roadrunner branch of the CFDNS code uses structure-of-arrays (SoA) to accomplish this vectorizing. Some of the particle-based codes (e.g., RRU) also use this type of data transformation. This method allows the SPEs to operate on the data without the need to shuffle data within the local store (see Figure 9.4). As a result, DNS and RRU have achieved acceleration of the local kernels by factors on the order of 100x.

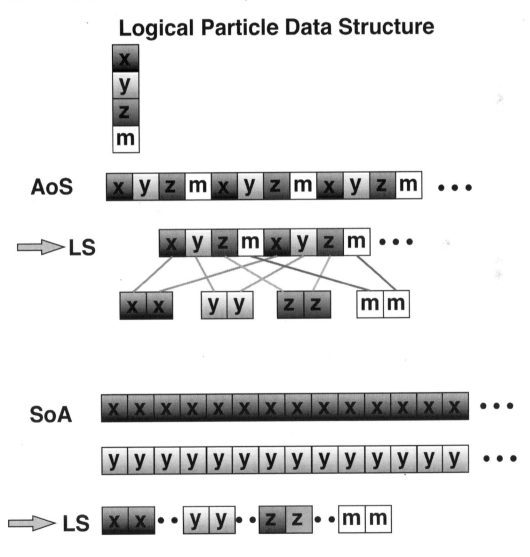

**FIGURE 9.4**: Comparison of Array of Structures (AoS) and Structure of Arrays (SoA) data layouts. If the data is stored as AoS, then values must be shuffled in local store to allow vector math operations. If the data is stored as SoA, then no reshuffling is required and the computation is significantly faster.

In contrast, some particle-based schemes retained the AoS data layout in order to minimize the amount of modification required to the original code. In these cases, they use the excellent shuffle intrinsics of the SPE, although there is still a performance penalty compared to fully vectorized code. Speedups of the local kernel in these cases appear to be on the order of 10x. SPaSM initially adopted a hybrid scheme, whereby the particle data was converted from AoS to SoA by the Opteron prior to being sent to the Cell, thus allowing more of the original Opteron code to be retained. A later version of the code resulted in a full redesign of the data structures.

### 9.2.5    Redesign of the Local Kernel

In addition to being a short vector processor, the SPE has other idiosyncrasies that have occasionally mandated modifications to the local algorithms. In particular, the SPE has poor branching performance, which affects the design of the particle-based kernels. Typically, these kernels involve a series of checks to determine if the particle has passed out of the grid cell, and a branch is then executed based on the result. Since a failed conditional check results in an 18-cycle stall, these operations can become extremely inefficient if executed on single particles. Instead, most of the particle codes have adopted strategies where all particles are treated as if they remain within a grid cell (and within the local domain) and then outliers are flagged and treated in a separate pass. Similarly, the SPaSM local kernel does not attempt to enforce reciprocity during the force calculation, since this complicates the data access patterns. This action results in doubling the number of flops, but has no effect on the total data movement, which is a more significant factor in the overall execution time.

In the IMC computation, for example, the computation of the intersection of a particle trajectory with a cell face has been completely recast to remove the conditional. Instead, the intersection of the particle path with all six faces of the cell is computed and then masking operations are applied to remove the negative values. Finally, the minimum of the remaining values is chosen. This procedure is significantly faster than the original algorithm, despite requiring six times the computational effort. The speedup comes from the nature of the instructions: the five discarded distance calculations can be pipelined, whereas the (possibly) five missed branches cannot.

In contrast, the grid-based code rarely requires conditional statements except at boundaries. In this case, the implementation of boundary conditions was performed by multiplying the field values by masking stencils that were determined and set by the Opteron at startup. Thus, the Cells executed some extra flops, but these are cheaper than failed branch checks. The only other conditional statements are those required for the time-stepping scheme. In that case, the logic is performed on the Opteron, which is natural since the time-step restriction is dependent on global values of the error, and these are only available on the Opteron. Additionally, the SPEs perform conditional checks on state flags set by the Opterons, but these are outside large work blocks so that the cost of the 18-cycle stall is amortized over several thousand or million cycles, depending on the local block size.

### 9.2.6    Strategies for Evaluating Future Codes

The changes made for Roadrunner have enabled the participating projects to port their codes to newer architectures more easily. Two cases in point are the Sweep3D code where the Roadrunner version was directly translated into a multi-threaded accelerated version for running on multi-core CPUs and on Intels MIC (Many Integrated Core) architecture, and the RRU project where many of the ideas behind the original MC3 code written for Roadrunner formed the basis for a new cosmological simulation framework, HACC (Hardware/Hybrid Accelerated Cosmology Code(s)). The highly integrated HACC family runs on all current supercomputer architectures (standard MPP clusters, Cell-and GPU-accelerated systems, IBM BG/P and BG/Q systems, Intel MICs, etc.) at very high performance levels and with scalability designed for the exascale. HACC is a Gordon Bell Award finalist for 2012, achieving greater than 50% of peak performance on the IBM BG/Q and attaining > 90% parallel efficiency at the million-core level.

Based on the experiences encountered with Roadrunner, we offer the following prescription for porting other codes to hybrid architectures. Foremost is identification of the kernels to be ported, based on the fraction of execution time in the original code and the amount of data movement required. Once these have been identified, it is safe to assume at least an order of magnitude speedup of the kernel execution time alone. The total serial wall-clock time improvement is then estimated based on the ability of the programmer to hide the data transfer and kernel invocation times by efficiently streaming work to the accelerator. At this stage, the serial speedup may inform the need to redesign the execution pattern of the parallel code in order to avoid poor scaling due to inter-node communication bottlenecks. This can be done either by overlapping the inter-node communication with local compute, or by redesigning the applications to require less data movement. Note that for some applications, the acceleration of local work will lead to the execution time being dominated by inter-node data movement, which will lead to poor scaling behavior, albeit with vastly reduced total execution time.

## 9.3   Open Science on Roadrunner

The sheer performance and size of Roadrunner enabled first-of-a-kind computer codes and science simulations of the biggest of the big and the smallest of the small during its first eight months of operation at LANL. From February to September 2009 Roadrunner was focused on a set of unclassified, open science projects, developing a new suite of hybrid computer codes for modeling and simulation in a wide variety of disciplines. The machine then switched to a classified mode for its intended mission, and since November 2009, codes and simulations are being used on Roadrunner to help assure the safety, security, and reliability of the U.S. nuclear deterrent.

This chapter details seven open science projects that were selected to be part of the stabilization and integration of Roadrunner. Selection was based on scientific quality and the ability to develop an accelerated science code within the allotted time, about six months. All of the projects described here were transformational, building computational scientific capabilities that did not exist before. Roadrunner's open science period had two interrelated purposes: 1) burn in, stabilize, and optimize the machine and its system software, and 2) develop several hybrid computer simulation codes in order to run full-scale science simulation studies for a set of peer-reviewed projects. Earlier work on a few computer codes had already proved the efficacy of the hybrid design of Roadrunner, thus there was great interest in using the enormous power of the machine to accomplish additional large-scale simulations of significant scientific value. Ten open science projects were selected from proposals drawn from within LANL for areas of important scientific merit and teams staffed with the appropriate mix of skilled subject matter experts, computational scientists, and programmers. A few projects would build on earlier code demonstration efforts, but for many projects the Roadrunner hybrid architecture would be completely new and would require an entirely new code base. Computational scientists engaged in the earlier demonstration codes worked directly on several of these projects. The range of science represented in these projects was extremely varied, as seen in this report.

During development, open science projects explored and exercised new programming techniques, system software, and tools for the hybrid Cell-accelerated Roadrunner architecture, demonstrating the usability and performance of the unique hybrid architecture across a broad range of disciplines. Once the code development effort was complete, these projects ran scientific studies, often comprising many large simulation runs, to examine important scientific questions or issues. Collectively, these runs provided an early and challenging workload on the system, enabling computer scientists to optimize the system and application software, and to work the kinks out of the operations as well. The projects are:

1. Laser-Plasma Interaction [(Section 9.3.1)]
   This work is focused on understanding the nonlinear aspects of fusion experiments in the National Ignition Facility (NIF) at LLNL by studying the physics of onset and saturation of stimulated Raman scattering (SRS) in the fundamental building block of a NIF laser beam, a single laser speckle.

2. Exploring Magnetic Reconnection [(Section 9.3.2)]
   Magnetic reconnection is a basic process that occurs within hot ionized gases known as plasmas. This process often leads to an explosive release of energy that is stored within the magnetic fields, and plays a key role in the Earth's magnetosphere, solar flares, magnetic fusion machines, and a variety of astrophysical problems.

3. Understanding the Largest HIV Evolutionary Tree [(Section 9.3.3)]
   Mapping Darwinian phylogenic evolutionary relationships for large numbers of HIV genetic sequences results in an HIV family tree that may lead researchers to new vaccine focus areas.

4. Modeling Tiny Nanowires at Long Time Scales [(Section 9.3.4)]
   Nanowires stretching and breaking under stress is simulated atom-by-atom over a period of time, which is closer than ever to experimental reality, to see how the movement of single atoms can change a material's mechanical or electrical properties.

5. How Shock Waves Cause Materials to Fail [(Section 9.3.5)]
   Physicists use the SPaSM (Scalable Parallel Short-range Molecular Dynamics) computer code to conduct multibillion-atom simulations of materials as extreme shockwave stresses break the materials into pieces. For the first time atomic-scale models reveal the detailed formation and transport of ejecta.

6. Direct Numerical Simulation of Reacting Turbulence [(Section 9.3.6)]
   In the field of fluid dynamics, understanding turbulence, the chaotic behavior of fluids, remains one of the unsolved problems in physics. This study focused on the complex interactions of flame and turbulence, as in the early stages of a type Ia supernova.

7. Origins of the Unseen Universe [(Section 9.3.7)]
   Cosmologists have created some of the largest high-resolution simulations of the distribution of matter in the Universe. These simulations model an expanding, accelerating Universe to better understand the structure of the Universe, dark energy, and dark matter.

### 9.3.1    Understanding the Nonlinear Physics of Laser-Plasma Interaction through "At Scale" Plasma Kinetic Simulations

In 2010, inertial confinement fusion (ICF) experiments commenced at the NIF. In these, over a million Joules of laser energy are focused within a gas-filled hohlraum. The hohlraum walls absorb the laser energy and re-radiate it as X-rays, which absorb in a spherical capsule at the hohlraum center. This causes the capsule to compress, bringing the deuterium-tritium fuel to the high temperatures and pressures required for thermonuclear fusion.

To prevent the hohlraum walls from ablating during the $\sim 10^{-8}$s laser drive, a fill gas of hydrogen or helium is used. As the laser propagates through the fill gas, laser-plasma instabilities (LPI) may arise, which scatter laser light out of the hohlraum, degrade capsule implosion symmetry, and preheat the fuel with hot electrons, making compression harder to achieve.

SRS, the resonant amplification of electron density fluctuations by a laser, is one of the LPI concerns in ICF. In ICF experiments, a roughly uniform laser intensity is maintained across the beam with random phase plates that break the beam into an ensemble of laser speckles. For the success of fusion experiments on the NIF, we must first understand the physics of onset and saturation of SRS in the fundamental building block of a NIF laser beam, a single laser speckle. In a laser speckle, SRS manifests as the amplification of a forward-directed electron plasma wave (EPW) and the backward scattering of laser light. Unlike the linear growth of SRS, the nonlinear physics was not well understood until recently [YAB+07]. Roadrunner has been used to assess the impact of the nonlinear SRS physics on laser penetration and energy deposition in fusion experiments. These fully kinetic plasma simulations employ the VPIC particle-in-cell code [BAB+08] and are performed in large plasma volumes in 3D at an unprecedented range of time and space scales.

Until recently it has not been possible to fully simulate the comparatively large 3D plasma volumes of laser speckles. With VPIC on Roadrunner, simulations of the NIF holhraum plasma have been done using 4096 Cell chips at a range of laser intensity values (see the graph in Figure 9.5). These simulations [YAR+09] showed that SRS reflectivity within a solitary speckle exhibits nonlinear behavior: a sharp onset at a threshold intensity, whereby reflectivity increases abruptly to a level orders of magnitude higher than linear theory predicts over a small range of intensity, with a plateau in reflectivity at higher laser intensity in which SRS nonlinearly saturates. This generic behavior matches that measured in single-speckle experiments at the LANL Trident Laser facility [MCF+02] with physics that cannot be captured by linear gain models of SRS growth within the speckle.

As a highlight of the unique simulations afforded by Roadrunner, the largest of these calculations was run on 16 CUs using 11,520 Cell chips and MPI ranks, nearly the full Roadrunner system, and employed a record 0.4 trillion particles, over 2 billion computational cells, and ran for nearly 58,160 time steps ($\sim 10^{19}$ flops), long enough for two bursts of stimulated Raman scattering to grow from noise to significant amplitude at a laser intensity near the SRS onset.

Figure 9.5 shows isosurfaces of the electrostatic field associated with these bursts; the wave fronts exhibit bending or bowing, arising from nonlinear electron trapping, as well as self-focusing, which breaks up the phase fronts. The essential nonlinear physics governing SRS saturation has now been identified. The scattering manifests as a series of pulses, each of which passes through four distinct phases: 1) SRS grows linearly from density fluctuations; 2) electrons trapped by the EPW reduce the wave frequency and phase velocity by an amount that scales with EPW amplitude; 3) near the speckle center, where the amplitude is highest, the EPW phase velocity is lower than at the speckle's edge; EPW phase front bending ensues as shown by the top image in Figure 9.6; 4) The EPW wave amplitude exceeds the electron trapped particle modulation instability (TPMI) threshold. TPMI generates waves off-axis from the laser direction and leads to EPW filamentation, self-focusing, and phase front breakup, shown by the bottom image in Figure 9.6. Self-focusing increases the transverse loss of trapped electrons and increases EPW damping.

From these basic science simulations, researchers are now able to better understand the essential nature of LPI nonlinear onset and saturation. Current research focuses on determining whether neighboring speckles can interact via exchange of hot electrons or

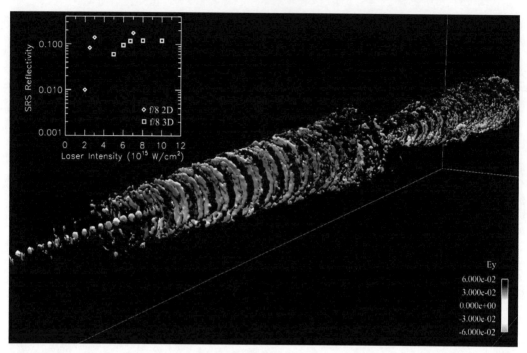

**FIGURE 9.5**: Single-speckle LPI calculations using 16 CU of Roadrunner (11,520 ranks), nearly the full system; this calculation employed a record 0.4 trillion particles, > 2 billion cells, and ran for nearly 58,160 time steps ($\sim 10^{19}$ floating point operations), long enough for two bursts of stimulated Raman scattering to grow from noise to significant amplitude at a laser intensity near the SRS.

waves to produce higher backscatter than they would individually, the kind of study only possible on Roadrunner, where at scale kinetic simulations of laser-plasma interaction in 3D at realistic laser-speckle and multispeckle scales can be prosecuted at unprecedented size, speed, and fidelity.

## 9.3.2    Understanding Magnetic Reconnection

Magnetic reconnection is a basic plasma process involving the rapid conversion of magnetic field energy into various forms of plasma kinetic energy, including high-speed flows, thermal heating, and highly energetic particles. This process is usually associated with changes in magnetic topology, giving rise to magnetic islands or more complicated flux rope structures. These types of dynamical changes are conveniently viewed in terms of the breaking and reconnection of magnetic field lines, thus explaining the origin of the term *magnetic reconnection*. The process is thought to play an important role in a diverse range of applications including solar flares, geomagnetic substorms, magnetic fusion devices, and a wide variety of astrophysical problems. Despite a great deal of effort, scientists are still working to understand a range of basic questions regarding the onset, structure, and dynamical evolution of magnetic reconnection in large-scale systems.

Many of the outstanding scientific challenges are related to the vast separation of spatial and temporal scales inherent to most applications. High-temperature plasmas are very good electrical conductors, which implies that the magnetic flux is constrained to move together with the plasma (commonly known as the frozen-flux constraint). For magnetic

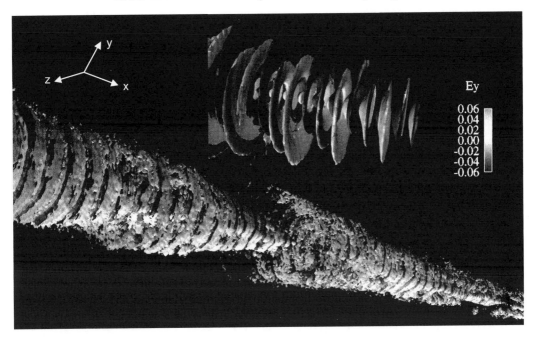

**FIGURE 9.6**: (Top) A snapshot taken from a 3D VPIC LPI simulation at SRS pulse saturation of a $f/4$ laser beam, showing bending of iso-surfaces of EPW electric field across the speckle. The iso-surfaces are colored by the laser electric field, graphically showing the source for SRS backscatter has become incoherent. (Bottom) Self-focusing and filamentation in two bursts of SRS, a snapshot taken from a 3D VPIC LPI simulation of a $f/8$ laser beam. The speckle volume is $16x$ larger than the $f/4$ simulation, permitting more transverse self-focusing modes to develop. This leads to chaotic EPW phase variation across the speckle. This further reduces SRS source coherence and increases wave damping, quenching the SRS pulse.

reconnection to proceed, it is necessary to break the frozen-flux constraint within so-called diffusion regions. This can occur either through collisional dissipation, which gives rise to electrical resistivity and viscosity, or through a variety of different plasma kinetic effects. In most applications, the diffusion regions are quite small in comparison with macroscopic scales, but play a critical role in the evolution. Thus researchers are working to understand the basic physics of these regions, as well as the coupling to the larger macroscopic systems. Due to the complicated nonlinear physics, simulations have played an important role in scientific progress. Most previous simulation studies have focused on 2D models using a variety of fluid and kinetic descriptions. With increasing computer power, these 2D simulations have progressed to larger-scale systems and raised a number of new questions. In particular, recent 2D kinetic simulations have demonstrated that diffusion regions often develop elongated current sheets that are potentially unstable to a variety of different plasma instabilities [DSK06]. Understanding the dynamical evolution of these layers in 3D systems is a formidable challenge that clearly requires petascale computing.

To address these questions, LANL scientists are utilizing the 3D kinetic plasma simulation code VPIC [BAB+08], which provides a first-principles description of the physics. The primary science goal is to better understand the role of plasma instabilities on the 3D evolution of reconnection layers in both space and laboratory plasmas. The simulations performed on Roadrunner were of unprecedented scale and complexity, using upwards of

4096 Cell chips and MPI, or message passing interface, ranks, ~200 billion particles, and requiring careful attention to boundary conditions, collisional physics and extensive new diagnostics. Despite these complications, the simulations achieved a factor of ~3x speedup using the Cell processors, and the results are leading to a variety of new insights into the influence of plasma instabilities on reconnection. Here we give a brief overview of these simulations and highlight a few key science results emerging from these efforts.

In space and astrophysical applications, magnetic reconnection typically occurs in highly collisionless parameter regimes and involves dynamical structures on both ion and electron kinetic scales. This is computationally challenging since the kinetic time scales are separated by the ion to electron mass ratio $m_i/m_e$ while the spatial scales are separated by $(m_i/m_e)^{1/2}$.

For example, in the most common case of an electron-proton plasma the electron cyclotron frequency is $m_i/m_e = 1,836$ times faster than the ion cyclotron frequency, while the electron gyroradius is ~43 times smaller than the ion gyroradius. Furthermore, the global scales of interest in astrophysical plasmas are vastly larger than an ion gyroradius. Due to this immense scale separation, it is not possible to study the global 3D evolution while simultaneously resolving the kinetic scales. To make progress, it is necessary to reduce the scale separation by employing artificial mass ratios $m_i/m_e \sim 100 - 300$ and furthermore to focus on the most interesting regions for reconnection, which are considerably smaller. These preferred sites for the onset and initial development of reconnection are thin current sheets, where the intense current density gives rise to a rapid rotation in the magnetic field. As reconnection develops, a flow pattern is set up that brings new plasma and magnetic flux toward a reconnection site and expels the reconnected plasma as a high-speed jet tangent to the initial layer. It is possible to accommodate these reconnection flows and effectively mimic a much larger system by employing a suitable set of open boundary conditions to permit plasma and magnetic flux to cross the boundaries [DSK06]. This approach was employed to study several types of initial conditions on Roadrunner, resulting in a wealth of interesting new results.

Several of these open simulations focused on neutral sheets, where the initial magnetic field reverses sign across an ion scale layer and goes to zero in the center. After the onset and initial evolution, the diffusion region features highly elongated electron scale layers that are unstable to several distinct secondary instabilities. As illustrated in Figure 9.7, these modes include an electromagnetic wave that gives rise to kinking of the electron layer and a secondary reconnection instability that gives rise to flux rope formation. The unstable kink wave propagates in the direction of the ion drift with a wavelength similar to recent predictions from kinetic theory [Dau03]. The flux rope instability is the 3D analogue of secondary island formation that has been previously reported in 2D [DSK06]. Although these processes are qualitatively similar to recent 3D electron-positron ($m_i = m_e$) simulations [YDK+08], this is the first time they have been observed for the high mass ratio limit $m_i/m_e = 300$ that is now feasible with Roadrunner. While researchers are still exploring the implications of these results, they are potentially of great interest from several perspectives. First, the kink instability is within a range of frequencies where both ions and electrons can exchange momentum through the wave, potentially giving rise to a wave-induced resistivity, a problem of long-standing theoretical interest in reconnection physics. In addition, flux rope formation provides one mechanism to control the length of the electron layer by breaking the diffusion region into two current sheets as illustrated in Figure 9.7.

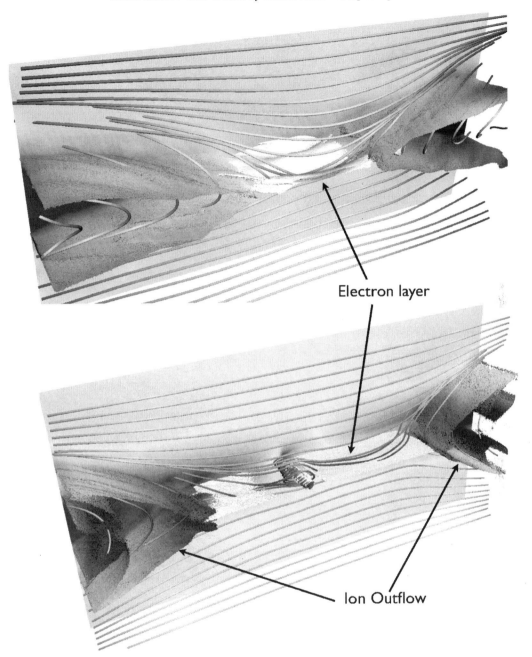

**FIGURE 9.7**: Open boundary simulations for neutral sheet geometry feature two types of secondary instabilities within the electron layer: an electromagnetic kink wave (top) and flux rope formation (bottom). The boundary conditions permit inflow of new plasma (the top and bottom) and outflow of reconnected plasmas (left and right). The outflow jets are visualized with a particle density isosurface colored by ion outflow velocity while the central electron current sheet corresponds to an isosurface of electron current density. Sample magnetic field lines are colored by the magnitude of the magnetic field. Simulation was performed with mass ration $m_i/m_e = 300$, using 4,096 ranks, 245 million cells, and 147 billion particles.

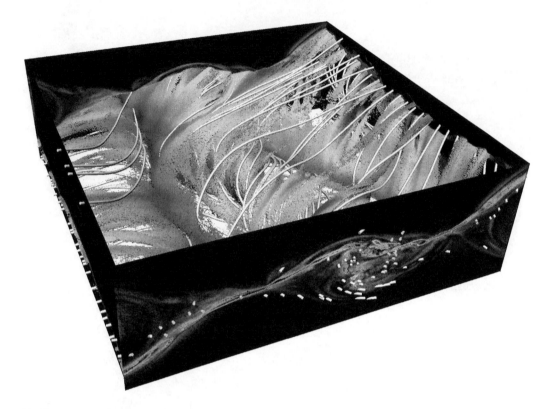

**FIGURE 9.8**: Open boundary simulations for guide field geometry feature highly elongated electron current layers that are unstable to flux rope formation over a wide range of angles. These plasma instabilities cause the sheets to break into filaments as illustrated by an isosurface of the current density colored by the plasma density. Some sample magnetic field lines are shown and cutting planes along the perimeter also show current density. This simulation was performed with a guide field equal to 50% of the reconnecting field, mass ratio $m_i/m_e = 64$, 2048 ranks, 360 million cells, and 72 billion particles.

The formation of flux ropes becomes significantly more complicated when a finite guide field is included in the initial conditions. In this limit, the magnetic field rotates across the layer but always remains finite. This type of initial condition is unstable to flux rope formation at oblique angles across the initial ion scale current sheet, leading to new electron scale current layers that are unstable to secondary flux ropes over a wider range of oblique angles. As illustrated in Figure 9.8, the current density forms intense filamentary structures leading to complicated magnetic field topologies. LANL scientists are presently working to understand how some of the main features in this complex evolution compare with predictions from kinetic theory and what role the flux rope interactions may play in the acceleration of highly energetic particles.

Magnetic reconnection is also of great interest in laboratory experiments, which offer the ability to study the structure and dynamics in a controlled setting. While there are good reasons to believe that the reconnection physics is similar in laboratory experiments, the plasma parameters and boundary conditions are quite different than in space. Three-dimensional kinetic simulations may serve as a bridge to help extrapolate ideas, which have been validated in the laboratory, to regimes of direct relevance to space and astrophysical plasmas.

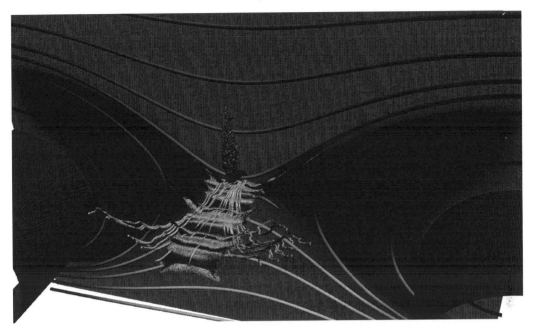

**FIGURE 9.9**: Simulations were performed on Roadrunner with geometry and boundary conditions relevant to the MRX experiment [YDK+08, DDR+08] including the influence of weak Coulomb collisions [DRA+09]. The reconnection process is driven by reducing the currents inside the flux cores (grey cylinders) which pulls magnetic flux inward toward the cores. The resulting ion flow velocity is illustrated on the back cutting plane along with characteristic magnetic field lines. The central electron current sheet is illustrated with an isosurface of the current density, colored by vertical component of the current density to show the plasma instability within the electron layer. Sample electron streamlines illustrate the electron flow from the upstream region through electron layer into the downstream region. This simulation was performed with mass ratio $m_i/m_e = 300$ using 2,880 ranks, 720 million cells and 144 billion particles.

The Magnetic Reconnection eXperiment (MRX) at the Princeton Plasma Physics Laboratory (PPPL) is one leading experiment that has reported detailed measurements of the diffusion region including the kinetic structure of the electron layer [RYJ+08]. In this experiment, magnetic reconnection is driven by reducing the current within two axi-symmetric flux cores. Weak binary Coulomb collisions are necessary to properly describe these plasmas, but the applicability of fluid models is questionable. The kinetic approach within the VPIC code includes experimental boundary conditions appropriate to MRX [DDR+08] and a Monte Carlo treatment of the collisions [DRA+09].

On Roadrunner, a series of simulations were performed to examine the influence of collisionality and plasma instabilities on the structure of the diffusion region. An example 3D simulation in Figure 9.9 illustrates an electromagnetic instability within the central electron scale current layer. This instability has certain similarities with the kink instability discussed in Figure 9.7, and it could potentially play a role in facilitating momentum exchange, or in broadening the electron layer.

Researchers at LANL are working with the scientists at PPPL to perform detailed comparisons with these new simulation results. These validation efforts will include the characteristic thickness and length of the electron layer as well as the observed electromagnetic wave spectra. Together with ongoing theoretical work, these efforts are expected to shed new light on the influence of plasma instabilities on magnetic reconnection.

### 9.3.3    New Frontiers in Viral Phylogenetics

Rapidly evolving viruses pose one of the major public health threats today. Among these, the Human Immunodeficiency Virus (HIV), the cause of the Acquired Immune Deficiency Syndrome (AIDS), is particularly devastating, infecting 33 million people with millions of AIDS-related deaths and new infections each year. Vaccines against such highly variable viruses have been unable to cope with the diversity of circulating strains. When a vaccine immunogen is presented to the human body, the elicited immune memory fails to recognize most other strains of the virus. This calls for both a thorough understanding of the adaptability of the virus in its war against the human host and an intelligent design of vaccines that would provide lasting immunity against the virus. Starting with the establishment of a central sequence repository for the virus, to establishing that the virus has been circulating in humans since the early part of the 20th century [KMT+00], LANL has been at the forefront of such theoretical biology research and has contributed substantially to the field. We also developed ideas of artificial immunogens that better capture the observed diversity of HIV strains than any natural strain can do [GTY+02, FPT+07]. While preliminary results on this research are sufficiently promising [BOS+10] to move to human trials, it is desirable to advance the field of vaccine design from such data-mining techniques to biological knowledge-based approaches.

The adaptive arm of the human immune system consists of three basic branches: the first is the Cytotoxic T Lymphocyte arm, which recognizes distinctive fragments of foreign proteins being manufactured in the body (i.e., viral proteins in infected cells) with very high specificity, the second is the Helper T Lymphocyte arm, which produces cytokines that orchestrate the immune response and have antiviral activity, and the third is the B-cell or antibody arm, which recognizes distinctive shapes on the surface of fully folded proteins.

Vast amounts of data on the interaction between HIV and all three arms of the human immune system are available, but the patterns of correlations are cryptic. Evolutionary systems are marked by long time scales, so that observed patterns in data can be due to correlations imposed by the initial historical emergence of a lineage of viruses, or founder effects, as well as due to biological interactions. In fact, not accounting for these effects leads to vastly erroneous statistical conclusions about the effect of the T-cell induced immunity on the evolution of the virus in populations [BDH+07]. But, whereas the sequence, that is the state of the virus, indeed depends on its evolutionary history, the changes that it undergoes are almost independent of changes in other lineages. Thus, true causal correlations are manifest also in correlations with these changes (see Figure 9.10), and in our work it was shown to detect effects that were validated experimentally. The separation of the two effects, i.e., a phylogenetic correction, thus needs access to these changes, and requires us to be able to statistically assess the genealogical relationships between the viruses and reconstruct the ancestral forms of the viruses.

Fortunately, evolution happens by the accumulation of random mutations, most of which are effectively neutral in that they do not much affect the fitness of the virus to live and infect its hosts. The covariation of these mutations, then, carries a signal of shared history. This can be used to construct a phylogenetic tree and evolutionary model that leads to random changes, and, simultaneously, the ancestral forms of the virus are also reconstructed statistically. But this reconstruction is technically challenging because the number of possible relationships grows factorially with the number of sequences sampled, and even heuristic searches fail to find reasonable models without extensive computations. For example, a vaccine needs to prepare the body for fighting an incoming virus that can establish

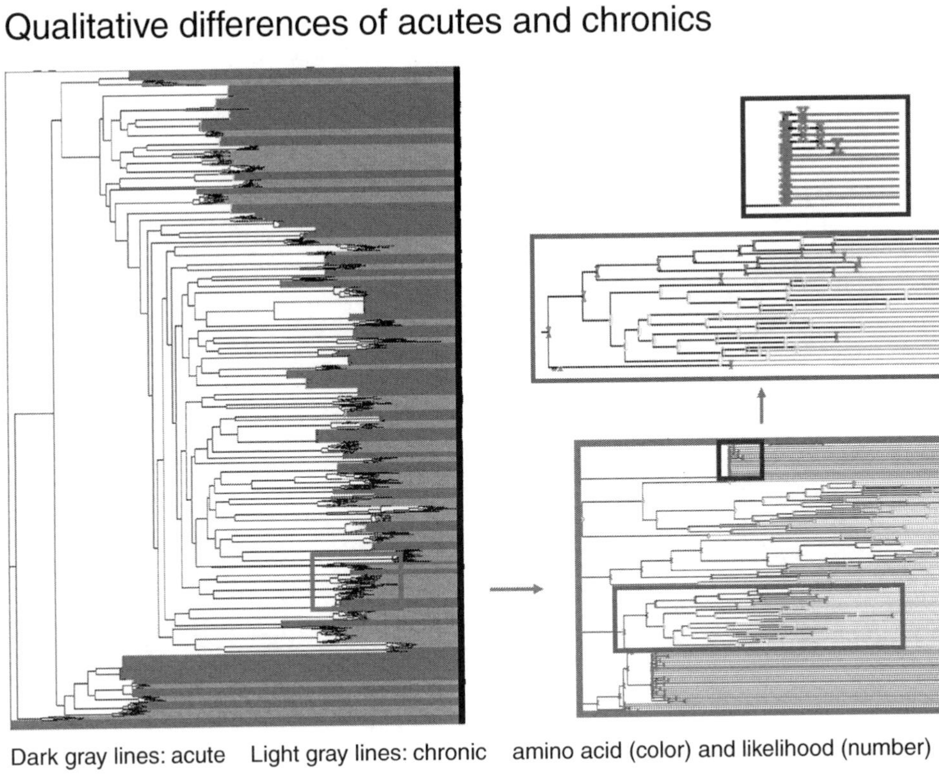

# Qualitative differences of acutes and chronics

Dark gray lines: acute    Light gray lines: chronic    amino acid (color) and likelihood (number)

**FIGURE 9.10**: Founder effects lead to entire clades sharing characteristics. If the sampling of the various clades is nonrandom, this leads to apparent correlations with traits of interest. True causal correlations, however, show up as correlations with changes (From [GBD+11]).

an infection in the healthy body. The virus that exists in a chronic patient, however, results from a long process of virus-host interaction and may be qualitatively different than the virus at the time of infection.

The characterization of these differences is a daunting task: the viral diversity in a chronic patient needs to be represented by at least three to four dozen sequences each, but to control for the phylogenetic effects, we need at least two to three hundred patients infected with various subtypes of the virus. This means that one needs to fit together some 10,000 HIV sequences into a giant family tree of HIV viruses, and find those patterns that distinguish acute and chronic viruses.

We had performed a preliminary study to look at only one subtype of the virus: the B subtype that is predominant in most of the developed world. What we found was that a particular site in the so-called signal peptide region of the precursor of the envelope glycoprotein, which coats the virus, was far more conserved in the early sequences than is expected by chance sampling. It was important to know whether this result is universal to all HIV strains, or specific to the B subtype. We therefore used Roadrunner to construct a phylogenetic tree of about 10,000 sequences from over 400 people (see Figure 9.11) and studied the variability of this site. In this much bigger tree, we did not find the site in the signal peptide region to be any less variable in the acute patients, and it is, therefore, likely that the signature we had found was subtype-specific.

We have since started analyzing data that directly measures the immunogenicity of

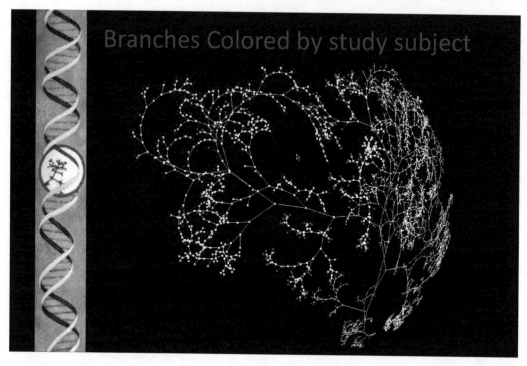

**FIGURE 9.11**: A phylogeny of about 10,000 HIV sequences colored by the study subject that was used to implement phylogenetic correction on the observed correlation between genotype and phenotype.

viruses by collecting antibody containing sera and viruses from the same patients. These sera are seen to cluster into groups with markedly different neutralization potencies [DRKM+09]. We then look at the sequences of viruses from the subset of patients who make potent sera that neutralize the activity of a vast panel of viruses, and compare them with those that make average or poor responses. Even though we did not know a priori whether the difference that we observe is due to host genetics, viral factors, or stochastic events, a preliminary analysis uncovered sites in the viral sequence where changes correlated with the induction of a good immune response. Interestingly, in a model structure, these sites clustered around the part known as the CD4 inducible region of the viral envelope that had long been suspected to be involved in the induction of beneficial antibodies. In the current analysis, however, we used a small number of sera; this analysis is being extended to a much larger panel.

Looking forward, technological advances are making it possible to get hundreds of thousands of sequences from each patient, providing a detailed view of the intrahost diversification in adaptation of the virus. Phylogenetic analysis of such datasets is still a challenge. More importantly, however, in current calculations we are looking only at the best possible phylogeny that we can resolve, and neglecting all the other possible phylogenies. To increase our confidence in the results, we will need to incorporate this phylogenetic *uncertainty*, and such calculations will stretch the limits of conventional computation even for a small number of sequences. The advent of petaflops-scale computing, exemplified by Roadrunner, is coming to the rescue, and in the near future we expect to see a fully detailed phylogenetic analysis of such problems with all sources of uncertainty correctly propagated to the final conclusion. Such computational techniques, complemented with our advance in experimental methods and theoretical understanding, we hope, will usher in a new era that finally stops this deadly epidemic.

### 9.3.4 Simulating the Mechanical Behavior of Metallic Nanowires over Experimentally Accessible Timescales

For many years now, we have witnessed explosive growth in our ability to control the structure of materials down to the atomic scale. For example, it is now possible to bring the tip of an atomic force microscope (which might be only a few atoms wide at the apex) in contact with a surface. In the case of a metal tip contacting a metal surface or another tip, a bonded contact forms, and if the tip is then lifted away from the surface, surface reorganization and diffusion often create a nanowire of metal that maintains a connection between the tip and surface. This process, as captured by high-resolution transmission electron microscopy (HRTEM), is shown in Figure 9.12 [Kiz98]. This kind of manipulation can be exploited for the intentional creation and study of nanowires, whose width can sometimes be reduced all the way down to a single atomic chain by continuing the retraction process.

These nanowires are an ideal probe of the nanoscale behavior of materials, be it mechanical [LZK05], or electrical [PMGH+95], and hence are of interest both for fundamental studies and because of their expected importance in various nanotechnology applications such as electrical conductors and electrical or mechanical switches. However, a deeper understanding of the fundamental nanoscale behavior of materials is required before these applications can become widespread. Indeed, experiments at the nanoscale are hard to control and sometimes lack the resolution necessary to fully understand how the systems behave. For example, metallic nanowires are often seen to completely disappear from one frame to another, leaving one completely in the dark about the basic mechanisms leading to their failure. Further, the act of imaging itself leads to an uncontrolled increase of the temperature of the wire, making it very difficult to perform these experiments under controlled and reproducible conditions.

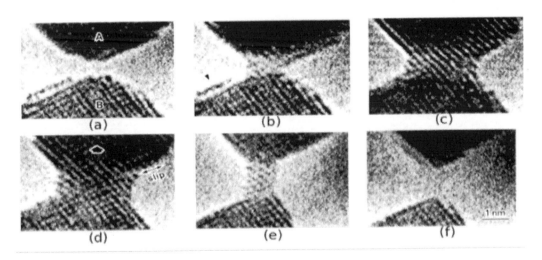

**FIGURE 9.12**: A series of high-resolution transmission electron microsope (HRTEM) images showing the contact formation - retraction - and rupture processes of two gold tips (a)-(c): contact formation process with (a) corresponding to $t = 0$ s, (b) $t = 3.7$ s, (c) $t = 4.3$ s, (d)-(f) retraction and rupture processes: (d) $t = 0$ s, (e) $t = 2$ s, (f) $t = 3$ s. [Kiz98]

There is thus a pressing need for atomistic numerical simulations to complement such experiments and help interpret and understand them. The most powerful tool for performing this kind of simulation is molecular dynamics (MD), whereby one integrates the equations of motion of all the atoms in the system, advancing the positions and velocities of the atoms by repeatedly taking small steps forward in time. In this way, one learns about the evolution of the system with full atomistic detail. However, for many systems and processes we would like to study, there is a serious problem with the mismatch in time scale. For example, the nanowire-stretching process discussed above usually takes place over seconds or, at the very fastest, milliseconds. In contrast, conventional MD simulations are limited to a time scale of about one microsecond, even on the fastest parallel computers, i.e., $10^3$ to $10^7$ times faster than the experimental reality. Because of this extremely large gap, physical arguments suggest that current simulations do not adequately represent reality.

The way to overcome these limitations is to use so-called Accelerated Molecular Dynamics (AMD) methods to reformulate the problem in a form that is more amenable to computer simulation. For example, the Parallel Replica Dynamics (ParRep) [Vot98] method developed at LANL generates a proper evolution of the system while allowing a parallelization of the problem in the time-domain. This allows one to make optimal use of massively parallel computers to reach time scales that are orders of magnitude longer that what could be done with conventional MD. When implemented on petascale supercomputers like Roadrunner, the ParRep method enables one to study the evolution of nanoscale systems (containing about a thousand atoms or so) over unprecedented time scales. Using 12,000 replicas on 12,000 out of the 12,240 Roadrunner Cell chips we obtained a simulation rate of about 0.1 ms per wall-clock hour, thereby allowing a direct connection between experiments and fully atomistic simulations.

Using ParRep on Roadrunner, we simulated silver nanowire stretching experiments similar to those illustrated in Figure 9.13 for different nanowire sizes, temperatures, and retrac-

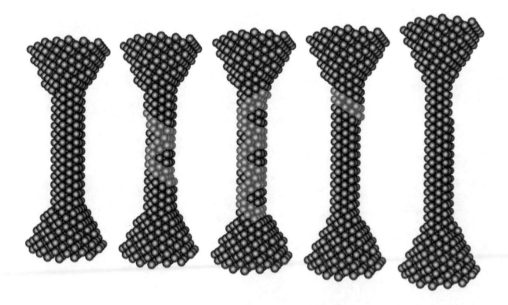

**FIGURE 9.13**: Early stage of a ParRep simulation of the stretching of a silver nanowire on Roadrunner at a temperature of 300 K and a retraction velocity of $10^{-5}m/s$. From left to right, $t = 0\mu s$, $t = 30\mu s$, $t = 60\mu s$, $t = 90\mu s$, $t = 150\mu s$. Defective sections of the wire are shown in lighter-colored atoms.

tion velocity, reaching more than one millisecond of simulation time in a few instances, more than a thousand times longer than conventional techniques would have allowed. Overall, we were able to study the change of behavior of these wires while varying the strain rate by more than four orders of magnitude, a feat that was unthinkable before the advent of Roadrunner.

Thanks to these simulations, a picture of the evolution of these systems is emerging. The basic plastic reaction of the system when subjected to strain is to create stacking faults along (111) planes. These stacking faults are highlighted in Figure 9.13. The formation of a zig-zag network of such stacking faults causes the release of internal stresses while leading to the elongation and narrowing of the wire. Interestingly, all wires, almost independently of temperature or strain rate, initially behave this way. As the wire is stretched further, given enough time, these stacking faults annihilate, leaving behind a defect-free wire that is uniformly thinned down relative to the initial configuration. These simulations illustrate the unique ability of these nanostructures to, under suitable conditions, heal themselves when subjected to severe external constraints. Note that this self-healing behavior emerges only on long time scales that are completely inaccessible to standard MD simulations.

The later stages of the simulation of the evolution of nanowires also revealed some completely unintuitive mechanisms by which plastic deformation occurs at the nanoscale. Shown in Figure 9.14, one of these mechanisms is the conversion of bulk-like segments of the wire into low-symmetry helical structures (here a fivefold-symmetric icosahedral structure). These structures appear to be extremely tolerant of mechanical constraints. Indeed, the conversion process between two relatively stable conformations offers a continuous pathway for the stretching to occur, in contrast with competing mechanisms that lead to the

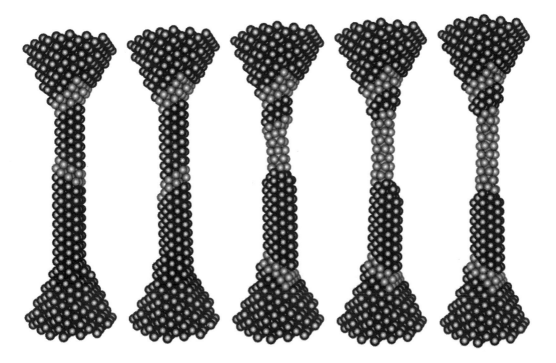

**FIGURE 9.14**: Late stage of a ParRep simulation of the stretching of a silver nanowire on Roadrunner at a temperature of 300K and a retraction velocity of $10^{-5}m/s$. From left to right, $t = 165\mu s, t = 180\mu s, t = 195\mu s, t = 210\mu s, t = 225\mu s$. Defective sections of the wire are shown in lighter-colored atoms.

accumulation of defects and ultimately to failure. Through this pathway, we have observed elongations in excess of 100% without failure. Once again this process, involving structures that are not allowed by the symmetry of the bulk crystal, demonstrates the unique ability of nanoscale systems to react to their environment in completely unintuitive ways.

The conjunction of innovative algorithms and methods with the unprecedented computational power of Roadrunner enabled us to simulate, for the first time, the mechanical behavior of metallic nanowires, which are widely foreseen as playing a major role in the next generation of nanodevices, on experimentally accessible time scales. With this new capability, it is now possible to directly assist in the interpretation of experiments as well as in the design of novel structures with precisely tailored properties.

### 9.3.5    Material Dynamics at Extreme Conditions

Dynamic loading, such as high-speed sliding friction or shock impact, can dramatically affect the microstructure and properties of materials on ultrafast time scales that are difficult, if not impossible, to probe experimentally. Because sound waves travel at a few km/s, or equivalently a few nm/ps, through a typical metal, they traverse the sub-nanometer interatomic lattice spacing in much less than a picosecond(ps). While experimentally challenging, processes occuring at such nm length and ps time scales are ideal for study by non-equilibrium MD simulations.

Over the past decade, large-scale MD simulations have provided significant insight into the microscopic pathways and kinetics of shock-induced plasticity and phase transformations in single-crystal metals. Sample sizes of a few million atoms are typically sufficient; representing a cube of material with edge lengths 10-100 nm, this can capture the emergent length scale (average spacing between dislocations or product phase nuclei). Such simulations first suggested that the polymorphic (bcc-hcp) transformation in shocked iron can take place on ps time scales [KGLH02]. The predicted orientation relationship, time scale, and product grain size were all subsequently confirmed by ultrafast in situ X-ray diffraction measurements on laser-shocked iron thin foils [KBC+05]. With advanced 21st century experimental facilities such as the Linac Coherent Light Source (LCLS) at Stanford, the National Ignition Facility (NIF) at LLNL, and the Matter-Radiation Interactions in Extreme Environments (MaRIE) at LANL becoming available in the next decade, we anticipate such simulation-led experiments will provide insight into even more complicated dynamic materials phenomena occurring at nm-$\mu$m length and ps-$\mu$s time scales.

The SPaSM code was originally developed in the early 1990s for the newly emerging era of massively parallel supercomputers such as the Thinking Machines CM-5, and achieved IEEE Gordon Bell Prize-winning performance by minimizing memory usage and floating-point operations. However, for the modern generation of heterogeneous, multicore architectures such as Roadrunner, it is data movement rather than storage or arithmetic operations that is increasingly the bottleneck. Thus, we have redesigned the entire communication infrastructure and data structures of SPaSM to allow for asynchronous interactions between the processors, in particular to accommodate the Cell processor and the unique multilayer hierarchy of Roadrunner's architecture. This effort has paid off, resulting in double-precision benchmark performance of 369 teraflop/s on the full machine [GKS09], and a ~5x speedup for the embedded atom method (EAM) potentials typically used to model simple metals such as copper, silver, and iron.

Using the SPaSM code on Roadrunner, we are investigating the ejection of material that can occur from shocked surfaces [GDH+09]. The goal of this work is to develop models that can predict the amount of mass ejected from a shocked interface with a given surface finish and loading history (peak shock pressure, either from a supported square-wave or explosive-driven Taylor wave). We would also like to understand how that mass is distributed, namely

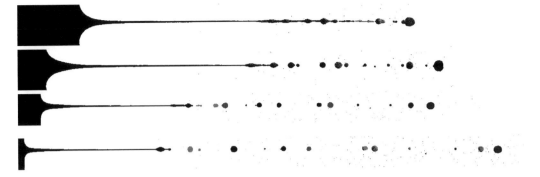

**FIGURE 9.15**: Ejecta particle formation by fragmentation of an expanding jet produced when a shock wave reaches a copper-free surface with a sinusoidal profile.

its particle size and velocity distributions, as well as evolutions and correlations, if any, between the two. Experimentally, the total mass can be inferred by measuring the resulting momentum transfer onto an Asay foil or piezoelectric probe at some standoff distance, while particle sizes larger than a micron can be imaged using holography or X-ray radiography. However, there is no direct experimental information on the distribution of particle sizes smaller than a micron, nor on the correlation between size and velocity distributions.

On such microscopic scales, MD simulations can complement experiments by providing unique insight into the material dynamics at submicron length and subnanosecond time scales, including key fragmentation and atomization mechanisms, but until now this problem had remained computationally intractable. The formation and transport of ejecta involves a complex range of physical processes, including Richtmyer-Meshkov instability (RMI) development in solid materials with dynamic material strength properties, classical and turbulent fragmentation and atomization, and particulate transport in a turbulent gas. We have carried out a systematic study of RMI development from a single sinusoidal surface perturbation in copper to test various RMI theories including material strength effects, which suppress the instability growth. We are using these simulations to study the evolution of the density and velocity distributions of the ejected mass, the modes of particle breakup, and ultimately to develop source theories of ejecta formation based on RMI growth, including material strength effects and transport models that describe the time-evolving particle size and velocity distributions. Earlier MD simulations were able to demonstrate the initial jet formation but could not reach time scales long enough to observe the subsequent necking instabilities leading to jet breakup and droplet formation that have now been revealed (Figure 9.15). These fragmentation and atomization processes are also difficult to study experimentally, although various theories have been proposed; atomistic-level simulations such as those presented here are contributing to the development of physics-based models at LANL.

Ejecta is only one form of shock-induced material failure, occurring when a shock wave reflects from a free surface to become an expanding rarefaction (or release) fan. When two such rarefaction fans (one from the impactor free surface, the other from the target) intersect in the interior of the material, they put the material into tension and can lead to spall failure [LGT09]. Ductile spall failure results from the nucleation, growth, and coalescence of voids. Models have been developed that account for each of these aspects, but without direct experimental information-due again to the ultra-fast time and ultra-small length scales.

Using Roadrunner, we have been able to study this process in copper bicrystals, revealing the competition between heterogeneous void nucleation at defects such as grain boundaries

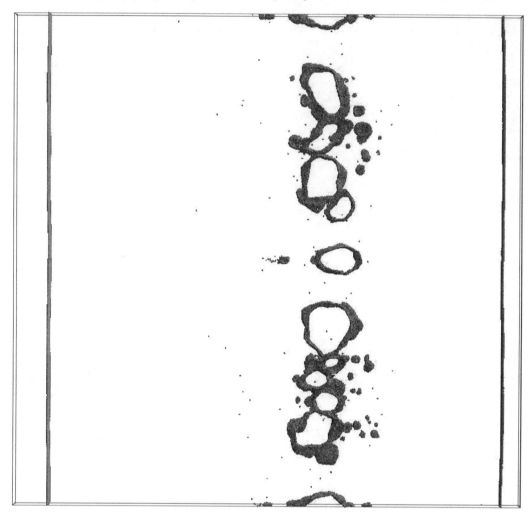

**FIGURE 9.16**: Incipient spall failure in a copper bicyrstal (shocked left-to-right) by homogeneous void nucleation along the (vertical) plane of maximum tensile stress. Only undercoordinated surface atoms are shown, so that one sees the free surfaces of the impactor and target and the voids which have begun to nucleate, grow, and coalesce. The (horizontal) grain boundaries, one in the center of the sample, and the other at the top/bottom periodic boundary, remain intact and are not visible.

and homogeneous nucleation within the bulk single crystal. Large system sizes are required to clearly separate the two processes, and long time scales to explore a wide range of strain rates. Figure 9.16 shows a copper bicrystal loaded parallel to the horizontal grain boundaries (one in the center and the other at the top/bottom periodic boundary), with 400 m/s impact velocity. The sample is 230 nm tall (i.e., each grain is 115 nm), 20 nm thick (into the plane, i.e., images are looking through the entire 20 nm thickness), and 205 nm long (54 million atoms in all). Following shock compression and release, dislocations and voids are produced that leave the sample in an incipient spall state; that is, with a number of voids that remain intact after growing and coalescing, but that have not caused complete fragmentation. In this example, the short sample length leads to a very high strain rate, with voids primarily nucleated homogeneously (within the grains) along the vertical plane of maximum tensile stress. On the other hand, a longer sample length (1 $\mu$m, 270 million atoms) leads to a lower strain rate and sufficient time for void nucleation to be localized at the grain boundaries, changing the failure mode from a vertical spall plane to a horizontal grain decohesion (Figure 9.17). These results indicate the interplay between grain size and the time scale for nucleation kinetics, with a competition between heterogeneous and homogeneous nucleation.

The materials science community is extremely excited about the discovery opportunities now presenting themselves with the Roadrunner-class petascale computers. In particular, we are starting to study polycrystalline materials with realistic grain sizes and interface structures at the relevant time and length scales. In addition, our redesign of the SPaSM code for Roadrunner enables us to optimize performance on the new generation of hybrid supercomputers with many-core nodes and/or GPU accelerators.

## 9.3.6 Direct Numerical Simulation of Reacting Compressible Turbulence

Although important progress has been made in recent years in our understanding of turbulence, complete quantification, description, prediction, simulation, and control still elude us. The problem is due in part to the very large range of spatiotemporal, dynamically relevant scales, but also to the multitude of problems that can be encompassed by the generic term "turbulence." If "ideal" turbulence is in a homogeneous, isotropic Kolmogorov steady state, then "nonideal" turbulence can occur due to many practically relevant effects: time-dependence, anisotropy, inhomogeneity, coupling with active scalars, shock waves, exothermic reactions, etc. Unlike kinetic theory, where significant departure from a weakly perturbed local Maxwellian is exceptional, the analogous state of nonideal turbulence is what is typical, yet the only successful turbulence theory so far is Kolmogorov's 1941 theory. It is then not surprising that the turbulence theory is still centered on the ideas of Kolmogorov related to the existence of inertial range dynamics (e.g., a -5/3 range in the isotropic turbulence energy spectrum) and small-scale universality. However, more and more evidence points to departures from universal laws in the energy spectrum due to

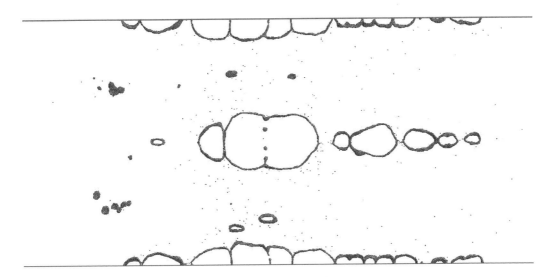

**FIGURE 9.17**: Incipient spall failure in a copper bicrystal by heterogeneous void nucleation along the (horizontal) grain boundaries.

intermittency and a direct connection between the small and the (nonuniversal) large scales, especially in the presence of strong gradients [LM04] or buoyancy [LR07, LR08, LRG+09].

Most of the turbulence research to date has been concentrated on several canonical flows with periodic boundaries or simple jets, wakes, or boundary layers. Numerous modeling strategies have been proposed, and, while there is no "best" strategy, each of the approaches has its own advantages and domains of applicability. Yet, most practical flows are not canonical. In many situations they are driven by acceleration, as in ICF or cosmic explosions, and may undergo exothermic reactions. In addition, radiation could have a significant effect, for example through heat gain or loss. For these complex flows, the limitations of the current modeling strategies, as well as the turbulence and mixing properties, are unknown.

Turbulence theory and the subsequent model development rely on experimental or high-resolution direct numerical simulation (DNS) data for development and verification and validation. This technique has emerged as a powerful research tool to study the physics of turbulence, for verifying and improving models, and for complementing and even guiding and helping the design of better experiments [MM98]. The DNS technique seeks "exact" solutions of the governing equations, so that all relevant scales are accurately solved, using high-resolution numerical simulations based on high-order accurate discretization algorithms. DNS relies on nondissipative high-accuracy schemes and is conducted without resort to subgrid modeling or the introduction of "artificial" numerical dissipation or other algorithm-stabilizing schemes. Such computations allow a degree of control in isolating specific physical phenomena that are typically inaccessible in experiments. With the recent advances in supercomputing technology and algorithms, it is now possible to perform simulations of simple flows at ranges of scales comparable or even larger than in typical laboratory experiments. Petascale computing is expected to further increase the range of scales of the simulations and allow accurate calculations of more and more complex flows.

This study represents the first successful implementation of a large structured fluid dynamics code (CFDNS) on the Cell processor architecture. The CFDNS code solves the compressible and incompressible Navier-Stokes equations in 3D using high-order compact finite differences or Fourier transforms in the periodic directions. Multiple species are allowed, each with realistic material properties equation of state (EOS), as well as Cartesian, cylindrical, and spherical grid geometries. The serial single processor speedup of the Cell version of the code is approximately 30x faster than the reference Opteron version, which is reasonable when considering the clock speed, parallelism, and vectorization afforded by the Cell. Notably, the excellent performance of the individual memory controllers is responsible for this, since the low arithmetic intensity of the algorithm does not allow the actual compute power of the SPEs to be utilized to their fullest. This serial speedup prompted us to perform significant modifications to the parallel code design, which lead to overall speedup in the range of 20x compared with the Opteron-only version [MYLK09b, MYLK09a].

The model problem addressed by the study is the flame-turbulence interaction under the complex conditions characterizing the early stages of a type Ia supernova. These conditions are novel and have no direct analogue on Earth. This makes them interesting for testing new physics, but it also means that our terrestrial intuition regarding flames can be misleading. For example, it is thought that laboratory flames in the $Ka \gg 1$ regime simply go out because they are unable to maintain their heat in the presence of so much turbulence. But the flame in a supernova can never "go out" until the star comes apart and, in terms of local flame variables, that takes a very long time. Although several mechanisms for detonation have been proposed, the debate around deflagration/detonation models is still not settled. Moreover, most turbulent flame simulations so far, under these conditions, are in the low Mach number approximation and no DNS have been performed for such flows.

Using the Roadrunner supercomputer, researchers have performed the largest reacting compressible turbulence simulations to date. The flow conditions considered for the reacting

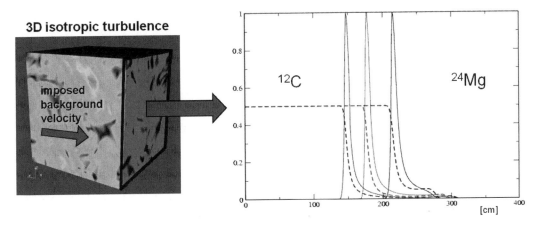

**FIGURE 9.18**: Schematic of the reacting turbulence simulations. The figure on the right shows the $^{12}C$ mass fraction and nuclear energy generation rate profiles through a laminar flame propagating to the left in a $C - O$ mixture. The fuel temperature and density are $6 \times 10^8\ K$ and $10^{10}\ kg/m^3$, respectively. The nuclear energy generation rate has been normalized to a peak value of 1.

simulations correspond to "well-stirred" single component burning, $^{12}C(^{12}C,\gamma)^{24}Mg$, relevant to Type Ia supernovae. The flame advances into the cold fuel ($^{12}C$) in a C–O mixture and leaves behind hot product ($^{24}Mg$). Inflow/outflow boundary conditions are imposed in the flame propagation direction. The physical transport properties are appropriate for the astrophysical situation investigated and are calculated within new modules added to the code. Thus, the thermal transport includes both radiative and electron transport (accounting for degenerate regimes) contributions. The equation of state considers radiative, ion, and electron contributions. To reduce the computational effort, precalculated tables for the transport properties, EOS, and nuclear energy rates are used.

The simulations were performed in three stages (Figure 9.18):

1. Generate 1D reacting flow profiles as initial conditions.
2. Generate inflow turbulence by performing triply periodic simulations with a background velocity matching the flame speed [PL10].
3. Simulate flame-turbulence interaction under supernova conditions.

To better study the flame characteristics, the reference frame was chosen such that the flame was stationary in the computational domain. The $3D$ reacting flow simulations were initialized using the 1D profiles and isotropic turbulence was introduced through the inflow boundary. To understand the effects of various parameters, most notably Da (Damkholer) and Ka (Karlovitz) numbers, as well as the effect of compressibility, several simulations were performed, on up to 20,483 meshes.

There is a complicated phenomenology associated with turbulent flames under type Ia supernova conditions, from the suppression of the smallest vortex tubes due to the flame "fire polishing," but enhancement of intermediate turbulent scales (Figure 9.18), to the rapid acceleration of the flame itself to large velocities, which is one of the important open questions related to the supernova modeling. In addition, the fully compressible simulations allowed considering the dynamics of the dilatational motions, neglected in previous studies. These motions are enhanced by the heat addition due to the flame and can cause shock waves that may lead to detonation (Figure 9.19). Current research focuses on the departures

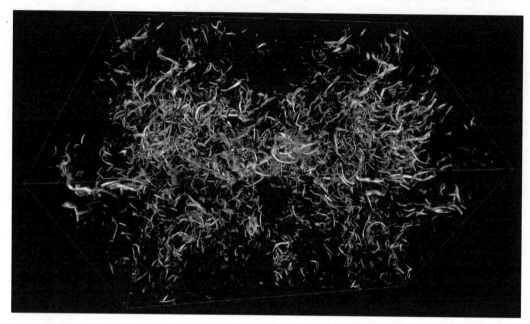

**FIGURE 9.19**: Entropy field in reacting compressible turbulence shows the rich phenomenology of the flame turbulence interaction. Across the flame, "fire polishing" damps the smallest turbulence scale; however, some of the vortex tubes are enhanced through baroclinic vorticity generation.

of the turbulence properties from the classical Kolmogorov picture and determining accurate turbulent flame speeds.

### 9.3.7 The Roadrunner Universe Project: Baryon Acoustic Oscillations in the Intergalactic Medium

Over the last two decades, critical observational advances in large-volume sky surveys carried out over a wide range of wavelengths, as well as over short time cadences, have revolutionized cosmology. Computational cosmology has emerged as an essential resource for providing detailed predictions for these observations, for providing essential data for assisting in the design of cosmological surveys, and as sophisticated tools for interpreting the final results.

Results from cosmological surveys have cemented a cross-validated cosmological "Standard Model" presenting a comprehensive picture of the evolutionary history of the Universe and its constituents: 1) its content is dominated by 23% in dark matter, which only interacts gravitationally (and a large fraction of which is localized in clumps called halos), and 72% in a smooth "dark energy" component described by a cosmological constant; 2) the initial conditions of the Universe are prescribed by adiabatic Gaussian random initial density fluctuations; and 3) the spatial geometry of the Universe is flat [KDJ+09]. Although this is a great triumph, it has exposed some of the biggest puzzles in physical science:

- What is dark matter?
- Why is the expansion of the Universe accelerating?
- Does general relativity need to be modified?
- What is the origin of primordial fluctuations?

To investigate these questions, the observational state of the art is rapidly advancing; surveys now coming on line and within the next decade represent an improvement in capability by roughly two orders of magnitude, translating into a determination of certain cosmological parameters at the 1% level. Remarkable as this is, the effort will only come to fruition if the accuracy of the underlying theory can be controlled to the sub-percent level. This severely demanding task will push the boundaries of computing for the foreseeable future.

Structure formation in the Universe is driven primarily by gravitational instability. Initial density perturbations collapse and merge in a hierarchical fashion to form dark matter halos within a global "cosmic web" structure (Figure 9.20). On scales smaller than several Mpc (megaparsec; 1 parsec=3.26 light-years), baryonic matter collects in halos, eventually forming stars and galaxies. The collisionless evolution of matter subject only to gravity is described by the Vlasov-Poisson equation in an expanding Universe, which can be solved in detail only by N-body techniques. Next-generation surveys demand simulations with multiGpc (gigaparsec) box-sizes and particle counts in the $10^{11-12}$ range, all with ~kpc force resolution (a force dynamic range of $10^6$). An overall 2–3 orders of magnitude improvement in throughput over the current state of the art turns out to be the minimal requirement.

To meet the challenge of next-generation simulations, the Roadrunner Universe project

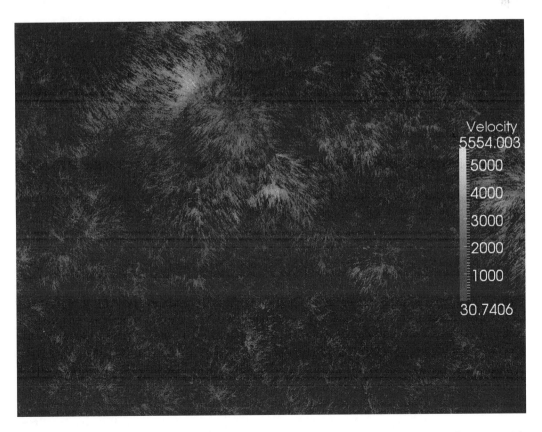

**FIGURE 9.20**: Dark matter halos from one of the large Roadrunner simulations, with 1/64 of the total $(750 \text{ Mpc}/h)^3$ volume displayed. The halos are shown as arrows, colored with respect to their velocity magnitude. This particular simulation was run with 64 billion particles, where each simulation particle has a mass of approximately one billion suns. The snapshot is taken at a redshift of $z = 2.5$.

code MC$^3$ (Mesh-based Cosmology Code on the Cell) splits the interparticle force problem into two parts, a medium resolution solver based on Fast Fourier Transforms (FFT) augmented by a direct particle-particle short-range solver. The biggest FFT provides up to four orders of magnitude of dynamic range, the remaining factor of 10-100 coming from the short-range force evaluations carried out on the Cell processors. The MC$^3$ algorithms match to the machine architecture, minimizing data transfer through the narrow communication pipe between the Opterons and the Cell. The global philosophy is to explicitly sacrifice memory and in-place computation to minimize communication and simplify communication patterns. Our approach has two key aspects:

1. Reduction of particle communication across the Cell layer using particle overloading, a mirrored particle cache.
2. Application of digital filtering and differencing in the spectral domain, allowing simplified computations at the Cell layer [PHL$^+$10].

The RRU runs on Roadrunner consisting of nine ultra-large simulations to study the imprint of oscillations in the baryon-photon plasma in the early universe, the baryon acoustic oscillations (BAO). Due to BAO, a distinct, but subtle, signature is imprinted on the large-scale distribution of matter and has been seen in the spatial statistics of the distribution of galaxies [EZH$^+$05], confirming one of the most important predictions of modern cosmology. BAO has now become one of the premier methods for determining cosmological distances and hence the expansion history of the Universe.

Traditional galaxy-based BAO surveys require a heavy investment in telescope time, especially as one goes to higher redshifts. Fortunately, there exist tracers of the mass distribution other than galaxies. Neutral hydrogen in the intergalactic medium (IGM) furnishes one such example. At redshifts of $z \cong$ 2-3, the gas making up the IGM is thought to be in photoionization equilibrium, which results in a tight density-temperature relation, with the neutral hydrogen density proportional to a power of the baryon density [Mei09]. Since pressure forces are sub-dominant, the neutral hydrogen density closely traces the total matter density on large scales. The neutral hydrogen density can be probed by obtaining spectra of distant, bright compact sources, the quasars, and studying the celebrated "Lyman–$\alpha$ forest" of absorption lines which map the neutral hydrogen along the line of sight to the quasar. The structure in quasar absorption thus traces, in a calculable way, slight fluctuations in the matter density of the Universe back along the line-of-sight to the quasar, with most of the Lyman–$\alpha$ forest arising from over-densities of a few times the mean density.

The upcoming Baryon Oscillation Spectroscopic Survey (BOSS) [SWE09] will provide an unprecedented number of quasar spectra for Lyman–$\alpha$ studies, motivating a major simulation effort at understanding the BAO imprint in the IGM. The set of Roadrunner simulations [WPC$^+$10] are the first to simultaneously resolve structure down to the Jeans scale of the gas (~100 kpc) as well as properly capture the acoustic scale (~100 Mpc). Using the results of the simulations (the density and velocity fields), mock quasar spectra were constructed by running lines of sight from quasar "sources" to an "observer." These spectra have properties close to those observed at $z \cong$ 2-3. Because these mock spectra will be very useful in testing observational data pipelines, calibrating analysis tools, and in planning future projects, they have been made publicly available.

Given the quasar spectra derived from the simulations, one can compute the flux-flux correlation function, which is related to the underlying nonlinear, redshift-space, mass correlation function. The characteristic BAO "bump" signal in the flux correlation function as measured from our simulations is shown in Figure 9.21. Although our total simulation volume is large (nine $750h^{-1}$ Mpc boxes,) covering effectively 1000 sq. deg. of sky, it is still only 10% of the area planned for BOSS. Thus the fractional errors in the flux correlation function as achieved by BOSS should be a factor of three better than in our simulations.

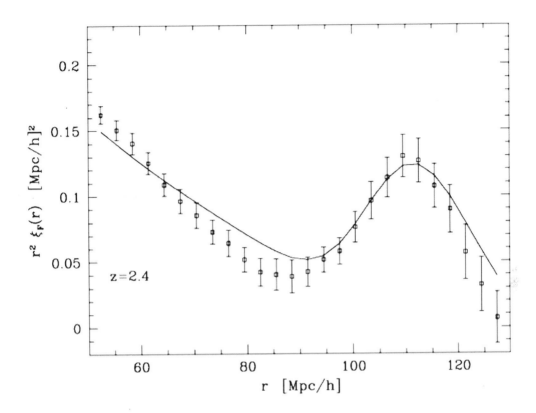

**FIGURE 9.21**: The redshift space flux correlation function, $\zeta_F$, as a function of the co-moving distance, $r$, measured in $Mpc/h$. The BAO feature is the "bump" centered around $110h^{-1}Mpc$. The error bars are derived from a bootstrap analysis. The solid line is a Gaussian-smoothed linear theory result multiplied by a scale-independent bias to match the simulations.

Once detailed simulations are available, several important effects can be studied, including key sources of systematic errors and bias in the observations. We carried out preliminary investigations of an evolving mean flux, fluctuations in the photoionization rate, and HeII reionization, which generate "extra" power on the acoustic scale and reduce the contrast of the acoustic peak. Gravitational instability produces a well-defined pattern of higher-order correlations, which is not obeyed by nongravitational contributions such as the above, allowing (in principle) a diagnostic of nongravitational physics in the forest. As an example, we demonstrated that the three-point cross-correlation function in models with HeII reionization has a different scale dependence than the three-point function in gravity-only simulations, regardless of the equation-of-state assumed in the latter.

As one part of the Roadrunner Universe project, future BAO simulations will be run with much larger boxes for an improved treatment of planned surveys. Additionally, the quasars will not be randomly placed in the simulation box but will follow the appropriate statistical occupation distribution for being hosted by dark matter halos.

## Contributors

This chapter contains the work of a number of authors in addition to the primary author. Andrew B. White, Kenneth R. Koch, Jamal Mohd-Yusof, and Sriram Swaminarayan of LANL contributed to Section 9.1. Section 9.3.1 represents the work of Lin Yin, Brian J. Albright, Benjamin K. Bergen, and Kevin J. Bowers of LANL. Section 9.3.2 represents the work of William Daughton, Vadim Roytershteyn, Lin Yin, Brian J. Albright, Benjamin K. Bergen, and Kevin J. Bowers of LANL. Section 9.3.3 represents the work of Tanmoy Bhattacharya, Marcus Daniels, and Bette Korber of Los Alamos. Section 9.3.4 represents the work of Danny Perez, Sriram Swaminarayan, and Arthur F. Voter of LANL, and Chun-Wei Pao of Academin Sinica, Taiwan. Section 9.3.5 represents the work of Timothy C. Germann, Sheng-Nian Luo, and Sriram Swaminarayan of LANL. Section 9.3.6 represents the work of Daniel Livescu, Jamaludin Mohd-Yusof, and Timothy M. Kelley of LANL. Section 9.3.7 represents the work of Salman Habib, Adrian Pope, and Katrin Heitmann of Argonne National Laboratory, David J. Daniel, Patricia Fasel, Chung-Hsing Hsu, and James Ahrens of LANL, Zarija Lukic of LBNL, Martin White and Jordan Carlson of University of California, Berkeley, and Nehal Desai of Aerospace Corporation.

The author would also like to thank Katherine Pallis, Sharon R. Mikkelson, and Susanne D. King of LANL for painstakingly proofreading this chapter.

# Chapter 10

## Blue Gene/Q: Sequoia and Mira

Anna Maria Bailey, Adam Bertsch, Barna Bihari, Brian Carnes, Kimberly Cupps, Erik W. Draeger, Larry Fried, Mark Gary, James N. Glosli, John C. Gyllenhaal, Steven Langer, Rose McCallen, Arthur A. Mirin, Fady Najjar, Albert Nichols, Terri Quinn, David Richards, Tom Spelce, Becky Springmeyer, Fred Streitz, Bronis de Supinski, and Pavlos Vranas

*Lawrence Livermore National Laboratory*

Dong Chen, George L.T. Chiu, Paul W. Coteus, Thomas W. Fox, Thomas Gooding, John A. Gunnels, Ruud A. Haring, Philip Heidelberger, Todd Inglett, Kyu-hyoun Kim, Amith R. Mamidala, Sam Miller, Mike Nelson, Martin Ohmacht, Fabrizio Petrini, Kyung Dong Ryu, Andrew A. Schram, Robert Shearer, Robert E. Walkup, Amy Wang, and Robert W. Wisniewski

*International Business Machines Corporation*

William E. Allcock, Charles Bacon, Raymond Bair, Ramesh Balakrishnan, Richard Coffey, Susan Coghlan, Jeff Hammond, Mark Hereld, Kalyan Kumaran, Paul Messina, Vitali Morozov, Michael E. Papka, Katherine M. Riley, Nichols A. Romero, and Timothy J. Williams

*Argonne National Laboratory*

## 10.1   Overview

The IBM® Blue Gene®/Q (BG/Q) supercomputer system was developed in partnership between IBM, the Argonne National Laboratory, and the Lawrence Livermore National Laboratory. It is funded by the National Nuclear Security Agency (NNSA) at LLNL and the DOE Office of Science at ANL. Its purpose is to serve a very broad spectrum of the nation's needs through numerical simulation. From maintaining and modernizing the nation's nuclear weapons capability, to developing new energy sources from nuclear fusion, to the design of the next generation of safe and efficient nuclear energy plants, to serving needs of the U.S. industry, to enabling medical and technological breakthroughs, and to serving basic science research, the Blue Gene/Q system is now ready to deliver. Its software and application base is already in place and growing, as are the delivered and operational hardware racks.

For NNSA and LLNL programs, a modern, responsive weapons complex demands a balanced and predictive simulation infrastructure to support Uncertainty Quantification

(UQ) and reduction in phenomenology (i.e., replacing calibrated models with physics-based models). To accomplish this effectively requires performance 12 to 24 times the delivered performance of design codes on ASC Purple (a 100 Teraflop/s IBM® POWER5™ system) and 20 times improvement over ASC Blue Gene/L (BG/L) for underlying materials studies. These performance measures have characterized the requirements for the Sequoia system.

BG/Q is the third supercomputer developed by this partnership during the past ten years. Its predecessors, Blue Gene/L and Blue Gene/P, have been widely successful and have resulted in a wealth of supercomputing awards including the National Medal of Technology and Innovation in 2009 by President Obama [nr09]. The BG/Q node is already on the top of the Green500 list as the most energy efficient node used in HPC. BG/Q was designed to reach 10 PetaFlops capability at the ANL Mira system and 20 PetaFlops capability at the LLNL Sequoia system in 2012 and it is on schedule to do so. BG/Q brings many innovations over the previous generations, including 16 cores per node, multithreaded cores, a 5-dimensional torus interconnect, water cooling, and optical fiber links. The system was designed for optimal power efficiency, reliability, and price-performance. The 20 PetaFlops system will have a staggering 1.6 million processor cores with a total possible of 102 million hardware threads all operating simultaneously without fail. This type of parallelism dictates new directions in supercomputing and enters a new regime of the possible physical systems that can be simulated numerically.

Blue Gene/Q is a bright example of the United States Department of Energy and IBM's capability and seamlessly brings together science and technology and the people that make this possible. This chapter is organized as follows: In Section 10.1 an outline of the sponsor, program, and timeline background is given. In Section 10.2 an overview and selected applications are presented. In Section 10.4 the benchmarks that were used for design and evaluation are described. In Section 10.5 the BG/Q hardware from chip to system is reviewed. In Section 10.6 the software system is described. In Section 10.7 the programming system is reviewed. Storage Visualization and Analytics is presented in Section 10.8. The facilities infrastructure is given in Section 10.9. The expected system statistics are described in Section 10.10. In Section 10.11 we describe one of the interesting features of BG/Q, the transactional memory hardware.

### 10.1.1 Sequoia Sponsor and Program Background

The National Nuclear Security Agency (NNSA) Defense Programs set forth the goal of transforming the nuclear weapons complex into a responsive, modern infrastructure while continuing to address needs in the existing stockpile. As weapons age and move further from the test base, the assessment of these weapon systems relies heavily on science understanding and the ability to extrapolate weapon performance using predictive capabilities. NNSA's Advanced Simulation and Computing (ASC) computational resources are essential to enable nuclear weapon scientists to fulfill stockpile stewardship requirements through simulation science in lieu of underground testing. The realism and accuracy of ASC simulations must increase through development of improved physics models and methods, which require greater computational resources. Problems at the highest end of this computational spectrum have been, and will continue to be, a principal driver for the ASC Program as highly predictive codes are developed.

"Predictive simulation" is the simulation of the performance of a nuclear weapon with quantified, useful uncertainties—the caveat being that these uncertainties are small enough to contribute to certification of devices without resorting to new underground tests. To quantify uncertainties and to predict with confidence, the ASC Program requires new computing resources to support uncertainty quantification (UQ) and reduction in phenomenology (that is, elimination of code "knobs," which are tunable parameters that calibrate the codes to tests but also mask a lack of understanding of the underlying physical processes). Predictive simulation depends on advances in the fidelity of physics, the accuracy of numerical methods, and the ASC Program's ability to assess uncertainty. In turn, these are dependent on the level of computing that can be brought to bear. For example, errors associated with numerical approximations may mask physical phenomena and shortcomings in physical models; and basic to the need for adequate numerical representations is sufficient computing power.

For these reasons, NNSA authorized and funded a UQ-focused computing system, named Sequoia, to be delivered to Lawrence Livermore National Laboratory in 2012. Sequoia will provide 12 to 24 times the sustained performance of ASC Purple (the IBM POWER5 based system sited in 2006) on integrated design code calculations and 20 times the sustained performance of ASC Blue Gene/L (IBM's first Blue Gene system, sited in 2005) on a weapons science materials calculation of importance to the Program. The fundamental benefits from successful implementation of Sequoia are agile design and responsive certification infrastructure, increased accuracy in material property data, improved models for understood physical processes that are known to be important, fulfilled programmatic requirements for uncovering missing physics, and improved performance of complex models and algorithms in integrated design codes within a framework of quantified uncertainty. All of these are necessary to achieve predictive simulation in support of nuclear weapons complex transformation.

### 10.1.2    Mira Sponsor and Program Background

The 2007 interim report of the landmark Department of Energy (DOE) Office of Science report "Facilities for the Future of Science Twenty-Year Outlook" ranked the nation's UltraScale Scientific Computing Capability among its highest domestic priorities. Earlier, starting in 2004, the Office of Science began to add dramatically to the supercomputing capabilities in the DOE National Laboratory complex, leading the way in developing the nation's supercomputing capabilities to enable researchers to model and simulate experiments that could never be performed in a laboratory and for U.S. industry to perform "virtual prototyping" of complex systems and products. Scientists and researchers are using the Office of Science's high-speed computational resources to understand combustion processes, model fusion reactions, analyze climate change data, reveal chemical mechanisms of catalysts, study the collapse of a supernova, and build better airplanes, among scores of other applications.

There are several large problems in DOE mission areas that can be advanced on today's systems, but whose major breakthroughs will be greatly accelerated on petascale systems and beyond. These areas are: astrophysics, biomass to biofuels, chemical catalysts, climate change science, economics of energy alternatives, efficient chemical separations, energy production and storage, fusion energy, nuclear energy, and phenotype from genotype. The upgrade of the Argonne Leadership Computing Facility (ALCF) to at least ten petaflops by the 2012 timeframe is vital to advances in those domains as well as to the nation's ability to retain its leading role in several important international programs, including the Intergovernmental Panel on Climate Change, the International Thermonuclear Experimental Reactor, and the Nuclear Energy Advanced Modeling and Simulation program. Moreover, the U.S. is facing serious economic, environmental, and national security challenges based on its dependence on fossil fuels. To address the scientific grand challenges identified by Office of Science programs alone would require a computing capability of at least 100 petaflops by 2015. The Mira Blue Gene/Q will provide a major advance toward meeting those needs.

ALCF's mission is to provide the computational science community with leadership class computing resources dedicated to breakthrough science and engineering. Consequently, these systems must support a workload that is primarily comprised of many very large jobs. The current ALCF system, Intrepid, a 557 teraflops Blue Gene/P, supports over 25 science applications whose simulations run on 124K or more cores. Mira's workload will include even larger simulations. These application codes frequently use most or all of the cores in the system, often involve intense communications among the nodes, and can generate massive I/O loads. Therefore, the system must have an interconnection network with low latency even for jobs that use the entire configuration; it must be sufficiently reliable that most long-running jobs will not be affected by system failures; its I/O speed and capacity must be high at the hardware level; and the filesystem must have high performance. In addition, the system software must also be able to support such a workload with high efficiency, and the software tools must be capable of processing and handling such demands. In summary, to fulfill its mission, the ALCF requires a system that was designed and implemented for leadership scientific computing applications. Mira is such a system, due in large part to the insights gained through years of partnership on the Blue Gene family among Argonne, Lawrence Livermore, and IBM.

### 10.1.3 Timeline

The IBM®Blue Gene®/L supercomputer debuted in November 2004, followed by the second generation three years later. Indeed, the second and third generations, called Blue Gene®/P and Blue Gene®/Q, respectively, were conceived before Blue Gene/L was formally announced. In August 2004, IBM, Lawrence Livermore National Laboratory, and Argonne National Laboratory formed an alliance. Together the three parties decided to develop two generations of HPC (High Performance Computing) platforms consecutively, with a single Blue Gene/PQ contract. The Blue Gene/Q project started to receive focus in late 2006 once the IBM Research team could finish up its efforts on Blue Gene/P. Thanks to the Blue Gene/PQ contract, which spanned across two generations, the transition was uninterrupted.

The historical trend of the Top500 lists [TOP11] indicates that HPC systems are advancing almost 2× in FLOPS (floating point operations per second) per year whereas the underlying silicon technology is progressing at 2× every two years. Thus, many innovations must be sought over and above the integration level of silicon technology. From 2007 to 2010, an intense joint effort in chip, packaging, and software research and development was undertaken by IBM Research in Yorktown Heights, NY, and IBM Systems and Technology Group in Rochester, MN. Highlights of this development are reflected in the major differences between Blue Gene/P and Blue Gene/Q: the processor core count jumped from 4 to 16, the processor cores became multithreaded, the network architecture expanded from a three-dimensional to a five-dimensional torus, water cooling was introduced inside the racks, the efficiency of power supplies was increased, and we introduced optical links between midplanes.

For Blue Gene/L, IBM used 130nm ASIC technology. Evolutionally, the Blue Gene/P system used 90nm ASIC technology. For the Blue Gene/Q Compute chips, described in Section 10.5.3, we skipped the 65nm generation and used 45nm technology.

The production phase of the Sequoia program began with the tape-out of the DD2.0 Compute chip in the fourth quarter of 2010. During the second and third quarters of 2011, prototype production racks were built and tested with early system software. It was determined that this revision of the Compute chip, along with the DD1.0 Link chip, was good to go for full production. The first production racks built by a qualified manufacturing process arrived in 4Q11 and entered System Test. Based on the positive results, IBM shipped the first Test and Development $1/2$-rack to LLNL in December 2011. The first 4 of 96 Sequoia racks were also shipped in December 2011, with the majority of the remaining racks shipping in the first quarter of 2012.

With the deployment of Sequoia in Livermore, and the Mira 48-rack system in Argonne, Blue Gene/Q began to accumulate its trophies. Among the early ones are:

- Green500 #1 November 2010 to June 2012, four times consecutively [GRE11].

- Graph500 #1 November 2011 to November 2012, three times consecutively [GRA11].

IBM is both proud and pleased to see the Blue Gene platform enabling its users to blossom in their respective application fields.

## 10.2    Sequoia Applications

### 10.2.1    Applications Overview

The NNSA ASC Program roadmap defines a path to predictive capability for the next decade while maintaining a constant emphasis on current mission deliverables. Its four focus areas are to address national security simulation needs, establish a validated predictive capability for physical phenomena, quantify and aggregate the uncertainties of simulation tools, and provide mission-responsive computational environments to meet stockpile stewardship needs. Production computing regimes (drivers) that were needed to meet these requirements included:

- Providing agile design and responsible certification infrastructure

- Creating increasingly accurate material property data

- Improving models for known physical processes that are recognized to be important

- Meeting programmatic requirements for uncovering missing physics

- Addressing security and surety concerns

- Improving performance of complex models and algorithms in integrated design codes

Scientists using Sequoia will guard the integrity of present predictions and guarantee their improvement into the future by focusing on Uncertainty Quantification (UQ) and calculations that lead to elimination of knobs through better understanding of underlying physics. To highlight the expected impact of Sequoia, a few selected examples from the six drivers are described below. This list is not exhaustive; rather, it is representative and intended to motivate intuition and a sense of the challenge.

Creating increasingly accurate material property data by investigating equation of state, melt curve, phase change, strength, and fracture properties using quantum and classical molecular dynamics, dislocation dynamics, and structural mechanics codes all have been demonstrated to scale effectively on Blue Gene/L and are also expected to scale well on Sequoia. These calculations are required to support integrated design codes through improved multi-phase data tables and sub-grid-scale models, essential for enhanced predictivity. The increased memory of Sequoia will allow a factor of 100 times increase in complexity (with between a factor of 20 to 40 speedup) over that captured by Blue Gene/L in materials studies. At the 50-billion-atom level, scientists demonstrated on Blue Gene/L that it was possible to capture the entire response of an evolving structure without any simplifying assumptions. [GRC$^+$07]. Alternatively, with Sequoia, scientists will be able to validate atomic-scale phenomena over macroscopic time scales. A million-time-step simulation could complete in a month or less on Sequoia. This is important as steady-state response in real materials can take from one nanosecond to one microsecond to develop, and these simulations represent an important step toward establishing validated predictivity.

Improving models for important physical processes, for example, high-explosive (HE) burn and turbulent mix, have been proposed. Both development efforts require significantly more data to better understand the physics. Nuclear tests and simulation are the only ways to generate needed data for an improved mix model; however, simulation creates data for the HE burn model much more easily and safely than experiments. These efforts will require quantum and classical molecular dynamics, structural mechanics, and high-accuracy hydrodynamics simulation codes. Improving turbulence models will require Sequoia-class resolution in addition to a significant number of smaller calculations. The HE models will be incorporated into the integrated design codes to meet NNSA goals.

Meeting programmatic mandates for uncovering missing physics is a major driver, from the perspective of both the magnitude of the calculations required and the importance of this work to transformation reflected in the ASC Roadmap and the rapidly evolving Predictive Capability Framework (PCF). The Roadmap and the PCF both describe the ultimate removal of the knobs (that is, the tunable parameters in the integrated design codes that calibrate the codes to tests but also mask a lack of understanding of the underlying physical processes). This lack of understanding can be serious if the intent is to certify, using simulation, a weapon whose characteristics, either from initial design intent or from aging, vary significantly from test-base neighbors. Via successful execution of the PCF, the complex will evolve from the ASC Program's current initial operational capabilities, to near-term objectives to meet initial capabilities for stockpile transformation and benchmarked predictive capabilities for the legacy stockpile. The ASC Program strives to deliver predictive capabilities for extrapolation and fulfill evolving requirements and emerging threats. In the future, the capabilities will be integrated for a responsive infrastructure.

Addressing security and surety concerns involving nuclear weapons has been made obvious by changes in the DOE's Design Basis Threat over the last few years. Empirical evaluation via testing of this new class of concerns has proved both costly and time-consuming. In addition, testing only partially reveals insights into the totality of the physics associated with this class of concerns. Performing credible, predictive vulnerability assessments through numerical simulation is essential for understanding consequences, quantifying risk, and determining effective mitigation strategies for a wide range of terrorist-delivered threats. Analytical results are urgently needed to address security/surety concerns throughout the entire lifecycle of fielded nuclear weapons, including manufacturing, transport, storage, staging, deployment, and dismantlement.

An emerging category of critical use is focused on uncertainties. While UQ is not separately listed as one of the six drivers, it is central to all of them. Prediction with certainty is no more than simulating with quantified and sufficiently small uncertainties. To significantly reduce uncertainty of simulated predictions, scientists will extend sensitivity analysis on Sequoia in the following significant ways: increase the number of parameters in the sensitivity analysis, increase from standard resolution to high resolution in 2D, move from 2D to 3D with standard resolution, and increase from a single system to a suite of over 20 systems in 2D with standard resolution. The critical importance of UQ for all of the mission elements stems from its ability to provide confidence. Uncertainties that are accurately quantified can be risk managed. Unquantified uncertainties create gaps in confidence that put NNSA's highest level certification responsibilities at risk, and increases the likelihood that serious, unforeseen problems will arise.

**TABLE 10.1**: Sequoia applications showcase.

| Application | Language | | | Parallelism | | | Application Characteristics |
|---|---|---|---|---|---|---|---|
| Code | F | C | C++ | MPI | OpenMP | Threads | |
| National Security Apps | ✓ | ✓ | ✓ | ✓ | | | Hydrodynamics, structural mechanics, multiphase fluid dynamics, heat transfer, chemistry, and electromagnetics Arbitrary Lagrange Eulerian, hybrid finite element + volume, unstructured grid with slide and open/closed contact |
| Laser Plasma pF3D | | ✓ | | ✓ | ✓ | | Paraxial wave optics, non-linear coupling between light and plasma waves, 2D FFT, 3D Cartesian grid |
| ddcMD | | ✓ | | ✓ | ✓ | | Classical MD with EAM, MGPT, Yukawa, Coulomb + quantum statistical potentials, particle-particle, particle-mesh, link cells, neighbor lists |
| Lattice Particle Physics | | ✓ | ✓ | ✓ | ✓ | ✓ | Beyond standard model, QCD thermodynamics, QCD Nuclear Physics, hybrid molecular dynamics, conjugate gradient, 4-dimensional regular torus grid |
| Qbox | | | ✓ | ✓ | ✓ | | Pseudopotential, plane wave Density Functional Theory (DFT), 3D FFT, dense linear algebra) |
| Cardioid | | ✓ | ✓ | ✓ | ✓ | ✓ | Cardiac electrophysiology simulation, 3D regular grid, finite volume, explicit Euler, fast communication and synchronization using SPI and L2 atomics |

Below we showcase six Sequoia applications with their main characteristics given in Table 10.1.

## 10.2.2    National Security Applications on Sequoia

ALE3D is a multi-physics numerical simulation software tool utilizing arbitrary Lagrangian-Eulerian (ALE) techniques. The code is written to address two-dimensional (2D) and three-dimensional (3D) physics and engineering problems using a hybrid finite element and finite volume formulation on an unstructured grid. The ALE and mesh relaxation capability broadens the scope of applications in comparison to tools restricted to Lagrangian-only or Eulerian-only approaches, while maintaining accuracy and efficiency for large, multi-physics and complex geometry simulations. Beyond its foundation as a hydrodynamics and structures code, ALE3D has multi-physics capabilities that integrate various packages through an operator-splitting approach (Figure 10.1). The flexible and extensible code framework supports additional fully-integrated features including heat conduction, chemical kinetics and species diffusion, incompressible flow, a wide range of material models, chemistry models, multi-phase flow, and magneto-hydrodynamics with mesh generation, visualization, and other code linkages. Also unique to ALE3D is the fully coupled explicit and implicit time integration allowing the evaluation of long (implicit) to short (explicit) time scale applications.

DOE, DHS, DoD facilities, and DoD contractors are utilizing ALE3D for a variety of

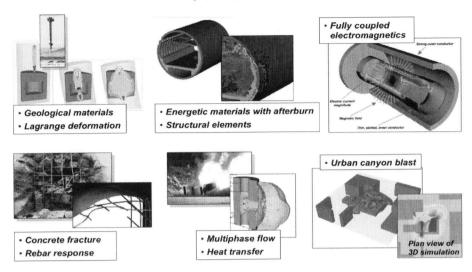

**FIGURE 10.1**: ALE3D is a single code that integrates many physical phenomena.

applications including the design of effective and insensitive munitions, evaluation of threats to structures, vehicles and personnel, and the design of useful and useable armor against blast and impact loads. ALE3D is supported by DOE Advanced Simulation and Computing (ASC) program, the DOE/DoD Office of the Secretary of Defense Joint Munitions Program, DoD HPC Institutes, and other DOE, DoD, and DHS national security programs.

Through our agile design and ability to scale to large simulations, scientists and engineers using Sequoia will directly simulate phenomena utilizing full 3D physics models, rather than empirical or experimentally calibrated model approximations. An example application is the critical need to accurately predict the conditions and physics drivers for shock initiation of high-explosives (HE). Solid plastic-bonded HE materials consist of crystals whose size typically ranges between 10 and 100 microns with micron-sized embedded impurities and air bubbles. These voids increase the ease of shock initiation by generating high-temperature regions during their collapse and these high-temperature regions can lead to ignition of the HE material. Understanding the mechanisms of hot-spot initiation in HE materials is of importance due to safety, reliability, and development of new insensitive munitions.

A computational study using ALE3D is being pursued to investigate the mechanisms of air bubble collapse and hot spot initiation in insensitive high-explosive (IHE). The current focus is on non-reactive dynamics to isolate the thermal and hydrodynamics effects. Three-dimensional (3D) high-resolution simulations are performed on systems with Sequoia's computational power to evaluate the parallel performance and gain insight on the 3D dynamics of pore collapse. The configuration investigated corresponds to a 3D pore collapse of a spherical air bubble in IHE in support of the ASC Grain-Scale Simulation Modeling effort (Figure 10.2). Several mesh resolutions are considered with 250M and 500M zones for over 30,000 BG/P processors.

### 10.2.3 Laser Plasma Interaction on Sequoia

The National Ignition Facility (hereafter NIF; [MBR+09]) is a large NNSA experimental facility that houses the world's most powerful laser. One of the key goals of the NIF is to compress a target filled with deuterium and tritium to a temperature and density high enough that fusion ignition occurs. The laser beams ionize the target and heat the resulting

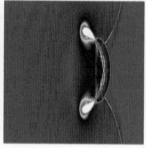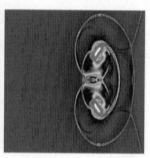

**FIGURE 10.2**: Numerical Schlieren (magnitude of density gradient) contours at three representative time instances, showcasing the pore collapse dynamics for 2 mm-diameter and 25-GPa shock. From left to right (a) pore front wall being pushed toward pore back wall; (b) pore collapsing and changing from a spherical shape to a torus; (c) pore collapsed, rotating and advecting in IHE and hot spots are seen to form in its vicinity.

plasma to a few tens of millions of degrees. The laser intensity is high enough that laser-driven plasma instabilities may backscatter some of the laser light.

pF3D ([BSWL98]) is a multi-physics code used to simulate interactions between laser beams and the plasma in NIF experiments. pF3D is used to evaluate proposed target designs and pick the ones with acceptably low levels of backscatter.

NIF experiments have shown that laser-plasma interactions occur in regions where multiple beams overlap. Our goal on Sequoia is to simulate the interaction of 5 beams over 3.5 mm of plasma. We estimate that this simulation will require one trillion zones and use roughly 300 TB of memory. This simulation can fit in roughly one fifth of Sequoia, but we hope to use half or more of the nodes to reduce the time required to complete the simulation.

pF3D uses spectral methods to simulate refraction, diffraction, and coupling between the laser beam and waves in the plasma. As a result, pF3D spends a significant amount of time passing messages as groups of processes carry out 2D FFTs. One of the key performance optimizations on Sequoia will be finding a way to place processes on the 5D torus so that they maximize the utilization of all 10 links on a node while keeping hop counts low.

Most pF3D simulations have been run in pure MPI mode. We believe that running in hybrid MPI/OpenMP mode will be a better choice on Sequoia. Using fewer processes will allow us to send larger messages and thus obtain higher message bandwidth. Work on adding OpenMP to pF3D has been under way for over two years.

The parallel filesystem on Sequoia should be fast enough that we can use application directed checkpoints to magnetic disk as a fault tolerance strategy. We also plan to investigate the use of SCR ([MBMdS10]). We can afford to checkpoint to RAM disk much more often than we can checkpoint to magnetic disk. When a system problem forces us to restart, we will have a much more recent checkpoint and will lose much less work due to the error.

### 10.2.4    ddcMD on Sequoia

ddcMD is a classical Molecular Dynamics code with the capability to simulate both condensed matter and high-energy plasmas. It has been used to investigate the kinetics of phase transitions, atomic scale formation of fluid instabilities, formation of defects under material deformation, ion-electron temperature equilibration, and stopping power in dense plasmas.

ddcMD computes particle interactions using Model Generalized Pseudo-potential Theory (MGPT), the Embedded Atom Method (EAM), as well as the Coulomb and Yukawa potentials for charged particles. Simulations using these potentials achieve efficiencies of up to 30% of peak. Communication between nodes is minimized by using a flexible particle-based domain decomposition. Each MPI rank is given a center point and particles are assigned to the rank in whose Voronoi volume they reside. Domain centers can be chosen to minimize the surface to volume ratio of the domains. As particles are evolved in time and diffuse out of the Voronoi volume of a given rank, they are not immediately reassigned to new ranks. This allows ddcMD to amortize the cost of computing communication lists by re-using them for many time steps.

ddcMD also serves as a test bed and demonstration platform for large-scale parallel programming and application design techniques. Highly tuned force kernels are an obvious necessity for high efficiency, but obtaining maximum performance requires a host of other optimizations such as scalable parallel I/O, application assisted fault tolerance, dynamic load balance, and heterogeneous decomposition.

When the number of MPI ranks in a parallel job reaches 100,000 or more it becomes obvious that the commonly used file per task I/O model is not scalable. The opposite approach, writing all data from all tasks in a single file, can serialize I/O also leading to poor performance. ddcMD was among the first application codes to demonstrate a solution to this problem using an I/O model that is a compromise between the two extremes. Each task in a ddcMD job is a member of an I/O group that typically contains 50–200 tasks. Each group nominates a single member as the I/O master responsible for all file I/O. Other group members exchange data with the group master using standard MPI point-to-point messages. On Blue Gene, I/O masters are chosen to ensure only one master per I/O node. This model allows ddcMD to perform I/O at rates that frequently approach the peak bandwidth of the filesystem.

On BG/L, ddcMD was used to demonstrate application assisted fault tolerance. The L1 cache on BG/L can detect, but not correct parity errors due to bit flips. On a system with over 200,000 cores L1 parity errors occur roughly every five hours. Operating in "write-through" mode ensures a clean copy of any corrupted data can always be found, but the performance cost is typically 20–30%. ddcMD preserves high performance despite faulty hardware by registering an interrupt handler that catches the parity error and triggers a rollback to a previously stored known-good configuration. The overhead of periodically storing such configurations is less than 1% in a typical run—a clear win compared to the alternative.

The flexible domain decomposition employed in ddcMD allows a simple approach to dynamic load balancing. Domain center positions are arbitrary so it is possible to manipulate the load on any task by changing the position of its domain center relative to its surroundings. Shrinking the Voronoi volume of a domain leads to a corresponding reduction in computational load. By adjusting domain centers in response to in-situ measurements load imbalances due to under-performing nodes (due for example to large numbers of correctable DRAM errors) can be automatically eliminated.

ddcMD has also been used to showcase the advantages of breaking free from the single program, multiple data (SPMD) organization commonly used in parallel applications. In simulations with charged particles, ddcMD uses the standard particle-particle particle-mesh (PPPM) method to compute the long-ranged coulomb potential. Because the PPPM method employs 3D Fast Fourier Transforms (FFTs) that require global communication, it presents a scalability challenge. To conquer this problem for large-scale runs, ddcMD divides the compute nodes into two pools: one for computing particle pair interactions and the other for computing FFTs. This so-called heterogeneous decomposition restricts the FFTs to only 5–10% of the compute nodes. The resulting alteration of communication patterns allows ddcMD to efficiently simulate charged particles at scales much larger than other MD codes which use more conventional approaches.

## 10.2.5    Lattice Particle Physics on Sequoia

Quantum Chromodynamics (QCD) is the theory of the strong nuclear force that is responsible for binding nucleons together to form the atomic nuclei of all elements in our world. QCD is responsible for almost all of the visible matter in the Universe and is the first-principles theory that describes a wide range of nuclear phenomena from light element fusion to fission. QCD is now very well established experimentally and the Nobel Prize for its discovery was awarded in 2004 [GPW04].

Nuclear particles such as neutrons and protons are not fundamental. Instead they are made up from smaller particles that are tightly bound together inside called quarks and gluons. The force that binds them is very strong and it increases linearly with distance so that one cannot separate a single quark out of a nuclear particle. The energy to do so is so high that it excites the vacuum and generates additional quarks that bind with it to form new nucleons. This property is called confinement. On the other hand, inside the nucleons, quarks move essentially free—a property called asymptotic freedom. At very high temperatures, 250,000 times larger than our sun's interior, nuclear matter "melts" into a quark-gluon plasma. This state of matter is believed to have existed a few microseconds after the Big Bang and has been recently reproduced in the Relativistic Heavy Ion Collider (RHIC). These are remarkable properties and QCD has been termed "our most beautiful physical theory" [Wil00].

QCD belongs to a larger class of theories that share this property of strong force dynamics that results in confinement and asymptotic freedom. These types of theories, sometimes referred to as Technicolor, can explain the origins of mass and they predict that a new force of nature and a wealth of strongly bound composite particles must be present at energies beyond what is currently known. These theories are prime candidates for explaining the experimental results currently being produced at these very high energies at the Large Hadron Collider (LHC) [CER12]. It is remarkable that some of these predicted particles are also prime candidates for making up Dark Matter. Dark Matter makes up about 83% of all matter in the Universe. We know it is there because it dramatically affects the galactic shapes through the force of gravity. However, it has no direct electromagnetic or strong nuclear interactions. This makes it invisible and virtually undetectable by us, although about a billion of Dark Matter particles are going through our bodies every second. As LHC continues to probe nature during the next several years it will point to the true theory.

But, in order to understand QCD and this larger class of strongly interacting theories, we need to be able to calculate the predictions they make and compare to experiment. Because of the strong interactions, these theories can only be simulated numerically using the most powerful supercomputers available. The numerical simulations are performed using a discretized 4-dimensional grid of space-time points called the Lattice. For the Blue Gene machines this grid is directly mapped onto the node grid of the nearest neighbor torus network. This is optimal because the typical communication pattern is nearest neighbor. At the same time, it is incredibly demanding because the Flop to data access ratio of the application is about one and it exposes all hardware latencies both in the memory system and the network. Because the application kernel is small (a few thousand lines), it is typically coded directly in assembly and low level SPI.

This effort results in high performance kernel execution (in the range of 20% to 30%). Because the kernel consumes more than 90% of cycles this directly results in very good time to solution properties. The application exhibits linear speedup with the number of nodes up to the full machine size and has won the Gordon Bell award twice; in 2006 for QCD on BG/L

[ea06] and in 1998 for QCD on the QCDSP supercomputer [ea98]. The QCDSP machine was built by a group of physicists at Columbia University in order to study QCD. This machine directly led to the design of the QCDOC by Columbia University and IBM, and, subsequently, to BG/L, BG/P, and BG/Q. The lineage of BG/Q is directly rooted to QCD, and some of the main architects and designers of these machines are also practitioners of LQCD. LQCD has served well both as a hardware and software guide in this line of machines.

### 10.2.6 Qbox on Sequoia

In computational materials science, it is often desirable to be able to compute the properties of a given system directly from first principles, without the need for experimental data or variational parameters. The Qbox code[Gyg08], a highly scalable first-principles molecular dynamics (FPMD) code developed at Lawrence Livermore National Laboratory and in collaboration with the University of California, Davis, is one such tool. The FPMD approach combines a quantum mechanical representation of electrons with a classical description of atomic nuclei. The electronic term is solved within the Density Functional Theory formalism to reduce the exponential complexity of the many-body Schrodinger equation to a more tractable $\mathcal{O}(N^3)$ scaling, where $N$ is the total number of electrons.

In general, the computational cost of FPMD is high, limiting most calculations to tens or hundreds of atoms. Periodic boundary conditions enable precise simulation of homogeneous or highly symmetric systems with a relatively small number of atoms, but many systems of interest require longer length scales. Due to the inherently nonlocal nature of quantum mechanics, it is not possible to do a simple domain decomposition to distribute work in parallel, and thus FPMD codes have to be carefully designed to avoid communication bottlenecks. Qbox uses a plane wave basis to represent electronic orbitals, and maps the problem onto one of dense linear algebra on a two-dimensional process grid. Terms in the Kohn-Sham equations are computed in either real or reciprocal space, requiring frequent 3D Fourier transforms. Constraints on orthogonality and orbital occupation require additional global dense linear algebra operations throughout the calculation.

Qbox has demonstrated excellent scalability and floating point efficiency, achieving 56.4% of peak performance on 131,072 cores of the LLNL Blue Gene/L system simulating a system of 1,000 molybdenum atoms (12,000 electrons)[GDS+05, GDS+06]. In addition to using well-optimized single-node kernels such as fast Fourier transforms and matrix multiplication to fully exploit the underlying hardware, it was found that mapping MPI tasks onto the physical compute nodes so as to optimize bandwidth and latency for the specific pattern of subcommunicators within the code was critical to achieving good strong scaling and parallel efficiency. It is expected that similar awareness of machine topology will continue to be important as hardware becomes larger and more inhomogeneous, and the ratio of compute to communication resources continues to grow.

### 10.2.7 Cardioid Heart Simulation on Sequoia

A team of scientists from Lawrence Livermore National Laboratory and IBM has developed a cardiac electrophysiology model designed to simulate the human heart in near-real time at realistic spatial resolution (0.1 mm) on the Sequoia machine. Compared to the current state-of-the-art, this represents a 15-fold increase in spatial degrees of freedom and a 100-fold increase in the length of time that can be simulated. Having this capability will better enable understanding of the detailed mechanisms that lead to sudden cardiac arrest and simulating drugs designed to counter arrhythmia.

We solve a reaction-diffusion equation for the cell membrane potential, where the reaction term [tTP06] models effects of ion currents on the cell potential, and the diffusion term models the traversal of the activation wave across the heart tissue. The reaction module utilizes source code from a medical software repository. A local linearization enables analytic integration of ordinary differential equations over a time step. The diffusion equation solver uses a finite-volume approach. The code is validated using an internationally accepted intercomparison benchmark.

We construct a Cartesian grid based on actual human heart data, taking fiber orientation into account. The computational domain is restricted to those grid cells that contain heart tissue. We apply a scalable 3-D domain decomposition and assign Message Passing Interface (MPI) tasks to subdomains in a one-to-one fashion. The diffusion term requires nearest-neighbor communication in each direction. We apply threading within a subdomain, using four (hardware) threads per core, for a total of 64 threads per MPI task.

Our optimization balances reaction, diffusion, and communication with a flexible scheme to distribute threads between the reaction and diffusion phases, and we overlap communication with computation. The SIMD units are applied to all phases of the discretization. We initialize threads at the start of the calculation and invoke a specialized fast barrier call for thread synchronization.

We approximate reaction terms having exponentials with Pade approximates of specified tolerance, and store the Pade coefficients in registers. The reaction phase is maintained largely within L1 cache. Most of the reaction terms use a functional decomposition for hardware threading; the remaining terms apply hardware threads to groups of grid cells. Unrolling of loops provides additional speedup. The diffusion equation in its natural form has an unfavorable ratio of memory references to arithmetic operations, so we rearrange the computation to mitigate that.

We find that MPI communication has an unacceptably large latency. This is exacerbated by the fact that our messages are relatively short. We therefore apply low-level primitives (SPI) to the nearest-neighbor communications and achieve a 20-fold reduction in communication time; this is at the cost of SPI being tedious to program. We also map the domain decomposition to the Sequoia network topology to further optimize performance.

Our initial application is to investigate the effects of a drug designed to be anti-arrhythmic but later shown to paradoxically increase arrhythmia. We compute ECG information that can be compared with actual human data. As this document goes to press, we are applying the optimizations and performing initial testing on BG/Q. We expect to report results by mid-2012 [tTP06].

## 10.3   Mira Applications

### 10.3.1   Applications Overview

The Mira workload will consist of applications from a broad spectrum of domains and utilizing essentially all the algorithms that are found in scientific and engineering codes. Projects are awarded time on Mira based on peer-reviewed proposals, with the key criteria for selection being high-impact potential, calculations that require systems of Mira's size, and whose codes scale to a significant fraction of the entire configuration. Based on early results, we expect that the Mira workload will mirror Intrepid's, much of which consists of jobs that each use 20% or more of the nodes, some even 80-100%: tightly-coupled calculations that involve extremely large meshes, for example. Such scaling is enabled by the Blue Gene architecture's high-dimensional torus network. Mira's applications use the

MPI and OpenMP programming models, the latter providing higher performance for codes that benefit from using up to 64 threads per node. The following brief descriptions of five applications provide a glimpse of the exciting scientific breakthroughs that will be tackled on Mira.

### Global Simulation of Plasma Microturbulence at the Petascale and Beyond

As scientists look for alternatives to fossil fuels to meet the world's energy needs, there is increasing interest in nuclear fusion, the power source of the sun. Of utmost importance in the design and operation of future fusion power sources is an understanding of turbulent transport losses. Acquiring this knowledge requires computational efforts at the extreme scale. Professor William Tang, Princeton Plasma Physics Laboratory, investigates the influence of plasma size on confinement properties in advanced tokamak systems, like ITER. This requires a systematic analysis of the underlying nonlinear turbulence characteristics in magnetically confined tokamak plasmas that span the range from current scale experiments, which exhibit an unfavorable scaling of confinement as the plasma radius increases, to ITER-scale plasmas, expected to be insensitive to size variations. Present-day tokamaks are not even one-third the radial dimension of ITER, making high-fidelity predictive simulations even more critical, since improvements in ITER-sized devices can only be validated after they are constructed and operational. The GTC-P and GTS codes, highly scalable particle-in-cell gyrokinetic codes, are used for simulating microturbulence-driven transport in tokamaks. GTC is a Gyrokinetic Toroidal Computation particle-in-cell fusion plasma simulation code that represents the state of the art in kinetic tokamak plasma simulations using particles. Mira will enable long-duration simulations of ITER plasmas that will demand $O(10^8)$ grid points and $O(10^{10})$ particles.

### Deepening the Understanding of Interactions between Quarks and Gluons

Quantum Chromodynamics (QCD) research plays a key role in the ongoing efforts to develop a unified theory of the fundamental forces of nature. While the behavior of atomic particles such as protons and neutrons is well understood, less is known about the interactions of subatomic particles like quarks and gluons, which compose the atomic particles. Paul Mackenzie from Fermilab leads the US-QCD INCITE project that studies these interactions. Logging over 800 million core hours on ALCF's Intrepid, scientists have generated gauge configurations with up, down, and strange quarks on lattices that are sufficiently fine-grained and have sufficiently small up and down quark masses to enable the extrapolation of key quantities to their physical values found in nature. The gauge configurations are being used to determine a wide range of physical quantities of importance in high energy and nuclear physics. Not only does this work directly impact the understanding of physics, but the research done on ALCF resources has a direct impact on large experimental programs. For example, Brookhaven National Laboratory's Relativistic Heavy Ion Collider used results from US-QCD computation to firmly constrain heavy-ion collision models for the first time. Fermilab has used calculations by US-QCD members combined with experimental results, that allow many of the fundamental parameters of the Standard Model to be determined more accurately than ever before. Mira will enable the generation of configurations that would support calculations of the spectrum, decay properties and internal structure of strongly interacting particles, and tests of the standard model, of unprecedented precision.

### Breakthroughs in Protein Structure Calculation and Design

Protein structure prediction is key to understanding the function and interactions of biomolecules and provides the insights necessary to design new molecules with novel and useful functions. Faster and more accurate predictions of structure can yield significant cost and time savings. In collaboration with other researchers, David Baker from the University of Washington has achieved several exciting breakthroughs in protein structure calculation and design that were enabled by a new approach they developed for computational analysis of Nuclear Magnetic Resonance (NMR) data that pushes the limits of protein size that can be structurally solved from NMR spectroscopy data. This is a very significant step forward since many of these larger proteins are not amenable to analysis by X-ray crystallography, and thus, NMR remains the only way to obtain their structure. The workload consists of large numbers of runs that are managed by an ALCF-developed system for automating ensemble runs. The project team also invented an approach in which electron density maps generated from molecular replacement solutions for each of a series of starting models are used to guide energy optimization by structure rebuilding, combinatorial side chain packing, and torsion space minimization. Despite these improvements, the workload generated by the desired range of biomolecules to be studied is very large for the current resources. Mira's powerful configuration will enable the understanding and design of many more protein structures, possibly including de novo computational design of antiviral proteins.

**Advanced Reactor Thermal Hydraulic Modeling** Advanced nuclear reactors are a key technology for providing power at a reasonable cost and with a low carbon footprint. This research project, led by Paul Fischer, Argonne National Laboratory, is focused on analysis of thermal-hydraulics (heat transfer and coolant flow) in next-generation sodium- and gas-cooled nuclear reactors. The project simulations span a broad range of modeling scales. An important role for the compute-intensive simulations is to provide validation data for lower-cost reactor design simulations based on reduced-order models or subchannel codes. This project's workload consists of tightly-coupled calculations that require large numbers of cores. As part of a worldwide validation effort for nuclear simulation codes, the Nuclear Energy Agency/Organization for Economic Cooperation and Development conducted a blind-benchmark study in 2010 that involved such jobs. Participants submitted computational results for velocity and temperature distributions in a T-junction (where streams of differing temperatures merge with limited mixing) that are important to understanding thermal-mechanical fatigue in light water reactors. Results were compared against experiments conducted for the benchmark. The Nek5000 code used up to 163,840 cores on Intrepid. Further scalability was demonstrated using the Jülich BG/P, where 19% of peak was realized on 262,000 cores. Runs from this project ranked first of 29 in temperature and sixth in velocity. Similar runs on Mira are expected to run on even larger numbers of cores and enable modeling reactor design simulations of greater complexity and fidelity.

**Intricate Climate Models Used to Study Global Warming** Global warming increases the occurrence of droughts, heat waves, wildfires, and floods. By improving the understanding of global warming's impact, society can optimally address climate adaptation considerations. Advanced computation allows the Climate Science Computational End Station (CCES) project led by Warren Washington (NCAR) to develop more complex and intricate climate models. The vital information these improved models provide will help guide environmental policy. The CCES is advancing climate science through both aggressive model development activity and an extensive suite of climate simulations to correctly simulate the global carbon cycle and its feedback to the climate system, including its variability and modulation by ocean and land ecosystems. Researchers are testing a new, highly scalable method for solving the fluid dynamics of the atmosphere for use in future climate simulations. This method, called HOMME, is included in the CAM-SE model and has run with a resolution as high as $1/8$th of a degree of latitude on more than 80,000 cores. Next, researchers will use CAM-SE to perform standard climate model benchmark simulations for comparisons with other models. The availability of Mira coupled with the enhanced scalability of the codes will enable the use of suites of simulations with higher complexity and greater resolution.

Below we showcase five Mira applications with their main characteristics given in Table 10.2.

**TABLE 10.2**: Mira applications showcase.

| Application | Language | | | Parallelism | | | Application Characteristics |
|---|---|---|---|---|---|---|---|
| Code | F | C | C++ | MPI | OpenMP | Threads | |
| MADNESS and MPQC | | | ✓ | ✓ | | ✓ | Dense eigensolve, matrix multiplication, tensor contraction |
| DFT to QMC | | ✓ | ✓ | ✓ | ✓ | | Stochastic sampling of many-body wave functions, C++ STL and custom C++ structures/templates |
| HACC | | ✓ | ✓ | ✓ | ✓ | | Particle-mesh, particle-particle, tree code, FFT, structured mesh, tree |
| Large Eddy | ✓ | | ✓ | ✓ | ✓ | | Finite Volume Schemes, unstructured and overlapping block structured meshes, basic integer/real arrays |
| HSCD | ✓ | ✓ | | ✓ | ✓ | | Multi-physics AMR direct numerical simulation of reactive gases, fully-threaded trees |

### 10.3.2 MADNESS and MPQC on Mira

MADNESS [Rob10] and MPQC [JNL+07] are two modern quantum chemistry applications that employ very similar designs and programming models; specifically software abstraction via objects and templates via C++ as well as asynchrony and hybrid parallelism using MPI and POSIX threads (Pthreads) [NJ00]. Together, they provide a wide range of molecular simulation capability, from multiresolution adaptive numerical basis set methods for density–functional [HFY+04, YFG+04] and wavefunction theory (MADNESS) and traditional (that is, using atom-centered Gaussian orbitals) implementations of these as well as explicitly correlated methods [VJ04] (MPQC). In addition to quantum chemistry capability, the numerical features of MADNESS also enable nuclear physics applications [FPH+09] and the solution of partial differential equations (PDEs) with irregular boundary conditions [RHH12].

Many aspects of MADNESS and MPQC are ideally suited for Mira as well as other modern HPC systems. In addition to relatively simple system software requirements (MPI, Pthreads, C++) both codes make use of automatic code generation for key kernels that are readily vectorizable. MPQC relies upon LIBINT [VF96] to automatically generate atomic integral recurrence relations [Gil94], as such functions are too numerous to optimize by hand. The primary kernel in MADNESS is

$$R_{pqr} = \sum_{i,j,k}^{N_i,N_j,N_k} s_{ijk}c_{ip}c_{jq}c_{kr} = \sum_{k}^{N_k}\left(\sum_{j}^{N_j}\left(\sum_{i}^{N_i} s_{ijk}c_{ip}\right)c_{jq}\right)c_{kr}, \qquad (10.1)$$

which is used to evaluate low-rank functions over discontinuous spectral elements. The dimensions $N_i$ are on the order of 20, meaning that this kernel is potentially evaluated using a DGEMM call with $(m,n,k) = (200, 20, 20)$, which is far from optimal in most implementations of the BLAS for modern architectures, although it can be assumed that all the dimensions are even and buffers are properly aligned. MADNESS employs automatic code generation to produce optimized assembly code for the relevant input arguments. This was first done for x86 using SSE vector instructions, then for Intrepid using the double hummer, and very recently, for Mira using the QPX instruction set.

For communication, both MADNESS and MPQC employ a communication helper thread (CHT), which allows them to provide portable active-message and one-sided communication using MPI send/recv. In MPQC, the primary communication is a one-sided accumulate, which is used to implement a distributed-memory container that resembles Global Arrays [NHL94]. MPQC has been shown to scale perfectly to 16,384 nodes of Intrepid and reasonably to 32,768 nodes. In MADNESS, the CHT provides active-messages, which are the basis for futures [Fri76, Bak77]. While MADNESS is a full-service quantum chemistry code, the runtime capability described here is useful in other contexts. For example, it has been used to implement a distributed tensor library [CV12], such as would be required for reduced-scaling quantum many-body methods.

### 10.3.3    DFT to QMC on Mira

U.S. Department of Energy (DOE) requisites for atomistic materials simulations are broad and span the gamut of accurate quantum mechanical methods to empirical interatomic potential methods. In the materials and chemistry arena, Density Functional Theory (DFT) calculations have been very prominent among users of DOE's Leadership Computing Facilities (LCFs). Several DFT codes (CPMD [HC05], GPAW [ERM+10], OpenAtom [BBK+08], and Qbox BGQ-Gygi2008) have demonstrated scalability in excess of 10,000 cores on Intrepid and other Blue Gene systems. They have been used to study fundamental physical phenomena such as the vibrational spectrum of liquid water as well as more applied material problems in Li-ion batteries and catalysis.

In sharp contrast to the computational science drivers for next-generation supercomputing architectures in other scientific domains, the materials and chemistry communities are focused on high accuracy methods and rational design strategies (e.g., machine learning [RTMvL12]) for materials instead of solely larger problem sizes. While several high-accuracy quantum many-body methods exist, a significant sector of the chemistry, materials science, and condensed matter physics communities have adopted the use of quantum Monte Carlo (QMC) methods due to their high accuracy and highly parallel nature. Although the computational complexity of QMC is similar to DFT ($N^3 - N^4$), the substantially larger computational prefactor has prevented the widespread adoption of QMC methods.

Petascale computational resources have allowed QMC to become a more mainstream approach in the scientific community, albeit for relatively small problems ($< 1,000$ electrons). QMCPACK [qmc12] and CASINO [GTA11] are examples of QMC codes that are presently used on DOE LCFs and scale to over 100,000 cores. Mira will allow routine QMC calculations of systems containing over 1,000 electrons. For the nanoscale regime ($> 10,000$ electrons), a 100 PF supercomputer is likely to be needed. Further down on the computational roadmap, an exaflop supercomputer will enable rational design of materials based on QMC methods and allow molecular dynamics based on QMC (called coupled electron-ion Monte Carlo [PC06]) to be used routinely for studying materials under realistic conditions.

In spite of QMC's ideal strong-scaling behavior, Mira will require developers of QMC codes to expose more parallelism in their algorithms. This is rather straightforward since the Blue Gene/Q architecture is well suited for nested OpenMP. Presently, such an effort is under way with the QMCPACK code as part of ALCF's Early Science Program. Mira will enable us to advance materials research based on high accuracy QMC calculations that were not possible with the previous generation of supercomputers.

### 10.3.4    Hybrid/Hardware Accelerated Cosmology Code (HACC)

The HACC framework [HACC12] simulates formation and evolution of structure driven by gravity in an expanding universe. Mass is represented by gravitationally interacting tracer particles, having masses $O(10^6 - 10^{11})$ solar masses (problem-dependent). The gravitational force is split into short- and long-range components. At short distances, $< O(1)$ Megaparsecs

(Mpc), the $N$-body problem is solved using some combination of two methods: (1) direct $N^2$ particle-particle interaction, (2) tree methods (low-order multipole expansion). At longer ranges, a grid-based spectral method is used: deposit particle masses onto a grid to form a density field, solve the gravitational Poisson equation using Fourier transforms and advanced spectral operations, interpolate the long-range force field from the grid to particle positions, move particles each timestep under long/short-range forces using timestep subcycling.

The simulation volume cube is typically a few Gpc on a side, corresponding to measurement volumes of current and pending state-of-the-art sky surveys. At this scale, the void-and-filament web-like structure of the universe repeats many times, giving a natural computational load balance when the domain is decomposed into $O(10^5 - 10^6)$ subdomains for parallel computation. The short-range force computation time strongly dominates the long-range computation time. So, most compute time is spent in parallel local force computations, giving both excellent scaling and local computational efficiency on the largest machines of today and tomorrow. HACC scales to full system sizes on today's machines, including Roadrunner (Cell/BE) and Intrepid —tens and hundreds of thousands of cores.

Current and near-future HACC simulations resolve structures down to the length and mass scale of single-galaxy dark-matter halos and subhalos. The length scale resolved is few Kpc. The minimum halo mass scale is $O(10^8)$ solar masses. Given the size of the whole simulated domain, these resolutions require $O(10^{10} - 10^{12})$ simulation particles. The next run campaign ($O(100)$ simulations) will generate a suite of cosmological observables (such as weak lensing maps) and mock galaxy catalogs, from which statistics such as the galaxy 2-point correlation functions can be measured. These results will allow studying effects on observable quantities of systematically varying cosmological parameters. This simulation database will be used to interpret and understand ongoing and forthcoming experimental results from sky surveys such as the Dark Energy Survey.

At length scales $< O(1)$ Mpc, hydrodynamic effects are important. HACC is incorporating new hydrodynamics capabilities, which will complete the capabilities needed in the next few years. HACC was designed looking toward exascale; the basic balance of underlying algorithms will remain unchanged. In the next 5-10 years, an expanded range of applications will demand extra capabilities such as "zooming in" on objects at extreme resolution. The aim is to do this using particle-information-based virtual local meshes. Lagrangian particle behavior makes the method naturally adaptive. Future sky surveys will demand very high accuracy simulations and codes within the HACC framework will be used to understand the measurements and match the highest observational resolutions.

### 10.3.5 Highly Scalable Structured Overset Grid and Unstructured Mesh Solvers for Large Eddy Simulations

Designing better jet engines and wind turbines requires understanding the source of noise generation in the devices. For jet engines, if the sources of noise are not well understood, design changes to lower the acoustic signature need to be made in an ad-hoc manner which could result in bulkier and less-efficient engines. A similar argument could be made for developing low noise and more efficient wind turbines. Current studies on Intrepid have shown that Large Eddy Simulations (LES) can predict the noise generated by an experimental jet nozzle. Studies, based on simulations on Intrepid, have also shown that low Mach number LES of high Reynolds number flows past a single wind turbine blade have been able to capture the physics of flow transition at the leading edge and separated flows at the trailing edge. Also, LES studies are currently under way to predict the broadband fan noise in turbofan engines. The simulations, at present, are on 125M - 350M grid points and larger simulations are planned on 600M - 1B grid points.

Jet noise simulations are currently being done using an overlapping, multi block, structured grid, compressible Navier-Stokes solver that uses higher-order compact schemes to improve the fidelity of flow field predictions. Since compact schemes require that blocks of banded matrices be solved, to compute the derivatives of flow variables, there is a need for sparse direct matrix solvers that scale well on Mira when the underlying grid has O(B) grid points. Researchers at ALCF have looked at the scaling of the MUMPS solver package, and the matrix solvers in PETSc, and are confident that the large jet noise simulations can be carried out on Mira. Likewise, a team of researchers at Stanford University and G.E. Global Research have looked at alternate finite volume formulations that can improve the performance and accuracy of wind turbine simulations with unstructured, low Mach number, incompressible, Navier-Stokes solvers with algebraic multi grid acceleration. The results of their findings indicate that it is feasible to do large O(B) grid point simulations, on Intrepid (and Mira), on highly anisotropic grids. Grid generation, remains another key challenge. Here again, researchers at Argonne have developed and enhanced the capabilities of mesh generation tools, such as the SciDAC funded ITAPS program (see, http://www.itaps.org/), that can generate large dense structured and unstructured meshes when provided with coarse meshes and STL files as inputs.

As the G.E. Global Research teams lead by Dr. Umesh Paliath and Dr. Giridhar Jothiprasad transition to doing these larger simulations on Mira, one can begin to expect that it will enable engineers at G.E. Global Research to better understand the role of chevrons in lowering the acoustic intensity of jet noise, in real jet engine geometries, and a better understanding of the trailing edge noise generation mechanism that could lead to better airfoil sections and turbine blades for wind turbines.

### 10.3.6    HSCD on Mira

Hydrogen is emerging as an important fuel across a range of industries as a means of achieving energy independence and as a way to reduce emissions. Deflagration-to-detonation (DDT) and the resulting detonation waves can have catastrophic consequences in a variety of industrial and energy producing settings related to hydrogen and nuclear power generation. The goal of the project is to create a direct numerical simulation (DNS) tool for fundamental first-principles understanding of high-speed combustion and detonation (HSCD) phenomena in reactive gaseous systems of engineering scale. The project's current focus is on complex multi-scale physics in the transitory regimes of rapid flame acceleration and the DDT in hydrogen-oxygen ($H_2 - O_2$) mixtures.

In the HSCD regime, fluid velocity ranges from subsonic to supersonic. Sound waves, compressible turbulence, and shocks are all important to the simulation. Many existing codes can treat low-speed combustion with Mach numbers less than one, but would have difficulties dealing with HSCD regimes. The HSCD physical model is based on reactive compressible Navier-Stokes equations, includes multi-species equation of state, viscosity, heat conduction, diffusion, radiation loss, and chemical kinetics, and uses a compressible fluid dynamics code with a Riemann solver to treat both continuous flow and shocks, with a dynamic adaptive mesh refinement (AMR) capability. The computational challenge is to resolve spatial scales from the viscous microscale, measured in microns, to the scale of a combustion apparatus, measured in meters, and resolve temporal scales spanning many orders of magnitude from time-scales of chemical reactions to a sound-crossing time of the apparatus, while taking into account all of the physics detailed above.

The HSCD code currently scales up to 128K cores of Intrepid. Using an INCITE allocation on BG/P, the team was able to simulate and reproduce a process of weak ignition in $H_2 - O_2$ in a 5 cm cross-section one-meter pipe — something that has not been possible in the past. The plan for Mira is targeting first-principles modeling of transient flame acceleration and DDT in the same pipe at atmospheric conditions. The transition to atmospheric pressure will place greater stress on the AMR code, specifically on the rebalancing operation that happens after refinement. Additionally, the code is currently hybrid MPI/OpenMP on Intrepid, but with a coarse-grained strategy that works well with the threading model on that platform. The CPU architecture on the Mira, however, will respond better to a re-architecture that emphasizes more fine-grained parallelism.

The project is a collaboration between The University of Chicago (PI Alexei Khokhlov), the University of Illinois at Urbana-Champaign (PI Joanna Austin), and Argonne National Laboratory (PI Charles Bacon).

## 10.4  Benchmarks

### 10.4.1  The Sequoia Benchmarks

The Sequoia Marquis benchmarks were selected to represent the broad spectrum of applications to be deployed. Each of the chosen applications covered one small domain of interest, had exhibited reasonable scaling on Blue Gene and Linux® systems, and did not pose any export control issues. To the extent possible, the codes were also chosen to provide the opportunity to investigate the utility of hybrid (MPI/OpenMP) programming models.

The codes included in the suite of primary applications include AMG, IRS, Sphot, UMT, and Lammps. A brief description of each of the benchmarks follows and the main characteristics are given in Table 10.3.

- AMG: (Adaptive Multigrid) is a stand in for the widely used Hypre solver package. The Hypre package provides components for a wide range of equation solving and preconditioning techniques. The AMG benchmark enables a user to create a weak scaling benchmark utilizing several preselected techniques that are the primary methods used in many of the physics codes in use at LLNL and elsewhere. The code scales up to large numbers of MPI tasks with a user selected communications/compute ratio as desired. The code can be run MPI only, or in a hybrid mode with a mix of MPI and OpenMP.

- IRS: (Implicit Radiation Solver) is a proxy for the solver in one of the most heavily used

**TABLE 10.3**: Sequoia benchmarks.

| Benchmark | Language | | | | Parallelism | | Description |
|---|---|---|---|---|---|---|---|
| Code | F | Py | C | C++ | MPI | OpenMP | |
| AMG | | | ✓ | | ✓ | ✓ | Algebraic multigrid linear system solver for unstructured mesh physics packages |
| IRS | | | ✓ | | ✓ | ✓ | Implicit Radiation Solver for diffusion equation on a block structured mesh |
| Sphot | ✓ | | | | ✓ | ✓ | Single physics package code, Monte Carlo Scalar PHOTon transport code |
| UMT | ✓ | ✓ | ✓ | ✓ | ✓ | ✓ | Unstructured-Mesh deterministic radiation Transport |
| LAMMPS | | | | ✓ | ✓ | | Classical molecular dynamics simulation code (as used) |

multiphysics applications at LLNL. The solution technique is based on the conjugate gradient method applied to the diffusion equation on a block structured mesh. The solution strategy employs MPI only, or a hybrid MPI/OpenMP approach.

- Sphot: (Single Physics Photon Transport) is an embarrassingly parallel, Monte Carlo Photon Transport code which can be used in MPI only mode or in a hybrid MPI/OpenMP mode. The size of problems on each domain is scalable and can be adjusted according to the memory footprint desired.

- UMT: (Unstructured Mesh Transport) is an unstructured mesh, deterministic radiation transport code. This particular code has a highly optimized computational kernel written in Fortran 90, driven by a Python-based MPI layer, and C++ code. It generally scales very well up to large MPI counts, but currently does not operate in a hybrid mode.

- LAMMPS: is a widely used, open source molecular dynamics (MD) code written in C++. It is the most general MD code used in the community. The current version of the benchmark has been modified to include OpenMP to improve scaling and single node performance. The simple Lennard-Jones and EAM potentials are utilized to investigate the single node performance.

The performance of each of the benchmarks is measured using a Figure of Merit. The FOM is based on the performance each of the simulation codes achieved on an 8192 MPI task Purple run, while the LAMMPS FOM is based on the performance of a run on the entire Blue Gene Machine located at Lawrence Livermore. The weighting for each of the applications is equivalent, and represents the rate in units of work/time for each application. This metric is used to enable comparisons of a wide range of hardware designs scaling from only a few nodes to Sequoia's millions of cores.

### 10.4.2   The Mira Benchmarks

A set of representative benchmarks was carefully chosen for Mira to test and measure the various features of the Blue Gene/Q system. Existing standard benchmarks were used wherever possible, but new ones were created where needed to benchmark Blue Gene/Q specific features and simulate real application behavior and workloads. The benchmarks are described below.

#### Standard Benchmarks

The ALCF relied on a couple of standard benchmarks to measure performance within a node of the Blue Gene/Q. These include **STREAM** to measure memory bandwidth and **SPEC OMPL2001** to measure scalability and OpenMP compiler and runtime performance on applications. To measure access latency of memory and all levels of caches a home-grown benchmark is used. To measure I/O bandwidth performance the **IOR** benchmark is used.

#### New Benchmarks

The ALCF created a couple of new benchmarks to measure performance of MPI and the 5-D torus interconnect, and the performance of the compiler in identifying and generating SIMD optimizations in applications.

- MPI: the ALCF created a new set of MPI benchmarks that is adapted from and simulates the behavior of ALCF applications to measure the performance, bandwidth, and latency, of internode and intranode communication for point to point messages, halo exchange in 3-D topology, and global operations and collectives for the 5-D torus network on Mira.

- QPX: the ALCF extracted kernels from three key applications — MILC, LS3DF and NEK 5000 — that would benefit from the quad floating point instructions extensions implemented on the PowerPC®A2 core. The benchmark measures the performance improvement of these kernels from SIMD optimizations generated by the compiler.

**Application Benchmarks**

ALCF created an application benchmark suite comprised of ten key science applications shown in Table 10.4 to measure single node performance and scalability of Blue Gene/Q and compare it to its predecessor.

The applications were selected while taking into account several criteria, including:

**TABLE 10.4**: Mira benchmarks.

| Benchmark | Language | | | | Parallelism | | Description |
|---|---|---|---|---|---|---|---|
| Code | F | Py | C | C++ | MPI | OpenMP | |
| FLASH | √ | √ | √ | | √ | √ | Multi-physics, block-structured oct-tree AMR |
| NEK5000 | √ | | | | √ | | Spectral element, algebraic multigrid, MMX kernel |
| MILC | | | √ | | √ | | DFT (Conjugate gradient), Divide and conquer, DGEMM, 3D FFT |
| LS3DF | √ | | | | √ | | Hybrid Monte Carlo, Krylov methods |
| DNS3D | √ | | | | √ | | Turbulence, spectral element |
| NAMD | | | | √ | √ | √ | Charm++, particle mesh ewald, 3D FFT |
| HIRAM | √ | | | | √ | √ | Non-hydrostatic, cubed-sphere, finite-volume, global atmospheric simulation |
| GFMC | √ | | | | √ | √ | Greens function Monte Carlo, master-slave |
| GTC | | √ | | | √ | √ | Particle-in-Cell, PETSc |
| GPAW | | √ | √ | | √ | | DFT, Projector-Augmented Wave (PAW) method. |
| ALCF MPI Bmks | | | √ | | √ | | Measures interconnect messaging rate, latency, bi-section bandwidth, collectives performance, etc. |
| STREAM | √ | | √ | | √ | √ | Measures sustainable memory bandwidth. |
| QPX App Kernels | √ | | √ | | | | Single core kernels that should benefit from compiler SIMD optimizations. |
| SPEC OMP2001 | √ | | √ | √ | | √ | Standard OpenMP based bmk suite; measures compiler and hardware performance. |

- Demand: DOE strategic science research, large current and potential applications, and a broad user base (community code) must be accommodated.

- Scalability: Science with large parallelism must be efficiently addressed on LCF resources.

- Breadth: A breadth of science demands and modeling approaches must be covered. The applications provide good coverage of the fundamental kernels/algorithms used including both structured and unstructured meshes, sparse and dense linear algebra routines, particles/ N-body problems, Fourier transforms, Monte Carlo techniques, etc., as well as a wide range of programming models and languages.

- Collaboration: Applications teams are motivated to collaborate with the ALCF teams.

The suite comes with source code, makefiles and input data sets of several sizes. Output data is also provided for validation. The suite measures performance improvements in hardware and software and to that effect, the run rules do not allow manual source code changes, except for pragma directives to aid the compiler. The performance metric is the per node performance improvement compared to a reference architecture (ALCF Intrepid BG/P) for each application.

**Other**

ALCF also wrote several other functional tests to check the capability of specific features in hardware. An example would include a number of performance counter tests to measure the capabilities of performance monitor and the BGPM API.

ALCF also used benchmarks from the Sequoia suite to supplement the Mira suite. An example would include the enhanced CLOMP benchmark to measure OpenMP runtime performance and new hardware features like memory speculation implemented in Blue Gene/Q hardware.

### 10.4.3    The IBM Benchmarks

The High-Performance Linpack (HPL) benchmark [PWDC08] is used to measure the performance profile of parallel computers in the factorization and solving of a large dense system of linear equations. The performance metric is double precision floating point operations per second (FLOPS). The Top500 list, presented at the twice-yearly Supercomputing conferences (ICS [ICS11] and SC [SC11]), ranks the fastest 500 supercomputers in the world according to their performance on the Linpack benchmark. The Linpack HPL characteristics are given in Table 10.5.

More recently, the Green500 List has combined the performance of these systems with their power consumption, creating a reordered list based on power efficiency, measured in FLOPS per Watt (FLOPS/W).

In June 2012 the Top500 list [TOP11] featured 20 Blue Gene/Q installations, of which

**TABLE 10.5**: IBM benchmarks.

| Benchmark | Language | | | | Parallelism | | Description |
|---|---|---|---|---|---|---|---|
| Code | F | Py | C | C++ | MPI | OpenMP | |
| Linpack HPL | | | ✓ | | ✓ | ✓ | Standard benchmark suite used to rank the top 500 supercomputers. |

the 96-rack Sequoia and 48-rack Mira systems were #1 and #3, with benchmark scores of 16.3 and 8.16 PFLOPS, respectively. Correspondingly, these 20 systems also occupied the top of the Green 500 list [GRE11] with power efficiencies over GFLOPS/W.

Multiple hardware features provided by the Blue Gene/Q architecture can be beneficially utilized by the HPL benchmark. These range from on-core features (QPX and L1P streaming prefetch), to shared on-node features (the L2 atomics), to the multi-dimensional torus that provides the communication backbone of the system. These hardware features are further discussed in Section 10.5.

Another benchmark that has been executed on Blue Gene/Q is the Graph500 [GRA11]. The Graph500 is a coordinated attempt to establish a set of large-scale benchmarks characterizing data intensive applications. Its specifications are the result of the efforts of a steering committee whose members come from academia, industry, governmental agencies, and national laboratories. Despite its recent introduction, the Graph500 is already becoming a widely recognized alternative to more traditional benchmarks that very often fail to capture the essence of big-data applications. At the time of this writing, the Graph500 specification defines one timed kernel, consisting of a Breadth-First Search (BFS) over a very large, randomly generated graph.

Our initial design and experimental evaluation has shown that Blue Gene/Q can efficiently support data-intensive applications, reaching the impressive processing rate of 254 Billion Traversed Edges Per Second (GTEPS) on a configuration with 4,096 nodes (4 racks), ranking first on the November 2011 Graph500 [GRA11]. As a direct comparison, the second ranking entry came in at less than half this processing rate, using a much larger machine. In June 2012 and November 2012, the Blue Gene/Q Sequoia and Mira installations continued their leading positions on this benchmark.

The Graph500 results are a clear testament to both the power efficiency and versatility of the Blue Gene family of supercomputers, and prove that Blue Gene systems can be successfully used to parallelize demanding data-intensive applications.

## 10.5 System Hardware

### 10.5.1 Overview of System Hardware Architecture

Blue Gene®/Q (BG/Q) is the third generation in the IBM®Blue Gene® line of supercomputer systems. As in the earlier Blue Gene systems, BG/Q aims to build a massively parallel high performance computing (HPC) system out of very power-efficient processor chips.[1,2]

Like the previous generations Blue Gene/L (BG/L) [GBC+05] and Blue Gene/P (BG/P) [Tea08], the system design goals for BG/Q are to optimize for price-performance, power efficiency, and reliability.

The heart of a BG/Q system is the Blue Gene/Q Compute (BQC) chip [HOF+12], which

[1]Sections 10.5.1 through 10.5.5 are based on *The IBM Blue Gene/Q Compute Chip*, by R.A. Haring, M. Ohmacht, T.W. Fox, M.K. Gschwind, D.L. Satterfield, K. Sugavanam, P.W. Coteus, P. Heidelberger, M.A. Blumrich, R.W. Wisniewski, A. Gara, G. L-T. Chiu, P.A. Boyle, N.H. Christ and C. Kim, which appeared in *IEEE Micro*, 32(2):48-60, March/April 2012. ©2012 IEEE and on *Design of the IBM Blue Gene/Q Compute Chip*, by the IBM Blue Gene team, which will appear in the *IBM Journal of Research and Development*, Jan 2013. ©2013 IEEE.

[2]IBM's work on the BG/Q project has been supported and partially funded by Argonne National Laboratory and the Lawrence Livermore National Laboratory on behalf of the U.S. Department of Energy, under Lawrence Livermore National Laboratory subcontract no. B554331.

combines processors, memory, and communication functions on a single chip. At 1.6 GHz, the chip will deliver a peak performance of 204.8 GFLOPS at about 55 W. Section 10.5.3 will describe the BQC chip design in more detail.

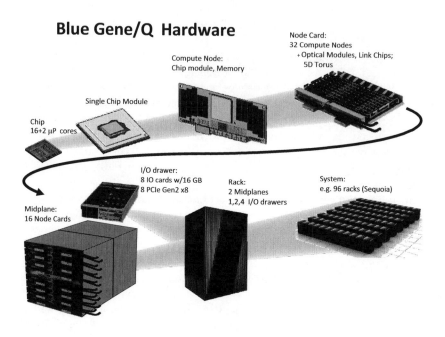

**FIGURE 10.3**: Blue Gene/Q system hierarchy. ©Springer-Verlag 2012. Reprinted with permission.

As shown in Figure 10.3 a *compute card* contains a BQC chip with surrounding DDR3 memory chips, currently 16 GB. Logically, this entity (chip + memory) is known as an *I/O node* when located in an 8-way *I/O drawer*, or as a *compute node* when located in a 32-way *node board* assembly,

Sixteen node boards are arranged into a *midplane*, which takes up half a rack. The 16 x 32 = 512 compute nodes in a midplane are electrically interconnected in a 4x4x4x4x2 configuration of a 5-dimensional (5D) mesh network, with all chip-to-chip communication links operating at a bandwidth of 2 GB/s in each direction. The final x2 dimension is wrapped within the midplane. The chip-to-chip links for the other 4 dimensions are routed through separate BG/Q Link (BQL) chips, which are also located on the node board assemblies. The BQL chips can be configured to either wrap any given link (completing a torus dimension), or to route the link through an optical fiber to a next midplane, thereby extending the torus in that dimension. Section 10.5.5 will describe the network in more detail.

Two midplanes are stacked vertically into a BG/Q rack. A rack therefore contains 1,024 compute nodes, with an aggregate peak performance of 209.7 TFLOPS. Thus the 96-rack Sequoia machine will contain 98,304 compute nodes with a peak performance of 20.1 PFLOPS. The 48-rack Mira machine will contain 49,152 compute nodes with a peak performance of 10.1 PFLOPS.

A subset of compute nodes in each midplane, called *bridge nodes* use an additional out-of-torus link to connect (again via fiber optics) to separately packaged I/O nodes. I/O nodes are located in 8-way "I/O drawers," which, dependent on the customer's I/O to compute ratio, are placed on top of the BG/Q racks or in separate racks. I/O nodes connect to a 10 Gbit Ethernet or InfiniBand data center network, and thereby to an external filesystem.

The BG/Q system is not only designed for performance, but also for power efficiency and reliability. These aspects permeate all levels of the hardware design. The integration of processors, memory subsystem and communication subsystems into a single chip eliminates chip-to-chip interfaces, and thereby increases the bandwidth between units, eliminates the power associated with off-chip drivers, and increases reliability (since fewer parts). The chip is designed with soft error reliability in mind, using techniques such as ECC (error checking and correction), hardened latches and parity detection/recovery, wherever most appropriate. The chip's built-in memory controllers control directly attached DRAM chips, that are soldered down on the same compute card as the BQC chip. This eliminates connectors, thus enhances reliability, and the resulting shorter connections reduce power. The memory has extensive ECC capabilities. Chip-to-chip communication links have multiple levels of error checking and correction.

Water cooling of the node board assemblies keeps temperatures low, enhancing reliability and reducing leakage power. Power supplies are N+1, or, in some cases, N+2 redundant. The fiber optic links between midplanes and between midplanes and I/O drawers have spare fibers with dynamic fail-over capability.

Power efficiency was proven on smaller BG/Q prototype systems to be about 2.0 GFLOPS/W, taking the top positions in the Green500 list since November 2010 [GRE11]. We therefore expect Sequoia and Mira to be both the most power efficient and the most reliable High Performance Computing systems currently available.

### 10.5.2 Processor Core and QPX Accelerator Design

The processor core on the BQC chip is an augmented version of the A2 processor core first used on the IBM PowerEN™chip [JAB+10][BWBJ11]. The A2 processor core implements the 64-bit Power instruction set architecture (Power ISA™), and is optimized for aggregate throughput. The A2 is 4-way simultaneously multithreaded and supports 2-way concurrent instruction issue: one integer, branch or load/store instruction, and one floating point instruction. Within a thread, dispatch, execution, and completion are in-order.

The first level (L1) instruction cache is 16 KB, 4-way set associative. The L1 data cache of the A2 core is 16 KB, 8-way set associative, with 64B lines. The 32B wide load/store interface has sufficient bandwidth to support the Quad Floating Point Unit discussed below.

The processor core has been re-synthesized to run at 1.6 GHz, at a reduced voltage (0.8V nominal) versus the original PowerEN chip design point. The lower voltage operation reduces both active and leakage power.

A Quad Processing eXtension (QPX) to the Power ISA was developed specifically for BG/Q. The BQC chip Quad floating-point Processing Unit (QPU) implements the new QPX instruction set, in addition to the Power ISA's scalar floating-point instructions. Each execution slot within the QPU embodies a Fused Multiply-Add (FMA) dataflow pipeline, which is the machinery that calculates the mathematical equation $\pm[(A \times C) \pm B]$, where $A$, $B$, and $C$ are the operands defined by the Power and QPX ISAs. The QPU instantiates four copies of the FMA pipeline, creating a 4-way SIMD floating-point microarchitecture. Complex arithmetic instructions can use data from two adjacent pipelines. A permute unit implements data shuffling across execution slots. Comparison, conversion, and move operations are also supported in the QPU.

The peak performance of the QPU is 4 FMA operations (i.e., 8 double-precision floating-point operations) per cycle. At 1.6 GHz, a single A2 processor core with QPU therefore has a peak performance of 12.8 GFLOPS. The aggregate peak performance of the 16 user-processors on the BQC chip is 204.8 GFLOPS.

More details on the A2 processor core and on the QPU will be described in [Tea13].

### 10.5.3  System on Chip Design

The BG/Q Compute (BQC) chip has been optimized for power efficiency, in terms of floating point operations per second, per Watt (FLOPS/W); for networking/connectivity; and for reliability with features such as redundancy, the usage of error correction and detection, and the minimization of sensitivity to soft errors.

The BQC chip [HOF$^+$12] is an 18.96x18.96 mm$^2$ chip in IBM's Cu-45HP (45 nm Silicon on Insulator, SOI) ASIC technology [IFB$^+$11]. The chip contains about $1.47 \times 10^9$ transistors and 11 layers of metal. It is a System-on-a-Chip design, integrating processors, memory subsystem, and networking subsystem on a single chip. A die photograph of the chip (Figure 10.4) shows 18 processor units (PUnits: PU00 - PU17) surrounding a large L2 cache that occupies the center of the chip. Functionally, the PUnits are intended to be used as 16 user processors and 1 processor for operating system services. The 18$^{th}$ PUnit is a redundant spare processor, that may be invoked for repair during the manufacturing test flow. The spared-out processor is shut down and not functionally available.

As described in Section 10.5.2 the processor unit (PUnit) is based on the Power A2 processor core, with a SIMD quad floating point unit. In addition, the PUnit also contains an L1 prefetching unit (L1P), which implements two types of automatic data prefetching. Data is prefetched as 128 byte L2 cache lines (twice the L1 cache line length) and stored in

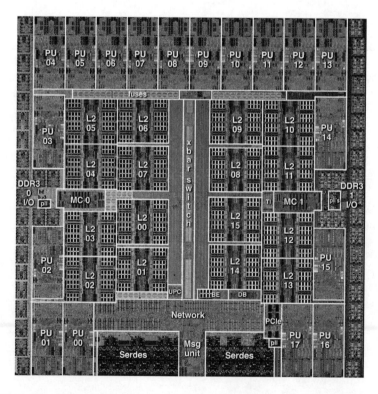

**FIGURE 10.4**: Blue Gene/Q Compute chip die photograph. ©IEEE 2012. Reprinted from [HOF$^+$12] with permission.

a buffer capable of holding 32 prefetch lines. Full coherency is maintained for all prefetched data lines.

The first of the L1P engines implements an adaptive stream prefetching algorithm. The engine assigns a variable depth to each established stream, up to a maximum of 16 streams. The largest supported depth is 8. Each stream begins with a default, preloaded depth that is typically small (like 2). When a stream is first established, data is prefetched up to this initial depth. Subsequent prefetches are triggered when an L1 miss address lies within the stream. Such hits on data that have not yet been retrieved from memory then trigger an adaptation event that increases the depth of that stream. That depth is stolen from the least recently hit stream, keeping the total depth for all active streams at or below the 32-line capacity of the prefetch buffer. With this demand-driven adaptation, buffer thrashing is reduced when many streams are active. The device will adapt to operate efficiently over a range of work loads; from a single stream from one thread, to multiple streams and multiple threads.

The second prefetch scheme targets repetitive, deterministic code, such as that in iterative solvers, in which the same sequence of addresses is accessed again and again. This new method requires the beginning and end of a repeating code segment to be identified in the application program. Once activated, each list prefetching engine (one per thread) will capture the subsequent series of L1 miss addresses. The captured miss addresses are packed in a list written to memory. On later execution of this repetitive portion of code, the recorded sequence is read from memory and the list of addresses is used to prefetch the needed data. The loading of the recorded list and the subsequent data prefetching is synchronized with code execution. On each iteration, the list is refined, adapting to missing or extraneous fetches.

The second level (L2) cache is 32 MB with 128 B lines, and is shared across all processor cores. To provide sufficient bandwidth, it is split into 16 slices, labeled as L2_00 - L2_15 in Figure 10.4. Physical addresses are scattered across the slices via a programmable hash function, to achieve uniform slice utilization. The interconnection between the PUnits/L1Ps and the L2 slices is via a crossbar switch that is located along the vertical centerline of the chip.

The L2 slices are 16-way set associative, operate in write-back mode, and have 2 MB capacity each. Data+ECC storage is implemented using 8 embedded DRAM (eDRAM) macros per slice for dense, power efficient, and high bandwidth storage.

The L2-cache serves as point of coherence and as point of control for atomic accesses, when using the PowerISA's LARX/STCX instructions. Given the large number of concurrent threads and the target of high aggregate performance, the L2 cache provides additional hardware assist features to accelerate sequential code and to help with thread interactions. Specifically, the L2 cache provides memory speculation support and atomic memory update operations. These features, described in detail in an upcoming article [OWG+13], provide effective hardware support for Transactional Memory (TM) and Speculative Execution (SE) programming models (also see Sections 10.7.2, 10.11).

L2 cache misses are handled by dual on-chip memory controllers (MC0, MC1 in Figure 10.4) that drive the DDR3 integrated I/O blocks located on the left and right edges of the chip. We elaborate on the memory subsystem in the next section.

The network and messaging unit occupies the south end of the chip. It is further described in Section 10.5.5.

## 10.5.4 External Memory System

Any memory accesses not found in the L2 cache are serviced by two memory controllers. Each memory controller interfaces to external SDRAM-DDR3 through a 16-Byte-wide (+2B overhead) channel.

As a system of 20 PFLOPs will contain over 7 million DRAM chips, the error checking and correction (ECC) system must be powerful. BG/Q uses 8B of check bits on a 64B data block. This ECC scheme offers double symbol error correct and triple detect, where a symbol is 2 bits wide by 4 beats. With a partial or full chip-kill (i.e., 2 or more bad symbols in one 8-bit-wide memory device), the code can correct one additional bad symbol. The ECC algorithm has two modes of operation, fast or slow. The fast mode is used for most accesses. If data is corrected on a read it is written back to memory. If the read has an uncorrectable error (UE), it is retried a programmable number of times, which often corrects data transmission errors. If still uncorrected then slow mode is invoked to correct the error using an advanced algorithm. The error is usually corrected, but a chip mark (indicating a bad RAM) may be set. To prevent errors from accumulating, the controller reads, corrects, and writes back the entire memory in about an hour as a background (scrubbing) operation.

The memory controllers are designed to support multiple DDR3 density/rank/speed configurations. BG/Q currently ships with 16GB of memory per BQC chip, using 2 ranks of 2Gb DDR3 DRAM at 1.333 Gb/s. In this configuration, the peak DDR bandwidth is 42.7 GB/s, excluding ECC. With 2 ranks of memory devices, the average sustainable bandwidth is slightly less than 70% of the peak bandwidth for a 1:1 write-to-read access ratio.

For high reliability the 1.35V DRAM chips are directly soldered onto the same Compute Card as the BQC chip. The data nets on the Compute Card are therefore quite short and can be left virtually un-terminated, saving power.

A large number of error counters were implemented to assist with identifying failures. At the end of an application run, these counters are logged to the control system database. An offline preventive maintenance program can scan this database and identify candidate memory replacements. With the combination of error correction and a preventive maintenance program we expect very few application fails due to memory errors, even in the largest systems.

## 10.5.5    Interconnect Design

A detailed description of the BG/Q interconnection network is given in [CEH$^+$11, CEH$^+$12], and only a brief description will be given here. As described in Section 10.5.1, the BG/Q compute nodes are connected in a five-dimensional (5D) torus configuration, in which each BQC chip uses 10 chip-to-chip communication links that each simultaneously send at 2 GB/s and receive at 2 GB/s. Point-to-point, collective and barrier messages between nodes are all implemented over this 5D torus network. A subset of the compute nodes, called bridge nodes, uses an 11$^{th}$ communication link to connect to I/O nodes. Thus, counting the I/O link, a BQC chip can support a total network bandwidth of 44 GB/s per node. The on-chip network logic that supports these 11 chip-to-chip communication links also supports collective broadcast and reduction operations, including integer and floating point sum, min and max. Such operations can therefore stay within the network logic and do not have to involve the PUnits.

The messaging unit (MU) provides an optimized interface between the network routing logic and the memory subsystem, with enough bandwidth to keep all the links busy. Using crossbar switch master ports to connect into the memory subsystem, the MU provides remote DMA capability, including remote puts, remote gets, and memory FIFO messages. The MU thereby offloads the most demanding aspects of messaging from the PUnits.

On BQC chips configured as I/O nodes, two of the 11 chip communication ports are repurposed and combined to form a PCIe Gen2 x8 (4GB/s) interface, supporting InfiniBand or 10 Gb/s Ethernet communication cards to the outside world. Two other 2 GB/s links connect back from the I/O node to two different compute bridge nodes, thus balancing the

4 GB/s PCIe port. On-chip, the PCIe interface logic is connected to the memory subsystem via a single crossbar switch master port.

### 10.5.6 System Packaging

All BG/Q midplanes and I/O drawers are clocked synchronously from a master clock propagated through up to 4 layers of low jitter 1-10 clock buffers. Within the midplane and IO drawer, more clock buffers deliver the clock signal to all compute and link chips. Thus all chips are frequency locked, but will have clock phase differences. This system-wide synchronous clock design simplifies the send and receive logic for all chip-to-chip communication links, maximizing bandwidth and reducing power.

As stated earlier BG/Q has a power efficiency of about 2.0 GFLOPS/W. With an aggregate peak performance of 209.7 TFLOPS/rack, a highly efficient application could consume nearly 100 kW/rack. This power is supplied by four air-cooled 26.5 kW bulk power enclosures (BPE) per rack. Each BPE contains $8 + 1$ (spare) independent 50 V DC bulk-power modules (BPMs) delivering 2.9 kW each, at 92.5% efficiency. Each BPE can source two connections to each of eight node boards, where each connection cable is capable of carrying the full 60 A at 50 V DC to power a 3 kW node board at full current. By delivering power in this way, resistive losses are greatly reduced. Each node-board assembly comprises two pluggable direct-current assemblies (DCA), only one of which is required. The DCA converts the 50 V DC from the BPE to a set of intermediate voltages that are supplied to the node board and converted to seven different low-voltage/high-current domains near the point of load. At least one and, for high current domains, two extra point-of-load converters will preserve voltage in the event of a supply fail.

The BPMs are cooled with an integrated fan whose speed varies with output current. Within the BG/Q compute rack, water cools all other heat-producing components. All water to the rack flows first through a system of sensors, electronics, and shut-off valves collectively called the *Coolant Monitor*, which measures a number of parameters such as water flow rates, temperatures, and pressures, as well as ambient-air temperature and relative humidity. If preset thresholds are violated a warning is issued or, if severe, power is turned off the rack and fast acting shutoff valves are automatically closed.

On a node board assembly, all major components (compute cards, power supplies, link chips, and optics) are cooled with water that flows through a single, continuous serpentine copper tube. This tube is formed, pressed into an extruded-aluminum rail, and then machined to make a flat-topped cold rail surface. This cold rail assembly is placed upon the node board power supplies and link chips, and is connected intimately to the node board optical transceivers to keep them at a stable temperature below 50°C. Finally the compute cards, covered by an aluminum heat spreader, are inserted into their node board power and signal receptacles while simultaneously making a thermal connection to the top side of the cold rail. There are 13 different thermal interface layers used in the node board assembly, each designed to keep their associated electronics well below its maximum allowed operating temperature.

Further details of the Blue Gene/Q system packaging may be found in [CHT+13].

### 10.5.7 Storage System

As stated earlier, a subset of compute nodes, called bridge nodes, in each midplane use an additional 11th out-of-torus link to connect to external I/O nodes located in I/O drawers. Compute nodes are diskless so all access to storage and external communication must follow this path. The midplane is designed such that as many as 128 of the 512 compute nodes can act as bridge nodes. However, more typical configurations are 8 or 16 compute nodes within the midplane. This is a cabling decision that is made when a system is built and installed.

Compute nodes that are not bridge nodes may communicate with an I/O node by directing their messages over the 5D torus to a bridge node which then relays the message to the I/O node on the 11th link. The MU will route the message without any involvement by the processors in the bridge node. The mapping of compute nodes to their bridge nodes is static and defined by the control system.

I/O drawers contain 8 I/O nodes and each I/O node has two out-of-torus links to the compute nodes. Therefore, an I/O node has two direct links to two different bridge nodes. I/O drawers contain a PCIe Gen2 x8 (4GB/s) slot for each of the 8 I/O nodes installed in the drawer. A typical system will have either QDR InfiniBand or dual 10Gbps Ethernet adapters installed in these slots. These adapters link to an external InfiniBand or Ethernet switch complex to provide access to an external parallel filesystem.

---

## 10.6    System Software

### 10.6.1    Overview of System Software

The system software objectives on Blue Gene/Q are ultra-scalability, high reliability, and delivering the full performance capability of the hardware to applications. The Blue Gene/Q system software has achieved these goals while adding functionality and flexibility over what was offered in previous versions of Blue Gene. Part of the software stack was improved with innovative evolutionary progress, such as unified sub-blocks and the ability to overcommit hardware threads. Other areas, such as Transactional Memory and Speculative Execution, represent a revolutionary step forward. In this section we describe the overall software architecture for Blue Gene/Q. We then describe each of the main components of the software stack. In each area, we focus on the major enhancements introduced in the Blue Gene/Q system software stack.

Over a decade ago, we began designing system software [MAA+05] for Blue Gene/L, the first generation of supercomputers in the Blue Gene line. At that time, large High Performance Computing (HPC) machines counted thousands of cores and we were designing a machine with a hundred thousand cores, roughly a two-orders-of-magnitude increase. There are two approaches on how we could make that jump. We could have taken an existing stack, evaluated the scalability challenges, fixed those, and iterated on this design. Instead we chose an approach to start with a clean slate design and to determine how to design system software for ultra-scalability. Since Blue Gene was at first a research project, the original system software stack was rightfully viewed as targeted at core HPC applications. It did not contain support for some common Unix type services. However, Blue Gene/L had much broader applicability than originally anticipated, and its success led to the following generation Blue Gene/P.

For Blue Gene/P, the system software made some significant strides forward in terms of generality and support of more common Linux interfaces such as glibc and pthreads. The larger team was able to build on the expertise, code base, and success from the first generation to implement these enhancements. As we began designing the Blue Gene/Q system software stack five years ago, we were facing the challenges of an HPC community needing a richer ecosystem and more complex hardware. Appreciating the value of the strides we made on Blue Gene/P, we designed the Blue Gene/Q system software stack to push toward greater flexibility and generality and increased open source (see Table 10.6 and Figures 10.5 and 10.6).

**TABLE 10.6**: A listing of the different components in the Blue Gene/L and Blue Gene/Q system software stacks demonstrating the increased generality provided in Blue Gene/Q.

| | **Property** | **BG/L** | **BG/Q** |
|---|---|---|---|
| Overall Philosophy | Scalability | Scale infinitely, minimal functionality | Scale infinitely, added more functionality |
| | Openness | Closed | Almost all open |
| Programming Model | Shared Memory | No | Yes |
| | Hybrid | 2 processes 1 thread (software managed) | 1-64 processes 64-1 threads |
| | Low-Level General Msg | No | PAMI, generic parallel program runtimes, wake-up unit |
| | Programming Models | MPI, ARMCI, global arrays | MPI, OpenMP, UPC, ARMCI, global arrays, Charm++ |
| Kernel | System call interface | Proprietary | Linux/POSIX system calls |
| | Library/threading | glibc/proprietary | glibc/pthreads |
| | Linking | Static only | Static or dynamic |
| | Compute Node OS | CNK | CNK, Linux, Red Hat |
| | I/O Node OS | Linux | SMP Linux with SMT, Red Hat |
| Control | Scheduling | Generic API | Generic and real-time API |
| | Run Mode | HPC, prototype HTC | Integrated HPC, HTC, MPMD, and sub-blocks, HA with job cont |
| Tools | Tools | HPC Toolkit | HPC Toolkit, Dyninst, Valgrind, PAPI |
| Research Initiatives | OS | Scaling Linux | ZeptoOS, Plan 9 |
| | Big Data | N/A | BGAS (Blue Gene Active Storage), Large memory nodes |
| | Commercial | N/A | Kittyhawk, Cloud, SLAcc |

## 10.6.2   Operating System

The operating systems for the Blue Gene/Q inherit the dual-kernel architecture of previous Blue Gene machines. I/O nodes run a Linux-based operating system and serve as a proxy to and from the external network. The compute nodes run a Blue Gene customized operating system called CNK (Compute Node Kernel). CNK connects to the I/O nodes for File I/O, sockets, and job and tool interaction. CNK on Blue Gene/Q has significant advances over previous Blue Gene kernels.

Increasingly, customers want to run more sophisticated and complicated applications on Blue Gene and with 64 hardware threads on a Blue Gene/Q node, the ability to handle complex threading applications is important. However, it is challenging to keep 64 hardware threads efficiently exploiting the full hardware. To achieve high utilization, it is critical to avoid serialization behind a single lock. For the design of the CNK scheduler, we considered various scheduler options such as global versus local and core-scoped versus hardware-thread-scoped. A hardware-thread scoped scheduler was chosen for implementation due to its characteristics of multiple software thread capability and lock-free contention. For each hardware thread, CNK allocates five slots for software threads and schedules work based on their relative priorities. The software threads are intended to provide simultaneous threads for XL OpenMP, GNU OpenMP, pthreads, and Speculative Execution, although they can be used for other purposes as well. The fifth thread is available so that the clone syscall can

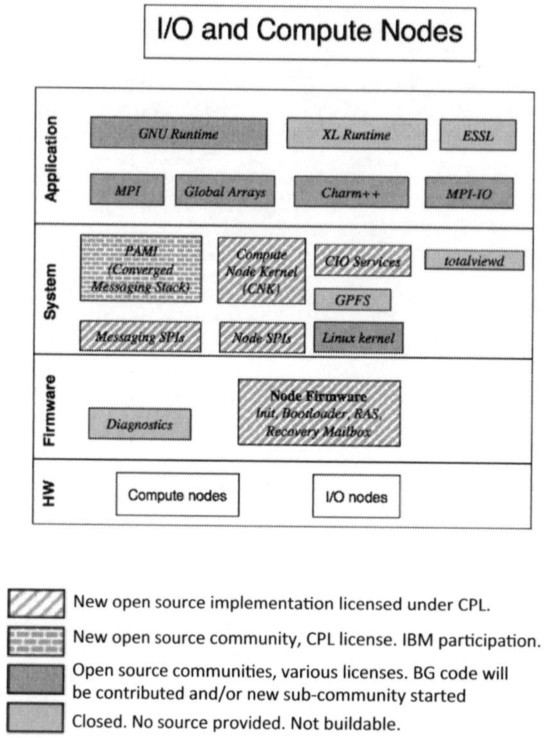

**FIGURE 10.5**: A depiction of the different components in the Blue Gene/Q system software stack and their open source status for the I/O and Compute nodes.

succeed placing a new thread before its new hardware thread affinity is assigned. We also had a design goal to minimize performance jitter introduced by operating system functions. Thus, the scheduler does not have timer ticks or round-robin pre-emption. As the application runs, it may use pthread_set_affinity() calls to migrate software threads from one hardware thread to another. Thread creation and migration are the only times in which the kernel threads block for threading operations.

CNK leverages a 17th core for operating system function to further isolate jitter. This core is used for control message processing, I/O messaging, special hardware event and error processing, debugger protocols, and application agent threads.

I/O scaling was also a challenging design problem for Blue Gene/Q. Common customer configurations have a compute node to I/O node ratio of 128 to 1. In that common configuration, each I/O node needs to accommodate 128 compute nodes communicating across the torus via an OFED verbs interface. If an I/O node fails, the control system routes around the failure and each remaining I/O node needs to handle the additional compute node load. Each compute node could have up to 64 processes running, and therefore an I/O node will serve up to 8,192 compute processes, in the normal case, and even more in the presence of a failed I/O node. On Blue Gene/P there was a one-to-one mapping of I/O processes to compute node processes. This simplified handling of process context and block-

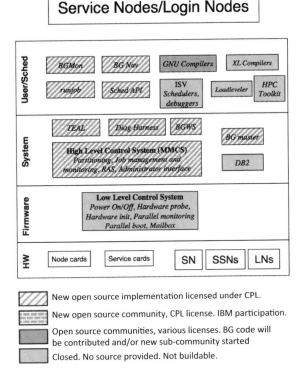

**FIGURE 10.6**: A depiction of the different components in the Blue Gene/Q system software stack and their open source status for the Service/Login nodes.

ing I/O by Linux processes. However, there was a concern about having a huge number of processes per I/O node this strategy implied. Thus we designed to minimize the number of processes needed to handle the compute nodes. Rather than 8,192 processes mirroring the compute processes, we spawn two processes per compute node (or 256 for the above case). A sysiod process filesystem and socket operations and a toolctld process handles tool or debugger connections. The sysiod daemon uses openat() functions in place of open() to avoid modeling current working directory state. Instead, each process on the compute nodes individually tracks their current directory and translates file descriptors between the ionode's file descriptor and the compute process' descriptor.

Another area of scaling optimization was improving the application load and application exit performance. For loading an application into memory, a leader node is selected within the compute block. The leader reads the executable and performs a collective broadcast operation to all the compute nodes on the Blue Gene/Q torus. Application exit performance is also important. To significantly enhance the exit performance, it is required to summarize the pass/fail status of the application via a unified exit code. The compute nodes use an L2 (Level 2 cache) atomic torus packet to quickly identify the maximum exit status across the entire application. Additionally, the first compute node to fail is obtained by performing an L2 atomic load-and-fetch operation across the torus. The Blue Gene control system is notified of the failure only by the first process to fail. Once all the exits have occurred, only the leader emits the final status to the control system. This architecture avoids the control system bottleneck in accounting for each process in the system.

Another design challenge was achieving reliability on the system with 1.6 million cores. To address issues with hardware reliability, we structured the kernel software such that the firmware resides in the on-die 256kiB BeDRAM (Boot embedded DRAM) and created machine check vectors to the BeDRAM-resident instructions and data. This removes the requirement for L2 cache and DDR (Double Data Rate) memory to be functional in order service a machine check, which diminishes the frequency of silent hangs. To address issues with software reliability, we use the Blue Gene/Q wakeup unit's address compare ranges to detect guard page violations between stack and heap. As the heap location grows, the kernel moves the guard page location. This allows the application to have both guard page protection and a pinned memory mapping without a page table and associated overhead.

One of the major features of the Blue Gene/Q chip is support for Transactional Memory and Speculative Execution. There is significant support in the kernel to implement the policy needed by the associated runtime library. Originally, we considered a design that would deliver a signal whenever a speculative violation occurred. This left the runtime software with the responsibility of determining the response. As we explored that option, it became apparent that there would be many potential timing exposures due to speculative memory conflicts or invalidations, which would be difficult to overcome. Instead, we structured the code such that the kernel always runs in non-speculative mode and does not access user memory speculatively unless requested. When a speculative interrupt occurs, the kernel executes a pre-arranged algorithm to determine whether the thread continues or rolls back. The runtime pre-defines parameters to determine conflict priorities and register state in the case of a rollback event. Jail mode, a protected mode that limits threads actions, and a specific list of allowable syscalls protects the application from performing operations that result in any I/O operations that cannot be rolled back.

Another challenge with the Blue Gene/Q chip was debugging a new design with 68 concurrent hardware threads (or hwthreads), transactional memory, and complex I/O. We developed a lockless flight recorder technology using the L2 atomics support. Each entry contains a message code, hwthread number, timestamp, and up to four 64-bit data words. The kernel code was heavily instrumented with these flight recorder entries. There are over 130 instrumentation points allowing for debug of complex timing problems as well as application optimization.

### 10.6.3   File Systems

Section 10.5.7 provided a description of the interconnect and configuration between compute nodes and I/O nodes. At assembly time, systems may be configured to have different ratios of compute nodes to I/O nodes with 64:1 and 128:1 ratios being the most common. The function shipping mechanism from CNK to the I/O node over this interconnect was described in the previous section.

The I/O nodes run a full Linux distribution. Blue Gene leverages Linux to provide access to external parallel file systems. Parallel file system client software may be installed and configured on all the I/O nodes to provide file system access to processes running on Linux. The sysiod daemons described in the previous section run as ordinary Linux processes under the credentials of the application user, thus providing access to these configured Linux file systems from CNK.

In the time frame of Blue Gene's development, parallel file systems have not been scaling to the number of clients needed by Blue Gene, were each compute node to have hosted its own file system client. The function shipping concept not only allowed CNK to remain simple and lightweight, but also addressed the file system client scaling problem by reducing the number of file system clients by two orders of magnitude. While this mechanism has reduced the number of clients, it has not necessarily reduced the number of files that might be opened simultaneously by an application.

Blue Gene/Q CNK introduced a simplified memory-based file system that may be accessed by processes local to the node. The file system is simplified for integration into a lightweight kernel, and it is simplified to allow efficient implementation of a remote access feature. The I/O node tools interface provides the ability to use torus RDMA to read CNK local files without communicating with CNK. This allows an application to write local data (e.g., checkpoint data) that may be transferred to remote storage in the background by I/O node software.

### 10.6.4 Control System

The Blue Gene control system is designed to seamlessly scale from a half rack of hardware (512 nodes), through greater than 256 racks (over 260 thousand nodes). On Blue Gene/Q we introduced several new capabilities to the control system. These include: high available through automatic failover with job continuation to remove a single point of failure, sub-block jobs for increased flexibility in job scheduling, a unified scheduling mechanism for simplified job control, and TEAL, an enhanced event analyzer.

The Blue Gene/Q control system uses a DB2 database for persistent storage of machine configuration, active and historical jobs, and operational status. The control system software runs on the Blue Gene/Q Service Node and manages the information stored in this database. Previous generation control systems for Blue Gene/L and Blue Gene/P had a single point of failure in the Service Node. Should this system become unavailable, any jobs running on the Blue Gene hardware were forcefully terminated. The Blue Gene/Q control system resolves this single point of failure by enabling job reconnection from a backup Service Node, which is automatically made active, when the primary node fails. This capability is largely transparent to applications, although some standard output may be lost during the failover process.

The control system on every Blue Gene/L, Blue Gene/P, and Blue Gene/Q system supports the concept of subdividing the machine's resources into logical entities known as blocks. These blocks are electrically isolated from each other and may be as small as 32 nodes, to as large as the entire machine. On a specific system the minimum block size may be larger as a block must have at least one connected I/O node. Larger blocks utilize optical cables to complete a multi-dimensional torus network, whereas smaller blocks are networked through their encompassing node boards and midplanes. Blue Gene/L supported a single job per block. Blue Gene/P extended this concept with High Throughput Computing (HTC) where a job can occupy a single node, though this decision had to be made at the time the block was booted. The single nodes for HTC jobs cannot communicate with one another. The Blue Gene/Q control system extends this capability by providing sub-block jobs. These jobs can range in size from a single node up to 512 nodes and a decision is made at job launch time, instead of at block boot time. The size of the job must be rectangular where each of the five dimensions can only be one, two, or four nodes. This allows greater use of the machine with less fragmentation for capacity workloads that do not occupy the entire system. It also preserves the HTC single-node type workloads that we enabled in BG/P, but extends the capabilities by not requiring a decision to be made at block boot time, but rather at job submission time.

The job submission architecture in the control system has changed significantly when compared to the previous generation systems. The most notable difference is the unification of the different job modes including HTC and HPC from BG/L and BG/P into a single consistent interface called runjob. Previous systems had different commands for different workloads, resulting in multiple and confusing interfaces. The unified runjob submission architecture presents a single consistent interface for both sub-block jobs and jobs using the entire block. The design provides a smooth path for moving work from the previous generations of Blue Gene systems to Blue Gene/Q.

As HPC systems move toward exascale, being able to detect, capture, analyze, and respond to errors is becoming increasingly important. On Blue Gene/Q we introduced the Toolkit for Event Analysis and Logging (TEAL), an event analysis framework based on the Blue Gene/P Event Log Analysis (ELA) and Federation ELA. It is designed as a pluggable processing pipeline that allows different components to use connectors to log events, analyze the events, create and log alerts, and deliver the alerts to interested parties. TEAL supports the processing of events as they occur, i.e., real-time analysis, and events that have occurred in the past, i.e., historic analysis. Analyzers specific to Blue Gene/Q look for events taking hardware offline, such as compute nodes, I/O nodes, bulk power modules, and cables. Events causing abnormal job termination are also analyzed. Listeners can be configured to send an email, write to a file, or invoke an external program.

## 10.7    Programming System

### 10.7.1    Programming Models, PAMI, and Messaging

The messaging layer on Blue Gene/Q maintains the philosophy of providing the full capability and performance of the hardware to user-space. Its primary realization is in the Parallel Active Message Interface (PAMI) illustrated in Figure 10.7. PAMI is a new high-performance and feature-rich set that serves as a common messaging layer across IBM's HPC platforms and is designed to be extensible to other platforms. PAMI is used as a foundation to support MPI (Message Passing Interface), which is the primary programming model being used in HPC today. However, it can also be used to support other popular programming models such as UPC (Unified Parallel C), ARMCI (Aggregate Remote Memory Copy Interface), and Charm$^{++}$. It improves upon the earlier DCMF (Deep Computing Messaging Framework) and LAPI (Low-level Application Programming Interface) facilities from which it was unified, by providing support for efficient point-to-point and collective communication.

PAMI allows for multiple independent communications incorporating new concepts for end-point addressing. It also supports non-contiguous data conversion. The API is non-blocking and supports integrated collectives that are optimized for the BG/Q platform. Many HPC applications exhibit locality with most of the communication occurring between neighboring peers. To support such communication patterns, PAMI supports low-latency and high-bandwidth messaging using shared memory within a node. The fundamental components used to support these operations are a) *BG/Q scalable atomic primitives* to support lockless queues and b) *Shared addressing in CNK (Compute Node Kernel)* that allows sharing of address spaces so that a process can directly read the memory belonging to another peer process sharing the same node. The lockless queues are used in the point-to-point protocols to enable low latency. Shared addressing is used to achieve high bandwidth for messaging and to provide optimizations for collectives such as broadcast and allreduce. These are explained below.

*BG/Q scalable atomic primitives*: BG/Q nodes support different atomic operations such as load-increment, store-update, etc., for 64-bit integer words in memory. These atomic operations have been implemented by special atomic addresses that are aliases to the L2/DDR memory. L2 atomics have significantly lower overheads than traditional mutexes. They are scalable with only a few extra cycles for each additional atomic request. The L2 atomics are used in several places including lockless queues and messaging counters that are used to track communication progress.

*Shared addressing in CNK*: To aid message passing within the node, CNK provides global virtual addresses within the node. These addresses are aliases to the virtual addresses of the processes and can be used by any process on the node to read the memory locations of its peers. CNK provides a separate global virtual to physical address translation table containing the global addresses of all the processes on the node. This capability eliminates extra copies in the message passing operations between processes on the same node, both for point-to-point and collective operations.

*Lockless queues*: The L2 Atomic operations provide convenient and scalable atomic constructs that can be used to design communication queues for different message passing operations. One of the supported L2 Atomics operations is "bounded increment." This combines an atomic load-and-increment with a compare against bounds, enabling atomic allocation of elements to a fixed-sized array used to implement a fast scalable queue. This fixed-sized array is enhanced with an overflow queue to handle cases when the array is full. The overflow queue is accessed through mutexes.

*BG/Q Collective network*: The BG/Q network supports hardware acceleration for collectives such as barrier, broadcast, reduce, and allreduce for both MPI_COMM_WORLD as well as rectangular subcommunicators. This is provided via a classroute that allows the user or library to program the routes of the collective tree. Each classroute specifies the links that are the down tree inputs to the router and the uptree output. The local contribution is also included, and the tree can skip the contribution from a node depending on whether this bit is on or off. The number of classroutes in which a node can participate is 16; however some are reserved for the system use. The collective network supports both integer and floating point operations such as add, min, and max.

*Shared Address Collectives over BG/Q*: As copy costs dominate the intra-node perfor-

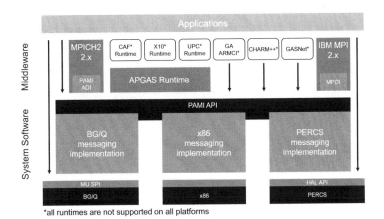

**FIGURE 10.7**: PAMI is a flexible and extensible messaging interface that is supported across IBM platforms including Blue Gene/Q.

mance of a collective with multiple processes per node, we deploy the "shared address" approach to reduce the data movement within the node. Using global addresses within the node, a process can read the data from its peers. This feature is used to efficiently implement collectives such as MPI_Bcast (Broadcast) and MPI_Allreduce. In MPI_Bcast, a master process from each node is designated to post RDMA (Remote Direct Memory Access) descriptors to the collective network and the data directly arrives to its own buffer. Thereafter, other peers on the node can directly copy the data arrived using the global virtual address of the master.

For MPI_Allreduce, there is an extra logical step of doing the local math within the node. Depending on the message size, we use two different approaches for performing math and pipelining with the network operations. For short messages, performing the local math is parallelized and a single network descriptor, which describes the entire local result obtained, is injected into the network. All masters from all nodes are responsible for injecting descriptors and polling on the counters, checking for the arriving data. The network sum from the collective network arrives directly into the master's receive buffer through the use of the RDMA write feature. The other peers wait for the master and copy the final result directly from the master's receive buffer. For large messages, we use pipelining across the local math, network allreduce, and local broadcast to achieve the best performance. To do this, each process operates on a slice of buffers and reports to the master after it is done. The master injects all the slices and the ordering of injection is maintained across all the masters of the nodes. The result is copied from the master's buffer in the same manner as described above.

*Performance results*: Using the optimizations described above, we achieve close to a micro-second latency for point-to-point operations intra-node using the lockless queues. The atomic operation finishes in much less time than a microsecond; the extra protocol overhead associated with active messages contributes most to the overall latency observed. For collectives, MPI_Allreduce over PAMI and for processes per node (PPN) counts of 1, 4, and 16, the respective latencies on 2,048 nodes are 5.5 microseconds, 5.0 microseconds, and 5.3 microseconds. We achieve a throughput of 1,704MB/sec (95% of peak) with a PPN of 1 for an 8MB allreduce. At PPN counts of 4 and 16, we achieve a throughput of 1,693MB/s (94% of peak) for a 2MB allreduce and 1,643MB/s (91% of peak) for a 512KB allreduce, respectively. For MPI_Bcast over PAMI, with a PPN of 1, we achieve a performance of 1,728MB/s (96% of peak) for a 32MB broadcast. At a PPN count of 4, the best performance is 1,722MB/s with a 4MB buffer size, while at PPN count of 16, we achieve a throughput of 1,701MB/s for a 1MB buffer.

## 10.7.2   Languages and Compilers

There are four key areas of innovation in the IBM XL C/C++/Fortran Compiler support for BG/Q. The first area is in the OpenMP Language Specification 3.1 support implemented in XL's SMP runtime. The implementation utilizes the hardware L2 atomics and fast wakeup mechanism.

The second area is in the exploitation of Quad Processing eXtension (QPX) to the Power ISA (Instruction Set Architecture)) instructions. This is accomplished by the optimizations of automatic vectorization and SIMDization (SIMD - Single Instruction Multiple Data). Both optimizations are part of the Toronto Portable Optimizer (TPO) of the XL compiler, which provides a high-order loop transformation framework. Automatic vectorization is capable of recognizing common usage of mathematical routines such as div, exp, and log, inside a loop. It transforms the loop into calls to vectorized routines, namely the vdiv, vexp, and vlog. It allocates temporary vectors when needed. The vectorized routines typically accept a trip count and references to data arrays as input parameters. The vectorized routines utilize QPX instructions to compute results in parallel. The compiler supports a stand-alone MASS (Mathematical Acceleration SubSystem) library tuned for optimum performance for BG/Q to which users can make direct calls. It includes 82 vector functions (single-precision or double-precision) as well as 4-way SIMD versions to be used by automatic SIMDization.

Automatic SIMDization is also a loop transformation where a floating point loop is typically blocked in groups of four such that the entire loop is transformed into a QPX loop. The optimizer is able to analyze and process the alignments of the references such that a prologue and epilogue section are generated to handle misalignment or runtime trip count. Versioning for alignments is also performed when needed. Intra- and inter-procedural alignment information reduces permutation instructions inside the SIMD loop. User-level alignment and iteration space independent directives also assist in better SIMD loop generation.

Programmers can also manually make use of QPX instructions by writing either inline assembly or using QPX intrinsics supported by the compiler. The QPX intrinsics approach is often encouraged as the code benefits from register allocation and instruction scheduling performed by the compiler.

The third key area is TM (Transactional Memory) support. To exploit this hardware feature, the compiler supports the following notation.

```
for C/C++:
#pragma tm_atomic [(safe_mode)]
{
        < code >
}
```

```
for Fortran:
!TM$ tm_atomic [safe_mode]
        < code >
!TM$ end tm_atomic
```

While the BG/Q hardware TM is bounded and can fail a transactional execution in various ways, a transaction defined by the above programming model can be arbitrarily large and is guaranteed to eventually succeed. The TM software, which includes the TM runtime and extension to the kernel and compiler support, is developed to bridge the gap between TM as a programming model and TM as a hardware implementation. The TM runtime is part of the XL SMP runtime.

The compiler is responsible for translating the tm_atomic enclosed region into two function calls to the TM runtime; namely, the tm_begin and tm_end routines surrounding the region. It is also responsible for generating register save and restore code in case a transaction is aborted and needs to retry.

The *safe_mode* clause serves as an assertion to the runtime that the TM region does not contain irrevocable actions. Irrevocable actions are actions that cannot be reverted or undone, such as a write to device I/O, and therefore needs to be protected.

The last key area is in the support for SE (Speculative Execution). The compiler supports the following speculative pragmas (or speculative directives in Fortran). The syntax mimics closely that of OpenMP parallel for-loop and sections. However, the SE programming model guarantees sequential equivalence semantics. That is, the results need to be identical as if the region is running using a single thread, sequentially. The supported clauses are private, shared, default, firstprivate, lastprivate, schedule, num_threads, and reduction which have the same meaning as the clauses supported for OpenMP.

```
for C/C++:
```

```
#pragma speculative for [clause[[,] clause]] new-line
for-loop

#pragma speculative sections [clause[[,] clause] ...] new-line
{
[#pragma speculative section new-line
structured-block]
[#pragma speculative section new-line
structured-block ]
  ...
}

for Fortran:
!SEP$ speculative do [clause [[,] clause]]
do-loop
[!SEP$ end speculative do]

!SEP$ speculative sections [clause[[,] clause] ...]
[!SEP$ speculative section
structured-block ]
[!SEP$ speculative section
structured-block ]
...
!SEP$ end speculative sections
```

Speculative Execution requires in order start, as well as in order commit of threads. The workload is split into a sequence of work units, namely chunks, and assigned to a team of n threads, in sequence. A complete round of allocation assigns work units to thread $T_0$, $T_1$, ...,$T_{n-2}$, $T_{n-1}$. By dispatching the threads in order, and committing them in order, program semantics is preserved.

The SE runtime is also part of XL's SMP runtime. When hardware speculation fails too many times, the SE runtime needs to revert back to use only a single thread to execute the remaining work in the region. The synchronization of speculative threads is managed by the SE runtime.

To assist users in understanding the behavior of their application, both the TM and SE runtimes collect a set of counters. The collection is done in a light-weight manner with as little application perturbation as possible. Users can print or query the contents of the counters. Information such as the total number of rollbacks and serializations is available for tuning purposes.

TM and SE runtimes both support up to 16 speculation domains per node, which allows the support of multiple MPI processes per node. When an application utilizes both TM and SE, the runtime provides a mechanism to reset the hardware speculation mode so that part of the application can benefit from the TM hardware and another part can benefit from the SE.

## 10.7.3   Tools — Correctness, Debugging, Performance

Over the past decade there has been an increase in the richness of the ecosystem for supercomputing. This has been motivated in part by increasing complexity in the hardware and in part by a user desire for more effective tools for programming, debugging, and performance tuning their applications. To meet this need on Blue Gene/Q we moved toward leveraging open source initiatives. As such, many tools for Blue Gene are developed by third parties. For Blue Gene/L and Blue Gene/P these developers had to wait for the IBM software to be made available before they could start working on their tools, and also had to rely more on their understanding of the released code. This meant that Blue Gene customers had to wait three to six months before they could start using these tools. For Blue Gene/Q we put in place a mechanism for providing expertise early on in the process, in order to provide a wider array of tools to be ready when the machine was available.

Significant legal complications were involved in working with third parties prior to the release of the hardware and software. However, many advantages were garnered by this process. In addition to the advantage of being able to provide the tools when the machine was released, there were others. There was additional benefit in early testing of the software stack by the tools that we intended to be on the machine. The third party tool providers could identify components missing from the software stack that their tool needed either for performance or functionality. The main ingredient for the success of this model was to maintain good communication between all parties and customers. This communication involved status updates, third party's needs, and an interlock on the schedule. The plan to open source the software stack provided additional advantage to the third parties as they knew they would be able to maintain ongoing interaction after Blue Gene/Q was released. The early and open exchange of information facilitated the tools' ability to react to the programming model of Blue Gene, finding effective alternate solutions. For example, Dyninst was able to find a different solution for the challenge that CNK does not support code relocation of static applications. They also were able to have access to all the new quad vector architecture (QPX) instructions that take advantage of Blue Gene/Q's quad floating point processor. Further, the CNK threading model introduced more flexibility than the previous solution and needed to be understood by the tool providers.

The information on how to interface with the Blue Gene software is described in the Code Development and Tools Interface Guide (CDTI). The CDTI provides the support for launching and controlling tools on a Blue Gene/Q system. A tool operates in the context of a Blue Gene job. It executes on the I/O nodes so it must be in a filesystem accessible from the I/O node. A tool can access and modify the processor state and process memory.

Tool launching has the following requirements. Up to four tools can be launched for a job. Tools can be launched on a subset of the I/O nodes servicing a job. Tools can be launched at the start of a job or they may be launched after a job has begun. This is also known as *tool attach*. Tools can be terminated before a job ends and can end at different times on different I/O nodes. Tools terminate when a job ends.

If the user wants to launch a tool during their job they need to tell the control system. The start tool command is used to tell the control system to start tools on all of the I/O nodes that are servicing the job with which they will interact. The tools communicate with the Common I/O Services (CIOS) daemons running on the I/O nodes to pass messages back and forth to the compute nodes, where the user code is running. No user code runs on the I/O node; the I/O node is just a proxy/manager for compute nodes.

## 10.8 Storage, Visualization, and Analytics

An overall view of the storage and viz system for Sequoia is shown in Figure 10.8 and for Mira in Figure 10.9.

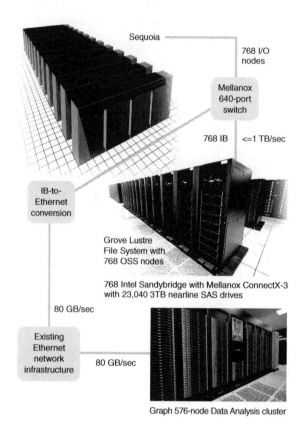

**FIGURE 10.8**: Overall view of the Sequoia storage and viz system.

## 10.8.1    Sequoia Storage Strategy

The 55-petabyte Sequoia filesystem hardware and its retooled Lustre filesystem software (together named Grove ) directly satisfy the parallel filesystem requirements of Sequoia. Users are able to rapidly store data to Grove and access or move this data to and from other platforms, visualization machines, or Lawrence Livermore National Laboratory's (LLNL's) High-Performance Storage System (HPSS) archive.

Grove's hardware base is comprised of 48 racks of NetApp E5400 storage arrays containing over 23,000 disks. Supporting this disk are 768 RAID controllers and an identical number of Appro International Green Blade-based Object Storage Servers. The entire Sequoia hardware infrastructure is tied together by a large QDR InfiniBand infrastructure. This hardware is capable of providing well over 1 terabyte per second of filesystem bandwidth to Sequoia.

Limitations of Lustre's underlying EXT-based filesystem implementation spurred LLNL software developers to replace Lustre's EXT underpinnings with ZFS, an alternate and much more scalable filesystem. LLNL and developers from Whamcloud retooled Lustre to establish the software infrastructure for Grove. This effort additionally established a canonical layering within Lustre that will allow for a wide range of alternate filesystems to exist under Lustre. ZFS' input/output (I/O) patterns, inherent scalability, and built-in integrity checking features allow high-performance Lustre operation at the scale of Grove.

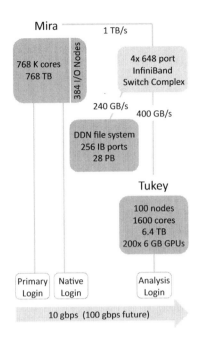

**FIGURE 10.9**: Overall view of the Mira storage and viz system.

## 10.8.2 Mira Storage Strategy

Mira, the single rack debug system named Cetus, and the associated visualization and analysis resource named Tukey will all access the same storage systems. There is a shared home filesystem. There is a pair of filesystems for programmatic access. Quotas will be set and enforced, but there is no "use it or lose it" policy, typical in scratch filesystems.

Mira will be using the IBM®General Parallel File System™(GPFS™) for the filesystems, Data Direct Network (DDN) Storage Fusion Architecture (SFA) 12Ke storage arrays for the storage hardware, and Mellanox InfiniBand cards and switches for the storage fabric. The e moniker in 12Ke indicates that the file servers are embedded inside the storage array controller running in virtual machines. This saves time, money, space, and power, since additional file servers and switches are not required. The home filesystem will have a raw capacity of 1.6PB, and a bandwidth of 60 GB/s. Dual parity RAID and filesystem level replication will be used for data protection. The filesystems for programmatic access will be an aggregate 28 PB raw with a minimum bandwidth of 240 GB/s, but a projected 300 GB/s. Dual parity RAID is used for data protection.

Advanced features being investigated include the use of HPSS (software for archival tape storage in common use in the national labs) as a hierarchical back end for GPFS and the use of asynchronous replication between the two parallel filesystems to minimize down time.

## 10.8.3 Sequoia Strategy for Post Processing, Visualization, and Analytics

Sequoia users will benefit from a suite of visualization and data analysis tools and techniques available on both Sequoia and specialized visualization platforms. The VisIt open source parallel visualization and graphical analysis tool will be available for viewing and analyzing large-scale scientific data. VisIt's viewer and engine components can be distributed across multiple machines, so users may run the client on a desktop or visualization server to leverage graphics cards for rendering while the server itself runs where data can be accessed without copying. ParaView, EnSight Gold, and other visualization and data analysis software will also be available on Livermore Computing platforms for operating on the massive datasets generated by simulations run on Sequoia.

In support of post-processing on Sequoia, LLNL deployed two visualization and data analysis machines. The interactive visualization machine Graph has 576 nodes, and the 1,296-node compute cluster Muir serves as an even larger resource for post-processing data. Graph and Muir were designed with high-speed bandwidth to the Lustre filesystem to provide users with zero-copy access to their files. Interactive exploration of large datasets requires a memory-rich environment. Therefore, Graph has more than 72 terabytes of memory (128 GB per node) and optimized input/output (I/O) to best support heavily I/O-bound post-processing tasks. Nodes will also be partitioned on Sequoia for visualization and data analysis, to be used by those whose analysis problems overwhelm the visualization platforms.

Beyond the traditional post-processing model, visualization researchers and developers will work with developers to instrument simulation codes to perform visualization and analysis operations in situ during data generation on Sequoia. For example, the VisIt Libsim library has been incorporated into several ASC codes, which will be able to take advantage of large-scale in situ operations on Sequoia. In this way, scientists will be able to operate on their simulation results as the simulation runs rather than solely depending on post-processing as a later step.

### 10.8.4   Mira Strategy for Post Processing, Visualization, and Analytics

Increasingly large and complex datasets dominate the dialog that informs design of new high performance computing systems. The image depicted in Figure 10.10, for example, comes from a national collaboration that has run large cosmological simulations on a Cray supercomputer (Jaguar at ORNL). Globus Online services have then been used to move tens of terabytes of data in tens of thousands of files to Eureka, a visualization and analysis system at ALCF. On Eureka, custom analysis software provides interactive visualizations that are remotely controlled and viewed from a large-format tiled display system at the San Diego Supercomputer Center.

Mira will be augmented by a high performance visualization and analysis cluster (named Tukey) with direct connection to both Mira and its parallel filesystem. This architecture enables a wide range of important scenarios, including: traditional post-processing on the dedicated GPU-accelerated visualization cluster; simulation-time analysis on Tukey with high bandwidth coupling to Mira; and accelerated apparent I/O on Mira by staging data to Tukey. The 100-port QDR InfiniBand network connection to Tukey provides balanced throughput to both the Mira and the filesystem ensuring performance matched to the data generation capacity of Mira.

Tukey comprises one hundred servers each configured with two 8-core AMD Opteron processors, two 6 GB Fermi 2070 GPU cards, 64 GB of CPU memory, and a QDR InfiniBand connection to the shared network fabric. Each of the processor sockets is connected to one of the GPUs and half of the memory to allow for optimal contention-free performance of demanding processes. Paraview and VisIt are open source, richly capable parallel visualization and analysis tools. They will provide Mira users with the means to interactively explore their data from remote workstations with Tukey as the rendering engine.

Support for strong compilers for mixed CPU, GPU, and GPGPU codes will let developers and users apply Tukey's computational power to problems not supported by more general purpose analysis environments like Paraview. Recent experience in developing custom high performance features for our users include: a volume rendering code with optimized GPU-based ray casting for high-speed handling of large data volumes, GPU implementation of most likely path algorithm for real-time proton tomography, and synchronized multiple-stream video for interactive visualization of large datasets over WAN.

## 10.9 Facilities

The main characteristics of the Sequoia and Mira systems are given in Table 10.7:

### 10.9.1 The Sequoia LLNL Facility

The facility that houses Sequoia–the Terascale Simulation Facility (TSF)–has 30 MW of computational electrical capacity with an ability to expand to 45 MW. The TSF has a dedicated 7,200-ton cooling tower and chilled water plant, a dedicated 2.6-million-cubic-feet-per-minute (CFM) air cooling system, and a newly installed liquid cooling process loop that is used to provide the liquid cooling solution for Sequoia. The facility consists of two 48,000-sq. ft. computer rooms. Sequoia resides in one of these rooms and encompasses about 4,000 sq. ft. of floor space. Sequoia is a small dense set of water cooled racks which are more cost and power effective to reach 20 PF than trying to accomplish a similar feat with a larger set of low power-density, air cooled racks. Sequoia exhibits high Flops/Watt coupled with low Square Foot/Flops and low Square Foot/Watt.

Sequoia has challenging mechanical, electrical, and physical requirements. Compartmentalized space planning for all utilities was required, and 3D modeling was performed to ensure the appropriate space for mechanical distribution, power distribution, network distribution, structural systems, and fire protection distribution were allocated.

The mechanical requirements for Sequoia required that the racks be 91% liquid cooled and 9% air cooled. The liquid cooling requirements required that the temperature of the

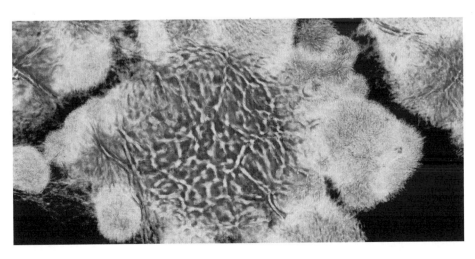

**FIGURE 10.10**: The effect of light from early galaxies on the gasses filling the universe. Image courtesy of Argonne National Laboratory.

**FIGURE 10.11**: Process tertiary piping loop and connections installed in the mechanical room.

water ranged between 64 degrees F to 74 degrees F. This requirement was met by the installation of a new tertiary loop (see Figure 10.11).

In addition to the liquid temperature requirements, the new tertiary process loop must maintain water pressure at 25 pounds per sq. in. (psi), handle water temperature rise of 20

**TABLE 10.7**: Main characteristics of the Sequoia and Mira systems.

| | Sequoia | Mira |
|---|---|---|
| CPU-core frequency | 1.6 GHz | 1.6 GHz |
| Peak speed per node | 204.8 GFlops | 204.8 GFlops |
| Compute nodes per rack | 1,024 | 1,024 |
| Peak speed per rack | 209.7 TFlops | 209.7 TFlops |
| Compute node memory | 16 GB | 16 GB |
| I/O node memory | 16 GB | 16 GB |
| Rack compute memory | 16.4 TB | 16.4 TB |
| Racks | 96 | 48 |
| Peak system speed | 20 PFlops | 10 PFlops |
| System compute memory | 1.6 PB | 787 TB |
| Compute to IO nodes | 128 to 1 | 128 to 1 |
| Filesystem | Lustre, 55PB capacity, 1 TB/sec peak BW | GPFS, Home 1.6 PB storage, 60 GB/s bandwidth, Data 28 PB storage, 300 GB/s bandwidth |
| Interconnect | 5D torus compute net, IB for I/O and storage | 5D torus compute net, IB for I/O and storage |
| Viz | Graph is the viz system it has 576 24 core AMD Istanbul nodes with 128GB memory per node | Tukey system is 100 nodes with dual-8 core AMD Opteron processors, 64GB cpu memory and two 6GB Fermi m2070 GPU cards |
| Footprint | 4500 Sq. ft. | 2,500 Sq. Ft. for Mira, and all support infrastructure |
| Operating ambient temp | 65 F - 70 F | 65 F - 70 F |
| Operating water temp | 62 F supply | 64 F |
| Water flow | AMB to supply: 30 to 35 gallons per minute | 25 gallons per minute at each rack |
| Rack booted/idle Watts | 58 KW | 58 KW |
| Rack running Linpack Watts | 93.75 KW | 93.75 KW . |
| Max watts per rack | 100 KW | 100 KW |
| Max system watts | 9.6 MW | 4.8 MW |

**FIGURE 10.12**: Custom underfloor power distribution unit.

degrees F, and provide 25 to 30 gal./min. (gpm) to each rack. This equates to about 2,800 gpm for the entire system.

The biggest challenge for the tertiary process loop was the requirement that all of the piping be either stainless steel or copper. Both of these are very expensive and drove project installation costs higher than originally anticipated. This led to striving to find alternate cost-effective piping materials. After much search and review, a polypropylene sustainable piping system was sourced instead of stainless steel or copper piping. This resulted in a 2M dollar net savings to the project. This sustainable piping system will also help the TSF maintain Leadership in Energy and Environmental Design (LEED) Gold Status; provide efficient flow, reduce heat gain and loss, and minimize environmental chemical impacts.

The electrical distribution requires 100 kW per rack for a total of 9.6 MW of power for the system. Each rack has four 480-V, three-phase, 60-A line cords. These requirements drove installation of an innovative electrical distribution to reduce the amount of conduit to minimize the under-floor congestion. The system engineers worked with a local vendor to provide a custom power distribution unit for each rack (Figure 10.12) that reduced the electrical distribution by 75% and resulted in a 1M dollar net savings to the project.

Each rack weighs 4,500 lb., which equates to about 210 tn. for 96 racks. This required a robust stand system to be engineered and fabricated to meet the dead load structural requirements, i.e., support the raised floor and spread the loading on the underfloor. Figure 10.13 illustrates the stands required to support the racks along with a compartmentalized view of the infrastructure to support Sequoia.

### 10.9.2 The Mira Argonne Facility

The Argonne Leadership Computing Facility (ALCF) will have 50 racks of BG/Q installed as three separate systems: Mira, Cetus, and Vesta. Mira is a 786,432 core, 48 rack, 10 petaflop peak, production resource that is used to support INCITE, ALCC, and Director Discretionary projects. Cetus and Vesta are non-production systems, each with 1,024 BG/Q compute nodes (one rack), used to support debugging for the science application code teams, system software research, and system management testing and development. All three systems will be installed in the 25,000 sq ft data center in the Theory and Computing Sciences building at Argonne National Laboratory. This two-year-old data center has a raised floor sitting 4 feet above the concrete floor, which sits on compacted earth. The mechanical rooms holding the supporting conventional facility infrastructure (power, UPS, AHUs, etc.) are located to either side of the data center. Upgrades to the TCS data center implemented to support the BG/Q systems, as well as future systems, included power, air and liquid cooling, redundancy improvements, and upgrades to a portion of the raised floor system. After the power upgrades, the TCS has 20MW of electrical capability in a redundant configuration (40MW in a non-redundant configuration). In addition, two 1,500 ton chillers (see Figure 10.14a) and cooling towers were installed at a new Argonne chilled water plant (CWP - located next to the TCS building) to support Mira.

As discussed in the LLNL facility section, deploying a large dense system such as Mira or Sequoia requires mechanical, electrical, and physical support. Specific BG/Q requirements are covered in some detail in the LLNL section; therefore the following focuses on the support provided for Mira and the two test and development racks.

**Floorspace:** Mira's compute and ION racks will encompass about 2,000 sq ft in the north half of the data center. The compute nodes will be laid out in 3 rows of 16 racks each, with 2 racks of I/O forwarding nodes (or IONs) located at the end of each row (for a total of 6 racks of IONs). The infrastructure (storage, management, network, and visualization system) for all three systems, along with Vesta and Cetus, encompasses an additional 500 sq ft of floor space.

**Floor Load:** The BG/Q racks are very dense; at Argonne they weigh around 4,300 pounds each. This is slightly less than the LLNL racks because the IONs are not located on top of each rack, but in separate racks located at the end of each row. A structural load analysis determined that the data center floor pedestals, as installed at the time the building was built, were not strong enough to support the BG/Q racks. The pedestals in the back half of the data center, where the new and future systems would be located, were upgraded to heavy duty pedestals. Figure 10.15 shows the pedestal replacement work in progress. In addition, load testing determined that the floor tiles with the cutouts for hoses and cables would not support the racks properly, consequently, all floor tiles around and under the BG/Q racks were upgraded to heavy duty floor tiles.

**FIGURE 10.13**: Underfloor infrastructure zoned for efficiency.

(a)                          (b)

**FIGURE 10.14**: a) Two 1,500-ton chillers installed in the new Chilled Water Plant. b) Cable trays and cooling process loop pipes under TCS data center floor.

**FIGURE 10.15**: Underfloor pedestal replacement in progress. Approx. 2,000 pedestals were replaced with heavy duty versions.

**Power:** The maximum electrical load for Mira, Cetus, Vesta, and all of the supporting computing infrastructure is 6MW of power, with an expected average load of 4MW.

**Cooling:** As discussed in the Sequoia section, the BG/Q compute racks are cooled primarily by liquid cooling. The other infrastructure and the IONs are all 100% air cooled. Mira, Cetus, and Vesta are the first water cooled computer systems in the TCS data center and they required the installation of a closed liquid cooling process loop that runs from the CWP underground to the TCS and back. Figure 10.14b shows a portion of the cooling process loop under the data center floor. To minimize the energy usage associated with producing chilled liquid to support both air handling units (AHUs) and the BG/Q process loads, a water side economizer design was used for the ALCF cooling systems installed at the CWP. This maximizes free cooling capabilities when weather conditions are favorable. We installed oversized cooling towers to increase the capacity of chilled water that could be produced via free cooling operation. Multiple blended modes were also designed into the CWP control sequences, allowing for partial free cooling and centrifugal chiller cooling operation simultaneously during high demand load scenarios. The two 1,300 ton chillers currently installed at the CWP are high efficiency chillers with 0.571 kW/ton performance at max load conditions. During days in which a 100% of the CWP capacity can be produced through free cooling modes, the chillers can be bypassed resulting in 17,820 kW-hr saved per day. During the winter season, when temperatures allow for optimal free cooling (December through March) the CWP can potentially avoid using 2,174,040 kW-hr by not operating the chillers.

## 10.10    Expected System Statistics

### 10.10.1    Sequoia System Statistics

Sequoia will be a national resource shared by the three NNSA laboratories: Lawrence Livermore, Los Alamos, and Sandia. It is expected to go into a production operating mode by February of 2013. Time on Sequoia will be managed via a process called "Capability Computing Campaigns" (CCC). Code teams or projects are awarded six-month allocations on the machine based on program priorities. These allocations are revisited every six months, and new projects and priorities are assigned. We expect to have as many as 20 projects or code teams with allocations during any six month period and expect at least 650 separate users over the life of the machine. Utilization of Sequoia is expected to be well above 90%. ASC Purple, the last CCC machine sited at LLNL, had an average utilization in the high 90% range. We expect Sequoia will also meet this high standard of effectiveness.

The primary Sequoia mission is uncertainty quantification (UQ)—the running of large suites of calculations employing integrated design codes to quantify the uncertainty in estimates of nuclear weapons performance. Sequoia will provide computational resources up to 24 times greater than Purple for UQ and up to 50 times more capable than Blue Gene/L for weapons science investigations—and it will do this simultaneously. An example of our Sequoia usage model (Table 10.8) shows we are running six 8-K MPI task jobs of four of the Sequoia benchmark applications at the same time as a 20X Blue Gene/L instance of LAMMPS, our benchmark ddcmd code. This suite of applications will be run as part of the machine acceptance test because it approximates Sequoia production usage models and addresses the two key Sequoia mission drivers.

Sequoia has a multitude of design features to increase its reliability both from soft and hard errors. There are far too many of these features to list all of them here, but they fall into three main categories: enhanced reliability without redundancy, enhanced reliability with redundancy, and hot pluggable and enhanced reliability with redundancy and not hot pluggable. There are hot pluggable, N+1 AC-DC bulk power supplies, fans, and DC-DC intermediate power supplies. There are redundant optical cable links with seamless failover, DRAM Kill + 1 additional error protected external memory interface, and N+1 redundant local DC-DC supplies (not hot pluggable). Memory retry on error is also provided. The contractual Mean Time Between Application Failure (MTBAF) due to a hardware failure

**TABLE 10.8**: Example of Sequoia usage model.

| LAMMPS | SPhot | SPhot | SPhot |
|--------|-------|-------|-------|
| LAMMPS | SPhot | SPhot | SPhot |
| LAMMPS | UMT | UMT | UMT |
| LAMMPS | UMT | UMT | UMT |
| LAMMPS | IRS | IRS | IRS |
| LAMMPS | IRS | IRS | IRS |
| LAMMPS | AMG | AMG | AMG |
| LAMMPS | AMG | AMG | AMG |

or hardware transient error on Sequoia is 72 hours (3 days). A hardware-induced application error is any hardware failure or transient error that causes an application running on the system to abnormally terminate.

As this document goes to press, 24 racks of the eventual final 96 Sequoia racks have been integrated in the Terascale Simulation Facility (TSF) at LLNL. What we know for certain is that our building name is out of date! The first known example of a message passing interface (MPI) job with over one million tasks was recently executed on 16 Blue Gene/Q racks, the first of what we hope are many positive experiences to come. A 4-petaFLOP/s Linpack result was achieved recently on 24 racks. Our code teams have begun the port of their codes to our half-rack system of 512 nodes. We expect Sequoia to enable unprecedented scientific achievement; however, it is too early in the integration to have seen many results. The 4D torus between midplanes and 5D torus within each midplane have been addressed by unique packing algorithms to make efficient use of nodes with varying job sizes. As applications and control systems are pushed into extreme scaling regimes, challenges will consume us and achievements will come.

### 10.10.2 Mira System Statistics

The ALCF hosts over one hundred projects, with over 800 users, each calendar year. Computer time is allocated at the ALCF through three separate programs: DOE Innovative and Novel Computational Impact on Theory and Experiment (INCITE) [INCb] at 60%, DOE ASCR Leadership Computing Challenge (ALCC) [ALC] at 30%, and the ALCF director's discretionary at 10%. Mira is expected to go into production in 2013, with a similar number of projects and users. Once Mira is in full production, it will be capable of providing well over 5 billion core hours per year to high impact open science projects; supporting science that has not been possible without a resource of this size and capability.

As a leadership computing facility resource, the INCITE jobs on Mira are expected to be primarily capability jobs and to utilize a large percentage of the system, anywhere from 20% to 100% of the cores. This capability requirement in the INCITE allocation program leads to a smaller number of projects. This requirement is in place due to specific HPC problems that require leadership computing resources. Leadership computing is computing that requires a significant portion of a large resource to produce meaningful science. Alternatively, leadership computing can also serve projects where there is a "time to discovery" requirement on the science. This is science that cannot be run on traditional, non-leadership computing resources.

ALCF expects that Mira usage patterns will follow that of Intrepid. During Intrepid's first year of operation, the majority of the INCITE projects were relatively small scale. Over time, they have grown and in Intrepid's fifth year of operations, more than 70% of the jobs are capability jobs, many of them utilizing the majority of the system.

These capability jobs could only run with a system as stable as Intrepid. On average there is a Blue Gene hardware failure once every 10 days. This is the result of both the reliability of the Blue Gene architecture (system on a chip, n+1, error detection and correction, etc.) and the management of the system. ALCF tightly reviews the weekly issues regarding hardware failures and job failures. This process discovers issues within the machine before they have global impacts to availability.

The deployment process of Mira also included standing up and testing science on early access hardware at IBM, and on test and development systems at Argonne. This provided the ALCF Operations team the opportunity to work out their understanding of the hardware and software infrastructure, and the ALCF computational scientists and performance engineers to benchmark and port critical code. Access to this early hardware also provided a test environment to vet the acceptance tests for Mira, many of which are real, leadership-computing class, scientific problems.

To accelerate early success on Mira, the ALCF created the Early Science Program (ESP). This is a group of 16 scientific application projects, selected by ALCF and DOE, to represent a wide spectrum of science and types of scientific codes. The projects in question have resources within their groups that are combined with dedicated ALCF resources to make this early scalability and performance tuning of computational science codes possible. ALCF and DOE created the ESP to facilitate the porting and scaling of a large body of scientific codes to Mira, to build a strong user community early, and to enable the ability to have production codes running production science on the system as soon as it is deployed and accepted. As a part of this process, the ALCF is working with IBM and the ESP projects to gather a store of knowledge that will be documented and available to future users of Mira. To further ensure the ability of the INCITE and ALCC projects to move their codes to Mira and get them up and running quickly, a Tools and Library Collaboration was created. This collaboration includes the developers of the core tools, debuggers, and libraries expected to be used on Mira. As a result of the collaboration work, these codes and libraries will be available to the users in a functioning state on day one.

## 10.11    Hardware Transactional Memory

We close this chapter by describing one of the interesting features of the BG/Q supercomputer to some detail. The primary pathway from petascale to exascale will be to increase the available concurrency in the computer system, from $O(10^6)$ to $O(10^9)$. Thus, applications must expose much more parallelism to scale efficiently by another factor of 1,000. Blue Gene/Q (BG/Q) has a number of architectural features that simplify effective exploitation of concurrency, including efficient locks, larger numbers of threads, a flat memory hierarchy, prefetch modes, speculative execution, and transactional memory. Altogether they represent an arsenal of tools for incorporating concurrency into applications. One of the most powerful and novel of these tools is BG/Q's hardware transactional memory (HTM), the first time that HTM has been incorporated into a commercially available computer system [Ht11] [Ot11].

Expressing parallelism and hiding latency on BG/Q's shared memory node involves management and correct synchronization of up to 64 threads, which can be a difficult and error-prone task. Consider the case where, occasionally, multiple threads seek to update the same memory location at the same time. Traditionally such conflicts have been avoided with lock-based synchronization schemes, which are available and efficiently implemented on BG/Q. However coarse grain locking schemes create substantial skew between processes when conflicts occur, and fine grain schemes accumulate considerable overhead and introduce semantic issues. Locks pessimistically assume contention and always incur the exclusion overhead, even when no conflict occurs.

Transactional memory (TM), first proposed in 1993, provides a high level abstraction for synchronization that avoids the complexity of other approaches [HM93]. TM encapsulates critical sections as transactions, which are optimistically executed by parallel threads that update values in the L2 cache. When no conflict occurs, the results are committed, but, when a conflict does occur, the transaction is either repeated or serialized after a set number of conflicts. Thus, application performance can be fully parallel, prorated by rare conflicting transactions. In addition BG/Q's large L2 cache supports large transactions, which provides the developer with a great deal of flexibility.

BG/Q's synchronization tools, including TM, locks, OpenMP, and barriers, provide a number of choices for the application developer. The introduction of TM creates the challenge of determining which approach is best for each type of parallel code segment, and that work is already under way. The insight gained with BG/Q is expected to provide deep insight into how all of these capabilities should be deployed and improved for exascale systems.For further details on the TM runtime see Section 10.7.2. Our early experiments are already uncovering valuable rules of thumb for applications.

BG/Q applications demarcate transactions with a `tm_atomic` directive that is similar to an OpenMP critical directive. BG/Q support for this directive involves three aspects. The BG/Q compute chip includes a versioning L2 cache that can associate version numbers with cache tags. Thus, the cache can contain multiple instances of the same address. The compiler translates the `tm_atomic` enclosed region into two function calls to the TM runtime, `tm_begin` and `tm_end`, as well as other bookkeeping required for when a conflict occurs.

The TM runtime implements two conflict detection schemes: eager and lazy. Users can choose which detection scheme to use via the `TM_ENABLE_INTERRUPT_ON_CONFLICT` runtime environment variable. In the eager scheme, threads receive interrupts upon WAW, WAR, and RAW conflicts. We base conflict arbitration on the age of the transactions to favor survival of the older one. In the lazy scheme, all transactions, including doomed ones run to the commit point at which arbitration and invalidation occur. When we abort a transaction, the thread rolls back to the start of the transaction and retries immediately.

BG/Q supports irrevocable actions inside a transaction as the runtime can revert to a single global lock when an irrevocable action occurs. The runtime also reverts back to a single global lock when a hardware transaction fails more than a configurable number of times. Users can adjust this threshold via the `TM_MAX_NUM_ROLLBACK` runtime environment variable. The runtime implements flat transaction nesting semantics in which commit and rollback are to the outermost enclosing transaction.

The BGQ L2 cache is 16 way set associative and the default configuration is to allow 10 ways to be used for speculative storage without an eviction. It is possible that a set contains more than 10 speculative ways if the speculative ways have been recently accessed and are not selected for eviction. Since the L2 is 32 MB in size and as such, it can buffer approximately 20 MB and potentially more of speculative state. Capacity overflow can also happen when the ways in a set are exhausted. When a transaction suffers capacity overflow, the TM runtime retries the transaction `TM_MAX_NUM_ROLLBACK` number of times; that is, in the same way as rollbacks due to access conflicts. The reason is that it is likely that capacity related rollbacks are transient, for example, due to too many concurrent transactions running at the same time.

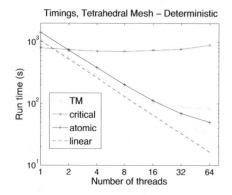

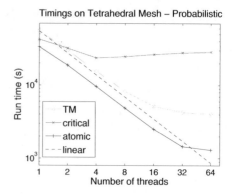

**FIGURE 10.16**: Deterministic mode run times.

**FIGURE 10.17**: Probabilistic mode run times.

Our early experiments focus on a benchmark that we implemented to compare HTM to two OpenMP synchronization constructs, `atomic` and `critical`, on BG/Q. Our tests with `atomic` protect individual updates but do not provide atomicity guarantees for transactions that modify more than one value. Thus, they provide a lower limit for performance under OpenMP. The BUSTM (**B**enchmark for **U**n**S**tructured-mesh **T**ransactional **M**emory) code supports deterministic and probabilistic modes that model conservative finite volume schemes and Monte Carlo applications on realistic meshes [Bih12].

Transactions of our deterministic mode experiments involve updates to three values while those of our probabilistic mode experiments only update one. Figures 10.16 and 10.17 taken from [BBC12] demonstrate some key observations about BG/Q's HTM support. First, we observe that it offers nearly linear speed up with up to about 16 threads. Further, it consistently outperforms OpenMP `critical` with more than one thread. It also outperforms OpenMP `atomic` for transactions with multiple updates and fewer than 16 threads. As another example for BG/Q's HTM providing a high performance and *convenient* synchronization mechanism, see also our work with CLOMP-TM as well as other codes presented in [MS12].

---

# Acknowledgments

**LLNL**

Disclaimer: This document was prepared as an account of work sponsored by an agency of the United States government. Neither the United States government nor Lawrence Livermore National Security, LLC, nor any of their employees makes any warranty, expressed or implied, or assumes any legal liability or responsibility for the accuracy, completeness, or usefulness of any information, apparatus, product, or process disclosed, or represents that its use would not infringe privately owned rights. Reference herein to any specific commercial product, process, or service by trade name, trademark, manufacturer, or otherwise does not necessarily constitute or imply its endorsement, recommendation, or favoring by the United States government or Lawrence Livermore National Security, LLC. The views and opinions of authors expressed herein do not necessarily state or reflect those of the United

States government or Lawrence Livermore National Security, LLC, and shall not be used for advertising or product endorsement purposes.

Auspices Statement: This work performed under the auspices of the U.S. Department of Energy by Lawrence Livermore National Laboratory under Contract DE-AC52-07NA27344.

## ANL

Auspices Statement: This work was supported by the Office of Science, U.S. Department of Energy, under Contract DE-AC02-06CH11357.

Government License: The submitted manuscript has been created by UChicago Argonne, LLC, Operator of Argonne National Laboratory ("Argonne"). Argonne, a U.S. Department of Energy Office of Science laboratory, is operated under Contract No. DE-AC02-06CH11357. The U.S. government retains for itself, and others acting on its behalf, a paid-up nonexclusive, irrevocable worldwide license in said article to reproduce, prepare derivative works, distribute copies to the public, and perform publicly and display publicly, by or on behalf of the government.

# Chapter 11

## "Lomonosov": Supercomputing at Moscow State University

**Victor Sadovnichy**

*M.V. Lomonosov Moscow State University*

**Alexander Tikhonravov and Vladimir Voevodin**

*Researching Computer Center of M.V. Lomonosov Moscow State University*

**Vsevolod Opanasenko**

*T-Platforms Company*

## 11.1 Background

### 11.1.1 HPC History of MSU

The history of High Performance Computing at the Moscow State University began with the creation of the Research Computing Center (RCC) in 1955. Since its inception, the MSU Computing Center was equipped with up-to-the-minute equipment. As early as December 1956, the "Strela" computer was commissioned (Figure 11.1) which performed complex calculations associated with the launch of the first Earth satellites, the first Soviet missiles to the Moon, as well as the first manned flight into space of Yuri Gagarin. In May 1961, the M–20 computer was installed; in 1966, BESM–4 arrived, and in 1968 "Strela" was changed to BESM-6, Russia's highest-performance computer at the time.

**FIGURE 11.1**: "Strela" computer installed at MSU computing center in 1956.

MSU developed its own computers too. Since 1959, an experimental model of a small computer "Setun" had been operating — the country's first machine made of tubeless elements, and the first one in the world working in the ternary numeral system. "Setun" was designed and manufactured at MSU RCC; in 1961, serial production of "Setun" computer began.

From 1955 until the beginning of the 1990s, more than 25 high-performance systems of different architectures had been installed and were actively being used at the Moscow State University. At the same time, a deep study of methods for solving applied problems using computers had been carried out, and these methods were introduced into the educational process at Moscow State University. In 1999, MSU Research Computing Center had chosen the cluster architecture as the basis for projected new computer systems. The first in-house assembled cluster (Figure 11.2) consisted of 18 nodes connected by SCI network. Each node contained two Intel Pentium III 500 MHz processors, and its peak performance was 18 Gflops. Then, in 2002, a cluster followed with a performance of 82 Gflops. In 2004, a cluster from Hewlett-Packard was installed with 160 AMD Opteron 2.2 GHz processors and InfiniBand network with a peak performance of 700 Gflops. In 2008 supercomputer "Chebyshev" entered into operation with a peak performance of 60 Tflops, which consists of 625 nodes and includes 1,250 quad-core Intel Xeon 5472 3.0 GHz processors. Almost immediately after its launch, the supercomputer was fully workloaded.

"Lomonosov" supercomputer (Figure 11.3) was installed at the M.V. Lomonosov Moscow State University in 2009. This supercomputer was created by the Russian company "T-Platforms." The official launch ceremony was attended by D.A. Medvedev, President of the Russian Federation, who proposed to name the supercomputer after the Great Russian scientist of the 18th century. At launch time, a peak performance of "Lomonosov" was 420 Tflops, which allowed the supercomputer to lead the list of the most powerful computers in CIS and Eastern Europe, and rank 12th in the global Top500 list in November 2009. By that time, the number of users of MSU supercomputing center had reached 250, and its resources were used by more than 50 organizations — MSU faculties, institutions of the Russian Academy of Sciences, and others. Only a year later, available resources of "Lomonosov," which became the flagship of MSU supercomputing center, were not sufficient to deal with all the necessary workloads.

**FIGURE 11.2**: The first computing cluster at RCC MSU, 2000.

## 11.1.2 "Lomonosov" Supercomputer: Timeline

2009 — the first stage: designing, installation, and commissioning of the base section of "Lomonosov." The main computational supercomputer's section consisted of 4,160 dual-processor diskless compute nodes based on quad-core Intel Xeon 5570 processors. The second section included 260 dual-processor compute nodes with quad-core Intel Xeon X5570

**FIGURE 11.3**: "Lomonosov" supercomputer, 2012.

processors and local hard drives. The total number of x86 processor cores was 35,360. In addition to x86 compute nodes, the supercomputer included 26 nodes based on PowerXCell8i accelerators. The total amount of memory was 56.5 TB, storage – 0.35 PB, and backup system capacity – 234 TB uncompressed. Supercomputer's power consumption was 1.5 MW. At the time, its peak performance was estimated at 420 Tflops, and Linpack performance – 350 Tflops which resulted in a very good efficiency of 83%.

In 2010, the second stage in the supercomputer creation process began. The system was supplemented with 640 diskless compute nodes based on TB2-XN computing platform and 40 compute nodes equipped with local HDD storage. Each of the new compute nodes was equipped with 6-core Intel Xeon X5670 processor as CPU. The total amount of RAM increased to 79.92 TB, storage — to 1.75 PB. Supercomputer's peak performance increased to 510 Tflops, and its Linpack performance was 397.1 Tflops. The efficiency was 77.8%. Its decline from the preceding year's level was caused by the system's heterogeneity, as compute nodes with different CPUs were used in the test.

2011 — the third stage: system expansion. Following the trend in the supercomputer industry, "Lomonosov" was additionally supplemented with 777 compute nodes equipped with GPU accelerators. As a hardware platform for nodes, a TB2-TL solution was used where each node has two Intel Xeon E5630 CPUs and two NVIDIA X2070 computing accelerators. A total peak performance of the computer system was 1.37 Pflops, and Linpack performance – 674 Tflops.

2012 — the fourth stage and yet another system expansion round. The supercomputer has been additionally equipped with 288 compute nodes with Intel Xeon X5570/X5670 processors and GPU accelerators. Its total amount of memory has increased to 92 TB, and now the computer consumes 2.6 MW. As a result of modernization, a peak performance of the computing system has been increased to 1.7 Pflops, and Linpack performance reached 901.9 Tflops.

### 11.1.3    Main Applications Highlights

At the beginning of 2012, MSU's supercomputing center based on "Lomonosov" had over 550 users from MSU, the Russian Academy of Sciences (RAS), and other organizations. Areas of research requiring the use of supercomputer processing power are magnetic hydrodynamics, hydro- and aerodynamics, quantum chemistry, seismic exploration, computer modeling of drugs, geology and materials science, fundamentals of nanotechnology, cryptography, ecology, astrophysics, engineering calculations, new materials design, and more (Figure 11.4).

### 11.1.4    Benchmark Results and Rating Positions

**Linpack and Top500**

Since its inception in 2009, "Lomonosov" has been included in a global Top500 ranking. In the November 2009 Top500 list edition, it ranked 12th with a peak performance of 420 Tflops, Linpack performance of 350 Tflops, and efficiency of 83%. Test was run on 4,160 TB2-XN nodes and 260 T-Blade1.1 nodes equipped with two quad-core Intel Xeon X5570 processors each.

In 2011, after the third expansion round, "Lomonosov" ranked 13th in the June edition of the Top500 list with the actual performance of 674 Tflops. To test the entire system and achieve this performance level, T-Platforms' experts developed their own implementation of High Performance Linpack test – standard implementation did not allow effective operation in a heterogeneous counting field where some of compute nodes were equipped with GPU

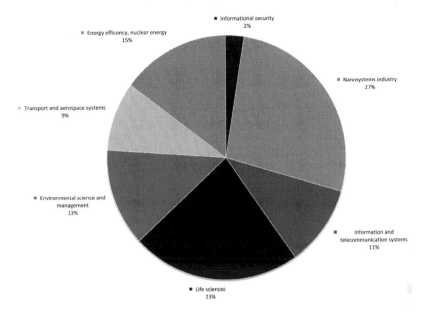

**FIGURE 11.4**: MSU supercomputing center's user priorities.

accelerators, and others not. It is worth noting that when we run a test on 6-core processors, only 4 cores were really involved.

At the time of this writing (spring 2012), "Lomonosov" ranked 18th in the Top500 list.

### Graph500

In June 2011, "Lomonosov" was included in the Graph500 list. According to test results, the system ranked third (positions were allocated depending on the workload), but showed the best performance among all systems in the list. During tests, a result of 43,471,500,000 TEPS (Traversed Edges Per Second) was obtained using 8,192 cores/4,096 nodes based on Intel Xeon 5570 processors. In testing, benchmark implementation was used based on in-house developed DISLIB library designed for parallelization of data-intensive applications.

The first DISLIB implementation was realized over the GASNet library. Subsequently, the library was optimized and ported over MPI library, and the InfiniBand network was further optimized too, which improved system performance in the Graph500 test. At the time of this writing, it was 103,251,000,000 TEPS, and the system was ranked 2nd in the November 2011 list edition. This result had been reached using 32,768 cores/4,096 nodes based on Intel Xeon 5570 processors.

### Top50

Since 2004, RCC MSU and RAS Joint Supercomputer Center have been keeping a list of Top50 most powerful computers in Russia and CIS (http://top50.supercomputers.ru). It is issued twice a year, in March and September. In its compilation principle, it is similar to the Top500 list — computers are ranked by their Linpack performance. Since spring of 2010, "Lomonosov" steadily has been ranking first, thus confirming its leading position in the Russian supercomputer industry.

To learn more about MSU Supercomputing Center, its facilities, projects, applications, and other activities, see http://hpc.msu.ru.

## 11.2  System Overview

### 11.2.1  Architecture

"Lomonosov" (Table 11.1) uses 8 types of compute nodes and processors of different architectures (Table 11.2); this allows us to obtain high sustained performance for the widest range of applications. The computing system is based on TB2 solution designed by T-Platforms. As classic multi-core supercomputer x86 nodes, TB2-XN solutions are used based on quad- and six-core Intel Xeon X5570 Nehalem and X5670 Westmere processors. The system also uses TB 1.1 platform with extended memory and local disk storage to perform specific workloads demanding these system resources. Supercomputer system also contains TB2-TL hybrid nodes based on Intel Xeon and NVIDIA Tesla processors. Another type of node is based on the multi-core PowerXCell 8i processor.

TB2 is built of compute modules based on a motherboard designed by T-Platforms (Figure 11.5). The unique computing density of the solution is achieved primarily by the innovative design of 14-layer PCB that contains four Intel Xeon 55xx or 56xx series processors, four triple-channel DDR3 memory modules designed by T-Platforms, and integrated QDR InfiniBand interconnect controllers.

Unlike standard DIMMs, original highly integrated memory modules designed by T-Plaforms (Figure 11.6) allow a very dense placement of compute blades within a chassis. Each chip integrates the functionality of three DIMMs and is placed horizontally on the motherboard allowing you to save space. Memory modules are effortless to remove and replace, making maintenance easier and cheaper compared to other compact solutions where memory is integrated onto the motherboard.

High-density motherboard releases about 570W of heat and requires efficient cooling. The optimal design for a heat sink to remove this heat was found by simulation on a supercomputer capable of 10 teraflops (Figure 11.7).

During two-month computer analysis, the best weight/energy efficiency ratio was chosen from six options. This is a composite aluminum radiator with copper accents that completely covers the board and provides effective air-cooling for the blade system.

Air cooling can take up to 65 kW of heat from each rack. The "Lomonosov" cooling system has three circuits based on air (within a chassis), water (in a building), and ethylene glycol (out-of-doors).

Dedicated backplane (Figure 11.8) interconnects all chassis (Figure 11.9) subsystems:

**FIGURE 11.5**: Blade module PCB.

**TABLE 11.1**: "Lomonosov" supercomputer highlights.

| | |
|---|---|
| Peak performance | 1.7 Pflops |
| Linpack performance | 901.9 Tflops |
| X86 compute nodes | 5 104 |
| GPU compute nodes | 1 065 |
| PowerXCell compute nodes | 30 |
| X86 processors | 12 346 |
| X86 cores | 52 168 |
| GPU cores | 954 240 |
| Compute node types | 8 |
| Main compute node type | TB2-XN |
| Main processor types | Intel Xeon X5570 / X5670 NVIDIA X2070 |
| Memory | 92 TB |
| Footprint (computer) | 252 sq.m. |
| Footprint (total) | 1376 sq.m. |
| Computer power consumption | 2.6 MW |
| System network | QDR InfiniBand |
| Service network | 10G Ethernet |
| Management network | Gigabit Ethernet |
| Specialized network | Barrier synchronization and global interrupt network |
| Storage system | Lustre parallel filesystem, NFS, StorNext hierarchical filesystem, backup and archiving system |
| Operating system | Clustrx T-Platforms Edition |
| Total equipment weight | More than 75 tons |
| Total cable length | More than 23.5 km |
| Coolant weight | 50 tons |

**TABLE 11.2**: Specifications of compute nodes.

| | |
|---|---|
| 2 x Xeon 5570 2.93 GHz, 12 GB RAM | 4160 |
| 2 x Xeon 5570 2.93 GHz, 24 GB RAM | 260 |
| 2 x Xeon 5670 2.93 GHz, 24 GB RAM | 640 |
| 2 x Xeon 5670 2.93 GHz, 48 GB RAM | 40 |
| 2 x PowerXCell 8i 3.2 GHz, 16 GB RAM | 30 |
| 2 x Xeon E5630 2.53 GHz, 2 x Tesla X2070, 12 GB RAM | 777 |
| 2 x Xeon E5630 2.53 GHz, 2 x Tesla X2070, 24 GB RAM | 288 |
| 4 x Xeon X7560 2.26 GHz, 512 GB RAM | 4 |

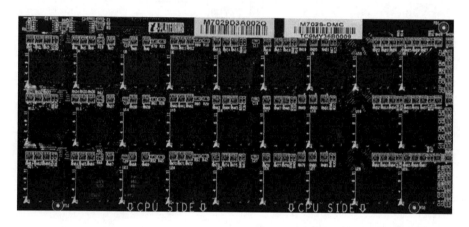

**FIGURE 11.6**: The original DDR3 memory module.

compute modules, power and cooling system, networking and control system. Backplane's compact design leaves plenty of space in the chassis for efficient air cooling of compute modules by fans located in the front chassis section. 24-layer PCB provides hot-swap of compute modules, as well as power supply and data signals to all subsystems.

All compute nodes and a storage system are connected by the QDR InfiniBand high-speed communications network with data throughput up to 40 GB/sec (Figure 11.10). As additional networks, 10G Ethernet and Gigabit Ethernet are used, as well as dedicated shared communications support networks developed by T-Platforms.

As the interconnect switch, TB2 solution uses T-Platforms' proprietary design based on the Mellanox InfiniScale IV reference design. Two integrated switches (Figure 11.11) provide interconnect non-blocking bandwidth sufficient for conflict-free data transmission in tens-of-thousands-nodes installations.

Two switches have 32 internal ports for connecting all compute nodes and 40 external ports.

A management module (Figure 11.12) consists of four functional units that provide system monitoring and management, as well as integrating management and supporting 10GbE/GbE/Ethernet networks, integrating dedicated barrier synchronization and global interrupt networks, and the external clock network for compute nodes. Dedicated networks

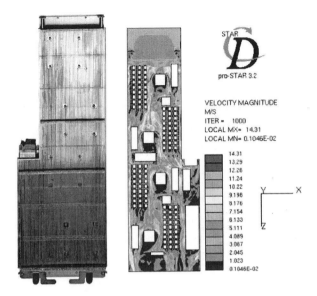

**FIGURE 11.7**: Motherboard heat sink.

driven by FPGA chip reduce delays that occur when synchronizing parallel operations in large installations.

The system network provides communication between parallel application processes in the compute nodes using MPI protocol, and an access to a parallel filesystem for the service servers and all compute nodes. The network is based on QDR InfiniBand technology. It has CLOS network topology with a network diameter of 5 and provides full bisectional bandwidth (FBB). Each x86-based compute node is connected to the system network through one QDR InfiniBand interface. Each PowerXCell-based compute node is connected to the system network via two QDR InfiniBand interfaces.

The management network provides communications between all compute nodes and service servers via TCP/IP. It is built based on 10G Ethernet and Gigabit Ethernet technology.

The service network provides communications between all compute nodes and service servers via TCP/IP. It provides the infrastructure to manage the following computer system components:

- Compute nodes

- Management servers

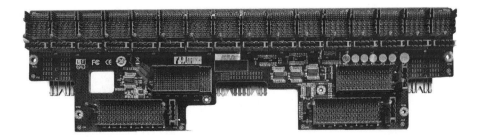

**FIGURE 11.8**: TB2 chassis backplane.

**FIGURE 11.9**: "Lomonosov" supercomputer chassis.

- Management network switches

- Storage servers

- Storage system main and metadata repositories

- Cluster statistics servers and switch

- Backup system server and tape library

- Air conditioning packs

- UPS uninterruptible power supplies

- Water-cooling units

The service network is built based on the Ethernet standards family and designed as a number of Ethernet segments independent from the management network with routing between them.

The barrier synchronization network (Figure 11.13) is designed to improve barrier synchronization operation efficiency when running parallel applications. The global interrupt network is used to synchronize OS kernel interrupts used for internal kernel timers in all compute nodes connected to the network. Barrier synchronization and global interrupt networks are implemented as a separate communication infrastructure distinct from the system, management, and service networks.

The barrier synchronization network provides a MPI_Barrier function response time of less than 20 $\mu s$ for all x86-based compute nodes.

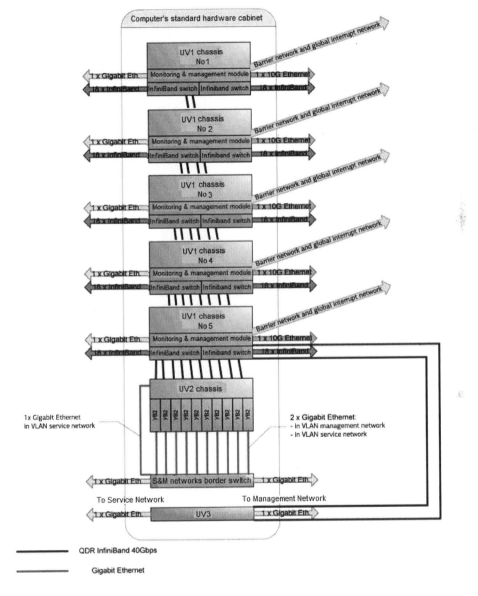

**FIGURE 11.10**: Wiring the equipment in the computer's standard hardware cabinet.

## 11.2.2 System Software

### Operating System

Not only hardware technology, but also new system software solves the task of accelerating real-world applications in the "Lomonosov" supercomputer. For centralized administration of the supercomputer, ClustrX series of special software solutions is used, developed

**FIGURE 11.11**: QDR InfiniBand switches for the blade system.

by T-Platforms Group. ClustrX contains the developer's proprietary code and open source code and does not depend on any outside commercial software that requires licensing.

ClustrX OS is a single set of software components that provide resource management, monitoring, and effective functioning of the service node in the computing system. The solution includes:

- Linux-based operating system for servers (CentOS 6.1)

- Linux-based OS for compute nodes

- A set of optimized math libraries

- Software development kit

**FIGURE 11.12**: Management module.

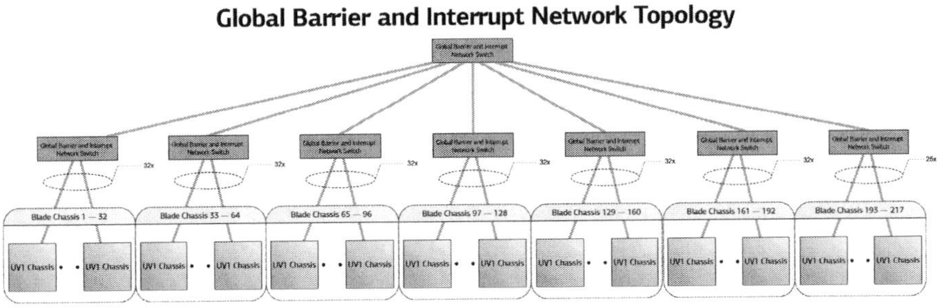

**Global Barrier and Interrupt Network Topology**

**FIGURE 11.13**: Barrier synchronization and global interrupt network topology.

- ClustrX Watch monitoring and management system

- Automatic equipment shutdown system

- Resource management system

ClustrX OS architecture is designed so that a computing cluster running under its control is a single supercomputer unit from the user viewpoint. A large number of compute and control nodes in the cluster is reduced to one scalable computing service managed from a single point. A key feature of the architecture that allows implementing this is the separation of a cluster to computing and management farms with the organization of the latter in a hierarchical structure for the purpose of monitoring and management.

### Service Servers

Each service server of the computer system may be configured to perform one or more of the following tasks:

- **Management server** — to perform administrative tasks for managing the computing system.

- **Boot server** — to support booting of compute nodes through the network.

- **Network services server** — to support DHCP and DNS network services.

- **Authentication server** — for user authentication and authorization.

- **User front-end server** — for remote user connections.

- **Monitoring server** — to accommodate cluster's monitoring and management system components.

### Automatic Equipment Shutdown System

The automatic equipment shutdown system is designed to provide high availability, reliability, and security of the computing cluster.

Automatic equipment shutdown pursues the follows goals:

- Continuous automated monitoring of the cluster survival equipment

- Shutdown of equipment in the case of a dangerous situation without an operator's direct supervision

- Timely alert of the staff, if such a situation arises

The automatic equipment shutdown system responds to events of varying criticality levels using administrator-defined reactions.

**Workloads and Resources Management System**

The workloads and resources manager of ClustrX OS has the following features:

- Based on SLURM

- Support of heterogeneous systems

- Integration with ClustrX Watch monitoring and management system

- Flexible workload management system

- Flexible access management system

Workloads and resources management is not the exclusive function of a single subsystem, but is integrated into the system and tied to ClustrX Watch monitoring and management system to make critical decisions.

### 11.2.3    System Programming

**Application Programming and Debugging**

The following compilers are installed on the supercomputer:

- C/C++/Fortran optimizing compilers with OpenMP support: GCC, Intel ICC/I-FORT, PathScale, PGI for Intel-based compute nodes — on compile and front-end servers. Provided licenses allow simultaneous use of the product by five users both on compile and front-end servers.

- C/C++/Fortran compilers: GCC for PowerXCell-based accelerator nodes — on compile servers for accelerators.

- C/C++/Fortran T-UTL optimizing compilers with automatic program parallelization for nodes with PowerXCell-based accelerators — on compile servers for accelerators. Licenses provided allow simultaneous use of the product by five users both on compile servers and accelerators.

The following performance analysis and debugging tools are installed:

- Intel VTune Performance Analyzer — performance analyzer

- Intel Trace Analyzer and Collector — MPI application performance analysis tool

- Allinea DDT (The Distributed Debugging Tool) — integrated graphical debugger for sequential, multi-threaded, and parallel applications written in C, C++, and Fortran

- RogueWav TotalView, and ThreadSpotter

The set of application development tools includes an optimized version of OpenMPI library supporting MPI 2.0, barrier synchronization network, hybrid applications, and Intel MPI.

System software mathematical libraries include:

- ScaLAPACK, ATLAS, IMKL, AMCL, BLAS, LAPACK, and FFTW optimized for x86 compute nodes

- BLAS, LAPACK, FFTW, SIMDMath, MASS, and MASS/V optimized for Cell-based accelerator nodes

- cuBLAS, cuFFT, MAGMA, cuSPARSE, CUSP, and cuRAND optimized for GPU nodes.

**Application Software Packages**

Users of the MSU supercomputing center may use the following software packages:

- VASP — a package for the study of electronic structure and molecular dynamics of condensed phase using the local density functional model in the plane wave basis.

- WIEN2k_08.3 — a package for solid-state calculations using local density functional model in the plane wave basis and local orbital basis, taking into account relativistic effects.

- CRYSTAL09 — a package for solid-state calculations of the electronic structure and dynamics of solids using local and hybrid density functional models with the ability of optimization and calculation of vibration spectra.

- Gaussian06 — a package for nonobservational calculations.

- MOLPRO — a package for ab initio calculations.

- Turbomole — a package for the electronic structure calculations.

- Accelrys Material Studio — a universal nanotechnology-oriented software package.

- MesoProp — nanotech-oriented package for the simulation of surface coatings, adhesives, elastomers, nanocomposites, gels, nano-structured polymer blends, membranes.

- MOLCAS — ab initio quantum chemical calculations for molecules in the ground and excited states.

In addition, MSU supercomputer system users use the following packages: Gromacs, FireFly, LAMMPS, NAMD, GAMESS, Quantum ESPRESSO, ABINIT, Autodock, CP2K, NWChem, PRIRODA, SIESTA, Amber, CPMD, DL_POLY, VMD, GULP, Aztec, Geant, OpenFOAM, PARMETIS, FDMNES, GSL, METIS, Msieve, Octave, OpenMX, PETSc, SMEAGOL, VisIt, VTK, WRF, and others.

## 11.2.4  Data Center/Facility

**Uninterruptible Power Supply System**

The uninterruptible power supply system of "Lomonosov" supercomputer (Figure 11.14) consists of:

- Two Symmetra MW 1600 modular uninterruptible power supplies (UPS) connected to the main switchboard circuit breakers. Each UPS includes the bypass mode service panel.

- Output switchboards of the uninterruptible power supply system (power clean system).

- Panels and the necessary cables to connect computer system equipment.

The total capacity of the uninterrupted power supply system is 2,800 kW with N+1 redundancy.

### Uninterruptible Power Supplies

As uninterruptible power supplies, UPS Symmetra MW from APC are used in configuration with eight power module bays. A capacity of each Symmetra MW UPS power module is 200 kW. Thus, in its full configuration the UPS provides 1,400 kW with N+1 redundancy.

### Climate System Structure

Cooling of the computing system is based on the use of in-row air conditioners. Equipment cabinets are placed in the computer room space in such a way as to form "hot" and "cold" aisles. Air conditioners are installed within rows of cabinets. They take hot air out of the "hot" aisle and fan chilled air into the "cold" aisle.

Two types of air conditioners are used. ACRC502 provides accurate maintenance of the set temperature in the area where computer equipment takes air for cooling. In addition, ACRP502, a second type of air conditioner, provides monitoring and maintenance of humidity in the room. In each "hot" aisle, air conditioners are grouped together ensuring synchronized operation.

To ensure optimal climatic conditions in the uninterruptible power supply system area, four grouped HPM M66UC air conditioners are used.

As a source of cold for the air-conditioning system, water chillers (Figure 11.15) are used which are mounted on an outside ground. To ensure the required redundancy level for HVAC equipment, a cluster of four water chillers is designed with a total cooling capacity of 4,000 kW. Three chillers of the cluster are operating, and the fourth one is used as a reserve. Total estimated cooling performance of the cooling system taking into account N+1 redundancy is 3,000 kW.

Water accumulator tanks (Figure 11.16) are designed to supply enough cold water to cool all computer system equipment for a time period of not less than 10 minutes followed by cooling of the critical computer system equipment for at least 20 minutes. The water loop pump group gets power from the uninterruptible power supply system. This ensures

**FIGURE 11.14**: Uninterruptible power supply.

complete computer system cooling during the time of the computer system operation from the UPS system's batteries.

### Placement of Equipment

All computer system, data storage system, switching, and service server equipment (Figure 11.17) is housed in 69 19" APC AR3100 cabinets that are constituents of the engineering infrastructure. These cabinets have 42 standard mounting positions (U) and a useful depth of 1,000 mm, which allows one to use them for any standard equipment designed for installation in 19" hardware racks.

## 11.2.5 Data Storage

### Lustre Parallel File System

For applications' IO operations, a parallel data storage system is used based on the Lustre filesystem (Figure 11.18). To store the object data, each of six LSI 7988 storage systems is directly connected to four object data servers by two FiberChannel 8 Gbit interfaces. Each LSI 7988 system includes four disk shelves for 60 drives each. In total, 1,296 500GB HDDs are used; in addition, each object data storage system has 16 hot spare drives. The total volume of Lustre parallel filesystem is about 500 TB; at the filesystem level, the storage system shows peak write performance of 24 GB/s and read performance of 30 GB/s. The architecture of the data storage system providing Lustre filesystem is implemented with no single point of failure that insures system fault tolerance both at the raid-arrays and data paths duplicating level, and at the level of file system object data and metadata service redundancy (object data and metadata servers are divided into failover-pairs).

Lustre filesystem is available on compute nodes and front-end servers over QDR InfiniBand network. Users can get access to the Lustre filesystem through a separate folder in their home directories on front-end servers.

### NFS File System

The main filesystem accessible to users is NFS that is provided by EMC Celerra storage system. The root part of a user's home directories is located just in NFS partitions that

**FIGURE 11.15**: Chillers on the outside ground.

**FIGURE 11.16**: Water accumulator tanks.

are accessible for front-end servers over 10G Ethernet management network. This scheme allows you to increase user data storage reliability and minimize the maintenance window. The total volume of NFS partitions is 240 TB; volume quotas policy is implemented for both individual users and user groups that work on a single research project.

**StorNext Hierarchical File System**

In addition to NFS partition, users have access to StorNext hierarchical file system based on EMC Cellera iSCSI partition and Quantum i6000 tape library partition. The total filesystem volume is 500 TB. The use of a hierarchical filesystem allows users to reduce their footprint on the underlying file system while maintaining a regular access to data at the filesystem level without the use of a backup system.

To control the amount of occupied space, a per user quota system is implemented; per

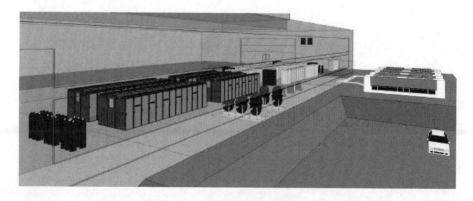

**FIGURE 11.17**: 3D-model of "Lomonosov" supercomputer equipment placement within the building.

group quota is also possible. The hierarchical filesystem available to users on the front-end servers as a separate directory in their home directories.

### Data Backup and Archiving System

In addition, the storage system includes a backup system archiving data on LTO-5 tapes within Quantum i6000 tape library. Data archiving system is designed for backing up system and user data, as well as for long-term storage of user data. The tape library has five LTO-5 tape drives connected to a storage area network (SAN) via Fiber Channel interfaces. The total volume of cartridges installed in the library is up to 500 TB. As backup system software, Symantec NetBackup is used and deployed in failover mode, ensuring no single point of failure throughout the data backup and archiving subsystem.

## 11.3 Applications and Workloads

This section presents some interesting results obtained by users of the MSU supercomputer center in 2010-2011.

Improving efficiency in the **oil and gas industry** directly depends on the power of the high-performance computing systems used. This is true both at the stage of prospecting and exploration for fossil fuels, and at the stage of their development and operation. In the process of extracting information from seismic data, it is necessary to suppress the interference waves, assess the media depth-velocity model, and build a depth image of a crust segment in the observation area. A special problem arises because the amount of data in one field can reach tens or hundreds of terabytes, which requires the application of the most powerful

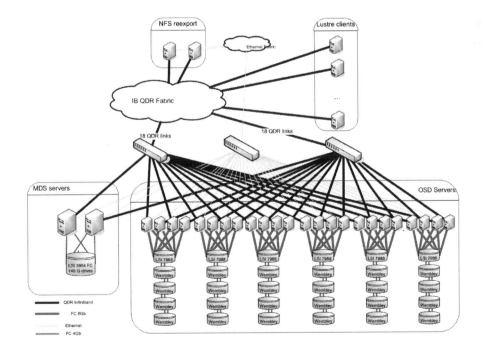

**FIGURE 11.18**: Lustre parallel filesystem schematic.

supercomputers. Currently, experts at MSU Research and Education Center "Prospecting, Exploration, and Development of Hydrocarbon Deposits" and "GEOLAB" are solving some important problems of seismic data processing using the "Lomonosov" supercomputer. In particular, using a high-performance 3D SRME method, they perform suppression of wave-interferences due to re-reflection from the free surface into the lower half-space and construct the media depth image using reverse time migration (RTM) method. Every calculation for each of these tasks requires several thousands of processor cores.

A team of MSU Mechanics and Mathematics Faculty's researchers delivered world-class results in the field of **cryptography**. Using "Lomonosov" supercomputer, they study the vulnerability of certain cryptographic algorithms with respect to different types of attacks. In particular, work is under way to study so-called hash functions and factorization of large composite numbers. In July 2010, a collision was built for SHA-1 with contractive function truncated to 72, and then to 75 rounds. Final calculations that led to collision discovery were performed on the GPU part of "Lomonosov" supercomputer.

Factorization is based on fundamental knowledge of the number theory and algebra. At the same time, it includes engineering features, as it often uses assumptions based on experiences that still have no theoretical justification. On the other hand, it is like art—algorithm execution duration and the result are often dependent on the successful choice of parameters. In the period from 10 May to 8 November 2010, a joint team of MSU and CWI (Netherlands) found prime factors of RSA-190, that filled the last gap in the section to RSA-200.

RCC MSU researchers used "Lomonosov" supercomputer for calculations in the process of developing a **new anticancer drug** based on new urokinase inhibitors. Blocking (inhibition) of urokinase stops tumor formation. In this development of new inhibitors, the central role is accorded to molecular modeling methods and supercomputers which can significantly reduce the time and expense of developing a new drug. The unique SOL docking program positions the candidate molecule in the urokinase proteolytic center and evaluates the energy of its binding to urokinase. The higher the energy of the candidate molecule binding with urokinase, the more effective an inhibitor it should be, and the more effective will be the new drug. The work is carried out in two directions. First is the search for new inhibitors in databases of existing compounds. Second is the construction of virtual libraries of new chemical compound molecules and the search for new inhibitors among them. During the development period from mid-2010 to spring 2011, docking for a total of about 1 million molecules was performed (at a cost of several hours per single molecule per CPU). Only "Lomonosov" supercomputer can perform this number of calculations. As a result, more than 100 compounds — candidates for new urokinase inhibitors — were selected, some of them synthesized, and these compounds have been tested experimentally. Thus, the conveyor development of new urokinase inhibitors has been launched: design — calculations — experiments.

A large amount of supercomputing has been carried out when using quantum chemistry and molecular dynamics methods, including those used to develop HIV integrase inhibitors (foundation for new AIDS drugs) and endothelin converting enzyme (drugs for the treatment of cardiovascular system diseases).

Currently, the issue of the relationship between dynamics of the **Earth's climate** and solar activity is being studied with the use of the climate model that was developed in close cooperation with MSU and RAS. At least several decades of calculation are needed to get a significant possible relation between the climate system parameters and solar activity indicators. Calculations of this kind are carried out on "Lomonosov" supercomputer. Solving the atmospheric boundary layer turbulence simulation problem requires the computational grid size from millions to tens of millions of nodes. In particular, such problems are being solved as estimating of the maximum wind gusts necessary for the design of architectural structures.

Investigation of changes in the **global ocean climate processes** is a complex interdisciplinary problem requiring the efforts of experts in the field of mathematical modeling, oceanography, and climate. The purpose of a joint project of MSU and Institute of Numerical Mathematics RAS is the creation in Russia of the modern mathematical model of the Global Ocean dynamics that describes the physics of ocean processes with a high degree of completeness and can effectively be run on high performance computer systems. The model includes a set of programs for solving three-dimensional large-scale thermo-hydrodynamic ocean processes equations sets, atmosphere and ocean interaction sub-model, sea ice dynamics and thermodynamics, sub-grid processes parameterization, and supporting procedures for working with data and computational grids. One of its applications is the study of the year-to-year variability of the thermohaline circulation of Global Ocean waters in the second half of the 20th century. In 2011, the first results were delivered reproducing within-year variability of Global Ocean water circulation using an eddy-resolving global ocean model with a resolution of $1/10°$ horizontally and 49 levels vertically.

MSU Chemical Faculty research is aimed at identification of mechanisms for the processes of relaxation of excited electronic states of biological chromophores in photoreceptor and fluorescent proteins that underlie their operation using modern combined methods of high-accuracy quantum and molecular mechanics. Interest in the **photoactive biomolecular systems** is due not only to their undoubted important biological function, but also to the opportunity to explore the basic physical and chemical processes which are the rate-determining steps in these systems, such as transfer of an electron or proton, and rupture and formation of a chemical bond. In this project, photoreceptor systems are studied: flavin-containing proteins, in which the local chromophore environment is undergoing changes as a result of photoreaction with the formation of new intermolecular bonds, and the process of relaxation of the excited state is accompanied by formation of a singlet biradical, as well as fluorescent proteins — green fluorescent protein (GFP) and GFP-like proteins, the photochemical features of which are associated with the formation of different protonated forms of the chromophore group and cis-trans isomerization. Calculations carried out using the MSU supercomputer system resources allowed us to identify primary relaxation process mechanisms in the functioning of two types of photoactive biosystems — flavin-containing photoreceptors and flare-up fluorescent proteins. Protein photoresponse on UV photon absorption was also investigated.

One of the main directions of drug development for the **treatment of Alzheimer's disease** is a search for noncovalent and weak covalent cholinesterase inhibitors. In the later stages of Alzheimer's disease, a sharp drop in the acetylcholine neurotransmitter concentration leads to cognitive impairment. Partial inhibition of acetylcholinesterase (AChE) and butyrylcholinesterase (BChE) can increase acetylcholine concentration and maintain cognitive function in patients. Work on this project is carried out in several directions. MSU in collaboration with the RAS Institute of Physiologically Active Compounds is looking for weak covalent inhibitors of AChE and BChE. One group of compounds is phosphorus-organic compounds with a P-C bond. Typically, such compounds are not reactive because this bond is very strong, and the interaction with the active site serine, which requires breaking this bond, is impossible. But insertion of fluorine or other strong electron-seeking groups in an atom group can activate this bond, making the compound a weak inhibitor. An important task is to assess the strength of this bond for a preliminary estimation of the compound's reactivity. The calculation is carried out using high accuracy ab initio quantum mechanical methods. Isodesmic false-reaction method is used that compares the strength of the bond in a series of similar compounds with different substituents.

MSU International Center of Biotechnology has carried out an in silico search of cyclooxygenase activity inhibitors for the prostaglandin-H synthase (PGHS, EC 1.14.99.1) enzyme. Nine new potential PGHS inhibitors were selected. In vitro experiments showed that five of them really are inhibitors of cyclooxygenase activity of PGHS enzyme.

RAS Keldysh Institute of Applied Mathematics is working on **creating a new parallel multigrid method**. The multigrid method is widely used in applications for modeling processes of diffusion, heat conduction, fluid dynamics, etc. But there are some difficulties in its parallel implementation. Quickly changing multiprocessor system architectures, hierarchical structure complication, and exaflop-scale computers looming ahead dictate high requirements to computer code scalability. The algorithm proposed in the work is a variant of the classical multigrid method and is designed to solve three-dimensional anisotropic diffusion equations on ultra-parallel computers in "three-dimensional processors grid" virtual topology. Scalability to a large number of processors is provided by the use of the Chebyshev iterative method on the coarsest grid with a special set of parameters for smoothing and a standard set to solve coarse-grid equations.

Tomographic studies, such as magnetic resonance and X-ray imaging, are widely used in medicine. The current trend is to reduce radiation exposure. In this regard, an urgent task is to develop **ultrasonic tomographic systems**. Ultrasonic tomography is primarily developed for the differential diagnosis of breast cancer. One in four cancers seen in the human population is breast cancer. MSU RCC examined the inverse ultrasonic tomography problem in three-dimensional nonlinear wave formulation. Problems of determining the optimal parameters of ultrasound scanners were solved in the mathematical modeling framework.

In joint work of the MSU Physics Faculty, Topchiev RAS Institute of Petrochemical Synthesis, and The Max-Planck-Institut für Eisenforschung (Dusseldorf, Germany), methods to **create new polymers** were investigated. As a rule, polymers of different chemical structures are not compatible, and mixtures thereof are being stratified. This problem of creating new polymeric materials can be solved by adding copolymers to the mixture: macromolecules of chemically related fragments of different natures are focusing on the interface and facilitate the mixing of other, incompatible macromolecules. In practice, it is more efficient to synthesize copolymers directly in the mixing process by adding to the melt of each polymer chemically active chains which form copolymers by reacting with each other. Such a reactive compatibilization has been studied in this work. It explains experimentally observed spontaneous dispersion of the mixture at the interface, as well as the autocatalytic reaction acceleration. Special cases of the formation of asymmetric copolymers, polydisperse copolymers, and the reaction in droplets were studied. The possibility of obtaining reactive compatibilization of complex nanostructures, including vesicles and structured micelles, was shown.

**Numerical laser optical field simulation** in scattering media is a mathematically complex and computationally time-consuming problem. The joint work of MSU Physics Faculty and the Institute of Atmospheric Optics (Tomsk) presents an effective approach to regularization and solution of this problem. The results of numerical modeling of the laser beacon's light field in the fog are shown based on parallel computing using the MSU supercomputer system.

MSU Physics Faculty, MSU International Training and Research Laser Center, and Lebedev RAS Physics Institute are implementing a project to create **compact laser-plasma charged particle accelerators**. The project aims to develop and optimize a new generation of accelerators based on particle acceleration in a plasma under the influence of an extremely intense ultra short laser pulse. Currently, the rate of particle acceleration in such accelerators is 4-5 orders of magnitude higher than the rate of acceleration in LHC and other modern linear accelerators, and in the short term, laser-plasma accelerators will be able to compete directly with conventional accelerators in energy, charge, and other beam characteristics. Moreover, laser-plasma particle accelerators have a simple, compact, and relatively cheap implementation and suggest a number of promising applications in nanophysics, medicine, and other fields. The project is based on the use of Mandor state-of-the-art parallel code and implements the large particles method to simulate the interaction of super intensive laser radiation with plasma. The calculations are carried out using "Chebyshev" and "Lomonosov" supercomputers.

A joint project of the MSU, RAS Institute of Organoelements Compounds, and RAS Keldysh Institute of Applied Mathematics is devoted to **supercomputer simulation of poliamfifils**. Synthetic polymers can self-organize into complex three-dimensional ensembles. This opens up prospects for the creation of ordered supramolecular nanostructures with controlled morphology. Supercomputers allow carrying out computational experiments on the mesoscopic level aimed at the prediction of new forms and new ways of polymer self-organization. By varying the macromolecule chemical structure, their nature, and distribution of functional groups, you can predict new ways and forms of molecular self-assembly. Of course, mesoscopic-level modeling cannot claim total and complete description of all interaction details. But as an auxiliary tool, this approach gives surprisingly good results, predicting the behavior of real systems with an unexpected accuracy. It should be emphasized that mesoscopic-scale phenomena can occur not only in systems with mesoscopic dimensions, but also in macroscopic systems. In many cases, the results of the virtual molecular design are the basis for in-depth understanding of the processes, subsequent chemical polymer synthesis, and preparation of nanostructured materials with unique properties.

RAS Nuclear Safety Institute has developed the technology **for simulation of turbulent flows** in complex technical devices by solving the problem of unsteady coolant flow in the heat exchanger. Geometry and mesh descriptions, particularly using the "CABARET" method, and the results of solving the problem of unsteady filling of the heat exchanger with the coolant (heat shock) have been provided. The study was conducted using "Chebyshev" and "Lomonosov" supercomputers.

Bauman MSTU in cooperation with TESIS LLC carried out a project to research starting a piston engine with the use of a perspective vortex turbine starter. Using FlowVision HPC software package, **modeling of gas flow and rotor movement** has been conducted for the vortex turbine which is a component of the engine-starter system. Vortex turbines are characterized by complex vortex gas flow, features of which are currently poorly understood. The complex configuration of the turbine model and the flow make high requirements on computer equipment. In the research process, calculations of gas flow valve, which is, in fact, the turbine starter model with a stopped rotor, are carried out, as well as a comparison with the experiment data. The calculation of the turbine in a stationary mode has been performed, and the results obtained are in good agreement with the experiment. TESIS LLC, which has a collaboration agreement with Moscow State Technical University, is the developer of the FlowVision hydrodynamics software package.

## 11.4 "Lomonosov" in Supercomputing Education

The power of the MSU supercomputer system is widely used for the Russian Federation Presidential Commission Project on the modernization and technological development of the Russian economy: "Supercomputing Education." Moscow State University plays a key role in the implementation of the project; academician Victor Sadovnichy, MSU Rector, is the project leader and Chairman of the Coordinating Council of the System of Research and Education Centers for Supercomputing Technologies (REC SCT) established for the project implementation. Research and education centers have been established at universities that

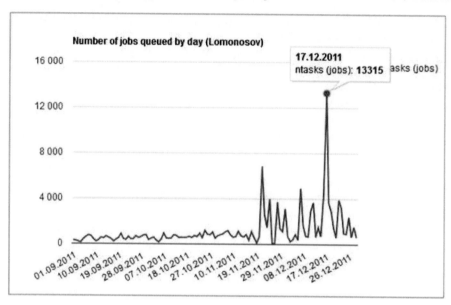

**FIGURE 11.19**: Number of jobs queued by day ("Lomonosov").

already have considerable experience in supercomputing technology. By 2012, eight RECs have been opened, covering all federal districts of Russia.

In the project framework, programs of mass entry-level supercomputing technology specialists training have been implemented. The program covers all REC SCT System's federal districts, 45 Russian universities, which in total amount to 1,824 specialists. In all REC SCT System's federal districts, the program has been implemented for retraining and professional development of teaching staff (72 hours), and 166 specialists from over 40 Russian universities have successfully passed the retraining.

The task of intensive training in the field of supercomputing technologies within 18 special teams in all REC SCT System's federal districts has been solved; 427 people successfully completed the training.

"Lomonosov" supercomputer is extensively used in the educational process at the Moscow State University. In 2011, more than 700 students passed through supercomputing training on the most powerful Russian supercomputer. Fifth-year students of the Computational Mathematics and Cybernetics Faculty launched more than 13,000 jobs in one day (Figure 11.19).

MSU Research and Education Center "Supercomputing Technologies" regularly conducts training sessions for users of the MSU supercomputer system dedicated to the efficient use of available computing resources, and learning to debug and optimize their own applications. The following activities in 2011-2012 must be highlighted:

- NVIDIA graphics processor programming technology schools

- A unique Intel training workshop dedicated to optimizing applications developed by MSU supercomputer system users

- Training for MSU supercomputer system users in operating Accelrys Material Studio software package installed on "Lomonosov" supercomputer. The audience for this four-day training course consisted of more than 60 people

- Youth summer school "Development of Superscalable Parallel Applications"

- A special training program "Supercomputer Simulations: Technologies, Tools and Applications"

- Training on RogueWave TotalView debugger and RogueWave ThreadSpotter software package.

# Chapter 12

## Pleiades: NASA's First Petascale Supercomputer

**Rupak Biswas, William Thigpen, Robert Ciotti, Piyush Mehrotra, Chris Henze, John Parks, and Bryan Biegel**

*NASA Ames Research Center*

**Robert Hood**

*Computer Sciences Corp.—NASA Ames Research Center*

**FIGURE 12.1**: The Pleiades supercomputer, located within the NASA Advanced Super-computing facility at Ames Research Center, Moffett Field, California.

## 12.1    Introduction

Since its installation in 2008, the Pleiades supercomputer (see Figure 12.1) within the NASA Advanced Supercomputing (NAS) Division at Ames Research Center has been integral to meeting the science and engineering goals of NASA's missions in space exploration, aeronautics, and science. By enabling advanced computational modeling, simulation, and data analysis for these missions, Pleiades plays a pivotal role for the Agency in its developing next-generation space launch and exploration vehicles, understanding complex aeronautical phenomena, and advancing Earth and space sciences. Pleiades is NASA's flagship super-computer and is funded under the High-End Computing Capability (HECC) project, which is chartered to develop and deliver the most productive high-end computing (HEC) environment possible to support each of the NASA Mission Directorates.

The unique analysis requirements of NASA's challenging missions have driven both NASA's fundamental need to develop world-class supercomputing capabilities, and the identification of specific system attributes to meet those needs. In the remainder of this section we present the key characteristics of NASA's HEC requirements and general background that influenced the acquisition and evolution of Pleiades.

### 12.1.1    Importance and Benefits of HEC to NASA Missions

NASA increasingly relies on computational modeling to achieve and enhance mission success. For example, over the years aerospace design and engineering efforts have relied on a combination of theory, experimental data, flight tests, and numerical modeling and simulation (M&S). Before modern HEC capabilities were widely and reliably available, the necessary design information was primarily obtained from heritage data, ground-based experiments, and flight tests. However, with the exponential advances in computing technology and capabilities throughout the 1980s and '90s, M&S began to provide extensive design and analysis support more efficiently than ever before.

Experiments, such as wind tunnel tests, are expensive and time-consuming, requiring maintenance of large, highly specialized facilities and construction of precisely instrumented models to make the needed measurements. These tests are also limited by the range and scale of conditions that can be accurately reproduced. While flight tests can better cover the relevant scales and conditions for a particular design, they are even more difficult, costly, and risky, and are only practical once a design is almost fully developed. In contrast, computational models can be generated within a matter of days and provide the necessary design and analysis data at a fraction of the cost. Furthermore, M&S provides scientists and engineers with predictive analysis capabilities, enabling them to be proactive and examine a much broader range of potential conditions and design variables than would be possible through testing alone.

HEC resources have also become increasingly important to NASA's research efforts. As scientific knowledge grows, researchers strive to understand ever more complicated systems and phenomena, requiring complex coupled models and high-fidelity computations. Multi-disciplinary, multi-physics, multi-phase, and multi-resolution time-dependent non-linear computations are now the norm rather than the exception. In addition, with the explosive growth of observational and simulation data, researchers in many domains, such as climate modeling and cosmology, must efficiently analyze multi-petabyte data sets to extract knowledge and accelerate scientific discovery.

## 12.1.2 HEC System Requirements to Meet NASA Needs

The Agency's space exploration, aeronautics, and science missions each require different types of analyses and applications that place specific demands on the selection of system architectures, processor types, memory hierarchies, interconnect fabrics, and so forth. In particular, NASA's missions drive three primary aspects of HEC system requirements: leadership-class *capability* to run very large-scale computations, high-throughput *capacity* to handle large numbers of simulations, and predictable *availability* to meet mission-critical deadlines.

The research-oriented science and aeronautics projects rely on very large-scale, high-fidelity simulations to advance the understanding of a broad spectrum of topics, such as Earth's weather and climate, galaxy evolution, heliophysics, and complex aircraft aerodynamics. Some of these intensive simulations require leadership-class system capabilities that can handle long-running computations using upwards of 50,000 cores each.

In contrast, NASA's engineering-oriented efforts, such as launch and crew exploration vehicle development, often require high-throughput system capacities to rapidly process large sets of moderate-scale computations (typically 500–4,000 cores each) that are needed to analyze a wide range of flight conditions and vehicle design variations. For example, extensive sets of analyses enable designers to generate detailed databases of aerodynamic and aerothermal conditions throughout launch and reentry, which they can use to optimize vehicle shapes, trajectories, and crew abort capabilities early in the design process.

Some of NASA's projects also have a significant need for high-availability systems to ensure that time-sensitive, mission-critical analyses can be performed on demand. For instance, HEC systems must be continuously available during space missions to perform immediate analyses of anomalous events (such as debris strikes) and ensure mission and crew safety during launch and reentry. Similarly, timely weather prediction analyses can help prepare communities for dangerous storms such as hurricanes and blizzards.

NASA's missions also use a wide range of specialized M&S applications that further drive requirements for an integrated HEC environment and its supporting infrastructure. The performance of key applications, such as those used heavily in aerospace vehicle design and Earth and space sciences research, must be taken into careful consideration when selecting system and processor types, parallel architectures, storage and filesystems configurations, and so on. Some of these driving applications are discussed in further detail in Section 12.9.

NASA's HEC users run well over 100 applications covering various programming paradigms and languages, and numerous classes of algorithms, data structures, and communication/memory access patterns. To enable broad mission success, the Agency's primary supercomputer must efficiently run this wide variety of codes. Furthermore, many of these codes are being continually enhanced, so the systems must also provide an environment that is productive for application development. In addition, the lifetimes of NASA applications are measured in years and often decades, and these applications grow to be very complex in order to handle the necessary physics and algorithms for accurate computations. Therefore, NASA HEC systems must maintain efficient performance portability between system generations.

A final factor that drives HEC system requirements is that NASA is a large, distributed Agency with users spread across the U.S. As of 2012, the NAS facility must deliver a productive and efficient supercomputing environment to more than 1,200 users from all NASA centers as well as from partner research and engineering organizations in academia and industry. The physical distribution of these users drives wide-area network latency, bandwidth, and efficiency requirements.

Collectively, these diverse NASA project needs, analysis applications, and access requirements drive many of the key decisions to procure, configure, and regularly upgrade the Agency's supercomputing systems and capabilities.

## 12.1.3   History behind Development of Pleiades at NAS

The advantages of computational analysis and the unique requirements of NASA missions made clear the need to aggressively develop and expand in-house HEC capabilities. The development of the Agency's supercomputing capabilities leading up to Pleiades began at NASA Ames Research Center in 1979, when a project that later evolved into the current NAS Division began to transform U.S. aerospace R&D from costly and time-consuming wind tunnel experiments to simulations that use computational fluid dynamics (CFD) models.

After establishing its pioneering leadership in HEC and expertise in CFD in the '80s and '90s, NAS experts were called on in February 2003 to conduct critical foam debris transport analyses to determine the physical cause of the Space Shuttle Columbia accident, and then to improve the shuttle's design for a successful return-to-flight. The large volume of analyses required for this effort strained the available NAS resources and prompted the purchase of additional supercomputing systems. By 2004, the importance of large-scale, high-fidelity simulations for aerospace and other missions was clear. The Columbia supercomputer was procured to enable NASA to pursue the new Vision for Space Exploration, while simultaneously conducting pathfinding research in Earth science, astrophysics, and aeronautics. In October 2005, the Agency committed to the long-term support of supercomputing with the formation of the HECC project within the Shared Capabilities Assets Program (SCAP), which ensures that NASA's critical technical assets are reliably available to support the Agency's mission requirements.

The NAS facility was chosen as the natural home for the HECC project due to its history in pioneering HEC capabilities and high-fidelity CFD tools. Even as Columbia was being expanded, NASA's computational demands were outpacing its capacity. It became clear that another new supercomputing system was necessary to keep up with demand and take advantage of emerging computing technologies. As a result, NAS began a comprehensive process in 2006 to research and select the next supercomputer for NASA, eventually leading to the Pleiades system.

### 12.1.4  NAS Technology Refresh Process

A key strategy for ensuring broad mission impact of the HECC project is the continual growth of NASA's supercomputing capability. Approximately a third of the annual HECC budget is spent on providing new capability to the user community. To guide this activity, the NAS Technology Refresh (NTR) process was created. NTR, modeled after the successful methods used to deploy Columbia, reduces risks and increases the probability of fielding systems that are productive and cost effective. The annual process includes a detailed requirements, options, and constraints analysis (ROCA) to determine if the technology landscape has changed sufficiently to warrant a comprehensive reexamination, or if the current system should merely be augmented. In the former case, one or more test systems are selected from the broad vendor community. The testbeds are installed and evaluated within the NAS environment, and the results are used to drive the competitive acquisition of the full system from among the testbed vendors. Each year, the NTR process is repeated to ensure that HECC's supercomputing resources align with NASA's evolving computational capability, capacity, and availability requirements and goals.

The NTR process for Pleiades began with a ROCA midway through Columbia's second year of operation. Studying usage patterns proved valuable in helping define near-term requirements. For example, it was determined that more than 65% of Columbia's jobs used a Message Passing Interface (MPI) library for interprocess communication and did not need the system's large shared-memory address spaces. The ROCA phase culminated with the release of a Request for Information (RFI) to the HEC vendor community in September 2006. The RFI included requirements for benchmarking using the HPC Challenge Benchmarks [DL05], the NAS Parallel Benchmarks [BHS+95], and a set of five applications that were representative of the anticipated workload. The vendor responses were received in December, and two selected test systems were installed in May and September of 2007. System evaluation was conducted on all existing platforms on the NAS computer floor, including the two testbeds as well as other machines acquired to meet immediate customer requirements. Testing concluded in December 2007; it was determined that three architectures were competitive for the build-out phase, and a Request for Proposal (RFP) was sent to the eligible vendors. The RFP included similar benchmarking instructions as the RFI. The applications currently used in benchmarking requirements are described in Section 12.7.1.

In March 2008, NAS selected an SGI Altix ICE architecture with 5,888 nodes in 92 racks as NASA's next primary supercomputer. Each node contained two Intel Xeon E5472 (Harpertown) processors and two double data rate (DDR) InfiniBand (IB) ports for communications and I/O. The system was interconnected in two independent (partial) 10-dimensional (10-D) hypercubes, with each hypercube connecting all of the nodes. The new system, named Pleiades, was integrated with an existing eight-rack SGI ICE system consisting of Intel Clovertown processors. Pleiades debuted in third place on the November 2008 TOP500 list, achieving 487 TF/s out of a theoretical peak of 609 TF/s on the Linpack benchmark [Topb].

Since its installation, Pleiades has undergone eight major compute enhancements and four major I/O infrastructure upgrades. Due to this evolution, the resulting system is heterogeneous. For example, it uses four different generations of Intel Xeon processors in its compute nodes. In addition, the IB technology used to connect the components has evolved over time, starting with DDR, then progressing to quad data rate (QDR), and finally fourteen data rate (FDR) links. As of June 2012, the system has 11,776 nodes in 181 compute racks. It achieved 1.24 PF/s on the Linpack benchmark out of a peak of 1.746 TF/s.

In the remainder of this chapter, we will examine Pleiades and how it is organized and run to meet NASA's HEC needs. We start with a detailed description of the system.

---

## 12.2    System Description

Pleiades is composed of several major subsystems—compute, storage, and graphics—connected using IB. Topologically, the system is two independent hypercubes. SGI refers to this organization as a "dual-plane" hypercube. In general, one plane of Pleiades is used for message passing and the other for I/O. Each system component is connected to one or both IB planes, depending on its connectivity requirements. High-speed local and wide area networking then provide access to local and remote users. This section starts with a discussion of the goals that drive the architectural and operational decisions. We then describe the compute and storage subsystems, the IB interconnect, local and wide area networking, and the system software used.

### 12.2.1    System Goals

High-level analysis of mission requirements identified three primary needs for NASA's HEC resources: *capability*, *capacity*, and *availability* (see Section 12.1.2). A more detailed analysis refined those three requirements into the five specific system goals listed below that NAS uses to guide decisions on system acquisitions and operations.

**Capability:** Some applications must be able to use a sizable portion (25% or more) of the system at one time. At a minimum, the system must be scalable across all compute resources of a given processor type.

**Capacity:** The system must support more than 1,000 users and be able to run hundreds of jobs simultaneously. In addition, individual jobs running on the system must not adversely affect the performance of other jobs that are also being executed.

**Availability:** The high demand for compute resources and the need to meet mission critical deadlines mean that any downtime related to maintenance activities must be minimized. Similarly, because of the productivity impact of draining the job queue, the number of scheduled outages should be minimized as well. Whenever possible, maintenance should be done while the system is in production.

**Versatility:** Since hundreds of projects, each with its own set of requirements, need to run on the system simultaneously, it must be designed to maximize workflow and minimize potential bottlenecks that could result in poor performance. In addition, the user environment must be configurable so that individual users can tailor it to meet specific project needs.

**Evolvability:** To handle an increasing workload over time, the system must be expandable while still providing a consistent user interface over its lifetime. Increases in system capability must allow for potentially large upgrades that augment rather than eliminate existing resources. This helps ensure that the lifetime of the system can extend much longer than that of its individual components. It also reduces lost user productivity typically associated with adapting to a new platform.

In the remainder of this chapter we will see how these goals have influenced the Pleiades system in its design, evolution, and operation.

**TABLE 12.1**: Details of Pleiades' four node types from the oldest Intel Xeon processors (Harpertown) to the newest (Sandy Bridge).

|  | Harpertown | Nehalem | Westmere | Sandy Bridge |
|---|---|---|---|---|
| # of racks | 64 | 20 | 71/2 | 24 |
| # of nodes | 4,096 | 1,280 | 4,544/128 | 1,728 |
| Sockets × cores | 2×4 | 2×4 | 2×6 | 2×8 |
| Total cores | 32,768 | 10,240 | 54,528/1,536 | 27,648 |
| Processor # | E5472 | X5570 | X5670/X5675 | E5-2670 |
| Clock speed (GHz) | 3.0 | 2.93 | 2.93/3.06 | 2.6 |
| Cache/socket (MB) | 12 | 8 | 12 | 20 |
| Memory type | DDR2 | DDR3 | DDR3 | DDR3 |
| Memory/node | 8–16 GB | 24 GB | 24–96 GB | 32 GB |
| Total memory | 32 TB | 30 TB | 106.5/3 TB | 54 TB |
| Dual-port IB HCA | DDR | DDR | QDR | FDR |

## 12.2.2 Compute Subsystem

The compute subsystem of Pleiades consists of the processing nodes, which are the primary resources for executing jobs; front-end nodes, which are used for program and data preparation, launching jobs, and post-processing; and bridge nodes that facilitate file transfers. Each Pleiades compute rack contains one of several classes of Intel Xeon processors. Numerous system expansions from 2008 to 2012 have resulted in the collection of nodes shown in Table 12.1. Nodes are arranged in racks consisting of four building blocks that are referred to as Individual Rack Units (IRU). Each IRU for the first three generations of Xeon processors contains 16 nodes. The newest Sandy Bridge IRUs are slightly different, with 18 nodes each. Each node has a dual-port IB Host Channel Adapter (HCA), which is used to connect to the two hypercube planes.

Of the 4,544 Westmere X5670 nodes, 64 are equipped with graphics processing units (GPUs) and 48 GB of memory per node. Each NVIDIA Tesla M2090 GPU has 512 processor cores, 6 GB of RAM, and operates at 1.3 GHz. Of the remaining Westmere nodes, 21 have 48 or 96 GB of memory instead of the standard 24 GB. These large-memory nodes accommodate post-processing work and jobs where a single large-memory node is needed for I/O performed by a master process.

The compute subsystem also consists of front-end and bridge nodes, whose architectures are similar to those of the compute nodes so that users can easily perform small tasks in an environment that closely resembles the one used for running their jobs. Currently, six SGI XE320 systems act as front-ends to Pleiades. Each XE320 contains two front-end nodes, each with two Intel quad-core E5472 (Harpertown) processors, 16 GB of RAM, and a dedicated DDR (HCA). New Sandy Bridge front-ends will be deployed in mid-2012. Four bridge nodes (two SGI XE250 and two SGI UV10) are available to transfer files between Pleiades and Columbia or the storage subsystem. These nodes have more memory (64 and 256 GB of RAM, respectively) and faster interconnects (QDR HCA and Chelsio 10 GigE adapter) than the front-ends. For user convenience, the bridge nodes mount all of Pleiades' home and scratch filesystems, along with the Columbia scratch filesystems.

## 12.2.3    Storage Subsystem

Users on Pleiades have access to a home filesystem that is backed up and a larger scratch filesystem that is not. They also have access to a long-term archive storage capability comprising both disk and tape. As with other components of the HEC environment at NAS, the storage subsystem has evolved over time to accommodate changing usage demands and to take advantage of technology advancements. The original Pleiades storage subsystem consisted of a single Network File System (NFS) server used for home directories and three Lustre filesystems used for scratch space. Over the past four years, the subsystem has increased to four NFS servers (three home filesystems and one scratch filesystem) and six Lustre filesystems for scratch—for a total online disk storage capacity of nearly 10 PB.

One of the four NFS servers is a 16-processor, 72 GB Itanium-based SGI Altix 4700 that serves a 59 TB scratch filesystem. It accommodates users whose applications perform better on NFS than on Lustre, for example, because they do many small I/O operations. The other three NFS systems are two-socket, Xeon-based servers that provide a total of 4.2 TB of storage. These systems are used for user home directories and system software repositories for compilers, MPI libraries, licensed software packages, and so forth. In order to improve performance, all four NFS platforms utilize multiple IB interfaces on the same subnet.

Lustre is used for the primary scratch filesystems on Pleiades. Each of the six filesystem complexes consists of one metadata server (MDS), an SGI IS220, and eight object store servers (OSS). To improve performance, each MDS and OSS is configured to preload metadata into memory. In addition, NAS system engineers have configured Lustre to disable read and write caching, and the block device read-ahead buffer. The async journal commit feature is enabled, along with adaptive timeouts and peer health detection. This configuration improves metadata performance by two orders of magnitude by reducing disk seeks through more effective metadata caching. The six scratch filesystems have names starting with "/nobackup" to reinforce the fact that users are responsible for copying their important data to the archive.

Pleiades users have access via 1 GigE and 10 GigE links to two SGI Altix 4700 systems used as archive servers. The first has 32 Itanium processors, 64 GB of memory, and 380 TB of disk. The second has 64 processors, 128 GB of memory, and 535 TB of disk. To balance the expected load between archive servers, users are assigned to one based on multiple factors, including NASA mission and anticipated usage characteristics. Each server runs an instance of SGI's Data Migration Facility DMF) software and is connected to either two or four Spectra Logic T950 tape libraries. The tape libraries use LT05 tape drives and media, and have an uncompressed capacity of 88 PB. Each server writes a copy of the data to two tape libraries that are located a kilometer apart to reduce the likelihood of data loss.

## 12.2.4    InfiniBand Networking

Pleiades uses a "dual-plane" IB hypercube to connect its components. The cabling and switches for the two planes are independent of one another. For simplicity, we limit the description here to a single plane. Each of the compute nodes shown in Table 12.1 is connected to an IB switch: 24-port DDR in the Harpertown racks, 36-port QDR in the Nehalem and Westmere racks, and 36-port FDR in the Sandy Bridge racks. Each of the switches is a vertex in the hypercube. Successively larger hypercubes are made by doubling and connecting corresponding vertices. For example, as shown in Figure 12.2, each IRU has two switches that are linked to each other, constituting a 1-D hypercube. The four IRUs in a rack link up to make a 3-D hypercube. Two racks are joined to form a 4-D hypercube. As indicated

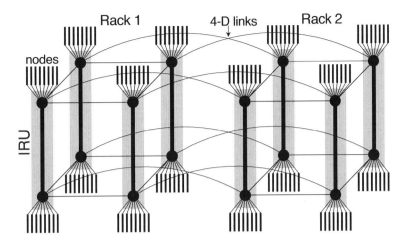

**FIGURE 12.2**: Hypercube building block: two racks are joined together to form a 4-D hypercube with switches at the vertices. Multiple compute nodes are connected to each switch. Within an IRU, the links between switches have up to four cables.

by the thick vertical lines in the diagram, the inter-switch links in each IRU are "enhanced" by adding up to three extra cables.

Before the integration of the Sandy Bridge racks, Pleiades was a partial 11-D hypercube. With the addition of the Sandy Bridge racks, Pleiades now has connections in the twelfth dimension as well. This was done to accommodate maximal future expansion without connecting FDR and DDR switches.

Pleiades uses the opensm IB subnet manager from OpenFabrics [Opeb], which provides Dimension Order Routing (DOR) for computing the switch-forwarding tables in the hypercube. It is based on the Min Hop algorithm, with ties broken by favoring lower-numbered dimensions. This strategy avoids deadlock cycles.

Each of the independent IB planes is managed by its own subnet manager. One plane is used primarily for MPI communication while the other is used for access to the NFS and Lustre, as well as to the hyperwall visualization system (described in Section 12.5.) It is possible, however, for an application to use both planes for message-passing traffic during a computation.

Pleiades' I/O IB plane is connected to six Lustre filesystems through a 2-D torus of nine 36-port QDR switches. These nine switches correspond to nine servers per Lustre filesystem—a total of 54 servers. This arrangement is illustrated in Figure 12.3. A second identical torus is connected to the hyperwall's compute nodes, except that a connection is made only to every second rack, instead of every rack. This torus enables concurrent visualization of computations on Pleiades using the hyperwall (see Section 12.5.2). Corresponding switches from the two tori are connected on port 36, allowing the hyperwall to access the Lustre filesystems for data post-processing.

In order to continue using opensm's DOR algorithm with the torus, NAS and SGI system engineers augmented DOR with a weight per port. Ports have a default weight of one in the outbound direction, and a configuration file is used to associate weights greater than that with particular switch ports. This makes the outbound path appear to have several hops (equal to the weight); thus, it is less likely to be chosen. By using this approach, potential deadlocks (or credit loops), such as those between a torus switch and a hypercube switch and back to the torus, can be avoided.

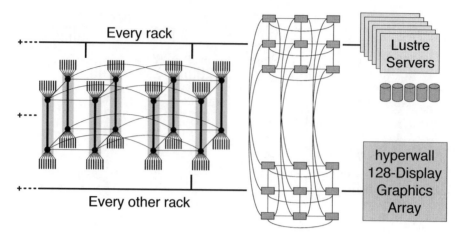

**FIGURE 12.3**: I/O fabric: two 9-switch tori provide connectivity for the Lustre servers and the hyperwall.

### 12.2.5 Local and Wide Area Networking

The NAS high-speed routed data network interconnects multiple components within the NAS facility and also provides system access to external users. Users move more than 170 TB of data into and out of the NAS high-speed routed data network each month. The network has three major elements: the Enclave, the Core, and the Border.

The **Enclave** directly interconnects the major Pleiades subsystems, supporting the overall administrative and IT security requirements. With the exception of a few management ports, jumbo frames are utilized with a maximum transmission unit of 9,000 bytes. The jumbo frame capability extends from the enclave to the Border and also to jumbo frame-enabled peer networks.

The **Core** provides high-speed Local Area Network (LAN) connectivity for users to access compute resources and services. It also contains private networks (e.g., for system administrator access), a perimeter network that has "demilitarized zone" (DMZ) filesystems to facilitate file transfers into and out of the Enclave, and public-facing networks such as web servers. This LAN has a 10 GigE backbone consisting of many subnets for NAS support functions. Hosts are connected to subnets at 1 GigE or 10 GigE.

The **Border** provides high-speed Wide Area Network (WAN) connections to NASA networks and external partner sites for access by remote users. This advanced peering environment includes 10 GigE connectivity to the NASA Integrated Communications Services (NICS) backbone, and dedicated 10 GigE connectivity to the Jet Propulsion Laboratory and the Goddard Space Flight Center. In addition, there is 10 GigE peering with Energy Sciences Network (ESnet), Pacific Wave (which includes many research networks such as Internet2), Corporation for Education Network Initiatives in California (CENIC), and other high-speed peering partners to ensure high-speed network connectivity between Pleiades and other supercomputing centers, academic institutions, and commercial partners.

### 12.2.6 System Software

All hosts on Pleiades run Linux. Some infrastructure hosts—such as those used for subnet managers, license servers, and PBSPro—run SUSE Linux Enterprise Server (SLES). The Lustre servers run CentOS, and compute nodes run either SLES or CentOS, as requested by the users' jobs. The compute nodes run a full operating system image, similar to that

**TABLE 12.2**: System software used on Pleiades (as of June 2012).

| | |
|---|---|
| *Operating Systems–Compute Nodes* | SLES11sp1; CentOS v6 |
| *Operating Systems–Lustre Servers* | CentOS v6 |
| *Operating Systems–Other Servers* | SLES11sp1 |
| *IB Software* | OFED 1.5.4.1 |
| *Filesystems* | Lustre 1.x, 2.x; NFS v3, v4; CXFS 5.x |
| *Hierarchical Storage Management* | DMF 4.4 |
| *Batch Scheduling* | PBSPro 10.2, 11.3 |

used on the front-end and bridge nodes, except for the omission of a few packages and the disabling of non-essential services and daemons. All of the InfiniBand software—e.g., the subnet manager, drivers, and libraries—comes from OpenFabrics Enterprise Distribution (OFED). Table 12.2 lists the most significant system software components used on the system.

## 12.3 User Environment

The user experience on Pleiades is largely determined by its software environment and the support services provided by NAS. In this section we discuss the software environment and how it influences two common user activities: programming and running jobs. We also describe the support services that are provided to ensure that users are getting the most out of Pleiades.

### 12.3.1 Programming Support Software

With about 500 active projects, Pleiades must support a diverse set of application characteristics. The execution models for the applications range from ensembles of small- to moderate-scale computations at one end, to tightly-coupled, distributed-memory computations scaling up to tens of thousands of cores at the other end.

Fortran is the programming language of choice for most NASA applications, with a small number of C and C++ codes as well. Some projects also use scripting languages such as Python to manage their computations. Since Pleiades is a large, distributed-memory cluster, most applications use the message-passing parallel programming model, with some version of the standard MPI library for inter-process communication. Because each node has multiple cores with shared memory, some codes use the OpenMP model to exploit these resources within a node, while others use a hybrid model (MPI across nodes with OpenMP within a node) to scale to a larger number of cores. With the addition of the GPU nodes in 2011, Pleiades also has some projects using CUDA to accelerate their codes.

Most of the application codes running on Pleiades are developed and maintained by small groups of researchers, but are used by a large community for NASA research and

**TABLE 12.3**: Libraries and tools available on Pleiades via Modules.

| | |
|---|---|
| *Compilers* | Intel, GNU, PGI |
| *MPI Libraries* | SGI MPT, mvapich2, Intel MPI |
| *Math Libraries* | Intel MKL, PETSc, GSL (GNU) |
| *Graphics & Visualization* | MATLAB, Tecplot 360, IDL, FieldView, Grace, gnuplot, NCL/NCAR Graphics, VisIt |
| *Third Party Libraries* | HDF4/5, netCDF, UDUNITS, ESMF, ParMetis, Gridgen |
| *Debuggers* | TotalView, GDB, valgrind |
| *Software Development* | CVS, Subversion, Eclipse |
| *Performance Tools* | PerfSuite, MPInside, Open\|SpeedShop, TAU |
| *Miscellaneous* | Java, Mathematica, Ruby, Gaussian |

engineering. These codes are continually upgraded to increase their fidelity or to add new physics models. A few projects use pre-packaged, third-party Independent Software Vendor (ISV) applications, but the percentage of such usage is extremely small.

The size of the user community and the diverse nature of their applications lead to a large set of requirements, sometimes necessitating multiple versions of various libraries and software packages to be simultaneously maintained on the system. The open source Modules package is the primary mechanism available for users to dynamically configure their execution environments. Table 12.3 shows the most significant libraries and tools supported on Pleiades.

### 12.3.2    Resource Allocation and Scheduling

As a NASA-wide resource, Pleiades is shared among hundreds of projects representing NASA's three Mission Directorates (MDs): Aeronautics Research (ARMD), Human Exploration and Operations (HEOMD), and Science (SMD). Each MD is assigned a percentage of the total annual node-hours available on the system, excluding a small fraction reserved for NAS internal engineering use. The MDs subdivide their allocations among their own projects, and NAS then tracks resource usage to ensure that projects do not exceed their allocations. The overall MD allocations are translated into share percentages to help the scheduler guarantee that each MD is given an appropriate amount of resources at any given time. The scheduler share percentages are adjusted as needed to ensure that compute cycles are not wasted, system utilization is high, and users receive the best possible turnaround for their jobs.

The PBSPro job scheduling software (originally developed at NAS and commercialized through a NASA technology transfer agreement with Altair) is used to manage batch jobs that run on Pleiades. Users specify the number and type(s) of node that are needed, and PBSPro handles the job scheduling and resource allocation. It takes into account numerous factors, including MD share, job priority within an MD, number of requested nodes, job wait-time, and so on. Once it starts, a job has exclusive use of the nodes allocated to it.

The determination of when to run a job is governed by a set of custom policies built into PBSPro that are not necessarily always in agreement. Because these general policies sometimes conflict, NAS operators have the ability to override them for a given job. For example, if a job requests more than 25% of an MD's current share, operators have the discretion to promote that job to the head of the queue. In addition, a few racks are set aside for short, one-job-per-user development work.

Advance reservations allow users to have a collection of compute resources set aside for their exclusive use for a period of time. This is helpful for debugging very large jobs because it allows multiple runs without waiting in the queue, thus facilitating a cycle of editing and execution steps. In addition, users are encouraged to request reservations when they need to run on 25% or more of Pleiades, because there is a small probability that any individual node could be up and responsive, but not functional. For example, this could be due to a memory error correction issue or the existence of unkillable processes left behind by a previous job. If some spare nodes were included in the reservation, they could be used in the place of any bad ones and the job could be re-run without waiting in the queue again.

### 12.3.3 User Support Services

To help NASA scientists and engineers take full advantage of Pleiades, NAS provides services to assist users through the entire lifecycle of their projects. A key strategy of the NAS approach to effective HEC operations is to form issue-focused, interdisciplinary teams as needed by engaging discipline-area experts, each with broad and deep knowledge of advanced systems and technologies. All of the following support service elements are critical to providing the HEC technologies and environments that improve user productivity, allowing them to focus their time and attention on NASA's current and future mission challenges.

**24 × 7 User Support:** The NAS user services team ensures that Agency scientists and engineers can make the most effective, productive use of Pleiades and associated systems around the clock. The control room operators provide immediate response to all user questions and coordinate end-to-end user services with other NAS teams to offer any custom support that is needed. The team continuously monitors and fine-tunes all systems, peripherals, and job processes to ensure a stable and secure supercomputing environment.

**Application Performance and Productivity:** The NAS application performance and productivity team helps users effectively port their codes to the supercomputers housed at the NAS facility, improve code scalability, and optimize their application performance. These support efforts often produce dramatic improvements in the performance of important NASA codes. In addition to the direct productivity impact for a code's user, optimization benefits the rest of the Pleiades community as well because of the increase in resource availability that results. The team also provides up-to-date documentation and regular training on best practices to assist users in making the most effective use of the system.

**Data Analysis and Visualization:** NAS visualization experts develop and implement advanced software tools and data analysis technologies that are customized to help scientists and engineers make new discoveries for Agency missions. This team's extensive repertoire includes a sophisticated concurrent visualization framework, which—together with the hyperwall visualization system—allows users to explore high-resolution results in real time and pinpoint critical details in large, complex datasets.

**Production Supercomputing and Archive Storage:** The NAS Division's expertise in developing and delivering HEC technologies is at the center of its integrated environment. To attain the highest possible HEC capability and capacity for the Agency, the systems team constantly evaluates, acquires, installs, and operates new systems, develops custom software tools, and implements advanced IT security methods. They also provide customized training and support to help users efficiently manage large amounts of data.

**High-Speed Networking:** NAS' high-capacity connections and network expertise enable users to transfer massive volumes of data—sometimes many terabytes in size—seamlessly between local and remote systems. The networks team works closely with remote users to optimize multiple aspects of data flows, select the most efficient transfer methods and protocols, and fine-tune their data transfer systems. The team is responsible for the end-to-end flow, acting as a single point of contact for resolving all networking issues.

## 12.4   Operations and Maintenance

This section provides an overview of the tools used to administer, debug, monitor, and correct problems on Pleiades. We also discuss the processes that are used to evolve the system while providing high availability to the users. Central to the operations and maintenance activities is the fact that all hosts in the system run Linux (see Section 12.2.6). Thus, there is a variety of open source tools that are available for the operations and maintenance activities. In the remainder of this section we discuss how NAS uses those tools and specialized processes to keep Pleiades running and to make any necessary changes.

### 12.4.1   Administration Tools

SGI provides a cluster administration package, called Tempo, based on open source tools such as systemimager, Oscar, C3, and pdsh. These tools have been extended with commands that customize them for the Altix ICE environment. One of the key elements in the administration of an ICE system is the Rack Leader Controller (RLC) in each compute rack. (Note that a Sandy Bridge RLC controls two racks, rather than one.) The RLC and compute nodes within a rack communicate over their own private 1-Gb Ethernet LAN. The RLC is responsible for all administrative functions within its rack. It provides the following: DHCP, NTP, DNS, and syslog services to the nodes; NFS, shared, read-only system images; and per-node, per-image writable space. The RLC uses the Intelligent Platform Management Interface (IPMI) to communicate with the baseboard management controller in each node to power the node up or down, reset it, and monitor its status. The RLC is also indirectly responsible for controlling the power to the IB switches in each rack.

These RLCs allow the system to scale. The load on an RLC is nearly independent of the total number of system racks, and racks do not compete with each other for LAN bandwidth since each has its own private LAN for administrative functions. A single "admin node" is used for overall administration of Pleiades. It communicates with the RLCs rather than the individual compute nodes. It provides DHCP, NTP, DNS, and syslog services to the RLCs and to other infrastructure service hosts, such as I/O servers and front-end nodes. All initial install images and updates are built on the admin node and then pushed out to the RLCs. Pleiades currently has 169 RLCs and more than 80 infrastructure hosts. This large number of hosts is starting to tax the admin node, and so a hierarchy of super-leader hosts and networks is being investigated as a possible solution to this impending scaling issue.

Configuration management is handled with CVS and Bcfg2, although there are some gaps in the tools. For example, while the infrastructure nodes can update themselves from the Bcfg2 repository automatically, updates to the compute nodes are more complicated. At NAS, the image on the admin node is first updated from the Bcfg2 repository. The changes are then pushed out to the images on the RLCs, and finally applied to each compute node's read-write area. The changes must be applied in such a way that running executables are not disturbed. If the changes require a daemon restart or a node reboot, these actions are delayed until any job using the node finishes.

### 12.4.2 Monitoring, Diagnosis, and Repair Tools

With more than 10,000 nodes on Pleiades, it is important that system health and status be monitored automatically and that the mechanism be scalable. System administrators currently use Nagios with several custom plug-ins to monitor all the infrastructure hosts and filesystems. The Nagios data is also used to provide status information in two ways: via an at-a-glance display used by the computer operators who monitor the NAS facility 24×7, and via the web for users and program managers.

With the current monitoring method, each node mostly runs its own diagnostic and repair tasks. To achieve this, the PBSPro batch scheduling system runs prologue and epilogue scripts at the start and end of every job. These scripts perform several diagnostic tests on each node used by the job to check for the following: correct amount of free memory in the node; adequate spool space; array services daemon; clock synchronized by the NTP daemon; and necessary filesystems. If a test fails, the node is marked as being offline, causing PBSPro to select other nodes for future runs.

In addition to system health monitoring, post-mortem analysis is also important. For instance, if a node experiences a problem, other nodes are likely to be similarly affected. Because of this domino effect, it is critical to analyze system crashes quickly and develop appropriate solutions. All hosts are therefore configured with kdb and crash dumps enabled. It is also fairly common for application codes to exhaust the memory on the nodes. The default behavior for Linux is to kill a process. Unfortunately, it does not kill the appropriate one. Thus, Linux on Pleiades is configured to reboot nodes when this occurs so that the error can be handled. A set of scripts using the Simple Event Correlator (SEC) tool monitors system logs and node consoles to detect such out-of-memory (OOM) reboots. SEC then identifies the job and instructs PBSPro to terminate it on the remainder of its nodes. The script also sends an email to notify the user. In addition, custom SystemTap scripts are used to examine other issues on running nodes and gather performance data for filesystems. Finally, to monitor the health of the approximately 3,000 IB switches, scripts fan out to have each RLC check the status and error counters of its nearest switches. Interpretation of these errors is still largely a manual process.

### 12.4.3 System Enhancements and Maintenance

To meet the availability goal for Pleiades, NAS has developed several operational processes to minimize the number of full system outages. For example, each compute node can be booted using one of several images. This facilitates a rolling update where the default OS of each compute node can be upgraded at the completion of the job executing on that node.

To maximize availability and allow for filesystem maintenance, each user is assigned to one or more Lustre scratch filesystems. When any job is considered for execution, the PBSPro scheduler checks for the availability of the required filesystems as a necessary resource. This allows operators to take a specific filesystem down for maintenance while the system can still be fully utilized by jobs that do not require the offlined filesystem. All NFS filesystems are hard mounted, and user applications can reliably withstand reboots (or crashes) of the NFS servers.

Pleiades is the first major supercomputer to incorporate *live integration*—the ability to augment the system while computational jobs continue to run on the existing hardware, greatly increasing overall availability. When new compute nodes are ready to be integrated with the existing system, they are powered down, the subnet manager sweeping is turned off, the new hardware is cabled to the existing hardware, the cabling is verified, and finally the new hardware is powered up and the subnet sweeping is restarted. The subnet manager sweep integrates the new hardware into the overall fabric and the new nodes are added to the PBSPro's list of available resources. While this approach works for integrating new compute hardware, most of the software maintenance on the IB network itself is too disruptive to attempt while Pleiades is operational. These include updates to the subnet manager and firmware updates to the switches.

As described in Section 12.4.1, each node mounts its OS image from an RLC. In order to update the RLC, all nodes in that rack must be idled. Over time, fragmentation occurs where many jobs end up running on a single rack. Since it is impractical to idle 181 compute racks, RLC updates require a full system outage. NAS is developing a method to eliminate this problem so as to allow an individual RLC to be passed over during resource allocation while it boots into an updated image.

## 12.5    Visualization

Scientific visualization is an integral part of the NASA HEC environment and is particularly important for the high-fidelity M&S projects that make up the dominant workload on Pleiades. At the same time, the continually increasing resolution and complexity of modern simulations that make visual methods so useful also make them increasingly difficult to deploy. Extremely large datasets with numerous components require effective data management strategies such as: parallel decomposition across hundreds or thousands of compute nodes provides challenging opportunities for efficient data retrieval; complex and adaptive discretization schemes create issues for data access and rendering; and time-varying multiphysics codes present difficulties for extracting and depicting salient information. Taking into account all of these factors, NAS has created a visualization environment for Pleiades that is tightly integrated with its major compute, interconnect, and data storage subsystems.

### 12.5.1    Rendering Platforms

Currently, there are two primary rendering engines in the Pleiades visualization environment. The first is the hyperwall, a custom-built, 128-node display wall. One of the largest, most powerful visualization systems in existence, the 128-screen wall is arranged in an 8×16 packed array of 20" NEC 2090UXi LCDs. The array measures 23 feet wide by 10 feet high, and has 245 megapixels (see Figure 12.4). Each LCD is driven by an individual graphics node with dual-socket, quad-core AMD Opteron 2354 (Barcelona) processors, 16 GB of RAM, 1 TB of local disk, a ConnectX DDR IB HCA, and either one or two NVIDIA GeForce GTX480 graphics boards. The hyperwall contains several additional console, service, and management nodes, as well as a metadata server and OSS nodes for its own local 350 TB Lustre filesystem. In addition, it mounts all of the Pleiades Lustre filesystems as described in Section 12.2.4.

The hyperwall uses a 288-port 4X DDR IB switch router (Voltaire 9288) for its local fat-tree interconnect, and nine 24-port QDR switches arranged in a torus for interfacing with the I/O plane of the Pleiades IB fabric, as shown in Figure 12.3. This configuration

**FIGURE 12.4**: The hyperwall can show a single image across all 128 screens or display multiple configurations of data on individual screens.

provides dedicated pathways and high bandwidth for processing data-intensive applications on the hyperwall while isolating Pleiades' compute subsystem from this traffic. The total unidirectional bandwidth between Pleiades and the hyperwall is more than 100 GB/s.

The second rendering engine consists of 64 Westmere nodes on Pleiades that are essentially identical to the other Pleiades Westmere nodes, but with local disk, enhanced memory (48 GB), and one NVIDIA Tesla M2090 GPU on each node. Unlike the hyperwall, the Pleiades GPU nodes have no attached displays. In fact, the M2090 cards lack a DVI port and are not externally accessible. Also, unlike the hyperwall, these GPU nodes are part of the Pleiades dual-plane hypercube, on par with any other Pleiades Westmere nodes.

## 12.5.2 Visualization Strategies and Deployment

Two types of visualization methods are used on Pleiades. The first is traditional post-processing visualization, which uses data stored on disk or written to the tape archive as input. Although it does not scale well to the largest time-varying calculations, this widely-used method is still the predominant type of visualization dataflow that is run on Pleiades.

Both the hyperwall and the Pleiades GPU cluster are well suited to post-processing dataflow, as their architectures allow highly parallel access over high-bandwidth IB links to Pleiades' Lustre filesystems and their underlying fast RAIDs. In fact, some of the highest performance obtained from the NAS Lustre filesystems (~20 GB/s) has been from simultaneous access by all hyperwall nodes in a data-limited rendering context. The high bandwidth to the graphics nodes supports both intra- and inter-frame parallel rendering. The local disk on each hyperwall node allows staging copies to be made, which is useful in some cases. However, recent improvements in Lustre read/write caching and current RAID performance have largely removed the advantages of the local disks on the hyperwall.

Applications on Pleiades are also able to do concurrent visualization (CV), where data from a running calculation are provided directly to analysis and rendering routines without being written to disk. Some approaches (usually described as in situ visualization) deploy rendering algorithms on the same nodes as the calculation producing the data, and may in fact use the source data structures themselves. However, in situ approaches interleave the calculation and rendering tasks, and typically have unwanted effects on memory footprints and caching. In the strategy used on Pleiades, the data are copied from the nodes producing them—typically at the completion of an iterative timestep—onto some collection of graphics nodes, where analysis and rendering take place as the compute nodes resume the simulation [EGH+06]. The data copies occur in parallel from a distributed application and are limited only by memory and IB speeds, both of which are so fast that the simple option of creating fully synchronous copies is adequate; it is unnecessary to manage the extra complexity of an asynchronous operation. For large unsteady calculations, CV has the primary benefit of providing very high-temporal-resolution analyses and visualizations with overhead so low that it does not impede the primary calculation. In some cases, for example with magnetohydrodynamics calculations that are used to resolve very fast dynamics, sampling every solver timestep is greatly excessive and one can choose a larger stride, which also reduces any interference.

CV requires that the relevant application code be instrumented, although the changes are generally minor. Most of the complexity occurs in the visualization clients on the receiving end, which typically must handle multiple incoming chunks of a domain decomposition. Some rendering techniques can exploit the application's parallel decomposition. For example, isosurfaces can be computed independently in each chunk, and then recombined in the framebuffer. However, other techniques, such as fieldline or particle tracing, may require adjacency information and knowledge of ghost cell schemes in order to essentially undo the parallel decomposition. Frequently, code to do this sort of domain reassembly can be found in the I/O routines of the program.

## 12.6    Facilities Infrastructure

Constructed in 1985 to house the computational assets of the original NAS program (see Section 12.1), Building N258 at NASA Ames Research Center has over the years hosted more than 25 separate supercomputers on its 30,000 sq. feet of raised floor. Built to sustain shear loads consistent with the force of a magnitude 8.0+ earthquake, the two-story building is a steel-frame structure with steel-reinforced concrete floors. The raised floor includes 15,000 sq. feet of primary computer floor (see Figure 12.5), 3,000 sq. feet of auxiliary floor that was originally designed as a secure processing facility, and 12,000 sq. feet dedicated to visualization workstations and networking laboratories. The building also houses more than 200 staff members of the NAS Division.

To eliminate the heat produced by the computational systems, N258 has a chiller system, which has a capacity of 1,800 tons and is capable of achieving a water temperature of 42° F. An intricate plumbing topology and a pumping system capable of sustained flow rates in excess of 2,200 gpm are used to deliver cooling in a precise and efficient manner. The heat load is ultimately ejected to the cooling tower, which uses evaporative and drip technology to lower the water temperature before returning it to the chillers.

Electrical consumption by HEC resources at the NAS facility hovers at the current building capacity of 6 MW. Electrical service arrives at the building at 13.8 kV, and is transformed and delivered to electrical switchgear at 480 V for the HEC systems and 2.4 kV for the chillers. The reliability of the electrical infrastructure is being augmented with a series of rotary uninterruptible power supplies (RUPS), scheduled for completion in early 2013. All electrical and mechanical infrastructure components, including chillers, pumps, and the cooling tower, are managed for electrical efficiency through switchgear, motor control centers, and variable-speed motors.

Currently, Pleiades is stressing the facility's engineering thresholds in almost every infrastructure category. With each system augmentation, the increased processor and memory density cause power, cooling, and floor loading requirements to grow. These demands have prompted engineering investigations into new heat ejection protocols and alternative equipment sites within Ames Research Center.

## 12.7 Performance Results

Despite having the capability to run applications at scale—most notably a LINPACK benchmark across the entire system for a sustained performance of more than 1.2 PF/s— Pleiades is not commonly used for applications running on more than 10,000 cores. Rather, the system's primary use is as a capacity resource for projects supporting NASA's future space missions, fundamental aeronautics applications, and Earth and planetary science research. In fact, Pleiades typically runs about 75,000 jobs each month, and about 85% of the resources are used by jobs requesting 4,096 cores or fewer.

Given this usage pattern, NAS concentrates its benchmarking and performance research activities on modest-sized computations that represent the actual NASA computational workload. In 2011, more than a year of past accounting data were used to identify six application codes that were heavily executed on Pleiades: three codes from SMD and three representing ARMD, HEOMD, and the NASA Engineering and Safety Center (NESC). This suite of codes makes up the application portion of benchmarking requirements in NAS' RFPs

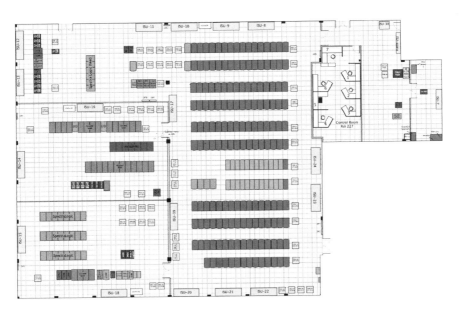

**FIGURE 12.5**: Schematic layout of the 15,000 sq. foot main computer floor housing the Pleiades supercomputer at the NAS facility. Each of the small squares in the diagram represents a two-foot by two-foot floor tile.

for supercomputers. In the remainder of this section we describe these applications and give a brief explanation of how they are used to establish charging rates for Pleiades' different compute resources (see Table 12.1). We then highlight some of the performance research conducted using these six codes.

### 12.7.1    Performance of the Pleiades Node Types

One of the benchmarking goals is to define a Standard Billing Unit (SBU), which reflects the amount of computing power needed to run a representative workload. Each Pleiades node type can then be tested to determine the amount of resources used to run the workload and establish its SBU charging rate. By using the relative computing power of each node type to set the SBU rate, users are encouraged to guide their jobs to those parts of the machine that execute their codes most economically, thereby improving overall system utilization.

The SBU is defined in terms of the following six representative application codes in such a way that a Westmere node has an SBU rate of one. All of these codes use MPI for interprocess communication.

**Enzo v2.0** is an adaptive mesh refinement, grid-based code, developed by a community of academic participants, that is used to simulate cosmological structure formation [Enz]. Appropriate input files are used to create data in HDF5 format representing initial cosmological conditions in the setup phase. When the benchmark is executed, the cosmos represented by these binary HDF5 files is allowed to evolve. This benchmark case uses 240 MPI ranks.

**FUN3D v11.3** is an unstructured CFD code from NASA Langley Research Center (LaRC) that is used for aerospace design analysis and optimization [Nie]. The code uses an adjoint-based error estimation to perform mesh adaptation. The benchmark grid is a wing-body geometry developed as a Common Research Model (CRM) for aerodynamic prediction validation studies of various CFD codes. The CRM consists of unstructured tetrahedral grids with about 100 million unknowns. This benchmark uses 960 MPI ranks.

**GEOS-5**, the Goddard Earth Observing System Model, is the atmospheric general circulation model from Goddard's suite of models to support climate and weather prediction, data analysis, Earth observing system modeling and design, and basic research [Rie]. The dataset used is benchmark case 4 with a resolution of 7 km, where all initial data are generated by the code itself. The physical problem that it solves is known as the Jablonowski & Williamson Baroclinic Test Case. This benchmark uses 1,176 MPI ranks.

**OVERFLOW v2.1ae** is a CFD code from LaRC for solving complex compressible flow problems. It is widely used to design launch and reentry vehicles, rotorcraft, ships, and commercial aircraft [NTB06]. The dataset used is a three-blade, generic rotor system with a fixed NACA0010 airfoil section and rectangular planform, similar to the UH-60 rotor system. The benchmark geometry consists of about 99 million grid points and uses 480 MPI ranks.

**USM3D v20100611** is an unstructured mesh code from LaRC used to calculate flows over complex geometries such as aerospace vehicles [PPF]. The dataset used in the benchmark solves the same CRM problem as FUN3D. This benchmark uses 480 MPI ranks.

**WRF v3.1**, the Weather Research and Forecasting Model, is the latest-generation, mesoscale numerical weather prediction system from the National Center for Atmospheric Research (NCAR). WRF is designed to serve both operational forecasting and atmospheric research needs [fARc]. The Typhoon Morakot (August 2009) dataset is a production run with a resolution of 2 km. This benchmark uses 384 MPI ranks.

In order to choose the number of MPI ranks to use for each application, the benchmarking team first conducted a strong scaling study on the Westmere nodes of Pleiades, shown in Figure 12.6. They then picked rank counts to reflect typical usage of each application and

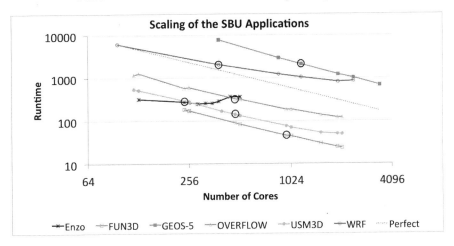

**FIGURE 12.6**: Westmere scaling results for the six applications used to define the SBU charging rates for Pleiades. The data points used in the SBU determination are circled.

verified that there was reasonable scaling behavior at that point. Choices for counts were limited to numbers that are divisible by both 8 and 12 so that the execution would exactly populate all of the nodes being used. Runtime parameters such as iteration counts were then adjusted so that the execution required about 30 minutes on the Westmere nodes.

To establish the SBU charging rates, each application was run on each Pleiades node type. The runtimes are shown in Table 12.4. This information is used to calculate the relative number of runs that each application can execute in one hour on 64 nodes (prorated both in time and space, as needed) compared to what could be run in an hour on the baseline 64 Westmere nodes. Those numbers are shown in Table 12.5. Note that although the Westmere runtimes are greater than those on Nehalem, the relative numbers are better on the Westmeres. This is due to the fact that Westmere nodes have 12 cores, compared to 8 cores on a Nehalem. For each node type, the SBU charging rate is a weighted average across all applications of the relative number of runs shown in Table 12.5. This calculation gives the SBU charging rate for each node type, as shown on the last row of the table. Note that the charging factor progressively increases with newer generations of the Xeon architecture.

**TABLE 12.4**: Runtimes (in seconds) for the SBU suite of six applications on different Pleiades processor types.

| Application | Harpertown | Nehalem | Westmere | Sandy Bridge |
|---|---|---|---|---|
| Enzo | 2,128 | 1,525 | 1,925 | 1,637 |
| FUN3D | 3,270 | 1,616 | 1,734 | 1,405 |
| GEOS-5 | 2,815 | 1,636 | 2,096 | 1,219 |
| OVERFLOW | 2,931 | 1,364 | 1,786 | 1,154 |
| USM3D | 3,954 | 1,596 | 1,802 | 1,499 |
| WRF | 3,404 | 1,775 | 2,036 | 1,500 |

**TABLE 12.5**: Relative number of runs for the SBU applications on different Pleiades processor types.

| Application | Weight | Runs relative to Westmere | | | |
| --- | --- | --- | --- | --- | --- |
| | | Harpertown | Nehalem | Westmere | Sandy Bridge |
| Enzo | 20% | 0.60 | 0.84 | 1.00 | 1.57 |
| FUN3D | 10% | 0.35 | 0.71 | 1.00 | 1.65 |
| GEOS-5 | 15% | 0.50 | 0.85 | 1.00 | 2.29 |
| OVERFLOW | 20% | 0.41 | 0.87 | 1.00 | 2.06 |
| USM3D | 20% | 0.30 | 0.75 | 1.00 | 1.60 |
| WRF | 15% | 0.40 | 0.76 | 1.00 | 1.81 |
| Weighted Average | | 0.43 | 0.81 | 1.00 | 1.83 |

## 12.7.2    Performance Research Using Pleiades

Most of the performance research performed at the NAS facility is focused on the efficient use of its HEC platforms. Since the installation of Pleiades, NAS has used representative NASA applications to understand the system's performance characteristics. Three such efforts are described below.

### Resource Contention in Multi-Core Systems

One study used differential performance analysis to investigate the impact of resource sharing in commodity, multi-core processors [HJM+10]. By comparing runs that bound MPI processes to cores in different patterns, the authors were able to quantify the performance penalty for sharing resources, such as cache and memory bandwidth, in four production applications, including OVERFLOW. The experiments were conducted on four different quad-core microprocessors: Intel Clovertown, Intel Harpertown, AMD Barcelona, and Intel Nehalem.

Results showed that the dominant contention factor for the applications tested was the available bandwidth on the memory channels for a single socket (for example, the front-side bus of the Harpertown processor). Contrary to previously held beliefs, that resource turned out to be a more important factor in explaining the superlinear scaling of OVERFLOW on Harpertowns than was the last-level cache. This research also revealed the performance advantage of moving from the Uniform Memory Access (UMA) model of Harpertown to the Non-Uniform Memory Access (NUMA) of Barcelona and Nehalem, where an integrated memory controller speeds access to local memory.

### Hyper-Threading and Processor Source Utilization

A second study investigated the impact of hyper-threading on processor resource utilization for production applications [SJH+11]. The goal of hyper-threading is to use processor resources more efficiently by making them available to two different hardware threads simultaneously, and therefore hide latencies related to data access. Four production applications were run, including OVERFLOW and USM3D, and data (such as instructions retired, cache hits/misses, and vector/scalar floating-point operations) were collected from the Performance Monitoring Unit of the Westmere processor. In comparing the times of a single-threaded run of $n$ MPI ranks to a hyper-threaded run with $2n$ ranks, only OVER-FLOW did not show a performance boost from the use of hyper-threading.

Using an efficiency metric to quantify processor resource utilization, the study found that the efficiency in hyper-threaded mode was higher than in single-threaded mode across all core counts in the applications studied. The fact that OVERFLOW did not demonstrate any improvement from hyper-threading meant that other factors were influencing its performance. In particular, the study found that vectorization played a key role, as OVERFLOW was by far the most vectorized of the four codes assessed. One of the key conclusions was that less vectorized codes could attain a performance boost from hyper-threading because the additional thread did not cause load instructions to go deeper into the memory hierarchy than they would have in single-threaded mode.

### Hybrid Programming Model for Multi-Core Systems

The third study investigated the use of a hybrid programming model that combines the message-passing paradigm of MPI with the shared-memory parallelism of OpenMP [JJM+11]. The authors examined the performance of two of the multi-zone NAS Parallel Benchmark codes and two production applications on three multi-core based systems, including Pleiades.

Results showed the usefulness of the hybrid approach for improving load balance and numerical convergence. It also demonstrated two primary limitations that impede wider adoption of hybrid programming: first, no well-defined interaction exists between MPI processes and OpenMP threads, and second, performance of OpenMP is limited, especially on NUMA architectures. The study also described an approach to extend OpenMP with the concept of location to improve performance of the resultant codes on NUMA systems. In addition, the work proposed the syntax of language extensions to express task-data affinity.

## 12.8   System Utilization Statistics

Since its installation in 2008, Pleiades has experienced extremely heavy utilization. Projects began using the system in earnest in November 2008, doubled their usage within one month, and reached the total allocation (i.e., 75% of the maximum available) by February 2009. This rapid adoption occurred despite the fact that most users had to port codes from the Intel Itanium-based Columbia shared-memory system to the Xeon nodes of Pleiades. Initially, system utilization was heavily focused on the engineering challenges associated with early design studies being conducted for NASA's Constellation Program.

Utilization closely tracked system expansions from 2009 through 2011, and has continued to rise in 2012. See Figures 12.7 and 12.8 for Pleiades compute and storage utilization, respectively. Astrophysicists and Earth scientists began to use the system heavily in summer 2011, coinciding with a drop in usage by spacecraft operations, due to the end of the Space Shuttle Program. In the fall of 2011, aeronautical engineers were also vying for compute cycles.

The Pleiades operational approach is designed to best meet the needs of NASA's users. For example, the configuration of the different batch queues gives users options for trading off maximum runtime versus likely queue wait time—longer job requests tend to wait longer in the queue. Most of the SBUs delivered on Pleiades are to jobs that run 24 hours or longer. Job queue limits allow runs of up to five days, and many users take advantage of that. When

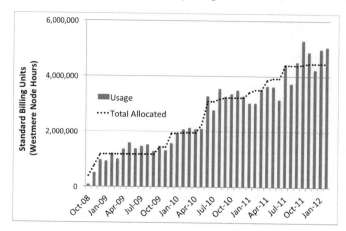

**FIGURE 12.7**: Pleiades compute capacity and utilization growth over the life of the system. The Total Allocated line represents 75% of the maximum theoretically available SBUs.

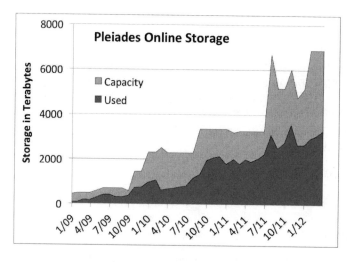

**FIGURE 12.8**: Pleiades storage capacity and utilization growth over the life of the system.

an application requires even more time, NAS allows jobs up to 16 days if there is a compelling reason and support from the project's MD.

In addition to its continual growth as a capacity resource, Pleiades has also seen an increase in its use as a capability resource. In June 2009, jobs requiring between 257 and 512 cores used more SBUs than jobs in any other category, and the widest jobs were under 8,192 cores. However, a year later, jobs between 512 and 1,024 cores represented the largest category of SBU usage, and the widest jobs were between 16,000 and 32,000 cores. Continuing the trend, by May 2012, jobs between 2,049 and 4,096 cores were the heaviest users of SBUs, 56% of the SBUs were used by jobs of 1,025 cores and over, and the widest jobs exceeded 65,000 cores.

## 12.9 Key Applications

From the approximately 500 science and engineering projects running on Pleiades, we highlight four significant applications representing NASA's three MDs. Each of these applications requires the supercomputing capability of Pleiades to achieve its scientific or engineering objectives. Across the board, researchers have repeatedly stated that these rapid solutions and advancements would not be possible without access to the computational power of Pleiades.

### 12.9.1 High-Fidelity Simulation of Rotor Wakes

There is a continued need to improve aircraft performance and safety while reducing the impact on the environment. NASA conducts fundamental, leading-edge research in new aircraft technologies in order to meet these challenges for the U.S. air transportation system. One of these challenges is the accurate prediction of aerodynamic and structural performance, and noise for rotorcraft used in many civil and military applications. Solving this problem requires a multi-disciplinary approach to account for rotor blade aerodynamics, blade flexibility, and blade motion for trimmed flight. Compounding the problem, rotor blades may encounter the tip vortices of other blades, resulting in very complex blade-vortex interactions and vortex wake structures. While traditional comprehensive codes provide fast multi-disciplinary engineering analyses for rotorcraft simulations, they utilize simplified aerodynamics models that typically include an inviscid lifting-line model, 2-D airfoil table lookup for additional viscous realism, and tip-vortex wake models. NASA is developing new physics-based computational tools to predict rotorcraft flowfields more accurately by using the nonlinear, three-dimensional, Navier-Stokes equations.

Using Pleiades, NASA researchers have obtained significantly improved results by loosely coupling OVERFLOW with CAMRAD II, a commercial, comprehensive rotorcraft code. This process replaces the simplified aerodynamics model in CAMRAD II with the OVERFLOW Navier-Stokes equations. For the first time, the figure of merit (a measure of rotor blade efficiency) for a V-22 Osprey rotor in hover was predicted within experimental error

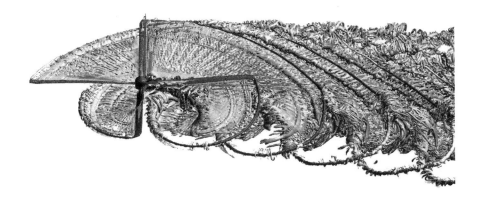

**FIGURE 12.9**: Navier-Stokes simulation of a UH-60 Blackhawk helicopter rotor in high-speed forward flight, using AMR and the Spalart-Allmaras/DES turbulence model.

using finer body grids, high-order spatial accuracy, and an improved turbulence model with detached eddy simulation (DES) [CB11]. A new dynamic adaptive mesh refinement (AMR) algorithm was also used to improve the resolution of rotor tip vortices by a factor of four, revealing previously unknown turbulent vortical worms. Moreover, CFD simulations of the UH-60 Blackhawk helicopter rotor in forward flight (see Figure 12.9) improved the prediction of rotor normal forces and pitching moments by almost 50% [CA12]. Each run of the forward flight simulation used 1,536–3,072 cores on Pleiades, enabling the completion of baseline grid solutions in one day and completion of AMR solutions in five days. In 2011, this project consumed 1.2 million SBUs on Pleiades, and required up to 100 TB of disk to store solutions for time-dependent flow animations.

### 12.9.2 Design Analysis for the Space Launch System

Coinciding with the final space shuttle mission in July 2011, NASA began to focus its efforts on space operations related to human exploration in and beyond low Earth orbit. Pleiades plays an important role in producing high-fidelity CFD simulations for design analyses of the upcoming Space Launch System (SLS), with the first developmental flight planned in late 2017.

These comprehensive aerodynamic simulations of SLS vehicle designs are used to predict aerodynamic performance, loads, and pressure signatures for design variations. The simulations include initial shape trade studies to help assess and compare various candidate designs; inviscid and viscous aerodynamic performance characterization for both crew and cargo vehicles; and computations of line loads and surface pressure signatures throughout ascent for preliminary designs (see Figure 12.10). Results from these ongoing CFD analyses enable NASA designers and engineers to enhance the vehicle's shape for better performance, and to assess SLS structural and acoustic loads during ascent.

As of June 2012, more than 3,300 cases for seven different SLS vehicle designs have been simulated on Pleiades using NASA's Cart3D and OVERFLOW CFD codes. A best practice protocol for simulating launch vehicle ascent using those codes was established during the Constellation Program [KHG+11]. Between May 2011 and February 2012, the SLS ascent aerodynamics project consumed over 356,000 SBUs on Pleiades. Extensive aerodynamic databases, comprising hundreds to thousands of simulations each, can be performed in less than a week on Pleiades—previous cases required two months on the Columbia supercom-

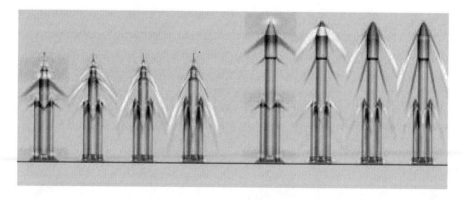

**FIGURE 12.10**: Contour plots of pressures on the vehicle surface and on a cutting plane for two early candidate crew (left) and cargo (right) SLS designs at four different Mach numbers.

puter. This fast turnaround of CFD data is crucial to streamlining the speed and cost of the SLS design process while ensuring the highest possible performance and safety standards.

### 12.9.3 Ocean-Ice Interactions in Earth System Models

Along with its partners in the science community, NASA uses space observatories to gain a deeper understanding of Earth and other planets, the Sun and its effects on the solar system, and the universe. One of the Agency's key Earth science goals is to increase our understanding of the role of oceans, atmosphere, and ice in the climate system, and to improve capabilities to predict the future evolution of these climate system components. The availability of Pleiades enables scientists supporting the Estimating the Circulation and Climate of the Ocean (ECCO) project to improve estimates and models of the general circulation of the ocean and its interaction with atmosphere, ice, and biogeochemistry [WHPF09]. ECCO circulation estimates are used to understand the recent evolution of the polar oceans [SMRS12], to monitor time-evolving property fluxes within and between different components of the Earth system [CTM11], and for many other science applications.

Pleiades dramatically increased the detail at which global ocean circulation can be simulated by the ECCO project. For example, Figure 12.11 shows a snapshot of surface current speed for a global ocean simulation carried out on a grid with horizontal spacing ranging from 1 km at high latitudes to 7 km at the Equator [HMCH07]. The computation involves time stepping 180 active, three-dimensional fields, each containing 1.25 billion cells for a total memory footprint of approximately 1.8 TB. Each model time step entails $4.5 \times 10^{12}$ arithmetic operations, a computation that is made possible by spreading the load on 2,000–4,000 Pleiades processors. Pleiades also allowed the ECCO team to run the massive minimization problems that must be solved in order to constrain the numerical model with observations. These nonlinear optimization problems are among the largest ever undertaken, involving billions of observations and control parameters, and trillions of predictive model variables. During the past year, the ECCO project used over 2 million SBUs on Pleiades and Columbia. At present, the project archives about 600 TB of data on NAS storage systems.

### 12.9.4 Search for Habitable Earth-Sized Planets

As part of NASA's science goal to achieve a deeper scientific understanding of other planets and solar system bodies, the Kepler spacecraft, launched in 2009, continuously monitors over 150,000 stars in the Milky Way to discover Earth-sized and smaller planets— especially those in the "habitable zone" of their stars, where liquid water might exist. Researchers at the Kepler Science Operations Center (SOC) calibrate and combine pixels to form light curves, correct for systematic errors, and search for the periodic dimming that may indicate the presence of a transiting exoplanet passing in front of a star. Figure 12.12 depicts the Kepler science data processing pipeline. The most computationally intensive portions of the pipeline are the Transiting Planet Search (TPS) and the Data Validation (DV) modules.

The computational power of Pleiades is essential to running Kepler's major analysis components. After the light curves are corrected, copies of the data are transmitted from the SOC to Pleiades where the TPS and DV modules are executed. Processing of light curves from all the observed stars typically utilizes about 36,000 Pleiades cores for 20 hours, versus more than a month on SOC computers. Select candidates that survive DV are carefully studied by the SOC team for confirmation as true planets. Candidates may be validated by a statistical code called BLENDER, which attempts to find astrophysical "mimics" that could produce light curves indistinguishable from a planetary transit. Typical BLENDER runs take about 10 hours on 2,500 cores; however, recent NAS optimization work has shortened

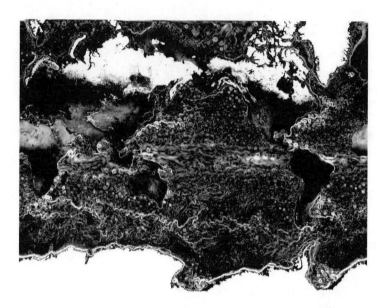

**FIGURE 12.11**: Visualization of surface current speed for a global ocean simulation carried out with 1/16-degree horizontal grid spacing on Pleiades by the ECCO project, capturing the swirling flows of tens of thousands of ocean currents.

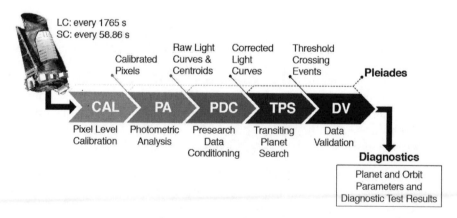

**FIGURE 12.12**: Kepler's science data processing pipeline (adapted from [RB]). The TPS and DV modules are executed on Pleiades.

these runtimes by two orders of magnitude. With the Kepler SOC team's interest turning to smaller planets in wider orbits, the increased efficiency of BLENDER will be critical to improving the scientific results by enabling exploration of more parameters, such as stellar ages and metallicity.

As of February 27, 2012, Kepler's discoveries include 2,321 new planet candidates with 61 confirmed planets, a new planetary system comprising planets orbiting two stars (circumbinary planets), and the first Earth-size planets orbiting a sun-like star outside our solar system [FTR+12].

## 12.10  Ongoing Impact of Pleiades

Apart from being one of the most powerful supercomputers in the world over the last five years, Pleiades has had major positive impacts on NASA missions in two key areas. First, by increasing the Agency's HEC capacity by more than 20-fold, it has played a significant role in the success of numerous NASA programs and projects. For example, Pleiades has enabled new understanding of the Earth system through very high-resolution ocean-atmosphere-cryosphere models; empowered aerospace engineers to develop best practices for high-fidelity simulation-assisted design and analysis for next-generation spacecraft and operations; allowed complex CFD computations of rotorcraft to set a new benchmark for accuracy; and critically supported the Kepler mission to search for Earth-like planets.

Pleiades has also impacted the supercomputing community through the pathfinding technologies, techniques, and processes developed by NAS and its partners. When NASA formulated the plan for implementing Pleiades in 2008, NAS faced substantial risks in realizing a productive, petascale system based on open source software, commodity hardware, an InfiniBand network, and the Lustre filesystem. To achieve the mission impacts noted earlier, Pleiades had to deliver the capability and capacity needed to serve NASA's broad array of user requirements while ensuring that the system could be efficiently administered and operated.

The NAS Technology Refresh process used to select and procure Pleiades has proven to be an efficient and effective approach for ensuring fairness while identifying the best candidate architectures to support NASA's computational requirements, conducting rigorous testbed evaluations, making optimal build-out decisions, and refining final system designs. Moreover, NAS' collaborative approach to reducing risk by partnering with vendors from testbed evaluations to phased expansions is highly effective at resolving complex issues, creating a world-class HEC environment, and minimizing capital and operations costs.

The result is that Pleiades has pushed well past previous benchmarks in the scale of major HEC components, including Linux, Lustre, PBSPro, InfiniBand, and commodity processors. The system's live augmentation capability, which enables new compute resources to be added while the system continues to operate, has saved tens of millions of compute hours for the users. The high-bandwidth connection established between Pleiades and the hyperwall makes possible innovations in concurrent visualization, which in turn accelerates scientific and engineering achievements across NASA's Mission Directorates. In addition, the NAS HEC environment's approach to providing user support services in areas ranging from networks to applications has made Pleiades a model of HEC productivity and efficiency.

To keep pace with NASA's emerging modeling and simulation requirements, NAS is preparing for a significant technology refresh that will soon increase its computational capability another tenfold. Storage will continue to expand to meet users' growing data repository needs, with an expected 400% increase over the next three years. NAS is also delving into technology advancements such as large accelerator-based clusters and streaming visualizations to remote users. Over the next few years, scientific visualization at NAS will continue to become more tightly integrated into the traditional environment of supercomputing, storage, and networks to offer an even more powerful tool for scientists and engineers. Together with its partners, NAS will power NASA's vision to conduct pioneering aeronautics research, design future crewed space vehicles, and increase our understanding of the Earth and the universe. This important work will be achieved through continuous innovations in supercomputing that expand scientific discovery and boost engineering productivity, helping to ensure the success of America's space program for generations to come.

---

## Acknowledgments

The authors would like to thank the many members of the NAS Division who contributed to the writing and editing of this chapter. We are also indebted to the entire Division for its hard work in acquiring and running Pleiades, helping users, and providing some of the applications that keep NAS focused on maximizing impact to NASA.

# Chapter 13

## The Blue Waters Super-System for Super-Science

**Brett Bode, Michelle Butler, Thom Dunning, Torsten Hoefler, and William Kramer**

*National Center for Supercomputing Applications, University of Illinois, Urbana-Champaign*

**William Gropp**

*Department of Computer Science, University of Illinois, Urbana-Champaign*

**Wen-mei Hwu**

*Department of Electrical and Computer Engineering, University of Illinois, Urbana-Champaign*

## 13.1     Background

Blue Waters is a very well-balanced sustained petascale system being deployed into the NSF Office of Cyber Infrastructure portfolio in 2012 for a diverse range of unique science and engineering challenges that require huge amounts of sustained performance. The Blue Waters project has used a number of principles, now frequently referred to as "co-design," to improve the ability of the science teams to use the technology.

### 13.1.1     Program Background

The National Science Foundation is the primary sponsor of the Blue Waters Project, along with substantial support from the state of Illinois and the University of Illinois at Urbana-Champaign (UIUC).

The NSF Office of Cyber Infrastructure initiated a three track organization of the computational and data resources in the U.S. academic community. Track 3 systems are modest to large-scale systems funded by academic institutions or regions. Track 2 systems are funded by the NSF as large-scale systems initially of the order of a peak petaflops/s. The plan calls for two or three such systems at any given time. NSF plans for one Track 1 system, typically ten to twenty times more powerful.

The original goals of the Blue Waters project and its systems are listed in the NSF Track 1 solicitation http://www.nsf.gov/pubs/2006/nsf06573/nsf06573.html to develop, acquire, deploy, and support a sustained petascale system that enables researchers to work on a range of computationally challenging science and engineering applications at the frontiers of research; incorporates reliable, robust system software essential to optimal sustained performance; provides a high degree of stability and usability; and, functions as a community-driven resource that actively engages the research and education communities in petascale science and engineering.

Despite the solicitation's focus on a single computational system, NCSA developed a broad-based plan to ensure the maximum science productivity would be possible by proposing an extremely well-balanced "super system" capable not only of sustained petascale computational performance for a diverse set of extreme scale science and engineering challenges, but also sustained petascale data-driven and analytics challenges. This chapter summarizes all the aspects of the project and provides the details of the Blue Waters system.

### 13.1.2     The National Center for Supercomputing Applications at the University of Illinois

NCSA was established in 1986 as one of the original sites of the National Science Foundation's Supercomputer Centers Program as a partnership of the University of Illinois, the state of Illinois, and the federal government. For more than 25 years, the center, located in Urbana-Champaign, has aided scientists and engineers across the country with powerful computers, innovative technologies and tools, and the support of its expert staff. Investment in NCSA continues to yield concrete dividends for scientists, government, industry, education, and society.

Scientists using NCSA's supercomputers have:

1. Simulated the nationwide spread of a flu virus—including every individual in the United States, every school and workplace, and the journeys people make in their daily lives.

2. Developed new methods of locating the source of contaminants in urban water distribution systems.

3. Modeled every step of the photosynthetic process, identifying proteins that could greatly enhance plant productivity.

4. Discovered how HIV protease changes between forms, pinpointing when this "starter molecule" for the virus that causes AIDS is most vulnerable to attack by drug treatments.

Blue Waters follows more than 20 high-performance systems that NCSA has deployed and supported for use by the national science and engineering community over its 25-year history.

NCSA also leads the National Science Foundation's Extreme Science and Engineering Discovery Environment(XSEDE), a five-year, \$121 million project to deliver advanced computing, data, networking, and collaboration tools and support to the nation's researchers.

As the role of computing in science and engineering has evolved, NCSA has broadened its mission to embrace the new opportunities and challenges this has created. Today, NCSA works closely with a broad range of science and engineering communities, enabling them to use the latest computing technologies to advance their research. Activities include the visualization of complex natural phenomena such as supernovae explosions and the changing climate to the management, analysis and visualization of massive data sets for astronomical, biological, biomedical and environmental research. In addition to its grant-funded activities, NCSA partners with industry, helping companies address modeling, simulation, code-optimization, data analysis, and visualization needs. Current partners include: Boeing, Caterpillar, John Deere, GE, Procter & Gamble, and Rolls-Royce.

## 13.1.3 Timeline

Blue Waters started with creating the response to NSF's Track 1 solicitation in 2006. The proposals were submitted to NSF in the first half of 2007 and NSF announced the award to UIUC in the second half of 2007. Contracts and agreements were negotiated and the Blue Water project officially began in August 2008. At that time, the computational system was to consist of an IBM Power7 IH system, with the near-line storage, networking and support services subsystems to be competitively selected. The major components of the project are shown in Figure 13.1.

In 2009, the first eighteen PRAC science teams were announced by NSF after a full peer review. Having actual teams with science goals shifted the project focus from generalized requirements to also have specific science-driven requirements developed from the goals of the science and engineering teams. This *co-design* phase of the project uses simulators, emulators, and existing hardware platforms coupled with in-depth analysis of codes to guide application transformation for petascale. Over time, NSF added ten more teams.

Design and demonstrations continued until mid 2011 when IBM informed Illinois it was no longer feasible to deploy the planned Power7 IH system as planned. In the summer of 2011, Illinois identified an alternative computational technology provided by Cray and

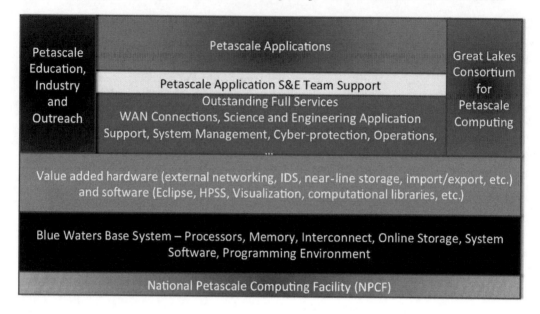

**FIGURE 13.1**: Blue Waters project components.

executed a project change to incorporate it. In November 2011, NSF approved the change and Illinois and Cray executed a contract to provide the system.

In December 2011, a small test and development system was delivered to the National Petascale Computing Facility, located on the UIUC Campus, followed in January 2012 by about 18% of the system named the Early Science System. The Early Science period lasted for three months until June 2012, as all the other equipment arrived. Then full integration and testing progressed into the fall of 2012 before acceptance and full service. Blue Waters will provide full service to the entire science community for five years after acceptance — 2013-2017. Throughout 2012, additional S&E teams were announced, now totaling 33 teams.

### 13.1.4   Applications and Workloads

#### 13.1.4.1   Partner Allocation Process and Assumptions

By agreement with the NSF allocations at least 80% of the Blue Waters resources are allocated via the Petascale Computing Resource Allocation process known as PRAC. This process involves a full peer review of both the proposed science, the unique need for such a large amount of resource, and the readiness of the proposer to use such a resource.

By NSF design, the Blue Waters partner community will consist of 30 to 36 active PRAC science projects that are engaged in transformative computational and data-intensive research. The number of PRAC science teams being supported should remain at about 36 throughout Blue Waters operations, with about one-third of the projects ending per year and new projects taking their place. The Blue Waters project collaborates with each science team with a "large allocation" (approximately to be 2–4% or more of the total Blue Waters resource) to identify requirements, create a support plan, and monitor progress. There are additional science teams from other allocation processes, as specified in the NSF Blue Waters award to NCSA. A summary of the science team characteristics is in Table 13.1.

**TABLE 13.1**: Breakdown of Blue Waters users and allocations.

| Type of Allocation | Percent of Allocation | Expected Number of Science Teams |
|---|---|---|
| NSF PRAC | 80 | 30–36 |
| NCSA industrial affiliates | 5–7 | 2–4 |
| Great Lakes Consortium for Petascale Computation | 2 | 10–20 |
| Educational efforts | 1 | 20 |
| Illinois allocations | 5–7 | 10–20 |
| Innovation and exploration | 5 | 5–10 |

### 13.1.4.2 Science Team Summary Characteristics and Requirements

The quantitative and qualitative requirements that drive the creation of the Blue Waters Service Architecture (BWSA) are based on the Blue Waters Directorate's assessment of both explicit and implicit requirements. The explicit requirements are expressed in the original Track 1 solicitation and, most importantly, in requirements from the science teams.[1] Implicit requirements derive from other expectations that may be assumed or are "state of the practice." Implicit requirements are necessary to make Blue Waters a highly successful system for the range of science projects that will be allocated time on the system. Activities based on these requirements will assist PRAC science teams in effectively exploiting the innovative, leading-edge features of the Blue Waters hardware and software. The performance and scalability needed for the science teams to fully exploit these features require substantial support from the Blue Waters Directorate. This support begins with the traditional aspects of facility services, such as system administration and consulting. But traditional support will not be sufficient to maximize the impact of the Blue Waters system on science and engineering, so the BWSA incorporates new approaches and services that should establish Blue Waters as a leading facility for services and support in the HPC community. Blue Waters is a fully open platform that must support a broad range of computational science and engineering research projects. Almost all of the PRAC science teams will have multiple researchers working with one or more community codes, averaging two codes per team. The teams are geographically distributed, and all use will be remote. It is expected that the experienced teams will be using other large-scale resources, at NSF, DOE, or other sites. However, since most of the teams will be actively using XdSEDE resources, compatibility with the XdSEDE environment is an implicit requirement. NCSA has analyzed the explicit requirements of the 27 PRAC science teams as an early indicator of science requirements. Many science team partners, in addition to their explicit requirements (software libraries, amounts of key resources) have many implicit requirements they expect, including excellent staff services, a reliable system, clear documentation, high performance, etc. A summary of

---

[1]Science team members are referred to as *partners* in this document to denote the intent to establish much more integrated working relationships with the teams than is found in traditional HPC facilities that have many "users."

the PRAC codes and their characteristics is shown in Figure 13.2. While each team has individual needs and desires, synthesizing their explicit needs shows that Blue Waters science partners require high availability storage for multiple 100–200 TB data sets per year because it is not practical to move 100+ TB data sets to remote sites due to network constraints on the remote end. Some science teams expect to generate approximately 5 PB of data during their project and many science teams expect to perform most post-processing on Blue Waters. Science teams need at least 10 Gb/s connectivity to their primary work places and some will eventually desire more bandwidth. Interactive visualization will be greatly improved by 100 Gb/s connectivity when this rate becomes available in network backbones and remote destinations. Job management requirements include quick turnaround for short but large benchmarking jobs that last no more than two hours while using 60,000 or more cores and 12–24 hour time limit for production runs at scale, possibly ramping to longer run times balanced with appropriate turnaround. Large blocks of dedicated time will seldom, if ever, be needed by the science teams but will be provisioned for critical needs.

Science teams need expert assistance to improve the ability for scaling to large numbers of cores and to re-engineer parallel I/O strategies to remove major bottlenecks and use more effective methods at scale. Re-engineering algorithms is needed to take advantage of new heterogeneous computing paradigms at scale: ranging from many-core to PGAS to heterogeneous processing. Also needed are re-engineering visualization tools for large, remote data display—including more inline visualization. Teams need assistance with techniques that provide the ability and improve the flexibility of application codes to better deal with node failures, components with different performance and bandwidth limits.

As part of the co-design efforts, the Blue Waters team analyzed the potential and current use of GPU accelerators by all the science teams in mid 2011. The summary of this study is that about half of the science teams have started initial exploration of GPU use and have some experimental or limited GPU implementations of their codes, but are not planning using GPUs for production science in the near to moderate term. About 20% of the teams, however, are able to use GPU implementations of their production science runs at least for some of the science areas they explore.

## 13.1.5    Highlights of Main Applications

There are currently 33 PRAC science teams approved by NSF to use Blue Waters that represent a very diverse set of science and engineering objectives. Below are very brief highlights of a few of the projects. Complete and current listing of all projects can be found at the Blue Waters web site (http://bluewaters.ncsa.illinois.edu).

Principal investigators Keith Bisset, Shawn Brown, and Douglas Roberts have a team focused on the simulation of contagion on very large social networks. Their goal is to use Blue Waters to create an agent-based model of global epidemics therefore providing crucial information for preparedness and emergency response. The computational challenges are to increase the scale of the simulations to the interactions of more than 6 billion people, rather than just a few hundred million, making work load balancing very challenging.

A team led by the University of Southern California's Thomas Jordan is creating a set of three seismic and engineering modeling codes to model fault rupture, propagate seismic energy through a detailed structural model of Southern California, predict ground motion, and model building response to earthquakes. The goal of this project is to combine the use of these codes to understand building damage likely to result from realistic, strong earthquakes. The improved earthquake simulations will provide better seismic hazard assessment and inform the design of safer building codes.

Formation of the first galaxies: predictions for the next generation of observatories. Principal investigator Brian O'Shea's team is studying the formation of the first galaxies

| Science Area | Number of Teams | Codes | Struct Grids | Unstruct Grids | Dense Matrix | Sparse Matrix | N-Body | Monte Carlo | FFT | PIC/Agent | Large I/O |
|---|---|---|---|---|---|---|---|---|---|---|---|
| Climate and Weather | 3 | CESM, GCRM, CM1/WRF, HOMME | X | X | | X | | X | | | X |
| Plasmas/Magnetosphere | 2 | H3D(M),VPIC, OSIRIS, Magtail/UPIC | X | | | | X | | X | | X |
| Stellar Atmospheres and Supernovae | 5 | PPM, MAESTRO, CASTRO, SEDONA, ChaNGa, MS-FLUKSS | X | | | X | X | X | | X | X |
| Cosmology | 2 | Enzo, pGADGET | X | | | X | X | | | | |
| Combustion/Turbulence | 2 | PSDNS, DISTUF | X | | | | | | X | | |
| General Relativity | 2 | Cactus, Harm3D, LazEV | X | | | X | | | | | |
| Molecular Dynamics | 4 | AMBER, Gromacs, NAMD, LAMMPS | | | X | | X | | X | | |
| Quantum Chemistry | 2 | SIAL, GAMESS, NWChem | | | X | X | X | X | | | X |
| Material Science | 3 | NEMOS, OMEN, GW, QMCPACK | | | X | X | X | X | | | |
| Earthquakes/Seismology | 2 | AWP-ODC, HERCULES, PLSQR, SPECFEM3D | X | X | | | X | | | | X |
| Quantum Chromo Dynamics | 1 | Chroma, MILC, USQCD | X | | | X | X | X | X | | |
| Contagion/Social Networks | 1 | EPISIMDEMICS | | | | | | | | | |
| Evolution | 1 | Eve | | | | | | | | X | |
| Engineering/System of Systems | 1 | GRIPS,Revisit | | | | | | X | | | |
| Computer Science | 1 | | | X | X | X | | X | X | X | X |

**FIGURE 13.2**: Comparison of the major algorithmic approaches by science area.

in order to simulate many more galaxies in much greater detail The project will increase learning about the earliest days of the universe's evolution as the team expects to use more than 1,000 times the mass resolution and 32 times the spatial resolution when compared to simulations from a decade ago, which translates into simulations of hundreds of thousands of galaxies instead of a thousand galaxies.

Principal investigator Klaus Schulten and his NAMD team use mathematical modeling as a "computational microscope" that allows unprecedented looks at how molecules behave, revealing the basic structures and processes of life. Prior to Blue Waters, scientists could simulate systems of several million atoms. With Blue Waters, Schulten's team is simulating more complex biological structures such as the full ribosome, the HIV virus, and chromataphores with resolutions of 1 nanometer and hundreds of millions of atoms. The team will be able to simulate (and watch via advanced visualization) biomolecular processes, like protein folding, leading to better understanding of these basic processes and structures which can lead to better understanding of diseases and new avenues for developing potential treatments.

There are several petascale computational chemistry projects. For example, Monica Lamm's team is improving the GAMESS and NWChem chemistry codes to enable them to effectively leverage Blue Waters and other extreme-scale supercomputers.

The initial PRAC teams include three that are investigating climate and weather at unprecedented scales. Principal investigator Robert Wilhelmson leads a multi-institution team that will use Blue Waters to better understand supercell storms and the dangerous tornadoes they sometimes spawn. The sustained petascale power of Blue Waters enables the team for the first time to capture some of the small-scale features that control tornado structure and evolution. The project will provide data that can help improve tornado forecasting.

Testing hypotheses about climate prediction at unprecedented resolutions is the focus of two teams. One, led by Cristiana Stan, Benjamin Kirtman, William Large, and David Randall uses Blue Waters to use sets of numerical experiments to test two hypotheses about Earth's climate system. The first hypothesis is that the transport fluxes and other effects associated with cloud processes and ocean large-scale eddy mixing are significantly different from the theoretically derived averages embodied in current-generation climate models, and that these differences explain a large portion of the errors in these models. The second is that a more faithful representation of these eddy-scale processes will increase the predictability of the climates generated by climate models. A team led by Don Wuebbles and Xin-Zhong Liang is using Blue Waters to address uncertainties in climate prediction both with higher resolution and with increased numerical experiments.

Principal investigator Ilias Tagkopoulos' team is investigating how an organism's environment influences it evolution and its adaptation. The team is modeling multi-scale biological systems where processes from gene expression and intracellular biochemistry to ecosystem dynamics are in play. The study will look at the influence of nutrient concentrations and mutation on adaptation, compare different strategies for survival in static and fluctuating environments, and examine how unicellular organisms modify their internal networks to facilitate such changes.

There are several astronomy and astrophysical projects ranging from simulation of turbulent stellar hydrodynamics to understand the helium flash events that occur in old, giant stars near the end of their lives and you begin to understand the origin of heavy metals flung throughout the universe. Two other projects are simulating and visualizing astrophysically realistic compact star system binaries that include the ability to characterize the events' gravity wave signatures and gamma rays. Two other teams are studying galaxy formation to help determine when and how galaxies form and how they evolved in the early universe. These projects also compare simulations that will be tested against a suite of cosmological data sets from new ground- and space-based observatories.

Principal investigator Peter Diener leads a team investigating and understanding gamma-ray bursts, thought to occur when a massive star collapses, creating a black hole. The resulting explosion sends bright flashes of gamma rays radiating across the universe. This team will prepare a code for Blue Waters that will improve the physics and add neutrino transport and interactions, radiation transport, the capability to handle ultra-relativistic flows, gamma-ray emission from relativistic plasmas, and afterglow photon emission.

---

## 13.2 System Overview

The Blue Waters System Architecture has six major subsystems, represented in Figure 13.3. These subsystems are the Cray XE6/XK7 computational, the Cray Sonexion on-line storage subsystem, the Spectralogic/HPSS near-line storage, the BW local server and network, the wide area network and the cyber-protection subsystems.

The key feature of Blue Waters is the very balanced investment strategy of the system, beginning with the XE6 Compute Node with the AMD Interlagos processor (shown in Figure 13.4), fast access to 4 GB/core module of RAM, high-speed 3D Torus interconnect with a total injection bandwidth of over 276 TB/s, and high-performance disk and tape storage subsystems able to achieve more than 1.1 TB/s aggregate, mea-

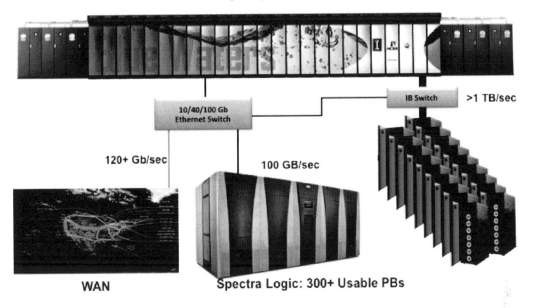

**FIGURE 13.3**: A high-level view of the Blue Waters system and subsystems.

sured performance. The configuration is based upon the tightly coupled Cray XE6/XK7 MPP (http://www.cray.com/Products/XE/Specifications.aspx) and (http://www.cray.com/Products/XK/Specifications.aspx) system complete with powerful parallel storage and filesystem capabilities.

The Cray XE6/XK7 is a hybrid system featuring AMD socket G34 Interlagos processors for x86 compute performance and NVIDIA Kepler GK110 GPUs with powerful acceleration

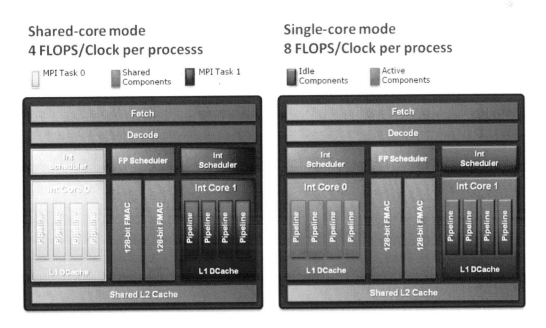

**FIGURE 13.4**: Comparison of Interlagos operating modes. (Courtesy of Cray Inc.)

capabilities. The Cray XE6/XK7 balance was determined by the mission of Blue Waters to support wide and diverse science applications at unprecedented scales and an in depth analysis of the known PRAC science teams assessing their current and planned experimental and production use of accelerated computing. Of the nodes 88% are XE6 all-CPU AMD Interlagos processor nodes, and 12% are the XK7 nodes with one AMD Interlagos processor module and one NVIDIA Kepler GPU in a single system using the Cray-designed Gemini router. It is important to note that if the Blue Waters funding was invested to target the highest possible peak performance by populating as many compute racks as possible with the NVIDIA GPUs, the peak performance of Blue Waters would approach 40 petaflops/s. However, this is contrary to the philosophy of Blue Waters and the needs of science and engineering teams. The investment strategy maintains one of the largest general purpose computational resources with one of the largest accelerated computational resources, the largest aggregate memory and the highest performance, largest capacity storage infrastructure, allowing BW to be very productive in addressing all computational and data-driven challenges.

### 13.2.1    Interlagos Processor

The Cray XE6/XK7 system uses the latest AMD Opteron Series 6000 model 6276 "Interlagos" die — 32 nanometer technology (socket G34) processor in both the Cray XE6 compute node and the Cray XK7 accelerator nodes. The Interlagos availability of four (4) memory channels and higher speed DDR3 memory DIMMs enables excellent bandwidth from memory to the x86 sockets. Sockets feature eight "bulldozer" core modules, each capable of eight floating point operations per clock. In addition the processor core is capable of running in a mode that shares the floating point unit between two integer units. Both these modes are shown below. These AMD processors include a L1 cache for each integer unit and a L2 cache for each core as well as two 6 MB L3 caches shared by all the cores of each of the two dies, DDR3 internal memory controllers and an HT3 HyperTransport interface that increase the injection bandwidth between the interconnect network and the compute processor.

The Interlagos socket is a dual-die multi-chip module. The XE6 compute nodes consist of two sockets each with associated memory and HT interconnection. The XK7 accelerator nodes having one Interlagos socket with the associated memory and one NVIDIA Kepler K20X GPU.

With four (4) DDR3 channels at 1600 MHz, each Interlagos processor has a global memory bandwidth of 51.2+ GB/s (4 x 1600 MT/s x 64 bits) and memory latency under 100 ns. Memory will be direct attached, with no FBDIMM or motherboard buffer chips. AMD's memory controller has many features, such as smart read-ahead, designed to hide memory latency. Aggregate memory per socket is 32 GB (4 GB per core) with 8 GB DIMMS. Each DIMM has 72-bit interfaces: 64 data bits and 8 error-correcting code (ECC) bits. All memory channels can be operated in parallel for a total bandwidth of 51.2 GB/s. Memory is protected using single-symbol correction/double-symbol detection (SSC/DSD) error-correcting code (ECC).

The Interlagos die presents several new challenges in how it is described in simple terms of clock rate and core, that is predictive of future generations of processing chips. For example, the Interlagos processor is capable of running in three energy states. The P2 (2.3 GHz) and P1 (2.6 GHz) states are the default states and the processor will move between these two states and average frequency will vary by application. The P0 state (3.0 GHz) is only entered if an application is using half of the available cores. In studying the planned applications using emulators and the actual processors, the majority of the applications run mostly at the 2.6 Ghz rates with only very intense (e.g., DGEMMN) computational kernels

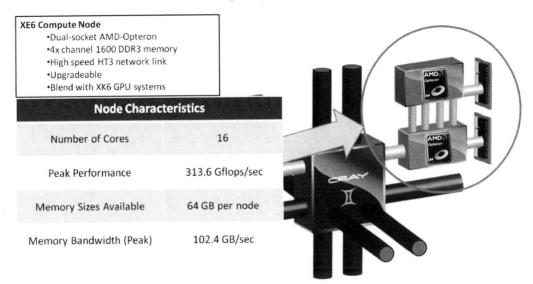

**FIGURE 13.5**: Cray XE6 compute node. (Courtesy of Cray Inc.)

running closer to 2.3 Ghz. Hence, for Blue Waters the average peak processor frequency is estimated as 2.45 GHz.

In summary, the Interlagos processor has a peak performance of 156.8 GFLOPS/s per socket at 2.45 GHz (average of P2 and P1. It can be used as two 4 cores modules with each core supporting two threads giving a total of eight results per clock per FMA. Each processor socket has four HyperTransport links, up to 5.2GB/s. The core module has shared fetch/decode units, shared I cache for each FPU.

### 13.2.2 The Gemini Interconnect

The Blue Waters system consists of 276 computational cabinets arranged in 12 rows, each with 23 cabinets. The interconnect topology is a 3D torus of dimension X=23, Y=24, and Z=24. All torus links run at a minimum bit toggle rate of 3.125 GHz. Figure 13.5 shows the configuration of the XE6 and XK7 nodes.

The resulting peak bisection bandwidth in each dimension is listed in Table 13.2.

It should be noted that the peak global bandwidth value is two times larger. This is due to the fact that in all-to-all communication patterns, only half of the total traffic crosses the bi-section in a 3D torus topology.

### 13.2.3 Cray XK7 Accelerator Blade

The Cray XK7 accelerator blade is similar to the Cray XE6 compute blade in form factor and placement of the Gemini network cards. It differs in that each of the four compute nodes on the blade consists of an AMD processor socket and a connection for a Kepler GPU (NVIDIA GK110 K20X) card. In addition to the 32 GB of Interlagos memory, these GPU cards each contain the accelerator chip and 6GB of GDDR5 memory and connect to the motherboard with a high reliability connector. These cards sit up off the motherboard to allow the necessary cooling on both sides of the card. The blade will be managed, monitored, powered, and cooled within the Cray XE6/XK7 infrastructure. A top view of the XK7 architectural diagram is shown in Figure 13.6.

**TABLE 13.2**: Data payload bi-directional bandwidth in X, Y, Z dimensions.

| X=23, Y=24, and Z=24 | X dimension | Y dimension | Z dimension |
|---|---|---|---|
| Dimension size | 23 | 24 | 24 |
| Bits per direction per link | 24 | 12 | 24 |
| Bisection bandwidth per link @ 3.125 Ghz | 18.75 GB/s | 9.375 GB/s | 18.75 GB/s |
| Number of links per dimension (includes torus wrap-around links) | 1152 | 1104 | 1104 |
| Total peak bisection bandwidth per dimension | 21.6 TB/s | 10.35 TB/s | 20.7 TB/s |

| | |
|---|---|
| Average bisection bandwidth | 17.55 TB/s |
| Minimum bisection bandwidth | 10.32 TB/s (Y direction) |

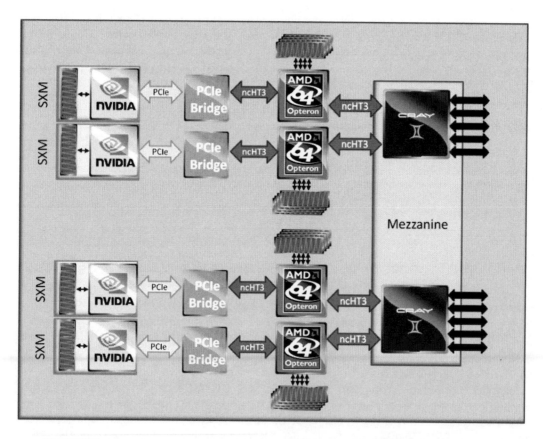

**FIGURE 13.6**: Compute blade: architectural diagram. (Courtesy of Cray Inc.)

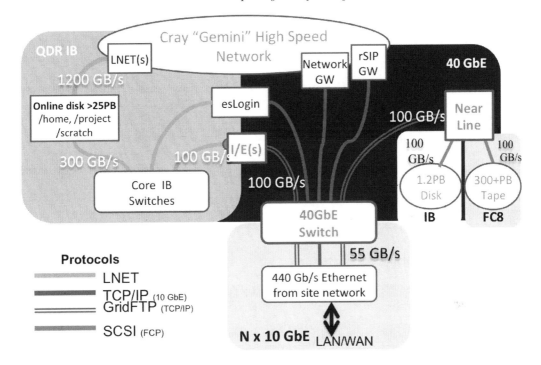

**FIGURE 13.7**: Blue Waters I/O subsystem.

## 13.2.4 Blue Waters Storage Subsystem

Blue Waters provides one of the most intense storage systems in the world using a combination of online and near-line storage devices and media. The storage subsystem is connected with an integrated InfiniBand fabric and 40Gbps Ethernet as shown in Figure 13.7.

### 13.2.4.1 Online Storage Subsystem

The building block of the online storage subsystem is the new Cray Sonexion CS-1600 (http://www.cray.com/Products/Storage/Sonexion/Specifications.aspx; note that the Sonexion 1600 is not announced at the time of this writing) which is a high-performance computing storage element designed and built to uniquely address Lustre scalability and performance. Four high level components (storage hardware, operating system, management user interface, and filesystem) are bonded in a synergistic manner to create a reliable, performant, and manageable HPC storage

The CS-1600 features an integrated Scalable Storage Unit (SSU). Each SSU supports two industry-standard x86 Embedded Server Modules (ESMs) based on the Intel Sandybridge processors, which connect directly through a common midplane to all drives in the SSU and share a redundant high-speed interconnect across the midplane for failover services. The ESMs run an industry-standard Linux distribution and each module has its own dedicated CPU, memory, network, and storage connectivity.

Each SSU contains eighty-two (82) 2 TByte 7.2K RPM NL-SAS disk drives housed in two (2) trays. Eighty (80) data drives are configured in four (4) RAID-6 (8+2) RAID arrays resulting in 64 usable data drives. The other two (2) drives are global hot spares. In addition, there are two (2) 100 GByte SSD for OSS metadata and two (2) OSS servers. Together, the metadata and object storage servers present file systems to clients.

The Management Server (MGS) stores configuration information for all Lustre filesystems in a cluster. Each Lustre server contacts the MGS to provide information. Each Lustre client contacts the MGS to retrieve information. Metadata Servers (MDS) make metadata available to Lustre clients from the Metadata Target (MDT). The MDT stores file system metadata (filenames, directories, permissions, and file layouts) on disk and manage the namespace. The MDS provides network request handling for the filesystem.

The Object Storage Servers (OSS) provide file I/O service and network request handling for one or more local Object Storage Targets (OSTs). The OST stores data (files or chunks of files) on a single LUN (disk drive or an array of disk drives). XE6 Lustre clients is the interface for user applications to the Lustre filesystem. The client presents a POSIX filesystem interface to user level applications and is responsible for routing I/O requests, data and metadata through the Cray XE6 system to the Lustre servers in the CS-1600 storage cluster. Crays XE6 Lustre Networking (LNET) implements the Lustre networking protocol between the Lustre client and the Lustre server. The LNET layer allows clients and servers to be executed on the same system (i.e., direct attached Lustre) or for compute clients to communicate with external Lustre servers or Lustre appliances.

### 13.2.4.2   Online Storage Performance

The online storage subsystem provides over 25 usable petabytes of storage to the science and engineering teams. The overall bandwidth exceeds 1.1 TB/s as measured by a range of IOR tests. Similarly, the measured metadata performance is over 25,000 mean creates/second of a single file from each node; 30,000 concurrent deletes/second and 40,000 stat()/second as aggregate rates using up to all XE6 client nodes in either a single directory or in separate directories.

### 13.2.5   Near-Line Storage

Blue Waters is enhancing the online storage with a near-line automated storage system composed of automated tape robots and caching disk under the control of the High Performance Storage System (HPSS) (www.hpss-collaboration.org). The system, which provided traditional archive function as well a new, closely integrated HSM between the online and near-line storage that is under development, is the largest system in the open science community.

NCSA will initially deploy four Spectra Logic 19-frame T-Finity tape libraries, which with a total 244 IBM TS1140 tape drives and house more than 15,000 media slots in each library. In 2013, NCSA will deploy two more libraries with an additional 122 tape drives. This environment will provide 380 petabytes of raw data slots. Each tape drive's performance is 240 megabytes per second. There will be 30 to 50 HPSS "movers" to move the data from one storage level to another. 1.3 PB of caching disk will be used for the traditional archive data movement and the system has two large core services to hold the metadata.

NCSA will use a RAIT (Redundant Array of Independent Tapes) technology developed by NCSA and the HPSS consortium—a new feature of HPSS that provides data integrity/protection through parity technologies for the tape subsystem. RAIT provides protection from single point failures while improving total cost of ownership.

### 13.2.5.1   Near-Line Storage Performance

The near-line storage subsystem provides over 300 usable petabytes of storage to the science and engineering teams with an aggregate bandwidth of 100 GB/s. The physical robotic units have a capacity of over 500 petabytes if needed. The Blue Water project is budgeted to provide 380 raw petabytes of tape cartridges. The implementation of RAIT discussed below will use about 22% of the raw capacity to provide protection from single points of

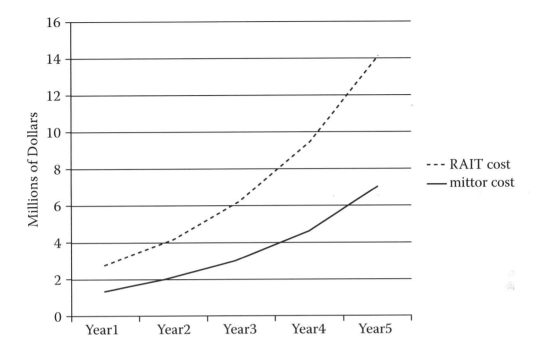

**FIGURE 13.8**: The estimated cost difference between RAIT and mirroring data on tapes. Both provide data loss protection from single points of failure.

failure, resulting in about 300 usable PBs of storage. Figure 13.8 shows the anticipated budget savings from using RAIT as compared to mirroring all data tapes.

### 13.2.6 Hardware Summary

Figure 13.9 provides a view of the hardware components of the system in a summary form. The system has a peak rate of 11.6 petaflops with all nodes. It has over 35 PBs of raw disk storage and the capability of upto 500 PBs of near-line storage capacity.

## 13.3 System Software

The software for the Cray XE6/XK7 is based upon an open software environment and integration of Cray enhancements for HPC and third-party tools to enable the best platform for development and implementation of scalable production applications including the Cray Linux Environment (CLE), the Cray Programming Environment (CPE), and tested third-party software tools. This ecosystem provides a single cohesive environment for developers and users. UIUC/NCSA has expanded the Cray software with software from other organizations and software developed and/or improved as part of the Blue Waters project.

The overall software components are shown in Figure 13.10. For the sake of brevity, this section will only discuss the new or novel aspects of the software environment.

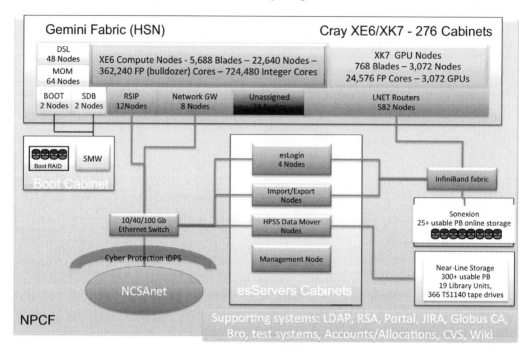

**FIGURE 13.9**: A logical diagram of the Blue Waters hardware components.

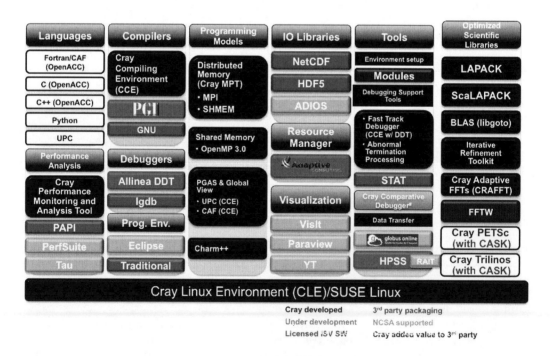

**FIGURE 13.10**: Blue Waters software ecosystem.

## 13.3.1 Cray Adaptive Software Ecosystem: Cray Linux Environment

The Cray Linux Environment (CLE) is a suite of high-performance software, which includes a Linux-based operating system, based on SUSE Linux™, and is designed to run large, complex applications and scale efficiently to more than a million processor cores.

Compute Node Linux (CNL), Cray's lightweight operating system for compute and accelerator nodes, was developed to provide support for application execution without the overhead of a full operating system image. When running highly scalable applications, CNL runs by default in Extreme Scalability Mode (ESM). ESM provides an optimized compute node OS environment where a minimum of essential OS services are configured. This lessens operating system interference with application scalability.

Among the features supported are the ability to set, on a job-by-job basis, the page size, access to dynamic libraries, and core specialization, which allows the user to specify that non-application work be performed on one or more specific cores, rather than distributed among all the cores.

To allow applications built for standard Linux clusters to run without modification on Cray XE6/XK7 systems, Cray developed Cluster Compatibility Mode (CCM). This execution environment gives processes compute nodes access to all standard Linux services and libraries. This provides the same environment for applications, including the MPI libraries (MPICH2, Platform MPI™, Intel, etc.) with which they are built, that would be present on a standard Linux cluster. To use CCM, the user specifies designated queue parameters, and includes CCM commands in the run script. CCM transparently configures the allocated nodes, and the job runs just as it would on a Linux cluster. When the job completes, the nodes are automatically returned to their default ESM state, and are available for any other job.

The Application Level Placement Services (ALPS) is a Cray-developed tool used to place and launch applications. It works in tandem with third-party workload managers, which make scheduling decisions and enforce site policy. ALPS also performs job launch functions.

The job scheduling (batch) system works with ALPS via an XML interface. This obviates the need for the batch system to link with proprietary libraries, and in turn enhances its extensibility. In addition to its interfaces with the batch system, ALPS includes a helper tool to provide entry points for debugging applications. This tool enables external components to interact directly with application processes. ALPS utilizes a scalable variable-radix tree based control structure to provide high-performance job-launch.

ALPS for the UIUC/NCSA Blue Water system will support new functionality which will cause ALPS to automatically restart the application when the application has terminated due to a compute node failure (no other failures will cause a restart). An environment variable is used to inform the application that it is being automatically re-run due to a node failure.

ALPS will support the following behaviors on a detected node failure: the application is terminated (default behavior); the application is relaunched using the same number of nodes (requires the job to have spare nodes); and the application is relaunched using fewer nodes (no spare nodes available)

The job schedule used by an application to be restarted must allocate one or more spare nodes which will be used to replace a failed node as described above. The number of spare nodes determines the number of concurrent failed nodes that can be tolerated. One spare node is the minimum number required to use this feature. Four spare nodes would be required to tolerate a complete compute blade failure.

After a compute node failure(s) and when requested by an aprun option, ALPS and PMI will rebuild their communication trees without the failed node(s). The remaining application processes will not be killed.

PMI will notify the application runtime of the failure. The runtime is responsible for notifying the application, and helping the application recover from the node failures.

#### 13.3.1.1    Topology Awareness

In order to increase the effective bandwidth of the interconnect, UIUC/NCSA and Cray are working to implement new topology aware features in the resource manager, the job scheduler, and the communication infrastructure.

### 13.3.2    Gemini Software

The Cray XE/XK architecture was designed for extreme scalability of real-world applications. The native messaging protocol for the Cray XE6/XK7 system is the Generic Network Interface (GNI), a low-latency, low-overhead message-passing interface ideal for scalable, high-performance network communication between nodes over a high-speed network. A second messaging protocol, the Distributed Shared Memory Application (DMAPP) interface, is also supported. GNI and DMAPP provide low-level communication services to user-space software. GNI directly exposes the communications capabilities of the Cray Gemini ASIC.

DMAPP is a communication library which supports a logically shared, distributed memory (DM) programming model. DMAPP provides remote memory access (RMA) between processes within a job in a one-sided manner. One-sided remote memory access requests require no active participation by the process at the remote node; synchronization functions may be used to determine when side-effects of locally initiated requests are available. The DMAPP API is used by one-sided communication libraries (such as Cray SHMEM), and PGAS compilers (such as CoArray Fortran and UPC) as well as user developed communication libraries.

The layering of the communication software is shown in Figure 13.11, which emphasizes both the interoperability of the different parallel programming models (because they use the same two low-level interfaces, uGNI and DMAPP), and the OS bypass features so that data moves directly between the user's application and the network.

The Cray Gemini based system interconnection network and its associated software provide excellent support for a variety of programming models. This includes support for message passing, one-sided (also called remote memory access), and global address space programming; collective communication and computation, and end-to-end data protection in hardware.

## 13.4    Programming Environment

The Cray Compilation Environment (CCE) includes optimizing compilers that exploit automatically the scalar, vector, and multi-threading hardware capabilities of x86 processors. These automatic optimizations are fully integrated with support for user directed programming models such as MPI and OpenMP. CCE (and Cray developed tools) is optimized for 64-bit AMD Opteron processors including support for AMD Interlagos-specific optimizations.

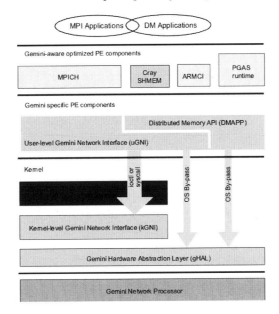

**FIGURE 13.11**: Layers of communication software. (Courtesy of Cray Inc.)

The Cray Compilation Environment provides support for optimized Fortran (including Co-Array Fortran), C (including UPC), and C++. Parallel programming models supported include OpenMP, MPI, Cray SHMEM$^{TM}$, and Partitioned Global Address Space (with the PGAS languages UPC and Co-Array Fortran).

Combined with the one-sided transfer capabilities of the Gemini interconnect, the availability of UPC and Fortran with coarrays facilitates effective scaling on complicated communication patterns resulting from adaptive mesh refinement applications and other applications that need to send large numbers of small messages around the system. CCE natively compiles UPC and Fortran with co-arrays which means that the remote loads and stores are translated directly to one-sided remote accesses on the Gemini interconnect. The compiler is able to pre-fetch operands and generally perform normal compiler optimization on both local and remote accesses. Remote loads and stores are automatically performed in parallel and overlapped with computation.

The Cray Message Passing Toolkit (MPT), derived from MPICH2, supports the Message Passing Interface (MPI) and Cray SHMEM parallel programming/distributed memory Models.

Use of the XK7 heterogeneous nodes will have special support that includes an expanded set of software tools, experience from best practices and new algorithmic methods for scaling in conjunction with heterogeneity. Blue Waters will be one of the few systems that provides thousands of accelerator-based nodes with an efficient interconnect so science teams can start to use accelerators at scale and in combination with the XE x86 nodes.

Both Cray and PGI compilers support the OpenACC standard (http://www.openacc.org/sites/default/files/OpenACC.1.0_0.pdf) that provides directive-based compilation for the NVIDIA accelerators. Using OpenACC as a basis for application development will speed the conversion of new applications as well as enhance the portability of applications to other systems and technologies. Blue Waters will also provide the CUDA and OpenCL libraries and the Thrust C+ template library from NVIDIA for applications. Cray and Blue Waters staff will also provide application level libraries that are specially tuned to use the Kepler

GPUs. Similarly, the complete suite of debugging and performance tools supports the XK heterogeneous nodes at full scale. Blue Waters will also explore the use of the GPUs for visualization by using Cray's Cluster Compatibility Mode (CCM), to support visualization applications that use the OpenGL library.

Besides the foundation components, Blue Waters provisions an advanced toolset based on the Eclipse Integrated Development Environment, specifically the Eclipse Parallel Tools Platform (PTP), to provide support for developing C/C++/OpenMP/UPC and Fortran/OpenMP/CAF applications. This will consist of a powerful, interactive desktop workbench interacting with the Blue Waters system remotely to manage source code development, compilation, linking, deployment, and execution. The Blue Waters workflow capability will support both Blue Waters and other virtual organization systems such as XSEDE, requiring only minimal software on the target systems (e.g., SSH or GSI-enabled SSH; GridFTP) for partners to orchestrate work on a variety of systems.

Blue Waters will offer training opportunities to enable our science partners to make the fullest possible use of these traditional and advanced tools. We will solicit feedback to ensure complete coverage of software capabilities and to determine improvements to the software environment.

Blue Waters is providing a multi-faceted user portal for partners. This portal is the point for information dissemination, as well as the host for other services such as the Blue Waters Import-Export facility and specialized visualization services. Blue Waters will work with XSEDE to configure the Blue Waters portal in the style of XSEDE information and will cross reference its user portal with the XSEDE User Portal in an effective manner and will share tools and methods where appropriate. BW is using portal infrastructure SW that is also used by XSEDE.

### 13.4.1    Performance Measurement and Analysis Tools

The Cray Performance Measurement and Analysis Tools (CPMAT) is the primary performance analysis toolset for Cray systems. The focus of functionality offered through the tools is to provide a productive environment that assists the novice user with application performance analysis and optimization. With ease of use and intuitive user interfaces, the tools help users identify important and meaningful information from potentially massive data sets instead of just reporting data, with a goal of bringing optimization knowledge to a wider set of users. It is an integrated infrastructure for measurement and analysis of computation, communication, I/O, and memory utilization. The toolset allows developers to perform sampling, profile, and trace experiments on single-processor or multiple-processor executables at the binary level with function and loop granularity. It supports Fortran, C and C++, the MPI, SHMEM, and OpenMP programming models (or combinations of these programming models), as well as the UPC, CAF, and Chapel parallel programming languages. CPMAT allows users to select the functions to be instrumented by group, by user function, or by name, without the need to modify the source code or the makefile. It also provides an API for fine-grain instrumentation at the basic block level — this API requires recompilation after the insertion of the API calls.

The toolset consists of components that prepare a program for performance analysis experiments, capture performance data during program execution, process and analyze the data, and present performance results to the user in both a text report and through an interactive graphical user interface.

CrayPat is the data capture tool, which is used to prepare user programs for performance analysis experiments, to specify the kind of data to be captured during program execution, and to prepare the captured data for text reports or for use with other programs.

Performance data is captured during application execution by sampling at intervals, or upon entry/return from traced functions, and is recorded in the form of a summarization of events over time (profile), or a sequence of events of time (trace). Each process collects its own performance data. Per process buffers in memory are used to temporarily store local collected performance data. The data in these buffers is later flushed to a performance log file or files on a parallel filesystem.

The user can optionally control the behavior of the instrumented program during execution through a set of runtime environment variables that affect what and how the performance data is collected. Examples of this include the enabling of predefined hardware counter groups that track chosen sets of hardware events, the ability to choose the mechanism to use to sample the application, and the ability to modify the number of data files that are written in parallel by the processes. By default, a runtime summarization of the data is provided, which involves aggregation of the data.

The pat_report utility available in the toolset performs two functions. It reads state and event data in the performance file created by the runtime library, and generates text reports according to the groups selected, presented in table format. Reports display such detail as hardware performance counters event values, call trees, and special processing for the function groups. One of the strengths of this utility is that it can be run several times against the same collected performance data to provide different combinations of data, so that users can choose the subset from the collected data that best suits their needs.

Through higher-level derived metrics, the toolset helps identify the "why" of unexpected performance, so the application developer can more quickly identify the source of intra-node performance bottlenecks. Examples of these metrics include load imbalance, and HW counter metrics such as computational intensity and D2_cache_hit_ratio.

*Loop Statistics* To help application developers transition their programs to take advantage of increased on-node concurrency, the Cray performance measurement and analysis tools have added loop statistics to help the user find additional parallelism. In addition to collecting sampling information to identify the top time consuming functions within a program, the user can collect timing and iteration counts for serial loops to get an estimate for the amount of work performed in a loop or multi-level loop nest. This can help determine whether or not a particular loop would then benefit from being parallelized for execution on the x86 in a multi-core environment and/or benefit from being executed on a GPU.

Loops are identified by the function where they reside, their nesting level and by their source line number. Loop statistics presented in the default report provide inclusive times shown as a percentage of the overall time, the number of times a loop is called during program execution, the average trip count, and optimization feedback/hints from the compiler which are defined in the table's notes section.

*Accelerator Performance Statistics* The Cray performance toolset provides statistics for accelerated regions. These statistics give the user feedback on how well an accelerated region performed within their overall application, and how well it performed on the GPU. Advantages that the Cray tools offer over GPU-specific profilers include summarized results that are consolidated in one place, statistics mapped back to the user source by line number and grouped by OpenMP accelerator directive, and statistics tied to the program as a whole.

Current development work is focused on providing performance statistics that include host time for kernel launches, data copies and synchronization with the GPU, GPU time for kernel execution and data copies, and the number of times each accelerated region was called during program execution. Events associated with an accelerated region are identified by the function where they reside, the type of event (async_copy, async_kernel, etc.), and by the source line number. And to better understand how an accelerated region is performing on the GPU, GPU hardware counter statistics are available.

When a program is built with the CCE compiler and contains accelerated regions through OpenMP directives, statistics are automatically collected for the user and presented in the default report.

---

## 13.5   Visualization and Analytics

Blue Waters supports a broad range of visualization by providing tools, assistance in migrating data to dedicated visualization resources, and in-depth consulting by visualization staff. Blue Waters provides a common suite of state-of-the-practice visualization tools that span the application requirements, from simple tools like gnuplot to advanced tools such as ViSit https://wci.llnl.gov/codes/visit/ and ParaView http://www.paraview.org/. Visualization support includes the determination and implementation of features that enable in-line visualization for applications as they are running as well as tools that enable post-processing of large amounts of data. The tools and processes will be refined as part of the science team requirements-gathering process. They will evolve with developments in the visualization community.

Visualization consulting is offered through this function and will range from simple assistance with tool use to in-depth assistance to science teams to integrate advanced visualization and data analysis tools into their computational workflow.

The visualization efforts will also explore the unique configuration of the XE6/XK7 system by looking for opportunities to use the NVIDIA Kepler GPUs in the visualization pipeline.

### 13.5.1   Data Management and Analysis

Blue Waters will have the most intense storage subsystems in open science with its combination of very large capacity and very high bandwidth storage. This makes BW an excellent system for large-scale data analysis and data management. BW will work with science teams who focus on these areas to evaluate, select, and implement appropriate data management tools and methods at scale in order to provided enhanced data analysis services.

#### 13.5.1.1   Storage Management

Another goal of Blue Waters is to have the right data at the right place at the right time for our partners. Blue Waters will proactively use new storage functions to implement new practices for HPC storage management. Data in this category will hereafter be referred to as "managed." The ultimate implementation of this goal will be to have one extremely large, single name space storage system—with online and near-line limits, but this will occur after deployment. For initial service, Blue Waters will provide a state of the practice storage infrastructure consisting of three online, parallel filesystems — /home, /project, and /scratch — and a large near-line storage archive.

In order to improve data access and reduce operating costs, all near-line media will be within data robots. The Blue Waters Directorate will craft a flexible data-retention and management policy and also create the tools to automatically repack data on tapes as a constant background task. All online storage is provisioned up front for five years. Near-line media will be provisioned in batches (from a master contract) in order to keep ahead of the increase in data needs (projected from past experience to be at least 75% per year).

*Filesystem and Data Management.* The storage services combine the ultimate goal with realistic limitations. Each filesystem will be tuned differently to match its targeted use. The "scratch" filesystem will be tuned for maximum sustained performance for large files, while the "home" file system will be tuned to deliver good performance and space efficiency for small files such as source code, binaries, etc. The "scratch" file system is where partners will store larger files, including input and output from computations, intermediate run data, and checkpoints. Files on the "scratch" filesystem can be expected to be more dynamic; thus tuning the management policies will be more critical to provide high performance. Space on this filesystem is expected to be a critical shared resource for both data and computational intensive work, therefore its usage will be supported as a dynamic resource.

The Blue Waters Directorate will use quotas on all filesystems. Quota values will be adjusted with experience and project needs with soft quotas to generate warnings to partners' jobs and hard quotas 5% greater. Project wide data storage areas, rather than individual partner areas, will be provided via a special service request of the science team PI. Each project will have an encompassing global quota (user and project folders) evaluated individually.

*Long-Term Storage Hierarchy Goals.* The Blue Waters' vision is to introduce a new storage paradigm that transparently combines online and near-line storage to a single namespace for all files whether they are resident on disk, tape, or both. Files would be transparently copied to tape and their data removed from disk based on policies created by the administrator. These policies would also coordinate with the job management system that will schedule the online storage as a consumable resource. The scheduler can invoke the policy engine to free up space for upcoming jobs by moving data to near-line tape. Partners would specify files required for jobs, which would transparently be staged to online locations prior to the job starting, as well as free space, which will be maintained as a finite consumable resource. Additional controls will allow the partner to push files to near-line storage, if the system policies have not moved them yet, for example, if a partner's online quota was reached. Basic data-migration policies will be based on file size and age, with additional rules available for more complexity. For example, most checkpoint files will never require migration.

This storage management approach is similar to implementations of virtual memory in that there are:

- Large virtual storage (combining online and near-line storage)

- Limited online work sets of data (on online storage)

- The capability to keep the data with the most temporal locality in the highest (fastest) levels of storage when it is needed

In order to realize this vision, Blue Waters will work with the Lustre open-source community and the HPSS community to develop, test, integrate, and deploy interfaces between the Lustre filesystem and HPSS. Work to develop this interface is already under way within the Opensfs and the HPSS communities. Blue Waters will be an active participant and contributor to these communities in order to accelerate this vision's implementation.

### 13.5.1.2 Cyber Protection

The National Petascale Computing Facility (NPCF) protection architecture is determined by Blue Waters being the primary and most valuable asset in the facility. The protection architecture needs to conform to relevant rules, laws, and policies but also provide the broadest possible access and partner flexibility. The defense in depth cyber-protection approach is guided by the axiom "monitor and react rather than restrict" wherever possible, recognizing that there will be unavoidable practices and restrictions for partners and peers.

Identity theft (stolen credentials/passwords) has historically been the most common form of compromise on open HPC systems. To minimize the likelihood of credential compromise resulting in an attacker gaining access to the system, all partner and administrator logins to Blue Waters will require the use of one-time passwords (OTP). Partners will be able to obtain short-lived certificates with their OTP, reducing usability concerns and increasing interoperability with XSEDE.

The Blue Waters security architecture will follow a defense-in-depth strategy, including host and network intrusion detection and prevention systems (IDPS), "choke points" for access to critical functions, up-to-date system management and procedures, system integrity checking and appropriate policies. Many of the security tools being used by the Blue Waters Directorate, such as the Bro Instruction Detection System http://bro-ids.org/, are on the leading edge and not yet vendor supported. The security staff will continue to develop and improve upon the existing tools to meet their needs and the results of these development efforts will be shared back to the main projects. The NCSA security team has a long history of working with trusted security groups, such as the TeraGrid/XSEDE Security Working Group, FIRST, REN-ISAC, and Infragard, to share information about ongoing threats, stay abreast of advances in detection and prevention techniques, and assist with multi-site response.

An often overlooked, but important aspect to a complete protection plan is the involvement of partners. Successfully recruiting partners to help rather than circumvent security is extremely valuable as they are the first line of defense for protecting their accounts from misuse. Partners are the best warning of common intrusions, such as inappropriate use or stolen credentials and, in the end, it is in their best interest that Blue Waters is protected. Partners will be regularly encouraged to contact the security team if they notice anything out of the ordinary. The Blue Waters Directorate will also provide security training for staff and partners, integrating with the Information Provisioning efforts discussed previously, and be open to partner suggestions in a risk-based security approach.

---

## 13.6    National Petascale Computing Facility

The Blue Waters super system is housed in the National Petascale Computing Facility (NPCF) on the University of Illinois Urbana-Champaign campus. The NPCF was created as part of the Blue Waters project to house Blue Waters and other systems. This unique facility — the only one of its kind on an academic campus — is more than 88,000 gross ft$^2$, 30,000 ft$^2$ with a 6-ft raised floor ready to house world-class computational systems. The computer floor includes a 20,000 ft$^2$ machine room gallery with no obstructions or structural support elements in a 2 by 1 aspect ratio.

The NPCF, shown from the outside in Figure 13.12, is one of the very first large-scale computational facilities to receive a LEED Gold rating. This means the facility was built and is operated in an environmentally friendly way. In particular, the Power Utilization Efficiency of the building is between 1.1 and 1.2, meaning that very little power is used for the building infrastructure. PUE is the ratio of the total power used by the building divided by the power that is available for the computational and data equipment.

The NPCF is supplied with and can use 24 megawatts of electrical power with three independent feeds. The actual feeds provide power to 4 8-megawatt 13.8 KvA substations

**FIGURE 13.12**: National Petascale Computational Facility at the UIUC campus.

located on the first floor of the NPCF, and the building design leaves a 25% surplus capacity from each substation. The substations feed 20 2-megawatt transformers that convert the power to 480 volts for distribution.

The NPCF is capable of cooling all the equipment either with air or water cooling but all major power drawing racks are directly connected to the chilled water piping. The NPCF has two sources of cooling water. It has three large evaporative cooling towers integrated into the facility that are able to cool the entire facility when the outside temperature and humidity allow, meaning the only energy used to cool the systems is pumping water. NPCF is connected to the university chilled water system that mechanically cools water for the entire campus for time periods when the outside temperatures are too high for efficient evaporative cooling. It is also possible to mix the two sources so when the outside temperature/humidity does not allow complete free-cooling the towers can be augmented with mechanically chilled water to the extent necessary. The University built a 6.5-million-gallon cool water holding tank both as a buffer and so it can mechanically chill water when energy rates are the lowest.

All 300+ racks (computational, storage, services) of the Blue Waters system are liquid cooled in order to increase the energy efficiency. Furthermore, the inlet water temperatures will dynamically vary between $42\,^\circ$ and $60\,^\circ$ Fahrenheit based on time of year. In the winter and hot summer, the water will be at lowest temperature. In the middle parts of the year, it will increase to the highest temperature. Being able to operate within this range provides the maximum efficiency.

The NPCF is highly instrumented and automatically controlled. Every circuit is monitored and power use measured. The automated controls also operate the cooling system.

## 13.7    Measuring Sustained Performance on Blue Waters

Assessing productivity and performance of large-scale supercomputers is a difficult task. Micro-benchmarks are often used as a proxy to evaluate how a computing system performs. One problem with this approach is that application performance is a very complex problem and microbenchmarks may overlook important features of the system. For example, operating system noise was only recently discovered [PKP03] and an analysis with microbenchmarks is very challenging [HSL10].

Those problems can be avoided by using the time to solution of application benchmarks to evaluate system performance. An application benchmark, in this case, is defined by a particular application code and a unique input set that represents a science problem of interest. The combination of the application code and input set defines a consistent code path that can be used to assess performance in a consistent manner.

As discussed above, the Blue Waters project strives to deliver sustained petascale performance for a variety of applications from the National Science Foundation (NSF). Ultimately, sustained performance is the time to solution to solve science problems. It is explicitly not a goal of the system to achieve highest possible HPL or other microbenchmark performance. Indeed, if the goal were the highest number of peak performance or the highest ranking on the Top500 list, the Blue Waters system could have been configured to have more than 40 peak petaflops/s by using all XK nodes and sacrificing the large memory and robust storage subsystems to add more XK nodes. Instead, the Blue Waters design strives to deliver the best balance between CPU, memory, network, accelerator, and I/O performance as supported by the Cray XE and XK series.

The heterogeneous design of Blue Waters requires an explicit analysis of how the XE (x86) and XK (x86+GPU) parts contribute to the sustained petascale performance of the overall system. It is also necessary to find the right application mix to accurately evaluate this heterogeneous system. Furthermore, the addition of the XK should improve the overall sustained performance of the system in a measurable manner.

To assess the capabilities and sustained performance of Blue Waters, the project team chose a set of twelve application benchmarks, eight to demonstrate x86 performance and four to demonstrate GPU performance. Each of these benchmarks represents a real science problem from beginning to end, and thus represents typical use of the system. Those benchmarks form the Sustained Petascale Performance (SPP) benchmark suite that represents the anticipated NSF workload.

### 13.7.1    The Sustained Petascale Performance Measure

The Sustained Petascale Performance (SPP) measure stems from the Sustained System Performance (SSP) metric defined by Kramer as part of the PERCU method of system assessment [Kra08]. According to this definition, a benchmark should serve four purposes: 1) enable one to compare two different computer systems, 2) enable one to verify system performance and numerical solution correctness, 3) enable one to monitor performance through the lifecycle of the system (regression testing) and 4) help to guide the design of future systems.

To represent the average workload of the Blue Waters system, we chose a suite of applications from a variety of disciplines important to the NSF: Lattice Quantum Chromodynamics (MILC, Chroma), Materials Science (QMCPACK), Molecular Dynamics (NAMD), Geophysical Science (VPIC and SPECFEM3D), Atmospheric Science (WRF), Astrophysics (PPM), and Computational Chemistry (NWCHEM, GAMESS).

We refer to the combination of code and computational input problems as a "benchmark configuration." Eight benchmark configurations represent the performance of the x86 part of the SPP metric solving one input problem for each of the eight applications: MILC, QMCPACK, NAMD, VPIC, SPECFEM3D, WRF, PPM, and NWCHEM. Four configurations represent the GPU part solving one input problem for each of the four applications Chroma, NAMD, QMCPACK, and GAMESS.

### 13.7.2 Reference FLOP Count

We define the common unit for work across the science domains by counting the floating point operations as reference FLOPS for the benchmark configuration (code + problem input set) and the according rate as FLOPS per second (FLOPS/s) where time is the wall clock time to solution for the benchmark configuration. The performance of the $i$-th benchmark configuration is derived from the total number of FLOPS required to solve the complete representative problem, the total number of processing elements used, and the total time. The required number of FLOPS for this specific problem, also called reference FLOPS, is ideally the minimal number of floating point operations required to solve the input problem on a single core. This avoids an artificial inflation of the FLOP count due to scaling (an inflated number of iterations or redundant computations).

If running the full problem on a single core is impossible or impractical, one can either run the full problem on multiple different core counts and show that the total number of FLOPS required is independent of the number of cores used, or one can extrapolate the reference FLOPS required to execute a large number of iterations (for an iterative application) from a smaller number of iterations. To demonstrate the former, we run the full application on at least three different core counts such that the minimum and maximum differs by at least three orders of magnitude. For the latter method, an accurate model for the required number of iterations and FLOP counts per iteration must exist and the pre- and post- processing of the algorithm must be taken into account separately.

### 13.7.3 The SPP Metric

To define the SPP of the Blue Waters system, we use the following definitions:

- node type $\alpha$: the system consists of two types of nodes $\alpha \subset \{XE, XK\}$.

- node counts $N$: the system has a specific number of nodes $N_\alpha$ of each type $\alpha$.

- benchmark configurations $C$: an application and an input set form a benchmark configuration. The ordered set $C_{XE}$ of eight configurations represents all XE benchmarks and the ordered set $C_{XK}$ of four configurations represents all XK benchmarks.

- per-node performance $P$: a configuration $i$ has a specific performance, $P_\alpha^i$, on each node of type $\alpha$.

- SPP contribution of configuration $i$: the SPP contribution of a configuration $i$ is the per-node performance $P_\alpha^i$ multiplied by the number of nodes $N_\alpha$.

The SPP performance of a homogeneous (single node type) system is defined as the geometric mean of the SPP contributions of all applications. The SPP performance of a heterogeneous system is defined as the sum of the SPP contributions for all node types. Each benchmark must be run on at least 20% of the total number of available nodes $N_\alpha$ of each type to measure $P_\alpha^i$, since this represents the anticipated system usage more closely than the unrealistic assumption that all science runs will only be at full-system scale.

The total SPP performance for the Blue Waters system is computed with

$$\sqrt[8]{\prod_{i=1}^{8} P_{XE}^i \cdot N_{XE}} + \sqrt[4]{\prod_{i=1}^{4} P_{XK}^i \cdot N_{XK}}$$

This number defines the sustained performance of the full system for a representative workload.

---

## Acknowledgments

The authors express their thanks to all the members of the Blue Waters Team. This work is part of the Blue Waters sustained-petascale computing project, which is supported by the National Science Foundation (award number OCI 07-25070) and the state of Illinois. Blue Waters is a joint effort of the University of Illinois at Urbana-Champaign, its National Center for Supercomputing Applications, Cray, and the Great Lakes Consortium for Petascale Computation.

# Chapter 14

## Kraken: The First Academic Petaflop Computer

**Mark R. Fahey**

*National Institute for Computational Sciences, Industrial and Information Engineering Department, University of Tennessee Knoxville*

**Lonnie D. Crosby, Gary L. Rogers, and Victor G. Hazlewood**

*National Institute for Computational Sciences, University of Tennessee Knoxville*

| | | |
|---|---|---:|
| 14.1 | Overview | 368 |
| | 14.1.1 Program Background | 368 |
| | 14.1.2 Plan and Timeline | 369 |
| | 14.1.3 Further Upgrades to Kraken | 371 |
| | 14.1.4 Integration Activities | 372 |
| | 14.1.5 Acceptance Testing | 373 |
| | 14.1.6 System Overview | 375 |
| 14.2 | Computer Center | 376 |
| 14.3 | Hardware Architecture | 377 |
| | 14.3.1 Processor | 377 |
| | 14.3.2 Node Design | 378 |
| | 14.3.3 Memory | 379 |
| | 14.3.4 Interconnect | 379 |
| 14.4 | System Software | 380 |
| | 14.4.1 Operating System | 380 |
| | 14.4.2 System Administration | 380 |
| | 14.4.3 Scheduling | 382 |
| | 14.4.4 Security | 384 |
| 14.5 | Storage | 384 |
| 14.6 | Programming System | 387 |
| | 14.6.1 Programming Models | 387 |
| | 14.6.2 Languages and Compilers | 388 |
| | 14.6.3 Frameworks and Libraries | 388 |
| | 14.6.4 Application and Library Tracking | 389 |
| | 14.6.5 Tools - Debugging and Performance | 389 |
| | 14.6.6 Grid Software and Gateways | 390 |
| 14.7 | Applications and Workloads | 390 |
| | 14.7.1 Workload | 390 |
| | 14.7.2 Benchmark Results | 392 |
| | 14.7.3 Visualization and Analytics | 392 |
| | 14.7.4 Continued Operation of the Cray XT4 | 394 |
| 14.8 | System Statistics | 394 |
| | Acknowledgments | 397 |

## 14.1   Overview

With the singular focus on empowering and preparing the U.S. academic research community for sustained petascale science and engineering, the University of Tennessee, Knoxville (UTK) Joint Institute for Computational Sciences (JICS) responded to the 2005 National Science Foundation (NSF) solicitation to deploy and support a world-class high-performance computing (HPC) environment of unprecedented capacity and capability. In particular, JICS proposed to deploy a 1-petaflop (PF) peak performance Cray XT5 system later named Kraken. Figure 14.1 shows a picture of Kraken.

**FIGURE 14.1**: Kraken.

In the following sections, we describe the program background, timelines, upgrades, integration activities, acceptance testing, and provide a system overview.

### 14.1.1   Program Background

In the 2006 report "Revolutionizing Science and Engineering Through Cyberinfrastructure," [NSF06], the NSF Blue Ribbon Advisory Committee summarized: "Environments and organizations, enabled by cyberinfrastructure, are increasingly required to address national and global priorities, such as understanding global climate change, protecting our natural environment, applying genomics-proteomics to human health, maintaining national security, mastering the world of nanotechnology, and predicting and protecting against natural and human disasters, as well as to address some of our most fundamental intellectual questions such as the formation of the universe and the fundamental character of matter." In response to this report, the NSF issued two major solicitations to prepare for (Track2: NSF 05-625 [NSF05]) and create (Track1: NSF 06-573) petascale computing environments for science and engineering.

The Track2 "mid-range" high-performance computer would bridge the gap between current HPC machines and advanced petascale systems. As such, the NSF 05-625 call [NSF05] solicited proposals for HPC systems that would have a petaflop of computational power by 2010.

---

**High Performance Computing System Acquisition: Towards a Petascale Computing Environment for Science and Engineering**

NSF's five-year goal [2006-2010] for high performance computing (HPC) is to enable petascale science and engineering through the deployment and support of a world-class HPC environment comprising the most capable combination of HPC assets available to the academic community. By the year 2010, the petascale HPC environment will enable investigations of computationally challenging problems that require computing systems capable of delivering sustained performance approaching $10^{15}$ floating point operations per second (petaflops) on real applications, that consume large amounts of memory, and/or that work with very large data sets. Among other things, researchers will be able to perform simulations that are intrinsically multi-scale or that involve the simultaneous interaction of multiple processes.

Exerpt from the Track 2 05-625 solicitation document [NSF05].

---

In August 2007, the NSF announced that the National Science Board approved funds for the acquisition of the Track2 system [NSF07], also known as Track2B since it was the second Track2 award. This second award of \$65 million for five years would fund the deployment and operation of an extremely powerful supercomputer at UTK JICS. With this award, UTK created the National Institute for Computational Sciences (NICS) project within JICS. Under the direction of Dr. Thomas Zacharia, the group would acquire a system with a peak performance of just under one petaflop, available to the research community with technical support from NICS and TeraGrid. The system would be nearly four times the capacity of the entire NSF-supported TeraGrid infrastructure at the time.

## 14.1.2 Plan and Timeline

The original UTK proposal was a staged deployment that would first install a 170-teraflops (TF) Cray XT4 system in November 2007, with an option to either operate it separately or use it as an upgrade to a 300-TF Cray XT4 system, thereby delivering 470 TF of compute, 80 TB of memory, and 1,000 TB of disk. This XT4 would be followed by a 1-PF peak performance Cray XT5 system by November 2008. This XT5 system would have 10,128 eight-core AMD Opteron$^{TM}$ processors operating at 3 GHz, 100 TB of memory (8 or 16 GB per socket), and 2.3 PB of disk space with 24 GB/s of I/O bandwidth to provide a balanced architecture for the user community. A quarter of the system would have 16 GB of memory per socket providing flexibility for applications as needed.

This sequence of systems was based on AMD's 2006 plan to deliver an eight-core Opteron$^{TM}$ processor. The system would have had a peak performance of 967 TF in 36 cabinets. After NSF's decision to negotiate an award for the Track2B solicitation, AMD made several changes to their roadmap, including changing both the physical size and power of the eight-core chip, and pushing the delivery into 2010. AMD offered a new replacement Opteron$^{TM}$ processor with six cores per processor available in the second half of 2009, as seen in Table 14.1.

Due to changes in AMD's roadmap, UTK and Cray proposed changing the deployment in two ways: (1) quickly deploy a 40-cabinet XT3 that would be upgraded to a 48-cabinet XT4 and (2) change the configuration of the XT5 system with its own staged deployment. The revised XT5 deployment was a system with 2.3 GHz four-core AMD Opteron$^{TM}$ processors delivered in November of 2008, followed by an upgrade to 2.4 GHz six-core AMD Opteron$^{TM}$

**TABLE 14.1**: Kraken configurations.

|  | XT3 April 2008 | XT4 July 2008 | XT5 Feb 2009 | XT5 Dec 2009 | XT5 Jan 2011 |
|---|---|---|---|---|---|
| Cabinets | 40 | 48 | 88 | 88 | 100 |
| System ft$^2$ | 768 | 1008 | 2,000 | 2,000 | 2,200 |
| Sockets | 3,676 | 4,512 | 16,512 | 16,512 | 18,816 |
| Cores/processor | 2 | 4 | 4 | 6 | 6 |
| Core GHz | 2.6 | 2.3 | 2.3 | 2.6 | 2.6 |
| GFlops/socket | 10.4 | 36.8 | 36.8 | 62.4 | 62.4 |
| Mem/socket GB | 2 | 4 | 4 or 8 | 8 | 8 |
| Memory type | DDR | DDR2 | DDR2 | DDR2 | DDR2 |
| Memory Mhz | 400 | 800 | 800 | 800 | 800 |
| Mem bndwdth/node GB/s | 6.4 | 12.8 | 25.6 | 25.6 | 25.6 |
| Peak TF | 38.6 | 166.5 | 615.5 | 1,030 | 1,174 |
| Total compute mem TB | 7.7 | 18 | 101 | 129 | 147 |
| Storage PB | 0.1 | 0.46 | 3.3 | 3.3 | 3.3 |

processor in the fourth quarter of 2009. (See Section 14.1.3 where we note how this changed again.) This system would be 88 cabinets and contain 16,704 AMD Opteron[TM] sockets. The peak performance of the four-core-based system would be 615 TF; the peak performance of the six-core system would be 962 TF.

The change in system configuration depended on keeping the M-value [oT08] metric the same or greater than the original configuration. The M-values are a metric based on the total delivered flops over the lifetime of Kraken weighted by Moore's law – flops later in the project are weighted less than flops early and are defined as

$$M = \sum_{i=0}^{47} a_i * b_i$$

where $a_i = (\frac{1}{2}^{\frac{1}{18}})^i$ and $b_i = \frac{(\text{Total cores in system})*3600}{\text{Benchmark}_i(\text{cores used})*\text{Benchmark}_i(\text{runtime(secs)})}$, for month $i$. M-values were calculated for the peak performance rating of the system, selected kernel benchmarks, and for a few applications. After the change to the system configuration, the M-values for the peak and High-Performance LINPACK (G-HPL) numbers were within 10% of the original contract, while the application projected numbers improved, thereby providing a total M-value metric for the newer contracted system that was close to the original contracted system.

In summary, the revised plan was that the initial system deployed would be a Cray XT3 system of 40 cabinets, which would be subsequently upgraded to a Cray XT4 system with 48 cabinets. The final system deployed for NSF would be an 8,256 node (16,704 compute socket) Cray XT5 system (88 cabinets), with 100 terabytes (TB) of memory and 2.3 petabytes (PB) of disk. In order to meet the technical requirements (M-values) for the XT5 portion, an additional phase was added that upgraded the system to six-core processors. The resulting proposed system then had 8,256 XT5 nodes, each with two processors (first

**TABLE 14.2**: Kraken project execution timeline.

| Milestones | Planned Date | Actual Date |
|---|---|---|
| Draft contract between awardee and primary vendor submitted to NSF | Dec 31, 2007 | Dec 31, 2007 |
| Cray XT3 Production | June 2008 | June 2, 2008 |
| Hardware acceptance of Cray XT4 four-core system | July 2008 | July 2008 |
| Final acceptance of Cray XT4 four-core system | July 2008 | July 2008 |
| Cray XT4 Production | Aug 2008 | Aug 18, 2008 |
| Hardware acceptance of Cray XT5 four-core system | Dec 2008 | Dec 2008 |
| Final acceptance of Cray XT5 four-core system | Jan 2009 | Jan 2009 |
| Cray XT5 Production (four-core) | Feb 2009 | Feb 2, 2009 |
| Hardware acceptance of Cray XT5 six-core system | Sept 2009 | Sept 2009 |
| Acceptance of upgraded Cray XT5 six-core system | Oct 2009 | Oct 2009 |
| Cray XT5 Production (six-core) | Nov 2009 | Oct 5, 2009 |

four-core processors with four cores at 2.3 GHz and later six-core processors at 2.4 GHz.) The memory was fixed at 100 TB over the 8,256 nodes; with only multiples of 4 GB possible per node, the memory per node was split into roughly half the nodes with 8 GB and the other half with 16 GB.

A detailed timeline in Table 14.2 shows how the team met and/or surpassed every milestone in deployment to full production. By doing so, UTK delivered all performance metrics on time or early and therefore the agreed upon M-values with NSF never had to be renegotiated.

### 14.1.3 Further Upgrades to Kraken

As noted above, Kraken was scheduled to be upgraded from four-core 2.3 GHz processors to six-core 2.4 GHz processors in August/September 2009. NICS' vendor partner (Cray) was able to work with AMD to procure faster 2.6 GHz six-core processors instead at no additional cost as part of the upgrade. Consequently, the peak teraflop rating went from 962 to 1,030 – making Kraken the **first academic petaflop computer.**

Before the six-core processor upgrade, Kraken had a total memory of 100 TB for the 88 cabinets as planned. Due to DIMM and node requirements, the arrangement of memory allotted approximately half of the dual socket, quad-core nodes (4,416) with 16 GB of memory and the remainder (3,840) with 8 GB of memory. With the planned upgrade to six-core processors in August/September 2009, the 8 GB nodes would provide less than 1 GB per core. NICS submitted an unsolicited proposal to NSF to obtain more memory so that all the nodes would have the same amount (16 GB.) NICS was awarded this proposal and minimized downtimes by working with Cray to simultaneously conduct the memory and six-core processor upgrades. The 2 GB DIMMS in half of the 8 GB nodes (1,920 nodes) were moved to the other half of the 8 GB nodes, and four 4 GB DIMMS were installed in the 1,920 nodes with no memory, which brought all nodes to 16 GB. This increased Kraken's total memory from 100 TB to 129 TB.

The memory upgrade allowed for simpler scheduling of smaller scale jobs as well. Because of the uneven memory configuration before the upgrade, the scheduler had to automatically detect the ratio of memory to processor cores on each compute node and assign one or more features based on that ratio. The batch environment was set up so that jobs would get the smaller memory nodes by default, but users could request the larger memory nodes as a feature (e.g., a user could select the "2gbpercore" feature). With the upgrade to six-core processors, the memory per core would not be simply 1 or 2 GB per core anymore, and feature names with fractional values were not desired. Thus, upgrading to uniform memory sizes across all the nodes simplified scheduling. With all nodes having 16 GB of memory, the wait times for these previously limited nodes was reduced because they were no longer the scarcer resource. While the total memory only increased by 29 TB, this upgrade nearly doubled the memory available to full-scale jobs–from 65 TB of memory (using 8 Gb per node) to 129 TB of memory thereby enabling new science at scale.

In early 2010, the NSF put out a "Dear Colleague Letter" and NICS responded with a proposal to extend the size of Kraken by 12 cabinets (as well as continue running the original Kraken XT4 cabinets for another year; see Section 14.7.4), which was awarded in late 2010. The Cray XT machines are typically configured as a 3D torus and can only be expanded by a whole number in either the row or column direction. In December 2010, NICS added 12 cabinets (3 to each of the 4 rows) consisting of only compute nodes; in particular, 12 (cabinets) × 24 (blades) × 4 (nodes/blade) = 1,152 compute nodes were added. The total increase in peak compute capacity was 1,152 × 12 (cores) × 2.6 GHz × 4 (flops/clock) = 143.7 teraflops. The total increase in memory was 1,152 × 16 GB = 18.4 TB. Interestingly, only Ranger at the Texas Advanced Computing Center (and Kraken itself) provided more capacity to the TeraGrid Resource Allocations Committee (TRAC) than just the increase provided by the 12 additional cabinets. By January 2011, all 100 cabinets of Kraken were in production for TeraGrid users. The addition of 144 TF to the largest NSF resource made it 14% larger and 13,824 additional cores (1,152 nodes) created more room to run smaller jobs alongside the larger capability jobs, with the potential for some smaller jobs to run for extended periods. The peak performance of the 100 cabinet XT5 system reached 1.17 PF with a total of 112,896 cores.

### 14.1.4   Integration Activities

For each system deployed and upgrade performed, a stringent set of tests was completed. First, the system was brought into the facility and assembled by Cray, and all hardware diagnostics were completed. During this burn-in period, the system was integrated into the software infrastructure of the facility (e.g., staff accounts, customization for the specific environment, and necessary TeraGrid services for acceptance). After all problems were resolved from hardware and software integration, the acceptance testing period began. Acceptance tests included not only hardware diagnostics, but also software tests that probed the functionality, performance, and stability of the system. The details of these tests and the criteria for machine acceptance are in Section 14.1.5. After acceptance but before general availability of the system to users, the system was hardened for production utilization. This transition-to-operations period typically included a friendly user group that would bring their applications online to allow for early evaluation of the system and the infrastructure. The friendly users were selected from the wider NSF computational science community. When the system became production ready, it was made generally available to the NSF user community.

During the operations phase, the allocation of available cycles, i.e., those cycles available for computation after allowing for downtime, are allocated as follows:

- At least 80% of the available cycles will be made available for allocation through a national resource allocation process that will be determined by NSF.

- Up to 5% of the cycles can be made available on a recharge basis to industrial affiliates through industrial partnership programs. Fees will be consistent with federal guidelines for as long as the federal government retains interest in the equipment.

- Up to 8% of the cycles will be available to users at educational, non-profit research institutions, or state or local agencies within the state of Tennessee, at the discretion of the PI.

- Up to 2% of the available cycles can be allocated outside of the national allocation process at the discretion of the PI. These allocations will be to projects that are national in scope, that integrate research and education in the national science and engineering community, or broaden participation of underrepresented demographic groups in science and engineering.

- Up to 5% of the available cycles at the discretion of the PI, will be allocated outside of the national allocation process provided that they are allocated to further research or education in the national science and engineering community and to broaden participation in high performance computing.

## 14.1.5 Acceptance Testing

Acceptance testing was a regular occurrence during the first four years of Kraken's deployment. An acceptance test was performed after every major upgrade and installation. These included the XT4 installation, XT5 installation, six-core processor and memory upgrade, and the upgrade to 100 cabinets.

A similar methodology was utilized in each of these acceptance tests. This methodology was based on the acceptance tests used for Oak Ridge National Laboratory's (ORNL) Jaguar and for Lawrence Livermore National Laboratory's ASC Purple and Blue Gene/L [Laba, Labb]. This methodology gauged the ability of the system to deliver science by [Kov]:

- testing the development and execution environment,

- testing that the system meets computational, communication, and I/O performance specifications, and

- testing that expected results are generated repeatedly and reliably over a period of time.

The acceptance test contains various phases that have both entrance and exit criteria. These criteria must be met in order to proceed to the next phase. Entry criteria generally include the correct installation, setup, and documentation of the system's environment which includes OS, compilers, tools, software, and libraries needed to perform the tests within the phase. Exit criteria generally include completing all tests within the phase, meeting predefined performance criteria, addressing all critical problems, and documenting software/environment changes, bugs, and fixes.

Three major test phases are utilized within the acceptance tests. These phases, in order, are functionality, performance, and stability [oT08].

1. The functionality test is designed to identify and fix problems which would prevent the successful completion of other test phases. Basic hardware and software functionality is tested by performing hardware diagnostics and testing the communication interconnect, I/O subsystem, code development environment, and job submission capability. Tests performed consistently over a period of time are used to prepare for the stability test and ensure system integration.

2. The performance test is designed to verify correct operation and suitable performance of the system. This includes performance tests on the I/O subsystem, communication interconnect, and various benchmark and application tests. Many of these tests have negotiated or otherwise pre-determined performance goals that must be met. These tests also verify the expected scaling behavior of benchmarks and applications by utilizing tests of various sizes. Tests performed consistently over a period of time are used to prepare for the stability test, ensure system integration, and test for consistent system performance.

3. The stability test is designed to ensure that system is ready to sustain a workload similar to what would be expected in production. This is accomplished by testing the development and submission environments continuously for a significant period of time. Benchmarks and application tests of various sizes are utilized during this phase to ensure system integration. During these tests pre-determined benchmark and application performance and functionality criteria must continue to be met.

The acceptance test harness was developed at ORNL [Tha] and is used to automate the above phases. This framework allows the controlled and automated deployment of a large number of tests. These tests are capable of automatically resubmitting themselves. This feature allows the testing of the continuous workload capability of the system without manual intervention. In addition, real-time test results can be obtained during the execution of tests. These results include the number of tests run and lists of tests which were successful, failed, or encountered other problems. Due to the structure of the harness framework, test results and tests are able to be easily archived for future reference and to fulfill documentation requirements.

The application tests prepared for acceptance testing were designed to demonstrate both the capacity and capability computing performance of the systems by using a range of test sizes. During the XT4 acceptance five applications were run using over 16,000 cores. These applications included DNS, MILC [Colb], LSMS [Thea], Chimera [Cola, BMH+10b, BMH+10a], and GTC [Labc]. During the XT5 acceptance test nine applications were run using at least 64,000 cores. These applications included those above and LAMMPS [Pli95], NAMD [PBW+05], SPECFEM3D [fGC], and HOMME [DLSC+]. The six-core processor upgrade allowed for seven applications to be run using more than 97,000 cores. These included MILC, LSMS, Chimera, GTC, LAMMPS, SPECFEM3D, and HOMME. During the 100 cabinet upgrade, six applications were run using more than 110,000 cores including GTC, LAMMPS, LSMS, MILC, NAMD, and SPECFEM3D.

A continuous operation test was performed at the conclusion of each phase of the acceptance test. Table 14.3 [KC] shows the number of unique applications, test cases, total runs, and success rate for the XT4, XT5 (four-core), XT5 (six-core), and XT5 (100 cabinet) systems. However, the length of time for these tests has changed. In general, a 12-hour continuous operation test was performed during the functionality phase and a 24-hour test was performed during the performance phase. However, for the 100 cabinet acceptance test a combined functionality-performance phase utilized a single 24-hour test. The most significant change occurred with respect to the length of time the continuous operation test was run during the stability phase. During the XT4 and XT5 acceptance tests this test was seven days in duration. Although the test allowed some reboots within the testing window, the test would sometimes need to be extended to meet the continuous operation requirements. For the XT5 six-core processor and 100 cabinet acceptance tests, the test duration was changed to three days. However, these tests did not allow for reboots within the testing window and would require the tests to restart if an unexpected down time occurred. Additionally, during the 100 cabinet acceptance test, this three day test was split between the two upgrade phases.

**TABLE 14.3**: Acceptance test statistics.

| XT4 | Functionality (12 Hr) | Performance (24 Hr) | Stability (72 Hr) |
|---|---|---|---|
| Applications | 18 | 15 | 12 |
| Test Cases | 144 | 131 | 95 |
| Total Runs | 1,648 | 4,794 | 34,679 |
| Successful Runs | 1,633 | 4,749 | 34,297 |
| **XT5 Four-Core** | **Functionality (12 Hr)** | **Performance (24 Hr)** | **Stability (72 Hr)** |
| Applications | 10 | 14 | 14 |
| Test Cases | 34 | 108 | 117 |
| Total Runs | 1,796 | 3,569 | 32,835 |
| Successful Runs | 1,784 | 3,547 | 32,686 |
| **XT5 Six-Core** | **Functionality (12 Hr)** | **Performance (24 Hr)** | **Stability (72 Hr)** |
| Applications | 20 | 16 | 13 |
| Test Cases | 75 | 61 | 81 |
| Total Runs | 861 | 1,014 | 17,782 |
| Successful Runs | 842 | 1,008 | 17,769 |
| **XT5 100 Cabinet Upgrade** | **Functionality-Performance (24 Hr)** | **Stability (48 Hr)** | **Stability (24 Hr)** |
| Applications | 18 | 12 | 28 |
| Test Cases | 62 | 47 | 89 |
| Total Runs | 1,687 | 11,518 | 513 |
| Successful Runs | 1,682 | 11,504 | 505 |

## 14.1.6 System Overview

Kraken is a series of Cray XT systems that culminated in a 112,896-core (9,408 dual six-core AMD Opteron$^{TM}$ processors) XT5 system that has 147 TB of memory and 2.4 PB of dedicated formatted disk space. The Kraken system has provided sustained application performance, scalability, and reliability, and has prepared the user community for sustained, high-productivity petascale science and engineering.

Kraken has been a resource for the NSF community since June 2008. During this time, Kraken has delivered well over 2 billion hours of compute time to the user community and has processed over 1.4 million jobs. Kraken has been available to the user community over 97% of its operational life with utilization consistently above 90% for the last 20 months. These statistics are just highlights from the System Statistics Section 14.8.

The rest of the document is organized as follows: the datacenter is described next in Section 14.2; the hardware architecture is described in Section 14.3; the system software is detailed in Section 14.4; the storage system is described in Section 14.5; the user environment is described in Section 14.6; a summary of the application workload is detailed in Section 14.7; system statistics are shown in Section 14.8.

## 14.2    Computer Center

UT and ORNL established JICS in 1991 to encourage and facilitate the use of high-performance computing in the state of Tennessee. When UT joined Battelle Memorial Institute in April 2000 to manage ORNL for the Department of Energy (DOE), the vision for JICS expanded to encompass becoming a world-class center for research, education, and training in computational science and engineering. In June 2004, JICS moved into a new 52,000 ft$^2$ building next door to the Oak Ridge Leadership Computing Facility (OLCF), which is located on the ORNL campus. The JICS facility represents a large investment by the state of Tennessee and features a state-of-the-art interactive distance learning center with seating for 66 people, conference rooms, informal and open meeting space, executive offices for distinguished scientists and directors, and incubator suites for students and visiting staff. Joint faculty, postdocs, students, and research staff share the building.

The OLCF is among the nation's most modern facilities for scientific computing. The OLCF includes 40,000 square feet divided equally into two rooms designed specifically for high-end computing systems. The ORNL computer facility staff provides continuous operation of the centers and immediate problem resolution. On evenings and weekends, operators provide first-line problem resolution for users with additional user support and system administrators on-call for more difficult problems. The facility has an electrical capacity of 20 MW and chilled water capacity of 6,600 tons.

The Kraken XT5 cabinets draw approximately 37 KW per cabinet when running a demanding application such as the high-performance Linpack benchmark, and are rated to as high as 42 KW per cabinet. The maximum power we have seen on the full XT5 system as configured is approximately 3.5 MW. With this power requirement, standard 208 volt power supplies were not an option. The 480 volt supplies that the XT5 uses allow a 100 amp branch circuit to each cabinet rather than a 200+ amp circuit needed at 208 volts.

With a peak power density of about 1,750 watts per square foot, Kraken could not operate without using some form of liquid cooling to manage heat dissipation requirements. At 2,200 square feet, the XT5 segment is half the size of an NBA basketball court. Traditional underfloor, forced-air distribution methods would be impractical across such a large area and heat load. Cray solves this problem by using their ECOphlex$^{TM}$ cooling technology [GL09]. This cooling system circulates low pressure, liquid R-134a refrigerant through three evaporators where the heat from the cabinet boils the R-134a absorbing the heat through a change of phase from a liquid to a gas. After leaving the cabinet, the gaseous R-134a and any remaining liquid are returned to a heat exchanger at the end of each row of cabinets. The heat exchanger is an enhanced version of Liebert's XDP [Pow] system in which Cray and Liebert teamed to increase the thermal capacity of each XDP unit. Cray's engineers designed the evaporators and distinctive stainless steel piping that connects each XDP unit to four or five XT5 cabinets. The result is not only a highly reliable cooling delivery system, but a 5% reduction, or more than 2.5 million kWh annually, in total consumed electricity versus a traditional forced-air cooling system.

## 14.3 Hardware Architecture

### 14.3.1 Processor

In Table 14.1, the various AMD Opteron^TM processors used in each Kraken instantiation are shown. This includes the memory upgrade and faster processor changes to the "Final XT5" (Dec 2009) system that were not in the "Revised Plan" and it also includes a 12-cabinet upgrade (Jan 2011).

In [BK11], it is clearly delineated why the AMD Opteron^TM was chosen:

- The processor featured the open, high-speed interface HyperTransport^TM that would allow the processor to be tightly integrated with a custom high-speed interconnect chip.

- Full support of the x86 instruction set.

- Extensions to the x86 instruction set that allowed 64-bit addressing.

- The memory controller is on the Opteron^TM itself, resulting in very low latency and high bandwidth to memory.

Figure 14.2 shows a diagram of the six-core AMD Opteron^TM processor used in the XT5 system.

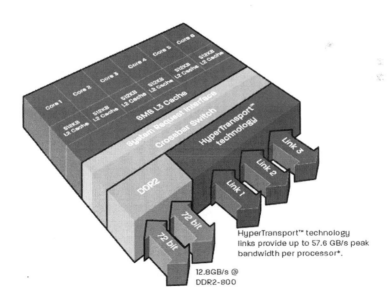

**FIGURE 14.2**: Six-core AMD Opteron^TM processor diagram [AMD].

In addition to the above reasons, Opteron^TM processors have other desirable features: out-of-order execution and the ability to issue instructions simultaneously, registers and a floating-point unit that support full 64-bit IEEE floating-point operations, an integer processing unit that performs full 64-bit integer arithmetic, performance counters that can be used to monitor the number or duration of processor events, a memory controller that uses

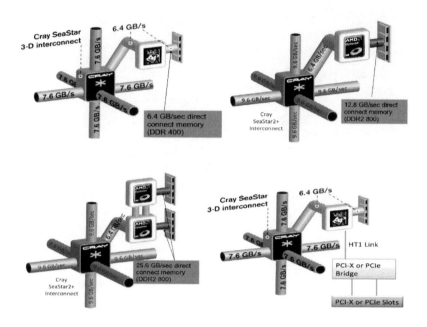

**FIGURE 14.3**: Cray XT3 (top left), XT4 (top right), XT5 (bottom left) compute and XT service (bottom right) nodes.

error correction code (ECC) for memory protection, and each core has its own execution pipeline and the resources required to run without blocking resources needed by other threads.

## 14.3.2   Node Design

The basic component of a Cray XT is the node. Because processors are inserted into standard sockets, customers can upgrade nodes as faster processors become available. There are two types of nodes. Service nodes provide support functions, such as managing the user's environment, handling I/O, and booting the system. Compute nodes run user applications. Each XT compute blade has four nodes, with two sockets on each node and four DIMM slots for its associated memory adjacent on both sides of the sockets.

Because of the many upgrades, Kraken has had three kinds of compute nodes: XT3, XT4, and XT5 all shown in Figure 14.3. The Kraken XT3 compute node had one dual-core processor, DDR1 memory, and a Cray SeaStar1 chip. The Kraken XT4 compute node had one four-core processor, DDR2 memory, and a Cray SeaStar2+ chip. The AMD Opteron$^{TM}$ is connected to the SeaStar chip via the HyperTransport$^{TM}$ 1 protocol.

The Kraken XT5 compute node consists of dual six-core processors, DDR2 memory, and one Cray SeaStar2+ chip. The dual six-core processors are connected by HyperTransport$^{TM}$ 1 links. Only one of these processors is connected by HyperTransport$^{TM}$ 1 to the SeaStar2+ chip. Each six-core processor and its associated DDR2 memory is referred to as a NUMA[1] node. This distinction arises due to the slight delay in accessing NUMA-node-remote versus NUMA-node-local memory. The XT5 compute node is composed of two such NUMA nodes.

---

[1]NUMA is an acronym for Non-Uniform Memory Access.

Service nodes (also shown in Figure 14.3) handle system functions such as user login, I/O, and network management. Each service node of Kraken contains one dual-core processor, DDR1 DIMM memory, and a SeaStar 1 or SeaStar 2 chip. In addition, each service node contains two PCI-X or PCIe slots for optional interface cards.

Cray XT systems include several types of service nodes, defined by the function they perform. Below are the kinds of services nodes found on Kraken.

**Login nodes:** Users log in to the system through login nodes. Each login node includes Ethernet network interface cards that connect to a local area network.

**Aprun nodes:** Batch jobs are run on aprun nodes (or batch nodes); parallel codes are launched using `aprun` from these nodes. This separation prevents interactive login use from interfering with running jobs.

**Gridftp service nodes:** Especially designed for large file transfers to/from Kraken using GSISSH. These have PCIe in the XT5 connections, while the XT3/4 had PCI-X.

**I/O nodes:** Each XT5 I/O node uses one InfiniBand card to connect to Lustre-managed RAID storage, while the XT3/4 I/O nodes used fibre channel.

**Boot nodes:** Each system requires one boot node. A boot node contains one fibre channel card which is either PCI-X or PCIe. The fibre channel card connects to the RAID subsystem, and an Ethernet network interface card connects to the System Management Workstation (SMW).

**Service Database (SDB) nodes:** Each SDB node contains a fibre channel card to connect to the SDB filesystem. The SDB node manages the state of the Cray XT system. The SDB node communicates to the SMW via the Hardware Supervisory System (HSS) network.

### 14.3.3 Memory

Cray XT systems use a simple memory model. Every instance of a distributed application has its own processors and local memory. The Kraken XT3 system used 2 GB DDR1-400 DIMMs for a 6.4 GB/s direct connect bandwidth rate. The Kraken XT4 system used 2 GB DDR2-800 DIMMs for a 12.8 GB/s bandwidth rate. The Kraken XT5 system, with 16 GB of memory per node, uses DDR2-800 DIMMs for an aggregate 25.6 GB/s bandwidth rate (12.8 GB/s per processor). Approximately 3/4 of the nodes are fully populated with 2 GB DIMMs while 1/4 are half populated with 4 GB DIMMs.

### 14.3.4 Interconnect

Kraken's interconnect is a high performance 3D torus based on Cray's SeaStar chip [Cra09a]. The Cray SeaStar application-specific integrated circuit (ASIC) chip is the system's message handler, offloading communications functions from the AMD Opteron$^{TM}$ processors. A SeaStar chip is connected to the AMD Opteron$^{TM}$ processor via HyperTransport$^{TM}$ 1. The SeaStar has a Direct Memory Access (DMA) engine that manages the movement of data to and from node memory. The DMA engine is controlled by an on-board processor. It also uses a low-level message passing interface called Portals, which provides a data path from an application to memory. Portions of the interface are implemented in Cray SeaStar firmware, which transfers data directly to and from user memory. The firmware runs on the embedded processor and RAM within the SeaStar chip. The chip has a link to a blade control processor (also known as an L0 controller). Blade control processors are used for booting, monitoring, and maintenance (see Hardware Controllers).

The Kraken XT3 used SeaStar1 chips, while the Kraken XT4 and XT5 used second generation SeaStar2+ chips. The service nodes are connected using the same SeaStar chips as the compute nodes. The SeaStar1 had an issue with its HyperTransport$^{\text{TM}}$ implementation that limited its injection bandwidth. The SeaStar2 corrected this issue, but otherwise was the same as the SeaStar1. The SeaStar2+ included a firmware upgrade and other policy channels that increased the bandwidth from 7.6 GB/s to 9.6 GB/s.

Peak transfer rates are shown in Figure 14.3. In particular, each of the six SeaStar1 and SeaStar2 links have a 7.6 GB/s signaling rate while the six SeaStar2+ links each has a 9.6 GB/s signaling rate. An Opteron$^{\text{TM}}$ processor is attached via HyperTransport$^{\text{TM}}$ 1 with a peak bidirectional bandwidth of 6.4 GB/s. For data on measured messaging rates, see [BPU05, AKB+07, ABE+08, WBK09].

## 14.4    System Software

### 14.4.1    Operating System

The Cray XT operating system, Cray Linux Environment (CLE), is a distributed system of service-node and compute-node components [Cra09a]. The CLE operating system includes Cray's customized version of the SUSE Linux Enterprise Server (SLES) operating system, with a Linux kernel. This full-featured operating system runs on the Cray system's service nodes. Service nodes perform the functions needed to support users, administrators, and applications running on compute nodes. Above the operating system level are specialized daemons and applications that perform functions unique to each service node.

Compute nodes run the Compute Node Linux (CNL) operating system, which runs a Linux kernel. The kernel provides support for application execution without the overhead of a full operating-system image. The kernel interacts with an application process in very limited ways. It includes a run time environment based on the SLES kernel with Cray-specific modifications. Cray has configured the kernel to eliminate device drivers for hardware not supported on Cray XT systems. Other features and services not required by applications have been taken out of the kernel. The kernel has also been configured to minimize processing delays caused by inefficient synchronization, thereby minimizing jitter [Wal07b]. It provides virtual memory addressing and physical memory allocation, memory protection, access to the message-passing layer, and a scalable job loader. Support for I/O operations is limited inside the compute node's kernel.

Kraken has run versions 2.0, 2.1, 2.2, and 3.1 of CLE.

### 14.4.2    System Administration

The management tools that power Cray XT systems help ease the task of administering large supercomputers. From low-level hardware details to high-level software configuration issues, Cray tools are present to make system administration easier. Figure 14.4 shows the components of a Cray system that an administrator manages. Portions of the remainder of this section are paraphrased from [Cra09a].

The HSS is an independent system of hardware and software that monitors system components, manages hardware and software failures, controls startup and shutdown processes,

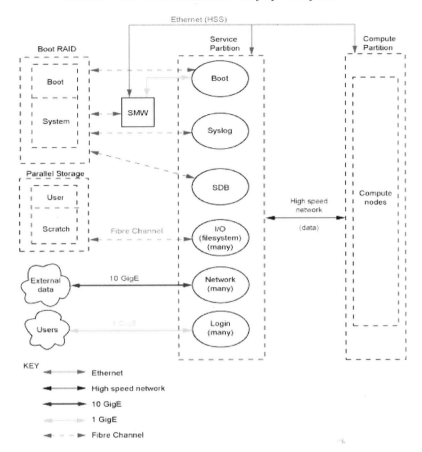

**FIGURE 14.4**: XT administrative components [Cra11b].

manages the system interconnection network, and displays the system state to the administrator. Because the HSS is a completely separate system with its own processors and network, the services that it provides do not take resources from running applications. In addition, if a component fails, the HSS continues to provide fault identification and recovery services and enables the functioning parts of the system to continue operating.

The SMW is a server and display that provides a single-point interface to an administrator's environment. Most system logs are collected and stored on the SMW. The SMW plays no role in computation. From the SMW, you can initiate the boot process, access the database that keeps track of system hardware, and perform standard administrative tasks. The `xtbootsys` utility orchestrates the entire boot process. Once the system is booted, console messages, kernel error messages, and panic messages are sent through the HSS and are logged on the SMW. System log messages generated by service node kernels and daemons are gathered by syslog daemons running on all service nodes. Initial system software installations as well as major software upgrades are performed on the SMW. A fibre channel storage device, called the boot RAID, is accessible both from the SMW and the boot node. Systems typically have multiple collections of storage partitions on the boot RAID, called system sets, on which the system software can be installed. This allows the administrator to keep a backup copy of the old system software during an upgrade, enabling the ability to roll back to the previous version if necessary.

The administrator uses the boot node to view files, maintain configuration files, and manage the processes of executing programs. Boot nodes connect to the SMW and are accessible through a login shell. The `xtopview` utility runs on boot nodes and allows the administrator to view files as they would appear on any node. The `xtopview` utility also maintains a database of files to monitor as well as file state information such as checksum and modification dates. Messages about file changes are saved through a Revision Control System (RCS) utility.

The Simple Event Correlator (SEC) package at NICS is used on the SMW to analyze the centrally collected log messages and take actions based on administrator-defined rules. It can cross-reference events from multiple log files and aggregate multiple similar events into a single alert. Alerts can be delivered via e-mail or sent to a central monitoring system, such as Nagios used on Kraken. Additional monitoring is typically implemented through a mix of active checks, such as SNMP queries or connection checks, and passive checks.

The Cray Node Health Checker (NHC) is run on the compute nodes after applications exit to ensure the node is still healthy enough to handle future jobs. The tests that NHC runs are configurable and check everything from memory utilization to filesystem availability. When NHC detects unhealthy nodes, they are marked as down in the system.

System administrators typically watch for nodes to be marked down and monitor for problems on compute or service nodes. If root cause cannot be easily determined, a full system or node-level dump can be initiated from the SMW with the `xtdumpsys` command. The dump process collects relevant logs and packages them into a convenient location for examination. Additionally, the `ldump` command can use either the SeaStar SSI channel to the ASIC chip or the HSS network, via a proxy, to read node memory and create a bit-for-bit image of the node's current state for later analysis.

The SDB, implemented in MySQL and accessible from every service processor, contains the following information: (1) node attributes used by `aprun` to schedule jobs and (2) system configuration tables that list and describe the configuration files.

The GNU 6.4 process accounting is enabled for XT service nodes. Comprehensive System Accounting (CSA) includes accounting utilities that perform standard types of system accounting processing on the CSA-generated accounting files. In addition, the project database used with CSA can utilize customer supplied user, account, and project information that resides on a separate Lightweight Directory Access Protocol (LDAP) server.

### 14.4.3    Scheduling

Kraken uses the TORQUE [Resb] batch environment. The following is taken from [Bae10].

> TORQUE is an open source resource management software package with a long and venerable history, being derived from Portable Batch System (PBS) and used on a large number of high performance computing systems over the years. Like all PBS variants, TORQUE is modular, consisting of three components: a queue server daemon (pbs_server), a scheduler daemon, and a machine-oriented mini-server daemon (pbs_mom). A typical TORQUE installation has one pbs_server instance, one scheduler instance, and as many pbs_moms as there are compute nodes. However, this arrangement changes slightly on Cray XT systems, as it is impractical to run a pbs_mom on every XT compute node; instead, pbs_moms run on a small set of dedicated service nodes, and jobs run on these service nodes spawn processes on the XT compute nodes by invoking the aprun command of the Cray Application-Level Placement Scheduler (ALPS) service [KLKA06].

The interface between the TORQUE pbs_server and scheduler is well defined, and while TORQUE includes a simple scheduler (pbs_sched), most sites choose to use one of the many available third-party schedulers. Like many large XT systems, Kraken uses the Moab scheduler. Moab [Resa] is an extremely powerful and flexible commercial scheduler software package that supports a wide variety of batch environments, including all PBS variants, LSF, LoadLeveler, and SLURM. Moab also supports a number of advanced scheduling capabilities such as advance reservations, quality of service (QoS) levels, consumable resource management, and a highly configurable priority and policy engine. On Cray XT systems, Moab communicates with ALPS as well as TORQUE, which is accomplished by interfacing to a native resource manager, a set of glue layer scripts that sit on top of ALPS and TORQUE services.

Prior to January 2010, Kraken was scheduled strictly on a priority basis, with jobs requesting large core counts receiving the highest priority to enable capability computing while servicing all job sizes. This posed several problems in terms of utilization of the machine from the operations perspective. Utilization would remain relatively high while processing capacity jobs, but when a capability job, (i.e., a job requesting more than 49,536 cores), entered the queue, the machine would immediately drain to accommodate it. This caused a dip in utilization while the machine was being drained. Utilization would peak again when the capability job was being processed. This resulted in frequent drains of the machine, creating frequent dips in the utilization that could last up to 24 hours (upper bound on requested job walltime).

When there were few large jobs, NICS recorded weekly utilizations of over 80%. On the other hand, when there were a number of capability jobs, the utilization would drop by 30% or more. These swings in utilization are the equivalent of a 300+ Teraflop computer, worth many millions of dollars. An approach followed by many centers to prevent such large drops in utilization has been to severely restrict the submission of large jobs. For example, a policy may be imposed that prevents a user from submitting jobs larger than 25% of the machine size without special arrangements. NICS has always eschewed such a policy, and any user (with sufficient allocation) has been able to submit a job of any size up to the complete machine capacity at any time. To this end, NICS implemented scheduling policies to improve utilization, maintain the ability to run large jobs, and provide reasonable service for all job sizes.

NICS instituted a demand-driven, machine-wide weekly reservation based on the promise shown by the previous simulations [AKHB10]. This reservation forced the clearing out of the entire machine once per week when there were capability jobs queued. Wednesday was chosen to coincide with the existing system drain for preventive maintenance, though this typically did not occur more than about once every third week. After the machine was emptied, large jobs (typically more than 85% of the machine) were run sequentially. Once the series of large jobs was completed, normal priority-based scheduling resumed, and capability jobs were not eligible to run again until the following week. In return for this restriction, a 50% capability discount in charging against their allocation was instituted. Charging at 50% was an incentive for the users to scale their codes up as large as possible, thereby ensuring a high utilization when capability jobs are running. This led to a stable, predictable scheduling system for capability users while still leaving the capacity jobs with reasonable throughput. NICS also instituted policies to allow debugging and other procedures to co-exist with large jobs, enabling users to prepare other jobs for submission while capability jobs were running.

There was some initial variation in utilization, but by June 2010, Kraken was consistently realizing over 90% utilization, as shown in Figure 14.5. Even more astounding is that the utilization has stayed near or above 90% since bimodal scheduling was implemented. These

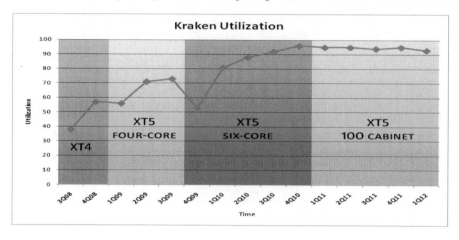

**FIGURE 14.5**: Kraken utilization before and after bimodal scheduling.

utilizations are excellent figures for any system approaching this size that also allows free submission of jobs ranging from 12 cores up to the full machine.

### 14.4.4    Security

Implementation of information technology security at NICS and on Kraken has followed a defense-in-depth methodology since NICS' inception. Many other academic supercomputer centers follow such a methodology and have been reasonably successful in limiting security incidents including root-level compromises. Due to the experiences with the Stakkato incidents of 2003-2005 [Sin05] of several of the management and staff at NICS who were former staff at the San Diego Supercomputer Center, NICS' management supported from the beginning the use of two factor authentication as one of the implemented authentication methodologies. Two factor authentication on Kraken was implemented by the use of RSA one time password (OTP) technology. Starting in August 2008, NICS allowed reusable passwords, ssh-keys, X.509 public key infrastructure, and RSA OTP authentication. By September 2009 NICS decided to improve its security posture by completely eliminating end-user reusable passwords and ssh-keys. There have been few end user account compromises and no known root compromise of NICS resources. The end user account compromises were account compromises outside of NICS that affected Kraken users and none were related to end user use of RSA OTP. It is believed that the low occurrence of security incidents is due to the defense-in-depth posture and the very tightly integrated use of OTP technology throughout NICS' resources including Kraken. Figure 14.6 shows the use of the different authentication types at NICS from August 2008 until March 2012.

## 14.5    Storage

Kraken has access to three major storage resources. These include a Network File System (NFS), Lustre filesystem, and High Performance Storage System (HPSS). The NFS filesystem is utilized primarily for user directories (i.e., home directories) and third-party software. The Lustre filesystem is the system's scratch area meant to provide a large, fast, and tempo-

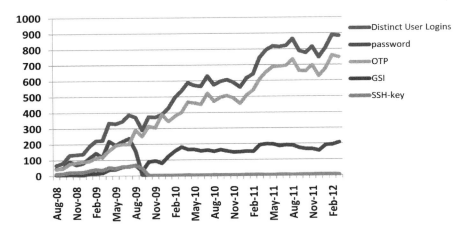

**FIGURE 14.6**: Kraken login types from August 2008 to March 2012.

rary filesystem for production workloads. The HPSS provides for Kraken's archival storage needs.

The data work flow on Kraken can be characterized by following the progress of a typical job. In general, a user's NFS home directories are used to store and maintain user executables, libraries, application source code, and input data. Initially these directories have a 2 GB quota which, depending on need, can be increased. In preparation for a batch job, any relevant input data is staged to the Lustre filesystem. This data can be copied directly from a user's NFS home directories or be obtained from HPSS or remote systems. The primary reason for this requirement is that the Lustre filesystem is the only filesystem accessible to applications running on Kraken's compute nodes. Batch scripts and executables may remain in the NFS home directories under usual circumstances. When a batch job is executed, all intermediate and output files (except potentially stdout and stderr which may be redirected through the batch script) must be written to the Lustre filesystem. At the conclusion of the batch job, this data may be processed in place by other batch jobs, moved to the NFS filesystem, archived via the HPSS, or moved to other resources.

The NFS filesystem is shared between Kraken and other resources at the center. Besides being used for user home directories, the NFS filesystem is utilized to organize and provide third-party applications and libraries to various computational resources. Additionally, this filesystem is periodically backed-up, which allows some level of data recovery.

All Kraken configurations have had a Lustre filesystem. Lustre is a scalable, high-performance POSIX-compliant filesystem that consists of software subsystems, storage, and an associated network [Ora]. One MetaData Server (MDS) and Target (MDT) plus one or more Object Storage Servers (OSSs) and Targets (OSTs) make up a single instance of Lustre and are managed together. There is no quota limit placed on Lustre; however, files older than 30 days are eligible to be purged — a NICS policy on file duration. Additionally, the Lustre filesystem is not shared between resources and not backed-up.

The XT3 had a 100 TB Lustre filesystem, the XT4 had a 300 TB Lustre filesystem, and the XT5 has a 3.3 PB filesystem. Only the XT5 filesystem is described in detail.

The planned XT5 Lustre OSS/OST configuration was to have 14 OSTs per OSS based on a configuration of 24 OSS service nodes. However, this configuration was not supported. Thus, 24 compute nodes were traded for service nodes resulting in 48 OSS service nodes and a configuration of 7 OSTs per OSS. This led to some difficult Lustre filesystem build problems discussed in [BHH+09].

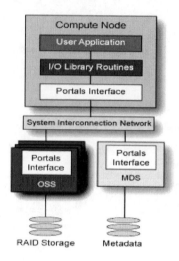

**FIGURE 14.7**: Lustre layout [Cra09b].

The 48 OSS nodes result from a DataDirect Networks (DDN) configuration of six cabinets with two S2A9900s each with four port controllers. Therefore, the aggregate theoretical peak burst rate for this Lustre configuration is approximately 1.6 GB/s per port × 4 ports × 2 controllers per cabinet × 6 cabinets = 76.8 GB/s. Assuming half of the bandwidth per port can be sustained, 0.8 GB/s, the estimated sustained performance is 38.4 GB/s. During acceptance testing, 30 GB/s was demonstrated using portions of the IOR [otUoC] benchmark application. No redundant controller paths exist in this configuration, meaning no failover is possible.

Kraken's archival data system is HPSS which is developed and operated by ORNL's National Center for Computational Sciences (NCCS). This system is shared between all NICS resources and resources at NCCS. The portion of the HPSS used by NICS users is

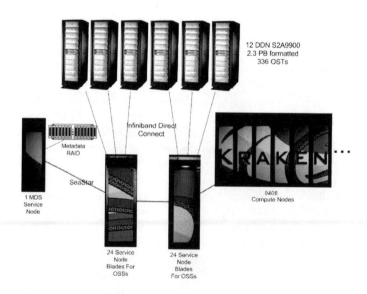

**FIGURE 14.8**: Kraken Lustre configuration [BHH+09].

organized as a separate branch. This partnership is facilitated by the purchase of tapes to hold data generated at NICS and the adoption of the same authorization protocol (OTP with RSA tokens) as NCCS. Additionally, users at NICS and NCCS must utilize different user names.

HPSS is capable of archiving hundreds of petabytes of data and can be accessed by all major leadership computing platforms. Incoming data is written to disk and later migrated to tape for long-term archiving. This hierarchical infrastructure provides high-performance data transfers while leveraging cost-effective tape technologies. Robotic tape libraries provide tape storage. The center has four SL8500 tape libraries holding up to 10,000 cartridges each. The libraries house a total of 24 T10K-A tape drives (500 GB cartridges, uncompressed) and 60 T-10K-B tape drives (1 TB cartridges, uncompressed), and 20T10K-C tape drives (5 TB cartridges, uncompressed). Each T10K-A and T10K-B drive has a bandwidth of 120 MB/s. Each T10K-C tape drive has a bandwidth of 240 MB/s. ORNL's HPSS disk storage is provided by DDN storage arrays with nearly a petabyte of capacity and over 12 GB/s of bandwidth. At the end of the 4th quarter in 2011, users on Kraken stored approximately 8.6 PB of data on the HPSS system at ORNL.

## 14.6    Programming System

### 14.6.1    Programming Models

Kraken, like all Cray XTs, supports both distributed memory, shared memory, and partitioned global address space (PGAS) programming models. In particular, Kraken supports the Message Passing Interface (MPI), SHMEM, OpenMP, pthreads, Unified Parallel C and Co-array Fortran implementations.

The Cray implementation of MPI is based on MPICH-2 and implements the MPI-2 standard, except for spawn support. It also implements the MPI 1.2 standard. The Cray MPI implementation on XT calls the Portals layer of software that has been specifically adapted for the XT architecture. The Portals interface is transparent to the application programmer.

The Portals data movement interface was developed at Sandia National Laboratories in collaboration with the University of New Mexico. Portals is intended to provide the functionality necessary to scale a distributed memory parallel computing system to thousands of nodes. Cray adopted Portals as the lowest-level network programming interface for their XT platform [BHP+05].

The shared memory access (SHMEM) library is a set of logically shared, distributed memory access routines. Cray SHMEM routines are similar to MPI routines; they pass data between cooperating parallel processes, but are considered one-sided in that a process puts or gets data without "handshaking" with another process. The Cray SHMEM library is implemented on top of the Portals low-level message-passing engine in a similar manner to MPI. The SHMEM API can be used either alone or in combination with MPI functions in the same parallel program.

OpenMP is a shared-memory parallel programming paradigm in C/C++ and Fortran and is only supported within a node on Kraken. Multiple threads of execution perform tasks defined implicitly or explicitly by OpenMP directives. By default, threads are pinned to a processor core, but the job launch utility `aprun` supports several options to control thread placement. Pthreads, a standardized C language threads programming interface often referred to as POSIX threads, are also supported only within a node on Kraken with the same runtime placement options.

Co-array Fortran (CAF) is a small extension to Fortran 95/2003. It is a simple, explicit notation for data decomposition based on the PGAS programming model and is supported natively by the Cray compiler.

Unified Parallel C (UPC) is a C language extension for parallel program development. The language provides a uniform programming model for both shared and distributed memory hardware and is considered a PGAS language. UPC is supported natively by the Cray compiler.

### 14.6.2 Languages and Compilers

The Cray XT system Programming Environment includes Cray Compiling Environment (CCE) and compiler suites from The Portland Group (PGI), Intel, the GNU Compiler Collection (GCC), and PathScale. All five of these compilers have been supported on Kraken. The PGI compiler has been the default during Kraken's deployment starting at version 7 going to version 12.

All five compilers support C, C++, and Fortran with support for MPI, SHMEM, OpenMP, and Pthreads. CAF and UPC are only natively supported by CCE. CAF can be mixed with MPI and SHMEM. Third-party downloads of UPC and/or CAF can also be built with one or more of the native compilers.

The command used to invoke a compiler is referred to as a compilation driver and supports any of the compilation options provided by the compiler suite. There are only three compilation drivers (cc, CC, and ftn) regardless of compiler suite for C, C++, and Fortran codes, respectively. The compilation drivers ensure programs are compiled with desired options (like target architecture) and also that the proper system libraries (like libmpich and libc) are linked into the executable to create a program that will run on the compute nodes. Modules are used to switch compiler suites and control the programming environment.

The vendor-specific compilers can be called directly to generate programs that will run on a login or service node. Creating programs that run on login nodes is useful for pre- or post-processing tools (like gnuplot), but these tools can easily become a problem when too many are running on the service nodes causing slowdowns or crashes due to out of memory problems. MPI programs cannot be run on the login/service nodes.

### 14.6.3 Frameworks and Libraries

In addition to the compilers, Cray provides several libraries that are integrated with the programming environments. Cray provides their own scientific library (libsci) that includes the Basic Linear Algebra Subroutines (BLAS), Linear Algebra Package (LAPACK), parallel LAPACK (ScaLAPACK), Basic Linear Algebra Communication Subroutines (BLACS), Fast Fourier Transform routines (FFT), Iterative Refinement Toolkit (IRT), Cray Adaptive Sparse Eigensolvers (CASE), and the Cray Adaptive Fast Fourier Transform routines (CRAFFT).

Cray also provides several more math libraries [Cra11a]: AMD Core Math Library (ACML), Portable Extensible Toolkit for Scientific Computation (PETSc), Fastest Fourier Transforms in the West (FFTW 2 and 3), fast math intrinsics (fast_mv), and a collection of Third-party Scientific Libraries (TPSL). TPSL contains Multifrontal Massively Parallel sparse direct Solver (MUMPS), serial and distributed sparse, direct linear-system solvers (SuperLU and SuperLU_dist), Parallel Graph Partitioning and Fill-reducing Matrix Ordering (ParMETIS), parallel multigrid preconditioners (HYPRE), SUite of Nonlinear and

Differential/ALgebraic equation Solvers (SUNDIALS), and another graph partitioning library (Scotch).

XT systems support two common IO libraries: NetCDF (Network Common Data Form) and HDF5 (Hierarchical Data Format). NetCDF and HDF5 provide a higher level of data abstraction than MPI-IO. NetCDF is a set of libraries and machine-independent data formats that are used to create, access, and share array-oriented scientific data [uni]. HDF5 is a library and multi-object file format used to transfer graphical and numerical data between computers. [Grob].

NICS installs and maintains a large number of third-party software packages. The software is maintained using the SWTools [Fah11] infrastructure. Approximately 140 third-party packages are maintained — from basic tools, to scientific applications, to parallel libraries, to profiling tools. For tools and applications, each package is built once with one compiler for every version; for libraries, each package is built with every compiler for every version. In this manner, the number of third-party builds supported on Kraken has been over 1,000.

## 14.6.4  Application and Library Tracking

NICS tracks application *and* library usage on Kraken in two ways. First, a copy of every job that is submitted is kept and subsequently parsed to look for known applications. In this way, every application (that we have registered) is identified, and the results are kept in a database. This method tracks every executable that is run in a batch job (whether or not it is run on a compute node). It has the drawback that the applications have to be known and put into the parsing process.

Second, NICS has implemented the Automatic Library Tracking Database (ALTD) tracking system [FJH10], which tracks library usage at compile time and tracks applications launched at runtime. ALTD tracks all library usage, which gives NICS' staff useful information on which libraries are used and which are not. For example, the data can be used to easily identify users using deprecated software. This also tracks executables, but only those launched to run on compute nodes, so it does not track everything in a batch job. On the other hand, it tracks everything without needing to know the applications beforehand.

## 14.6.5  Tools - Debugging and Performance

Cray provides a variety of tools for debugging. In particular, Cray has debugging options ranging from simple command-line debuggers to separately licensed third-party GUI tools, and these tools are capable of performing a variety of tasks ranging from analyzing core files to setting breakpoints and debugging running parallel programs. As it is on most systems, codes must be compiled with the "-g" option before the debuggers can provide meaningful information.

The Cray-provided debugging collection is referred to as the Cray Debugger Support Tools [Cra11a], but interactively they are loaded and used as individual modules. These packages are lgdb, atp, MRNet, and STAT. lgdb is a modified version of gdb that interfaces with aprun and works on compute nodes. atp is a system that monitors user applications and replaces the core dump with a more comprehensive stack backtrace and analysis. MRNet is a software overlay network that provides multicast and reduction communications for parallel and distributed tools and systems. And STAT is a stack trace analysis tool.

TotalView [Rog] is a debugger installed on Kraken that provides source-level debugging of applications running on multiple compute nodes. TotalView is compatible with the Cray, PGI, GCC, PathScale, and Intel compilers. TotalView can be launched in either of two modes: in GUI mode (using the `totalview` command), or in command-line mode .(using the `totalviewcli` command). TotalView is typically run interactively.

Cray provides its own performance analysis tool appropriately called the Cray Performance Analysis Tools (CrayPAT) [Cra11c]. CrayPAT is a suite of optional utilities that enable you to capture and analyze performance data generated during execution. The Cray Performance Analysis Tools suite consists of three components: CrayPAT, Cray Apprentice2, and PAPI [Inn]. CrayPAT is used to instrument a program and capture performance analysis data, and Cray Apprentice2 can be used to visualize and explore the resulting data files. Cray Apprentice2 can be run either on the Cray system or, optionally, on a stand-alone Linux desktop machine. Cray Apprentice2 can display a wide variety of reports and graphs, depending on the type of program being analyzed, the way in which the program was instrumented for data capture, and the data that was collected during program execution. PAPI is a standard API for accessing microprocessor registers. CrayPat uses PAPI to interface to the Cray system hardware. The interface between PAPI and CrayPat is normally transparent to the user. However, advanced users may want to bypass CrayPat and work with PAPI directly.

### 14.6.6   Grid Software and Gateways

Use of Kraken for science gateways was provided a few months after the Kraken XT4 was accepted. A science gateway is a web-based portal that provides a set of tools and applications for computational and data-enabled science and engineering to meet the needs of a specific community. Science gateways allow researchers to focus more on their scientific goals and less on assembling the cyberinfrastructure they require. Kraken supported the Globus Grid Resource Allocation and Management version 4 (GRAM4) software until GRAM5 replaced it in October 2010. Additional security capabilities were provided by integration of commsh, the community shell, with Globus GRAM [HW11]. Globus GRAM provides remote job submission, execution and job management capabilities for grid enabled applications. The following gateways have been implemented on Kraken: the Asteroseismic Modeling Portal (https://amp.ucar.edu/), Southern California Earthquake Center Petashake project (http://scec.usc.edu/research/cme/projects/petashake), nanoHUB (http://nanohub.org/), Network for Earthquake Engineering Simulation (http://nees.org), Center for Multiscale Modeling of Atmospheric Processes (http://www.cmmap.org), and Uintah (http://www.uintah.utha.edu).

---

## 14.7   Applications and Workloads

### 14.7.1   Workload

Projects relating to various NSF disciplines have been allocated resources on Kraken throughout its development. A majority of these allocations have occurred through quarterly resource allocation committee meetings. Although the deployment schedule for Kraken has been defined previously in Table 14.2, Table 14.4 shows the quarters in which each Kraken phase was allocated.

Figure 14.9 shows the percentage CPU hour utilization by each of the top eight NSF disciplines for each phase of Kraken. Collectively, these account for 90% of all utilized CPU hours. The top eight scientific disciplines, in order from most to least utilized, are

**TABLE 14.4**: Quarters allocated to each Kraken phase.

| Quarter | Phase | Allocated | Utilized |
|---------|-------|-----------|----------|
| | | (millions of CPU hours) | |
| 3Q08 - 4Q08 | XT4 | 141 | 31 |
| 1Q09 - 3Q09 | XT5 (four-core) | 294 | 229 |
| 4Q09 - 4Q10 | XT5 (six-core) | 1031 | 851 |
| 1Q11 - 1Q12 | XT5 (100 cabinet) | 1,134 | 1,097 |

physics, astronomical sciences, atmospheric sciences, molecular biosciences, chemistry, earth sciences, chemical and thermal systems, and materials research.

The total allocated and delivered CPU hours in each phase is given in Table 14.4. The amount of CPU hours allocated and utilized per quarter has increased during the various phases of Kraken. The allocated and utilized CPU hours both have gradually increased on average per quarter.

Most of the CPU hours utilized on Kraken originate locally on the resource. However, some jobs are submitted remotely through science gateways and Globus GRAM. In particular, the gateways enabled on Kraken have collectively utilized about 3.25 million CPU hours which is about 0.15% of all utilized hours on the Cray XT5 (1Q09 - 1Q12). The majority of these CPU hours (2.81 million) have been utilized by the Asteroseismic Modeling Portal.

There are various methods to categorize the most utilized applications on a computational resource. Previous analysis performed for Kraken for a portion of 2010 [HFJ10] and the 2011 calendar year [HFRR12] gave the usage of various compilers, libraries, and ap-

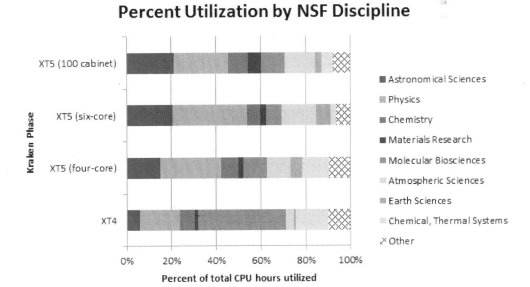

**FIGURE 14.9**: Discipline utilization of Kraken.

plications. Listed below are eight applications which comprise the top five applications by instances of use and by CPU hours consumed in 2011.

NAMD [PBW+05, Theb] is the most heavily utilized application by instance, is ranked second based upon CPU hour utilization on Kraken, and was a recipient of a 2002 Gordon Bell Award. NAMD is a molecular dynamics code designed for the simulation of large biomolecular systems. This parallel code is based on Charm++ parallel objects [PPL].

The Advanced Regional Prediction (ARPS) [Cen] is the second most utilized application by instance. ARPS is a regional to stormscale atmospheric modeling and prediction system. It includes a realtime data analysis, assimilation system, a forward prediction model, and a post-analysis package.

Amber [CDC+12, CDC+] is the third most utilized application by instance on Kraken. It is composed of a suite of programs for molecular dynamics simulations of biomolecules.

Hybrid Monte Carlo (HMC) [CJKS10] is the fourth most utilized application by instance and fifth by CPU hour usage on Kraken. This quantum chromodynamics (QCD) application is used to generate lattice configurations including the effect of dynamical fermions.

The Weather Research and Forecasting (WRF) [fARc] Model is the fifth most utilized application by instance. WRF is a mesoscale numerical weather prediction system. It is designed for both operational forecasting and atmospheric research. Featured in WRF are multiple dynamical cores, a 3-dimensional variational (3DVAR) data assimilation system, and a software architecture which allows for computational parallelism and system extensibility.

GADGET [Spr] is the most utilized application by CPU hour usage on Kraken. This application is a cosmological simulation code which performs N-body/smoothed particle hydrodynamics (SPH) calculations. An explicit communication model implemented with a standardized MPI communication interface is used. GADGET can be utilized to investigate a number of problems including colliding/merging galaxies and the formation of large-scale structure in the Universe.

Enzo [LfCA, OBB+04] is the third most utilized application on Kraken by CPU hour usage. Enzo is designed for simulations of cosmological structure formation using adaptive mesh refinement (AMR) and hybrid (N-Body and hydrodynamic) calculations.

The Community Climate System Model (CCSM)[fARa] is the fourth most utilized application on Kraken by CPU hour usage. It is a coupled climate model including atmosphere, ocean, land surface, and sea-ice models. CCSM is a subset of the Community Earth System Model (CESM) [fARb].

## 14.7.2    Benchmark Results

Benchmarks have been run and reported during the various phases of Kraken since 2008. Table 14.5 shows the TOP500® [TOPa] list rankings for Kraken and the HPL [PWDC00] result. In addition, the HPC Challenge benchmarks [DL05] were run after the XT5 six-core processor upgrade in November 2009. Table 14.6 shows both the base and optimized results for Kraken. Of particular interest are the G-HPL and G-FFT results. Kraken placed 2nd in G-HPL and G-FFT during SC 2009 and 2010. At SC 2011, Kraken placed 3rd in G-HPL.

## 14.7.3    Visualization and Analytics

Visualization tools are used to understand the massive data sets that result from simulations. The tools help scientists to understand, analyze, and glean insight from their data. VisIt and ParaView are two of the primary tools enabling scientific visualization and analytics on Kraken. These tools provide large-scale high-performance parallel visualization with real-time interaction. Parallel rendering capabilities are also provided to handle very

**TABLE 14.5**: TOP500® list: HPL results.

| List Date | System | Rpeak (Gflop/s) | Rank | Rmax (Gflops/s) |
|-----------|--------|-----------------|------|-----------------|
| Jun-08 | XT3 | 38,906 | 57 | 32,826 |
| Nov-08 | XT4 | 165,195 | 15 | 125,128 |
| Jun-09 | XT5 (four-core) | 607,200 | 6 | 463,300 |
| Nov-09 | XT5 (six-core) | 1,028,850 | 3 | 831,700 |
| Jun-10 | XT5 (six-core) | 1,028,850 | 4 | 831,700 |
| Nov-10 | XT5 (six-core) | 1,028,850 | 8 | 831,700 |
| Jun-11 | XT5 (100 Cabinets) | 1,173,000 | 11 | 919,100 |
| Nov-11 | XT5 (100 Cabinets) | 1,173,000 | 11 | 919,100 |

large data sets. Also, both of these scientific visualization tools have extensive libraries of data reader plugins that can handle hundreds of different formats for a wide variety of applications.

Both VisIt and ParaView use a client-server architecture. A client with a graphical interface can be run locally while connecting to a parallel server that runs on Kraken. Typically, the parallel rendering is hidden from the user experience on the local machine. In this way, users can run interactive sessions with these tools from their local machines to explore their data residing on Kraken. Job submission is handled automatically within the application.

Using the Python scripting capabilities of VisIt or ParaView, users can run visualization jobs in batch mode on Kraken as well. A typical workflow involves exploring the data interactively until a suitable rendering is achieved, constructing a Python script to reproduce the image, running the script in batch mode to produce a series of images, and finally combining the images into a movie.

**TABLE 14.6**: HPC challenge benchmarks (Nov. 2009).

| | G-HPL (Tflop/s) | G-PTRANS (GB/s) | G-Random Access (Gup/s) |
|------|------|------|------|
| Base | 736.301 | 1821.07 | 15.6789 |
| Opt. | 657.625 | 1559.64 | 18.4965 |
| | **G-FFTE (Gflop/s)** | **EP-STREAM Sys (GB/s)** | **EP-STREAM Triad (GB/s)** |
| Base | 3786.1 | 128281.331 | 3.8859 |
| Opt. | 7529.5 | 127201.772 | 3.8819 |
| | **EP-DGEMM (Gflop/s)** | **RandomRing Bandwidth (GB/s)** | **RandomRing Latency ($\mu$sec)** |
| Base | 28.8056 | 0.059316 | 15.588 |
| Opt. | 28.8195 | 0.055852 | 15.450 |

Many different scientific domains utilize parallel visualization tools to gain insight from massive datasets. Some examples include simulations of core-collapse supernova, scalar field visualizations of radiation dose levels around reactor cores, volume rendering and STL generation from CT scan data, and streamline generation with AMR meshes [CPA+10].

### 14.7.4    Continued Operation of the Cray XT4

The Cray XT4 instance of Kraken was a completely separate system than the Cray XT5 instance. Both Kraken systems ran as parallel production systems for two months, February and March 2009, while users migrated to the Cray XT5. The XT4 was taken out of general availability at the end of March 2009 and was renamed Athena.[2]

From April 2009 to October, it was primarily used as both a test vehicle for problem fixes on Kraken; and a resource for some NSF user groups who have been willing to live with its operational uncertainty and who required little support after other users were transitioned to the XT5. From October 2009 to March 2010, Athena was dedicated to the Center for Ocean-Land-Atmosphere Studies (COLA). The center simulated select climate problems at the highest resolution ever. For the months of April through June 2010, support was provided to three projects. Two of these projects involve new research in Quantum ChromoDynamics (QCD) with teams led by Bob Sugar at University of California Santa Barbara and Colin Morningstar at Carnegie Mellon. Finally, the Center for Advanced Prediction of Storms (CAPS) at University of Oklahoma conducted real-time severe storm forecasts nightly during the spring tornado season. All of the projects kept Athena at well over 90% utilization for the entire period.

In response to the NSF "Dear Colleague Letter" in 2010, NICS submitted a proposal and won an award to continue running Athena as a TeraGrid resource. The idea was to bind specific allocated projects to the most appropriate resource: smaller, longer running jobs on Athena, and larger, shorter running jobs on Kraken, thus maximizing the utilization of both systems in a way that conforms to the scientists' methodologies. The possibility of running modest-sized jobs that would otherwise be on Kraken made it easier to schedule full machine jobs on Kraken because jobs requiring 96,000 or more cores could not be run anywhere else in the TeraGrid. With Athena available as a general purpose resource for modest sized jobs, NICS concurrently ran large-scale jobs on Kraken thereby assuring jobs of all sizes ran in a timely manner. As a result of this extension, a wide variety of scientific disciplines including climate, lattice QCD, weather, molecular dynamics, materials science, and astrophysics made great use of Athena from July 2010 to June 2011.

---

## 14.8    System Statistics

Kraken has served as a supercomputing resource for more than 4,000 users on more than 1,000 projects. On average, 284 new users and 78 new projects were created each quarter. The majority of projects were allocated through the TRAC and the remaining projects were allocated at the discretion of the NICS' director as outlined in Section 14.1.4. The total number of computation hours, both allocated and utilized, is listed in Table 14.4.

Jobs submitted to Kraken were placed in one of six different queues: small, medium, large, capability, dedicated, and hpss. Placement into the compute queues is based strictly on the number of requested processors. Table 14.7 provides the different sizes of queues

---

[2]The Greek goddess of wisdom who burst forth fully grown from the head of Zeus.

**TABLE 14.7**: The processor threshold level that separated the different queue sizes scaled with the different machine phases.

| Phase | small | medium | large | capability | dedicated |
|---|---|---|---|---|---|
| XT4 | 1-512 | 513-2K | 2K-8K | 8K-18K | 18K |
| XT5 (four-core) | 1-512 | 513-8K | 8K-32K | 3K-66K | 66K |
| XT5 (six-core) | 1-504 | 505-8K | 8K-49K | 49K-98K | 98K-99K |
| XT5 (100 cabinet) | 1-504 | 505-8K | 8K-49K | 49K-98K | 98K-112K |

over the different phases of Kraken. Charges for these jobs are calculated by multiplying the number of processors by the wall clock (in seconds). The capability queue is reserved for large computation jobs requiring the use of more than half of the machine. The dedicated queue is reserved for full machine runs. Jobs that are in either the capability or dedicated queue receive a discount of up to 50% in order to incentivize the use of large runs. Details of this policy and the resulting positive effects on machine utilization were discussed in 14.4.3. Finally, the hpss queue is available to give users a batch method to access the HPSS without having to allocate Kraken compute nodes to initiate data transfers either before or after a compute job. This frees up the compute nodes to do computational jobs while relying on non-compute nodes to move data.

Figure 14.10 illustrates the breakdown of the jobs submitted to the different queues and the respective number of compute hours derived from each of the queues. Kraken has processed over 1.4 million jobs and delivered approximately 2 billion computation hours. Over 83% of these jobs were submitted to the small queue, but the jobs in the small queue account for only 17% of the compute hours. Jobs in the medium queue account for only

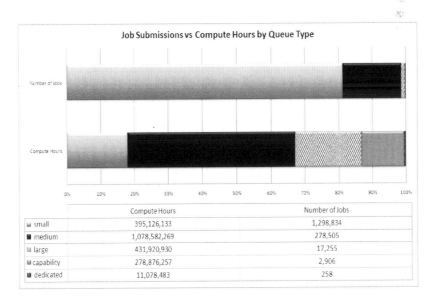

| | Compute Hours | Number of Jobs |
|---|---|---|
| small | 395,126,133 | 1,298,834 |
| medium | 1,078,582,269 | 278,505 |
| large | 431,920,930 | 17,255 |
| capability | 278,876,257 | 2,906 |
| dedicated | 11,078,483 | 258 |

**FIGURE 14.10**: Kraken was created to provide a platform to scientists to scale codes to petascale computers. As seen here, codes are initially ported to Kraken and tested in the small queue before scaling codes up to take advantage of Kraken's large core count.

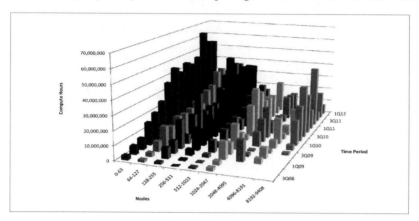

**FIGURE 14.11**: The overwhelming majority of compute hours are consumed by jobs that request fewer than 512 compute nodes.

16% of all submitted jobs, but are responsible for nearly half of all computation hours. Interestingly, the top 10 users of Kraken have consumed approximately one quarter of all hours, while the top 40 users have consumed almost half the available compute hours. A breakdown of the jobs completed on Kraken based on the node count is shown in Figure 14.11. A comprehensive analysis of the Kraken workload characteristics can be found in [ZY12].

During the many upgrades of Kraken from the XT4 to the final XT5 (100 cabinet) machine, Kraken has been resilient in terms of availability to users as seen in Figure 14.12. Kraken has been available to users for a total of 97% of the time that Kraken has been in production, approximately 29,000 hours. This includes 460 hours of scheduled downtime for preventative maintenance and 420 hours of unscheduled downtime due to system errors. Table 14.8 lists the mean time before failure (MTBF) and the mean time between interrupt (MTBI) for each phase of Kraken. An in-depth review of the particular causes of failure and the respective fixes can be found in [KEB12]. One particular change to Kraken's hardware that increased the stability was the slight change in the rectifier DC voltage during the 3rd

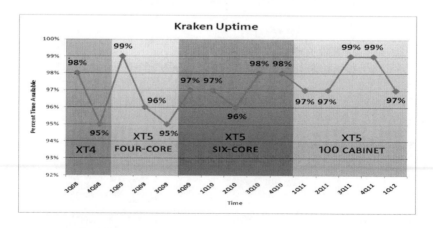

**FIGURE 14.12**: Kraken's uptime continues to increase with the addition of hardware and software patches.

quarter of 2011. As a result, Kraken's uptime during the remainder of the year was at an all-time high when, over a span of more than 2,200 hours, Kraken was unavailable for only 20 hours, including scheduled downtimes. The combination of Kraken's perpetually high utilization, see Figure 14.5, and high availability made Kraken one of the most productive academic supercomputers for open science.

**TABLE 14.8**: MTBF and MTBI numbers for Kraken's four major phases.

| Phase | MTBI (hours) | MTBF (hours) |
|---|---|---|
| XT4 | 115.7 | 191.1 |
| XT5 (four-core) | 74.4 | 106.4 |
| XT5 (six-core) | 138.4 | 201.5 |
| XT5 (100 cabinet) | 155.6 | 207.4 |

*Note*: The MTBI numbers included both scheduled and unscheduled downtimes, while the MTBF numbers exclude any scheduled downtimes.

## Acknowledgments

This material is based upon work supported by the National Science Foundation under Grants No. 0711134, 0933959, 1041709, and 1041710.

We would like to acknowledge all the NICS staff past and present who have contributed to the successful deployment and operation of Kraken, the world's first academic petaflop supercomputer.

Phil Andrews, the first NICS project director, was instrumental in the success of the Kraken project (Figure 14.13). He served as director of NICS from the very beginning until he unexpectedly passed away in February 2011.

**FIGURE 14.13**: Phil Andrews — the first NICS project director.

# Chapter 15

## Titan: 20-Petaflop Cray XK7 at Oak Ridge National Laboratory

**Arthur Bland, Wayne Joubert, Don Maxwell, Norbert Podhorszki, Jim Rogers, Galen Shipman, and Arnold Tharrington**

*Oak Ridge National Laboratory*

## 15.1 Overview

The U.S. Department of Energy (DOE) mission is "to ensure America's security and prosperity by addressing its energy, environmental, and nuclear challenges through transformative science and technology solutions." Among the department's targeted outcomes is to "continue to develop and deploy high-performance computing (HPC) hardware and software through exascale platforms." The value of computational approaches to complex problems is widely recognized by virtually every major study group. Together with theory and experimentation, computational science now constitutes the "third pillar" of scientific inquiry, enabling researchers to build and test models of complex phenomena. In January 2009, then Undersecretary for Science Dr. Raymond Orbach signed a mission needs statement describing the present and growing gap between requests versus allocations for leadership computing time within the Department of Energy Office of Science (DOE-SC) for such applications as climate change, chemical catalysis, economics of energy alternatives, energy production and storage, fusion energy, nuclear power, and bioenergy.

Oak Ridge National Laboratory's (ORNL's) Leadership Computing Facility (OLCF) delivers the most powerful resources in the United States for open science. Over the past decade, the OLCF has provided increasingly powerful machines to support its mission (Table 15.1). At 2.33 petaflops peak performance, the latest in the series, the Cray XT Jaguar, delivered more than 1.4 billion core hours in 2011 to researchers around the world for computational simulations relevant to national and energy security; advancing the frontiers of knowledge in physical sciences and areas of biological, medical, environmental, and computer sciences; and providing world-class research facilities for the nation's science enterprise. The OLCF continues to fulfill this mission through its fielding of a 20-petaflop Cray XK7 system named Titan.

In 2011 ORNL began an upgrade to Jaguar to convert it from a Cray XT5 into a Cray XK7 system named Titan. This upgrade is being accomplished in two phases. The first, which was completed in early 2012, was to replace all of the XT5 node boards with XK7 boards, including the AMD Opteron 6274 16-core processors, 600 terabytes of system memory, Cray's new Gemini network, and 960 NVIDIA X2090 Tesla processors. In the second phase, ORNL will add NVIDIA's next-generation Tesla processors to increase the combined system peak performance to more than 20 petaflops.

## 15.1.1   Sponsor/Program Background

Leadership computing is listed as the highest domestic priority in the DOE-SC report *Facilities for the Future of Science—A Twenty-Year Outlook*. Upgrade of the leadership computing facilities (LCFs) to tens of petaflops by the 2011–2013 time frame is vital to the United States' playing a leading role in several important international programs, including climate science (Intergovernmental Panel on Climate Change), fusion energy research (ITER), and the Nuclear Energy Advanced Modeling and Simulation program. Moreover, the United States faces serious economic, environmental, and national-security challenges based on its dependence on fossil fuels. To address the scientific grand challenges identified by DOE-SC programs alone would require a leadership-class computing capability of at least 100 petaflops by 2015. In the near term, based on the requirements for making incremental steps in application software and the projected availability of technology, DOE-SC has a mission need for a total leadership-class computing capability of 20–40 petaflops in the 2011–2013 time frame.

To allow substantial advances on near-term requirements in numerous mission-relevant science domains, the OLCF will deliver a 20-petaflop computing capability as part of a DOE-SC strategy that requires architectural diversity of computer systems to minimize risk within the program.

The OLCF has a proven track record of designing, constructing, and operating purpose-built, leadership-class computing systems to serve the open scientific user community and applying these systems to solve the most challenging and significant science and engineering problems of our time. The OLCF leverages massive data storage, high-bandwidth network connectivity, and advanced visualization resources to deliver the world's leading science cyberinfrastructure. The key measure of the OLCF's success is its ability to deliver transformational solutions in science and engineering, such as improving our understanding of high-temperature superconductivity, developing high-efficiency solar cells and other new energy technologies, improving fuel combustion in engines, understanding global climate change, and advancing biology and medicine.

**TABLE 15.1**: OLCF systems, 2009–2011.

| Description | Cabinets | Type | Nodes Number | Nodes Type | Processor Number Cores/Processor | Total Cores | Total | Memory Per Node | Memory Per Core | Peak Performance | HPL | Rank | Interconnect |
|---|---|---|---|---|---|---|---|---|---|---|---|---|---|
| Initial XT3 | 56 | XT3 | 5,294 | 2.4 GHz AMD Opteron | 1 | 5,294 | 10 TB | 2 GB | 2 GB | 25 TF | 20.5 TF | #10 (June 2005) #13 (November 2005) | SeaStar |
| Dual-core | 56 | XT3 | 5,294 | 2.4 GHz AMD Opteron | 2 | 10,588 | 20 TB | 4 GB | 2 GB | 54 TF | 432.5 TF | #10 | SeaStar |
| Addition of XT4 | 124 | XT3 and XT4 | 11,706 | 2.6 GHz AMD Opteron | 2 | 23,412 | 46 TB | 4 GB | 2 GB | 119 TF | 101.7 TF | #2 (June 2007) #7 (November 2007) | SeaStar2 |
| Quad-core | 84 | XT4 | 7,832 | 2.1 GHz AMD Opteron 2352 | 4 | 31,328 | 62 TB | 8 GB | 2 GB | 263 TF | 205 TF | #5 (June 2008) #8 (November 2008) #12 (June 2009) #16 (June 2009) #20 (June 2009) #30 (November 2010) | SeaStar2 |
| Initial XT5 | 200 | XT5 | 18,688 | 2.3 GHz AMD Opteron 2356 | 4 | 149,504 | 300 TB | 16 GB | 2 GB | 1,375 TF | 1,059 TF | #2 (November 2008 and June 2009) | SeaStar2 |
| Six-core upgrade | 200 | XT5 | 18,688 | 2.6 GHz AMD Opteron 2435 | 6 | 224,256 | 300 TB | 16 GB | 1.3 GB | 2,332 TF | 1,759 TF | #1 (November 2009 and June 2010) #2 (November 2010) #3 (June 2011 and November 2011) | SeaStar2 |

The ORNL Jaguar 2.3-petaflop system has been one of the top three systems for seven releases for the TOP500 list (twice the #1 system), at 1.759 petaflops total high-performance Linpack performance. In four HPC Challenge competitions, it has won seven first-place awards as well as six runner-up awards. Over its three-year lifetime, it has hosted three Gordon Bell Prize winners (DCA++, WL-LSMS, MoBo), four finalists (OMEN, AWP-ODC, AMR, NWChem), and one honorable mention (DRC). Jaguar has five applications that have sustained performance of more than 1 petaflop on full applications: DCA++ at 1.9 petaflops, LSMS at 1.8 petaflops, DRC at 1.3 petaflops, NWChem at 1.39 petaflops, and OMEN at 1.03 petaflops.

The mission of the OLCF over the next several years will be to further accelerate scientific discovery by providing multipetaflops sustained performance on a wide variety of high-impact applications and broaden the use and applicability of HPC at the highest level of capability and with exceptional price performance. To achieve this goal, the OLCF will construct and operate the next generation in a series of ever more powerful computing resources leveraging a more than half-billion-dollar investment by the Department of Defense and DOE in the Defense Advanced Research Projects Agency's (DARPA's) High Productivity Computing Systems (HPCS) program. DOE-SC is a mission partner in the DARPA HPCS program in funding, overall guidance of the requirements, and deployment through ORNL's partnership with Cray, Inc., in its Cascade program. These computational resources will enable and deliver productive petascale science results in support of the science mission of DOE. They will be built and operated by an experienced team that fully understands the challenges of massively parallel systems and has successfully moved applications through more than two orders of magnitude of system performance, as demonstrated by deployment of new or upgraded systems between 2004 and 2009.

## 15.1.2    Timeline

The OLCF conducted extensive surveys of both the science needs of the user community and the technical realities of building a leadership computing system in 2011–2013. Titan meets the technical needs of the science programs to accomplish DOE-SC goals over the useful life of this computer system and has a long-term architecture that will allow the investment in application software to be used over several generations of computer systems. Titan system design was initiated in April 2009, upgrades of the Cray XT5 resource were accomplished in 2011, and acceptance will be completed in 2013.

The existing Cray XT5 was upgraded from AMD Opteron 1354 quad-core processors to AMD Opteron 2435 six-core processors, providing a 50% increase in the resources available for OLCF users. Through the period ending October 9, 2011, the underlying Cray XT5 hardware configuration remained unchanged, with steady-state operation delivering well over 1.4 billion compute hours in 2011.

The OLCF subsequently upgraded the Cray XT5 to an XK7, causing operational impacts to a portion of the existing Cray XT5 beginning in October 2011 as a partition of the existing system was upgraded with the XK compute blades, Fermi GPUs, and Gemini interconnect. This new XK7/Gemini partition was released to users for the second half of December 2011 to allow the OLCF to upgrade the remaining XT5 partition. This strategy for partitioning the system and validating the upgrade process and architecture for a portion of the existing system was approved by the DOE-SC Office of Project Assessment as part of the formal Critical Decision process. The full Cray XK6 system entered production in February 2012 after completing its acceptance test.

The upgrade from XK6 to XK7 will occur when NVIDIA Kepler accelerator cards are added increasing peak performance to more than 20 petaflops.

System acceptance is expected to be completed and Titan resources allocated to users in 2013.

### 15.1.3   Applications and Workloads

The Titan science workload is driven by the mission objectives of DOE's Office of Advanced Scientific Computing Research, including

- **Energy Security** – computer simulation to help ensure America's energy security by enabling researchers to understand combustion, improve fuel cells, develop fusion energy, and develop other technologies.

- **Scientific Discovery and Innovation** – hosting the most powerful open computing systems in the world, key to scientific discovery and economic competitiveness and leading to improvements in quality of life through innovation.

- **Environmental Responsibility** – computer simulations to help researchers understand mechanisms of environmental contamination and develop appropriate remediation technologies.

**TABLE 15.2**: Representative science drivers for the Titan workload.

| Science Area | Science Driver |
|---|---|
| Astrophysics | Determine the explosion mechanism of core-collapse supernovae and Type Ia supernovae |
| Biology | Determine whether efficient ethanol production can offset the current oil and gasoline crises |
| Chemistry | Understand catalytic transformation of hydrocarbons; research clean energy and hydrogen production and storage |
| Climate | Predict future climates based on scenarios and anthropogenic emissions |
| Combustion | Develop cleaner-burning, more efficient devices for combustion |
| Fusion | Understand and control plasma turbulence fluctuations in ITER |
| High-Energy Physics | Find the Higgs particles thought to be responsible for mass; find evidence of supersymmetry |
| Nanoscience | Design high-temperature superconductors and magnetic nanoparticles for ultrahigh-density storage |
| Nuclear Energy | Design all aspects of the nuclear fuel cycle virtually, including reactor core, radiochemical separations reprocessing, fuel rod performance, and repository |
| Nuclear Physics | Describe nuclei whose fundamental properties we cannot measure |

Representative science drivers to fulfill these mission objectives are shown in Table 15.2. To achieve the goals specified by these science drivers, computer time is competitively awarded on OLCF leadership-class computer systems, primarily through the Innovative and Novel Computational Impact on Theory and Experiment (INCITE) program [INCa]. Through INCITE and other programs, teams of scientists develop and deploy science applications to address these pressing science issues using OLCF resources.

The vehicle through which these science drivers are met is the slate of science applications that are developed and executed by the INCITE project teams. Analysis of the application workloads of these systems reveals how science is currently being done and also what hardware and software are required for future systems in the 100-petaflop to 1-exaflop range.

The complement of projects awarded time on OLCF systems includes new projects added yearly as well as continuing multiyear projects and projects that have successfully competed for time over several award periods. Because the application mix over time is relatively stable, the characteristics of the anticipated science application workload over Titan's lifetime can be in large part inferred based on the workload of its immediate predecessor, the ORNL Jaguar system.

A study of Jaguar's application workload reveals that usage is concentrated in a relatively small number of applications, with 50% of the core-hours over a two-year period used by 20 science applications, and nearly 80% consumed by the top 50 applications [Joubert/Su[JS12]]. Figure 15.1 shows the cumulative usage of Jaguar core-hours ranked by science application. OLCF workloads are based on a small set of well-focused science teams, each using one or a small number of highly scalable codes as the focus of development, performance tuning, and science output. This narrow focus is strategically important due to the increasing level of effort required to deploy well-optimized applications to scale on leadership-class systems and will be even more important as science models and computer hardware become increasingly complex going forward.

Titan is designed to support science applications deployed across the entire range of scalability regimes required by the respective science codes, from thousands to hundreds

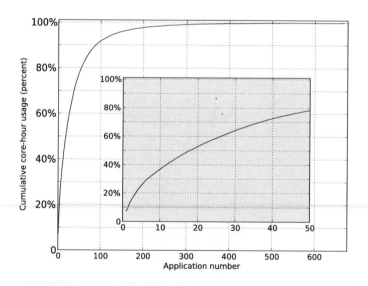

**FIGURE 15.1**: Cumulative core-hour usage by application.

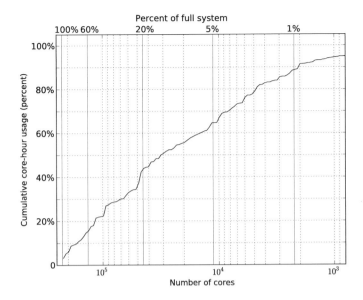

**FIGURE 15.2**: Cumulative core-hour usage by job size.

of thousands of cores. Figure 15.2 shows the number of core-hours consumed by users of the Jaguar system for jobs across a range of job sizes (as measured by core count). Usage is fairly uniform from jobs requiring 1,000 cores to ones requiring the maximum 224,256 cores. Different science domains and applications require different job sizes to produce the targeted science. Titan design and usage policies are constructed to support these kinds of workloads.

### 15.1.4 Highlights of Main Applications

Table 15.3 shows application codes expected to be heavy users of Titan over the production lifetime of the system. These applications account for more than 50% of the workload of the Jaguar system over the two-year period immediately previous to its upgrade to Titan. These codes represent a diverse range of science domains, models, and algorithms, accenting the importance of Titan being architecturally well-balanced, deploying hardware features and a software stack capable of efficiently running a diverse set of algorithms.

Titan is among the world's first multipetaflop systems to deploy heterogeneous compute nodes. It is recognized that science applications must undergo substantial changes to prepare for the exascale challenge of billion-way parallelism, memory wall, power wall, and fault tolerance issues [KBB+08], [ADD+09], [STBdf]. As a first step to exascale and to prepare for the heterogeneous compute environment of Titan, a set of leading OLCF applications was chosen as the focus of a porting effort to prepare for the new system (Table 15.4). The applications represent a diverse set of programming models, languages, algorithms, data structures, and library requirements. As such, they represent a broad cross section of the challenges expected to be faced by users as they prepare applications for the Titan system and systems beyond.

Titan represents a paradigm shift in hardware and programming models for HPC systems, similar to the previous transitions to vector computing, shared memory and distributed memory programming, and reduced instruction set computing-based architectures. New coding styles are required to obtain high efficiency on the new heterogeneous hardware.

**TABLE 15.3**: Selected OLCF applications.

| Application | Primary Science Domain | Description |
|---|---|---|
| NWChem | Chemistry | Large-scale molecular simulations |
| S3D | Combustion | Direct numerical simulation of turbulent combustion |
| XGC | Fusion Energy | Particle-in-cell modeling of tokamak fusion plasmas |
| CCSM | Climate Research | Climate system modeling |
| CASINO | Condensed Matter Physics | Quantum Monte Carlo electronic structure calculations |
| VPIC | Fusion Energy | Three-dimensional relativistic, electromagnetic, particle-in-cell simulation |
| VASP | Materials | Ab-initio quantum mechanical molecular dynamics |
| MFDn | Nuclear Physics | Many Fermion Dynamics code |
| WL-LSMS | Materials | First-principles-based ground state and statistical physics of magnetic materials |
| GenASiS | Astrophysics | Adaptive mesh refinement neutrino radiation magnetohydrodynamics |
| MADNESS | Chemistry | Adaptive multiresolution simulation by multiwavelet bases |
| GTC | Fusion Energy | Gyrokinetic toroidal momentum and electron heat transport |
| OMEN | Nanoelectronics | Multidimensional quantum transport solver |
| Denovo | Nuclear Energy | Three-dimensional discrete ordinates radiation transport |
| CP2K | Chemistry | Atomistic and molecular simulations |
| CHIMERA | Astrophysics | Modeling evolution of core-collapse supernovae |
| DCA++ | Materials | Many-body problem solver with quantum Monte Carlo |
| LAMMPS | Chemistry | Molecular dynamics simulation |
| DNS | Fluids and Turbulence | Direct numerical simulation for fluids and turbulence |
| PFLOTRAN | Geological Sciences | Multiphase, multicomponent reactive flow and transport |
| CAM | Climate Research | Global atmosphere models |
| QMCPACK | Materials | Diffusive quantum Monte Carlo simulations |

To port the early readiness applications to Titan's GPU-equipped nodes, several approaches were used, which we expect to be representative of software development approaches for the

**TABLE 15.4**: Titan early readiness applications.

| Science Area | Science Objective |
|---|---|
| WL-LSMS | Role of material disorder, statistics, and fluctuations in nanoscale materials and systems |
| S3D | Turbulent combustion through direct numerical simulation with complex chemistry |
| LAMMPS | A molecular description of membrane fusion, one of the most common ways for molecules to enter or exit living cells |
| CAM-SE | Answers to questions about specific climate change adaptation and mitigation scenarios |
| Denovo | High-fidelity radiation transport calculations that can be used in variety of nuclear energy and technology applications |
| NDRF | Nonequilibrium radiation diffusion |

wider scope of applications going forward. One approach is an application programming interface (API) such as CUDA [CUD], in which explicit function calls are made to launch computational kernels on the GPU and perform data transfers. An alternate approach is compiler directives to annotate parts of existing source code to be executed on the GPU [Opea]. Regardless of the approach, experience has shown that achieving realistic performance gains requires substantial restructuring of the algorithms and application codes to expose new parallelism and improve locality of memory reference. Each of the early readiness applications has presented its own unique challenges to moving the code toward exascale, as indicated in Table 15.5.

The performance gain manifested by these applications on Titan as a result of these efforts has been substantial. First, the applications now make significant use of the computational resources of the GPU-equipped compute nodes. Second, the porting effort has also significantly improved performance on traditional multicore CPU-based systems by improving the patterns of data access. This early readiness work, in addition to efforts over the

**TABLE 15.5**: Porting approach for Titan early readiness applications.

| Application | Porting Challenges | Programming Approach |
|---|---|---|
| WL-LSMS | Mapping code hotspot, a small dense BLAS-3 operation, to GPU; associated code restructurings | GPU Library |
| S3D | Coarse-scale code restructuring to expose more usable thread parallelism with proper data locality | Directives |
| LAMMPS | Porting short-range force calculations to GPU; implementing MSM algorithm for scalable long-range force calculations | CUDA |
| CAM-SE | Code and data restructuring to map multiple distinct code loops to the GPU | CUDA Fortran |
| Denovo | Rewrite of code hotspot sweep kernel to expose more thread parallelism and data locality | CUDA |

past several years in the broader community to port other leadership-class science applications to accelerator-based hardware, will ensure that the full capabilities of Titan will be effectively deployed to accelerate computational science when system delivery is complete.

## 15.2    System Overview

Titan, a hybrid Cray XK7 system, is the third generation of major capability computing systems at the DOE OLCF at ORNL. It is an upgrade of the existing Jaguar system first installed at the OLCF in 2008. The initial upgrade from Cray XT5 to Cray XK6 compute nodes was accepted in February 2012 and consists of 18,688 compute nodes for a total of 299,008 AMD Opteron 6274 "Interlagos" processer cores and 960 NVIDIA X2090 "Fermi" GPUs. The peak performance of the Opteron cores is 2.63 petaflops, and the peak performance of the X2090 GPUs is 638 teraflops. In late 2012 the 960 NVIDIA X2090 processors will be removed and replaced with 18,688 of NVIDIA's next-generation "Kepler" processors with a total system peak performance of the GPUs in excess of 20 petaflops.

ORNL is deploying Titan in 2012 as part of the DOE-SC's LCF program in support of its basic and applied science missions. Examples of specific modeling and simulation areas in which Jaguar and Titan are being and will be used include better understanding turbulent combustion; creating biofuels from cellulose; designing more efficient materials for photovoltaic cells; understanding the role of turbulence in combustion turbines; building a virtual nuclear reactor to increase power output and longevity of nuclear power plants; modeling the ITER prototype fusion reactor; predicting impacts from climate change, earthquakes, and tsunamis; and improving the aerodynamics of vehicles to increase fuel economy. Access to Titan is available through several allocation programs. More information about access is available through the OLCF website at http://www.olcf.ornl.gov/support/getting-started/.

The OLCF worked with Cray to design Titan to be an exceptionally well-balanced system for modeling and simulation at the highest end of HPC. The AMD Opteron processors double both the memory bandwidth and memory capacity per node as compared to the Jaguar Cray XT5 system it is replacing. The system will be linked to its filesystem by twice the number of I/O nodes and will use InfiniBand cards that provide at least twice the bandwidth of the InfiniBand cards in Jaguar. The file storage system is being acquired independently from the Titan system and will have at least twice the bandwidth and capacity of Jaguar's filesystem. The key, new component of Titan is that most of the Cray XK7 nodes have an NVIDIA GPU application accelerator. In the November 2011 TOP500 list of the world's most powerful computers, 39 of the 500 computers on the list used application accelerators, including three of the five fastest computers.

## 15.3    Architecture

### 15.3.1    Processor and Accelerator

The XK6 node consists of an AMD Opteron 6274 Interlagos 16-core processor linked to an NVIDIA X2090 Fermi GPU. The AMD Interlagos processor is the first to use the new "Bulldozer" [BBSG11] module, each of which contains two integer processor cores that share a floating point unit capable of generating eight 64-bit results per clock cycle. With eight floating-point units per processor and eight operations per clock cycle, each of the 2.2-gigahertz processors in Jaguar has a peak performance of 140.8 gigaflops. Each processor has four separate memory channels connected to DDR3-1600 memory, providing up to 102.4 gigabytes per second of memory bandwidth. The Interlagos processor connects to the NVIDIA GPU through a HyperTransport-3$^{TM}$ to PCI-express version 2 conversion chip. The bidirectional bandwidth between the Interlagos processor and the GPU is 10.4 gigabytes per second.

The NVIDIA GPU is mounted on an SXM form factor PCI-express card along with 6 gigabytes of GDDR5 memory. In the first phase of the upgrade to Jaguar, there are 960 compute nodes with NVIDIA Fermi GPUs [ND10]. The SXM module is a different form factor but functionally equivalent to the NVIDIA M2090 [NVI]. The Fermi GPU has 16 streaming multiprocessors and a peak performance of 665 gigaflops. The Fermi implements memory error correcting codes that can correct single-bit memory errors and report double-bit errors, but at a cost of storing those codes in the GDDR5 memory. The codes decrease the available memory to approximately 5.25 gigabytes. The memory bandwidth between the Fermi GPU and the GDDR5 memory is 177 gigabytes per second with error correction turned off and approximately 140 gigabytes per second with error correction enabled.

In late 2012, the NVIDIA Kepler will be available and will replace the Fermi GPUs in Titan. It will use the same SXM form factor board with 6 gigabytes of GDDR5 memory. The specific details of the HPC version of the Kepler GPU architecture have not been released; however, an architecture document [wu] describing the GeForce 680 version of the Kepler GPU shows the single precision floating point performance as almost twice that of the Fermi processor and describes some of the features of the Kepler architecture.

### 15.3.2 Node Design

The Cray XK7 is a descendant of the Red Storm system developed by a partnership between Cray and Sandia National Laboratories. Unlike Red Storm, however, the Cray XK7 system uses the Gemini network rather than SeaStar. In contrast to traditional networks that separate the network interface card (NIC) from an external switching system, Gemini is an integration of the NIC and the network switch.

Each node in the network is made up of a single Gemini application-specific integrated circuit (ASIC) that is comprised of two Gemini NICs and a 48-port "YARC" router. Each NIC is connected to the YARC router on the network side and to the compute node through a HyperTransport-3 link. The network is organized into a three-dimensional (3D) torus that has been shown to balance performance, scalability, and cost. Gemini is, thereby, a networking technology that combines high-speed serial links with a router ASIC wired into a 3D torus topology.

Gemini provides a number of advanced features not common in other networking technologies. Adaptive routing allows it to distribute traffic over lightly loaded links, improving total use of the network and helping avoid contention on the network. Gemini also provides the more common dispersive routing in which streams are deterministically hashed to specific routes, ensuring that ordering of delivery within the stream is preserved. The system can reroute traffic in the event of a network link failure, preventing system outages during such occurrences.

The Gemini network achieves unidirectional bandwidth of 4.7 gigabytes per second in the Y-axis of the torus and 9.4 gigabytes per second in the X- and Z-axes of the torus. This bandwidth is a result of the YARC router providing 12-bit links in the Y-axis and 24-bit links in the X- and Z-axes. Link injection bandwidth is limited to 6.1 gigabytes per second for any one compute node. Best-case latency (compute node to compute node) is 1.3 microseconds, and the 8-byte message injection rate is more than 4.75 million messages per second.

### 15.3.3   Interconnect

One of the key differences between the Cray XK7 and prior-generation XT systems is the Gemini interconnect [ARK10]. Instead of a SeaStar ASIC for each node, each Gemini custom ASIC connects two nodes to the 3D torus interconnect. All of the cables and backplane interconnections between node boards are the same for the SeaStar- and Gemini-based systems. The only difference is the mezzanine card on the node boards. The mezzanine card is a separate printed circuit board that plugs into the base XK7 node board and contains either the SeaStar or Gemini ASIC along with any support circuitry and the interconnections between the SeaStar or Gemini chips. This feature allowed ORNL to upgrade from an XT5/SeaStar system to an XK7/Gemini system while reusing the cabinets, cables, and backplanes.

### 15.3.4   Storage System

Intended for the write-heavy workloads found on scratch filesystems, Spider, the ORNL center-wide data storage system is designed for high performance in a small footprint and built from scalable building blocks. Each building block is comprised of two DataDirect Networks (DDN) S2A9900 storage controller [DDN], driven by four Lustre Object Storage Servers (OSSs). S2A9900 controllers are configured to run in pairs for increased reliability. Each pair is configured with five high-density drive trays, with 300 drives housed in 20U of rack space. For Spider, ORNL populated those trays with 280 SATA drives, each with a capacity of 1 terabyte. Write-back caching is disabled to prevent unrecoverable data loss in the event of a controller failure. These drives are grouped into 28 DirectRAID tiers (RAID3 with two parity drives), with seven 7.2-terabyte logical unit numbers (LUNs) exposed over double-data-rate (DDR) InfiniBand for each OSS. Each OSS is a Dell PowerEdge 1950, with 16 gigabytes of memory and two quad-core Xeon E5410 running at 2.3 gigahertz. Each OSS serves seven object storage targets (OSTs). This building block is capable of delivering more than 5.5 gigabytes per second of raw block storage.

There are 48 of these building blocks in the Spider system, giving it an aggregate of 13,440 terabytes of raw storage, or more than 10 petabytes of capacity after accounting for the parity overhead of DirectRAID. There are 192 OSS servers, providing 14 teraflops of compute capability and 3 terabytes of memory dedicated to the Lustre filesystems. This aggregate capability is broken up into four independent chunks to spread the metadata load. Widow 0, 1, 2, and 3 each have 336 OSTs.

Metadata services are provided by three identical metadata servers (MDSs). Each MDS is a Dell R900 with 64 gigabytes of memory and four quad-core Xeon E7330 processors running at 2.6 gigahertz. The metadata target (MDT) for each filesystem is stored on a shared NetApp Engineo 7900 (XBB2) storage system, connected via four 4-gigabit-per-second Fibre Channel connections to each MDS. Each MDT is configured as a RAID10 volume on the XBB2 with 80 SATA 1-terabyte drives, formatted to provide an 8-terabyte LUN.

As ORNL transitions to the heterogeneous Titan platform, the storage system will be upgraded to support higher-aggregate I/O bandwidth as well as scalable metadata performance. This upgrade will include an aggregate performance increase to 500–1,000 gigabytes per second as well as increased filesystem capacity. While the current storage system is divided among four parallel filesystems to improve aggregate metadata performance, horizontally scalable metadata performance through Distributed Namespace will allow higher aggregate metadata performance by distributing metadata workload based on namespace hierarchy. To support this approach, the OLCF plans to deploy multiple MDSs and distribute the namespace based on distinct users and project directories across these servers. Other changes in the Lustre software stack that improve vertical scalability of the MDS may allow higher-performance storage media technologies such as Flash-based MDTs to improve single-server metadata performance.

## 15.4 System Software

### 15.4.1 Operating System

The Jaguar Cray XK7 system runs an HPC-optimized Linux environment based on the SUSE distribution that Cray has dubbed the Cray Linux Environment (CLE). CLE has been designed to scale to very large systems and supports the Cray XK7 at the OLCF with nearly 300,000 compute cores. It provides a nearly full-featured operating system (OS) environment, thereby easing porting of applications to Jaguar. In most cases applications that run on a commodity cluster environment can quickly be ported to CLE, allowing the computational scientist to focus on scalability rather than simply porting. Transitioning to the Titan platform from Jaguar will require only modest changes to CLE, most notably support for the NVIDIA Kepler GPU.

Scalability of CLE is achieved through elimination of unneeded systems services that may impact application performance through OS noise. Such noise has been demonstrated to impact some classes of tightly coupled parallel applications as scale increases due to system interrupts impacting collective communication. Reducing the impact of OS operations on application scalability is generally achieved either by eliminating all heavyweight OS operations through use of a lightweight operating system or by isolation of OS services to a dedicated processing core. When run in core-specialization mode, CLE will bind OS services to a dedicated processing core to isolate OS services from the application. This approach allows for a nearly full-featured OS environment for the application at the cost of consuming dedicated CPU resources.

### 15.4.2 File System

The Spider system at the OLCF is the one of the world's largest-scale Lustre parallel filesystems [SDOW09], [WOS+09]. Envisioned as a center-wide shared parallel filesystem capable of delivering both the bandwidth and capacity requirements of the OLCF's diverse computational environment, the project had a number of ambitious goals. To support the I/O workloads of the OLCF's diverse computational platforms, the aggregate performance and storage capacity of Spider exceed that of ORNL's previously deployed systems by a factor of 6–240 gigabytes per second and 7–10 petabytes, respectively [KGS+11]. Furthermore, Spider has supported more than 26,000 clients concurrently accessing the filesystem, which exceeds the lab's previously deployed systems by nearly four times.

Spider is deployed as a center-wide filesystem, and ORNL designed its Scalable I/O Network (SION) to support its performance goals. SION is deployed as a multistage DDR InfiniBand fabric and provides more than 889 gigabytes per second of bisectional bandwidth. The network infrastructure is based on 288-port Cisco 7024D DDR InfiniBand switches. Two switches are dedicated to providing connectivity between Jaguar and Spider, while other switches provide links to the MDS and management services, as well as the smaller compute resources in the center.

The Lustre networking software stack (LNET) [Mic08] provides communication among Lustre servers and between Lustre servers and clients. Most importantly, LNET supports routing between different networks such as Cray's Gemini and InfiniBand. This capability allows Lustre to achieve very high performance while transparently bridging multiple networks.

To support the dramatic increase in system capability as the Cray XK7 system is upgraded with GPU-based accelerators, the filesystem will also be upgraded. This upgrade will target 500–1,000 gigabytes per second of aggregate bandwidth to accommodate the increased total memory footprint and compute capability of Titan. In addition to dramatically increasing bandwidth, this upgrade will include enhancements to the Lustre parallel filesystem such as improved system recovery performance in the event of storage server failure and better metadata performance and scalability.

### 15.4.3    System Administration

System administration has certainly been an evolutionary process from the first Jaguar cabinet that arrived at ORNL in January 2005 running the DevHarness OS to today and the latest OS, which supports a more resilient network and GPUs. With the arrival of that first, very immature OS, methods had to be developed to detect and remove bad hardware from the pool provided to the users. Until ORNL developed such methods, computing jobs would hang with no indication to the user as to the cause of the problem. In addition, no batch system was available in the beginning to coordinate work among multiple users.

Over time both ORNL and Cray have learned more about the system and its behaviors and had the opportunity to develop new system administration software to assist in monitoring and troubleshooting the system. ORNL developed a set of rules using an open-source package called the Simple Event Correlator, which provided monitoring and alerting of events found in console logs. This improvement enhanced the avenues by which bad hardware could be removed from the pool of resources available to users while the system was running. Shortly thereafter Cray developed a diagnostic tool now called NodeKARE that provided a mechanism to check the health of nodes after each job completed. These examples are just two instances of ways in which systems software has matured during the lifetime of Jaguar and will continue to do so in the Titan system.

Another area of improvement with the Titan system is the more resilient Gemini interconnect network. With the capability to dynamically route the system, which the Jaguar SeaStar interconnect network did not have, system uptimes will be dramatically improved. The failure of a single module could render the SeaStar network dead, requiring a system reboot. However, the same failure in the Gemini network is survivable due to its dynamic rerouting capability, which also enables improvement of the number of scheduled downtimes for hardware repair. With the ability to remove modules from the system without taking the machine down, hardware repairs can be performed while the system continues to run. All nodes on a particular module needing repair can be drained of jobs and the module physically removed from the system, repaired, and then reinserted into the system.

While administering a system the size of Jaguar and now Titan presents new challenges on a regular basis, the software and hardware have matured over the years to provide a more resilient and manageable system.

### 15.4.4    Scheduler

The OLCF has specific requirements for job scheduling to meet DOE-SC goals. To maximize investment in very-large-capability machines, metrics are set that require certain percentages of jobs to use a significant portion of the machine. The OLCF has contracted with Adaptive Computing to use its Moab workload management product to accomplish these goals. Jobs are categorized according to size using Moab job templates and assigned an increasing priority and maximum walltime relative to job size. Using these parameters compute cycles are committed to larger jobs on the machine, thereby maximizing the investment. Moab has also implemented dynamic backfill to maximize use and turnaround time for jobs. By filling in the holes left in the machine by completed jobs but continuing to honor the highest-priority jobs, use is maximized while fairly honoring the start time of jobs that are ready to run next in the queue.

Moab also provides several other features that assist with the management of INCITE allocations. Using the identity manager, Moab imports priorities for each INCITE project to provide a sliding negative priority once the project has reached its allocated hours. Using this method projects over allocation are not prevented from running, but will run only if no other projects with allocated hours remaining are running. Projects can easily be given reservations or priority boosts based on upcoming deadlines or debugging needs.

Another key feature being employed to provide partitioning of the system for scheduling nodes with GPUs is called standing reservations. By using a standing reservation, separate scheduling policies are being used to provide quicker turnaround time for application development on nodes with GPUs as preparations are under way for Titan. This standing reservation allows more jobs per user to be considered for scheduling compared to the standard production policies applied to other jobs that are using nodes with only CPUs. Standing reservations can also be used to schedule future events such as maintenance periods and dedicated runs.

The scheduler is critical software necessary for getting work done on the machine and providing the mechanisms for controlling job policies important to the site. Getting it wrong can certainly lead to an unhappy set of users, while getting it right maximizes the investment and provides fairness to each of the users.

## 15.5 Programming System

### 15.5.1 Programming Models

The Titan Cray XK7 system currently has 18,688 compute nodes. Each node contains a single 16-core AMD processor with 32 gigabytes of shared memory and a Kepler GPU. This gives Titan a peak performance of more than 20 petaflops. A significant number of flops will come from the GPUs, with a nontrivial portion residing on the CPUs. Making effective use of Titan will require CPU and GPU programming languages and compilers as well as scientific applications with programming models that can effectively exploit the multiple levels of parallelism within the system.

The current dominant programming model on Jaguar is the traditional all-message passing interface (MPI), in which each assigned core is assigned an MPI task. The all-MPI model exploits only the CPUs, which leaves all Jaguar's GPU resources unused. Obviously this programming model will not be ideal for Titan. The second-most-popular programming model is the hybrid MPI/OpenMP. Each node is generally assigned a single MPI task to exploit the inter-compute-node parallelism, and OpenMP is applied within each node to exploit the intra-compute-node parallelism. Not all of the GPU resources of Jaguar and Titan are used, however, which is undesirable. Currently the third-most-used programming model on Jaguar is the hybrid model of MPI/GPU. Each node is assigned MPI tasks with each MPI task performing GPU calculations on the node. And finally, the fourth-most-used programming model on Jaguar is the MPI/OpenMP/GPU model, in which each node is assigned an MPI task, OpenMP is done within each node, and GPU computations are done within each OpenMP thread.

These hybrid MPI/GPU and MPI/OpenMP/GPU programming models make effective use of Jaguar, and future Titan resource allocations will strongly favor projects with scientific allocations that use these hybrid GPU/CPU models. Use of GPUs in HPC is a relatively recent advance, and consequently the number of scientific applications using hybrid CPU/GPU programming is relatively small. Therefore, to prepare the scientific community for Titan, the upgrade of Jaguar was not limited to just hardware, but also included programming languages and compilers to facilitate the development of hybrid CPU/GPU–enabled programs.

## 15.5.2   Languages and Compilers

The primary CPU programming languages on Jaguar are FORTRAN, C, and C++, of which FORTRAN is the most commonly used. To this extent Jaguar has available the PGI, GNU, and Cray compilers, of which PGI is the default. All support the OpenMP extensions. C++ is currently the least used language on Jaguar, but its use is increasing.

With respect to GPU programming on Jaguar, there are three ways to program or exploit the accelerator that broadly differ due to the levels of interface with the GPU: GPU accelerated libraries, accelerator directives, and high-level GPU languages. GPU accelerated libraries are the highest level of interface to the GPU device. A few examples are Magma, a dense linear algebra library designed for hybrid architectures; CULA, a set of GPU-accelerated linear algebra libraries; and CuBLAS, an implementation of Basic Linear Algebra GPU-enabled algorithms.

Accelerator compiler directives provide a way of describing the parallelism in an application so that the compiler can generate the appropriate instructions for the underlying hardware. The emerging standard set of directives, called OpenACC, was announced at the SC11 conference. Cray, PGI, and CAPS all have compilers that can interpret OpenACC directives and generate code for the NVIDIA accelerators.

The lowest-level interface to the GPU is accelerator programming languages, which come in three types. The first type is NVIDIA CUDA C/C++, which extends C and provides control over the accelerator without directly interacting with it. The second is PGI CUDA FORTRAN, which enables CUDA programming directly in FORTRAN. Finally, an OpenCL programming interface exists with support for PGI or GNU compilers.

## 15.5.3   Tools

A programming environment (PE) is defined as the software stack that supports the application development cycle for one or more programming models. A typical PE consists of compilers, programming languages, libraries, debuggers, and performance tools unified within a common infrastructure.

During the design of ORNL's Cray GPU-based system, Titan, ORNL tools developers encountered several challenges. First, there was no production-ready PE for rapidly porting codes to a hybrid GPU-based system that could meet petascale-level performance. Second, it was not clear what the right programming model was and what tools would be necessary to support a massive, hybrid architecture like Titan's. As a result developers were tasked with assessing the current state of the art in the area of tools to select the suite of them that would be necessary to build an effective PE ecosystem to meet the demanding needs of OLCF-3 applications. In addition to commonly available commodity tools, the ecosystem consists of highly customized compilers, performance tools, debuggers, source-code analyzers, and GPU libraries specifically built for Titan. Table 15.6 provides a list of tools in the Titan PE, and an asterisk indicates tools that were customized and enhanced specifically for Titan.

After giving careful consideration to both productivity and performance, the tools developers decided that a hybrid programming model, one in which programs can be written to support different levels of abstraction in terms of communication libraries (or PGAS languages), combined with shared memory directives (e.g., OpenMP) and/or accelerator-programming APIs (OpenACC) and languages (OpenCL, CUDA) would allow application developers to take maximum advantage of Titan with minimal porting effort. The most technically challenging aspect was to design a standard de facto GPU accelerator directive API, as none existed when the effort began. To accomplish this feat the ORNL team worked closely with the Cray compiler group, CAPS-Enterprise, and PGI. Their effort led to the de facto standardization of OpenACC, a set of compiler-based directives targeted at NVIDIA GPUs. As a result Cray, CAPS, and PGI support OpenACC, with NVIDIA strongly supporting this effort. Of the three compiler vendors, the OLCF opted to work closely with CAPS-Enterprise because its GPU directive solution, which uses a source-to-source strategy for the translation of GPU directives, was the most advanced in terms of features, functionality, performance, and portability across compilers. CAPS also provided ORNL with a framework for the lab's scientists to help them understand how the directives are translated to OpenCL, CUDA, or other future accelerator standards. Enhancements to the CAPS-Enterprise GPU directives included support for data distribution and unified virtual addressing among GPUs/CPU, pointers inside GPU kernels, interprocedural data mirrors, C++, OpenMP, and GPU library compatibility. These enhancements stemmed from application studies and their needs.

The other challenge for Titan's PE was to provide a scalable, hybrid-aware debugger. The goal was to provide a debugger capable of handling petascale runs, while summarizing (reducing) and presenting meaningful information to the user. By employing sophisticated tree topologies, Allinea, working with ORNL, deployed the first petascale-level debugger, DDT, for Titan. Field tested on actual development codes at ORNL, DDT has been shown to scale to more than 200,000 cores. Allinea has applied a codesign methodology, working closely with compiler vendors that support the languages for Titan, to include GPU directives and languages. As a result DDT was designed from the ground up for large-scale hybrid systems. In addition to MPI/OpenMP parallel programs, DDT is fully supported on NVIDA GPUs and capable of stepping into GPU kernels with multiwarp stepping abilities. A scalable mechanism was designed to debug and visualize stacks and to merge variable stacks with the same values. In addition, DDT is now capable of stepping into GPU directives regions. The debugger was extended with CUDA memory-debugging capabilities, allowing the user to visualize the physical memory layout of his or her codes and its distribution over both the host and device memory.

The main performance-analysis tool for hybrid parallel applications is the Vampir toolset and CrayPat. The Vampir toolset consists of three major components: the Open Trace Format (OTF) library, VampirTrace, and Vampir. VampirTrace is used in the prerun phase to prepare the application source code to gather events during a run. At runtime VampirTrace processes the events and passes them to the OTF library. The visualization and analysis components of the Vampir toolset are the Vampir client and server, respectively. The purpose of the server is to analyze the trace in parallel and aggregate enough main memory on the compute nodes to open/load the trace. The client visualizes the data analyzed and transferred by the server and offers a variety of methods to interact with the trace (e.g., scrolling, zooming, and highlighting areas of interest). Developers selected the Vampir toolset for Titan's PE because its framework was designed to be highly scalable. To enhance the Vampir toolset for Titan, they identified four major areas of improvement: (1) support for GPU performance tracing, (2) improved I/O, (3) tracing scalability, and (4) the user-interface presentation of traces of large-scale runs. One of the more important enhancements has been improving MPI behavior of VampirServer, which now enables a user to effectively analyze a trace of an application that utilizes the entire Titan system.

**TABLE 15.6**: Tools supported in Titan's programming environment.

| Compilers | Performance Tools | GPU Libraries | Debuggers | Source Code Analyzers | Operating Systems | File Systems | Scheduler |
|---|---|---|---|---|---|---|---|
| Cray (*) | CrayPAT (*) | MAGMA (*) | DDT Debugger (*) | HMPP Wizard(*) | CLE | Lustre NFS | Moab |
| PGI | Vampir Trace/ | CULA (*) | NVIDIA gdb | Wizard (*) | | NFS | |
| CAPS/HMPP(*) | Vampir (*) | Trillinos (*) | Parallel NSIGHT | Apprentice(*) | | | |
| PATHSCALE | TAU | | | | | | |
| NVIDIA | HPCToolkit | | | | | | |
| GNU | CUDA Profiler | | | | | | |
| INTEL | | | | | | | |

* Tools customized and enhanced specifically for Titan.

Furthermore, a new display was implemented to directly compare two or more traces. This display enables the time-wise alignment of the traces and visualization of common Vampir displays next to each other.

## 15.6  Storage, Visualization, and Analytics

**High-Performance and Archival Storage.** Spider, a center-wide, shared filesystem provides disk storage for most OLCF systems. This shared filesystem is based on Lustre, DDN, and InfiniBand and provides centralized access to petascale data sets from all major computational platforms. Past experience showed that many data transfers were performed between the supercomputer and satellite clusters where users processed the results. The shared workspace provided by Spider has eliminated the need for manual transfers and multiple copies of large data volumes.

Delivering more than 240 gigabytes per second of aggregate performance, scalability to more than 26,000 filesystem clients, and storage capacity of more than 10 petabytes, Spider is one of the world's largest-scale Lustre filesystems. It consists of 48 DDN 9900 storage arrays managing 13,440 1-terabyte SATA drives and 192 Dell dual-socket quad-core I/O servers providing more than 14 teraflops of performance and more than 3 terabytes of system memory. Metadata are stored on two LSI Engino 7900s (XBB2) and served by three Dell quad-socket quad-core systems. ORNL systems are interconnected to Spider via a DDR InfiniBand system area network that consists of four 288-port Cisco 7024D InfiniBand switches and more than three miles of optical cables.

The work filesystem provides temporary storage, and the center regularly purges it of files more than two weeks old. Users are reminded to use the High Performance Storage System (HPSS) for archiving their important data. HPSS is capable of archiving hundreds of petabytes of data and can be accessed by all major leadership computing platforms. Incoming data are written to disk and later migrated to tape for long-term archival storage. This hierarchical infrastructure provides high-performance data transfers while leveraging cost-effective tape technologies. The center has four SL8500 robotic tape libraries, holding up to 10,000 cartridges each, and has plans to deploy a sixth SL8500 this year. The libraries house a total of 24 T10K-A tape drives (500-gigabyte cartridges, uncompressed), 64 T10K-B tape drives (1-terabyte cartridges, uncompressed), and 36 T10K-C tape drives (5-terabyte cartridges, uncompressed). Each A and B model drive is capable of reading/writing at a rate of 120 megabytes per second, whereas each C model drive is capable of 240 megabytes per second. ORNL's HPSS disk storage is provided by DDN storage arrays with more than 2 petabytes of capacity and greater than 12 gigabytes per second of bandwidth. This infrastructure has allowed ORNL's archival system to scale to meet increasingly demanding capacity and bandwidth requirements with more than 29 petabytes of data stored as of October 2012.

ORNL has several levels of support to facilitate efficient use of the storage system. First, the OLCF provides I/O libraries (e.g., ADIOS [LZKS09], HDF5, NetCDF) and tools as modules for all supported compilers. User Assistance helps users with problems using these modules. However, as applications run at scale, they run into I/O scaling problems they have not faced before. On the second level, members of the Scientific Computing Group, which provides liaison personnel to each project using OLCF resources, help users identify and fix their problems. On the third level, the Scientific Computing Group has a special team, called End-to-End Task, to address the I/O needs of the largest applications. This team has developed the ADIOS I/O framework that scales well on parallel systems.

The OLCF designed an application I/O solution for parallel filesystems. It has been developed based on constant interaction with developers of large-scale simulations from many domains, such as computer science, nuclear physics, combustion, and astrophysics. The primary focus was ultimate performance for typical I/O scenarios while maintaining a simple API for a self-describing data format. The result is ADIOS, a modular I/O framework, which provides several methods (different strategies) for performing I/O, which allows users to choose the best-performing one for their needs. The file format aligns well with parallel filesystems, avoiding much of the interference caused by the large number of data producers accessing a limited number of disk resources. It also provides a self-describing data format (i.e., one can discover the content of a file [variable names, types, and array sizes] and query arbitrary subsets of it). The End-to-End team has helped dozens of applications running at OLCF improve their I/O performance, typically with a ten-times improvement for applications that had already tried various solutions and even more improvement for other applications that were facing the I/O bottleneck for the first time.

**Visualization and Collaboration.** The Visualization Task was created to help researchers gain a better understanding of their data through visualization techniques. It seeks out and engages with projects at the OLCF and with collaborators who might benefit from applying visual data-understanding techniques to scientific data and to find ways of doing visualization that are different, are more effective, and better integrate with other research activities at the center.

ORNL's state-of-the-art visualization facilities can be used on site or accessed remotely. ORNL's **E**xploratory **V**isualization **E**nvironment for **RE**search in **S**cience and **T**echnology (EVEREST) is a large-scale venue for data exploration and visualization. The EVEREST room is undergoing renovation and will be completely reconfigured by January 2013. The EVEREST room contains two large-format displays. The primary display is a 30.5′ × 8.5′ tiled wall containing 18 individual displays and an aggregate pixel count of 37 million pixels. It is capable of displaying interactive stereo 3D imagery for an immersive user experience. The secondary display is a 13.5′ × 7.6′ tiled display containing 16 individual panels, and an aggregate pixel count of 33 million pixels. Both displays may be operated independently, providing the ability to view two or more sources of information simultaneously. The EVEREST displays are controlled by both a dedicated Linux cluster and by "fat nodes" allowing the display of information from commodity hardware and software. The diversity of display and control systems allows for a wide array of uses, from interactive and deep exploration of scientific datasets to engaging scientific communication to the public. A dedicated Lustre filesystem provides high bandwidth data delivery to the EVEREST power wall. ORNL also provides Lens, a 77-"fat node" cluster dedicated to data analysis and visualization. The Lens cluster has been demonstrated with a variety of commercial off-the-shelf software and open-source visualization tools including VisIt, Paraview, CEI Ensight, and AVS-Express. The Everest cluster rendering environment utilizes Chromium and Distributed Multi-Head X (DMX) for tiled, parallel rendering. The Lens cluster cross mounts the Center-wide Lustre filesystem to allow "zero copy" access to simulation data from other OLCF computational resources. The EVEREST facility will complete a significant upgrade late in 2012 that will provide state-of-the-art visualization and rendering facilities to the user community.

The OLCF formed a dedicated visualization team to assist users in solving visualization and data-interpretation issues. Support ranges from assisting users in displaying data on the EVEREST PowerWall to writing custom visualization tools for specialized needs to producing production-quality images and movies for publications and public relations.

As scientific simulations scale up exponentially, so does the pressure on processes and tools for making use of the data. Even with the largest and fastest filesystem, shared between multiple resources through a fast network infrastructure, the users increasingly face bottlenecks in their post-processing pipeline. Analysis and visualization tasks are spending an increasingly larger ratio of their runtime reading data from files. Also, users have to avoid producing all the data they would potentially like to in the first place to be able to scale their application and produce results with their post-processing pipeline. Because I/O bandwidth is growing much more slowly than computing performance, this problem is becoming more prevalent among users with each update of the computing resources.

The OLCF is committed to developing tools that enable researchers to efficiently manage, analyze, and visualize simulation results. Current development efforts aim at creating a unified analytics and visualization framework that integrates application I/O; analysis; and interactive, parallel visualization within the staging (memory-to-memory) environment provided by ADIOS. Users will be able to schedule analysis tasks that process the output of the simulation on the fly as well as perform exploratory visualization with VisIt or ParaView without creating files. This approach will enable production of orders of magnitude more data than is currently processed before a filtered, smaller data set is written to files on disk.

## 15.7   Computing Facility

ORNL operates three petascale computing facilities: the OLCF manages the computing program at ORNL for DOE, while the National Institute for Computational Sciences (NICS) runs the computing facility for the National Science Foundation. ORNL also manages the National Climate Computing Research Center (NCRC) for the National Oceanographic and Atmospheric Administration (NOAA). Each has a professional, experienced operational and engineering staff composed of groups in HPC operations, technology integration, user services, scientific computing, and application performance tools. The ORNL computer facility staff provides continuous operation of the center and immediate problem resolution. On evenings and weekends, operators provide first-line problem resolution for users, with additional user support and system administrators on call for more difficult problems.

The facility contains 40,000 square feet of raised floor computer room space in two equally spaced areas. Total electrical capacity to computer and related systems in this facility is 25 megavolt-amperes. Six thousand six hundred tons of chilled water in the primary central energy plant provide chilled water in a highly flexible configuration to cooling systems and directly to the largest computer systems. The electrical distribution system is hardened, with multiple 161-kilovolt-ampere feeds from the power utility, and multiple 13,800-kilovolt-ampere utility feeds from separate substations to the facility. The chilled water distribution system is hardened, with five separate chillers in one facility and large-capacity connections to two adjacent facilities such that chilled water can be distributed among other computing facilities as needed.

To prepare for the Titan system, the original electrical distribution system was revised from a total of three 2.5/3.5-megavolt-ampere transformers to four transformers. The new transformer provides an additional 3.5/4.5-megavolt-ampere. These changes will accommodate an anticipated short-term application-based load of up to 53 kilowatts per cabinet and a steady-state load of more than 44 kilowatts per cabinet. The increase in generated heat load required a small adjustment to the chilled water system that increased the maximum chilled water flow rate to Cray ECOphlex cooling system. Each of the 48 Liebert XDPs is now rate-limited to 130 gallons per minute at 42 degrees Fahrenheit.

The addition of the Kepler-based accelerator also necessitated physical changes to a number of components, including the internal power supply system, blower assembly, and physical plenum that delivers inlet air to the system.

**Physical and Cybersecurity.** ORNL has a comprehensive physical security strategy including fenced perimeters, patrolled facilities, and authorization checks for physical access. An integrated cybersecurity plan encompasses all aspects of computing. Cybersecurity plans are risk-based. Separate systems of differing security requirements allow the appropriate level of protection for each system, while not hindering the science needs of the projects.

**Network Connectivity.** The ORNL campus has access to every major research network at rates of 10 gigabits per second or greater. Layer 1 connectivity to these networks is provided via optical networking equipment owned and operated by UT-Battelle LLC that runs over leased fiber-optic cable. This equipment has the capability of carrying multiple 10-, 40-, or 100-gigabit-per-second circuits and is used extensively as the last-mile solution to connect the LCF to major networking hubs in Nashville, Atlanta, and Chicago. Currently, twenty of the 10-gigabit circuits and two of the 40-gigabit circuits are committed to various purposes, providing virtually unlimited expansion of the networking capability. ORNL is participating in the DOE/ESnet Advanced Networking Initiative (ANI) that provides a native 100-gigabit optical network connection among DOE-SC sites including ORNL, Argonne National Laboratory, Lawrence Berkeley National Laboratory, and other facilities in the northeast. The 100-gigabit connection will become primary in late 2012. Additional connections into ORNL include the National Science Foundation XSEDE and the University of Tennessee. To meet the increasingly demanding needs of data transfers between major facilities, ORNL has provisioned extra capacity into the border and wide-area-network infrastructures to accommodate substantial growth.

The local-area network is a common physical infrastructure that supports separate logical networks, each with varying levels of security and performance. Each of these networks is protected from the outside world and from each other with access control lists and network intrusion detection. Line rate connectivity is provided between the networks and to the outside world via redundant paths and switching fabrics. A tiered security structure is designed into the network to mitigate many attacks and to contain others.

# Chapter 16

## Blacklight: Coherent Shared Memory for Enabling Science

**Nick Nystrom, Joel Welling, and Phil Blood**

*Pittsburgh Supercomputing Center*

**Eng Lim Goh**

*SGI*

## 16.1    Background

### 16.1.1    Motivation

Data-intensive analysis and simulation are essential for advancing our understanding of science, engineering, the environment, health, public policy, sociology, and the interactions of complex systems. Prodigious volumes of data are created by simulations, stream from instruments, and arise from complex networks. Date-intensive science is widely recognized as a new paradigm for discovery [HTT09], complementing the prior cornerstones of theory, experiment, and simulation. Many important classes of data-intensive analyses and simulations require large shared memory.

Also critical to many analysis tasks is human productivity. This element takes several forms. First, various communities have not traditionally used HPC because they work with large, complex code bases written in Java. They build on robust class libraries to advance their fields of research, and they benefit greatly from large amounts of memory and large numbers of threads to handle data sets that would otherwise be intractable. Second, high-productivity programming models and languages such as OpenMP, MATLAB, Python, and R allow rapid prototyping, efficiently testing algorithms, and scaling workstation-sized applications to larger data sets. Third, large shared memory allows execution of ISV and third-party applications, for example in engineering and quantum chemistry, to scale to more memory and more threads.

Taking those factors into account, the Pittsburgh Supercomputing Center (PSC) designed Blacklight,[LRN10] an SGI® UV-1000 consisting of 4,096 Intel® Xeon® Nehalem-EX cores and $2 \times 16$ TB of hardware-enabled, cache-coherent shared memory connected by a full bisection bandwidth NUMAlink$^{TM}$ 5 interconnect, both to enable memory-intensive computation and to increase users' productivity. Memory-intensive computation can change the way we interact with data through graph analytics, machine learning, scaling out shared-memory applications, and interactive data exploration and visualization. Increasing users' productivity reduces the time from concept to implementation, allowing rapid testing of hypotheses. Extending existing code bases to new, large analyses, rapidly prototyping and developing algorithms, and running ISV applications at larger scales each extend researchers' capability at essentially no effort beyond that which would be required for similar activities, but at drastically smaller scale, on a workstation.

Blacklight was acquired as part of an NSF technology refresh program, replacing PSC's Pople, an SGI Altix 4700 having 1.5 TB of hardware-enabled, cache-coherent shared memory. Pople had been extremely popular with users for its shared memory and ease of use. Blacklight took those features to a new level, increasing shared memory from 1.5 TB to $2 \times 16$ TB, hardware threads from 768 to $2 \times 4,096$, and transitioning from the ia64 (Itanium) instruction set to x86 (Xeon). The scope of the technology refresh solicitation that led to Blacklight was of moderate size, allowing optimization of the architecture's unique quality, namely coherent shared memory, rather than peak flops.

### 16.1.2    A Brief History of PSC

The Pittsburgh Supercomputing Center is a joint effort of Carnegie Mellon University, the University of Pittsburgh, and Westinghouse Electric Company. PSC was founded in 1986 by Ralph Roskies (co-Scientific Director and Professor of Physics, University of Pittsburgh), and Professor Michael Levine (co-Scientific Director and Professor or Physics, Carnegie Mellon), and Jim Kasdorf (then, Westinghouse; now, PSC Director of Special Projects).

**FIGURE 16.1**: Blacklight, in PSC's machine room.

PSC's offices are on the Carnegie Mellon campus, and it operates a remote machine room (Figure 16.1).

PSC provides an integrated, flexible environment for solving large-scale computational problems, advances science and technology through collaborative and internal research, educates researchers on the benefits of HPC and data-intensive computing, and improves competitiveness of industry through use of computational science. To support those activities, PSC provides both general and domain-specific training in computational science, technology briefings, and other forms of outreach.

PSC is a founding member and service provider in XSEDE, the Extreme Science and Engineering Discovery Environment (http://www.xsede.org). In XSEDE, PSC currently co-leads (with SDSC) the Extended Collaborative Support Service (ECSS) and leads Novel and Innovative Projects (NIP; part of ECSS), the Technology Insertion Service (TIS), Allocations, and Security. PSC's emphasis on user support greatly enhances researchers' ability to achieve breakthroughs on its leadership-class computational resources, which are carefully tailored to meet upcoming requirements.

PSC also houses the National Resource for Biomedical Supercomputing (NRBSC; http://www.nrbsc.org), which advances biomedical research and provides outreach to the national biomedical research community. Research at NRBSC is currently centered in three areas: computational structural biology and bioinformatics, computational microphysiology and cell modeling, and large-scale volumetric data visualization and analysis. Through the NRBSC, PSC operates Anton, a special-purpose supercomputer for molecular dynamics simulation designed by D. E. Shaw Research (DESRES). Allocations on this 512-node

Anton machine were made available without cost by DESRES for non-commercial research use.

Throughout its 26 years, PSC has deployed many very early HPC platforms, often "serial number 1," as illustrated in Figure 16.2; each of those systems has led to scientific breakthroughs. These systems have included the following:

- Cray X-MP: Air quality control strategies for Los Angeles (Gregory McRae, Armistead Russell, and Jana Milford).

- Cray Y-MP: Protein-DNA recognition in Eco RI endonuclease (John Rosenberg).

- TMC CM-2: Oil reservoir simulation (Ernest Chung).

- TMC CM-5: Parallel solution of the phase problem in X-ray crystallography (Herbert Hauptman and Russ Miller).

- Cray T3D: First application of PME to treat electrostatics in DNA (Peter Kollman and Thomas Cheatham).

- *LeMieux*: Operation of the bacterial large conductance mechanosensitive channel (Klaus Schulten and Justin Gullingsrud).

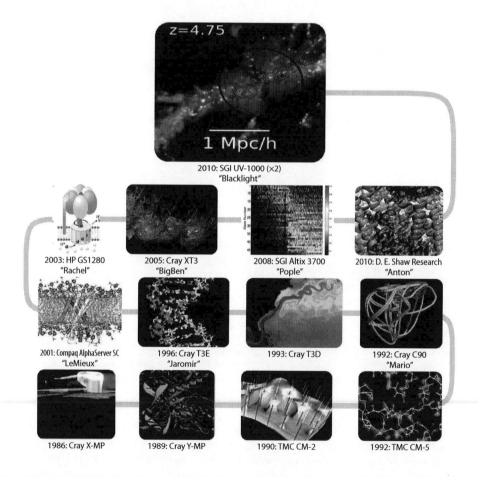

**FIGURE 16.2**: PSC system history. Details for these projects and others are available in PSC's *Projects in Scientific Computing* (http://www.psc.edu/science/).

- *Jaromir*: First correct prediction of the Gulf Stream in modeling the Atlantic Ocean (Matt O'Keefe and Aaron Sawdey).

- *Mario*: A fully functioning 3D computational model of the heart, its valves, and nearby major vessels (Charles Peskin).

- *Rachel*: Understanding the role of ATPase in metabolism (Klaus Schulten and Markus Dittrich).

- *BigBen*: Strong scaling and interactivity for understanding turbulence (Paul Woodward and David Porter).

- *Pople*: Exposing vulnerability in online information (Alessandro Acquisti and Ralph Gross).

- *Anton*: Water, along with a galactose substrate molecule, passing through a membrane transporter protein (Emad Tajkhorshid).

- *Blacklight*: Understanding rapid formation of supermassive black holes (Tiziana Di Matteo, Rupert Croft, Yu Feng, and Nishikanta Khandai).

The computational resource is only one factor in enabling those breakthroughs: other factors include PSC enhancements to let users realize the new system's full potential and in-depth consulting to maximize performance and to streamline challenging workflows. For example, in the context of Blacklight, PSC led optimization of I/O through use of memory-resident filesystems and developed the Data Supercell (Section 16.7.1) to provide high-bandwidth, low-latency, long-term storage, thereby breaking away from the "write-once, read never" model that often applies to magnetic tape. Also on Blacklight, tight collaboration with PSC allowed researchers to build an interactive, terapixel visualization of the MassiveBlack simulation of the early universe [FDMC11].

### 16.1.3 Blacklight Timeline

PSC's Blacklight system was designed in early 2010, following earlier consideration of the SGI UV architecture for its applicability to NSF's diverse workload.

For any new or unique supercomputer, it is vital to begin testing, integration of the site-specific production environment, and application development well ahead of system deployment. Proactively beginning those activities very early exposes and allows the resolution of issues that otherwise would go unnoticed until delivery of the production system.

To streamline bringing Blacklight into production, PSC installed a precursor system, "Herbie," on July 12, 2010. Herbie consisted of 160 cores and 640 GB of shared memory, corresponding to 4% of Blacklight's total cores and 4 GB of memory per core (half the memory per core of Blacklight). Although only a small fraction of Blacklight's 4,096 cores and 16 TB of shared memory per SSI (32 TB total), Herbie proved invaluable for integration with other PSC systems, early applications work, conducting a "friendly user" period in which external users could gain experience with the architecture, and configuring an effective production environment. Herbie ran the full software stack that would be on Blacklight, including OpenMP, p-threads, UPC, MPI, C, C++, Fortran, Java, etc. Herbie also ran PSC's *Simon* scheduler, accounting systems, and *modules* environment.

Following one day of installation and system testing, Herbie was opened to PSC staff on July 13. Within five minutes of announcing Herbie's availability, Shawn Brown ran the first application on PSC's UV. That application "FRED," is an agent-based epidemiology code used to model, for example, the spread of H1N1 influenza. Shortly thereafter on the same day, several of the other applications run on Herbie were MILC (quantum chromo-dynamics), NAMD (molecular dynamics), GAMESS (quantum chemistry), GADGETGPM (cosmology), and FLUENT (computational fluid dynamics).

On July 14, two days after installation, the first "friendly user" was granted access to Herbie. There were 43 additional friendly users granted access from July 14 through September 14.

Blacklight was delivered and installed on September 15, 2010, by which time 79 friendly users had begun work on Herbie. Friendly users were transitioned from Herbie to Blacklight on October 25.

Herbie traveled to New Orleans for SC10, running a suite of applications in PSC's booth from November 15–18.

Blacklight entered production on January 18, 2011.

## 16.2    Applications and Workloads

Blacklight is a resource on XSEDE. XSEDE allocations are to be awarded preferentially to projects that can make appropriate use of each resource, which in the case of Blacklight typically entails needing some element of large shared memory, many threads, and/or high-productivity programming models.

Many leading applications on Blacklight are from communities that have not traditionally used HPC. This is an excellent outcome, given that Blacklight was designed to support new kinds of research. The new uses of Blacklight include, for example, assembly of very large genomes, machine learning to automate generation of inferences from data found on the Web, natural language processing, development of strategies for games that are characterized by incomplete knowledge, quantum chemistry calculations requiring terabytes of memory from modest numbers of threads, and analysis of stock trading data. These applications have one or more of the following characteristics:

- **Large, coherent shared memory**
  Hardware-enabled, large, coherent shared memory allows low-latency access to remote memory with cache-line (64B) granularity. This is very powerful for dynamic, irregular algorithms such as are found throughout graph analytics. In addition to accelerating that difficult class of algorithms, 16 TB of coherent shared memory allows analyses that would otherwise be intractable, for example, genome sequence assemblies requiring 5 TB or more.

- **High thread count**
  Up to 4,096 hardware threads can be run on each of Blacklight's 2,048-core SSIs. This has proven valuable, for example, for sophisticated game-theoretic analyses to determine effective strategies in multiagent, stochastic environments with hidden information.

- **High-productivity programming languages**
  Many novel, data-intensive applications, especially in computer science, leverage substantial code bases written in Java. While Java is not a "traditional HPC" language, its value for human productivity is substantial due to the powerful class libraries that have emerged. Blacklight uniquely enables capability Java applications in at least two ways. First, any Java application can access 16 TB of memory, greatly accelerating

complex graph analytics on large data sets, for example, ClueWeb09 [Cal], which requires $\tilde{5}$ TB in compressed form or $\tilde{2}5$ TB uncompressed. Other projects rely on R, MATLAB, Python, and other languages for important parts of their analysis workflows. Of particular note, a commonly cited limitation of R is that its data must fit in RAM. Clearly, $2 \times 16$ TB on Blacklight significantly extends what is possible.

- **Rapid prototyping**
  OpenMP is widely used on Blacklight for rapidly testing ideas and algorithms and for conducting one-time analyses. When the highest performance is not critical, many developers find OpenMP to be easier to use than MPI. An example of OpenMP use on Blacklight is for developing and testing new algorithms for cosmology.

- **ISV applications**
  Blacklight's x86 processors and standard Linux operating system support an extremely broad range of independent software vendor (ISV) applications. Even more important is the additional value that Blacklight lends to those applications. Modifying commercial or other third-party applications is often impossible, impractical, or disallowed, but by running them on Blacklight, more ambitious simulations and analyses immediately and transparently become possible through accessing more memory and/or more threads. This is especially true for applications having their roots in the workstation market, for which scalable distributed-memory implementations often have not yet been developed.

The overall workload of Blacklight is highly diverse. Applications using the largest amounts of memory include (among others): genome sequence assembly (many projects), quantum chemistry, machine learning, social science, mesh generation, materials science, quantum physics, cosmology, optical properties of nanoparticles, natural language processing, convection in the Earth, genome sequence annotation, algorithms for image and video analysis, malware triage, financial analysis, and epidemiology. Considering also applications that use significant time, molecular dynamics, climate change, neuroscience, neural networks, carbon sequestration, weather, data preparation for terascale visualization, and many other fields also figure prominently.

## 16.2.1   Highlights of Main Applications

The following sections describe Blacklight's value for several repesentative applications where large shared memory, threaded programming models, and human productivity are enabling data-intensive analysis.

### 16.2.1.1   Genomics

Rapid advances in DNA sequencing technologies (next-generation sequencing [SJ08]) together with advances in *de novo* genome assembly algorithms are creating unprecedented opportunities to, among other things, determine the genome sequence of new organisms [Gen], understand the basis of human disease [LZR$^+$10], and uncover microbial diversity in human beings and the environment [QLR$^+$10]. In next-generation sequencing, DNA is broken into many short segments, which can be read by automated sequencers. The *de novo* genome assembly problem then entails reassembling millions or billions of short sequence reads into a single, large genome. Current *de novo* genome assembly applications, such as Velvet [ZB08] and ALLPATHS-LG [GMP$^+$11], do this by building a de Bruijn graph of short sequences of length $k$ ("$k$-mers") and using the sequence reads to trace paths through the graph. The massive amounts of memory required to construct these large graphs has presented a major obstacle to large-scale genome assembly. SGI Altix UV systems with several terabytes of shared memory are helping remove barriers to large-scale genome assembly in several important areas of genomics research. This section will highlight three areas of genomics research that are beginning to benefit from the UV architecture: *de novo* assembly of large genomes, metagenomics, and transcriptome assembly from RNA sequence data.

### *De novo* assembly of individual genomes

With the low cost of sequence data, there has been a push to sequence the genomes of thousands of organisms [Gen, I5k], including thousands of different human genomes [100]. This creates two analysis bottlenecks: first, the number of large genomes that need to be assembled is a challenge, and second, many important genomes simply require too much memory to attempt on lab resources. Currently, if they are fortunate, labs doing genome assembly have access to large workstations with 48 cores and 512 GB of RAM. On such a workstation, in takes about a month (and all available memory) to assemble the genome the size of the human genome (3 gigabase pairs, or 3 Gbp). The availability of a large shared memory UV system enables researchers to process many large genomes simultaneously, relieving a significant analysis bottleneck. Blacklight, with 16 TB of shared memory, can enable the assembly of important genomes that are much larger than human genomes. To assemble the 16 Gbp wheat genome, for example, would require approximately 5 TB of RAM. The loblolly pine, an important tree species that provides 16% of the world's lumber [Nea04], is even larger, at 22 Gbp. Beyond the memory required solely for assembly, additional RAM, readily available on Blacklight, is valuable for greatly reducing I/O times by staging files to memory-based filesystems.

### Metagenomics

The field of *metagenomics* aims to help address health, environmental, energy, and other pressing issues by more completely characterizing and understanding the microbial diversity in various environments on the planet [WGF10, QLR$^+$10, HSE$^+$11]. The initial step in this process is the sampling of microbes in their native environment and directly sequencing and then assembling all the genetic material in that sample into a *metagenome*. Metagenome assemblies are particularly memory-intensive due to the wide variety of species in the sample. One reason for this is that the size of de Bruijn graphs grows with the number of unique $k$-mers, which is larger for a highly diverse microbial sample than for a single organism. In addition, a vast amount of sequencing data must be generated to properly sample rare species in a given microbial community. Recently researchers completed a metagenome assembly of several billion reads on Blacklight using Velvet, which required 3.5 TB of memory; however, given an architecture like UV, it is conceivable that researchers might eventually try to assemble terabases of metagenomics data using many terabytes of memory.

### Transcriptomics

Next-generation sequencing technology can be applied to obtain the sequences of the total set of RNA molecules expressed in a given cell or collection of cells under certain conditions: the transcriptome [WGS09]. This methodology, termed RNA-Seq, can illuminate what factors control specific responses in cells, including the causes of disease. In particular, de novo assembly of RNA-Seq data has become a powerful tool for obtaining and studying transcriptomes since it can be used when a reference genome for the organism of interest is not available. Like de novo genome assemblers, the Trinity [GHY$^+$] de novo RNA-Seq assembler builds de Bruijn graphs to generate complete RNA transcripts from short read data. As in de novo genome assembly, this approach requires vast memory. Some researchers are even looking at taking metagenomics one step further and sampling the total gene expression of multiple organisms at once, yielding metatranscriptomics. Once again, in many cases the limiting factor in these projects is the availability (or knowledge) of large platforms with sufficient shared memory to tackle these tough problems. Indeed, since the availability of Trinity on Blacklight was posted on the Trinity website, Trinity has become one of the most requested applications for new allocations.

As researchers have become aware of the Blacklight UV system at PSC, they have begun to attempt projects that would have previously been unimaginable, but there is much more potential yet to be unlocked. So far, next-gen sequence assembly codes have been written primarily for large SMP workstations with tens of cores. As noted above, large assemblies on these workstations take weeks. Although larger assemblies (and greater quantities of assemblies) are possible on a large UV system, individual assemblies do not finish any faster than on a regular workstation due to the limited scalability of current codes. The Pittsburgh Supercomputing Center is working with application developers and researchers and other partners to improve the scalability of these codes. Once more scalable codes are available, the UV architecture will not only enable larger assemblies, it will significantly reduce the time required to assemble genomic and transcriptomic data.

### 16.2.1.2   Machine Learning

The large memory arena and traditional Linux operating system of the UV architecture make it a good match to the technical needs and traditional methods of the machine learning community. Codes from that community are often written in Java, a language with little penetration in the traditional supercomputing environment but with excellent support for thread-level parallelism. The ability to scale codes to large sizes without rewriting is a great help to an academic community that is only recently moving into the high performance computing environment. Traditional machine learning codes run on small department-level SMPs, or are distributed over clusters using MapReduce methods if the single SMPs prove inadequate. The use of MapReduce with large data corpora and iterative algorithms leads to poor performance as the data is repeatedly streamed from disk to the MapReduce processes.

Consider three tasks involved in machine learning from text, each at a different level in the data processing pipeline. A large text corpus must first be annotated, for example identifying noun phrases. Once annotations are available semantic information can be extracted, for example by looking for specific patterns relating noun phrases. Alternatively, processing of large sparse matrices of statistical data extracted from the corpus may be used for analyses like clustering and logistic regression.

The task of text annotation involves the training of classifiers in iterative cycles of testing against known examples, and the application of those classifiers to infer labels from much larger bodies of unlabeled text. For example, a Viterbi algorithm might assign labels, and then a global measure of the success of that assignment might be used to tune the weights used by the Viterbi algorithm. Keeping the full text in memory greatly speeds this iteration, and parallelization across threads within the memory arena is a natural way to accelerate the calculation of metrics like entropy across the many examples in the training data. Research codes written in Java already exist for these tasks, MinorThird being one example. The UV enviroment allows this process to be scaled up without recoding or retraining.

Given annotations and candidate patterns, relationships can be inferred between entities in the text. For example, "Sidney Crosby plays for the Penguins" matches the pattern "AthleteName plays for TeamName." If semantic data is available indicating that "Sidney Crosby" is an entity of type AthleteName, an inference can be made about the nature of the entity "the Penguins," and vice versa. Obviously not all references to penguins refer to athletes, however, so statistical methods must be used to combine multiple items of evidence discovered in a large database. It is this statistical synergy which makes analysis of large bodies of text so successful. The semantic ontologies used for this kind of inference are represented as large directed graphs. As inferences are made, the ontology graph is repeatedly accessed in response to patterns in the body of text. The Never-Ending Language Learner is a software system which uses these methods, simultaneously adding new beliefs to its ontology based on known patterns and inferring new patterns based on its known beliefs. The UV architecture is an excellent match to the needs for rapid graph traversal and rapid access to large bodies of text.

Operations on large sparse matrices are other tasks typical of machine learning. Typical example matrices might represent the number of times two words occur together in a large body of text, or the likelihood that a given person will like a given movie. Algorithms like logistic regression, singular value decomposition, or cluster analysis are then performed on these matrices. The sparsity of the matrices makes linear algebra methods developed for traditional supercomputing unsuitable. One tool developed for this class of problems is the GraphLab library. GraphLab exists in both shared-memory and distributed-memory versions, but the shared-memory version is better supported, more complete, and under more rapid development. This is an artifact of the programming environment in which the machine learning community is comfortable — large department-level SMPs — but it means that software developed for machine learning algorithms of this sort is a better fit for UV-type architectures than for more traditional supercomputers.

### 16.2.1.3   Interactive Analysis and Visualization

Blacklight is also valuable for interactive analysis and visualization where the appropriate algorithms traverse large memory in irregular ways. An example is tracing flux lines in 3D volumes, for which concurrency may be relatively modest, but the amount of data can be quite high.

Figure 16.3 is an example of a visualization performed on Blacklight by Homa Karimabadi (UCSD), whose petascale simulations on Kraken achieved, for the first time, realistic 3D modeling of magnetic reconnection [DRK+11]. To enable this work, PSC visualization staff produced a custom build of ParaView including Prof. Karimabadi's plug-ins. After transferring approximately 50 TB of data from Kraken, the Cray XT5 at the National Institute for Computational Sciences (NICS), reservations were made in PSC's scheduler to allow interactive, remote access. It was found that the required algorithms in ParaView worked well only when supplied with all 8 GB per core.

## 16.3   System Overview

Big data is characterized by its high volume, velocity, and variety. Volume is simply size, which today tends to range from tens of terabytes to petabytes. This will increase rapidly, with instruments that will produce petabytes per day already planned. Velocity refers to the high memory and I/O bandwidths that are required to process the high volumes. Computational intensity, the number of compute operations per byte of data, can be relatively low, reducing the opportunities for overlap. Variety refers to the many forms in which big data is produced and consumed: structured (e.g., in well-defined simulation data and certain data in databases), semi-structured (e.g., in databases containing certain text or blob data), or unstructured (e.g., loose collections of text, images, videos, and mixed-media documents).

Unstructured big data have been effectively analyzed via MapReduce, operating on a Hadoop scale-out platform that is typically low-cost servers connected by GigE or 10 GigE. With more structured data, and especially if low analysis latency is also required, computing

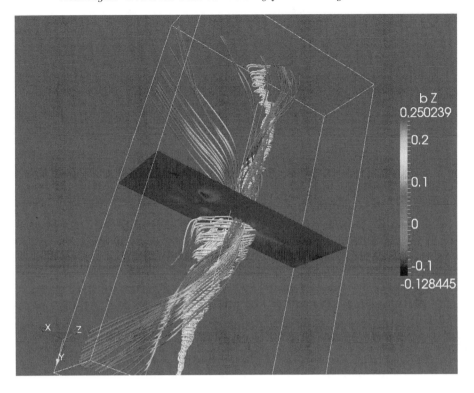

**FIGURE 16.3**: The role of electron physics in development of turbulent reconnection in collisionless plasmas. This visualization, produced on Blacklight by Homa Karimabadi (UCSD) using data from running his simulations on Kraken, shows magnetic field lines (shades of gray) and associated tornado-like streamlines (white) of a large flux rope formed due to tearing instability in thin electron layers [DRK+11].

architectures that are more tightly bound are required. The table below lists, in ascending order, how structured the analyzed data is and how low an analysis latency is required.

| Architecture | Interconnect | API | Primitive | Node-Node Latency |
|---|---|---|---|---|
| Distributed memory | GigE, 10GigE | TCP/UDP Socket, MPI | SEND/RECEIVE | mid-low 1000s ns |
| Shared memory non-coherent | IB-FDR with RDMA | MPI, UPC, CAF | GET/PUT | high-mid 100s ns |
| Shared memory coherent | Intel®QPI to 8skts/1TB | OpenMP, Pthreads | LOAD/STORE | mid-low 100s ns |

## 16.3.1 SGI® Ultraviolet Architecture

When the Big Data is structured and when low analysis latency is required a coherent shared memory or scale-up system is a suitable platform, albeit limited to 8-processor sockets connected to a coherent shared memory of the order of 1 TB. As Big Data to be analyzed grows, yet at low latencies, there is a need to scale up higher. Consequently the

SGI® Ultraviolet System was developed. It has a proprietary NUMAlink interconnect that is currently in its fifth generation, i.e., NUMAlink 5 or NL5. This interconnect comprises

- NL5 Hub: aka a NIC, Network Interface Chip

- NL5 Router

Together, they scale up the first generation Ultraviolet or UV1 architecture to a maximum of

- 256 Intel® Nehalem or Westmere processor sockets

- 4,096 threads or cores, including hyper-threading

- 16 TB of coherent shared memory

The limit of 16 TB limit is attributed to the 44-bit physical address space of the Intel® Nehalem and Westmere sockets. The next-generation UV2 System uses Intel® Sandybridge and Ivybridge sockets. They have an increased 46-bit physical address space and therefore UV2 can technically support up to 64 TB of coherent shared memory. The limit of 256 sockets is attributed to the UV1 architecture. The next-generation UV2 architecture increases this to 512 sockets. The limit of 4,096 threads/core is attributed to the current Linux kernel. There is currently no plan to increase this for the immediate next generation.

### 16.3.2    How It Works

In UV1, a node comprises two Intel® Nehalem or Westmere sockets connected via QPI to the NL5 Hub. To these two Intel® sockets, the Hub represents the remaining 254 sockets in the system. The Hub is responsible for maintaining coherency across the entire system, leveraging the one or two directory DIMMs connected to it. In a 256-socket UV1 System, there are therefore 128 Hubs. In UV2, the Hub will use a small portion of the socket memory to store Directory information. As such, there will no longer be the need for separate Directory DIMMs, thus reducing system cost.

### 16.3.3    Blacklight: A Very Large Shared Memory System for Science and Engineering

Blacklight constitutes the first time that a truly large, coherent, shared memory system is available to the national research community. It has enabled the community to expand many diverse and important fields of research such as the analysis of complex networks, natural language processing, epidemiological modeling, and graph-based methods for understanding condensed matter physics. Also, the availability of hardware-based coherent shared memory is allowing comparison of performance versus other software-based shared memory technologies and development of NUMA algorithms, which can inform future hardware and software architectures.

## 16.4    Hardware Architecture

Blacklight comprises 512 eight-core Intel® Xeon X7560 (Nehalem-EX, 8-core, 2.27 GHz) processors with a total of 32 TB of memory and a custom, high-performance, fat-tree, NUMAlink 5 (NL5) interconnect, supporting both coherent and non-coherent memory traffic.

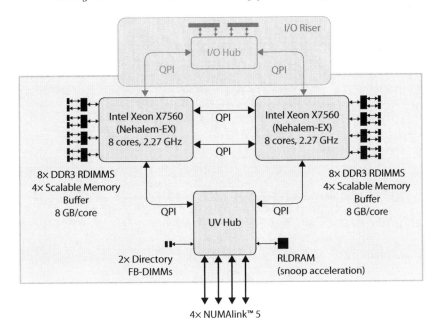

**FIGURE 16.4**: Each Blacklight compute node consists of two Intel Nehalem-EX 8-core processors running at 2.27 GHz, a UV Hub, 128 GB of memory, and four NUMAlink$^{TM}$ 5 connections to the rest of the system.

It is operated as two large, shared-memory single-system images (SSIs), with non-coherent communications between SSIs. At 72.6 Gf/s per socket, Blacklight has a peak 64-bit floating-point performance of 37 Tf/s.

Blacklight is housed in eight air-cooled cabinets. Each cabinet contains two chasses, and each chassis contains 16 compute nodes and 4 network modules. Each compute node contains 2 Nehalem-EX 8-core processors and a NL5 Hub, all connected by Intel® QuickPath Interconnects (QPI). Each node also contains 16 DDR3 DIMMs (8 GB each, 1,066 MHz) and an optional PCI Express Gen2 (PCIe2) I/O interface (Figure 16.4). The 8-core processors run at 2.27 GHz for 72.6 Gf/s per processor peak performance. Memory bandwidth is 35 GB/s aggregate per processor socket.

## 16.4.1 Topology

Blacklight has a full fat-tree topology within each SSI and also connecting its two SSIs. Nodes pairs are connected by NL5 to form 4-processor "quads" (Figure 16.5), which are then interconnected by 4 multi-level fat-trees, one for each upward-pointing NL5 line of Figure 16.5 (Figures 16.5 and 16.6).

## 16.4.2 Interconnect

The NL5 16-port router sustains 7.5 GB/s/direction along each link with latencies of only 1.7 $\mu$s. Separate routing tables for each port ensure that the worst-case latency is uniformly low. The cut-through latency is 22 ns within a quad and 37 ns on a router. The router also offers transparent multicast for synchronization.

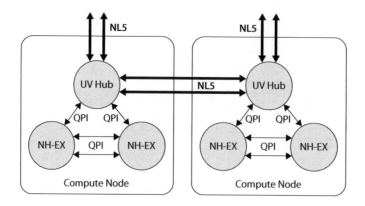

**FIGURE 16.5**: A "quad" consists of two compute nodes and has four NL5 links to a fat tree.

The Global Reference Unit (GRU), 2 per UV Hub, provides high-bandwidth, low-latency communication, scatter/gather operations, an update cache for atomic memory operations (AMOs), efficient byte copy operations, an external translation lookaside buffer (TLB) with large page support, and enhanced message sends. The GRU also functions as the master for the MPI Offload Engine (MOE), which improves performance while reducing load on the CPUs. Each GRU can have 128 references in flight, almost tripling the 48 references that a Nehalem-EX processor can maintain alone.

The Active Memory Unit (AMU) provides rich atomic operations, transparent multicast for synchronization, page initialization, and message queues in coherent memory (thereby supporting the MOE).

Together, these features greatly accelerate MPI. GRU-assisted message queues greatly reduce MPI latency and increase message throughput. The GRU byte copy provides sustained bandwidths of 3.41 GB/s/GRU for stride-1 loads, totaling 6.82 GB/s per GRU pair

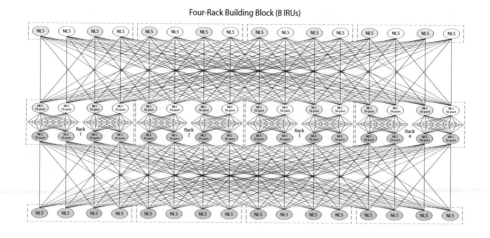

**FIGURE 16.6**: Lower levels of the 4-plane NL5 fat-tree interconnect, showing half of the full system.

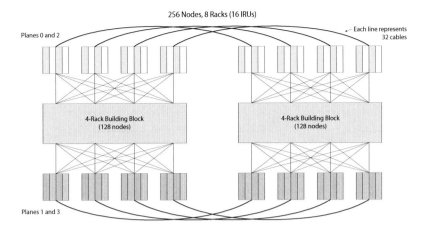

**FIGURE 16.7**: Upper-level, fat-tree, full-system (32 TB) interconnect. Each high-level line represents 32 NL5 paths.

(i.e., the "long path performance"), and vector gathers run at 1.05 GB/s/GRU. GRU updates provide exceptionally fast barriers of 3 $\mu$s for up to 4,096 threads.

### 16.4.3  Processor

Each 8-core, 2.27 GHz Nehalem-EX processor (72.6 Gf/s peak) contains 24 MB shared L3 cache, 256 kB L2 cache per core, and 32 kB instruction + 32 kB data L1 cache per core. Each processor also drives 4 FBD2 memory channels (6.4 GT/s each) and 4 full-width Intel® QPI links (6.4 GT/s each).

Cache line length is 64B, and both QPI and NL5 are designed for efficient fine-grained transfers of single cache lines.

Nehalem-EX, like all Xeon processors, runs the x86 instruction set. It also supports SSE 4 and 4.2, which add new instructions significant for technical computing: dot products for arrays of structures, population counts, type widening and rounding, etc. Hyperthreading allows 2 hardware threads per core, for which the larger cache sizes reduce cache thrashing and benefit long, dependent chains of operations.

The NH-EX processor connects to other sockets, the UV Hub, and I/O hubs using 4 bidirectional QPI links, each running at 6.4 GT/s (12.8 GB/s, peak, per link per direction). Nehalem-EX also supports 4- and 8-socket configurations without an external controller.

### 16.4.4  Memory

Each of Blacklight's 512 compute nodes contains 16 DDR3 DIMMs (8 GB each, 1066 MHz). Nehalem-EX processors each have 4 memory channels, yielding aggregate memory bandwidth of 35 GB/s per processor (70 GB/s per node).

Although each Nehalem-EX memory channel can drive up to two DIMMs, on Blacklight, only one DIMM per channel is populated because doing so maximizes memory bandwidth, and the total memory is already at its 16 GB limit as determined by the processor's 44-bit physical address space.

## 16.5    System Software

Blacklight runs a robust, familiar, and fully featured user environment.

The operating system is Novell SUSE Linux Enterprise Server 11 (SLES11) with SGI ProPack 6 on SUSE Linux Enterprise Server. The OS includes full support for threaded programming models, general interprocess communication, and interaction with external services, resulting in a fully flexible environment that makes applications unusually easy for users to install and execute.

PSC's *Simon* scheduler runs atop Torque, allowing administrators to maximize job performance and throughput by leveraging the resource management tools for NUMA systems. Simon assures a robust solution for facilitating CPU sets, for scheduling runs having certain requirements such as interactivity or integration into distributed workflows, and for prioritizing capability (full-machine) runs with minimal disruption to overall throughput. On systems other than Blacklight where topology is more important to job performance (e.g., a 3D torus), Simon supports customized job placement to minimize contention for shared interconnect links.

Administration of Blacklight is done using a combination of SGI's system administration tools plus other tools that PSC has developed for its many HPC systems. SGI tools include the Embedded Support Partner (ESP), a set of tools and utilities in the SGI Linux ProPack release that can monitor a system for events, software and hardware failures, availability, performance, and configuration changes, and then perform actions based on those events. ESP can detect system conditions that indicate potential problems, and then alert appropriate personnel by pager or e-mail.

Accounting is managed using PSC's own tool suite, which has been enhanced for Blacklight to monitor different forms of memory usage such as directly allocated RAM versus RAM disk.

Software environments are managed using the *modules* utility, and there is also support for the XSEDE Common User Environment (CUE).

PSC filesystems that are normally used by Blacklight are /brashear (Lustre, 292 TB), /home (NFS, 4 TB), and /arc (SLASH2, 4 PB). Filesystem /arc, designed for both ongoing projects and archiving, is implemented using PSC's Data Supercell, which is described in Section 16.7.1.

## 16.6    Programming System

Blacklight runs a standard Linux operating system, so the programming models that it supports are unusually rich. At the time of this writing, they include message passing (MPI), coherent shared memory (OpenMP, p-threads, Java threads), distributed shared memory (shmem), and partitioned global address space (PGAS; UPC).

Compilers on Blacklight include Intel and GNU C, C++, and Fortran, Sun and IBM Java, and SGI UPC. Naturally, C, C++, and Fortran support OpenMP, and C and C++ support POSIX threads ("p-threads"). Threading models are heavily used on Blacklight. The SGI Message Passing Toolkit (MPT) provides an MPI-2 implementation that is optimized to use to the sophisticated hardware features of the UV-1000. Blacklight supports a full complement of scripting languages, including Python, Perl, and shells.

PSC supports the suite of performance tools developed under the POINT[MSK$^+$] project, specifically PAPI, TAU, Scalasca, and PerfSuite, plus IPM. The programming environment also supports a full range of editors, version control systems, and utilities.

SGI MPI leverages the MPI Offload Engine (MOE) in the Altix UV_Hub ASIC to accelerate barriers and reductions (SUM, MAX, etc.), lowering latency and increasing scalability. MPI_Send performance is enhanced by the message_send instruction in the Global Reference Unit (GRU), which takes over and transmits data to a hardware-managed, memory-resident message queue slot on the destination blade, thereby reducing the load on the sending CPU.

PSC supports state-of-the-art database technologies as required by various projects, for example, the Tokyo Cabinet key/value store and the Neo4j graph database. These are particularly valuable to machine learning, natural language processing, and semantic web communities.

A large number of community applications, libraries, and utilities are supported, including multiple versions (managed by the *modules* utility). A few examples with noteworthy relevance to Blacklight workloads are as follows:

- GraphLab: a scalable framework for machine learning

- R and Rmpi: statistics

- Python, Scientific Python, etc.: high-productivity scripting

- ABySS, SOAPdenovo, Trinity, Velvet: genome sequence assembly

- ParaView: visualization and analysis

- Tokyo Cabinet and Kyoto Cabinet: key/value databases

- Neo4j: graph database

- HDF4, HDF4, NetCDF: data storage format

- PETSc, Hypre, IT++, etc.: math libraries

- Gaussian, MolPro, GAMESS, ABINIT, Siesta, etc: quantum chemistry and materials science

- MATLAB: high-level language and environment for numerical computing

## 16.7 Storage, Visualization, and Analytics

PSC's storage strategy centers on data-intensive computing. Recently, to address the need for ever-higher bandwidth to, and especially *from*, long-term storage, PSC designed and implemented the *Data Supercell* (described briefly below). Moreover, Blacklight specifically targets memory-intensive computation, placing visualization and analytics at the forefront of its use cases.

**FIGURE 16.8**: PSC's Data Supercell delivers a high-performance, cost-effective approach to long-term, petascale storage.

### 16.7.1    The Data Supercell

The Data Supercell (Figure 16.8) is a PSC-developed, groundbreaking, disk-based data management system for low cost, high bandwidth, low latency, high reliability, and high capacity. As cost-effective as tape, the Data Supercell combines scalable, cost-effective hardware with both community and PSC-proprietary software to provide exceptionally high, configurable performance and the reliability that is needed for petascale data sets.

The Phase 1 Data supercell is in production as filesystem "/arc," accessible directly from PSC computers and via GridFTP and Globus. Initially, the Data Supercell is configured at 4 PB, which will easily be expanded as additional capacity is needed. PSC's SLASH2 filesystem allows federation of Data Supercell units, which can be co-located or geographically distributed. SLASH2 includes optimizations for data replication and data movement. Latency of the Data Supercell is approximately 10,000 times better than tape, and at the same price point, its bandwidth is approximately 24 times better than tape.

### 16.7.2    Visualization and Analytics Applications

PSC support common community codes and applications for data visualization and analytics such as VisIt, ParaView, R (and Rmpi), and MATLAB. Many researchers also bring their own applications for statistics, machine learning, visualization, and other types of analysis.

### 16.7.3    Enabling Analysis Workflows

Creating effective data-intensive workflows often requires careful coordination of networking, storage, and computing capabilities. PSC is well-connected to research and education networks (XSEDE, National Lambda Rail, Internet2, and ESnet) as well as to the commodity Internet. To help users move data, PSC-developed networking diagnostics and tools suchs as Web10G, NPAD, and hpn-ssh are applied to optimize end-to-end file transfer rates. Sufficient space on /brashear (Lustre) for the project, which is backed by /arc for long-term, near-line storage and archiving. Batch analyses are handled normally through the queuing system. Interactive analyses and visualizations are either requested dynamically ("qsub -i") or, especially for larger requirements, reserved through PSC consultants. To accommodate reservations, the scheduler allows partial drains to ensure that the required resources are available at the scheduled times.

## 16.8 Computing Facility

Blacklight is housed in PSC's machine room, located in Monroeville, Pennsylvania, together with PSC's other computing platforms, storage, and some networking. The "dark" facility is operated remotely from PSC's offices, which are on the Carnegie Mellon campus, approximately 13 miles to the west. The PSC facility has dual power feeds, a UPS for critical infrastructure, and chilled water, with excess heat recycled during cold periods to heat office spaces on upper floors. Other networking, including a regional GigaPOP, is served from PSC facilities at other sites. Figure 16.1 shows Blacklight, shortly after installation, in PSC's machine room. Blacklight entailed no particular installation challenges.

## 16.9 System Statistics

At the time of this writing, 626 projects have been allocated on Blacklight, serving 2,321 researchers working in the following fields of science: advanced scientific computing, astronomical sciences, atmospheric sciences, behavioral and cognitive sciences, biological and critical systems, chemical and thermal systems, chemistry, CISE cross-disciplinary activities, computer and computation research, design and manufacturing systems, Earth sciences, electrical and communications systems, environmental biology humanities, information, robotics, and intelligent systems, integrative biology and neuroscience, materials research, mathematical sciences, mechanical and structural systems, molecular and cellular biosciences, networking and communications research, ocean sciences, physics, polar programs, science and engineering education, small business innovation research, and social and economic sciences.

Notably, 68 projects (117 of the total) are for training, testifying to the valuable role that Blacklight is serving for outreach. Training projects include, for example, development of HPC expertise across colleges and universities through the XSEDE Campus Champions program and the NRBSC's MARC (Minorities Accessing Research Careers) Summer Institute in Bioinformatics at PSC.

## 16.10 Summary

Blacklight provides the U.S. national research community with the largest possible ($2 \times 16$ TB) hardware-enabled, cache-coherent shared memory, limited only by the processor's physical address space. Blacklight also provides a fully featured user environment without limitations on programming models, applications, or workflows. Together, Blacklight's shared memory and flexible user environment are uniquely enabling for many researchers who are doing fundamental research in computer science, algorithms for diverse fields, and data-intensive analysis, as illustrated by the examples in Section 16.2.1. The diversity of research being achieved on Blacklight and the heavy demand for allocations both confirm that coherent shared memory serves a valuable, unique role in the HPC ecosystem.

# Chapter 17

## Gordon: A Novel Architecture for Data Intensive Computing

**Pietro Cicotti, Michael Norman, Robert S. Sinkovits, and Shawn Strande**

*San Diego Supercomputer Center*

**Allan Snavely**

*Lawrence Livermore National Laboratory*

## 17.1 Introduction

### 17.1.1 Sponsor/Program Background

In 2008, the National Science Foundation (NFS) released solicitation NSF 08-573, which sought systems in three distinct categories: 1) a data intensive, high performance computing system; 2) an experimental high performance computing system; and 3) a high performance grid test-bed. With regard to the first, the solicitation requested proposals for, "*...systems with designs that are optimized to support research with very large data-sets or very large input-output requirements. The total peak computing capacity of the system should be at least 200 teraflop/s. Such a system will be a production resource in the TeraGrid. (Up to 4 years duration. Up to $10,000,000 in acquisition costs and up to $3,000,000 per year, after acceptance, for operations and maintenance, including user support.)*"

The San Diego Supercomputer Center (SDSC) at the University of California, San Diego (UCSD) responded to this call with a proposal called Flash Gordon: A Data Intensive Computer. The proposal abstract provides the motivation for the design: "This project supports the acquisition, deployment and operation of a new supercomputing system suitable for data-intensive applications. The system, to be known as Flash Gordon, will be deployed by the University of California at San Diego at the San Diego Supercomputer Center and integrated into the TeraGrid. The system, which has been designed by Appro International Incorporated, with partners Intel and ScaleMP, seeks to bridge the widening latency gap between main memory and rotating disk storage in modern computing systems. It uses flash memory to provide a level of dense, affordable, low-latency storage that can be configured as either extended swap space or a very fast filesystem. The system will consist of very large shared virtual-memory, cache-coherent *supernodes* to support a versatile set of programming paradigms. Peak performance will exceed 200 teraflops/s in double precision. Flash Gordon's large addressable virtual memory, low-latency flash memory, and user-friendly programming environment will provide a step-up in capability for data-intensive applications that scale poorly on current large-scale architectures, providing a resource that will enable transformative research in many research domains. Even sequential codes will be able to address up to terabytes of fast virtual memory."

## 17.1.2   Design Highlights and Philosophy

How should the capabilities of systems such as Gordon be measured in this age of data exploration? LINPACK performance is widely used to rank HPC systems but does not address an important property of a data intensive (or any) computer, namely its ability to store and rapidly access large amounts of data [Kog08]. This attribute can be quantified by the metric Data Motion Capability (DMC) [Ama09], defined as the sum of the capacities divided by the latencies at each level of the data hierarchy:

$$DMC = \sum_{i=0}^{levels} \frac{capacity_i}{latency_i}$$

where i is the number of data hierarchy levels (including registers, caches, DRAM, SSD, HDD, etc.) in the data hierarchy of the machine; capacity has units of bytes, and latency has units of processor cycles (or seconds if preferred). DMC thus expresses the combination of the system's data capacity and speed for accessing data at every level. These two attributes are paramount for data intensive computing, as data intensive computations read and write large amounts of data and accesses must be fast.

Figure 17.1 depicts the DMC of Gordon, Kraken, and Ranger, systems that are currently available in the NSF open computing program. Gordon has a DMC of 1.84 TB/cycle, while the Kraken and Ranger systems have DMCs of 1.86 TB/cycle and 1.47 TB/cycle, respectively. By contrast, the LINPACK performance of Gordon, Kraken, and Ranger are 341 TFlops, 1.2 PFlops, and 580 TFlops, respectively. So while Gordon has a lower performance as measured by this traditional HPC benchmark, and is smaller in terms of core counts, it is better equipped to handle challenges associated with data intensive computing. In a nutshell, this is the motivation for the Gordon design.

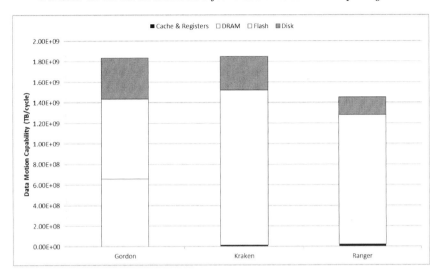

**FIGURE 17.1**: DCM of Gordon, Kraken, and Ranger.

Gordon achieves this breakthrough performance by combining several highly innovative technologies.

- 64 I/O nodes with an aggregate of 300 TB of high performance flash memory (also known as solid state disk, or SSD). Gordon features 1,024 Intel 710 series flash drives (code named Lyndonville), a new breed of SSD that uses eMLC NAND, but achieves performance levels comparable to much more expensive Single Level Cell (SLC) drives.

- Dual-socket compute nodes based on Intel's Xeon E5 Processor (code named Sandy Bridge). These processors implement the Advanced Vector eXtensions (AVX) instruction set and are capable of eight floating-point operations per cycle per core. With four memory channels per socket, the compute nodes have a theoretical memory bandwidth of 85 GB/s when populated with DDR3-1333 memory.

- Dual-rail, 3D torus interconnect based on Quad Data Rate (QDR, 40 Gb/s) Infini-Band.

- Virtualization using ScaleMP's vSMP Foundation software delivers large, shared memory *supernodes* which provide programming environments well-suited for data intensive applications.

- High-performance parallel filesystem that delivers sustained rates of 100 GB/s and a capacity of 4 PB.

At the time Gordon was proposed, most of these technologies were either not yet available or in early stages of development.

- SSD technology was in a state of rapid development, which meant that many vendors had products with varying claims of performance and endurance. Products with high performance come with hefty price tags and expected drops in flash prices did not materialize as rapidly as predicted, partly due to the huge demand for NAND in the consumer market (cell phones, MP3 players, etc.).

- The Sandy Bridge processor had been demonstrated, but was not projected to be available until early 2011.

- vSMP was a new technology that had not yet been demonstrated in multi-user high performance computing environment like that expected for Gordon. Furthermore, a device porting effort was required in order for vSMP to function on the Gordon-specific hardware.

- Deploying a high performance filesystem is a major undertaking in its own right, but integration with the Gordon I/O node architecture, and the requirement that it support multiple HPC systems simultaneously, put additional demand on the design, test, and deployment schedule.

From a project perspective, these represented significant risks to successful deployment. The combination of new technologies, uncertain product launch dates, and market dynamics meant that all stakeholders had to be willing to take risks and work together to deploy a system that the research community would find useful for doing data intensive research. The Gordon design philosophy and project was structured to achieve this:

- Rigorous schedule of milestones and demonstrations. These included: interim vSMP acceptance tests; flash testing; 3D torus prototype testing; applications studies; and critical design reviews.

- Substantial and meaningful engagement with the NSF, the sponsoring agency. The NSF program officer played a critical role in the process and provided important feedback and recommendations for addressing risk and keeping the project moving in the right direction.

- The combination of new technologies that could not be purchased off-the-shelf. The system was therefore a co-design effort between Appro, the system integrator and prime vendor, and SDSC. At its core, Gordon is a commodity cluster built with high performance technology.

- The project included a significant amount of prototyping and early testing to be sure that the technologies could be integrated into a functioning whole. SDSC carried out the lion's share of testing and provided information to the vendor that helped shape the design. This was most notable in the design of the I/O nodes and the selection of the flash drives.

- A highly competent, nimble, and focused project team that was committed to the project and always willing to put in the extra effort to overcome challenges and get the work done.

Gordon is one of the most innovative HPC systems to be deployed in the NSF's open computing program. Thanks to the willingness of all the stakeholders to accept a significant amount of risk in exchange for the reward of doing something truly unique, Gordon advances the state of the art in computing and in doing so, provides an important capability to the national research community.

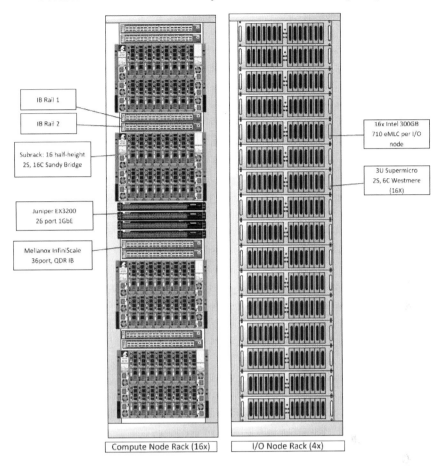

**FIGURE 17.2**: Gordon compute and I/O node racks.

## 17.2 Architecture

### 17.2.1 Overview

Gordon is a 1,024 node Appro cluster, based on an 8-core, 2.6 GHz Intel Xeon E5 processor (Sandy Bridge). The Xeon E5 is capable of executing eight operations per clock cycle, and therefore the dual-socket, 16,384-core system has a theoretical peak performance of 341 TFlops. There are 64 I/O flash-based nodes, each with sixteen 300 GB Intel 710 Series SSDs, for a total of 300 TB for the full system. In addition to their role as storage servers for the flash memory, each I/O node is a gateway to the high performance Lustre-based parallel filesystem, called Data Oasis.

The basic architectural unit is an Appro Greenblade 8U subrack containing 16 half-height blades and 5 power supplies in an N+1 redundant configuration. There are 4 subracks per 48U rack and a total of 16 compute node racks. Each of these racks also contains the Mellanox InfiniBand switches and Juniper edge ethernet switches. Figure 17.2 provides an overview of a compute node and I/O node rack.

Figure 17.3 provides a high level overview of the Gordon architecture. A few key features of the architecture include:

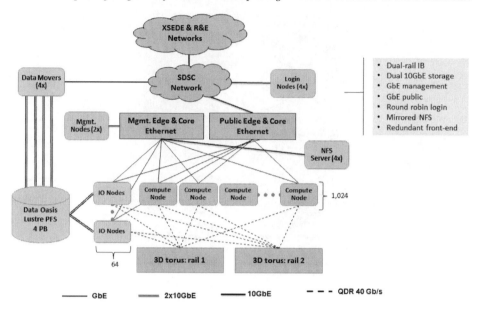

**FIGURE 17.3**: Gordon architecture.

- Each compute node and I/O node are connected via dual-rail QDR InfiniBand, 3D torus interconnect. The network is based on Mellanox technology.

- Each compute node and I/O node are connected via a dual-rail 1GbE network. One of these is used for the cluster management and the other for public access to the nodes for applications that require this. The network is based on Juniper technology.

- Each of the I/O nodes is connected to the Data Oasis Lustre-based parallel filesystem (described below) via two 10GbE connections.

- There are four login nodes that users are assigned to in a round robin manner, but the system is operational with only one if necessary. The login nodes contain the same processor as the compute nodes to allow for user compilations.

- There is a mirrored pair of NFS servers. These are shared with other HPC systems at SDSC to allow for cross mounting of user home directories for those who compute on multiple systems.

- SDSC's network is connected to several research and education networks, including CENIC, Internet2, and XSEDE. The latter is a dedicated 10GbE network that connects all major NSF computing centers.

- There are four data mover nodes that are used for high-speed data transfer between XSEDE sites. This is essential for many researchers who carry out simulations on one system, say Kraken, but want to do analysis on another, like Gordon.

Table 17.1 summarizes the major architectural features, memory and storage capacities, and the theoretical performance for the compute, vSMP and I/O nodes, interconnect, Data Oasis, and the system as a whole.

**TABLE 17.1**: Gordon hardware summary.

| Intel Xeon E5 (Sandy Bridge) Compute node | |
|---|---|
| Sockets & Cores/node | 2 & 16 |
| Clock speed | 2.6 GHz |
| DRAM capacity and speed | 64 GB DDR3-1333 |
| Local system disk (SSD) | 80 GB |
| **Intel Xeon 5650 (Westmere) Flash I/O Node** | |
| Sockets & Cores/node | 2 & 12 |
| Clock speed | 2.66 GHz |
| DRAM capacity and speed | 48 GB DDR3-1333 |
| Intel 710 eMLC SSD | 16 |
| SSD capacity per drive & per node | 300 GB  4.8 TB |
| **vSMP supernode** | |
| Compute nodes / I/O Nodes | 32 / 2 |
| Addressable DRAM | 2 TB |
| Addressable memory including flash | 11.6 TB |
| **Gordon** | |
| Compute Nodes | 1,024 |
| Total compute cores | 16,384 |
| Peak performance | 341 TFlops |
| Aggregate memory | 64 TB DRAM; 300 TB flash |
| Flash memory nodes | 64 |
| **InfiniBand Interconnect** | |
| Topology | Dual-Rail, 3D torus |
| Link bandwidth | QDR (40 Gb/s) |
| Aggregate torus bandwidth | 9.2 TB/s |
| **Lustre-based Disk I/O Subsystem** | |
| Total storage | 4 PB (raw) |

## 17.2.2 Compute Nodes

The Gordon Sandy Bridge compute nodes are hot-swappable, half-height blades based on the Intel Jefferson Pass motherboard, and Patsburg C600 series chipset. There are several features of the compute nodes that make them ideally suited for data and numerically intensive computing:

- Each of the 1,024 nodes contains two oct-core, 2.6 GHz Intel Xeon E5 processors capable of issuing 8 floating-point operations per clock cycle. This results in a performance of 333 GFlops per node.

- Each node has 64 GB of DDR3-1333 memory, which is 4 GB per core. This is currently the largest per core memory available on the XSEDE computing platforms (not including physical shared memory with Non-Uniform Memory Access (NUMA) systems such as the SGI UV Altix [Sil09]).

- Processors are connected via two 8 GT/s QPI (Quick Path Interconnect) links, which provides excellent memory bandwidth when accessing a remote processor's memory.

- Large dedicated and shared caches: L1 is 32 kB per core; L2 is 256 kB per core; and the shared on-chip L3 is 20 MB, or 2.5 MB per core.

- PCIe Gen3 support.

- Each compute node has a local Intel 80 GB SSD. This is primarily intended for hosting the operating system, but has also been used successfully as scratch space for user applications.

- Each compute node is equipped with two QDR InfiniBand Host Channel Adapters (HCA), one for each rail of the 3D torus.

- Each compute node has two 1 GbE adapters. One is used by the management network to distribute the cluster images and for supporting related monitoring and administration tasks; the other is used for public access to various file systems and, if required, by specific applications (e.g., Hadoop).

### 17.2.3  I/O Nodes

One of Gordon's most distinctive features, and the one that is generally cited as its most innovative, is the flash based I/O nodes. As noted above, Gordon has 64 I/O nodes that serve two purposes: 1) they serve an aggregate 300 TB of high performance flash to the compute nodes; and 2) they act as gateways to the Data Oasis Lustre-based parallel filesystem.

Given the significant role that the I/O nodes play in Gordon and the risk associated with them, the project plan called for them to be deployed many months before the Sandy Bridge processor was available to allow for flash testing, vSMP porting, and integration with Data Oasis [He,10b, He,10a]. Consequently, the I/O nodes use the Westmere processor and a different motherboard. Each of the 64 nodes contains:

- Two hex-core, 2.66 GHz Intel Xeon 5650 (Westmere) processor.

- Sixteen, 300 GB Intel 710 eMLC SSDs per node, for a total of 4.8 TB p n, or 300 TB for the full system.

- 48 GB of DDR3-1333 memory. The original design called for 24 GB, but after running some database tests, and doing combined I/O to flash and Lustre, this was increased to 48 GB.

- Dual port, 10GbE network interface card for access to the Data Oasis parallel filesystem.

- PCIe Gen2, which was tested to ensure that this would not be a bottleneck for exporting flash performance.

- Local Intel 80 GB SSD for the operating system and applications.

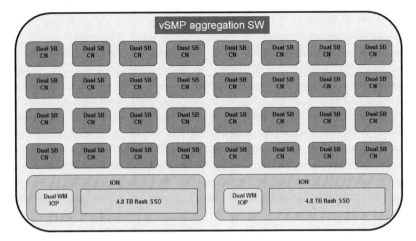

**FIGURE 17.4**: High-level view of vSMP node built from 16 compute nodes and one I/O node.

- Two QDR InfiniBand Host Channel Adapters (HCA), one for each rail of the 3D torus.

- Two 1 GbE adapters.

- 4 LSI SAS9211-4i controllers (one for every 4 SSDs).

The flash drives in Gordon deserve special mention. SSDs have much lower latency than spinning disks (less than 100 $\mu$s for SSD vs. 10 ms for HDD) and are therefore particularly well-suited for random data access, precisely the sort seen in data intensive computing applications. The original plan of record for Gordon called for a 256 GB SLC flash drive that was to be manufactured by Intel. A 64 GB version of this was used in the Dash prototype, and was found to meet all required acceptance criteria. However, midway through the pre-production phase of Gordon, Intel made some major changes to their flash roadmap which effectively eliminated SLC drives from their product offering. In its place, Intel proposed an alternative drive, code named Lyndonville, which was based on MLC NAND flash and appeared to meet the required performance of Gordon. This drive was not yet available, and uncertainty in the launch date added a new element of risk to the project. To mitigate this risk, a significant effort was undertaken to look at other vendor products to identify alternatives should the Lyndonville SSD not materialize in time. SDSC, working closely with Appro, tested approximately five different drives, and performed paper studies of another 15. This effort identified a handful of SSDs that, while not perfect in all dimensions, did meet the required performance. However, making a major change to the flash vendor would have required a formal project change request, with hard data to back up the choice.

As it turned out, the Lyndonville drive was formally launched at the Intel Developer Forum in September 2011. Early engineering samples were provided that allowed for verification testing, and quantity was available for the early delivery of the I/O nodes.

### 17.2.4 vSMP Virtualization

Gordon uses ScaleMP's vSMP Foundation software to aggregate up to 32 distributed memory compute nodes into a single virtual SMP image, called a *supernode*.[1] The compute nodes in these supernodes are connected by the dual-rail QDR InfiniBand network.

---

[1]SMP images of up to 64 nodes (4TB) have been tested on Gordon.

vSMP leverages the InfiniBand network to virtualize the underlying topology and set up a supernode with shared memory and I/O address spaces. With this capability up to 32 compute nodes with a total of 512 cores share a common 2 TB memory address space and provide access to the SSDs (Figure 17.4). Benchmarks studies now under way with Gordon and other hardware-based SMP solutions indicate that performance varies by application and that vSMP on Gordon is actually faster than other systems in some cases. Differences in processor and interconnect performance between Gordon and other systems account for some variation, but experience thus far is that vSMP provides an important capability without a large penalty in performance. Importantly, it is much less costly and allows multiple partitions of a large cluster to be used as SMP virtual machines only when needed. This capability makes a large cluster an even more general purpose computing environment. The large memory SMP capability and a very fast random access SSD disk capability combined with the best capabilities of a large unified distributed memory cluster provides the flexibility to handle a wide range of use applications, something that is important in the XSEDE, multi-user context. As part of the vSMP tool suite, Gordon also offers a unique application profiler that enables tuning of application to scale better on its unique architecture supporting closed-loop performance analysis for home-grown applications.

### 17.2.5   Interconnect

Gordon uses a dual-rail, hybrid tree/3D torus interconnect where each node on the torus is a 36-port, QDR InfiniBand switch. The switches in the dual-rail interconnect network are configured as a 4x4x4 torus topology with switches as vertexes. The switches are interconnected by three 4x QDR InfiniBand links that each have a peak full duplex bandwidth of 8 GB/sec, for a total 24 GB/sec full-duplex bandwidth for each rail (48 GB/sec aggregate). The bisection bandwidth for the two rails is 1536 GB/s and the aggregate peak bandwidth for all of the cross sections across the torus is 9.2 TB/s.

The 4x4x4 3D Torus network has a diameter of 6 hops, which corresponds to a maximum of 8 hops when including the HCA-to-switch and switch-to-HCA hops. Latencies were projected to be less than 1.25 $\mu$s between nodes on the same switch and less than 2.5 $\mu$s between the furthest nodes across the torus. Actual measured values are presented in Section 17.5.1. Figure 17.5 shows one of the two tori. Each of the squares shown represents a switch node. The total number of IB switches is 128 (64 for each tori):

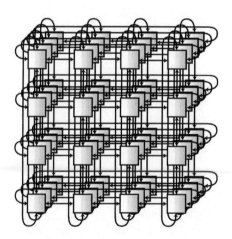

**FIGURE 17.5**: 4x4x4 torus of switches (one torus shown; links in the third dimension omitted for clarity).

The 3D torus was selected for Gordon for several important reasons:

- Lower cost: 40% as many switches, 25% to 50% fewer cables when compared to full bisection bandwidth fat free.

- Works well for localized communication. Given the design of 32 node vSMP super-nodes, and the expectation that non-vSMP jobs would generally have modest core counts, the torus delivers excellent bandwidth, while minimizing contention on the interconnect.

- Short cables minimize the number of fiber optic cables required.

- Linearly expandable. Future additions to the cluster could be made by breaking open the torus and adding another plane of switches.

- Simple wiring pattern since all compute nodes are cabled into the local switch.

- Reduced power and cooling requirements due to lower switch count.

- Fault tolerant within the mesh with 2QoS Alternate Routing. The loss of a switch is not fatal. The only impact is to the 16 compute nodes and 1 I/O node on the downed switch.

- Fault tolerant with Dual-Rails for all routing algorithms. New versions of MPI are under development that will allow MPI traffic to reroute over the other rail in the event that a switch node goes down.

Each switch node has connections as follows:

- One for each compute node (16).

- One for the I/O node (1).

- Three in each $+/-$ x, y, z direction (18).

- One open port per switch.

This is repeated for the second rail. The connectivity for a group of 32 compute nodes and 2 I/O nodes is shown in Figure 17.6.

The switches that connect the I/O nodes to the compute nodes are part of the overall interconnect fabric, which makes all of the I/O nodes accessible to all of the compute nodes in the system. Furthermore, each torus is an independent network, but with dual connections into each compute node and I/O node traffic can traverse from one rail to the next by passing through a compute node. This is the case as deployed, since Gordon uses rail 1 for user MPI traffic and rail 2 for I/O traffic to the Lustre parallel filesystem and the I/O node flash filesystem. Finally, for vSMP, the group of 32 compute nodes and 2 I/O nodes constitutes a supernode as described above.

## 17.2.6 Data Oasis Lustre File System

The Lustre-based parallel filesystem, Data Oasis, was designed to meet Gordon's 100 GB/s aggregate bandwidth requirement. It is composed of 64 storage servers, each connected through dual-10GbE links to the Gordon I/O nodes. As shown in Figure 17.7, Data Oasis provides high performance storage for three HPC systems at SDSC. While no single system can access the full 100 GB/s performance, in the case of Gordon, the 64 I/O nodes access 32 Data Oasis OSSs (object storage server) as a scratch filesystem at sustained rates of 50

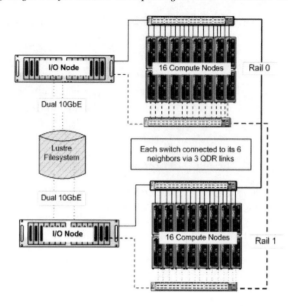

**FIGURE 17.6**: Compute and I/O node network topology.

GB/s. There is also a shared projects filesystem between Trestles and Gordon (not shown), which gives Gordon access to an additional 8 OSSs. Thus the aggregate bandwidth available to Gordon is approximately 64 GB/s.

The ratio of I/O bandwidth to Flops is useful for characterizing Gordon as a balanced system for data intensive computing. Gordon has a peak performance of 341 TFLOPS, and the ratio of I/O performance to FLOPS is 0.187 GB/TFlop. By contrast, Kraken, a system targeted at highly scalable applications, has a peak performance of 1.2 PFlops and a Lustre filesystem that performs at roughly 30 GB/s, resulting in an I/O to Flops ratio of 0.025 GB/TFlop [Tro09]. This is an important indicator of Gordon's ability to support data intensive computing. At this time, Gordon has the highest ratio of I/O to FLOPS of any system deployed in the NSF's XSEDE program.

### 17.2.7    Facility and Power

Gordon is physically located on the UCSD campus in SDSC's 19,000 square foot climate-controlled secure datacenter. The facility is equipped with 13 Megawatts of power, multiple 10GbE network connections and a 24/7 operations staff.

As noted previously, the full system consists of 16 compute node racks, 4 I/O node racks, and a service node rack that houses the login nodes, front end nodes, NSF servers, and management switches. All racks are 48U providing a compact design that minimizes floor space and cable lengths. Power distribution is via two 60A PDUs per compute node rack and two 50A PDUs per I/O node rack. The service node rack is on UPS which allows for graceful shutdown in the event of a power outage. Under full load the system consumes approximately 500 kW of power. Each subrack has six high efficiency fans, which provide excellent cooling and contribute to the overall energy efficiency for the system. In-floor cooling is provided with hot-aisle containment between the two rows. Gordon ranked 30th on the November 2011 Green500 list at 865 MFlops/W. Excluding the Blue Gene/Q and GPGPU based systems, Gordon ranks a close second on this list to another Sandy Bridge system at Sandia National Laboratory.

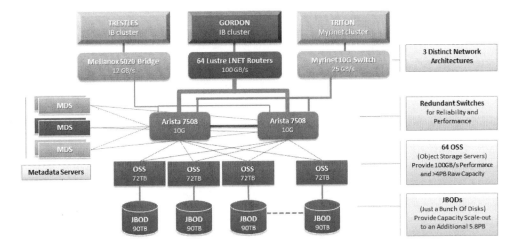

**FIGURE 17.7**: Data Oasis parallel filesystem.

One of the unique requirements for SDSC's datacenter is that all racks must be sited on earthquake isolation bases. The bases sit on top of the datacenter floor, which requires the racks be elevated approximately 2 inches. Since the racks were delivered fully populated, and weighed in at approximately 1,500 pounds each, their placement on the isobases required careful procedures and safeguards to ensure that there was no damage to the equipment. The rack layout is shown in Figure 17.8.

## 17.2.8 Project Timeline

The Gordon project officially started in September 2009. The project was structured in two major phases: preproduction and operations. Preproduction was structured around a rigorous set of design, prototype, and demonstration milestones that were intended to reduce risk in key technological areas and give users the opportunity to explore the use of flash and vSMP in their applications. A Gordon prototype system, Dash, was deployed in late 2009 and made available to users of the NSF TeraGrid program in April 2010. The prototype was instrumental in several important ways. First, it provided a platform for testing the performance of flash and vSMP from an applications perspective. Second, it allowed for systems development activities including exporting flash and development of system management processes for deploying vSMP nodes and networking. Finally, because the system was procured from the same vendor as Gordon, the use of a prototype was helpful in establishing effective communications and project practices that carried through the entire project.

The overall Gordon timeline and key milestones are given in Figure 17.9. A few interesting points should be noted in this schedule:

- Early versions of vSMP were tested on the Dash prototype beginning in late 2009.

- Early engineering work on the 3D torus led to a demonstration and acceptance milestone in November 2010, a full year ahead of the arrival of Gordon.

- 16 I/O nodes were delivered early using interim flash drives that had roughly the same performance, although much lower endurance, as the final drives. This allowed for early benchmarking of user applications and acceptance testing of some of the components in the I/O nodes.

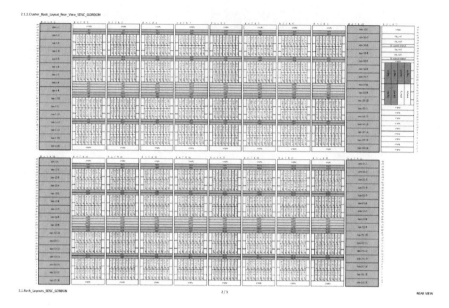

**FIGURE 17.8**: The full Gordon system consists of 21 racks, including 16 compute node racks, four I/O node racks, and one service rack.

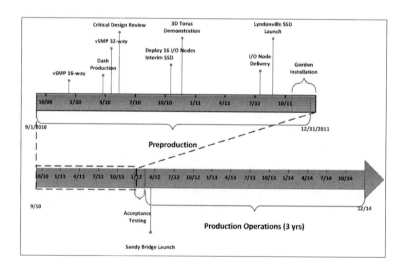

**FIGURE 17.9**: Gordon project timeline.

- The Intel Sandy Bridge launch was released late, pushing back the delivery of Gordon by several months. Whereas the original launch date of Gordon was July 1, 2011, the actual formal start of production operations was February 25, 2012. However, Gordon was delivered ahead of the Sandy Bridge launch and allowed production operations to begin about the time the Sandy Bridge formal launch occurred in March 2012. Gordon was the first system in the NSF open computing program that featured the Sandy Bridge processors.

- The Intel SSDs selected for Gordon were available in August of 2011, allowing early deployment of the I/O nodes ahead of the formal launch.

**TABLE 17.2**: Gordon software stack (version numbers as of 6/13/2012).

| Cluster management | Rocks 5.4.3 |
|---|---|
| Operating System | Modified for AVX |
| InfiniBand | OFED 1.5.3 Mellanox Subnet Manager |
| MPI | MVAPICH2 (Native); MPICH2 (vSMP) |
| Shared Memory | vSMP Foundation 4.0.225.18 |
| Flash | iSCSI over RDMA (iSER); Linux SCSI Target (tgt); XFS |
| User Environment | Rocks Rolls |
| Parallel File System | Lustre 1.8.7 |
| Job Scheduling | Torque, Catalina with enhancements for topology aware scheduling |

## 17.3 System Software

The Rocks cluster distribution software was chosen for the Gordon cluster to leverage SDSCs experience with previous Rocks installations and existing base of applications and system software. However, the version of the Rocks distribution available only supports CentOS up to version 5.6 and required two significant customizations: a backport of AVX and iSCSI over RDMA (iSER) support in the Linux kernel. AVX support was added by packaging a more recent release of the Linux kernel in a custom RPM, while iSER support was added by a custom backport provided by Mellanox of the upstream iSER module. An important lesson from this experience is that deploying a system like Gordon based on cutting edge technology requires compromises and additional work to fill gaps in various levels of the hardware and software stack. A summary of the Gordon software stack is shown in Table 17.2.

## 17.4 Programming Environment

### 17.4.1 Programming Models

Gordon supports the standard HPC programming models and we have installed the expected suite of compilers (Intel, PGI, GNU), interpreted languages (R, Python, Perl, Octave), and numerical libraries (e.g., FFTW, ScaLAPACK, PETSc) together with widely used chemistry, engineering, and visualization applications. While Gordon can support a wide range of users, it is targeted mainly at data intensive and shared memory applications as we describe below.

Gordon was designed primarily for applications that need to work with large amounts of data. This includes not only traditional data intensive applications that involve reading and processing enormous data sets, but also programs that generate substantial scratch or output files. At every step in the Gordon design, careful attention was paid to ensuring that data could be moved quickly from one level of the memory hierarchy to the next. The processors, memory, network, flash storage, and parallel filesystem were all chosen to ensure that the system as a whole would have a good balance between compute power and bandwidth while at the same time avoiding data motion bottlenecks.

Gordon is a general-purpose machine that can be used to run standard distributed-memory codes (e.g., developed using MPI), but its main strength lies in its support for a shared-memory programming model. With 64 GB of DDR3-1333 memory and 16 Intel Sandy Bridge compute cores, each Gordon compute node can serve as a powerful shared-memory resource. Gordon should also be ideal for hybrid codes (MPI + OpenMP) with large per-process memory footprints. To accommodate applications that need more cores or memory than is available on a single compute node, groups of 16 or 32 compute nodes and their associated I/O nodes can be aggregated using ScaleMP's vSMP Foundation software into logically shared-memory nodes with 1-2 TB of DRAM.

Many interesting and important problems do not lend themselves to a distributed memory approach. This can stem from the need to deal with irregular geometries and complex data structures or simply the requirement that each thread or process have access to the entire memory space. Even for applications that in theory could be parallelized with MPI, the required effort may be too great to be practical. Shared-memory parallelization has the advantage that it can often be implemented incrementally one loop or function at a time and without significant modifications to the underlying data structures. By embracing the shared-memory model, Gordon enables many researchers to finally make the leap from desktop computing to supercomputing.

## 17.4.2 I/O Models

Gordon provides multiple storage options depending on the persistence, performance, and capacity requirements. We describe these here in decreasing order of speed and increasing order of capacity.

The fastest option, available only on the vSMP nodes, is to use a RAM file system (ramfs). At the start of a job, the Torque prologue script automatically creates a directory on the ramfs belonging to the user and corresponding to the user name and job ID (e.g., /ramfs/$USER/$PBS_JOBID). At the conclusion of the job, the Torque epilogue script automatically deletes this directory and the user is required to copy all files that must be retained to a permanent location. While ramfs do give the best performance, this comes with a price since users of the vSMP nodes are charged based on compute core or memory usage, whichever is greater. For highly scalable jobs with relatively small per-core memory requirements, it would make sense to make at least limited use of ramfs. Jobs are charged based on the number of cores and the remaining space on the ramfs essentially comes for free. On the other hand, if a job requires more than 4 GB of memory per core, the user would likely want to first run benchmarks to determine whether or not the performance advantages of using ramfs are worth the extra charges against the allocation.

The next fastest, and more frequently used option, is to employ the flash storage as temporary scratch space. In a manner analogous to the management of ramfs on the vSMP nodes, the Torque prologue and epilogue scripts automatically create and destroy temporary directories corresponding to the user and job ID (e.g., /scratch/$USER/$PBS_JOBID) and the user is required to copy all files that must be retained to a permanent location. For regular compute nodes, we generally export a single 300 GB flash drive to each compute node. Recently though we have configured a small number of compute nodes to have exclusive access to all 4.8 TB of flash storage on an I/O node. In the near future we expect to deploy a shared flash filesystem so that all 16 compute nodes that are connected to a single switch will have shared access to all of the flash on the corresponding I/O node.

The situation is somewhat simpler for the vSMP nodes where all compute cores within a vSMP node have access to all of the corresponding flash storage. The only complication is that drives cannot be aggregated from across multiple I/O nodes so that for large vSMP nodes (e.g., more than 16 compute nodes and one I/O node) the flash appears as multiple filesystems named /scratch1, /scratch2, and so on. To simplify things for users who need less than 4.8 TB of flash or who will be moving between regular compute nodes and vSMP nodes, a symbolic link /scratch is always created that points to /scratch1.

An exception to flash purge policy is made for dedicated I/O node projects where a researcher is granted exclusive use of an I/O node for up to one year. In this case, data can be maintained persistently on the flash drives. Note that to maximize both performance and capacity, the flash drives for these projects are normally configured as a 16-drive RAID 0 device.

The largest capacity storage option is the Lustre-based parallel filesystem (Data Oasis). While slower than either ramfs or flash, it does have the advantage of being persistent and providing a degree of data integrity. Data Oasis contains a total of 64 Object Storage Servers (OSSs), each of which supports four Object Storage Targets (OSTs). Since each OST is a RAID 6 device with an XFS filesystem, up to two drive failures within an OST can be tolerated without a loss of data. Users have access to both project space and scratch space on the Data Oasis. The former is shared across SDSC's two nationally allocated resources, Gordon and Trestles, and provides each project with a minimum of 500 GB of space. Storage allocations policies are under development and users will be able to obtain multiple terabytes of project storage if sufficient justification is given. Separate scratch filesystems are mounted on each machine. While this scratch space is persistent, it is subject to purge once the total amount of stored data begins to impact performance.

### 17.4.3   Profiling

Several tools are available on Gordon for profiling I/O. These include PEBIL [M. 10], a lightweight tool developed at SDSC that keeps track of the number of times that each basic block is executed, and TAU [S. 06], a general purpose profiling and tracing tool that is useful for collecting statistics on parallel applications. The following example illustrates the use of PEBIL to profile a Reverse Time Migration code (RTM), an acoustic imaging and seismic application used to determine the structure of geological sub-surface features. As shown, for small problem sizes, there is little advantage to using SDD, but for larger problems speedups as large as 1.4x were obtained (Figure 17.10 and Figure 17.11). In this test case, replacing hard disks with flash drives improves write performance by about 10%, but reduces the time spent in reads by 2.5x. The use of SSDs also increased the fraction of time spent in computation rather than I/O. Hard disks are still susceptible to long write delays even though the average time spent in writes is relatively unchanged.

To profile and analyze the performance of applications running on vSMP, users have access to standard Linux tools as well as ScaleMP tools. Particularly useful non-proprietary tools are *top* and *vmstat*, which report information about processes, memory, paging, block IO, traps, and CPU activity. For example, Figure 17.12 shows a screenshot taken while running top during execution of the Velvet de novo genome assembly code. In this case *top* shows the memory usage and which processor the application is using.

ScaleMP provides two tools to collect performance events traces: *vsmpstat*, for a system-wide view, and *vsmpprof*, for an application-wide view. Both tools collect traces of relevant events such as memory usage and data movement between boards. Figure 17.13 shows some information collected with *vsmpstat* while an application (Velvet) is running. For example, we see that Velvet is running on board 1 (labeled bbc:01 in first column) and using all of the memory on that board (99.9 in final column), with additional memory supplied by other boards.

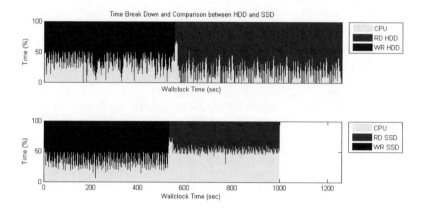

**FIGURE 17.10**: Breakdown of time into I/O and computation on the execution timeline. The area occupied by I/O is smaller with flash, and therefore the same amount of computation can be completed in a shorter period of time resulting in faster execution. (Figure generated using SDSC's PEBIL software.)

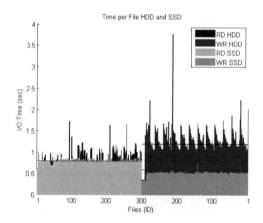

**FIGURE 17.11**: I/O time per file using disks and flash. The comparison illustrates how in the write phase the performance of both technologies is comparable although disks occasionally suffer high delays. (Figure generated using SDSC's PEBIL software.)

*vsmpprof* can collect events generated by a specific application, thereby enabling a more detailed analysis. Using the *logpar* post-processing tool, a trace can be summarized into tables or plots, showing timings or events counts. Tables can relate events to memory addresses and the routines responsible for the events. This information can then be used as a starting point for low-level performance tuning. Plots show a timeline of the events to give a sense of the behavior of the application and its interaction with the system. Figure 17.14 and Figure 17.15 show event counts and CPU usage for both Velvet and the system collected over the entire run.

```
top - 21:58:53 up 132 days, 10:31,  1 user,  load average: 1.31, 1.25, 1.39
Tasks: 1877 total,   2 running, 1875 sleeping,   0 stopped,   0 zombie
Cpu(s):  0.6%us,  0.2%sy,  0.0%ni, 99.2%id,  0.0%wa,  0.0%hi,  0.0%si,  0.0%st
Mem:  661804524k total, 230784280k used, 431020244k free,   305480k buffers
Swap: 16386292k total,        0k used, 16386292k free, 75798856k cached

  PID USER      PR  NI  VIRT  RES  SHR S %CPU %MEM    TIME+  P COMMAND

19489 pcicotti  20   0  139g 132g 1236 R 100.0 21.0 162:14.58  8 velvetg
```

**FIGURE 17.12**: Screenshot of Linux top command on vSMP node during single-core Velvet run.

```
Board Basic Counters:
bbc:Bd     Time %VMM  %Brd  %Sys     #Brd    #Sys #TLB Flush   #PTW %PTEm  #PTf     #4kCL  %Use
bbc:00       96 31.6   1.1  30.5    14380    2201     1799      27  29.6   141  12032713  16.3
bbc:01      100 64.1  27.0  37.1    38276    7862     7362       8   100     4  12033473  99.9
bbc:02       98 17.0   1.0  16.0     8739     456      372       0   0.0    21  12033463  42.1
bbc:03      100 24.8   6.7  18.1    34812    2044     2761     666  50.0    26  12033467   1.2
bbc:04       95 21.5   0.8  20.7     7482     595      451       0   0.0   109  12033477   8.7
bbc:05       93  7.0   1.2   5.8    13112    1307     1317      44  47.7   160  12033466  55.8
bbc:06       96 19.5   5.6  13.9    21907    3279     2740      83  97.6   170  12033476  24.9
bbc:07       95 12.4   0.9  11.4    12184    1653     1063     199  88.4   145  12033346  23.9
bbc:08       97 18.3   0.7  17.5     7974     984      775       0   0.0   161  12033466  20.9
bbc:09       97 18.1   0.6  17.5     7915     923      715       0   0.0 16365  12033454  18.9
bbc:10       91 28.3   1.6  26.8    11991    1523     1283       0   0.0   147  12033462  17.8
bbc:11       94 13.2   0.7  12.5     8053     899      666       0   0.0   212  12000600  23.4
bbc:12       95 25.7   2.0  23.7    11179     982     1054       0   0.0   164  12033470  15.4
bbc:13       93 10.6   4.3   6.3     5723     500      389       0   0.0   182  12033485  49.7
bbc:14       95  8.0   0.7   7.3     8553     890      772       0   0.0  2612  12033480  20.8
bbc:15       99 19.5   0.5  19.0     7414     933      742       0   0.0  1587  12033489   8.2
```

**FIGURE 17.13**: Screenshot of vsmpstat command on vSMP node during single-core Velvet run.

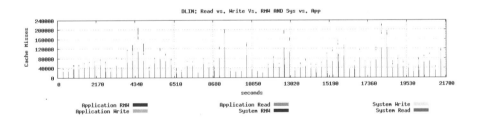

**FIGURE 17.14**: Event counts for Velvet run on vSMP node. Profiling information obtained using vsmpprof and display generated using the logpar post-processing tool.

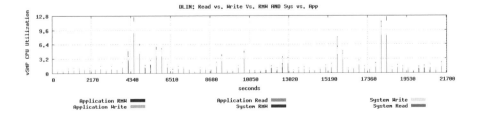

**FIGURE 17.15**: CPU utilization for Velvet run on vSMP node. Profiling information obtained using vsmpprof and display generated using the logpar post-processing tool.

## 17.5    Benchmarks and Applications

Approximately 80% of the total available compute cycles on Gordon are awarded on a competitive basis through the Extreme Science and Engineering Discovery Environment (XSEDE) allocations process. Preference is given to those projects that can make use of Gordon's unique features, namely the large memory vSMP nodes and flash memory. Priority is also given to researchers with large per-core memory requirements, heavy I/O needs, and codes that can effectively use the AVX instruction set to achieve up to eight floating point operations per cycle per core on the Sandy Bridge processors. By June 2012, Gordon had only been available for two XSEDE quarterly allocations cycles and in production for a little over three months. As a consequence, the user base is expected to evolve at least until the end of 2012, by which time most long-term XSEDE users will have had a chance to apply for time.

Although Gordon is still relatively new, some trends are already emerging. For example, the heaviest users so far have been computational chemists. Many of the chemistry codes need to write large integral files to scratch and then subsequently access them in a random manner. As would be expected, these codes can spend much of their time waiting for disk I/O. Since the latency for the flash drives (Intel 710 series specifications: 75 $\mu$s read, 85 $\mu$s write) is roughly two orders of magnitude faster than that for hard disks, substantial speedups can be obtained by using flash. Neither the Gordon I/O nodes nor the compute nodes contain local hard drives, so it is not possible to isolate the impact of the flash drives, but users of Gaussian, GAMESS, and other chemistry applications have been very satisfied with the performance. Researchers in physics, quantum chromodynamics (QCD) in particular, are the next heaviest Gordon users. Although these are distributed memory applications, the specific calculations tend to have large per-core memory requirements and are therefore well suited for Gordon.

Several shared memory applications have made excellent use of Gordon's vSMP nodes. Genome assembly codes such as Velvet, ALLPATHS, and SOAPdenovo tend to have limited scalability, but need hundreds of gigabytes of memory when working with large chromosomes. The Abaqus software suite and Gaussian 09 used large amounts of both memory and flash on the vSMP nodes to solve problems that could not be solved on standard machines. These are described in more detail below. Other problems run on Gordon include simulations of materials (traditional molecular dynamics, embedded atom methods, and QM/MM calculations), severe weather prediction, asteroid tracking, analysis of stock market activity, astrophysics, time-series classification and the construction of phylogenetic trees.

### 17.5.1    Benchmark Results

#### 17.5.1.1    Standard HPC Benchmarks

Standard applications benchmarks were run to characterize Gordon's compute, I/O, and networking performance on realistic workloads. These benchmark suite included LINPACK, STREAM [Joh95], HPCC [DL05], HOMME, WRF, PARATEC, and MILC.

The LINPACK benchmark was run on a configuration of 1,010 nodes hosting 16,160 MPI processes arranged as an 80 by 202 process mesh. The benchmark resulted in a measured 285.8 TFLOPS, which corresponds to 83.9% of the theoretical peak performance of the entire machine (285.8/340.8 x 100 = 83.9) or 85.0% of the theoretical peak for the 1,010 nodes. Note that 1,010 nodes were used rather than the 1,024 of the entire system as the result of a selection process aimed at finding an optimal process layout. An early result of

**TABLE 17.3**: HPCC benchmark results.

| Cores | G-HPL | G-PTRANS | G-FFTW | G-Rand Access | EP-DGEMM | Rand Ring BW | Rand Ring Lat |
|---|---|---|---|---|---|---|---|
| | **TFLOPS** | **GB/s** | **GFLOPS** | **GUPS** | **GFLOPS** | **GB/s** | **$\mu$s** |
| 128 | 2.25 | 27.0 | 85.4 | 0.904 | 19.34 | 0.374 | 4.3 |
| 256 | 4.50 | 57.0 | 150.3 | 1.595 | 19.30 | 0.345 | 5.6 |
| 512 | 8.77 | 98.1 | 264.2 | 2.706 | 19.41 | 0.261 | 5.9 |
| 1,024 | 17.02 | 196.3 | 464.7 | 4.883 | 19.21 | 0.241 | 6.3 |
| 2,048 | 36.67 | 327.3 | 627.8 | 8.347 | 19.38 | 0.199 | 6.7 |
| 12,288 | 218.5 | 710.3 | 968.7 | 22.302 | 19.27 | 0.050 | 11.8 |

218.1 TFlops using 788 nodes (77% of Gordon) was achieved during the initial integration of the system and resulted in a placement at number 48 in the November 2011 Top500 list [TOPa].

The STREAM benchmark was executed on every node of the system as part of acceptance testing. By running the test with ECC disabled, we were able to simultaneously verify the performance and identify defects in the memory subsystem. The bandwidth measured with the Triad micro-benchmark varied from 59.8 GB/s to 69.6 GB/s per node, which in the worst case corresponds to 70% of the 85 GB/s theoretical peak bandwidth for a node.

The HPCC benchmarks were run at different scales using both 16 and 12 cores per node (the results for the 12 cores per node runs are given in Table 17.3) in order to satisfy the acceptance criteria based on the expected count of 6 cores per processor. The results demonstrated both the strengths of Gordon, such as floating point operations per second, point-to-point communication, and memory bandwidth; some benchmarks also showed the effect of contention on over-subscribed switch-to-switch links.

The Double precision GEneral Matrix Multiply (DGEMM) micro-benchmark reflects the FLOPS capability of the Sandy Bridge processor core and its AVX instructions achieving more than 90% of the outstanding theoretical peak of 20.8 GFLOPS. The High Performance Linpack (HPL) benchmark results confirm the outstanding FLOPS of the processor and of Gordon, with 80% or more of the peak performance achieved in all cases.

By design, parallel jobs running on nodes that are all connected directly to the same switch enjoy very low latencies and high bandwidth, while larger jobs running on nodes that span multiple switches may suffer from the effects of over-subscription on inter-switch links. The network topology of Gordon is a hybrid torus topology in which each switch connects 16 compute nodes to the torus, and the switches are connected by 3 links. As a consequence, there is a ratio of 16:3 compute nodes to inter-switch links (the ratio is also aggravated by the higher than expected core count). The effect on performance is particularly noticeable in problems that are sensitive to bisection bandwidth, such as the FFT and the parallel transpose benchmarks (shown in Figure 17.16). Performance scales well up to 2,048 cores, at which point the switch-to-switch bandwidth is saturated for some paths and becomes a communication bottleneck.

The impact of the over-subscription is also seen in the random ring bandwidth benchmark and latency tests; in the latter, contention introduces delays affecting also the transfer latency (Figure 17.17).

Despite the limited scalability in these specific cases, the projected performance was met

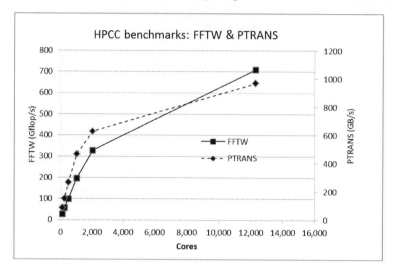

**FIGURE 17.16**: FFTW and PTRANS performance.

or exceeded in most cases. In addition, this limitation is not a flaw in the design of Gordon but rather an inherent characteristic of the topology, and the performance achieved is indeed extremely competitive. While this limitation can be reduced or eliminated by changing the ratio between compute node links and switch-to-switch links, Gordon's design strikes an optimal balance between costs and performance at various scales while delivering very high performance for small and medium size jobs (e.g., 16 to 128 compute nodes).

As part of acceptance, the system had to meet projected performance requirements for four standard HPC applications — HOMME, MILC, PARATEC, and WRF. For these applications, results on the benchmark test cases are given in Table 17.4, together with the corresponding target performance numbers. In every case, the measured time for the benchmark was below or within a very small tolerance of the projected value. Note that the

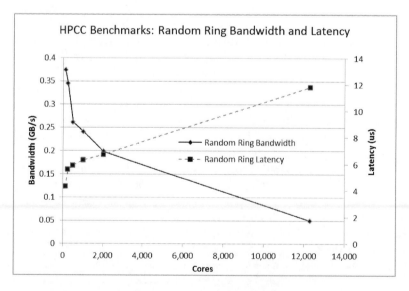

**FIGURE 17.17**: Random ring bandwidth and latency.

TABLE 17.4: Application benchmarks.

| Application | Problem size | Cores | Projected Time(s) | Measured Time(s) |
|---|---|---|---|---|
| HOMME | standard | 512 | 5609 | 5014 |
| | large | 2,048 | 61,790 | 52,471 |
| MILC | medium | 64 | 131 | 134 |
| | large | 256 | 1,034 | 982 |
| | xl | 2,048 | 1,441 | 1,255 |
| PARATEC | medium | 64 | 283 | 279 |
| | large | 256 | 388 | 424 |
| WRF | standard | 128 | 374 | 343 |
| | large | 512 | 1,279 | 1,304 |

applications were all run using 16 cores per compute node whereas the estimates were based on 12 cores per node according to the original plan of record. As mentioned previously, the final processor design was an 8 core chip. Given that the number of memory channels per processor remained unchanged from the initial Sandy Bridge design, the memory bandwidth available per core is only 75% of the original estimate and some relative loss of performance was expected.

### 17.5.1.2 I/O benchmarks

The architecture of Gordon has two storage layers: a flash-based scratch space and a global Lustre-based parallel filesystem. The flash-based layer is intended to be a scratch space for temporary data. The flash layer can be configured for either exclusive or shared access: a single drive filesystem per node (non-shared) and a 16 aggregated drives filesystem shared by 16 compute nodes. In both cases, I/O Operations Per Second (IOPS) as well as bandwidth are the relevant metrics. Flash performance was measured both locally on the I/O nodes,[2] and remotely from the compute nodes. Under a workload generated using the FIO benchmark running on the I/O nodes, the flash drives exceeded their nominal peak bandwidth for sequential workloads and their nominal peak IOPS for random workloads (the results of the benchmarks are reported in Table 17.5). The aggregate IOPS that the whole system can deliver has been of particular interest because it gives a sense of Gordon's capabilities and performance in supporting data intensive workloads. At a demonstration offered at SDSC's booth during SC11, the random workload benchmark was scaled to all the I/O nodes reaching an aggregate of more than 35 million IOPS.

In the production configuration, the flash drives are remotely mounted using iSER over one rail, of the IB network with XFS as the filesystem. Access to flash from the compute nodes incurs several overhead and performance penalties that are not present when accessing locally. From a single node, the sequential access bandwidth is reduced by 17% and 13% for read and write operations, respectively. The aggregate performance is reduced even more due to the limited bandwidth of a single rail. Similarly, high contention impacts the deliverable IOPS, with the aggregate rate dropping to 25% of the local read IOPS. However,

---

[2]To accommodate data intensive applications with persistent data sets, I/O nodes can be allocated and scheduled as dedicated resources and host computations.

**TABLE 17.5**: I/O node local flash performance.

| Drives | Operation | KIOPS | Bandwidth (GB/s) |
|--------|-----------|-------|------------------|
| 1 | Read | 37.6 | 0.27 |
| 1 | Write | 2.3 | 0.21 |
| 16 | Read | 601.9 | 4.34 |
| 16 | Write | 37.1 | 3.37 |

**TABLE 17.6**: Remote flash performance.

| Drives | Operation | KIOPS | Bandwidth (GB/s) |
|--------|-----------|-------|------------------|
| 1 | Read | 10.7 | 0.23 |
| 1 | Write | 2.2 | 0.19 |
| 16 | Read | 152.7 | 2.67 |
| 16 | Write | 34.3 | 2.60 |

the lower write IOPS rate is better supported by the network and is only marginally reduced (Table 17.6).

The Lustre-based filesystem is a global parallel filesystem to which all compute nodes have access and is base storage for persistent and very large data sets and the key performance measure is bandwidth. Lustre performance was measured using the IOR benchmark, with one compute node per I/O node and scaling from one to 48 compute node and I/O node pairs. The results (see Table 17.7) showed that a single compute node can obtain 1.8 GB/s for read operations and 1.7 GB/s for write operations. In addition, bandwidth scaling to 48 IO nodes was achieved with a relative efficiency of more than 86%. Scaling to 64 pairs effectively using all the IO nodes was not possible since the Lustre filesystem was in production and shared with another HPC system at the time of testing, and such a performance test would have required an interruption in service. However, based on the observed scaling, the projected performance at full scale would approximate 100 GB/s for both reads and writes.

**TABLE 17.7**: Lustre parallel filesystem performance.

| IO Nodes | Write GB/s | Read GB/s |
|----------|------------|-----------|
| 1 | 1.7 | 1.8 |
| 2 | 3.4 | 3.4 |
| 4 | 6.0 | 6.7 |
| 8 | 11.3 | 13.0 |
| 16 | 24.7 | 23.7 |
| 32 | 50.7 | 50.8 |
| 48 | 75.4 | 74.5 |

## 17.5.2  Highlights of Selected Applications

Researchers Matthew Goff and Chris Hernandez at Cornell University used the Abaqus finite element software to simulate the response of trabecular bone to mechanical stress. In particular, the work investigated how small variations in the boundary conditions affected the high strain regions of the model. Their research has relevance across a variety of fields. Paleontologists can gain insight into the locomotion of ancient people and animals, while medical specialists can use the results to develop strategies for dealing with the challenges faced by the elderly and other populations with fragile bones.

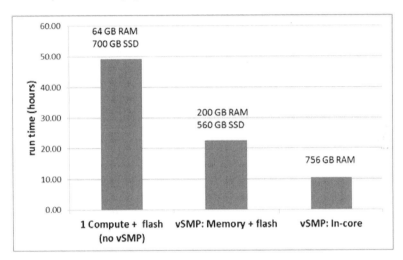

**FIGURE 17.18**: Abaqus benchmarks for large memory simulation of the response of trabecular bone to mechanical stress.

Because many finite element calculations have very large memory footprints, Abaqus provides capabilities for running out of core. The user will generally choose to use all of the available memory and make up the remainder using scratch space (Figure 17.18). Running on a single Gordon compute node with 64 GB of memory and using 700 GB of flash storage for scratch, a simulation of a bone model with five million 8-noded elements was still not completed in 1,023 hours. Although we could have repeated this calculation writing to the parallel filesystem, the already long run time using flash made this infeasible. Running on a vSMP node using 200 GB of DRAM and 560 GB flash reduced the run time to just over 20 hours, while running entirely in memory dropped the wall time to ten hours. In all three cases, just 16 compute cores were used due to Abaqus licensing restrictions and it is likely that even better performance could be obtained by using more cores. When choosing a balance between flash and DRAM, the user should take into account the number of underlying compute nodes that are used and the relative importance of minimizing the time to solution. The job run on the vSMP node using a combination of memory (200 GB) and flash (700 GB) spanned four node worth of memory and was charged accordingly. Using vSMP in this way clearly pays off since the run time was at most one fifth that needed when using just flash for scratch space. On the other hand, the fully in-core job used 13 boards worth of memory, but only ran 2.2x faster than the mixed job and was ultimately charged more.

Another example highlighting the capabilities of Gordon is a Gaussian MP2 gradient calculation on the digoxin molecule, an extract from the foxglove plant that is used to treat a variety of conditions including diseases of the heart. Using 64 compute cores and 700 GB of memory on a Gordon vSMP node, the simulation was completed in slightly

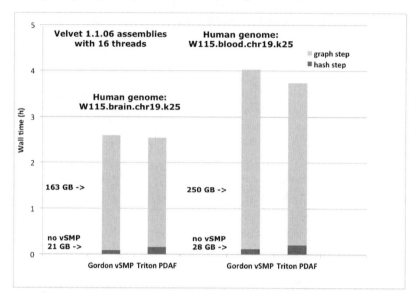

**FIGURE 17.19**: Assembly of human chromosome 19 from brain and blood samples using Velvet. The results compare performance on a Gordon vSMP node and on UCSDs PDAF (Petascale Data Analysis Facility), a large physically shared memory system.

less than 12 hours. What is notable about this result is that the run time was nearly identical to that obtained on SGI UV Altix system, thereby demonstrating that vSMP can provide performance at least as good as that obtained on hardware shared memory machines. Scalability studies on a smaller system (diporphyrin test problem with a 100 GB memory footprint) showed super-linear scaling when going from 32 to 64 cores, most likely due to cache effects.

A final example demonstrating the capabilities of Gordon is de novo genome assembly. For simple organisms with smaller genomes, the assembly process can often be done on standard desktop systems. For larger and more complex genomes though, large shared memory resources are often needed. Several programs, including SOAPdenovo, ALLPATHS, and Velvet, are widely used for genome assembly. Each of these has its own strengths and weaknesses in terms of accuracy and computational requirements. In this study, we evaluate the performance of Velvet when assembling human chromosome 19 using reads from brain and blood samples. The run times are compared using results obtained on Gordon and UCSD's Petascale Data Analysis Facility (PDAF) nodes, which are populated with 512 GB of physically shared memory (Figure 17.19). The first step of the process, known as the hash step, has a small memory requirement and can be run on a single Gordon compute node. The lower run times on Gordon simply reflect the difference in the processor performance on Gordon and the PDAF node. On the memory intensive graph step though, one might expect to see the advantages of physical shared memory, but the Gordon vSMP node performs nearly as well. Given that vSMP provides flexibility in how the nodes are deployed and is a less expensive solution than large physically shared memory, it can be a viable solution for many problems requiring large memory.

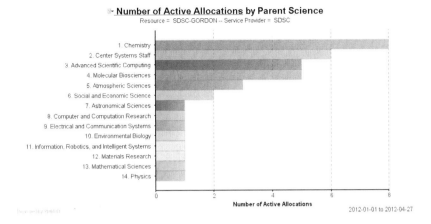

**FIGURE 17.20**: Number of Gordon allocations by domain.

## 17.6   System Statistics

Deciding which NSF allocation cycle to bring a system like Gordon into production is tricky. If allocated too soon, the system may not be fully stable and therefore be less productive for users. On the other hand, waiting too long could add a delay of 3-6 months after acceptance until the first allocated users get on the system. Given the expectations in the community for access to a major new platform like Gordon, there was a sense of urgency to get the system deployed. Working closely with the vendors,[3] it was determined that system delivery and testing would allow Gordon to be available to users in Q1 2012, which meant it needed to be an allocable platform in the proposal cycle that opened on September 2011 for a start date of January 1, 2012. As it played out, Gordon was delivered to SDSC on November 17, 2011,[4] two months after users submitted the first round of allocation requests. The subsequent build and acceptance process continued through mid-February, and Gordon was made available to early users on February 25, 2012. Job accounting became active on March 5. Although Gordon was not available on January 1, 2012, users were still able to access the system in Q1 2012 as originally planned. There are currently users from two XRAC cycles on the system, with a large outstanding request under review for projects beginning on July 1, 2012.

The XDMoD resource is useful in characterizing how Gordon has been used thus far [Fur11]. As Figures 17.20 and 17.21 show, computational chemistry and physics are the top two allocated fields, and have accordingly used the most time to date. There is an interesting project related to financial markets that has done quite a bit of computation as well which is reflected in the social and economic parent science. Notably, vSMP has been used for projects in astronomy and genomics with several allocations and recent transfers in the latter.

---

[3]The Intel Sandy Bridge processor availability slipped by 6 months from original projections.
[4]Incidentally, the same week as SC'11.

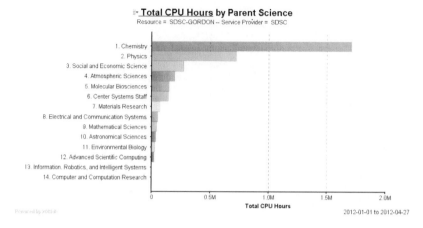

**FIGURE 17.21**: Service units (compute core hours) allocated on Gordon by domain.

## 17.7    SDSC — A History of Innovation and Discovery

SDSC was founded when General Atomics, then a division of General Dynamics, won a cooperative agreement in collaboration with the University of California, San Diego to establish a supercomputer center on the UCSD campus. SDSC opened its doors in 1985 with Dr. Sid Karin as the founding director (Figure 17.22).

On November 14, 1985, the San Diego Supercomputer Center opened its doors on the northwestern corner of the UC San Diego campus and showed off its first supercomputer, a CRAY X-MP/48 clocking at what one newspaper article called a "mind-boggling" billion calculations per second... a gigaflop. Actually, the peak performance was closer to 800 million calculations per second, but still pretty fast then. Some 100 researchers – all from traditional disciplines such as astrophysics, biochemistry, geology, and oceanography – applied for time on the new supercomputer, which promised to usher in a new era of scientific discovery. Since that day, scientific and technological advances made possible, and/or created by SDSC staff and resources like the original CRAY, have made a major mark in academia, industry, and society-at-large "turning data to discovery," a phrase that has become associated with SDSC. The Center has brought together researchers at UC San Diego and across the nation and world, in partnerships and collaborations that now are the hallmark of today's scientific enterprise. SDSC also has proven to be a good neighbor, providing its expertise and considerable resources to local educators and students, firefighters and other "first-responders," families of military serving overseas, and others in time of need. Over the last 25 years SDSC has deployed 22 high performance computing systems to the national research community. Starting with the Cray X-MP/48 in November 1985 with 800 million words (6.4 GB) of memory and a peak performance of 800 MFLOP/s, up to the most recent Gordon data intensive system in 2011 with 64 TB of memory and a peak performance of 341 TFLOP/s, SDSC's has a long tradition of innovation in HPC architectures (Table 17.8).

**TABLE 17.8**: SDSC HPC systems over the last 25 years.

| Date deployed | System | Characteristics |
|---|---|---|
| November 1985 | Cray X-MP/48 | 4 vector processors |
| July 1986 | Scientific Computer Systems SCS-40 | 1 vector processor |
| June 1988 | Supertek S1 | 1 vector processor |
| December 1989 | Cray Y-MP8/864 | 8 vector processors |
| September 1990 | Intel iPSC/860 | 32 nodes; 64 nodes in August 1991 |
| November 1990 | nCube 2 | 64 nodes 128 nodes in May 1991 |
| February 1993 | Intel Paragon | 192 nodes; 400 nodes in June 1993 |
| November 1993 | Cray C90 | 8 vector processors |
| September 1995 | Cray T3D | 128 processors |
| December 1996 | Cray T3E | 272 processors |
| October 1997 | Cray T90 | 4 vector processors; 14 processors in December 1997 |

**FIGURE 17.22**: SDSC Founding Management Team. Pictured left to right: Wayne Pfeiffer (manager, User Services), Chuck Fox (deputy director), Sid Karin (director), Fred McClain (manager, Programming and Software), Dan Drobnis (manager, Engineering and Operations), and Dan Bender (program manager), 1985.

Table 17.8 Continued.

| November 1997 | IBM RS/600 SP | 128 processors |
|---|---|---|
| December 1997 | Tera MTA | 1 multi-threaded processor; 2 processors in April 1998, 4 processors in December 1998 and 8 processors in June 1999. |
| November 1999 | IBM Blue Horizon SP | 1,152 processors; upgraded to faster processors in October 2000 |
| June 2003 | IBM/IntelIA-64 Phase 1 | 256 processors |
| December 2003 | IBM/IntelIA-64 Phase 2 | 512 processors |
| January 2004 | IBM DataStar SP | 176 8-way p655s and 11 32-way p690s; 272 8-way p655s and 11 32-way p690s in September 2005 |
| December 2004 | IBM Blue Gene | 2,048 processors; 6,144 processors in November 2006 |
| | Appro Nehalem cluster (Triton Resource) | 512 processors |
| August 2009 | Sun Shanghai cluster (Triton Resource) | 224 processers |
| September 2009 | IBM iDataPlex Nehalem cluster (Thresher) | 272 nodes |
| October 2010 | Appro Magny-Cours cluster (Trestles) | 1,296 processors |
| November 2011 | Appro Sandy Bridge cluster (Gordon) | 2,048 processors |

## Acknowledgments

A project like Gordon cannot succeed without the support and expertise of a great team. Jim Ballew was a primary system architect and remains an important advisor to the project. Special thanks are in order to Jiahua He and Jeff Bennett for their early work on Dash and Wayne Pfeiffer for his work with genomics applications under vSMP. Kenneth Yoshimoto, Diane Baxter, Susan Rathbun, Bao Nguyen, Tom Hutton, Phil Papadopoulos, Richard Moore, and many others at SDSC were critical in getting Gordon into production.

Greg Faussette, Steve Lyness, Adrian Wu, and Roland Wong from Appro were instrumental in the design and in working with technology partners. Shai Fultheim and Nir Paikowsky and the team from ScaleMP worked around the clock to bring vSMP to Gordon to meet the production schedule. This work was supported by NSF grant: OCI #0910847, Gordon: A Data Intensive Supercomputer.

On July 14, 2012, Allan Snavely passed away following a bicycle ride to the top of Mount Diablo in Northern California. Allan was an avid cyclist, and his energy and drive came through in everything he did. As the co-PI of Gordon, and the founding director of SDSC's Performance, Modeling and Characterization Lab, Allan's enthusiasm, expertise, and commitment to advancing the art of HPC design were an inspiration to everyone on the Gordon team. He was a mentor and friend to many in the community and will always be remembered as a visionary and true pioneer in HPC.

# Chapter 18

## Monte Rosa: Architectural Features and a Path Toward Exascale

**Sadaf R. Alam, Gilles Fourestey, Maria Grazia Giuffreda, and Colin McMurtrie**

*Swiss National Supercomputing Centre (CSCS)*

## 18.1 Overview

This chapter overviews a Cray XE6 platform [cra], which exhibits a number of architectural features and programming methodologies of multi-petaflops systems, and potentially serves as a testbed for developers of Exascale applications. A 1,496 nodes Cray XE6 platform has been recently deployed at the Swiss National Supercomputing Centre (CSCS) to support the scientific simulation needs of researchers at Swiss and international institutions. The system is composed of the latest generation of the AMD Opteron Interlagos processors,

Gemini interconnect, and has been connected to a parallel filesystem and other operational and management infrastructure of CSCS. At the node level, there is a total of 32 cores, which can be clocked to two levels of higher clock frequencies with the AMD Turbo Core feature. Moreover, the dual-socket node features four non-uniform memory access (NUMA) domains, two for each socket. Hence, in order to exploit the performance capabilities of the node, code developers must exploit the underlying architectural characteristics, especially the memory hierarchy, which is critical for Exascale application performance and power efficiencies. In addition, the applications must exploit multiple levels of parallelism, using available paradigms such as MPI and OpenMP as well as emerging parallel programming techniques. The Cray Gemini interconnect [ARK10], which provides support for MPI and remote memory access programming models (for example Coarray Fortran), enables code developers to optimize applications that demand high communication bandwidth to tens of thousands of nodes. Another important consideration for CSCS as a supercomputing and datacenter hosting site is the integration of parallel filesystems and other operational and management resources. At Exascale, there are additional considerations including fault tolerance, resiliency, and manageability. The Cray XE6 system offers scalable and resilient parallel file I/O and system management interfaces and in this report we provide current configuration details and discuss paths to extend the setup to multi-Petascale and Exascale platforms. Since development of scalable applications is an integral part of the strategy to deploy multi-Petascale and Exascale platforms, we outline initiatives and projects in Switzerland that have been funded since 2009 to pursue high risk and high reward high performance computing (HPC) challenges in different scientific domains.

### 18.1.1    CSCS Misson and Supercomputing Platforms

The mission of CSCS is to develop and promote technical and scientific services for the Swiss research community in the fields of high performance computing. To fulfill this mission, the flagship system has been deploying production and early access prototype systems as we explain in the next section. The current flagship production system for scientific simulations is a Cray XE6 platform. In addition there are systems for research and development, Meteoswiss and CHIPP clusters, and data analytics and visualization systems. There are infrastructure elements that are shared among these systems, job submission and accounting, etc., and the Cray platforms are integrated in the ecosystem and its operation and maintainability are ensured. In this chapter, we discuss some of these elements as integration of future Exascale systems to existing ecosystems of data, and HPC centers is a critical requirement.

### 18.1.2    Timeline: Cray Platforms at CSCS

The November 2011 TOP500 list of supercomputing platforms showcased High Performance Linpack (HPL) efficiency of over 10-Petaflops [TOPa]. Since June 2011, the first ten entries include systems that exceed 1 Petaflops. Two systems on this list are Cray XE6 systems while one is a Cray XT5 system. This chapter provides an overview of the Cray XE6 platform that has been recently deployed at CSCS. Over the past several years, CSCS has deployed a range of Cray XT series platforms; some were new deployments and others were upgrades of individual components. Hence, one of the advantages of Cray XE and XT series platforms is their potential for upgradability, where capabilities of a platform can be increased by orders of magnitude without full-scale hardware investment. Figure 18.1 shows the timeline of CSCS Cray XT and XE series platform evolution over the years. In 2005, CSCS installed a Cray XT3 system with a single-core and single-socket AMD Opteron processor. Later the system was upgraded to a dual-core processor. In 2009, a SeaStarII

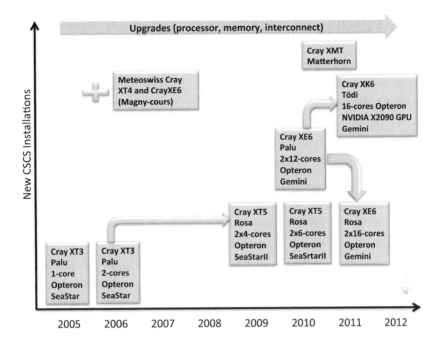

**FIGURE 18.1**: History of CSCS Cray XT and XE Series flagship systems. The upgraded components within a system include processor, memory, and interconnect infrastructure as well as operational hardware stack. For example, for the upgrade of the Cray XE6 platform, the processor, memory, and interconnect of the Cray XT5 system were upgraded, within existing cabinets.

based, dual-socket AMD 4-core processor based flagship platform named "Monte Rosa" was installed. This platform was upgraded twice, first with 6-core processors and later it went through a major upgrade where processors, memories, and the interconnect were upgraded. In addition to the flagship systems for production projects, CSCS introduced prototypes of two new generations of Cray MPP platforms. In 2009, CSCS introduced the first prototype, which was based on the Cray Gemini interconnect, with a dual-socket, 12-core AMD processor [BWM+12]. In 2010, a hybrid node system with CPU and GPU accelerator devices called the Cray XK6 platform was installed at CSCS. During this time frame, the core technologies were upgraded by the availability of socket compatible multi-core processors, memory technologies upgrades, and finally the network upgrade from the SeaStar to the Gemini interconnect [BPUH06][ARK10].

CSCS was one of the first sites in Europe to install a Cray XT3 system and since that time we have expanded, upgraded, and installed several newer Cray systems. In summary, at the time of writing, we have the following Cray systems at CSCS:

- Our flagship system, called Monte Rosa, which is a 16-cabinet Interlagos-based XE6 with 1,496 compute nodes and 47,872 compute cores. This system is used for production science projects and applications.

- A single cabinet Interlagos-based XE6 which is partially populated with compute and service blades. This system is our Test and Development System (TDS) for the the production XE6 machine. We install operating system patches and updates on this system and test them as thoroughly as possible before deploying them to the production environment.

- An advanced prototype system which is a three-cabinet XK6, called Tödi. Two of the cabinets of this system (i.e., 176 compute nodes) contain NVIDIA X2090 GP-GPU cards (one per compute node) and one Interlagos CPU per node while a third cabinet contains 96 compute nodes without any GPU card. This system is used by advanced research teams to experiment with this new architecture. We plan on upgrading the system as the new generation of accelerator devices become available.

- A three-cabinet XE6 system containing AMD Magny-cours (12-cores) processors. This system is partitioned into two parts, one partition containing two cabinets and the other the third cabinet. This system was installed new from Cray when CSCS shifted into the new datacenter just before Easter 2012 and will be the new weather simulation system for the MeteoSwiss. At the time of writing the system is fully operational and undergoing testing by the MeteoSwiss in parallel operation with the main production MeteoSwiss systems (described below).

- Five cabinets of Cray XT4 which are configured as one stand-alone system of three cabinets and one of two cabinets. These systems are the primary and secondary failover system in production use for the MeteoSwiss service. Once the new XE6 MeteoSwiss systems have proved themselves these aging XT4 systems will be shut down and decommissioned.

- One cabinet of Cray's next generation XMT. This system was purchased as a test and development system for large data-analytics services.

### 18.1.3    Characteristic Features of Cray X* Series Systems

The key feature of the X* lineup from Cray is the versatility and modular nature of the system design. For example the Monte Rosa system was upgraded in November 2011 from a 20-cabinet, water-cooled, XT5 system. All 20 cabinets were upgraded with the necessary components to make them function as liquid-cooled cabinets but only 16 of them had the upgraded compute blades put in them, containing the Gemini interconnect NIC and AMD Interlagos Opteron processors. Furthermore two cabinets' worth of the compute blades actually came from the predecessor of the Tödi system which had the AMD Magny-cores 12-core Opteron processors. Now located in the new CSCS datacenter the Monte Rosa system has the running 16 cabinets of XE6 and the non-functioning four cabinets all connected together in two rows each with two cooling units (XDPs) connected to five running cabinets and three running cabinets and two non-functioning cabinets, respectively. We could consider populating the four non-functioning cabinets with compute blades and add them to the system in order to expand it. This ability to expand and shrink the system as the product line evolves is a key feature of the Cray design and makes it very convenient for HPC sites to keep pace with the ever-evolving and ever-changing face of the HPC industry.

As another example of the versatility of the system design and integration, the three-cabinet XK6 system (two cabinets with GP-GPUs and one without) along with the one cabinet XE6 TDS system and the next-generation XMT were all converted from air cooling to liquid cooling and connected to the same XDP liquid cooling unit as part of the move to the new CSCS datacenter. This work was completed in a matter of days and makes the process of managing the building infrastructure components associated with these systems far easier and more cost effective. The machines all continue to function as independent systems however, with their own boot RAIDs, management workstations, etc.; it is just the same cooling infrastructure that they share.

This ability for HPC datacenter managers to carefully manage their system upgrades in a modular and flexible fashion has also been taken advantage of at other sites around the world and will likely play a part in the management of HPC systems as we move toward the Exascale regime.

## 18.2 Applications and Workloads

Almost all of the computational resources available on the current CSCS flagship Cray XE6 platform, Monte Rosa, are distributed to researchers who have successfully applied for them with regular Production Project Proposals. In summer 2009, CSCS has established an improved review process that entails the solicitation of two detailed expert reviews per proposal, two in-house technical reviews, and a final evaluation through a panel review committee. Reviewers have been drawn almost exclusively from academic institutions abroad, with European and U.S. institutions contributing 45% and 42% to the reviewer base in 2011, respectively. An additional 10% has been recruited from Australia, Japan, and Canada. A fairly large reviewer base is needed since it is CSCS policy to assign different proposals of the same scientist, also those submitted in subsequent years, to different reviewers in order to minimize the possible risk of undue personal conflict. The overwhelming number of proposals (92% in 2011) has received marks from the two reviewers that differed by no more than one unit on the scale 5 "outstanding," 4 "excellent," 3 "good," 2 "fair," 1 "poor." Substantial disagreement between reviewers opinions was found in only 8% of the cases, and in all these cases the opinion of a third reviewer was solicited. The regular Production Projects are thus the most common types of projects on the Cray XE6 platform. Currently there are 88 of them with a total users base of 605 scientists.

### 18.2.1 Requirements Analysis

CSCS supports and maintains a full range of software on the Cray XE6, Monte Rosa, ranging from programming tools (compilers and libraries) to often-used scientific software packages. Many users, however, contribute their own scientific codes, and they can draw upon a number of different parallel programming styles, all supported on Monte Rosa, including MPI, OpenMP, hybrid MPI/OpenMP, Global Arrays, and simple Pthreads. Next to the open-source GNU compiler collection, Monte Rosa also offers the Cray Compiler Environment (CCE), the Portland Group Compiler (PGI), the Intel Composer Suite, and the PathScale Compiler [HFRR12]. As expected for a scientific environment, Fortran (F90) and C (and C++) are the most-used programming languages. Various debugging and profiling tools are installed, as are a large number of numerical libraries, including ParMETIS [par], LAPACK [lap], FFTW [fft], ScaLAPACK [Sca], PETSc [pet], Trilinos [tri], and GA [NPT+06], to just name a few. Special-purpose I/O libraries are also provided, these include NetCDF, HDF5 [hdf], pNetCDF [pne], MPI-IO.

CSCS application analysts install third-party scientific codes for which there is a large need in the user community. This entails of course careful optimization for highly parallel execution and performance analysis using all the available compiler suites. Currently there are two major codes supported for the climate sciences (COSMO [RWH08], ECHAM-HAM) [ZOK+12] and a number of quantum-chemical (CP2K [cp2], Q-Espresso [qua], NWChem [BdJK+06], CPMD [AC00]) and classical molecular-dynamics codes (LAMMPS [Pli95], GROMACS [groa], AMBER [CCD+05]) for disciplines as diverse as chemistry, biology, ma-

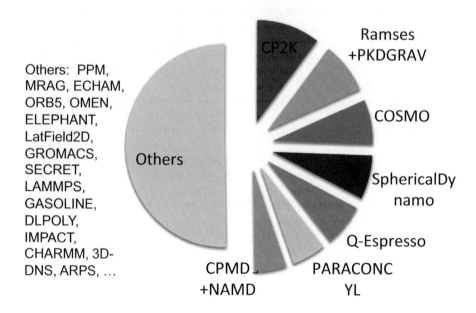

**FIGURE 18.2**: System allocation by application names for 2011 (approximated values).

terials science, and nanoscience. The two most-used codes, CP2K and NAMD [KHZ$^+$08], were the workhorses of 17 projects in 4 disciplines in 2011; they accounted for a total of about 50 mio core-hours or roughly 25% of the resources available on Monte Rosa.

The resource distribution by domain is shown in Figure 18.2.

### 18.2.2  Statistics

Currently there are 88 projects with a total user base of 605 scientists. Resources are distributed over many disciplines, including materials science and nanoscience (19% each), chemistry (18%), fluid dynamics (17%), astrophysics (16%), climate research (10%), biology (8%), geoscience (6%), phyics (5%), and finally applied mathematics (1%). The usage of different generations of the Cray platforms for the production science projects is shown in Figure 18.3 for different domains. Over this period of time, the system size and its capabilities have increased by an order of magnitude. Applications that are capable of exploiting both multi-core nodes and scalable interconnect effectively tend to use a large fraction of compute resources.

### 18.2.3  Production Projects and Applications

In this section we comment on some of the largest projects currently running on Monte Rosa, in order to give an impression of the wide range of research being conducted at CSCS. Fluid dynamics is one of the traditional disciplines of computational science. It is based on numerical solutions of the Navier-Stokes equation. Projects carried out at CSCS cover both fundamental aspects such as the evolution of flow structures and those with a very practical engineering background. Prof. P. Koumoutsakos (ETH Zurich), e.g., using his in-house developed code, investigates the dynamics of single and multiple aquatics swimmers such as

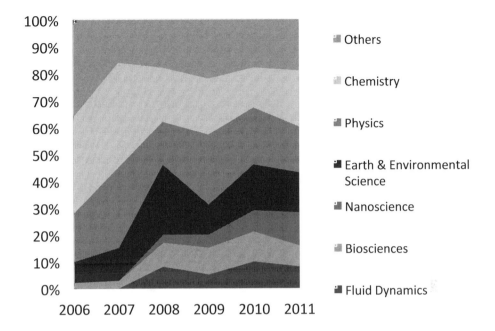

**FIGURE 18.3**: System usage by domains on the CSCS Cray platforms (from 2006 to 2011).

fast swimming fish, trying to assess optimal shape and motion patterns, with applications in robotics and energy harnessing (e.g., wind turbine farming) in mind.

The COSMO (COnsortium for Small-scale MOdelling) model, initially introduced by the German weather service as a "Local Model," has formed the basis of much of the European weather forecast and climate research. MeteoSwiss uses it at CSCS to prepare weather forecasts, and a number of projects at CSCS are based upon its "Climate Mode" version (COSMO-CLM, CCLM) for climate research. Continuing challenges addressed by a project of C. Schär include quality improvements in climate change projections for Europe as well as simulations at high resolution ("cloud-resolving," 2 km grid spacing) for the alpine region [ZOK+12].

CP2K is a code for massively parallel ab initio (density functional) molecular dynamics simulations. Developed by Prof. J. Hutter (University of Zurich) and collaborators, it has continuously been improved, lately, e.g., by the inclusion of Hartree-Fock exchange that allows for the use of more accurate functionals. Further code improvements geared toward applications to extremely large systems are ongoing and use Monte Rosa as their major testing platform. A number of challenging applications are currently pursued on Monte Rosa as well, and they include the computational engineering of dye sensitized solar cells (Prof. J. Vandevondele, ETH Zurich) and the investigation of boron-nitride nano meshes and their adsorption patterns (J. Hutter). Figure 18.4 demonstrates the potentials of CP2K scaling on the Petaflops-scale Cray XT5 platform at the Oak Ridge National Laboratory Leadership Computing Facility.

QuantumEspresso is another popular and well-parallelized density functional code specifically designed for materials modeling at the nanoscale. One large project (A. Hauser) uses it to study the photophysics and photochemistry of crystalline compounds containing transition metals such as rhodium.

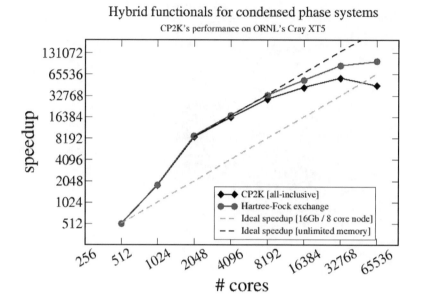

**FIGURE 18.4**: CP2K with hybrid MPI/OpenMP programming exceeding ideal scaling up to 32,768 cores on a CRAY XT5 platform (details at: http://www.pci.uzh.ch/researchgroups/vondele/research.html)

Details of production projects and their accomplishments can be found at: http://www.cscs.ch/newsroom/science/index.html.

## 18.2.4   High Performance and High Productivity (HP2C) Initiative

In order to prepare applications for Petascale systems and beyond, the HP2C initiative was launched in 2009. A number of application development teams were funded to pursue high rick and high reward HPC challenges in various domains. Project details are available at: http://www.hp2c.ch. The following projects were selected through a scientific review process:

- BigDFT - Large scale Density Functional Electronic Structure Calculations in a Systematic Wavelet Basis Set (PI: Prof. Stefan Goedecker, University of Basel)

- Cardiovascular - HPC for Cardiovascular System Simulations (PI: Prof. Alfio Quarteroni, EPF Lausanne)

- COSMO-CCLM - Regional Climate and Weather Modeling on the Next Generations High-Performance Computers: Towards Cloud-Resolving Simulations (PI: Dr. Isabelle Bey, ETH Zurich)

- Cosmology - Computational Cosmology on the Petascale (PI: Prof. George Lake, University of Zurich)

- CP2K - New Frontiers in ab initio Molecular Dynamics (PI: Prof. Juerg Hutter, University of Zurich)

- Ear Modeling - Numerical Modeling of the Ear: Towards the Building of New Hearing Devices (PI: Prof. Bastien Chopard, University of Geneva)

- Gyrokinetic - Advanced Gyrokinetic Numerical Simulations of Turbulence in Fusion Plasmas (PI: Prof. Laurent Villard, EPF Lausanne)

- MAQUIS - Modern Algorithms for Quantum Interacting Systems (PI: Prof. Thierry Giamarchi, University of Geneva)

- Neanderthal Extinction - Individual-based Modeling of Humans under Climate Stress (PI: Prof. C. P. E. Zollikofer, University of Zurich)

- Petaquake - Large-Scale Parallel Nonlinear Optimization for High Resolution 3D-Seismic Imaging (PI: Prof. Olaf Schenk, University of Basel)

- Selectome - Selectome, Looking for Darwinian Evolution in the Tree of Life (PI: Prof. Marc Robinson-Rechavi, University of Lausanne)

- Supernova - Productive 3D Models of Stellar Explosions (PI: Prof. Matthias Liebendorfer, University of Basel)

These project teams, in collaboration with CSCS, are investigating the production Cray XE6 platform and early access Cray XK6 prototype system to prepare applications for the Petascale and Exascale platforms, as these systems expose critical programming and scaling challenges of Exascale platforms.

## 18.3   System Overview

Although the path to the Exascale technologies, according to [BBC⁺08], is not going to be an incremental variant of the existing platforms, some components such as expected number of cores, processor frequencies, and memory hierarchies are already represented in the Cray XE6 architecture. Table 18.1 lists and compares characteristic features of the aggressive strawman system and the Cray XE6 and Cray XK6 platforms at CSCS. For instance, one of the architectural features of the 2015 strawman system is a large number

**TABLE 18.1**: Comparing CSCS Cray XE6 and XK6 systems with the Exascale software report's strawman system configuration for 2015.

|  | Aggressive Strawman (2015) | CSCS Cray XE6 (2011) | CSCS Cray XK6 (2011) |
|---|---|---|---|
| Number of cores per socket | 742 | 32 | 16 (CPU) + 512 (GPU) |
| Clock frequency (GHz) | 1.55 | 2.1 (3.0 with AMD Turbo Core) | 2.1 (CPU) and 1.15 (GPU) |
| Gflops per node | 55,205 | 268.8 | 164.4 (CPU) + 665 (GPU) |
| GBytes per node | 192 | 32 | 32 (CPU) + 6 (GPU) |

of cores. For a projected 2015 system, an aggressive design projects the number of cores per node to be over 700. In terms of the number of cores and other performance features, there is quite a significant difference. However, the hybrid node of a Cray XK6 platform that has a GPU device along with an Interlagos socket offers a similar level of concurrency per node. However, the two systems, Cray XE6 and Cray XK6, share almost all of their programming and operating infrastructure except the GPU related tools. Another important feature of the Interlagos system is an ability of the system to operate at higher clock frequencies. This will be explained in subsequent sections. One of the main reasons for considering the Cray XE6 platform as a path to an Exascale system is performance sensitivities of the architecture to the memory locality. This feature has been highlighted in the Exascale report. With four non-uniform memory access regions or domains, performance tuning on the Cray XE6 system is highly sensitive to the placement and locality of memory. This is true not only for computation on node but also off-node communication operations. Hence, applications developed and tuned for the platform could be ported to an Exascale technology where memory locality is critical for performance and power efficiencies.

The CSCS Cray XE6 platform is composed of dual-socket, AMD Bulldozer 6272 16-cores CPUs, 32 GB memory per compute node, and a proprietary, switchless interconnect called Gemini, which is connected in a class 2, 3D torus topology [gem]. There are in total 1,496 compute nodes or 47,872 cores, with a theoretical peak performance of 402 TFlops.

### 18.3.1    Node Hardware

1. Processor: The Cray XE6 system at CSCS is composed of AMD Opteron 6272 processors, which is based on the AMD Bulldozer micro-architecture (shown in Figure 18.5). The Bulldozer processor introduces the concept of a compute module, where each module is composed of two cores. Individual cores have their individual integer cores and L1 cache while they share the instruction dispatch unit and the floating point unit. The floating point unit has been an innovative feature of the Bulldozer micro-architecture. This 256-bit floating-point unit can be used as two 128-bit vector instructions, namely

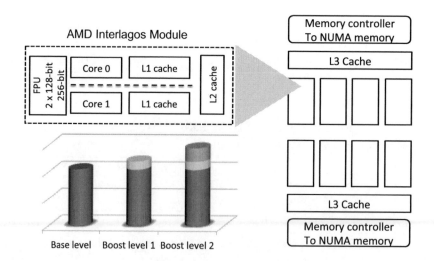

**FIGURE 18.5**: Bulldozer micro-architecture and processor setup. The basic unit is a module and there are two processors on a socket. AMD clock boost features are also shown in the figure.

SSE and AVX (Advanced Vector Extensions), while it can also perform a combined 256-bit AVX operation. AVX instructions have been introduced to take advantage of wide, 256-bit register file. Performance features are highly workload dependent. Additional features include two-levels of clock boost, where clock frequencies of applications can be increased by up to 1 GHz above the nominal frequencies. The first level of efficiency can be achieved depending on the processor workload, while the second level can only be achieved when only half of the modules are active. For example, to observe the maximum boost in clock frequency, only two of the modules can be active at a time. An application with four MPI tasks can be mapped onto two modules or four cores per processor. If the application instead is mapped onto one core per module on all four modules, this performance boost feature may not be activated. Each compute core has a separate 16 KB data cache, two such caches per module. A compute module shares L2 cache of 2 Mbytes. L3 cache is shared across four modules of a Bulldozer processor and there are two L3 caches per socket. There is a memory controller for four modules, each connected to a NUMA domain. Each Interlagos socket therefore has two such NUMA domains, which are connected through the Hypertransport links.

2. Node design: Each node of CSCS Cray XE6 platform is composed of two AMD Opteron 6272 processors, 32 GBytes of memory, and a link to the Gemini interconnect. Each AMD Opteron processor has 32 cores, where each two cores form a compute module. The architecture is 4-way NUMA as shown in Figure 18.6. Each memory controller is connected to two DDR3-1600 channels. The communication be-

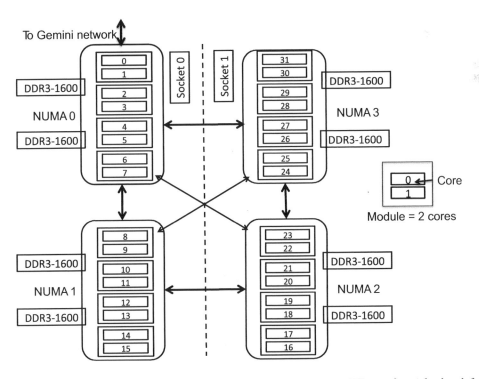

**FIGURE 18.6**: Layout of the 4-way NUMA domain of a Cray XE6 node with the default MPI and thread binding onto 32 processor cores. Hypertransport topology on the node results in different memory bandwidth for different NUMA domains.

tween the NUMA domains take place through the Hypertransport links. The Hypertransport has an interesting topology, where each NUMA domain has high bandwidth connections to the two other NUMA domains but a slightly low bandwidth connection to the third one. Figure 18.6 shows the default 32 threads or MPI task mapping on a Cray XE6 node. Each MPI thread or OpenMP task is assigned to a single core. This default binding can be changed by the users using simple runtime flags.

3. Memory: In addition to the 3-level cache hierarchy of the AMD Interlagos processor, the system has 32-GBytes of DDR3-1600 memory, which is organized in 4-way NUMA domains. Hence, each socket has 2-way NUMA and overall the 2 sockets have 4 NUMA localities that influence latencies and bandwidth for not only memory operations but also for MPI communication and file I/O operations. For example, memory access times can be considerably different for a process or thread mapped onto NUMA socket 0, if the target data resides on any of the given NUMA regions. Using the Cray compiler, we ran the stream benchmark on one NUMA domain (half a socket):

   - Copy: 18 GB/s
   - Scale: 11 GB/s
   - Add: 12 GB/s
   - Triad: 12.0 GB/s

Theoretical bandwidth on one chip within a socket is 26.6 GB/s, and the results demonstrate that 67% of theoretical peak performance can be achieved for the copy operations. Note that maximum performance is reached using three threads. Using more than four threads per NUMA domain shows no significant signs of improvement. The peak memory bandwidth of the Cray XE6 Interlagos node is 102.4 GB/s and we observed a large fraction of this peak performance by careful mapping of threads onto the NUMA domains. We also confirmed that a non-optimal mapping onto the NUMA regions can result in significant slowdown in performance. Results are listed in Table 18.2, which demonstrate not only the impact of the NUMA affinity but also impact of sharing the L2 cache on a single module. The single thread results with different NUMA bindings demonstrate the range of bandwidth available between two NUMA domains. These results also highlight how many threads are needed to saturate the memory bandwidth of a NUMA domain and of a socket. In practice, on the Interlagos processors, applications performance can demonstrate sensitivities to the NUMA and thread mapping schemes. This is more evidence of memory locality awareness, which is one of the key requirements for the Exascale systems.

## 18.3.2    Interconnect

The distinguishing feature of the Cray XE series platforms is the Gemini interconnect, which is a custom-built system-on-a-chip, like its predecessor called the SeaStar [VRB+11]. SeaStar has been optimized for 3-dimensional torus topology. In order to maintain upgradeability from the Cray XT to a Cray XE platform in a 3-dimensional torus topology, the Gemini chip has necessary ports available in the X, Y, and Z dimensions. The main distinction between the two network chips is the number of nodes. There is one SeaStar chip for each Cray XT dual-socket Opteron node while there are two nodes for each Gemini chip as shown in Figure 18.7. As a result, each chip has twice as many sets of links in two dimensions, X and Z, while one set of links in the Y dimension. In fact, the Y dimension is available within a Gemini chip and within a system design, a compute blade, which is composed of two nodes, provide 1 x 4 x 1 topology parameters of the network.

**TABLE 18.2**: Stream (copy) benchmark experimental evaluation with different thread and NUMA mapping schemes.

| Number of threads | Thread placement | Memory binding | Bandwidth (MB/s) |
|---|---|---|---|
| 1 | Core 0 | NUMA 0 | 12900.58 |
| 1 | Core 0 | NUMA 1 | 9013.58 |
| 1 | Core 0 | NUMA 2 | 6418.12 |
| 1 | Core 0 | NUMA 3 | 8894.06 |
| 3 | Core 0-2 | NUMA 0 | 15527.98 |
| 3 | Core 0,2,4 | NUMA 0 | 16832.34 |
| 4 | Core 0-3 | NUMA 0 | 16647.57 |
| 4 | Core 0-3 | NUMA 1 | 10451.38 |
| 4 | Core 0,2,4,6 | NUMA 0 | 16641.58 |
| 4 | Core 0,2,4,6 | NUMA 1 | 10512.12 |
| 8 | Core 0-7 | NUMA 0 | 15691.73 |
| 8 | Core 0,2,4,6,8,10,12,14 | NUMA 0,1 | 33267.49 |
| 16 | Core 0-15 | NUMA 0,1 | 31403.30 |

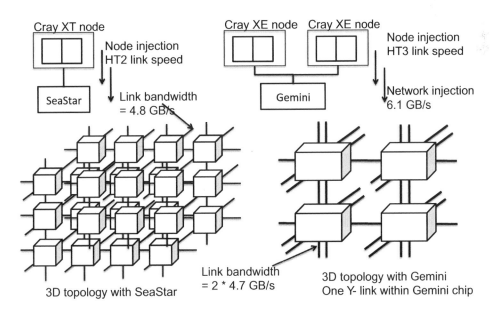

**FIGURE 18.7**: Comparison of the Cray Gemini networking technology with its predecessor. The SeaStar chip is connected with one node vs. two nodes per Gemini card. As a result, one dimension, the Y axis, is within the Gemini card. The injection and link bandwidths are also different. The Gemini chip has two links each in the X and Z directions, providing almost twice the bandwidth.

**FIGURE 18.8**: Layout of the physical topology is shown in terms of the basic building blocks, namely the blade, chassis, and racks.

The topological connections for a multi-rack system, which is composed of multiple rows is shown in Figure 18.8. The CSCS system has two rows of 8 racks, a total of 16 racks. According to Cray system specifications, the system is cabled using the class 2 topology, which means that there are no Y cable links [gem]. The highest bandwidth is available on the backplane, the Z-dimension, while the double cables in X and Z dimension and the Y in the mezzanine card are about the same. For systems composed of more than 2 rows of racks or cabinets, the reduced bandwidth in the Y dimension could be an issue. This issue can be resolved by carefully managing resources through a resource management system, scheduler, and the Cray ALPS interface. The Cray ALPS interface can be configured for different packing schemes.

A summary of the key distinct features of the Cray Gemini chip as compared to its predecessor, the SeaStar interconnect, are listed in Table 18.3. Note that the high rate of Gemini node injection bandwidth depends on the Hypertransport frequencies. In addition to significantly lower latencies and higher bandwidth, the Gemini router supports adaptive routing and has significantly higher messaging rates as compared to SeaStar. On the Cray XT series systems, both the network and routing chip as well as the communication API called Portals was optimized for the message passing communication paradigm. On the Cray XE6 system, there is an additional interface for global shared-memory address programming called DMAPP and Cry programming environment provides PGAS compilers, CoArray Fortran and Unified Parallel C (UPC) [VBO11].

## 18.4    System Software

Cray XT and XE series systems have a customized operating environment called the Cray Linux Environment (CLE) for compute or back-end nodes [Lar08]. The login nodes and service nodes have stock Linux operating systems. The early generations of the Cray

**TABLE 18.3**: Comparison of two generations of Cray proprietary ASIC based interconnect technologies from Cray: SeaStar (Cray XT series) and Gemini (Cray XE series).

|  | SeaStar 2.2 | Gemini |
|---|---|---|
| Interface | HyperTransport 2 | HyperTransport 3 |
| Adaptive routing | No | Yes |
| Latency | 5.5 usec | 1.3 usec |
| Node injection bandwidth | 4 GB/s | 20 GB/s |
| Network injection bandwidth | 2.2 GB/s | 6.1 GB/s |
| Peak link bandwidth | 4.8 GB/s | 4.38 and 9.37 GB/s |
| Communication API | Portals | uGNI and DMAPP |

XT platforms have a light-weight system called Catamount [KB05]. Both Catamount and CLE have been developed to minimize the jitter while offering the essential Linux operating system environment that most developers and end users are familiar with. The OS jitter is a well-known issue in high-end HPC systems [FBB08] and can cause bottlenecks especially for MPI collective communication operations at scale [Bec06]. A number of applications that have been extensively used by different production projects on the CSCS platform, most notably CP2K, depend on the availability of high network bandwidth.

CLE has been introduced to offer additional functionality to the users that was not available in Catamount. This includes multi-threading, I/O buffering, and sockets interface. CLE was introduced as the Compute Node Linux (CNL) [Wal07b]. The key features include scalability to tens of thousands of nodes, very small memory footprint, quick boot times, and essential Linux functionality to the code developers without compromising on overheads and noise. The number of system- related interrupts has been minimized while keeping all essential software stack components necessary to support multiple programming paradigms including MPI, OpenMP and PGAS, and parallel file system interfaces. Through the Data Virtualization Service (DVS) software, Cray XT and XE6 series systems can provide I/O forwarding to any file system client. Both scratch (Lustre) and site-wide, global (GPFS) parallel file systems are mounted on the CSCS Cray systems. Further details are provided in the storage section.

In order to guarantee optimal availability and utilization of supercomputing resources and to ensure that stakeholder criteria are met efficiently and effectively, CSCS has developed a highly customized resource management, scheduling, and accounting environment. Since early 2010, CSCS has been porting and testing SLURM on various XT, XE, and non-Cray cluster systems, with cluster dimensions ranging one or two nodes with a few cores up to a 20-cabinet Cray XT5. Patches evolving from this development have been reviewed and accepted by the main SLURM developers, who continue to evolve the interface and provide active and ongoing support for the Cray port of this modern, multi-threaded resource manager and scheduling system. SLURM offers the flexibility of encoding in-house algorithms that offer the following characteristics:

- Aggressive backfilling to ensure high system utilization

- Bottom-feeder policies (users can still run in a very low priority mode even after exhausting their quota)

- Extensions to support a key customer (MeteoSwiss) with specific scheduling policies tailored to the demanding requirements of operational weather forecasting and on-demand operation.

- Robustness extensions (scheduler health monitor)

Further details of the SLURM implementation and extension for the Cray XT and Cray XE platforms can be found in [RSH+11].

## 18.5    Programming System

On the Cray XE6 platform, like its predecessors the XT series systems, an integrated software development and execution environment is available to the code developers and end users to allow for straightforward migration from existing parallel platforms. This includes a number of compiler options, availability of tuned and optimized communication libraries, numerical libraries, parallel file I/O interfaces and debugging and performance tools. The Cray XE series system provides the *module* environment to users to enable them to specify their programming and runtime options using a single command. The module commands typically set all the necessary environment variables for the users.

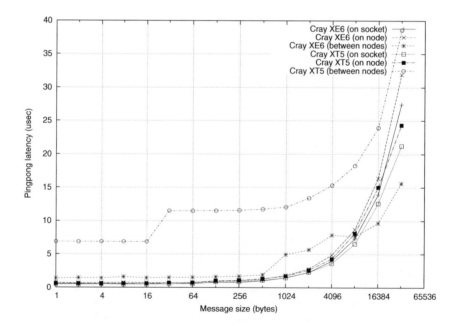

**FIGURE 18.9**: Inter and intra node performance on the Cray XE6 platform with Gemini interconnect as compared to a Cray XT5 platform with SeaStarII interconnect.

### 18.5.1    Programming Models

Due to the hardware features of the Cray XE6 platform, multi-core processing nodes and an interconnect, which supports both message-passing and remote memory access operations, a number of parallel programming techniques and models are supported on the platform. The distributed-memory message-passing MPI model is supported through an optimized MPI implementation, which is multi-core aware. The results for the Intel MPI benchmarks' pingpong benchmark in Figure 18.9 demonstrate the superior performance on and off node as compared to its predecessor system [imb]. Note that both systems have multi-core aware MPI; therefore, the latencies between two MPI tasks on a single socket or node are comparable. However the biggest improvement comes from the Gemini interconnect implementation, which is evident in the figure. The Gemini latencies are an order of magnitude smaller than the SeaStar and all MPI operations, particularly the latency and bandwidth sensitive collective communication operations greatly benefit from the Gemini interconnect.

As mentioned earlier, a network API called DMAPP, is available for the Gemini network to allow for global or partitioned-global (PGAS) shared-memory programming models [BR10]. Cray compiler environment (CCE) has built-in Coarray Fortran (CAF) and Unified Parallel C (UPC) compilers as well as support for the SHMEM library. These parallel programming interfaces are supported by the Cray code development environment and performance tools. All these programming environments are interoperable with the shared memory OpenMP programming, which is supported on individual nodes.

### 18.5.2    Languages and Compilers

A number of compilers for the 64-bit x86 platform are supported on the Cray platform for Fortran, C, and C++ applications. In fact, Cray programming environment provides wrappers for Cray, Intel, PGI, and GNU compilers for seamless compilation of parallel applications for cross-compiled compute nodes. Compiling and linking for OpenMP and MPI are enabled for all compilers. Cray compiler environment has embedded compilers for PGAS languages, Coarray Fortran and Unified Parallel C (UPC). These can be invoked using a compiler flag.

Since the Cray XE6 platform has a new generation of micro-processor, performances are very different with respect to the compiler and the test (read or write). It seems that Cray and PGI use different assembly strategies (load-op-store for Cray and register blocking for PGI) which directly influence the performance with respect to L1 cache for the read test. Note also that L3 cache bandwidth is slightly better than that of main memory. This behavior was demonstrated through the cachebench benchmark results shown in Figure 18.10 [cbe]. Multiple levels of cache bandwidth are evident in the performance of the read operations for both compilers but for the write operations, we observe only the main memory bandwidth for the Cray compiler, which is currently being resolved by the Cray compiler development teams. Hence, the availability of different multi-platform compilers on the Cray XE6 platform offers a wide range of opportunities for code development and tuning.

### 18.5.3    Optimized Libraries

A number of applications that rely on highly tuned numerical libraries for linear algebra target the Cray optimized scientific library called libsci. On the Cray XE6 Bulldozer processor, performance is highly sensitive to the placement of threads on cores and modules as well as the cache and NUMA memory hierarchy. The DGEMM test was run on a single node of the Interlagos processor, which is composed of two sockets. A socket is composed of eight modules. Each module packs two cores and one 256-bit wide FPU (which can be split into two 128-bit FPU). Theoretical performance is therefore 8*(4*2)*2.1=134.4 Gflops per socket, and 268.8 per node.

Using the Cray libsci (multi-threaded version) and using different thread mapping schemes, we demonstrate different architectural features of the Interlagos processor (refer to Figure 18.11). For example, On a single core, the observed peak performance is over 12 Gflops. The behavior becomes more interesting when two threads are mapped onto a single module vs. two modules, where we observe potential of multiple FPUs. Similar behavior is observed when mapping 8 or 16 threads in a similar manner. However, we also note that the full node performance is not twice as much as a single socket performance; it is a little bit lower. Best practice seems to show that it is more efficient to use the FPU in its dual 128-bit mode (i.e., MMX registers) with VEX instructions.

### 18.5.4    Tools

A number of tools are supported on the Cray XE6 platform. For debugging of parallel MPI and hybrid (MPI and OpenMP) applications, TotalView is available. We are also investigating Allinea DDT parallel debugging tool [ddt]. For performance measurements and analysis, an extensive toolset by Cray called perftools is available as part of the Cray programming environment. Since performance and scaling efficiencies on the Cray XE6 platform can be sensitive to the mapping and placement of jobs due to non-uniform bandwidths across the three dimensional torus network, user level utilities are available to inspect the placement of user jobs onto the available node. Partial output of the tool showing a subset of the CSCS Cray XE6 cabinets is illustrated in Figure 18.12. Jobs are denoted by different

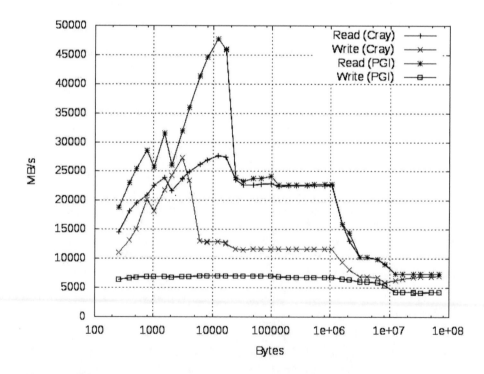

**FIGURE 18.10**: Performance of the cachebench benchmark highlighting the impact of the different compilers for utilizing the Interlagos cache and memory hierarchies.

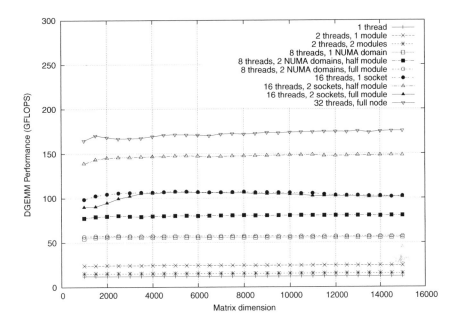

**FIGURE 18.11**: Performance of a multithreaded DGEMM using Cray libsci on a Cray XE6 Interlagos node with different numbers of thread and thread placement schemes.

pairs of letters. For example, job "aj" is allocated on 200 nodes. Some of these nodes are in different cabinets or rows (C0-0, C0-1, etc.), where 0-0 means rack 0 of row 0 or the x-dimension. Jobs that are mapped onto the backplane are likely to benefit from a higher bandwidth. Currently, work is in progress to interface with the ALPS node ordering schemes with SLURM, which will allow for the node placements according to topological configurations. There are also some third-party multi-platform performance tools, for example, TAU and Vampir, that are also available on the system [SMM07][BKMN09].

### 18.5.5 Execution Environment

Placement of executable MPP codes onto Cray XT/XE compute nodes is handled by the Cray Application Level Placement Scheduler (ALPS) whose interface to third-party batch scheduling systems is specified by the Cray Batch and Application Scheduler Interface Layer (BASIL). SLURM job scheduling system is available on the CSCS Cray XE6 platform [JG03]. The operational details of this interface are proprietary, but some details have been published [KLKA06]. The user level command for executing an application is called aprun. There is a wide range of parameters that users can specify including the mapping on MPI tasks on compute nodes, sockets and cores, mapping of OpenMP threads and mapping of Coarray Fortran images and UPC threads as well. For instance, due to the 4-way NUMA region and a Hypertransport connected network interface (Gemini) placement of MPI tasks on different NUMA regions can influence communication performance. Network bandwidth results depicting this behavior are shown in Figure 18.13. An MPI task that is mapped onto the NUMA region closest (cc_0) to the network interface has about 40% more bandwidth

```
      C0-0              C0-1              C1-0              C1-1
 n3 am--aMam--aDamaK ajarajatajaoamau abakbQambIbJavaj amakambm--ayaIbw
 n2 am--aMaL--aDamaK asarajatajaoamak abakbQambIbJavaj amakam----ayaIav
 n1 am--aHaB--aDamac asaraqapajaoamak abakbQambIbJXXaj amakam----ayaIav
c2n0 amaGaHaB--aDamac asaraqap--anamak abaka7am--bJamaj amakamaJ--avaIav
 n3 amayaza8--aDaFaj ajarajaEajak--aD amaka7am--bJamaj amakambm--ayaIbH
 n2 amayazaBavaDaFaj ajarajaEajak---- amakaGam--bvamaj amakambm--ayaIbw
 n1 amayazaBavaDavaj ajarajaEajakam-- amakaMam--bvamaj amakambm--ayaIbw
c1n0 amaj--aBaCawavaj ajarajatajaoamau amakaMam--aPamaj amakambm--ayaIbw
 n3 SSaj--adaxawavaj amakajaJaGavaISS amakSSam--aHamac akajambmakSSajaj
 n2 SSaaacadaxahaiaj amakajaJaGavaISS amakSSam--aHamac akXXambmakSSajaj
 n1 SSaaacadafahaiaj amakajaJajavaISS amakSSam--aHama7 akakambmakSSajaj
c0n0 SSaaabadaeagaiaj amarajaEajakaISS amaQSSam--aDama7 akakambm--SSajaP
   s0011223344556677 0011223344556677 0011223344556677 0011223344556677


      C2-0              C2-1              C3-0              C3-1
 n3 aaabadakagaiaOak ajasakaj--akavaj --akakacajajaUa4 akajajbmamay--av
 n2 aaabad--aNaF--ak ajaGakae--akavaj --akakah--ajaUa4 akajajbmamay--av
 n1 aaabad--adaF--ak ataGakae--akavaj --bOakahbLajaUa4 akajambmakayaeaj
c2n0 abaQadaPadaG--ak ataGakaj--akavaj --bOakambLajaea4 akajambmakayajaj
 n3 ahaQadaPadaj--SS ajasakajap--anam bGbOakambLajbNa4 akajajbmamaubzaD
 n2 awaQadaxadaj--SS ajasakajapakanam bGbOakambLaCbNa4 akajajbmamaubzaD
 n1 ajaQadaxadaj--SS ajasakajaGakanaj bG--akambLaubNa4 akajajbmamay--aD
c1n0 ajaQajaxadaj--SS ajasakajaGakaPaj bG--akambIbMaua4 akajajbmamay--av
 n3 ajaQajaxadaT--ak ajSSaraqap--anam bGauakambIbKbHa4 ak--ajXXama8--aD
 n2 ajaQajaxadaT--ak ajSSaraqap--anam bGbHakambIbJbra4 ak--ajaeama8bPaD
 n1 ajaQajaxadaT--ak ajSSaraqap--anam bGbHakambIbJbra4 ak--ajbmamaubzaD
c0n0 aVaQaTaUadaTaDak ajSSakajap--anam bGakakambIbJava4 akajajbmamaubzaD
   s0011223344556677 0011223344556677 0011223344556677 0011223344556677


      C4-0              C4-1              C5-0              C5-1
 n3 awaQaTaUadaTaDad a6akakaDava5a7ad abamaCSSajadbb-- aC--br--SSbzaoam
 n2 awaQaTaUadaT--ad a6akaka3ava5abad abamaPSSajadbb-- aC--br--SSazaoaK
 n1 awbdaTaUadaT--ad a6akaka3ava5abad abakaPSSajadbb-- ak--ajaGSSaz--aK
c2n0 bcbdbbaUadaT--ad a6akaka3aka5abad bxakbBSSajadaCaP ak--ajaGSSaD--aD
 n3 bcajbbaUadba--ad atakSSajaLakajaj bCakbDboajadaPaP au--braubqbza7am
 n2 a2ajazaUaKbaaDad atakSSajaLakajaK bCakbDboajadaPaj au--brauambza7am
 n1 a2ajazaUaKbaaoad atakSSajavakajaK bCakbDboauadbnaj au--brauambzaoam
c1n0 a2ajazaUa9baaoad a6akSSXXava5a7ad bCakbDboajadbnaj au--brauambzaoam
 n3 a2XXa8aUaGSSaoad atakakajavakajaj ajakbDboajbEbnaj ----braobqbpajam
 n2 a2XXagajaPSSaoa4 atakakajavakajaj ajakbDboajbEaUaj ----braobqbzajam
 n1 a2XXagajaPSSaba4 atakakajavakajaj ajakbDboajbEaUaj ----braobqbza7am
c0n0 a2XXa3ajabSSaba4 atakakajavakajaj ajakbDacajbEaUbF ----braobqbza7am
   s0011223344556677 0011223344556677 0011223344556677 0011223344556677
```

**FIGURE 18.12**: A utility called xtnodestat can be used to find out mapping of user jobs on to the physical resources. Out of CSCS 16 Cray XE6 racks, 12 are depicted in this picture showing the 3D torus configurations along the two rows (C0-0, C1-0, etc.), 8 cabinets in each row (C0-0, C1-0, etc.), 8 blades in each chassis (doubled for job IDs) (s001122...), and 3 chassis in a cabinet (c0n0, n1, n2, n3, c1n0, n1, n2, n3, ...).

than a task that is placed onto a NUMA region that is farther away from the Gemini interface of a node (cc_16).

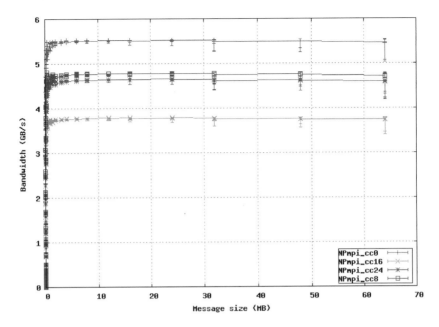

**FIGURE 18.13**: MPI bandwidth results demonstrating the impact of NUMA placements. Cray aprun flags enable users to control the placement and mapping of MPI tasks as well as memory affinities.

## 18.6 Storage, Visualization, and Analytics

At CSCS, we use Lustre as a parallel scratch file system on all of our Cray systems, and this temporary storage file system has been tuned for jobs that have high bandwidth requirements when writing large blocks of data [Ora]. In addition we have deployed a site-wide accessible, centralized storage facility with a current capacity of 1.9 PetaBytes and using GPFS [gpf]. This project file system serves as a longer term storage for a diverse range of computing, data analytics, and visualization platforms, including the flagship system, and is also used for staging data analytics and visualization jobs. Setup of CSCS storage resources is depicted in Figure 18.14.

### 18.6.1 Scratch File System

The Monte Rosa system was delivered by Cray with a Lustre scratch file system hosted by the service nodes internal to the machine (a so-called internal Lustre file system). The initial version of Lustre that came with the earlier versions of the system software stack were various dot releases of v1.6. Following the upgrade of the system to an XE6 in November 2011 and the move to CLE4 the Lustre version changed to v1.8.3. The Cray system engineering team are normally very conservative when it comes to changing any components of the system software stack and therefore the version of Lustre that they release is normally many months (or possibly a year or more) behind the version available on the Lustre website (http://wiki.lustre.org).

In terms of storage hardware the scratch file-system was initially built with 5 LSI7900 controller couplets each connected to 10 enclosures, each of which contained 16 512GB 7200rpm SATA drives. File system LUNs were built using 10 drives distributed across the 10 enclosures in RAID6 8+2PQ arrays as specified by Cray's storage engineering group. Consequently there was a total of 80 LUNs or Object Storage Targets (OSTs) for the Lustre file system, i.e., 4 OSTs per Object Storage Server (OSS). Each controller contained 4Gbit/s Fiber Channel (FC) cards and there was a total of 80 direct FC connections to the Cray service nodes (i.e., 16 per controller couplet, 4 per Lustre OSS) for a total aggregate throughput of 40GB/s. In this configuration the expected throughput bandwidth for each controller was 3.5GB/s for a theoretical aggregate peak throughput performance of 17.5GB/s. However the measured performance was somewhat less than this; monitoring of the controllers using LSI's monitoring tools indicated that the maximum sustained throughput of each controller couplet was more like 2.6 GB/s and this agreed with the measure performance of application I/O on the system.

Part of the reason for the lower than expected file system performance was attributed to the connection of 10 enclosures to each controller couplet because this caused imbalance in the internal data channels within the controllers. Consequently, as part of the upgrade of the system in November 2011, it was decided to add a 6th LSI7900 controller couplet and connect 8 enclosures per controller couplet. This lowered the total number of enclosures (and therefore drives) from 50 (i.e., 800 drives) to 48 (i.e., 768 drives) but this trade-off was seen as acceptable given the fact that 8 enclosures per controller is optimal in terms of balancing the internal data channels of each controller. Furthermore the 512GB, 7200rpm drives were replaced with 2GB, 10K rpm SATA drives which have slightly higher IOPS

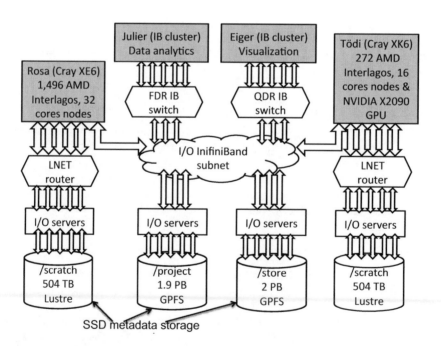

**FIGURE 18.14**: Scratch and project file systems storage setup and integration of data analytics and visualization resource.

count so this would offset the loss in drives spindles when going from 800 down to 768 drives.

Furthermore, as part of the storage upgrade all 4GBit/s FC cards in the 6 controllers would be upgraded with 8Gbit/s. However the number of OSSes was reduced to 12, each having two 8Gbit/s FC connections to the controllers for a total aggregate throughput of 24 GB/s. Each controller couplet is configured with 12 8+2PQ RAID6 LUNs (OSTs) so that there are 6 OSTs per OSS. Again the expected throughput bandwidth for each controller couplet was expected to be 3.5GB/s for a total expected aggregate bandwidth of 21GB/s. However, as before the measured performance fell somewhat short of this figure and was similar to the performance of the old file system configuration. The reason was likely due to the reduction in the number of Lustre OSSes (from 20 down to 12) and the resultant increase in the number of OSTs per OSS (which consequently puts more load on each OSS).

However, before there was time to adequately investigate the situation with the file system performance another issue of far greater importance arose. Specifically the stability of the internal Lustre file system and therefore the stability of the entire machine began to be a problem. The root cause of this issue was a problem with the Node Voltage Regulating Modules (NVRMs) on the service nodes which on the newer Cray XE6 design were slightly different from the old XT5 modules. Unfortunately these new NVRMs started failing regularly over the space of a few weeks. There are 4 nodes on a Cray XE6 service blade and if an NVRM failed on the blade it could affect some of the other nodes on the blade as well so that one or more of the nodes on a service blade would power down. On the older Cray XT5 system there had been very few problems of this type but these problems on the newer hardware highlighted a real problem with the design of the file system. Cray was quick to identify the problem with the NVRMs. In the meantime at CSCS we deployed an external Lustre based solution, which has been in production since June 2012.

## 18.6.2 Resiliency and Fault Tolerance

The Cray XE6 architecture is designed to be fault tolerant so that if compute nodes (or blades) or service nodes (or blades) fail, the Gemini High Speed Network (HSN) will dynamically route around the lost nodes; this behavior was not possible in the older SeaStar network available in the XT5 architecture where only static routing was supported. In fact we had experienced great success with entire compute blades and service blades needing to be powered down and serviced while the machine was in full operation, except if the service blade hosted Lustre OSSes. In the case that a service blade hosted a Lustre OSS, because there was no failover redundancy configured within Lustre, the complete file system would crash and this would of course kill all running jobs on the machine. Clearly this was not a good situation because we had essentially introduced multiple single-points-of-failure within an otherwise fault tolerant system design. The situation was compounded by the fact that several other systems also mounted the internal Lustre scratch file system in order for jobs running on these systems to access data contained there. Clearly, when the internal Lustre file system crashed it also killed jobs on these external systems.

Rather than investigate the option of configuring the internal Lustre file system with redundant failover, which was seen as adding yet more complication to an already complex system and was known to not work particularly well in Lustre (especially in the versions available with the Cray software stack), we decided to follow the lead of other large Cray sites (most notably Oak Ridge National Laboratory) and build a stand-alone external Lustre file system hosted by its own server cluster. Key features of this new external Lustre cluster are:

- 12 of the latest Intel Sandy Bridge servers as OSSes

- 2 AMD Opteron servers with 64 GB RAM as the Metadata servers (configured as a redundant failover pair)

- SSD storage for the metadata targets (MDT) storage

- FDR InfiniBand connections to the client systems

- Independence from the release schedule defined by Cray's engineering team so that we have the option to choose a later version of Lustre (we chose version 2.2, which is compatible with version 1.8.6 clients in the CLE 4.0)

- The same data storage as described above, namely LSI7900 controllers and storage enclosures

The above case study serves to highlight some important factors in the design and deployment of production HPC systems. Although not always given adequate attention during the procurement process, the design and implementation of the scratch storage subsystem is a non-trivial exercise that has multiple layers of complication. Particular attention needs to be given to designing a storage subsystem that delivers the expected throughput (and IOPS) capability and is fault tolerant. Some key factors in this regard are:

- The lack of clustered metadata capability within Lustre is a serious limitation and needs to be addressed if this file system will survive into the Exascale era.

- As the capacity of hard drives increases the length of time it takes for RAID array rebuilds, following a drive failure, is becoming increasingly important. The longer it takes for a RAID6 array to rebuild increases the possibility of additional drive failures with the risk that the RAID array will fail completely before it has had a chance to rebuild, resulting in the loss of user data. This situation will only get worse as we move toward the Exascale era and therefore needs to be addressed.

- As storage file systems get larger and the amount of data stored there increases there is a need to introduce end-to-end data integrity into either the underlying hardware or the file system itself. This issue has yet to be adequately addressed by the HPC industry.

## 18.7    Computing Center

In 2012, CSCS moved to a purpose built facility in Lugano, Switzerland (illustrated in Figure 18.15). The new computer center is a highly flexible building, well thought-out down to the last detail and future-proofed in its design, so that it will be able to support the supercomputers for the next 40 years. The hydraulic system alone, the main element of the innovative cooling system for the IT infrastructure, the supercomputers, and the building itself comprise several kilometers of pipework, three dozen pumps, and thousands of measuring points which have to be monitored and maintained. The machine room is shown in Figure 18.16.

**FIGURE 18.15**: CSCS' new building, data center (right), and offices (left).

### 18.7.1 Integration

CSCS also has a number of other general-purpose Linux clusters which provide High Throughput Computing (HTC) capability, large memory data analytics capability, as well as small-to-medium size parallel computing on Intel CPUs. We also have various file system clusters for global file systems (based on IBM's GPFS technology [gpf]), tape libraries for data backup and recovery functionality (using IBM's Tivoli Storage Manager/TSM technology) as well as external scratch file system clusters for various systems including the Cray platforms (as described earlier) and a multitude of servers which make up the entire ecosystem of the HPC datacenter operations. This entire infrastructure is contained within one new 2,000 square Meter facility not far from downtown Lugano. The cooling for the new datacenter comes by way of cold water pumped some 2.8 km from Lake Lugano. This use of passive cooling from the lake water makes for far greater cooling efficiency than previously achievable in the old building where traditional electrically powered cooling units provided the necessary chilled water. The new facility has a day-one power and cooling envelope of

**FIGURE 18.16**: Machine room with supercomputers in the foreground and cooling islands for additional hardware in the background.

12 Megawatts and this can be easily increased to 25 Megawatts with the addition of the necessary power and cooling infrastructure within the building basement.

## 18.7.2   Power and Cooling

The ability to easily add power and cooling infrastructure will also be a key feature in building designs as we move to the Exascale regime. Building a new datacenter is a massive public works undertaking which takes many years to fund and implement and involves a complex building consent process which cannot be expedited. Furthermore, as other authors have previously pointed out, one major limiting factor on the path to Exascale will be the availability and affordability of the necessary electrical power. For a nation the size of Switzerland it is hard to imagine the feasibility of a datacenter with more than 25 Megawatts capacity. Although the limits may be somewhat higher for nations the size of China, the U.S.A., or Japan there will still be a practical limit above which it is not feasible to build an HPC datacenter and this therefore puts a hard limit on the computational efficiency of any system that will reach the Exascale regime.

# Chapter 19

# Tianhe-1A Supercomputer: System and Application

**Xiangke Liao, Yutong Lu, and Min Xie**

*School of Computer Science, National University of Defense Technology*

## 19.1 Background

TianHe-1A(TH-1A) system [YLL+11] has been developed by the National University of Defense Technology (NUDT). It is the first petaflops system in China, and also in Asia. With the CPU and GPU hybrid architecture, the experiences of developing TH-1A have somehow impacted the succeeding HPC architecture and technology development.

One of the TH-1A systems, with peak performance of 4,700 TFlops, has been deployed at the national supercomputer center in Tianjin (NSCC-TJ) since November 2010, and another one, with peak performance 1,300 TFlops, has been deployed at the national supercomputer center in Changsha (NSCC-CS) since July 2011. Both systems are online providing High Performance Computing (HPC) services for users from different areas in China.

### 19.1.1    Program Background

Breaking the barrier of petaflops has been a grand challenge in high-performance computing for the last decade. In order to provide competitive HPC resources to China researchers and industries, the National High-tech Research and Development Program (also known as the 863 Program), managed by the Ministry of Science and Technology (MOST), launched a major project on petaflops HPC systems and grid service environment during the 11th five-year plan period (2006-2010). The 863 Program sponsors the NUDT, in collaboration with Tianjin Binhai New Area, to develop the petaflops supercomputer in China. NUDT has undertaken HPC research activities for several decades, and developed a famous series of domestic YH/TH supercomputing systems in China.

### 19.1.2    Timeline

The research and development of the Tianhe-1 system consisted of four stages: preliminary research, proof of concept, system implementation, and application exploitation. The development team in NUDT has been engaged in HPC studies for a long time, and has extensive experience in HPC technologies, including but not limited to chip design, high-speed interconnect communication technology, operating system, and heterogeneous parallel algorithms. The preliminary research started in 2005, and has been focused on investigating new HPC architecture based on stream processing technology. The first stream processor, named FT-64, was designed and tested in 2006. A proof-of-concept prototype was built during 2007 and 2008 to demonstrate the feasibility of our design [YYX+07]. We used general processors to construct a small-scale system with 1,024 compute nodes. System implementation began in 2008 and includes two phases. The first phase involved the implementation of the first petaflops hybrid system Tianhe-1 based on the prototype, and it was accomplished in September 2009. Tianhe-1 has 6,250 nodes connected by DDR InfiniBand. Each node has two Intel processors and one ATI GPGPU. The theoretical peak performance of Tianhe-1 is 1.206 petaflops and its Linpack test result reaches 0.5631 petaflops. The focus of the second phase is to enhance and upgrade the existing Tianhe-1 into TH-1A, and it was installed and deployed at the national supercomputer center in Tianjin in August 2010. TH-1A contains 7,168 compute nodes, and each node has two CPUs and one NVIDIA GPU. TH-1A adopts a proprietary interconnect network TH-net with a higher bandwidth than InfiniBand QDR. The theoretical peak performance of TH-1A is 4.7 petaflops, and its Linpack test result is 2.566 petaflops. It was ranked first on the TOP500 list [MSDS06] issued in November 2010. Subsequent to the completion of system installation and testing, TH-1A began to explore its scientific, industrial, and commercial applications, and is currently playing an important role in many domains.

### 19.1.3    Applications and Workloads

TH-1A supercomputer system began to run large-scale test applications and programs in November 2010, and then opened online to general users to provide high performance computing services. Now there are more than 300 users and groups from universities, in-

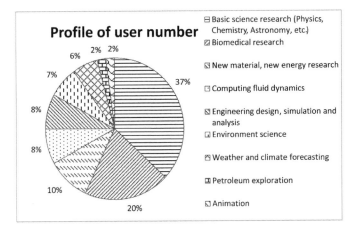

**FIGURE 19.1**: Profile of user number.

stitutes, and industries on TH-1A. The application areas span from petroleum exploration, bio-medical research, climate, new material, to Computational Fluid Dynamics (CFD), fusion, engineering, fundamental science (such as high energy physics, astronomy). In the past 18 months, more than 130,000 jobs have been launched on TH-1A. The utilization of the system is about 76%.

According to the entire design and deployment of economic construction of the Tianjin Binhai new area, five application platforms around the TH-1A supercomputer have been built, including petroleum exploring data processing platform, biological medicine development platform, 3D animation rendering and design platform, high-end equipment design and simulation platform, and geographic information service platform. In addition, the national science and technology innovation platform has been established lately aiming to support X research areas, mainly for national high-tech programs (such as 863, 973) and the application of national key areas. Those are colloquially referred to as the "five plus ×" scheme. Figure 19.1 and Figure 19.2 illustrate the profile of user numbers and resource usage.

We have also established the cloud computing center and industry zone for Binhai new area so that TH-1A supercomputer could provide computing service through the above five

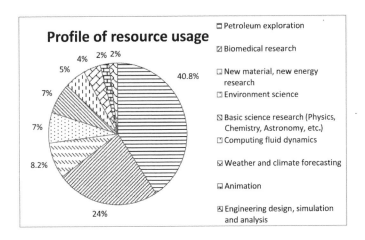

**FIGURE 19.2**: Profile of resource usage.

application platforms as well as the cloud computing center. There were many enterprise users on TH-1A all over the country by the end of 2011. Statistical data suggests that more than 100 million RMB have been saved from the cost of infrastructure upgrades or investment in hardware and software for these enterprises by using TH-1A in NSCC-TJ.

## 19.2    System Overview

On the design of a high productivity petaflops system, we face many great challenges, including high computation performance, low latency and high bandwidth communication, high throughput and large capacity I/O operations, low power consumption, and easy use and maintenance. The balance among the performance of computation, communication, and storage is one of the key factors affecting the efficiency of large-scale parallel applications. Based on the advanced research on the stream processing architecture, high-speed interconnect and large-scale parallel I/O technology, TH-1A system adopts hybrid MPP architecture with CPUs and GPUs. It consists of five subsystems, namely, compute, service, interconnection network, I/O storage, and monitor/diagnose subsystem, as shown in Figure 19.3.

TH-1A system consists of 7,168 compute nodes and 16 commercial service nodes. Each compute node is configured with two Intel CPUs and one NVIDIA GPU. There are 186,368 cores, including 14,336 Intel Xeon X5670 CPUs (6 cores), and 7,168 NVIDIA M2050 GPUs (14 Stream Multi-processors/448 CUDA cores). The total memory of the system is 262 TB, and the disk capacity is 2 PB. There are 120 compute racks, 6 communication racks, and 14 I/O racks in the entire TH-1A system, as shown in Figure 19.4. The overall system occupies 700 $m^2$. The power consumption at full load is 4.04 MW, the power efficiency is about 635.1 MFlops/W.

The interconnection network is a proprietary high-speed network, named TH-net, providing low latency and high bandwidth communication between all kinds of nodes in the TH-1A system. Two chips, including high-radix Network Routing Chips (NRC) and high-speed Network Interface Chips (NIC), as well as the high throughput switch, are designed by NUDT for constructing the TH-net. The interconnect topology is an optoelectronic hybrid fat-tree structure.

The monitor and diagnoses subsystem is constructed with control nodes, monitor network, and sensors on the node boards. Each node contains a Giga Ethernet interface for

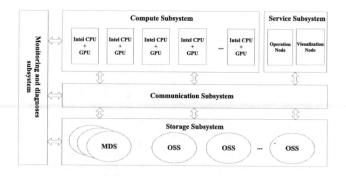

**FIGURE 19.3**: Structure of TH-1A system.

**FIGURE 19.4**: TH-1A system.

monitor and diagnoses subsystem connectivity, supporting a custom protocol for booting and IPMI protocol for controlling and monitoring of the system.

The I/O storage system of TH-1A adopts object storage architecture, supporting the custom Lustre filesystem [BZ02][LUS], with 6 I/O management nodes, 128 I/O storage nodes, and 2 PB storage capacity. There is another InfiniBand network for sharing the storage system with visualization clusters, and an ethernet network for connecting with external services such as the cloud computing environment.

In addition, the infrastructure design of the TH-1A system takes high power efficiency and low cost into consideration. TH-1A uses a high-density assembling technique, in which every eight mainboards can be plugged into a double-side backplane. There are 128 Xeon processors and 64 NVIDIA GPUs in each rack. The peak performance of one rack is about 42 TFlops. Unlike traditional air cooling system, TH-1A adopts a full obturation water cooling air-conditioning system, with two liquid cooling air-conditioners on each side of the rack, so that the cooling air may cycle in the rack to dissipate heat loads from chipsets. With these techniques, the power consumption of a compute rack is about 32 KW, thus the cost and complexity of TH-1A racks is acceptable.

The parallel software stack of TH-1A includes operating system, compiler system, parallel developing tools, virtualization, and visualization environment. The operating system of TH-1A is 64-bit Kylin Linux. It is designed and optimized for high-performance parallel computing, which supports power management and high-performance virtual zone. The Kylin Linux operating system is compatible with a broad range of third-party application software.

The compiler system supports C, C++, Fortran, and CUDA languages [CUD], as well as MPI and OpenMP parallel programming model. In order to develop applications on the hybrid system efficiently, TH-1A introduces a parallel heterogeneous programming framework to abstract the programming model on GPU and CPU.

The parallel application development environment provides a component-based network development platform for programming, compiling, debugging, and submitting jobs through the LAN or WAN. Users can also integrate different tools into this platform dynamically, such as Intel Vtune, TotalView, etc.

## 19.3    Architecture

We have designed two kinds of ASICs, four types of nodes (compute node, service node, I/O management node, and I/O storage node), two sets of networks (communication network, monitor and diagnostic network), and fifteen kinds of Printed Circuit Boards (PCB) for the TH-1A system. There are more than 40,000 PCBs in the whole system.

### 19.3.1    Node Design

Each compute node in TH-1A is configured with two Intel Xeon CPUs and one NVIDIA GPU. It has the 655.64 GFlops peak double precision computing performance (CPU has 140.64 GFlops and GPU has 515 GFlops) and 32 GB total memory.

The M2050 GPU integrates 3 GB GDDR5 memory, with a bit width of 384 bits and peak bandwidth of 148 GB/s. All the register files, caches, and specific memories support ECC, which improves the reliability of GPU computation.

The main task of the CPU in compute node is running the operation system, managing system resources, and executing general purpose computation. GPU mainly performs large-scale parallel computation. Facing the challenge of hybrid CPU and GPU architecture, we have to address some key issues, such as improving the efficiency of CPU and GPU cooperative computing, reducing energy consumption, and data communication overhead between CPU and GPU, to effectively accelerate many typical parallel algorithms and applications.

The main board structure of compute node is shown in Figure 19.5. The two processors in one compute node construct a SMP system using Intel Quick Path Interface (QPI). QPI is a platform architecture that provides high-speed (up to 25.6 GB/s), point-to-point connection between processors, and between processors and the I/O hub. Multiple processors can be connected directly to form a SMP node without a cache coherence chip. Furthermore, QPI interface supports adjusting link bandwidth dynamically and hot plugging. The IOH chip in compute node bridges the QPI interface and PCI-Express 2.0 interface, so that the NIC card can access the processor main memory effectively.

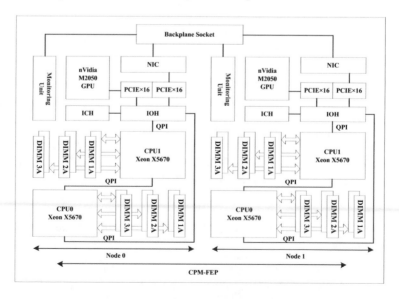

**FIGURE 19.5**: Architecture of compute node.

The physical package of the main board is constructed with two levels, the lower level and the upper level. The lower lever is the Compute Process Motherboard (CPM), and the upper level is the GPU board. The GPU is connected with the CPM via GPC, a PCI-E 2.0 bridging card. Each of the compute node main boards is constituted by two compute nodes (B0 and B1) with the same structure. Each compute node has its own CPU, memory, high-speed connection, IOH, and power supply. To be specific, there are 2 CPU sockets, 12 memory sockets, 1 GPU, and 1 NIC communication chip in each compute node.

## 19.3.2 Interconnect

In TH-1A high-speed communication network [XLW+11], the NRC is used for packet switching and routing, and the NIC is used for interfacing compute nodes and service nodes into the interconnect network.

1. NRC

   Facing some requirements of the large-scale interconnect network in TH-1A, such as reducing the hops, lowering communication latency, and improving the reliability and flexibility, we use high radix routing techniques [SAKD06] to design the NRC. As shown in Figure 19.6, the NRC contains 16 switch ports. Internally, NRC uses a tile-based switching structure to simplify the design of a 16x16 crossbar. There are 16 tiles which are arranged in a 4x4 array, and each tile is a 4x4 subcrossbar. The transmission rate of each serial link in NRC is 10 Gbps, and each port integrates eight serial links, thus each port can provide 160 Gbps bidirectional bandwidth.

   Besides using CRC on data packets, internal buffers in the NRC are ECC protected. The links of the NRC also support working at full-speed or half-speed mode, and can negotiate the bit-width statically or dynamically. With these supports, the NRC is able to isolate the failure links and improve the reliability and usability of the interconnect fabric.

2. NIC

   Figure 19.7 shows the internal structure of the NIC. It integrates a 16-lane PCI-Express 2.0 interface, and connects with the NRC via 8 10 Gbps links. There is also

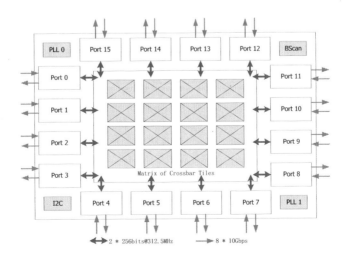

**FIGURE 19.6**: Structure of NRC.

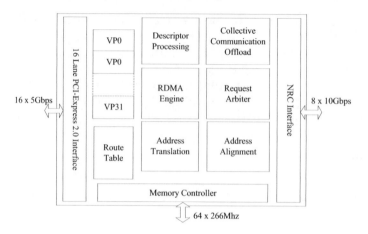

**FIGURE 19.7**: Structure of NIC.

an ECC protected 64bits@266Mhz memory controller interface to on-board memory whose function will be explained below.

The NIC utilizes user-level communication technique, and supports the overlap of computation and communication. Each NIC implements 32 virtual ports (VP). Each VP is a combination of a small set of memory-mapped registers and a set of related in-memory data structures, and the address range of registers in different VP are spaced out at least the length of the physical page. All of which can be mapped to user space, so that it can be accessed in user space concurrently and with protection.

To remove the overhead of data copy and achieve maximum bandwidth, the NIC support zero-copy of RDMA between process buffers. In TH-1A, RDMA access memory through Address Translation Table (ATT) [SH98], which is implemented in the on-board memory of a NIC card and managed by kernel module. Using ATT, we can construct a virtual address in the NIC so that non-contiguous physical pages can be merged into a contiguous virtual address range. NIC virtual address of buffer is used in the RDMA request. The NIC uses ATT to translate the virtual address into the PCI address of physical pages. An address aligning module is used in the NIC to byte-align the local and remote buffer of RDMA. Furthermore, several offload mechanisms have been developed to optimize collective communication, a set of important routines in MPI standard, which largely affects the performance of large-scale parallel applications.

Both the NRC and the NIC adopt the 90 nm CMOS fabrication and array flip-chip package. The substrate of the NRC chip contains 0.46 billion transistors and 2,577 pins, while the substrate of the NIC chip contains 0.15 billion transistors and 657 pins.

3. Topology

Based on NRC and NIC, we designed a high-speed, high-density, balanced, and scalable interconnection network. Figure 19.8 shows the topology which is a hierarchical fat-tree.

The first layer consists of 480 switching boards distributed in computing and service racks. Every 16 compute nodes connect a switching board through backplane, and communication on the switching board uses electrical transmission.

The second layer is composed of eleven 384-ports switches, which are fully connected using QSFP optical fibers. Each 384-port switch contains 12 leaf and 12 root switch

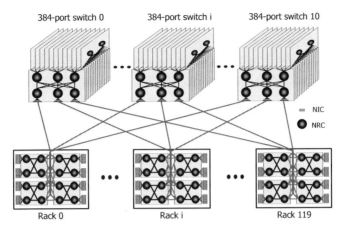

**FIGURE 19.8**: TH-1A interconnection network.

boards which are connected by a high-density backplane board in an orthotropic way. All of the rack-mounted switching boards have an optical-fiber connection to the 384-ports switches. The throughput of one 384-port switch is 61.44 Tbps. The whole system aggregate bandwidth is 1146.88 Tbps, the bisection bandwidth is 307.2 Tbps.

4. Communication software

The basic message-passing infrastructure on the NIC is what we call the Galaxy Express (GLEX). Based on the NIC virtual port, GLEX encapsulates the communication interfaces of NIC, and provides both user space and kernel space programming interfaces which can fulfill the function and performance requirement from other software modules.

GLEX consists of a kernel module for managing NIC and providing kernel programming interfaces, a network driver module for supporting TCP/IP protocol, a user-level communication library for providing user space programming interfaces, and management tools for system administration and maintenance. GLEX is also used in the preboot execution environment to boot diskless computation nodes in order to lower the overhead of system booting and maintenance.

GLEX implements reduced communication protocol, and provides zero-copy RDMA transfer between user space data buffers. By utilizing virtual memory protection and memory mapping in CPU, GLEX permits several processes to communicate simultaneously and securely in user space and bypass the operating system kernel and data copy in communication operations. We also implemented GPU-Direct which permits zero-copy RDMA of CUDA pinned memory; this improves data transfer bandwidth for applications that utilize GPU.

## 19.3.3 Storage System

The TH-1A storage system is a large-scale shared storage system equipped with different types of storage servers and disk arrays. All of the storage servers connect into TH-net, InfiniBand, and Gigabit Ethernet for sharing of its storage targets to both compute nodes inside and data processing facilities outside, constructing a shared object storage system based on a custom Lustre parallel filesystem. It provides parallel access with high aggregate bandwidth within the TH-1A system and centralized access to petascale data sets from

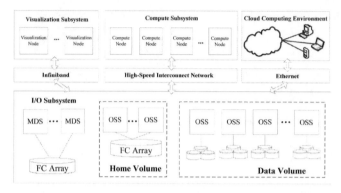

**FIGURE 19.9**: Architecture of TH-1A storage system.

other center-wide platforms to eliminate islands of data. The architecture of the TH-1A storage system is shown in Figure 19.9.

The TH-1A storage system can provide storage in aggregate over 100 GB/s of I/O bandwidth and over 2 petabytes capacity from above 16,000 SATA drives. Performance benefits from the custom I/O protocol based on GLEX, which can fully exploit the performance of TH-net and the advantage of object-based architecture. The TH-1A storage system provides multiple filesystem volumes for data storage. The default setting is one user HOME directory called HOME-volume and another one for large simulation data sets called DATA-volume. The multiple volume management in TH-1A storage system, guided by hints from upper level software, can greatly reduce the interference from various applications I/O workload and metadata bottleneck. The DATA-volume consists of 110 embedded RAID enclosure storage servers. Each OSS server is equipped with two PCI-E connected RAID controllers attached with an 8-disk enclosure capable of above 600 MB/s raw device I/O bandwidth. For user HOME-volume, there are four OSS servers connected to a FC-shared two-controller RAID array with high capacity and high hardware reliability support. In this configuration, each storage server controls 4 LUNs and provides an aggregate raw write performance of up to 500 MB/s.

All of the volumes store their metadata into a two-controller FC array called metadata disk array, equipped with SSD and FC disks to improve metadata storage performance. Two pairs of the four MDS servers connect directly to a RAID array to provide shared metadata access for all kinds of filesystem clients. The TH-1A metadata storage system is designed to eliminate single point of failure. A pair of high-availability metadata servers are both connected to a pair of 12-disk dual-controller RAID enclosures to maximize availability.

TH-1A is designed for large-scale and high-accuracy numerical applications, such as numerical weather prediction, high-energy physics, and so on. The model of the application is complex and the scale of the resulting data is large (TB or even PB), which introduces a new requirement and great challenges for the high performance visualization environment of TH-1A. The storage system also connects the external visualization clusters through the InfiniBand network, to share the data produced by massive compute nodes in TH-1A, supporting the online and offline application visualization efficiently.

The storage system has a third network connection through Ethernet, which can let the center and wide-area network system access the data from the TH-1A storage system. The cloud computing environment around the TH-1A has been established.

**TABLE 19.1**: System software stack.

| Operating system | Kylin Linux |
|---|---|
| Compiler | Intel 10/11, Gcc 4.2, Cuda 3.0/4.0 |
| MPI | MPICH2 + custom GLEX |
| Parallel filesystem | Lustre + custom over THNET protocol |
| Job batch and scheduler | Slurm + custom modules |
| System management | THRMS |
| Debugger | GDB, STAT, STDump |
| Performance tool | PAPI, TAU, IDE |
| Virtualization | HPUC |
| Visualization | TH-DPVS |

## 19.4 System Software

TH-1A provides a conventional HPC system software stack (Table 19.1), including Kylin operating system, global parallel filesystem, resource management and scheduling system, administration, as well as the virtualization and visualization environments.

### 19.4.1 Operating System

The operating system of TH-1A supercomputer is Kylin Linux. According to the architecture of TH-1A and user demands, the kernel of the Kylin Linux is optimized to support multi-core and multi-thread processors, heterogeneous computing synchronization, power management, system fault tolerance, and data security protection, which provides users an execution supporting environment with high efficiency, reliability, security, and usability.

Kylin Linux for the TH-1A supercomputer utilizes a coordinated heterogeneous architecture, running on each node. The basic service kernel contains the hardware abstraction layer, memory management module, task management module, interrupt management module, and the device management module. Above the basic service kernel, there is an extra support layer which provides the software and hardware coordinated power management, and the high performance user contains (HPUC). HPUC is used for quality of service, security, and environment customization.

The architecture of Kylin Linux in the TH-1A supercomputer can also be customized to fulfill the different requirements of the running environment. The operating system on service nodes provides each user an independent virtual environment based on the HPUC. The operating system on service nodes also implements the dynamic schedule of node access to balance the load between multiple service nodes. The compute nodes in the TH-1A system are diskless, thus the initial root filesystem is provided by a ram disk linked against the Kylin Linux kernel. The ram disk contains shells, simple utilities, shared libraries, network driver, custom Lustre client, etc. There is a quality of service module in the operating system on compute node, which avoids the excessive resource usage by malicious users or the faults in applications. We have designed and implemented the unified low power management techniques in the operating system of compute node, which can lower the power consumption through adjusting the running level of CPU and also control the state of GPU. This can reduce the maintenance cost when the system is deployed.

### 19.4.2    File System

High bandwidth I/O on TH-1A systems is provided by the object-based storage architecture powered by a deeply optimized Lustre filesystem. Lustre is an object-based parallel filesystem suitable for the I/O patterns typically seen in scientific applications and designed to provide large, high-bandwidth storage on large-scale supercomputers. Lustre is a Linux-based filesystem that uses the portals open networking API. TH-1A implements a native GLEX Lustre Network Device(GLND) designed to make Lustre run well with the TH-net GLEX communication system and Kylin OS, providing scalable high-throughput I/O on the TH-1A system.

The TH-1A system provides a consistent global name space that allows for identical pathnames to be used, regardless of which node on the system the application is running, whether Intel CPU compute nodes, FT CPU service nodes, or other service nodes. TH-1A has its custom design on its overall high-throughput storage solution. High data transfer throughput between clients and Luster OSSs is achieved by a carefully tuned RDMA transfer pipeline inside GLND. GLND can also set a balance between different RDMA policies, such as storage side push and client side pull, for better RDMA efficiency to achieve scalability for typical I/O communication patterns but with relatively lower consumed NIC resources. In the TH-1A storage system, each application can create files distributed or striped across OSTs within one filesystem volume. Any file that has a stripe count setting is broken into objects distributed on OSTs and a single client can gain high aggregated bandwidth above 2 GB/s.

The Metadata Server (MDS) is a central place that holds the file metadata for the entire filesystem. TH-1A has a carefully optimized MDS design. For the Lustre filesystem, metadata operation rate is restricted for its single metadata server design, which can result in a parallel I/O performance bottleneck at large scale. For this reason, all OSTs in TH-1A can be partitioned into multiple filesystem volumes served by multiple MDS to release the MDS load from the burden of a single server. The responsibility of the TH-1A upper level HPUC system is to help the users find their correct volume transparently or let them decide according to their special requirements. Latency also plays a key role in improving metadata operation efficiency. To reduce latency of each metadata operation, small or medium-sized metadata requests are encapsulated into one or multiple Mini-Packets for low latency transfer instead of using the handshake protocol seen in large data transfer modes with extra round trip overhead. SSD attached to MDS acting as MDT back-end filesystem external journal also plays an important role in metadata access optimization.

For I/O resilience, TH-1A is dependent on filesystem high availability (HA) support and hardware RAID support. Besides that, TH-1A has a central storage management system, which integrates both Lustre filesystem and storage hardware monitor facilities and can mask degraded storage target LUN from filesystem namespace to prevent further performance slowdown or data loss.

### 19.4.3    System Administration and Schedulers

The TH-1A system employs THRMS (Tianhe Resource Management System) for integrated system administration and unified jobs scheduling.

System administration of THRMS supports the system booting, interconnection network configuration, resource partition, node state monitoring, and temperature, voltage, and power monitoring. Medley methods including probe, registration, and health checking are used to ensure the accuracy of system state. There is a database to store information and variation of the whole system, which supports system diagnoses and data mining for maintenance.

The scheduler subsystem of THRMS is in charge of global resource allocation and task scheduling. It is customized based on SLURM for heterogeneous resource management and some adaptive scheduling mechanisms. A custom parallel job launcher is implemented to reduce the startup time of large-scale parallel jobs.

The scheduler subsystem provides common job scheduling policies including priority queuing, backfill, fair-share, and advance reservation. Topology-aware and power-aware node selection and allocation strategies are provided. Partitioned resource use and job QoS are also supported. A partition is equivalent to a job queue, which has availability state, access control, scheduling priority, and resource limits attached to it. Each job submitted to TH-1A has a QOS level associated with it. Different QOS levels differ in resource limits, job priority, and preemption relation.

Job logging and accounting is an important part of THRMS. Detailed information of jobs run on TH-1A is recorded in a database. Compute resource state changes are also logged in the database. The database stores account based resource limits and access control policies as well. Job accounting reports and system utilization analysis reports are generated from the log data.

THRMS supports event triggers which can be used for automatic administration. On hardware or software events like compute node state change, job state change, configuration modification, and daemon process failure, configured script programs will be executed automatically to perform predefined operations.

### 19.4.4 Virtualization

To improve the usability and security of the system, TH-1A utilizes virtualization techniques, i.e., the High Performance User Container (HPUC) technique which supports dynamic environment customization. Figure 19.10 shows the architecture of HPUC, which consists of three parts, virtual computing zone on the service nodes, high performance computing zone on the compute nodes, and task management system oriented virtual zone. Based on the high performance virtual zone technique, TH-1A can construct custom virtual running environments for various users, and enable data isolation between zones.

The virtual computing zone on the service nodes supports multiple users run in independent runtime environments on a single OS simultaneously. To reduce performance loss, the HPUC technology uses a lightweight security filesystem to reduce the overhead of constructing multiple running environments, and localize the file position to reduce the overhead of remote file access. The task management system oriented virtual zone is the linkage between the virtual computing zone on the service nodes and the high performance computing zone on the computing nodes, which couple the virtual zones on compute nodes and service nodes according to the configuration of the user runtime environment.

HPUC in the TH-1A system has two-levels to fulfill various user requirements, the common HPUC (CUC) and the specialized HPUC (SUC). The CUC environment is constructed during system initialization. It is the main working environment for most common users which provides basic tools for application programming, compiling, and debugging, as well as task submitting. The SUC environment is designed for users with special demands. When constructing an SUC, the system manager provides users a basic SUC template. Based on this template, users can construct their own running environment according to their own demands in this SUC.

### 19.4.5    Visualization

A distribute and parallel visualization system (TH-DPVS) is developed to accelerate the large-scale data visualization. TH-DPVS is a tool for visualizing two- and three-dimensional data sets, aimed at scalability, platform independency, and distributed computation models.

TH-DPVS uses Client/Server mode to implement remote visualization, and applies a desktop deliver strategy. The client of TH-DPVS can be deployed on various OS platforms. The server processes of TH-DPVS are distributed on the visualization clusters. TH-DPVS introduces a hybrid method to partition the workloads, that is, it first performs data division to parallelize data streams, and then an image space based partition method is used to accomplish task parallelism. This hybrid method is implemented just like the strategy of the hybrid sort-last and sort-first rendering mode.

TH-DPVS exploits both a static and dynamic load balancing strategy. In the case of static load balancing, both space partition based and scalar sorting based data structures are used, such as quadtree, octree, kd-tree, interval tree, B-like tree, and so on. These data structures can guarantee that nearly the same number of data cells is distributed to all server processes. In the case of dynamic load balancing, a work-stealing strategy has been employed for TH-DPVS. Therefore, TH-DPVS can achieve high performance by both the static and dynamic methods.

The visualization modules in TH-DPVS include a geometric rendering module, a volume rendering module, a texture rendering module, and a feature extraction and interactive analysis module. The geometric rendering module provides traditional visualization technologies, such as color map, iso-contour line, streamlines, iso-surface, and so on. Besides the mainstream volume visualization methods, a direct visualization method is employed in the volume rendering module to visualize the unstructured cell-centered data more precisely. In the texture rendering module, an adaptive sparse texture rendering technology is proposed to overcome the occlusion problem in three-dimensional vector data visualization. Furthermore, two cool/warm illumination methods are proposed and implemented to enhance the direction representation of the vector field. TH-DPVS provides powerful tools for feature extraction and data analysis. Besides the traditional methods, a fuzzy-based feature definition language (FFDL) is also implemented in TH-DPVS, which can visualize the uncertainty of the scientific data.

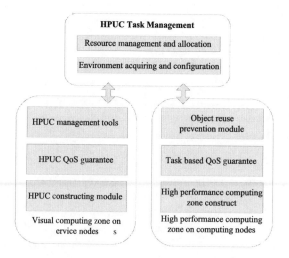

**FIGURE 19.10**: Architecture of HPUC.

TH-DPVS can also integrate many existing visualization toolkits (e.g., VTK, VisIt, ParaView), making it able to deal with various file formats.

## 19.5 Programming System

The programming system of TH-1A supports a hybrid programming model, provides serial programming languages such as C/C++, Fortran77/90/95, Java, and the parallel programming languages such as OpenMP, MPI, and OpenMP/MPI. TH-1A can use CUDA or OpenCL for GPU programming, and supports a hybrid programming model to fit the hardware architecture. TH-1A also provides various programming tools, including debugging, performance, etc.

### 19.5.1 Hybrid Programming Model

To fully exploit the computing ability of a petascale heterogeneous CPU/GPU supercomputing system, we employ a hybrid programming model consisting of MPI, OpenMP, and CUDA, which efficiently explore the task parallel, thread parallel, and data parallel of the parallel application as Figure 19.11 shows.

For the heterogeneous CPU/GPU supercomputer system, we map one MPI process on each compute element, which is the hardware model of the basic computing unit of TH-1A. These compute elements connect each other with TH-net. There are two CPUs as the host and one GPU as the accelerator in a compute element. The host controls the communication with others and the compute-intensive tasks are performed by the host and the accelerator cooperatively.

To parallelize the computation-intensive tasks, we use an OpenMP programming model on the host and configure 12 threads spawned at runtime when the progress enters into the parallel region. OpenMP dynamic scheduling is in charge of dynamic task assignment on CPU and GPU in one compute node. Each thread is bound with one core of the CPU. One of the 12 threads controls the GPU to finish the major part of the computing workload, and the other 11 threads consume the remaining fractions. Synchronization is performed at the end of all the OpenMP threads.

With powerful arithmetic engines, GPU devices can run thousands of lightweight threads

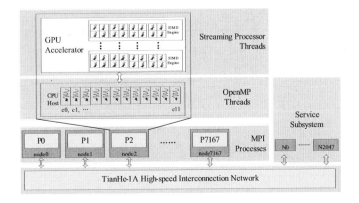

**FIGURE 19.11**: Hybrid programming model for the TH-1A system.

in parallel. Powerful data parallel capability makes them well suited to computations. In order to facilitate scientists to program the scientific applications for better performance from the NVIDIA GPU, NVIDIA builds an easily used GPU programming model called CUDA. In the CUDA model, the SIMD engine is regarded as the streaming multi-processor (SM), among which the basic unit of execution flow is the warp, a collection of 32 threads. These 32 threads execute the same instruction with different data. In one SM, multiple warps are allowed to be concurrently executed in the way of groups called blocks.

### 19.5.2    Languages and Compilers

The compiler on TH-1A supports multiple programming languages, from C, C++, Fortran77/90/95, and Java languages, to OpenMP API3.0 and global MPI library based on TH-net. TH-1A also uses CUDA toolkit and libraries for GPU programming and optimizations.

The TH-1A MPI, which we've named MPICH2-GLEX, is an optimized port of the Argonne National Laboratory's MPI-2 implementation: MPICH2. Currently, we've implemented software code that uses GLEX in the nemesis channel layer of MPICH2 [BGG+09]. It provides high performance communication within and between compute nodes. It also contains optimized MPI-IO interfaces.

In MPICH2-GLEX, we've implemented the short message eager protocol with two kinds of channel: shared RDMA channel and exclusive RDMA channel, to optimize the performance and memory usage. For the implementation of long message rendezvous protocol, we use zero-copy RDMA data transfer. There are also some optimized collective interfaces, such as MPI_Barrier and MPI_Bcast, which utilize the offloaded collective mechanisms the NIC provided.

### 19.5.3    Domain-Specific Software Infrastructure

The exponential growth of computer power in the last 10 years is now creating a great challenge for parallel programming toward achieving realistic performance in the field of scientific computing. To help the traditional program with a large amount of numerical simulations, TH-1A adopts an efficient heterogeneous programming infrastructure, J Adaptive Structured Meshes applications Infrastructure (JASMIN) [MZC+10][IAP].

JASMIN is developed by the Institute of Applied Physics and Computational Mathematics (IAPCM), with higher levels of abstraction and parallelism extraction of applications.

The programming challenges mainly arise from two types of increasing complexity. The first lies in the computer architecture. More and more cores are integrated into each CPU, and more and more CPUs are clustered into each computing node, and hundreds or thousands of nodes are interconnected. Parallel algorithms should have sufficient parallelism to utilize so many cores. The design of such data structures and parallel algorithms is too professional for the application users. The second complexity is in the application system. Large-scale simulations are mainly used to study the characteristics of the complex systems. With increasing computer capabilities, the complexity of the application systems should also increase simultaneously.

JASMIN is a new program design method based on the adaptive structured meshes applications. A large amount of common data structure, algorithm, and libraries are integrated into the software infrastructure. Using these data structures and programming interfaces, the user can easily develop parallel programs for complex computers. JASMIN simplifies and accelerates the development of parallel programs on the heterogeneous CPU/GPU supercomputer systems like TH-1A.

### 19.5.4 Tools

To assist users in developing correct and efficient parallel applications, a range of programming tools are offered on TH-1A, including a set of debuggers, performance analysis tools, and an easy-to-use IDE, which can help users to explore the available computing power and parallelism.

1. Debugger and performance analysis tools

   Several serial and parallel debuggers are offered on TH-1A, including GDB, STAT, and STDump (Stack Trace Dump) to help users to quickly locate, identify, and fix application bugs. After complex parallel applications have been running for a long time, it would be highly preferred to locate the context of the potential problems when applications are terminated exceptionally. STDump is a lightweight tool we developed to serve this purpose. It dumps stack traces of a parallel application in case of exceptional termination caused by asynchronous signals, such as SIGSEGV, SIGFPE. STDump installs a signal callback into the target application, which dumps the call stacks in case of invalid address access or floating point exception. STDump works using the LD_PRELOAD mechanism and does not require any change to the application source code. STDump stores the dumped stack trace into a human readable log file. By providing a separate log file for each individual task/thread, STDump provides support for large-scale MPI/OpenMP parallel applications.

   The commonly used performance tool on TH-1A is TAU. The OS kernel of TH-1A compute nodes is also enhanced to provide the necessary support for obtaining PMU statistics. An application's performance data can be visually analyzed via TAU's ParaProf GUI tool. The installed version of TAU on TH-1A has been updated to support the performance analysis of CUDA applications. Various performance analysis tools can run on TH-1A, including gprof, Vtune, Oprofile, PAPI, Open SpeedShop, Perfsuite, SCALASCA, etc., to help users identify the performance bottlenecks and hot spot code regions of applications.

   Apart from the aforementioned tools, TH-1A also provides some correctness tools, such as Valgrind and Marmot, to make user applications faster, safer, and correct.

2. Integrated development environment(IDE)

   TH-1A provides a parallel application integrated development environment (IDE) based on the Eclipse parallel tools platform (PTP). This IDE fully supports application editing, compiling, linking, launching, debugging, and performance analysis in a unified, standard GUI interface. By enriching PTP's support for TH-1A resource management system, a graphical job submission and monitoring environment is provided within this IDE. Through the GUI interface, the job submission process is greatly simplified. TH-1A IDE can remarkably improve the efficiency of parallel application development and greatly simplify the end-user interaction with TH-1A.

## 19.6 System and Application Statistics

TH-1A has been deployed in NSCC-Tianjin, in Tianjin Binhai new area district since November 2010.

### 19.6.1    Facility Statistics

NSCC-TJ occupies 8,500 square meters of floor space. There are two large computer rooms with total area of 3,600 square meters; one room hosts the TH-1A supercomputer and the other the cloud computing and system extension. NSCC-TJ is provided with one power station and one cooling station. The capacity of power equipment and cooling equipment is 13,600 KW and 9,600 KW, respectively, sufficient to meet the needs of NSCC-TJ.

TH-1A occupies 700 square meters of floor space, and its computer room has approximately 1,200 square meters and is equipped with a safety monitoring system consisting of smoke detectors and temperature sensors. Peak power consumption under a full CPU/GPU load is 4.04 MW. Short-term emergency power is served by an uninterruptible power supply (UPS). The computer room offers an environment of constant temperature and humidity. The temperature is 20 degrees centigrade and the humidity ranges from about 30% to 40%. The cooling system is equipped with a fully water-cooled air conditioning system. The monitoring facilities provide 24-hour monitoring services for the cooling system, power system, air-conditioner, and computer room environment.

### 19.6.2    Application Statistics

TH-1A has been providing HPC services for more the 300 users for the past 18 months. The scientific opportunities include energy assurance, earth science, material science, fundamental science, biology and medicine, engineering design, etc. Based on TH-1A, a creative scientific research platform is constructed through the collaboration between universities and institutes; a novel technology developing platform is also constructed through the collaboration between industry enterprises. These efforts aim to improve and boost the development of HPC applications in China.

The characteristics of some main applications are categorized as follows:

1. Energy assurance

   To address the key scientific issues related to energy, such as fusion, combustion, nuclear fuel cycle, renewables (wind, solar, hydro), energy efficiency, storage and transmission, the research has been done on simulation of electronic pulse complex cavity coupling, eradiation dynamic particles transportation, neutron dynamic transportation, laser solid reaction, and unstructured MC computation. The main scalar algorithms include 2D convective diffused equations, low latency parallel SN scan, 3D particles simulation of overlap of the computation and communication, Fokker-Planck parallel algorithm, non-stationary MC simulation, etc.

   These kinds of applications on TH-1A can scale from thousands to ten thousands CPU cores, with performance from teraflops to petaflops, supporting the simulation from 2-dimensional, partial 3-dimensional, to fully 3-dimensional.

2. Climate

   To address the key scientific issues related to weather and environment, the climate research has been conducted to establish the efficient numerical forecast business systems for medium-term numerical weather forecaster, high-resolution borderline weather forecaster, and global ocean marine environment forecaster. The main algorithms include multi-measurements multi-patterns scalar parallel algorithm, tangential concomitant mode, spherical syntonic pedigree transformation based 3D data transpose, 3D complex Helmholtz equations, 4D alternated assimilation frame, divisional parallel algorithm of directed assimilation, etc.

These applications usually scale to thousands of cores; the largest one scales to 20,000 CPU cores. The applications' running time can last a few days or even one week, with computation intensive, data intensive, and collective communication. These applications have used about 7% of the CPU time resource of TH-1A, supporting research and business services for global and area climate changing model, including ocean, atmosphere, terrene, zoology, and multiple model coupling.

3. Petroleum exploration

To address the petroleum exploration integrative process, the seismic exploration method is widely used in hydrocarbon energy development to improve the exploration efficiency. The fine simulations of multimillion dimension gridding have been done to improve the precision and resolution of petroleum seismic data processing. The main algorithms focus on the collection equips, array disposal methods, and fine description of style layers, for example, the 3D prestack depth migration.

These kinds of applications usually scale thousands of nodes; the largest one scales to all 7,168 nodes, 86,016 cores in the system. The applications' running time can last tens of hours to a few days. The applications are custom Geoeast, iCluster software, and some other software with hybrid parallel model including data parallelism and task parallelism, with high requirements for the capability and performance of memory and I/O accessing. By now, these kinds of applications have used about 40% of the CPU time resource of TH-1A, supporting the actual businesses.

4. Biomedical research

The research work in the biomedical field has been focused on high-resolution analysis of population genomics, AIDS and senile dementia research, new immunity drug design, and Molecular Dynamics methods to elucidate the relationship of structure and function of biological macro molecules. This kind of research can provide a theoretical reference for further study under conclusions and methods used in the design, and help us to design and synthesize new drugs, and expand the breadth and depth of life science research.

Applications cover from life science, new medicine development, gene sorting, protein folding, to molecule juncture. These kinds of applications scale from hundreds to ten thousands of cores, implementing the virtual filtration of 100 thousands of chemical combinations per day. The software includes open source software, such as Gromacs, NAMD, and some custom MD and gene sorting software. The running time usually lasts a few days or weeks. These applications have used about 24% CPU time resource of TH-1A, supporting either research work or businesses.

5. Materials

Materials science, especially the area of nanoscience and nanotechnology, is an interdisciplinary field applying the properties of matter to various areas of science and engineering. The research has been focused on addressing the key issues related to nanoscience, material life cycles, response, failure, and manufacturing. The algorithms used in these types of applications are mainly molecular dynamics, with intensive computation and frequently collective communication. The data scales to gigabytes or terabytes.

These types of applications usually scale to hundreds and thousands of cores. The largest one, the trans-scale simulation of the silicon deposition process, based on self-developed scalable bond-order potential (BOP) code, scales to all 7,168 nodes, using more than 180,000 hybrid CPU and GPU cores, with the performance reaching

1.87 Pflops in single precision (SP). The application softwares include Vasp, NAMD, Gromacs, and some custom software. These applications have used about 8.2% of the CPU time resource of TH-1A, supporting a wide range of research work.

6. Engineering

The main focus of the research on engineering is to address the design, deploy, and operate safe and economical structures, machines, processes, and systems with reduced concept-to-deployment time. Vehicle design uses more than tens of millions grid, high-precision simulation on structure modeling and collision testing to improve the performance and safety of vehicles. Aviation and space applications support low mach number flow for aviation and hypersonic flow for space. Civil engineering and structure simulation support the design, aseismatic and safety analysis of large-scale dams, subway tunnels, and flyover bridges.

These types of applications scale tens to thousands of cores. Structure design scales tens to hundreds of cores, and fluent design and simulation scales hundreds to ten thousands of cores. The largest parallelism algorithm now uses 12,375 cores, with more than 300 million grids simulation for aircrafts, with about 70% parallel efficiency. These kinds of applications are computation intensive, various communication intensive, and I/O intensive among different areas. Pre- and post-processing need nodes with large memory capacity, and use differential finite elements methods as the main algorithms. The applications include custom software and commercial software (such as Ansys, Ls-dyna, CFX, Fluent, etc.). Those applications are both for research and business use.

7. Animation

The Chinese government strongly supports the culture creative industry to drive the boom of Chinese culture. Supercomputer is a good mainstream choice in massive animation manufacturing. Large-scale heterogeneous supercomputers such as TH-1A could improve the capability of the Chinese animation and image industry.

These kinds of applications are task parallel and data parallel; the largest parallelism now needs 2,000 nodes; running time is from hours to days. The characteristics of these types of applications are computation intensive and I/O intensive, which perform frequently file read and write, with little collective communication. The main algorithm is ray-track. The applications include custom software (with sound scalability) and commercial software (such as 3DMAX, Maya, etc., with weak scalability). These applications are mainly for business use.

## 19.6.3    HPL Benchmark Result

Linpack is a widely recognized benchmark for system-level performance of high performance computing systems. We used High Performance Linpack (HPL), and developed the Level 3 Basic Linear Algebra Subprograms library for the TH-1A system (THBLAS3) [WYD+11] and optimized for GPU accelerated heterogeneous architecture.

For the Linpack benchmark we focused on the DGEMM and DTRSM which are the main time-consuming functions. To accelerate the DGEMM and the DTRSM, all the computing capacities including the host and the accelerator were used. The load balance and data exchange are the key issues to achieve high performance. We developed some novel methods and used some other well-known optimizations to solve or release these problems.

1. Two-level adaptive task mapping

We measured the performance of GPUs and CPUs in GFLOPS and used it to guide the split of the next workload. The optimal split by the GPU can be obtained by this formula:

$$G_{split} = \frac{P_{GPU}}{P_{GPU} + P_{CPU}}$$

$P_{GPU}$ and $P_{CPU}$ are the results of the workloads (the amount of floating-point operations) divided by the execution time of the GPU and the CPU, respectively. The performance of the GPU varies with the workload. So we store the $G_{split}$ in a database called *database*$_g$ which is indexed by the workload.

The second level is the mapping of the computations of CPU part to each CPU core, which is different with the GPU and the CPU split. The split fractions are stored in the database named *database*$_c$ and are indexed by the core number $i$, instead of the workload. Suppose that the total number of CPU cores executing the DGEMM is $n$, the split fraction of the *ith* CPU core is:

$$C_{split_i} = \frac{P_{CPU[i]}}{\sum_{j=1}^{n} P_{CPU[j]}},$$

where $P_{CPU[i]}$ is the performance of the *ith* CPU core.

When DGEMM and DTRSM are invoked in the Linpack, the whole workload is calculated first. The split ratio across the CPU and GPU can be obtained from *database*$_g$ indexed by the workload. The split ratio of the CPU cores can be got from *database*$_c$ indexed by the core number. After all the DGEMM parts are finished, the split ratios in *database*$_g$ and *database*$_c$ are tuned according to the above equations, and then are stored into the databases. The overhead of the whole procedure is almost negligible compared with the execution time of the DGEMM or DTRSM.

2. Software pipelining

On the CPU/GPU heterogeneous platform, the communication bandwidth between the CPU and GPU is much lower than the bandwidth of the device memory. We propose a neat software pipelining method that can overlap the kernel execution and the data transferring between the CPU and GPU.

In the Linpack, a large matrix-matrix multiplication can be split into a series of tasks that form a task queue. For example, the matrix multiplication $A \times B = C$ can be split to $\begin{pmatrix} A_1 \\ A_2 \end{pmatrix} \begin{pmatrix} B_1 & B_2 \end{pmatrix} = C$ and four tasks are formed $T_0 : C_1 = A_1 \times B_1$, $T_1 : C_2 = A_1 \times B_2$, $T_2 : C_3 = A_2 \times B_1$, and $T_3 : C_4 = A_2 \times B_2$. To optimize the data-transfer time, we implemented the software pipelining among the tasks. Since the same matrix between tasks can be reused, the order of the four tasks is like $T_0, T_1, T_3, T_2$ by using the "bounce corner turn" method. When $T_1$ is executed, matrix $A_1$ does not need to be transferred, so neither does $B_2$ for $T_3$ and $A_2$ for $T_2$. In all, the entire matrix $A$ and matrix $B_1$ are skipped. In each task, the input phase is responsible for transferring the matrix from the CPU to the GPU. Then the execution phase finishes the matrix multiplication. At last, in the output phase the result of the multiplication is transferred to the CPU.

**TABLE 19.2**: Linpack evaluations.

| Matrix size ($N$) | 3600000 | Panel broadcast | 2ringM |
|---|---|---|---|
| Block size ($NB$) | 512 | Look-ahead depth | 1 |
| Process mapping | Row-major | Swap | Mix (threshold=768) |
| process grid ($P \times Q$) | $64 \times 112$ | Matrix form | L1:no-trans, U:no-trans |
| Panel factorization | Left-looking | Equilibration | no |
| NBMIN, NDIV | 2,2 | Alignment | 8 double precision words |

3. Traditional optimizations combination

Apart from the optimizations methods mentioned above related to the hybrid nature of the TH-1A system, we employed a combination method consisting of some traditional and important optimizations for homogeneous systems. These optimizations are processes and threads affinity, streaming load/store, memory management strategy tuning, look-ahead technology, and large block size, etc.

4. Linpack evaluations

The configurations of the full compute nodes are shown in Table 19.2. HPL provides many tuning parameters, such as broadcast topology and block size, which have to be carefully tuned in order to achieve the best performance. For the TH-1A system, $N$, $NB$, $P$, $Q$, and look-ahead depth significantly impact the HPL performance whereas the others play relatively minor roles. With the coefficient matrix size $N = 360,000$ on $P \times Q = 64 \times 112 = 7,168$ processes, the final result was 2,566 TFLOPS. The progress of Linpack executing on the TH-1A system is shown in Figure 19.12.

## 19.6.4    Highlights of Main Applications

To accelerate the development and deployment of parallel applications on the heterogeneous CPU/GPU supercomputer system TH-1A, we introduced the domain-specific parallel programming frameworks, for example, JASMIN.

In the field of scientific computing, a mesh is the base representation of a set of non-overlapping zones partitioning the computational domain. On a mesh, a discrete system results from the discretization of differential equations and may be solved by parallel algorithms. Many types of mesh have been used, but the structured mesh and the unstructured

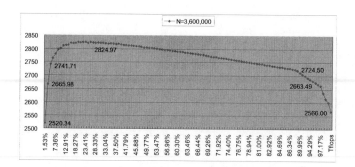

**FIGURE 19.12**: Linpack result on TH-1A.

mesh are the most important. JASMIN is aiming to improve on the traditional program for numerical simulations of laser fusion in inertial confinement fusion (ICF), and also could support various applications in the field of global climate modeling, CFD, material simulations, etc.

JASMIN promotes a new paradigm of parallel programming, which integrates the common algorithms and technologies to hide the parallel programming, support the visualization of computing results and tolerance computing, and so on. JASMIN enables domain-specific experts to develop the high-efficient parallel applications without learning many details of the parallel programming paradigms, which greatly reduces the developing difficulty of parallel programs and improves the developing efficiency of the large-scale parallel applications. Now JASMIN has released version 2.0 and has achieved its original objectives. A large amount of parallel programs have been reconstructed or developed on thousands of CPU/GPU nodes.

Aiming at the problems of large-scale heterogeneous parallel programming, such as program segmentation, data distribution, processes synchronization, load balancing, and performance optimization, JASMIN uses three layers: top layer for interfaces, middle layer for numerical algorithms, and supporting layer for SAMR meshes, shown in Figure 19.13.

The supporting layer for SAMR meshes contains three sublayers: toolbox layer, data structure layer, and mesh adaptivity layer. Toolbox provides the basic tools for object-oriented program design; the data structure layer provides the packages of managing patch data structure to divide the user program area into many data patches. Because of these packages, the details of parallel computation and the communication between nodes can be hidden from users. Users only need to emphasize the inner-patch calculations. The mesh adaptability layer implements the data copy among the data pieces of memory variables and completes data communications between processors. The middle layer for numerical algorithms supplies the common solvers for computing methods and numerical algorithms by the geometry method, which also provides the convenient numerical computing toolbox. The top layer for interfaces provides developing interfaces for user applications. These interfaces help the user to make full use of the infrastructure. They also guide the user to parallelize the calculation kernel by creating a nested threading model to control the cores of CPUs and GPUs on each node.

JASMIN provides the users a suite of C++ interface through encapsulating the above three layers to develop the parallel applications. Domain-specific experts mainly focus on the physics model computing methods without being concerned about parallel implementation.

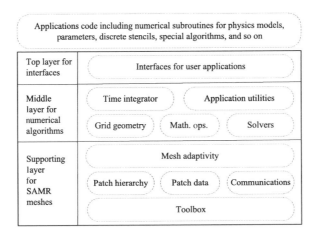

**FIGURE 19.13**: Software architecture of JASMIN.

Task partition, data distribution, and communication are all automatically implemented by JASMIN.

Tens of large-scale application programs have been reconstructed or developed on JAS-MIN. These programs are suitable for different numerical simulations arising from multi-material hydrodynamics, radiation hydrodynamics, neutron transport, hydrodynamics in-stability, laser plasma interactions, materials science, climate forecasting, and so on.

The following five complex application programs based on JASMIN could easily scale to tens of thousands of cores on TH-1A. These programs are developed for high performance computation arising from inertial confinement fusion and material science as well as high-power microwave. Their complexities are characterized by multi-physics coupling, extreme physical condition simulation, complex three-dimensional spatial configuration, etc.

In our tests [GCZ+11], the problem size for each program is fixed and various numbers of cores (5,250, 10,500, 21,000, 42,000, 84,000) are used. The number of cores is the product of the process number and the thread number per process. In the case of 84,000 cores, 12 threads are used on each process; in the other cases, 6 threads are launched on each process. One new feature of JASMIN 2.0 is the encapsulation of the MPI/OpenMP mixed programming while the users are free to direct it. The parallel efficiency is compared to the case of 5,250 cores. In the following, we present these five application programs and their test performance in more detail.

1) LARED-P is a three-dimensional program for the simulation of laser plasma intersec-tions using the method of Particle-In-Cell (PIC). Electrons and ions are distributed in the cells of a uniform rectangular mesh. The Maxwell electromagnetic equations coupled with particle movement equations are solved. Particles intersect with the electromagnetic fields. For this simulation, efficient load balancing strategies are essential for successful executions. LARED-P achieves a parallel efficiency of 73% for a typical test using 76 billion particles and 768 million cells on 84,000 processors.

2) LAP3D is a three-dimensional program for the simulation of filament instabilities for laser plasma intersections in the space scale of hydrodynamics. A uniform rectangular structured mesh is used. Euler hydrodynamics equations coupled with the laser broadcasting equations are solved. LAP3D achieves a parallel efficiency of 63% for the test using 300 million cells on 42,000 cores.

3) LARED-S is a three-dimensional program for the simulation of radiation hydro-dynamics instabilities occurring in the process of radiation-driven compression explosion. While the radiation effects are enforced, the implicit discrete stencils should be used. So, the performance of the sparse linear system solver is pivotal in large-scale simulations. For a typical test of Richtmyer-Meshkov hydrodynamics instability, LARED-S has a parallel efficiency of 47% for a single patch level using 300 million cells on 84,000 processors.

4) MD3D is a three-dimensional program for the short range molecular dynamics simula-tions of fusion material. A typical simulation using 512 million molecules achieves a parallel efficiency of 47% on 84,000 cores.

5) FDTD3D is a three-dimensional program for the time-domain simulation of the cou-pling and scattering of electromagnetic waves in the PC chassis. This program needs to handle the complex three-dimensional spatial configuration for the PC chassis. So it results in a very large amount of data, which challenges the bandwidth. FDTD3D has a parallel efficiency of 21% for a typical test using 1.7 billion cells on 42,000 cores.

These tests can be summarized as in Table 19.3. It can be shown that, based on the programming framework JASMIN, the scalability and performance of application programs could be extended and developed further.

**TABLE 19.3**: Results of selected applications based on JASMIN.

| Program | Application domain | #Cores | Parallel efficiency |
|---------|-------------------|--------|---------------------|
| LARED-P | Inertial confinement fusion | 84,000 | 73% |
| LAP3D | Inertial confinement fusion | 42,000 | 63% |
| LARED-S | Inertial confinement fusion | 84,000 | 47% |
| MD3D | Material science | 84,000 | 47% |
| FDTD3D | High-power microwave | 42,000 | 21% |

## 19.7 Discussion on Hybrid Computing

TH-1A aids in the exploration of the petaflops scale CPU-GPU hybrid computing. It demonstrates that this architecture is proper for large-scale scientific applications apart from graphic processing. GPU as the computing accelerator brings a series of problems, such as performance, efficiency, reliability, programming, etc. Nowadays, in designing the hardware, we need to make a choice for GPU which has memory ECC protected and can provide higher peak performance of double precision float computing based on benchmarks, decide the proper proration of CPU and GPU in a node, and consider the PCI-Express channel performance and cooling capacity for the main board design. In designing the software programming environment, we need to reduce the complexity of multi-level hybrid parallel programming for users and provide abundant optimization mechanics for improving the performance of the CPU-GPU hybrid applications. We have provided a parallel programming framework to support usable hybrid parallel application development, which is also capable of adapting to various types of system optimization and fault tolerance mechanics in the future.

The advances in hardware and software push the heterogeneous architecture to becoming an important way toward extreme large-scale computing systems, which looks like a pretty feasible choice to achieve success at present. The experiences from the exploration of hybrid computing in TH-1A show many achievements, but also show some problems which need to be continually improved in the design of future systems and applications The following are some points for future consideration:

(1) The hybrid structure of CPU-GPU can reduce the power consumption and the total cost of the HPC system, compared with the pure CPU homogeneous system. We believe that the heterogeneous architecture is one of the promising approaches to break the power wall and finally achieve the next-generation extreme large-scale supercomputer.

(2) The architecture of GPU still needs to be improved to target more complex problems in HPC fields. So far GPU has illustrated overwhelming advantages on some structured problems. However, the current architectures of GPUs are not suited for some irregular problems, in which the global memory is accessed discontinuously and different threads execute different control flow divergences. To solve these problems, more coalesced data access patterns on the global memory should be supported, and the bank conflict removal of the shared memory is expected to be more efficient. In addition, the bandwidth of data moving between CPUs and GPUs, GPUs and GPUs, still needs to be improved through some new mechanisms.

(3) Continuous efforts should be devoted to the programming languages and developing tools on the GPU platform. Most of the real-world applications running on the GPUs

are tuned manually now to achieve high performance by empirical search. The automated optimizing compilers are desired to help programmers prune the searching space. More accurate performance models and profile tools are required to help people understand and find the bottleneck of the GPU programs easily.

(4) On the CPU-GPU hybrid systems, the algorithms of the applications need to be redesigned and reconstructed carefully to maximize performance. We have to fundamentally rethink the algorithms of the applications from parallel paradigms, data structure, data access pattern, to load balancing, which could fully exploit the large data parallel metric of GPU-class processors. Creative designs of algorithms may take quite a long time with efforts by scientists from various application areas.

(5) The domain-specific programming framework is becoming an accelerator to boost the developments of large-scale heterogeneous applications. With the help of the programming frameworks, on the one hand, the application developers could focus on the algorithm depiction, utilize the efficient stencils and libraries, supporting code reuse and aiming to improve productivity. On the other hand, the system software developers could focus on the organization of communication operations, data distribution, task allocation, load balance, and even fault tolerant mechanics fitted to different system structures, to optimize the performance and reliability of the applications.

---

## Acknowledgments

The authors want to thank Zeyao Mo and Xiaolin Cao from the Institute of Applied Physics and Computational Mathematics for their contributions to the JASMIN framework. The authors also thank Wei Zhang, Feng Wang, Hongjia Cao, Enqiang Zhou, Chun Huang, and Kai Lu from NUDT for their contributions to this chapter. This work is supported in part by the National High Technology Research and Development 863 Program of China under grant 2009AA01A128 and 2012AA01A301, and the National Natural Science Foundation of China under grant 61120106005.

# Chapter 20

## TSUBAME2.0: The First Petascale Supercomputer in Japan and the Greatest Production in the World

Satoshi Matsuoka, Takayuki Aoki, Toshio Endo, Hitoshi Sato, Shin'ichiro Takizawa, Akihiko Nomura, and Kento Sato

*Global Scientific Information and Computing Center, Tokyo Institute of Technology*

## 20.1    Overview

TSUBAME2.0, successor to TSUBAME1.0 that superseded the Earth Simulator as Japan's fastest supercomputer in Spring 2006, became Japan's first muti-petascale supercomputer in history. TSUBAME2.0 embodies various innovative, forward-looking architectural properties as well as software features, such as extensive use of GPUs, highly scalable and optical high-bandwidth node and network design, along with massive utilization of silicone I/O technologies such as SSD. TSUBAME2.0 went into production operation as of early November 2010; thereupon TSUBAME2.0 became the fourth fastest supercomputer in the world on the TOP500, as well as being awarded the "Greenest Production Supercomputer in the World" award on the Green500 in November 2011, as well as the ACM Gordon Bell Prizes for 2011.

### 20.1.1    Program Background

In the year 2001, Global Scientific Information and Computing Center (GSIC) was formulated at the Tokyo Institute of Technology (Tokyo Tech), the leading science and engineering university in Japan, conjoining the two preceding organizations at Tokyo Tech, namely the Titech Computer Center and the International Cooperation Center for Science and Technology. Indeed, the former, which was founded in 1971, had been hosting supercomputers for the campus and for national usage since 1988, starting with the CDC ETA 10. However, the Titech Computer Center was sorely understaffed, not being able to procure nor operate the latest and the greatest supercomputer of the time to be competitive with other national supercomputer centers in Japan nor internationally. Such was the motivation to revitalize the center by conjoining the organization and attract supercomputing and other IT experts. For several years various research regarding building scalable commodity clusters had been conducted in our department laboratories, where, in research collaborations with the Japanese Real World Computing Partnership national project, we continued to build out new generations of clusters with increasing sizes yearly, eventually superseding the performances of the production supercomputers at the GSIC center that only accumulated to be 350 Gigaflops, whereas the lab experimental cluster was exceeding a Teraflop. This culminated in Tokyo Tech proclaiming to have built the second fastest cluster on the TOP500 in June, 2002, being ranked 47th overall with 716 Linpack Gigaflops. Moreover, other application workloads also exhibited impressive speedups.

It was clear that massive parallel processing, likely in the form of high-quality clusters would be the choice as the successor to the existing underperforming supercomputers, and that the intent was not to merely buy out of a vendor product catalog. The challenge was to migrate the technologies in cluster building for true-life production, so it was absolutely necessary to have our real user base attempt to migrate to the new parallel environment, while not compromising their existing day-to-day workloads on the production machine. So, as we continued our basic research of system software in clusters, we began a preparatory production project, "Titech Campus Grid Project" whereby we constructed a distributed set of clusters of varying sizes and populated various parts of the campus network with them, conjoining their unified operations using distributed computing as well as grid middleware. Various laboratories that had been conducting research with highly parallel applications at Tokyo Tech. were recruited to take part in the production experiment for a total of 400 nodes/800 processors/1.3 Teraflops total infrastructure initially, eventually growing to nearly 2.5 Teraflops in total over the four years of the experiment. Based on the experiences, we were able to determine the TSUBAME1 specifications, to be effectively jointly designed

**TABLE 20.1**: Power consumption and efficiency: TSUBAME2.0 x24 improvement in 4.5 years... $\Rightarrow$ x1000 over 10 years.

| Machine | CPU cores | Watts | Peak GFLOPS | Peak MFLOPS/ Watt | Watts/ CPU Core | Ratio c.f. TSUBAME |
|---|---|---|---|---|---|---|
| TSUBAME(Opteron ) | 10,480 | 800,000 | 50,400 | 63.00 | 76.34 | |
| TSUBAME2006 (w/360CSs) | 11,200 | 810,000 | 79,430 | 98.06 | 72.32 | |
| TSUBAME2007 (w/648CSs) | 11,776 | 820,000 | 102,200 | 124.63 | 69.63 | 1.00 |
| Earth Simulator | 5,120 | 6,000,000 | 40,000 | 6.67 | 1,171.88 | 0.05 |
| ASCI Purple (LLNL) | 12,240 | 6,000,000 | 77,824 | 12.97 | 490.20 | 0.10 |
| AIST Supercluster (Opteron ) | 3,188 | 522,240 | 14,400 | 27.57 | 163.81 | 0.22 |
| LLNL BG/L (rack) | 2,048 | 25,000 | 5,734 | 229.38 | 12.21 | 1.84 |
| Next Gen BG/P (rack) | 4,096 | 30,000 | 16,384 | 546.13 | 7.32 | 4.38 |
| TSUBAME 2.0 (2010Q3/4) | 160,000 | 810,000 | 1,024,000 | 1,264.20 | 5.06 | 10.14 |

and developed with supercomputing manufacturers. In fact, since the revamping as GSIC we have continued to operate and refine a mode of operation that effectively merges the research, experiment, and production phases, or to be more precise: (1) basic research in supercomputing and system software design, (2) experimental production of nascent hardware and software at GSIC and their assessment, (3) development and determining the specifications of a production machine, as well as feedback to a new cycle re-starting with (1). Such "waterfall" development model was our strategy for TSUBAME1.0 as well as TSUBAME2.0 and beyond. After several years of research and planning, GSIC, in collaboration with various industrial partners, constructed the supercomputer TSUBAME1.0 as a supercomputer for everyone; the goal of this system was to make supercomputing available even to non-specialist users. TSUBAME1.0 was ranked 7th immediately after it had started production operation in June 2006, and became the No. 1 supercomputer in Asia from June 2006 to November 2007. By carefully reflecting the needs of the user base of the Titech Campus Grid as well as our existing supercomputer, TSUBAME1.0 became extremely popular, widely used by a user base of approximately 2,000 both inside Tokyo Tech. as well as other academic institutions and the industry. In parallel to the operations, we continued our research for next-generation TSUBAME, to be designated TSUBAME2.0. In particular, even as the TSUABME1.0 design was nearing completion, we were assessing the power requirements of our facility. Since it was not practical to increase our absolute power budget, which was already over 10% of the overall campus electrical power usage, we had to sustain our power budget. However, as seen in Table 20.1, although TSUBAME1 already embodied top-of-the-class power efficiency compared to comparable supercomputers of similar timeframe (the peak MFLOPS/Watt column), we needed to improve this by a factor of 10. This was well beyond the power efficiency of not only the Blue Gene/L, the world's most power efficient supercomputer of the time, but over a factor of two compared to its successor, Blue Gene/P. Unless this technical challenge was resolved, we would not be able to achieve the target performance of over a petaflop for the successor to TSUBAME2.0.

## 20.2 Technological Developments toward TSUBAME2.0

The predecessor of TSUBAME2.0, i.e., TSUBAME1.0, (Figure 20.1 and Figure 20.2) was inaugurated in April 2006. It was a combined fruition of a series of various research on cluster computing at Tokyo Tech over the years, as well as experiences in fielding production supercomputers for over 20 years, in addition to experimental production operation projects such as Titech campus grid as mentioned earlier (April 2002 until March 2006).

**FIGURE 20.1**: The old computer room that housed TSUBAME1.

Based on these experiences, various design studies were conducted, resulting in a 655-node supercomputer that embodies over 10,000 CPU cores, exhibiting 50 Teraflops in total with 21 terabytes of memory, in addition to 1.1 Petabytes of hard disk storage, interconnected by dual-rail SDR (10Gbps *times* 2) InfiniBand. The compute nodes are augmented with 360 ClearSpeed Accelerator cards (later expanded to 648 cards) well-suited for dense matrix operations, providing an additional 30 Teraflops of compute power. TSUBAME in a way became a template architecture for large-scale cluster-based supercomputers for its follow-ons, as it possessed architectural parameters not seen in clusters in those days, and matched the best supercomputers in the world. In particular, circa 2006, a typical cluster might sport 2

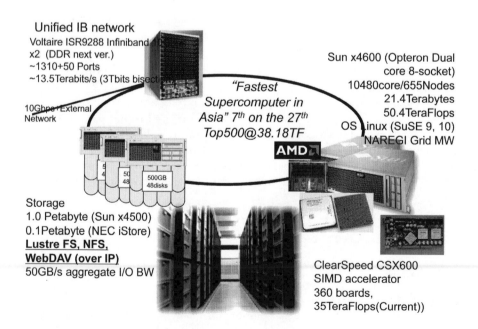

**FIGURE 20.2**: The TSUBAME1.0 supercomputing grid cluster: (production) spring 2006 NEC/Sun.

to 4 CPU cores per node with 1-4 Gigabytes of memory, whereas TSUBAME1 utilized the "glue-less" multi-socket capability of the latest AMD Opteron 800 series to implement a so-called "fat node" with 16 CPU cores and 32-128 Gigabytes of memory each, with (80+80) gigaflops peak performance from the CPUs and the ClearSpeed, respectively, interconnected by a dual-rail InfiniBand fabric for 20 Gbps bandwidth. Such a configuration allowed for both stability (smaller number of nodes) as well as provided extremely high ease-of-use as a supercomputer, as well as offering an environment where one's applications might not execute otherwise. The evidence of this is that TSUBAME1 is still highly competitive and in very high demand, even as it nears its retirement well beyond its initial designed shutdown in the Spring of 2010.

## 20.2.1    TSUBAME1 — The "Pros"

Here we list the technological points that led to its success, and carried over to TSUBAME2.0:

1. **Significant adoption of industry standard technologies such as high-performance x86 processor and Linux-OS**: Reports of PC clusters due to the adoption of x86 as well as its PC and server industry "ecosystem" have been reported a number of times, such as just-in-time adoption of high-performance and cost-effective technologies, as well as stability of quality achieved in the quantity due to mass production. In addition, continuity of the software and programming models from the usual laboratory PCs, workstations, and small clusters all the way up to supercomputing scale is a major benefit, as the increasing complexity of simulation software has transcended simulation work from being done on a single supercomputer, but rather, the mainstream usage model is for the same software to run seamlessly in a variety of environments from small to extremely large ones. Finally, it would be desirable to offer an easy path for a typical novice PC simulation user to their eventual use of supercomputers by allowing such step-by-step advances in the most transparent fashion. To become "Everybody's Supercomputer" was the main goal of TSUBAME1, and the most critical of the qualities to reach such a goal were achieved through the aggressive adoption of both hardware and software standards as much as possible.

2. **Implementation of "fat-node" architecture with mainstream x86 CPUs**: Almost being an antithesis to the previous point, supercomputers are meaningless without being associated with the unique value of their use. In particular, a supercomputer would be a big attraction in solving problems not just in acceleration of time-to-solution, but also being able to solve problems that were previously capacity-constrained. Thus, not only are total processor count and aggregated memory capacity for the entire system important, but also core counts and shared memory capacity inside a node would also be significant if problems are constrained at that level as they often are. In the past such "fat-node" design called for customized and expensive supercomputer design; for TSUBAME1, we were able to exploit the first generation of the latest technology x86 at the time, which sported high-bandwidth processor-to-processor interconnect as well as to memory in a glueless fashion, namely the AMD Opteron 800 series processors, which allowed up to 8 sockets or 16 CPU cores, largely matching the numbers for dedicated supercomputer design of the time. Fat node design not only benefits the users, but also helps to reduce the number of "moving parts" in the system allowing for higher reliability. Moreover it eases the redundancy and safety in the design, such as redundant power supply and fans, over ten thermal as well as other sensors, and comprehensive IPMI-based monitoring and control network

intended for large-scale server farms, etc. Augmented with adoption of efficient cooling with clever configuration of servers versus the CRC units, as well as well-attuned operations, it was possible to build and operate an 80 teraflop supercomputer that became the 7th fastest supercomputer in the world at the time.

3. **Accelerator for dense matrix computation**: Based on the technology at the time of TSUBAME1, it was already difficult to achieve 100 Teraflops given the constraints of space, power, costs, etc. As a result, we had decided to experiment with acceleration technologies that demonstrated reasonable results within the research lab of our center. Considering several candidates for actual production usage, the ClearSpeed SIMD accelerator was chosen, due to its favorable performance in dense matrix-type operations at very low power levels. For large dense matrix operations using the BLAS library, user performance nearly doubled with a mere command line switch, without modifying the source code, or adding significant power or space to the infrastructure. However, although it also contributed significant performance gains for our Linpack it was necessary to conduct research and development of a new heterogeneous algorithm to maximize their contributions [EM08].

4. **Multi-rail InfiniBand-based fat-tree network using large switches, and integration of I/O storage network**: Another important element of the supercomputer is a high-speed network interconnection between nodes. In particular, in addition to bandwidth available to a single node (called the injection bandwidth), latency between the nodes must be very low, in the order of several microseconds, while the bisection bandwidth, or the bandwidth available to the entire set of nodes when they conduct all-to-all communication, needs to be extremely high. By all means, low space overhead, low number of cables, low cost, and high reliability are required simultaneously, and many of these elements are sometimes contradictory in nature. TSUBAME1 employed a set of eight large 288-port InfiniBand switches configured in a two-tier fat-tree, six switches in the lower edge layer and two on the top layer. Also, each node had two rails of network ports. This allows each node to achieve 20 Gbps bandwidth with approximately 5 ns end-to-end network latency, matching the performance of supercomputers with dedicated networks.

5. **High-performance storage achieving high performance, high density, and low cost, with a parallel filesystem**: The oft-forgotten part of supercomputers is storage; for TSUBAME1-level simulation and processing capabilities in the 100 teraflops, it was judged early on that sub-petabyte class data handling capabilities would be of absolute necessity. As with compute nodes, the storage subsystem required high-performance, low cost and low power consumption, high reliability and scalability that coincided with the parallelism in the system. It became clear that traditional enterprise IT systems and technology-based storage systems were inadequate. Rather, a cluster-based approach was taken, where a powerful "fat" storage server that embedded 48 HDDs (24 Terabytes raw capacity) along with a powerful storage and network controller in a mere 4-U chassis, namely the Sun x4500 "Thumper," served as the basic building block; 42 of them (later 20 more were added) were clustered and also connected directly to the main InfiniBand network of the compute nodes allowing gigabyte level data transfer capability per each node. On top of this we implemented the Lustre parallel filesystem so that access could be done in parallel and very large files could be handled. This allowed us to achieve over 10 gigabytes per second I/O performance, in 1.0 (later 1.5) petabyte storage of compact dimensions.

6. **A batch scheduler that is fair and easy to understand, assuming simultaneous use by hundreds of both capacity and capability users**: TSUBAME's user

base of 2,000 typically had 100 or more users logged into the system and running jobs at the same time. The annual number of jobs exceeded a million in count, and varies greatly in usage patterns — number, memory size, time (makespan), parallelism, I/O performance, required QoS, I / O performance, etc. Moreover, there was a need to support both experts with highly-parallel, "capability" jobs versus novice users sometimes with parameter survey "capacity" jobs. Despite the large computational capacity of Tsubame1, it possessed nowhere near the amount of resources to satisfy all of these requirements. So, it was essential to adopt an easy-to-understand and seemingly-fair scheduling policy that would satisfy the above goals, such as co-existence and QoS control of pay-per-use versus flat-rate usage models, pay-for-priority-QoS, as well as later introduction of a job reservation for very large jobs, etc. All such requirements were incorporated as customization modules of the Sun GridEngine batch scheduler, and were continuously updated and improved due to user feedback.

## 20.2.2 The Dark Side of TSUBAME1.0 and Improvements in TSUBAME2.0

Some of the problems identified in TSUBAME1's performance and operations were more fundamental, and found not to be solvable with only the superficial improvements described above. Moreover, supercomputing is a field where the average performance of a machine increases by approximately 180-200% each year, well beyond Moore's law. As such it was obvious that there is a need for continuous research and development of various technologies merely to sustain such a growth level. Below we present the shortcomings in TSUBAME1, and how they were analyzed and attempts made to solve the problems for TSUBAME2.0:

1. **Drastic improvement of power/performance**: TSUBAME1.0 consumed a peak of about 1 MW electrical power, or 10% or more of the entire power usage of the Tokyo Institute of Technology's Oo-okayama main campus, or about 100 million yens per year. Since TSUBAME2.0 was initially planned to be deployed in the early part of 2010, its target performance would be about 10 times speedup at 1 petaflop while maintaining the power usage as we have seen in Table 20.1. However, recall that the power/performance ratio for TSUBAME1.0 was already very efficient for a supercomputer of that time, thanks to the ClearSpeed card for dense linear algebra operations. Thus, in order for TSUBAME1 to maintain international competitiveness, it became necessary to improve the power performance ratio significantly. Fortunately, the project sponsored by the JST-CREST program, called "ULP-HPC: High Performance Ultra Low-Power" was approved, with the aggressive goal of improving the power efficiency of supercomputers by $times 1000$ in 10 years. Such a boost in basic research accelerated our understanding of low power design of supercomputers, and some of the research results were applied to TSUBAME2.0.

2. **Widening the applicability and use of accelerators (GPUs)**: In related terms, we found that acceleration using GPUs was the key to low power and high performance; however, early accelerators lacked the applicability to a wide range of existing applications. Some resulted from the lack of algorithms and software, but some from the hardware architecture itself. In fact, early accelerators were quite limited in their applicability due to their hardware limitations; for example, ClearSpeed excelled in dense matrix type problems, but was found to be poor at bandwidth-hungry problems. This was principally due to the lack of memory capacity and a shortage of available hardware memory bandwidth as well as programming difficulties, and as a result narrowed its applicability quite a bit. Fortunately, GPUs sporting both high

**FIGURE 20.3**: (Left): NVIDIA Tesla s1070 GPU retrofitted to TSUBAME1; (right): NVIDIA Tesla M2050 GPU used in TSUBAME2.0; 3 cards per node, over 4,000 cards in total.

computational density and high memory bandwidth, as well as being low cost, were rapidly becoming general purpose in terms of both its hardware and software, and in the labs we had already demonstrated its advantages and flexibilities in many real-world HPC situations. Therefore, the question was how much GPU technology would be applicable to TSUBAME2.0; Fortunately, we had initiated technical partnerships and discussions in 2007 with two key companies, namely NVIDIA and Microsoft, and we were able to conduct projects which resulted initially in a 128 GPU prototype cluster in late 2007, and based on the results from that machine, we were able to augment TSUBAME1 with 680 cards of the latest NVIDIA Tesla GPU (Figure 20.3) in October 2008. The resulting supercomputer, TSUBAME1.2, formed a platform which allowed a variety of experiments in our preparations for TSUBAME2.0 which was to become extremely GPU centric due to many positive results we were obtaining and the problems we encountered and solved in its operations.

3. **Lack of memory and network bandwidth in the node**: With the local bandwidth resolved by GPU, another problem was the overall bandwidth of the system being somewhat deficient in TSUBAME1 than we initially anticipated. CPU memory bandwidth was affected by two negative factors, the decline of the memory bus clock with a larger number of multi-channel memory; also there was an inherent limit for the Socket 940 and Socket F generations of the AMD CPU design, where the total memory bandwidth of the shared memory was limited to approximately 20 GB/s due to memory coherency traffic. As for the network, InfiniBand theoretical channel performance of 1 GB/s was seeing a strong decrease to half or less due to overlap with other activities within the node. Thus, in TSUBAME2.0's design, increase of bandwidth exceeding the increase in compute FLOPS was absolutely necessary, and deemed to be the most important technological improvement; this was one of the major reasons an entirely new node design was mandated, instead of using existing products.

4. **The lack of width of the entire network bisection bandwidth**: In addition, bisection bandwidth in TSUBAME1 was lacking; whereas the aggregate injection bandwidth at the endpoint was 13 terabits/s, due to the constrained fat-tree bisection bandwidth, which was approximately 2.8 terabits/s, or about 5 to 1 oversubscription ratio. This has resulted in the weakness (e.g., in comparison to the Earth Simulator) in supporting various global-style algorithms such as global FFT, in which the communication bottleneck becomes the dominant performance inhibitor. Therefore, it was imperative to achieve high bandwidth across the network. A new network design was needed to achieve full bisection in the same manner as the Earth Simulator, while sporting more than twice the number of nodes. As a result of various design studies, combined use of smaller leaf switches with very large centralized core switch fabric

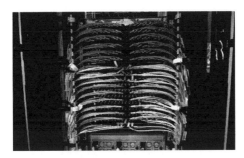

**FIGURE 20.4**: Fiber optic cables are aggregated into the large InfiniBand core switch fabric from the lower-tier edge switches.

that are physically clustered, with optical fiber connection in-between comprising a full fat-tree configuration, was deemed to be the smallest, most cost effective, and the most reliable (Figure 20.4). One requirement was to make the system as small as possible to shorten the fiber cable length.

5. **Cooling efficiency issues**: TSUBAME1.0 employed an advanced cooling strategy for its time after over a year of study and given the physical confines of the relatively small space we had for our computer room, such as achieving the hot-row vs. cold-row separation using specially placed CRC units as well as ducts in the ceiling instead of floor cooling, etc. The achieved PUE (Power Usage Effectiveness) was approximately 1.44, which was a reasonably good measure at the time. However, it is a fact that the cooling power consuming 44% beyond the machine power was not ideal indeed, and moreover, we knew that some of the recent advances would allow us to achieve much lower PUE. As a result, hybrid water- and air-cooled technology, where the individual rack would be cooled by water, and the circulatory air would be sealed and contained to cool the nodes, with an aim to achieving PUE as good as 1.2.

6. **Machine size and weight problems**: TSUBAME1 occupies nearly 80 racks in its entirety, occupying most of the computer room floorspace of GSIC's facilities building. This seriously compromised our ability to scale further, as well as complicating the wiring and control logistics spanning two floors. For these and other reasons we have mentioned, constructing a machine that is dense and with a very small resulting footprint was becoming an important issue. Making a machine smaller not only reflects in cost, but improves our ability to construct full bisection and fat networks, as the machines need to be located as close as possible to the central switch fabric. Fortunately, to accommodate multiple GPUs for high bandwidth fat-node configuration necessitated an entirely new node design, and the major technological goal of node implementations was set to achieve unprecedented levels of density (Figure 20.5). The result achieved is 50 teraflops per rack performance density, i.e., each rack being approximately the compute performance of the entire Earth Simulator, while the entire TSUBAME2.0 occupied about 60 racks, or about 3/4th of TSUBAME1 despite the 30-fold increase in computational performance.

7. **Lack of operational storage capacity**: The storage capacity of TSUBAME1 was significantly improved over its predecessor, but still the actual production capacity was lacking. This depended on various factors: tertiary storage systems and tapes or MAIDs were lacking, and moreover, all the storage was uniformly high-performance and somewhat expensive as a result, despite some being used purely for backup. Secondly, there were various single points of failure in the storage, including the Lustre

**FIGURE 20.5**: Individual compute nodes in TSUBAME2.0 are 1/4th the size of TSUB-AME1 nodes, despite being 10 times more computationally powerful.

parallel filesystem, necessitating duplication in various parts of the storage system. However, this resulted in an entire Thumper box used up for metadata management—expensive in terms of required capacity and sacrifices in performance. Thumpers were consumed for other service requirements; moreover, we had to deploy RAID6 with relatively small number of stripes, further constraining space. As a result of all these requirements, the capacity of high performance Lustre storage area shrank to be minuscule—less than 100 terabytes out of the original 1 petabytes. In 2007 we alleviated the problem somewhat by adding 20 more Thumper units, and the total raw physical capacity was raised to 1.6 petabytes; still the total Lustre capacity including the scratch space for Gaussian was only about 200 terabytes in total. Therefore, TSUBAME2 storage was designed to retain as much space as possible for operational Lustre and GPFS storage by extensive streamlining of storage management, and improving the reliability through redundancy and elimination of single point of failure without sacrificing storage capacity. In particular, we had started improving TSUBAME1's storage fabric in 2009 in preparation, incorporating dedicated storage management servers, as well as introducing a large capacity tape system that has the ability to be extended to beyond 10 petabytes, to better match the operational disk capacity of 7 petabytes for TSUBAME2.0 (Figure 20.6 A, B, C).

8. **Lack of storage bandwidth**: In order to achieve the initially determined performance goal of 2-3 petaflops, it was deemed that we would require I/O speeds of several hundred gigabytes per second of I/O performance. However, implementing such I/O performance would require a huge number of spinning disks and storage servers. Fortunately, studies indicate that major portions of I/O writes are stream writes for checkpoints, or local scratch writes for simple scratch files or more serious data structures for out-of-core algorithms [YVO08, BOS+09]. Assuming that approximately 80-90% of I/O workload are of such a nature, the achieved speed of hundreds of MB/s by a new breed of SSDs with their improved capacity, cost performance, and reliability seemed a perfect for the task to relieve the parallel filesystems of such loads

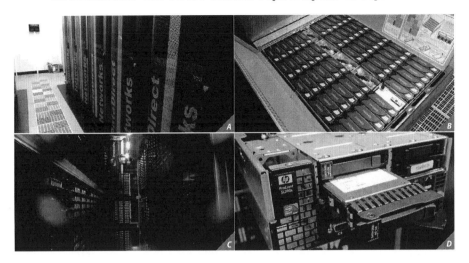

**FIGURE 20.6**: (A) Various storage servers in TSUBAME2.0 for Lustre, GPFS, NFS, CIFS, etc. (B) Each disk enclosure contains 60 units of 2 terabyte SATA HDDs. (C) TSUBAME2's SL8500 tape drive system, embodying over 10,000 tape slots and located in a separate building. (D) TSUBAME2.0 embeds two or more SSD drives on each node of 60 GB, or 120 GB, depending on the node memory capacity.

and effectively attain x5-x10 effective improvement in I/O performance. In practice, the aggregate I/O performance of two or more SSDs equipped in every node of TSUBAME2.0 (Figure 20.6 D) totals more than 660 gigabytes/s. TSUBAME2.0 embeds two or more SSD drives on each node 60 GB, or 120 GB depending on the node memory capacity.

9. **Further improvements in reliability**: TSUBAME1 was already designed with high reliability in mind. In fact, the entire history of failure and repair log is made constantly accessible via a web page of the GSIC center, and the system was entirely down only twice in 4.5 years, once when a major power outage occurred around a small area south of Tokyo where Tokyo Tech just happened to be affected for two hours. However localized faults that affect sizeable portions of the system did occur occasionally, including those that would affect one of the batch queues entirely. Significant lessons had been learned for TSUBAME2.0 design as a result, eliminating wherever possible single points of failure in batch queues, storage/parallel file system, various service nodes, etc. Despite the costs incurred by such redundancies, it was deemed that the user's lost time due to failures outweighed the costs, especially as the faults themselves would become bigger hindrances as we move on to future machines that will be more error prone.

## 20.3   The Total Picture of TSUBAME2.0

Given the observations and a variety of research conducted, in November 2010, GSIC started operation of the new supercomputer TSUBAME 2.0 with computing performance of 2.4 petaflops, which was about 30 times larger than TSUBAME 1.0. This new system was designed based on our research findings and operational experiences with TSUBAME1.0/1.2, and was co-designed in collaboration with NEC, HP, NVIDIA, Microsoft, and other partner companies.

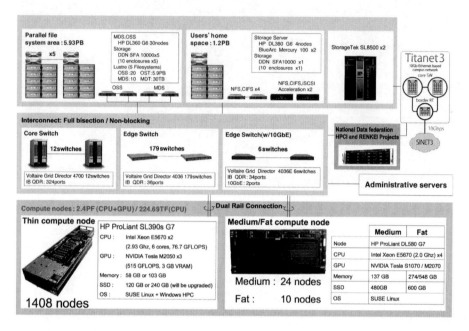

**FIGURE 20.7**: TSUBAME2.0 system configuration.

## 20.3.1   The TSUBAME2.0 Architecture

Basically TSUBAME1.0/1.2 and 2.0 are supercomputing clusters, which consist of a large number of the usual processors such as Intel compatible CPUs. Additionally, they are equipped with accelerators to significantly improve performance of scientific applications based on vector computing. We had experiences in operating ClearSpeed accelerators on TSUBAME1.0, and 680 NVIDIA Tesla GPUs in TSUBAME1.2, and learned various technologies for energy-efficient high-performance computing with accelerators. However, in terms of the number of processors, CPUs have been much more dominant. In TSUB-AME2.0, each node is equipped with three GPU accelerators, which enable a great leap not only in performance but also energy efficiency. TSUBAME2.0's main compute node, manufactured by Hewlett-Packard, has two Intel Westmere EP 2.93 GHz processors, three NVIDIA Fermi M2050 GPUs and about 50 GB of memory. Each node provides computation performance of 1.7 teraflops (TFLOPS), which is about 100 times larger than that of typical laptop PCs. The main part of the system consists of 1,408 computing nodes, and the total peak performance reaches 2.4 PFLOPS. Each CPU in TSUBAME2.0 has six physical cores and supports up to 12 hardware threads with the hyper-threading technology, achieving up to 76 gigaflops (GFLOPS). Each GPU sports NVIDIA's many-core processor architecture called Fermi and contains 448 small cores with 3 GB of GDDR5 memory with 515 GFLOPS performance and 150 GB/s of memory bandwidth.

In general, efficient use of GPUs requires different programming methodologies than CPUs. For this purpose, CUDA and OpenCL are supported so that users can execute programs designed for TSUBAME1.2 on the new system. Also Tesla M2050 GPUs have advantages both in performance and programmability; the adoption of the true hardware cache will be to make performance tuning of programs much easier. One of the key features of TSUBAME2.0 architecture is adopting hardware with highly improved bandwidth in order to enable data communication efficiently. To keep performance of intra-node communication high, the memory bandwidth reaches up to 32 GB/s on CPU and 150 GB/s on GPU. Communication between CPUs and GPUs is supported by the latest PCI-Express 2.0 x16 technology with bandwidth of 8GB/s.

As the interconnect that combines more than 1,400 computing nodes and storage described later, TSUBAME2.0 uses the latest QDR InfiniBand (IB) network, which features 40 Gbps bandwidth per link. Each computing node will be connected with two IB links; thus communication speed of the node is about 80 times larger than typical LAN (1 Gbps). Not only the link speed at endpoint nodes, but network topology of the whole system will heavily affect performance of large-scale computations. TSUBAME2.0 adopts full-bisection fat-tree topology, which accommodates applications of a wider area than others such as torus/mesh topology; the adopted topology will be much more advantageous for applications with implicit methods, such as spectral methods. Despite the significant improvements in performance and capacity, the power consumption of TSUBAME2.0 turned out to be smaller than TSUBAME2.0 despite a factor of 30 increase in performance, thanks to research and engineering advances in power efficiency. Cooling is also greatly improved by exploiting much more efficient water-cooling systems. The power usage effectiveness, or PUE, of TSUBAME2.0 turned out to be approximately 1.2 on the average.

### 20.3.2 Large-Scale Storage for e-Science

As a supercomputing system that supports e-Science, a large scale-storage system that supports fast data access is necessary. TSUBAME2.0 includes a storage system with a capacity of 7.1 petabytes (PB), which is six times larger than that of TSUBAME1.0. Users can store large-scale data used by their tasks; additionally, the storage system is used to provide Web-based storage service, which users in Tokyo Tech can use easily.

The storage system mainly consists of two parts: 1.2 PB home storage volume and 5.9 PB parallel filesystem volume. The home storage volume is designed so that it provides high reliability, availability, and performance based on redundant structure. Especially, it provides up to 1,100 MB/s of accelerated NFS performance, via QDR IBs and 10 Gbps networks. The volume also supports other protocols, such as CIFS and iSCSI in order to support transparent data access from all computing nodes running both Linux and Windows. It is also used for various storage services for educational and clerical purposes at Tokyo Tech. The center component of the home volume is a DDN SFA 10,000 high-density storage. It is connected to four HP DL380 G6 servers and two BlueArc Mercury servers that accept access requests from clients.

The focus of another volume, the parallel filesystem volume, is scalability so that it accommodates access requests from a large number of nodes smoothly. Based on our operational experience with TSUBAME1.0/1.2, it supports the Lustre and GPFS protocols, with three Lustre and two GPFS volumes of approximately 1 petabyte each. The aggregate read I/O throughput of each subsystem will be over 100 GB/s. Like the home volume, each subsystem contains a DDN SFA 10,000 system. To achieve high performance, each SFA 10,000 is connected to six HP DL 360 G6 servers.

Data on these TSUBAME2.0 storage systems will be backed up to 4 PB (uncompressed) Sun SL8500-based tape libraries running Tivoli as the HFS.

In addition to these system-wise storage systems, each compute node of TSUBAME2.0 has 120-240 GB solid state drives (SSD) instead of hard disk drives. They are used to store temporary files created by applications and checkpoint files. It is very challenging to introduce SSDs to large-scale supercomputers, and our innovative research on this topic has been leading the international efforts in reliability, in such work as [BGKM+11].

### 20.3.3    System Software

TSUBAME2.0 provides both Linux and Windows operating systems on its compute nodes. While the typical usage of computing power of TSUBAME2.0 remains to be submitting jobs via a batch queue system, it supports not only Linux OS (SUSE Linux Enterprise 11), but also Windows HPC Server 2008. The volume also supports other protocols, such as CIFS, iSCSI in order to support transparent data access from all computing nodes running both Linux and Windows.

This new operation is supported by virtual machine (VM) technology. We continue the hosting service using VM technology on the Tokyo Tech campus. Additionally, with VM technology, we plan to improve the efficiency of computing resources by suspending some low-priority jobs and dividing a single node into several virtual nodes.

We provided the large computing service (HPC queue) for so-called capability jobs where a user group can use up to 1,000 CPU cores and 120 GPUs exclusively in TSUBAME1.2. For TSUBAME2.0, we further enhanced this feature, providing up to 10,000 CPU cores and thousands of GPUs to selected user groups under regulated reservation and/or peer review process. We federate a web portal, called the TSUBAME portal with the Tokyo Tech portal to enhance usability such as paperless account application. For Tokyo Tech users, TSUBAME accounts are unified with the accounts of the Tokyo Tech portal. Additionally we provide account services across Japan as one of the nine leading National University supercomputing centers and its national alliance.

A network storage service is provided to Tokyo Tech users by using the large-scale storage of TSUBAME2.0. Users can easily utilize the storage from their PCs without recognizing the existence of TSUBAME. We promote data-oriented e-Science using TSUBAME2.0s high-end storage resources, which has been difficult for traditional Japanese supercomputing centers. For this purpose, TSUBAME2.0 and national supercomputing centers are tightly coupled with 10 Gbps class networks, called SINET. This enables data sharing and transportation service via GFarm filesystem and GridFTP using our newly developed RENKEI-PoP technology which is now being deployed at various national supercomputing centers.

### 20.3.4    Programming System

Available programming models and languages on TSUBAME2.0 are summarized in Table 20.2. In addition, we developed domain-specific language called *Physis* [MNSM11], which is a compiler-based programming framework that automatically translates user-written structured grid code into scalable parallel implementation code for GPU-equipped clusters such as TSUBAME2.0. The framework automatically translates user-written stencil functions to GPU execution code as well as message passing parallel code for inter-node parallelism. It also includes several optimizations for better scalability with a large number of GPUs, such as compute and communication overlapping.

### 20.3.5    Datacenter/Facility

TSUBAME1 occupied nearly 80 racks in its entirety, occupying most of the computer room floorspace of GSIC's facilities building. This seriously compromised our ability to scale further, as well as complicating the wiring and control logistics spanning two floors.

**TABLE 20.2**: TSUBAME2.0 programming system.

| | |
|---|---|
| Programming models | MPICH , MVAPICH , OpenMPI , OpenMP , Pthreads SHMEM Intel TBB |
| Programming languages | C, C++, F77, F90/95, F2003, Python, Java |
| Compiler | GNU, Intel, PGI |
| Library/Frameworks | BLAS (MKL, GOTO), FFTW , LAPACK, ScaLAPACK |
| Accelerator support | CUDA, OpenCL, PGI |
| Debugger | TotalView, Intel Threadchecker |
| Performace tools | gprof, Intel Vtune, PAPI, Valgrind |

For these and other reasons we have mentioned, constructing a machine that was dense with a very small resulting footprint was becoming an important issue. Making a machine smaller not only reflects in cost, but would improve our ability to construct full bisection and fat networks, as the machines need to be located close to the central switch fabric. Fortunately, to accommodate multiple GPUs for high bandwidth fat-node configuration necessitated an entirely new node design, and a major technological goal of node implementations was set to achieve unprecedented levels of density. The result achieved is 50 teraflops per rack performance density, i.e., each rack being approximately the compute performance of the entire Earth Simulator, while the entire TSUBAME2.0 occupied about 60 racks, or about 3/4th of TSUBAME1 despite the 30-fold increase in computational performance (Figure 20.8).

TSUBAME1.0 employed the advanced cooling strategy of the time after over a year of study and given the physical confines of a relatively small space we had for our computer room, such as achieving the hot-row vs. cold-row separation using specially placed CRC

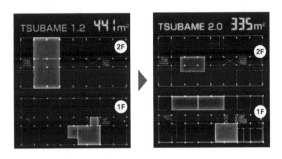

**FIGURE 20.8**: Despite the fact the performance boost is more that 30 times compared to TSUBAME1.2, the space required for installation has narrowed down.

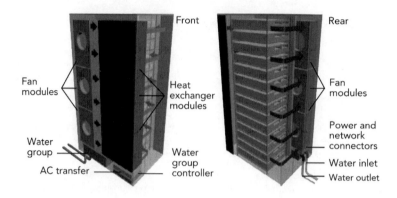

**FIGURE 20.9**: Cooling: modular cooling system.

units as well as ducts in the ceiling instead of floor cooling, etc. The achieved PUE (Power Usage Effectiveness) was approximately 1.44, which was a reasonably good measure at the time. However, it was a fact that the cooling power consuming 44% beyond the machine power was not ideal indeed, and moreover, we knew that some of the recent advances would allow us to achieve much lower PUE. As a result, hybrid water- and air-cooled technology, where the individual rack would be cooled by water, and the circulatory air be sealed and contained to cool the nodes was employed, with an aim to achieving PUE as good as 1.2. Figure 20.9 shows the cooling system. The rack-contained water-cooling system with a built-in heat exchanger is employed, allowing high-density cooling up to 35 kW per rack (it is the world's top class, being 10 times larger than what is used in typical datacenters). Homogeneous cooling air is provided through the inlet of the server with automatic open/close doors where a humidifier is unnecessary. Power consumption is minimized with a completely automated temperature control to enable heat removal from 95% to 97% by water cooling. Moreover, polycarbonate doors contribute to noise reduction. In addition, temperature, power consumption, etc., are observed in real-time not only in the computer room but also in compute nodes and in each rack.

TSUBAME1.0 consumed a peak of about 1 MW electrical power, or 10% or more of the entire power usage of the Tokyo Institute of Technology's Oo-okayama main campus, costing about 100 million yens per year. Since TSUBAME2.0 was initially planned to be deployed in the early part of 2010, its target performance would be $(1.8)^4$, or about a 10 times speedup at 1 petaflop while maintaining the power usage. However, recall that the power/performance ratio for TSUBAME1.0 was already very efficient for a supercomputer of the time, thanks to the ClearSpeed card for dense linear algebra operations. The University of Tokyo's T2K supercomputer that came out two years later but without using any type of accelerators, consumed about the same power as TSUBAME2.0, while in Linpack being only about 20% faster, instead of being over 3 times faster as the 180% growth should indicate. Thus, in order for TSUBAME1 to maintain international competitiveness, it became necessary to improve the power performance ratio significantly. Fortunately, the our project sponsored by the JST-CREST program, called "ULP-HPC: High Performance Ultra Low-Power" was approved, with the aggressive goal of improving the power efficiency of supercomputers by x1000 instead of x100 as is with Moore's law, in 10 years. Such a boost in basic research accelerated our understanding of low power design of supercomputers, and some of the research results were applied to TSUBAME2.0.

## 20.3.6 Benchmark Results

The first challenges for the newborn TSUBAME2.0, at its installation in October 2010, were large-scale benchmarks that would use the entire machine, such as Linpack. Such all-machine benchmarks in the early days of supercomputer inception are fairly commonplace and important for the following technical reasons:

1. The number of components embodied in a large supercomputer such as TSUBAME2.0 is several thousands of times greater than a standard PC. Even if we count merely the number of sockets of compute elements, namely the GPUs and CPUs, TSUBAME embodies over 7,000, whereas a standard PC only would have one or two. Memory on PCs would usually be a few gigabytes, whereas TSUBAME2.0 embodies nearly 100 terabytes, several tens of thousands greater. For such numerous components to perform under prolonged stress is one of the most important factors in attaining stable and reliable operation, as the failure rates are roughly proportional to the number of components in the system; that is to say, a PC which only fails once a year would fail more than three times a day if enlarged to the size of TSUBAME2.0.

2. At the same time, it is very important to confirm that expected design performance is being met in reality for supercomputers, as the slightest deviation could profoundly deteriorate overall performance of the system. It is quite common in a supercomputer that a component will function but not up to its specs and thus become the critical performance bottleneck. For example, the InfiniBand network employed in TSUBAME has several speed specs, and the system automatically detunes itself to the lowest mutual common denominator between the endpoints, so that communication can be established. However, when some glitch occurs that compromises a connection, and for some reason the established communication is of much lower specs, it would be more difficult to detect such anomalies. Automated means of detecting and compensating for such performance anomalies are strongly required.

3. In addition, large-scale supercomputers require constant monitoring by tens to hundreds of thousands of sensors, as well as proactive means for allocating resources to its numerous simultaneous users with extremely large-scale requests—users may submit tens of thousands of jobs at the same time, for example. If any portion of the job allocation algorithm embodies $O(n^2)$ behavior, then scaling of the machine would be catastrophic—a 100 times scaling would manifest in a 10,000-fold increase in overheads.

It is important not just for operations, but also from an academic Computer Science perspective, to determine how much we would be on target with the designed performance, and/or what the unexpected overhead would be. The computational science users would only benefit from the exercise, as various factors including performance but also reliability and usability at scale would greatly affect their actual usage.

With such a set of objectives, a series of large-scale, whole-machine benchmarks were conducted just before the operational commencement of TSUBAME2.0 on November 1, 2010, mostly throughout late October just after the machine was born:

(a) Linpack —the benchmark employed by the famous TOP500 [TOPa] supercomputer performance ranking. Basically, it computes the LU-decomposition of a very large dense matrix. For an n-by-n matrix, the computational complexity can be given as $2/3n^3 + O(n^2)$. This means that, the larger we can make the problem, up to the point where the entire matrix fits within the memory of the supercomputer, the more efficient the computation becomes due to the communication and other costs becoming relatively minimized. As a result, top-level supercomputers employ extremely large matrixes namely n=several million, and subject the CPUs/GPUs to the ultimately high workload for a long duration. The solution algorithm is delicate with no margin of error—even a single numerical error for its total $O(10^{19\ 20})$ operations would result in an error in the residual check, which would nullify the entire result. On the other hand, since the communication complexity is relatively low at $O(n^2)$, a reasonable supercomputer network would incur less than 10% network overhead. An extremely slow network such as the Gigabit Ethernet would end up having the network cost being dominant. Finally, memory bandwidth requirements are also fairly low.

(b) GPU Version of ASUCA—ASUCA is the next-generation weather forecast code for extremely large machine, being developed by Japan's Meteorological Agency. In collaboration with the Agency, a group at Professor Aoki's laboratory succeeded in full porting of ASUCA on a multi-GPU heterogeneous supercomputing environment [SAM$^+$10, SA10]. The principal computational kernel of ASUCA is the finite difference transport code, requiring extremely high memory and network bandwidth, quite contrasting to Linpack. Previously, such high-bandwidth application was perceived to be best served by custom-design, high-end vector supercomputers, but demonstrating that such code would perform extremely well on TSUBAME2.0, whose chief compute element GPU embodies extremely high bandwidth as a modern-day vector processor, was deemed important. Indeed we expected ASUCA on GPUs to achieve world's top-level performance on TSUBAME2.0, as the theoretical memory bandwidth of TSUBAME2.0 is approximately six times greater than the Earth Simulator, and ASUCA on GPU was demonstrating to be quite efficient and scalable on our preliminary tests on TSUBAME1.2. Such tremendous performance was expected to allow real-time weather prediction at unprecedented resolution and precision.

(c) Also, a set of benchmarks was performed as a part of an acceptance test of TSUBAME2.0.

### 20.3.6.1   TSUBAME2.0 Linpack —"The Greenest Production Supercomputer in the World"

The whole-machine benchmarks commenced in mid-October 2010, immediately after the initial deployment tests of TSUABME2.0 were completed. We first commenced the Linpack efforts spearheaded by the two teams running two different heterogeneous Linpack programs as described above in (a). Due to the unprecedented load imposed on the machine not possible on initial tests, we found a number of minor problems as expected, and resolved the issues one by one to attain stability. The Linux team at Tokyo Tech and the Windows HPC team sent from Microsoft took turns running their respective benchmarks. Both were very closely matched, but in the end the Linux team's heterogeneous edged the latter (Figure 20.10). It is important to note however that under slightly different conditions it would be quite possible that the results could have been the opposite.

As a result, TSUBAME2.0 recorded 1.192 petaflops, achieving approximately 52% of the theoretical peak performance. This is lower than the typical 70-90% achieved by Linpack on CPU-based supercomputers. However, it is not technically correct to simply assume that GPU-based machines are inherently less efficient compared to CPU-based ones. For our particular case, the lower efficiency is due to combination of the following performance degradation factors:

1. Firstly, the current NVIDIA Fermi GPU as employed in TSUBAME2.0 embodies a set of design bottlenecks that are not fundamental to GPU computing but rather a

```
--------------------------------------------------------------------------
- The matrix A is randomly generated for each test.
- The following scaled residual check will be computed:
   ||Ax-b||_oo / ( eps * ( || x ||_oo * || A ||_oo + || b ||_oo ) * N )
- The relative machine precision (eps) is taken to be       1.110223e-16
- Computational tests pass if scaled residuals are less than         16.0
==========================================================================

T/V              N    NB    P    Q              Time              Gflops
--------------------------------------------------------------------------
WR15R2R16   2490368  1024   59   69            8639.84           1.192e+06
--------------------------------------------------------------------------
||Ax-b||_oo/(eps*(||A||_oo*||x||_oo+||b||_oo)*N)=   0.0008911 ...... PASSED
==========================================================================

Finished      1 tests with the following results:
              1 tests completed and passed residual checks,
              0 tests completed and failed residual checks,
              0 tests skipped because of illegal input values.
--------------------------------------------------------------------------

End of Tests.
==========================================================================
```

**FIGURE 20.10**: TSUBAME2.0 begins the long road from TSUBAME1.0 to 2.0 (Part Two) TSUBAME2.0 Linpack Execution Output. Here we see that the Linpack run involved the matrix of n= 2.5 million squared elements, and the run was completed in 2.4 hours, resulting in 1.192 petaflops which ranked TSUABME2.0 to be fourth fastest in the world on the November 2011 edition of the TOP500. Notice that the residual computation is within the proper error bounds, which is a required property of the run.

result of particular design decisions. Although sufficient for graphics as well as for high-bandwidth applications where the GPUs are being used in a manner similar to a traditional vector processor, for dense matrix multiply (Level 3 BLAS) which is the principal kernel of Linpack, we only achieved 70-75% efficiency. This is substantially lower than the efficiency achieved by CPUs that exhibit more than 90% efficiency. However, with architectural as well as algorithmic improvements we expect future GPUs to match CPU efficiency in this regard, if not greatly exceed it.

2. For our Heterogeneous Linpack on Linux, CPUs are not utilized for BLAS kernel computation; however, the TOP500 results mandate us to incorporate the CPU peak performance in determination of the theoretical peak performance of the machine. For TSUBAME2.0, the two CPUs on each compute node (Intel Xeon Westmere 2.93Ghz) constitute approximately 8% of the peak performance, which we cannot utilize at all, but nonetheless by rule incorporated into the denominator on actual versus the theoretical peak efficiency ratio calculations. By all means we could conceive an algorithm that does utilize the CPU, and in fact we did so for TSUBAME1.2 [ENMM10], but that particular version proved to be less efficient due to various issues such as load balancing.

3. Our Heterogeneous Linpack effectively utilizes GPUs as a matrix multiply engine, where we send the sub-matrices of the matrix which is stored in CPU memory in stream pipelined fashion, perform the multiplication, and stream the matrix back. For normal applications where we typically transfer data in bulk to the CPU, dense computing algorithms such as matrix multiply where the compute overhead is $O(n^3)$ as opposed to the transfer overhead being $O(n^2)$, enlarging the matrix size n for pragmatic applications would hide most of the transfer latency. However, for HPL

the sub-matrix size is rather small, with n being 100-1,000, resulting in non-negligible transfer overhead.

The combination of all the factors above results in approximately 30% overhead. With advances in the GPU/CPU architecture as well as algorithms to utilize them efficiently we believe that the overhead could be effectively eliminated. By all means they are subjects of future research.

### 20.3.6.2    The Greenest Production Supercomputer in the World

On the 36th edition of the TOP500 which was announced during IEEE/ACM Supercomputing held in New Orleans, USA, during November, 2011, TSUBAME2.0 was ranked number 4 in the world. This was higher than TSUBAME1.2's initial appearance in June 2006, which was 7th in the world. The exhibited 1.192 petaflops was six times greater than the second ranking machine in Japan. Moreover, on the Green500, which ranks supercomputers based on their power efficiency, the average power consumption of 1243.80 KW during the TOP500 run resulted in 958.35 Flops/W, which ranked TSUBAME2.0 second in the world on its initial November announcement. More importantly, TSUBAME2.0 was recognized to the "Greenest Production Supercomputer in the World" (Figure 20.11), as other top machines on the Green500 were largely prototypes in nature.

The high rankings of TSUBAME2.0 on both lists simultaneously have an important technological significance. According to the current rules, it is difficult for a machine to be high on both lists; in practice, the top supercomputers of the TOP500 are extremely large-scale production supercomputers, whereas the top ranks of the Green500 are smaller-scale prototypes and/or special-purpose machines (Figure 20.12). Only TSUBAME2.0 is ranked in world's top five on both lists. Here is why such difficulty exists:

1. Since the top supercomputers on the TOP500 are large-scale, general-purpose production machines worth 10s to 100s of millions of dollars, they typically embody numerous elements that are necessary for production runs but will be detrimental to power efficiency. For example, such machines incorporate 100s of terabytes of memory which is necessary for practical high bandwidth/memory applications, but does not

**FIGURE 20.11**: November 2011 Green500 Special Award for "Greenest Production Supercomputer in the World."

**FIGURE 20.12**: The top ranking machine of November 2010 TOP500 and Green500 and their corresponding rankings on the other list. (At the very end of 2010 a revised list ranks Japan NAO's Grape-DR 2+ on the TOP500 at 1448.03 and Top500 at 383; this did NOT change the status of TSUBAME2.0 as being the most power-efficient production supercomputer in the world.)

contribute much to increasing the performance of Linpack. On large machines DRAM power consumption could be as much as 20-30% of the entire machine. On the other hand, to shoot for power efficiency on Linpack the best strategy would be to have rather small memory, but this would limit the scope of the machine to a very small number of specialized (typically compute intensive) applications.

2. The top rank of TOP500 often is of extreme logistical importance for computing centers and even countries, and as a result, all other factors could become sacrificed just to go up a notch in the rankings, including power efficiency in the Linpack algorithm and settings. On the other hand, if one would shoot for top rank on the Green500, going down in ranking on the TOP500 does not matter—all that matters is that the machine is on the TOP500. Such a difference in objectives is difficult to achieve especially at the top of each list.

3. The TOP500 runs of Linpack involve a matrix size of n=a few million, with tens of thousands of processor cores. Unfortunately, by the nature of the algorithm Linpack is inherently more efficient on smaller machines. For example, one typically sees a 5-10% drop in performance just by going multi-node, with increasing overhead proportional to machine size [ENMM10].

Despite such disadvantages, TSUBAME2.0 being ranked highly on both lists was the reason for the award in Figure 20.11. This was not achieved by simple employment of GPUs, as other GPU machines did not achieve similar results. Rather this is the result of years of basic research on low power, high performance computing at Tokyo Tech GSIC, including the JST-CREST Ultra Low Power HPC (ULP-HPC) project.

### 20.3.6.3  Memory and Network Benchmarking in a Real Application — GPU Porting of ASUCA Weather Code and Its World Record Performance

Although Linpack TOP500 is a significant metric for supercomputer performance measurement, for numerous applications that are largely memory or network bandwidth bound, the TOP500 numbers are not effective metrics. That is to say, for many important simulation applications such as computational fluid dynamics, structural simulations, and even modern apps such as Internet page rankings, how much effective bandwidth is achieved governs the overall performance, not how much Flops. As a result, the baseline availability of theoretical peak bandwidth as well as the ease at which major fraction of the peak bandwidth could be achieved, become the dominant performance factors. Unfortunately, in recent supercomputer architectural trends, the amount of available bandwidth relative to the machine size, as well as its ratio to compute, is on constant decrease due to various physical limitations. Vector supercomputers of the past, such as the Cray X series and the NEC SXes were built precisely with this purpose in mind, i.e., increase the memory bandwidth during the days where achieving high compute flops was technologically difficult, achieving in high computational efficiency as a result.

Such glory days are over, and in fact we must really re-think our notion of efficiency for modern machines in terms of efficiency over the dominant performance bottlenecks, in this case the memory/network bandwidth, not compute. So, the true "efficiency" metric is how much the application is utilizing the memory/network bandwidth in the system relative to the theoretical peak available, and has no correlation to the peak FLOPS of the machine.

In fact, in this regard we must point out that high computational efficiency that was apparently achieved in classic vector machines was rather artificial and misleading, the result of a technological trend of the times, and not an effective metric in modern times. That is to say, such vector machines that under-provisioned the computing resources did not properly exploit the available opportunity presented by dense problems and the available locality (e.g., due to the lack of cache memory), and as a result, their efficiency might seem extremely high, but the resulting absolute performance is low relative to the size/cost of the machine.

Exactly the same argument applies to GPUs versus CPUs, but often the same mistakes are made. As has been mentioned, GPUs exhibit extremely high memory bandwidth per socket compared to CPUs, but at the same time, also embody much higher (and effectively overprovision) compute as well. In fact, on TSUBAME2.0, the per-socket peak compute capability of each GPU is approximately 7 times that of CPU, but at the same time, measured effective memory bandwidth is also 6-7 times per socket. So if CPU-based implementation on TSUBAME2.0 would obtain 5% of peak, then it is likely that a GPU-based implementation would obtain similar computational efficiency, while being 6-7 times faster with the same number of sockets.

This in effect allows us to conjecture that TSUBAME2.0 would be comparable to x86 CPU-based machines of similar peak performance, or those with socket counts that are 7 times greater, if no artificial bottlenecks are imposed as was the case for Linpack. That is to say, TSUBAME2.0 with 4,200 GPU and 2,800 CPU sockets would be roughly equivalent to a 30,000 socket/200,000 core x86 CPU-based supercomputer, which would largely equal the size of ORNL Jaguar. In fact we can expect that Jaguar would have an advantage in compute but might not perform as well on high bandwidth code, as the older-generation x86 it employs is much less efficient in memory but similar in FLOPs utilization.

The ASUCA benchmark was important in this regard to determine if such performance estimations would hold for high-bandwidth applications. In particular, since finite difference solvers for transport codes are known to be mostly pure memory-bandwidth limited, the issues are whether (1) GPUs would be able to efficiently utilize the available memory bandwidth, (2) whether we achieve 6-7 times speedup per socket as discussed above, and finally (3) how the performance would compare as a whole to Jaguar in executing the same or at least very similar weather code.

For details of the ASUCA code itself the readers are referred to [SA10]; the result achieved largely confirmed our conjectures (1)-(3) above. The GPU version of ASUCA on TSUBAME2.0 scaled up to 3,990 GPUs [SAM+10] almost linearly in weak scaling (the problem size proportionally increasing relative to the machine size), and achieved 145 teraflops in single precision, and 76.1 teraflops in double precision (Figure 20.13). The per-

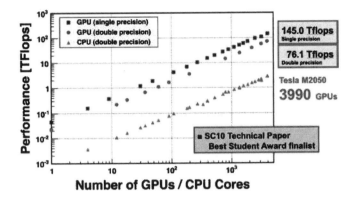

**FIGURE 20.13**: ASUCA benchmarking on TSUBAME2.0 (1). Notice that performance scales almost linearly to 3990 GPUs.

socket performance is approximately 6 times that of CPUs (Figure 20.14), confirming our conjecture in real, production-level code.

Moreover, the previous world record holder was the WRF code, a weather code similar to ASUCA, on Jaguar at approximately 50 teraflops (double precision); so ASUCA was even faster, by a factor of 10; we might attribute this to less efficient memory bus of the older-generation AMD processors in Jaguar, but since the applications are different, this result should be taken as preliminary, and more rigorous benchmarking should be done using the same applications under a controlled environment.

## 20.4    Applications and Workloads

We are conducting R&D related to advanced applications of high-performance computing on TSUBAME supercomputer and aiming at scientific outcomes and public contribu-

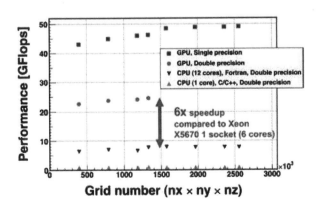

**FIGURE 20.14**: ASUCA benchmarking on TSUBAME2.0. The per-socket performance difference is approximately a factor of six, confirming the relative difference in peak achievable memory bandwidth.

**FIGURE 20.15**: Snapshot of the dendritic solidification growth.

tions. These applications include numerical weather prediction, large-scale simulation for multi-phase flow, large-eddy simulation of turbulent flow, study of fluid-structure interaction, tsunami simulation, and geo-mechanics simulation such as physical phenomena and modeling of granular media, stability analysis of landslide. In addition, the large-scale data processing group, along with the application scientists, are tackling the increasingly difficult problems of the so-called big-data science, such as large-scale environmental simulations or life science simulations, utilizing the supercomputing power of TSUBAME2.0 extensively.

The following are applications that are respresentative of TSUBAME2.0. For their details refer to the TSUBAME E-Science Journal (ESJ) volumes we publish at GSIC [ESJ].

### 20.4.1 GPU Computing for Dendritic Solidification Based on Phase-Field Model

The mechanical properties of metallic materials are strongly characterized by distribution and morphology of the microstructure in the materials. In order to improve the mechanical performance of the materials and to develop a new material, it is essential to understand the microstructure evolution during solidification and phase transformation. Recently, the phase-field model [TFT05] has been developed as a powerful method to simulate the microstructure evolution. In the phase-field modeling, the time-dependent Ginzburg-Landau type equations which describe interface dynamics and solute diffusion during the microstructure evolution are solved by the finite difference and finite element methods. This microstructure modeling has been applied to numerical simulations for solidification, phase transformation, and precipitation in various materials (Figure 20.15). However, large computational cost is required to perform realistic and quantitative three-dimensional phase-field simulation in the typical scales of the microstructure pattern. To overcome such a computational task, we utilize the GPGPU (General-Purpose Graphics Processing Unit) [EM08], which is developed as an innovative accelerator [Cor08] in high performance computing (HPC) technology.

We study the growth of the dendritic solidification of a pure metal in a super cooling state by solving the equations derived from the phase-field model. The remarkably high performance is shown in comparison with the conventional CPU computing. Although most GPGPU applications run on a single GPU, we exploit a multiple GPU code and show the strong scalability of large-scale problems. For details refer to [ESJ10a].

## 20.4.2 Multi-GPU Computing for Next-Generation Weather Forecasting

Weather forecasting is an indispensable part in our daily lives and business activities, not to mention for natural disaster preventions. The atmosphere is very thin compared with the Earth's diameter. In the previous atmosphere code, the force balance between the gravity and the pressure gradient in the vertical direction was used to produce a hydrostatic model. Recently it has become widely recognized that the vertical dynamical processes of water vapor should be taken into consideration in cloud formations. A three-dimensional non-hydrostatic model describing the up-and-down movement of air has been developed in weather research.

For weather simulations, the initial data is produced by assimilating many kinds of observed data and simulation results based on the four-dimensional variational principle. Since the weather phenomena are chaotic, the predictability period is less than several days for one set of initial data so jobs run sequentially to update the initial data.

In recent years, detailed weather forecasts, such as unexpected local heavy rain, and high resolution non-hydrostatic models have been in demand on fine-grained grids. The next generation weather prediction model and program, called ASUCA, is being developed at the National Meteorological Agency of Japan, and incorporates such a model for high-resolution simulations of local weather phenomenon. ASUCA has been effectively ported to TSUBAME2.0 in collaboration with the Agency to achieve world records in weather simulation performance (Figure 20.16). For details refer to [ESJ10b].

## 20.4.3 Computer Prediction of Protein-Protein Interaction Network

Living matter is maintained and developed by various molecular interactions. Elucidation of the regulatory relations among the thousands of protein species working in a human cell is crucial for understanding the mechanisms that underly diseases and for development of drugs. We are working on the problem of predicting the Protein-Protein Interaction (PPI) network (Figure 20.17), which is one of the main topics in systems biology, by using bioinformatics methods. Conventionally, computational methods have been used mainly to analyze the mechanism of individual known protein interactions in detail. Those methods are not applicable to a large-scale analysis such as in the systems biology field. In this work, we developed a method that can be applied to PPI prediction problems of mega-order data. For details refer to [ESJ10b].

**FIGURE 20.16**: ASUCA real operation to describe a typhoon with $4792 \times 4696 \times 48$ mesh using 437 GPUs of TSUBAME 2.0.

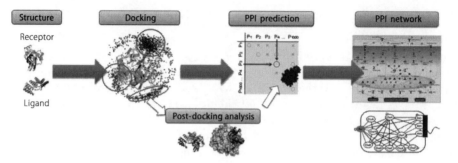

**FIGURE 20.17**: PPI network prediction.

## 20.4.4   GPU Computing for Interstellar Atomic Hydrogen Turbulence

Human beings have sent astronauts to the moon and unmanned probes to the end of the solar system. But to visit neighboring stars and collect evidence will remain a very hard job for generations. To overcome the limitations and understand the mystery of the universe, we have to collect observational evidence while on Earth, and carefully construct the reasoning based on scientific laws.

We use TSUBAME2.0 to determine the mass of the stars (Figure 20.18). Stars are born from fragmentation and condensation of the interstellar gas in the galaxy, which is as thin as one hydrogen atom per cubic centimeter. If the typical stars are ten times lighter, the nuclear fusion will not ignite and our galaxy will remain dark. If they are ten times heavier, they will much more rapidly burn hydrogen than they do today and our galaxy will be filled with black holes. The mechanism that sets the adequate initial masses for the stars is the interstellar turbulence driven by the thermal instability.

Interstellar hydrogen has two stable phases determined by the balance of various heating and cooling processes such as star irradiation and molecular line emission. Triggered by supernova shock waves, the interstellar medium makes phase transits from the warm, low

**FIGURE 20.18**: Interstellar atomic hydrogen turbulence.

density phase to numerous clumps of the cold, high density phase. It takes several more steps until stars and planetary systems are formed from these clumps. There is a lot of detective work left to do in the universe. For details refer to [ESJ11a].

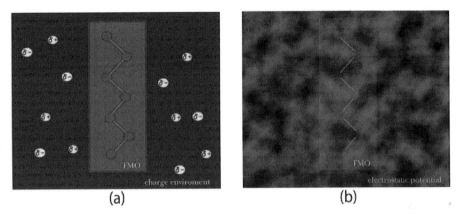

(a)                                          (b)

**FIGURE 20.19**: Illustration of the FMO-NMR calculation concept. Chemical shifts of target fragment (lighter gray, inner rectangular region) are calculated by using surrounding point charge (Model-I (a)) or charge density distribution (Model-II (b)) to represent the effects of surrounding chemical.

### 20.4.5   Ab Initio NMR Chemical Shift Calculations for Biomolecular Systems

In NMR spectroscopy, the chemical shift describes the dependence of nuclear magnetic energy levels on the electronic environment in a molecule. In other words, it is a parameter that corresponds to the difference in resonance frequency between nuclei placed in different molecular environments. This means that the chemical shift is sensitive to various physico-chemical factors such as molecular conformation, configuration, chemical composition, and surrounding solvent. Thus, observation of chemical shift, usually combined with those of other NMR parameters (i.e., J-coupling, relaxation time, and NOE), can provide invaluable information on the three-dimensional structures of molecules, especially in solution.

However, for large molecules like proteins, it is difficult to correctly assign their chemical shifts to corresponding 3D structures only by using experimental approaches. For accurate structural analysis based on the chemical shift observation, it is necessary to obtain information on how the electronic wave function of a molecule is perturbed by its conformational and other structural changes. Therefore, theoretical approaches play an essential role in determining and refining molecular structures in the framework of NMR spectroscopy. This work is concerned with the development of chemical shift calculations for protein on the basis of quantum mechanics.

Chemical shift in large molecular systems has long been considered too complicated, or even impossible to be studied by conventional quantum chemistry calculations. The major problem concerns the computational cost of calculating chemical shift. For reliable estimates of chemical shifts, high-level quantum chemical calculations, based on coupled perturbed methods, are required. Unfortunately, these methods are computationally very inefficient and can be applied to small isolated molecules only.

This work combines well-established ab initio methods for chemical shift calculation with the FMO method, which allows for a rapid calculation for a large molecule by dividing it into small fragments. In particular, we have used this combined method to predict the total chemical shifts of ubiquitin, a small (76 residues) and highly-conserved regulatory protein. Furthermore, to improve the accuracy of this FMO based NMR chemical shift calculation method, we develop a method capable of defining an appropriate fragment size, i.e., a cutoff distance, to better reproduce the chemical shift values (Figure 20.19). For details refer to [ESJ11b].

**FIGURE 20.20**: (Left): Simulation. (Right): Experiment for dam-break problem.

### 20.4.6    A Large-Scale Two-Phase Flow Simulation on GPU Supercomputer

Recently movie scenes of violent flows mixing air with water have been produced by computer graphics in Hollywood film productions. It is notable that they carry out larger-scale computations with higher-resolution than those of scientific and engineering works. For two-phase flows, particle methods such as SPH (smoothed particle hydrodynamics) have been used due to the simple algorithm and success of astrophysical N-body simulation in the beginning of GPU computing. Each particle interacts with all particles within the kernel radius to compute the particle motion. In three-dimensional simulation, the number of interacting particles increases, and particle methods have disadvantages from the viewpoints of numerical accuracy, random memory access, and amount of computation. In particular, the sparse matrix for the pressure Poisson equation has a wide bandwidth of non-zero elements in the semi-implicit time integration and is inefficiently solved in such memory distributed systems as multi-node clusters or supercomputers. In addition, there are problems involving non-physical oscillation at the gas-liquid interface, inaccurate evaluation of the surface tension, and large numerical viscosity.

In mesh methods such as FDM (finite difference method), FVM (finite volume method), and FEM (finite element method), the computation for a mesh point, a cell, or an element requires only accesses to some neighboring points. Higher-order numerical schemes are easily applicable to the FDM in structured meshes. In Hollywood film productions, they have changed the particle methods to mesh methods to make realistic water scenes. In a mesh method, the gas and liquid phases are treated as one fluid with different material properties: density, viscosity, and surface tension. It is necessary to introduce an interface capturing technique to identify the different properties. The density changes 1,000 times from the gas to the liquid at the interface, and the profile is expressed with a few meshes.

This work shows a large-scale gas-liquid two-phase simulation by full GPU computing, which has never been achieved before (Figure 20.20). For details refer to [ESJ11b].

**FIGURE 20.21**: Images of a material microstructure.

### 20.4.7 Evolutive Image/Video Coding with Massively Parallel Computing

In image/video coding schemes such as JPEG and AVC/H.264, the prediction mode, quantization parameter, prediction coefficients, context grouping thresholds, etc., are adaptively chosen to optimize the compression performance. So are motion vectors and prediction modes in video coding. In current image/video coding schemes, these coding parameters are dynamically optimized. However, the coding algorithm itself is never altered within the scheme. In other words, there has been no way to develop a new coding scheme other than by human implementation via the trial and error approach. Therefore, codec complexity cannot exceed what humans are capable of. Furthermore, it has not been realistic to develop content-specific (not even image-category-specific) coding algorithms. Our target then is to develop a scheme that allows a computer to generate content-specific image/video coding algorithms. In this overview, we introduce several latest activities on this evolutionary approach. For details refer to [ESJ11b].

### 20.4.8 Petascale Phase-Field Simulation for Dendritic Solidification

The development of new strong and light materials contributes greatly to transportation systems with high fuel efficiency. The strength of a metal depends on its microstructure, which is, in turn, determined by the solidification process of the metal (see Figure 20.21). However, determining material properties (such as strength) requires millimeter-scale macroscopic study.

The phase-field model [Kob93] is a physical theory describing the evolution of complicated material morphologies on the meso-scale, namely, between the molecular scale and the macroscopic scale of materials. It is a powerful numerical tool for studying the dynamics of phase transformations such as solidification. The derived equations are partial differential equations in time and space and often discretized by FDM (finite difference method) or FEM (finite element method). The phase-field equations include many complex nonlinear terms, and the amount of computations per mesh or element becomes large compared to normal stencil applications. Furthermore, the phase-field model assumes a narrow-thickness interface between liquid phase and solid phase, so the time integration requires high spatial resolution and short time step, and phase-field simulations remain restricted to two-dimensional or small three-dimensional computations due to their large computational cost.

This work carries out a large-scale phase-field simulation for the aluminum-silicon dendritic growth during directional solidification on the GPU supercomputer TSUBAME2.0 (Figure 20.22). The simulation code is developed in CUDA, and almost all the capability of TSUBAME2.0 is used for the simulation, which uses a domain decomposition and inter-node communications with an MPI library. Such a large-scale phase-field simulation has not been done before and will have a big impact on material science. For details refer to [ESJ12].

### 20.4.9    Large-Scale Biofluidics Simulations

Transport phenomena are ubiquitous in living systems, underlying muscle contraction, digestion, the nourishment of cells in the body, blood circulation, to name but a few. Blood is a reference biofluid, being the carrier of those biological components that fuel the most basic physiological functions, such as metabolism, immune response, and tissue repair. Building a detailed, realistic representation of blood and the vasculature represents a formidable challenge since the computational model must combine the motion of the fluid within an irregular geometry, subject to unsteady changes in flow and pressure driven by the heartbeat, as coupled to the dynamics of red and white blood cells and other suspended bodies of biological relevance.

Large-scale hemodynamic simulations have made substantial progress in recent years [VSE01, QVZJ02, GAC09], but until now the coupling of fluid dynamics with the motion of blood cells and other suspended bodies in vessels with realistic shapes and sizes, has remained beyond reach. Owing to non-local correlations carried by the flow pressure, the global geometry plays a significant role on local circulation patterns, most notably on the shear stress at arterial walls. Wall shear stress is a recognized trigger for the complex biomechanical events that can lead to atherosclerotic pathologies. Accurate and reliable hemodynamic simulations of the wall shear stress may provide a non-invasive tool for the prediction of the progression of cardiovascular diseases.

We illustrate here the first multiscale simulation of cardiovascular flows in human coro-

**FIGURE 20.22**: (Left): Solidification process of an alloy observed at SPring-8 (courtesy of Professor Yasuda). (Right): Solidification growth simulated by the phase-field model using GPUs.

nary arteries reconstructed from computed tomography angiography. The coronary arteries form the network that supply blood to the heart muscle and span the entire heart extension. Spatial resolution extends from 5 cm down to 10 $\mu$m, while a red blood cell has a diameter of about 8 $\mu$m.

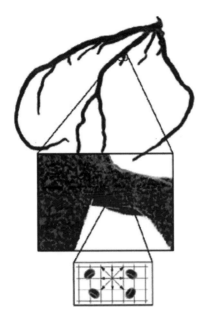

**FIGURE 20.23**: Geometry of the simulated coronary arteries, with the underlying level of red blood cells embedded in the lattice Boltzmann mesh.

The simulations involve up to a billion fluid nodes, embedded in a bounding space of about a 300 billion voxels, with 10-450 million suspended bodies, as shown in Figure 20.23. They are performed with the (MUlti PHYsics/multiscale) MUPHY code, which couples the lattice Boltzmann method for the fluid flow and a specialized version of molecular dynamics for the suspended bodies [BMSea09, MBea10]. The simulation achieves an aggregate performance in excess of 600 teraflops, with a parallel efficiency of more than 90% on 4000-GPU of the TSUBAME2 system. For details refer to [ESJ12].

# Chapter 21

# HA-PACS: A Highly Accelerated Parallel Advanced System for Computational Sciences

**Taisuke Boku, Toshihiro Hanawa, Yoshinobu Kuramashi, Kohji Yoshikawa, Mitsuo Shoji, Yuetsu Kodama, Mitsuhisa Sato, and Masayuki Umemura**

*Center for Computational Sciences, University of Tsukuba*

## 21.1 Overview

### 21.1.1 Sponsor/Program Background

1. The system is based on a program titled "Advanced interdisciplinary computational science initiative by development of exascale computing technology" to develop the next-generation scientific codes and algorithms based on accelerated computing facilities in fundamental scientific fields.

2. The project is sponsored by the Ministry of Education, Sports and Culture, Science and Technology, Japan.

3. The project name "HA-PACS" stands for Highly Accelerated Parallel Advanced System for Computational Sciences [UTb].

### 21.1.2    Timeline

The project has a term of three years from fiscal year 2011 to 2013 for base cluster development and installation as well as TCA (described in Section 21.11) prototype system development. The base cluster procurement procedure started in early 2011, the vendor was decided on August 2011, and the system was delivered in January 2012. The system started to be used in test mode in February 2012 followed by its full operation in October 2012.

## 21.2    Applications and Workloads

HA-PACS base cluster is mainly used for fundamental physics and advanced scientific code, mainly by academia. The primary target area in the first stage includes particle physics (Quantum Chromo Dynamics), astrophysics, and bioscience (QM/MM mixture). It also includes geoscience (large eddy simulation), nuclear fusion simulation, and more.

Basically, we have developed a large-scale accelerated code based on multi-GPUs per node and multi-nodes up to hundreds of nodes or thousands of GPUs. Astrophysics code is especially suited to GPU computing because of its dense computing amount compared with relatively small amount of I/O for accelerated devices (GPUs).

The primary scientific targets of these fields are as follows:

(a) Particle physics: Large-scale configuration of Quantum Chromo-Dynamics and finite temperature phase transition based on the theory.

(b) Astrophysics: Collisional N-body simulation, black holes, and first objects in the universe.

(c) Bioscience: The combined simulation of quantum mechanics and molecular dynamics for the mixture of fundamental atomic level simulation of biophenomena as well as molecular level macrosimulation.

(d) Geoscience: A global-scale atmospheric simulation and the regional detailed simulation by large eddy simulation with basic physics, cloud physics, building structure, and moisture conditions, etc.

(e) Nuclear fusion: The 5-dimensional magnetic fluid simulation for productive level of Tokamak toward exascale simulation.

### 21.2.1    Benchmark Results

1. HPL Linpack: 421.6 TFLOPS (power consumption: 366.00 kW, performance/power: 1151.91 MF/W, efficiency: 54.18%).

2. Ranked No. 41 in TOP500 list and No. 24 in Green500 list, both on June 2012.

## 21.3 System Overview

The system is constructed as a large-scale GPU cluster based on Appro International's Xtreme-X GreenBlade with two CPU sockets and four GPUs per node. The total count of computation nodes is 268 which are connected by the InfiniBand QDR dual rail system with two single stage InfiniBand QDR switches with full-bisection bandwidth. All HCAs and switches are provided by Mellanox. Intel E5 (SandyBridge-EP) CPU is employed both to provide the latest IA32 technology for high performance and to support four NVIDIA Tesla M2090 which requires x64 lanes PCI Express generation2 bus ("PCIe gen2," hereafter). Each Intel E5 processor supports up to x40 lanes of PCIe gen2, and a dual-sockets system can support four Tesla GPU without PCIe bottleneck.

A system rack is a standard 19-inch 40U rack, and each rack contains 12 computation nodes, 288-port single stage InfiniBand switch, or 500 TB Lustre filesystem. The total number of racks is 26, and the installation footprint is very compact at 5.5 m × 10 m.

For more detail of HA-PACS system, see [UTb].

## 21.4 Hardware Architecture

The block diagram of a computation node is shown in Figure 21.1.

1. Processor on node

   - Main processor: Intel Xeon E5-2670 (8 core, 2.6 GHz) dual socket
   - Accelerator: NVIDIA Tesla M2090 × 4

2. Node design: Blade configuration for 8U blade chassis, 4 blades per blade chassis

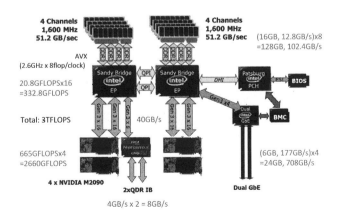

**FIGURE 21.1**: Block diagram of computation node.

3. Memory

- Memory on CPU: DDR3 128 GB, 1,600 MHz × 4 channel × 2 socket, 102.4 GB/s peak
- Memory on GPU: GDR5 6 GB per GPU = 24 GB total
- Total memory capacity in system: 34.3 TB (main), 6.4 TB (GPU)

4. Interconnect: Mellanox Connect-X3 QDR InfiniBand × 2 rails, Fat-Tree network with full bisection bandwidth. Aggregated system network bandwidth: 2.14 TB/s.

5. Storage system: Lustre cluster filesystem via InfiniBand QDR, directly accessible from all computation nodes, with Data Direct Network SFA 10000 RAID-6 file server, 500 TB user space.

## 21.5   System Software

1. Operating system: CentOS based on Linux 2.6.32

2. File system: Lustre filesystem

3. ACE (Appro Cluster Engine) cluster management system

4. Sun Grid Engine

5. No virtualization

## 21.6   Programming System

1. Programming models: OpenMP, MPI, CUDA

2. Compiler: Fortran90, C, and C++ by Intel and PGI

3. Libraries: BLAS, LAPACK, SCALAPACK, Gaussian90

4. Debugger: Allinea DDT

## 21.7   Storage, Visualization, and Analytics

The Lustre filesystem provides a flat view of shared filesystem accessed by any computation node through InfiniBand QDR.

## 21.8 Datacenter/Facility

1. System installation site: Center for Computational Sciences, University of Tsukuba, Japan [UTa].

2. Facility

   - Floorspace: 10 m × 5.5 m = 55 m$^2$
   - Power consumption: 410 kW
   - Cooling: Air cooling

3. Facility challenge: HA-PACS base cluster is challenged to provide a very compact and well-balanced large-scale GPU cluster supported by the latest CPU (Intel E5) for a balanced number of the latest GPUs with plenty of I/O bandwidth. A computation node with two CPU sockets provides enough PCIe bandwidth to support four NVIDIA Tesla M2090. A blade server node provides approximately 3 TFLOPS of peak performance (332 GFLOPS by CPU and 2,460 GFLOPS by GPU) with approximately 1,400 kW of peak power consumption. The entire system achieves very high performance/watt efficiency by HPL, 1,035 MFLOPS/W, which is the highest level in the world for a GPU cluster as of June 2012.

4. Figure 21.2 shows the full system view and computation node.

## 21.9 System Statistics

As of October 2012, HA-PACS base cluster was in full operation.

1. Number of users and projects: approximately 110 users and 25 projects

2. Reliability: overall MTBF in 4 months of operation is approximately 90 hours

3. Utilization: average utilization ratio is over 90%

## 21.10 Focused Scientific Applications

While the HA-PACS project targets a wide variety of scientific fields, it focuses on the following application fields in the early stages of the project.

### 21.10.1 Elementary Particle Physics — QCD

QCD (Quantum Chromo-Dynamics) is one of the toughest and most challenging applications in the state-of-the-art high-end systems so far. Since the application is originally computation bound with high memory bandwidth requirements, the potential performance

(a)

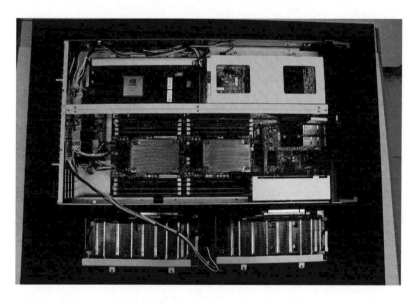

(b)

**FIGURE 21.2**: System view of HA-PACS base cluster (a) and computation node blade (b).

and bandwidth of GPU is expected to provide great power for this application. The simulation for generating QCD configuration requires a large-scale parallel computation, and it is needed to provide short latency communication as well as high bandwidth for strong scaling solutions. This computation characteristic is satisfied partially by the TCA feature of HA-PACS (described in Section 21.11).

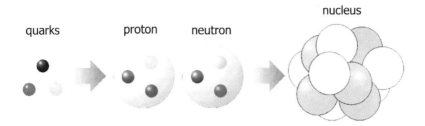

**FIGURE 21.3**: Hierarchical structure from quarks to nuclei. There are two kinds of nucleons: proton and neutron (middle). Three quarks (left) are bound to form a nucleon, and nucleons are in turn bound to form the nucleus (right).

For the early stage computation on HA-PACS, we focused on two special calculations.

1. Multi-scale physics:

   In the history of theoretical studies of the atomic nuclei the nuclear shell model has achieved great success in explaining the nuclear magic numbers and detailed spectroscopy since 1949, which established that protons and neutrons are very good effective degrees of freedom at the nuclear energy scale of a few MeV. Sixty years later, however, we know for certain that protons and neutrons are made of quarks and gluons whose laws are governed by QCD. The strong interaction dynamically generates a hierarchical structure: three quarks are bound to form a nucleon with an energy of 1 GeV, and nucleons are in turn bound to form nuclei with a binding energy of 10 MeV or so per nucleon (Figure 21.3). This is a multi-scale physics that computational physics should explore, and it is a great challenge to quantitatively understand the structure and property of nuclei based on the first principle of QCD. This direct approach will be more important and indispensable if we are to extract reliable predictions for experimentally unknown nuclei in the neutron rich regions of the nuclear chart. We now have a possibility that the physics of the nuclei, which has been investigated with the effective theories for almost 100 years, could be completely rewritten in terms of QCD. As a first step we address the fundamental question in the research in this direction, namely the binding energies of nuclei. These quantities are extracted from the time dependence of the nuclear correlation functions composed of the quark propagators, which require solving large sparse linear systems of equations. This calculation dominates more than 80% of all the computational cost and GPU works for it.

2. QCD at finite temperature and density:

   It is an important task for lattice QCD to establish the QCD phase diagram on the $T$-$\mu$ plane with $T$ the temperature and $\mu$ the quark chemical potential (Figure 21.4). We can understand the early universe and the inside of neutron stars by investigating the phase structure and the equation of state. The Monte Carlo simulation technique, which has been successfully applied to zero density studies in lattice QCD, cannot be directly applied to the finite density case due to the complexity of the quark determinant for finite $\mu$. Recently we have investigated the phase of the quark determinant with finite chemical potential in lattice QCD using both analytic and numerical methods. Applying the winding expansion to the logarithm of the determinant, we have shown that the absolute value of the phase has an upper bound that grows with the spatial volume but decreases exponentially with an increase in the temporal extent of

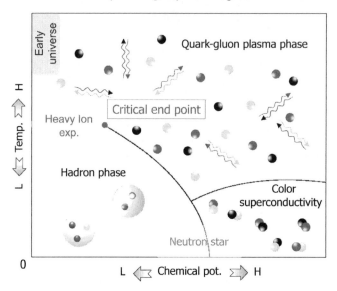

**FIGURE 21.4**: Expected QCD phase diagram on $T$-$\mu$ plane with $T$ the temperature (vertical) and $\mu$ the quark chemical potential (horizontal).

the lattice. This analytic result is confirmed with a numerical test in 4 flavor QCD. We have observed that the phase is actually suppressed as the temperature $T$ decreases with the chemical potential $\mu$ fixed. The winding expansion allows us to explore the high density region of the QCD phase diagram at low temperatures. The analysis of the phase diagram requires a number of relatively small system size simulations. GPU works for a high-speed implementation of the matrix-matrix product of dense matrices, which is the most time-consuming part of the calculation. Further acceleration is expected by low latency communication among multi-GPU.

## 21.10.2   Astrophysics

Gravitational interaction and radiation transfer are among the most important physical processes in the dynamics and the formations of almost all astrophysical objects. Since their numerical computations have high concurrency and require fairly compute-intensive workloads, it is expected that the numerical simulations of these two physical processes can be efficiently accelerated with the aid of GPUs. In the early stage of HA-PACS use, we specifically focused on the following astrophysical applications:

1. Collisional N-body simulation: The target of this application includes research on the formation and the time evolution of the globular clusters and the super-massive black holes in galaxies using N-body simulations. There are a number of studies in which N-body simulations are accelerated by GPUs. However, most of them are "collisionless" N-body simulations, where a single particle is a super-particle of stars and dark matter elementary particles, and utterly different from "collisional" N-body simulations. In collisional N-body simulations, each particle is a counterpart of a single star or a single black hole, and it is necessary to simulate the complicated gravitational interactions between stars and black holes much more precisely than collisionless N-

body simulations. To achieve high precision, we have to resort to the direct (brute force) calculations of gravitational accelerations and jerks (time-derivatives of acceleration) in double precision. For more than two decades, the GRAPE-4 [MTES94] and GRAPE-6 [MFKN03] accelerators have been utilized for these kinds of studies. In this application, GPUs are utilized as a substitution for the GRAPE accelerator family. With a unprecedented high performance density per node of the HA-PACS system, we perform the full-scale simulations of globular clusters and investigate the formation and evolution of the sources of gravitational waves such as binaries of black holes and neutron stars inside globular clusters.

2. Radiation transfer simulation: The most efficient way to transfer energy in the universe is by radiation, or the electromagnetic wave. Thus, the radiation transfer is an indispensable ingredient to understand the formation and the evolution of astrophysical objects. Since the radiation emitted by radiation sources such as stars and quasars can affect very distant matter owing to its high propagation speed, its numerical calculation has a non-local feature and a quite huge workload. Due to the huge computational costs of the radiation transfer, so far, it is treated in a rather phenomenological manner. In this application, we accelerate the calculations of the radiation transfer based on the ray-tracing method with the aid of GPUs. In the ray-tracing method, the calculation along individual rays can be done in an independent manner, and thus it is possible to drastically accelerate the most compute-intensive part of the radiation transfer using GPUs. Furthermore, we perform radiation hydrodynamic simulations, in which hydrodynamics of the gaseous matter in the universe and the radiation transfer through it are simultaneously computed in a self-consistent manner. Actually, such treatment of the gaseous matter in the universe is necessary to simulate the formation of stars and galaxies and re-ionization of the intergalactic medium in the early universe in the first-principle approach, though it is yet to be performed due to its huge computational costs. With the advent of the HA-PACS system, we, for the first time, can perform self-consistent radiation hydrodynamic simulations of galaxy formation and obtain a realistic picture of galaxy formation in the ancient and current universe.

### 21.10.3 Life Science

In the bioscience field, computational simulations are increasingly important for the detailed analysis of vital phenomena. One of the typical theoretical methods is the molecular dynamics (MD) method based on classical mechanics for the component atoms. The MD simulations allow us to study the dynamical mechanism underlying biomolecular functions; however, large computational costs are required for their realistic models, and there are still limitations for the total simulation time. For example, in traditional supercomputers such as PACS-CS, nanoseconds are the simulation-limit for typical protein systems composed of 50,000 atoms. For biological functions microsecond simulations are required to search the large-scale conformation changes (Figure 21.5).

Thus, utilization of a GPU for the speed up of MD simulations is very attractive. Currently, major MD program packages such as AMBER, Gromacs, and NAMD, support GPU accelerations for the non-bonded interactions. Using HA-PACS, replica exchange MDs (REMDs) were performed for the benchmark study. The system consists of 30,000 atoms with 128 replicas. Execution times of the MD simulation showed that 3.0 and 2.6 times accelerations are observed for the hybrid usage of GPUs and CPUs in the 32 and 64 nodes, respectively, where the speed up is compared to that of the CPU only usage (2 Sandy-Bridge CPUs with 16 cores per node) (Figure 21.6). The high-speed execution of HA-PACS

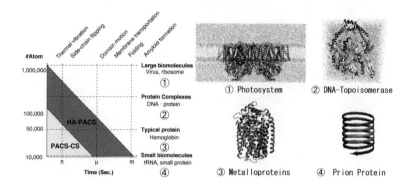

**FIGURE 21.5**: Targets of molecular dynamics (MD) simulations in the computational bioscience fields from macromolecule systems to small proteins (1-4).

corresponds to a 2 microsecond MD simulation per day for a 30,000 atom system using the 64 nodes.

It is to be noted that current GPU accelerations are limited for large systems composed of over 200,000 atoms. For a large system composed of 1,600,000 atoms, GPU speed up is 2.4 times; however, for less than 20,000 atoms, GPU usage only slows down the runtime. Though current GPU supports are still limited, a variety of GPU accelerations and the improvements will be expected.

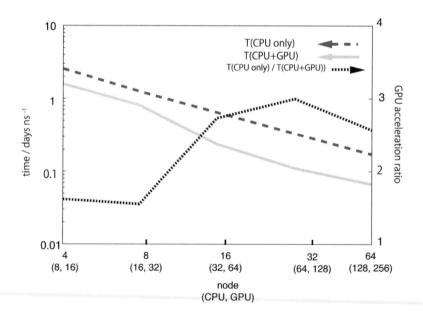

**FIGURE 21.6**: Performance of GPU accelerated MD using NAMD@HA-PACS. Replica Exchange MD (REMD) for a system composed of 30,00 atoms and the 128 replicas were performed. The left vertical axis shows the required time (day) for 1 ns simulation, and the right vertical axis shows the GPU acceleration ratio calculated from the ratio between the simulation times of CPU only and CPU+GPU.

Hybrid supercomputer based on CPU and GPU processors, HA-PACS, brought a dramatic speed up for the computation rate. Using HA-PACS, ten microsecond MD simulations can be easily performed, where the timescale is suitable for general functions of standard proteins. Utilization of GPU becomes increasingly important for large-scale computational simulations in the bioscience field, and further improvements of GPU acceleration and novel algorithms are required to achieve efficient performances.

## 21.11   Research and Development on Communication System for Accelerated Computing

HA-PACS project is not just the construction of a large-scale GPU cluster to run large-scale parallel codes, but also focuses on the research and development of new technology to support parallel accelerated computing. In this project, we have been developing a new technology to enable GPU-GPU direct communication over computation nodes. Currently, NVIDIA's CUDA 4.0+ programming framework enables the direct communication among multiple GPUs on a computation node; however, our goal is to establish a sophisticated interconnection network system among a number of system-wide GPUs. This technology is named "TCA (Tightly Coupled Accelerators)."

TCA is based on the concept to utilize the PCIe communication link as the direct network among CPUs and GPUs over multiple nodes. PCIe is a fast serial I/O interface to connect the device to the CPU. At present, PCIe is the standard I/O interface for the PC, and various I/O devices, such as Ethernet, InfiniBand, and GPU, are connected via PCIe. PCIe Base Spec. Rev. 3.0 (Gen 3)[PCI10] is the latest specification with 8 Gbps as well as 2.5 Gbps in Gen 1 and 5 Gbps in Gen 2. Moreover, multiple lanes can be bundled in order to expand the bandwidth required for the I/O performance. Originally, PCIe mainly performs memory read/write operations between the Root Complex (RC) at the host side and the Endpoint (EP) at the device side. However, the actual behavior is simply point-to-point bidirectional packet communication. Therefore, we proposed PEARL, which can extend PCIe packet transfer to inter-node communication [HBM+10]. To realize this feature, we are developing a new chip which works as an intelligent communication hub for PCIe bus with a feature of "flipping" of Root Complex and End Point roles on any edge of a PCIe facility connected to the chip. This chip is named "PEACH2 (PCI Express Adaptive Communication Hub ver.2)" since the original prototyping was performed in another research project [Oe11].

Figure 21.7 briefly sketches the concept of PEACH2 and the direct communication between GPUs through the CPU memory. In the conventional GPU cluster, the communication between GPUs across the different nodes includes three copies as follows:

1. Copy from GPU memory to CPU memory through PCIe bus at the source node

2. Copy from CPU memory to another CPU memory through the network

3. Copy from CPU memory to GPU memory through PCIe bus at the destination node

PEACH2 can replace the network to PCIe, and it enables the direct communication between GPUs over the nodes with zero-copy by using PCIe technology entirely. This technology is named "True GPU Direct."

TCA is applied for the application demanding low latency and high bandwidth, and is adapted for the small-scale cluster, such as 8 to 16 nodes, since the hop count among the nodes increases as the number of nodes becomes larger. All the nodes in the TCA part

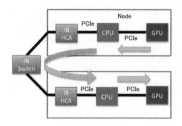 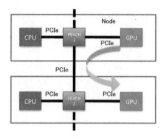

**FIGURE 21.7**: Difference between original GPU-GPU communication among nodes through CPU memory and network card (left) and Tightly Coupled Accelerators architecture with PEACH2 technology (right).

are also connected with InfiniBand similar to HA-PACS base clusters. Thus, the TCA part can provide the hierarchical network with the combination of both the local communication with high performance and the global communication with a large number of nodes for GPU application.

The purpose of TCA development is (1) investigate the technology to enable the direct communication over any PCIe device, and (2) application and algorithm development based on the TCA concept which enables ultra low latency communication especially required for strong scaling parallel processing in the near future of accelerated computing.

Figure 21.8 illustrates the block diagram of the PEACH2 chip. The PEACH2 chip includes four PCIe ports with Gen2 x8 lanes, internal memory, DMA controller, embedded processor, and DRAM interface. One PCIe port is dedicated to the connection to the host (CPUs and GPUs), and the other three ports can be used for communicating with the adjacent node. Internal memory is used for a temporary packet buffer. DMA controller provides chaining function for low-latency PCIe packet transfer. It enables the bulk transfer for several segments with discontiguous addresses. PEACH2 also employs an embedded processor which is used for monitoring the PCIe network and maintaining network connectivity by changing the routing table.

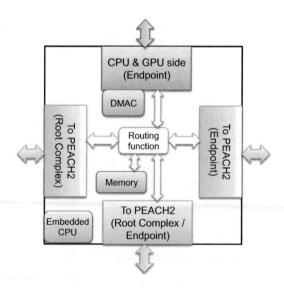

**FIGURE 21.8**: Block diagram of PEACH2 chip.

**FIGURE 21.9**: Photo of PEACH2 board. (The board consists of two layers at left, and there are two cable ports on the lower board.)

Currently, the PEACH2 chip is designed by Altera Stratix IV GX FPGA with four PCIe hard IPs. In addition, the PEACH2 board is implemented as the PCIe standard card, and tested in small-scale cluster. Figure 21.9 shows the photo of a PEACH2 board. The board is full-sized in PCIe specification with a PCIe edge connector and three PCIe cable connectors at the left side. It also has a DDR3 SO-DIMM memory, debug and management facilities, such as display module, Gigabit Ethernet port, and JTAG port.

TCA part will be delivered in October 2013 with an extension of HA-PACS base cluster and be called HA-PACS/TCA. We expect to provide additional performance of 350 TFLOPS at least by this extension, which extends the total performance of HA-PACS system to 1.15 PFLOPS peak.

## 21.12 Research and Development on Parallel Programming Language for Accelerating Devices

In the Center for Computational Sciences, University of Tsukuba, we have been developing a parallel programming language for accelerating devices such as GPU, named XcalableMP Accelerating Device Extension, or "XMP-dev" for short [LTO+11]. It is based on the original parallel programming language XcalableMP [NLBS10] for large-scale distributed memory systems toward post-petascale programming. XMP-dev is an extension of XcalableMP for a hybrid PC cluster, where each node is equipped with accelerated computing devices such as GPUs, many-core environments, etc. While XMP-dev is designed for a general accelerated computing environment, currently we have implemented the prototype compilers for CUDA and OpenCL.

### 21.12.1 XcalableMP

The details of XcalableMP (XMP) are described in [NLBS10], so here we explain only the essential XMP features required to understand XMP-dev.

XMP is a Partitioned Global Address Space (PGAS) style of language for describing large-scale scientific code for parallel systems with distributed memory architecture. With simplification for easy understanding, XMP is a directive-based parallelizing language with grammar similar to the grammar of OpenMP. The most important difference between XMP and OpenMP is that XMP supports a distributed memory system to provide data distribution and synchronization features as well as work sharing and task dispatching, whereas

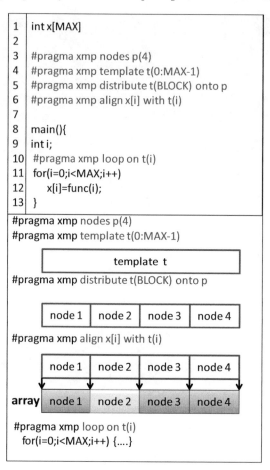

**FIGURE 21.10**: An example code segment of XMP.

OpenMP primarily focuses on task scheduling for multi-thread support by hardware-shared memory. It is possible to parallelize the target code with just a few changes of the original sequential code, thus significantly reducing the programming effort compared with many additional lines in MPI programming. The target systems of XMP are widely spread from small-sized PC clusters to massively parallel processors (MPPs). A reference implementation of version 1.0 with C language for a Linux PC cluster has already been published, and the implementation for the K Computer is underway now.

Figure 21.10 shows an example code segment in XMP. This figure shows data parallelization, which is executed on a PC cluster. First, the programmer states the "nodes" directive that declares the number of nodes that will execute the program. In this example, four nodes are used. Then the "template" directive describes the size and layout of the global data by using a virtual array called a template. In this case, we use the template $t$. The "distribute" directive is used to map the template $t$ to each node. In this case, the template $t$ is divided into four parts and mapped to the nodes. The "BLOCK" option means that each node gets a consecutive section of data. Finally, the "align" directive maps each distributed template to the array data. Here, an array named $x$ is distributed and mapped to the nodes and the elements of the partial array $x$ are allocated in the local memory of each node.

The "loop" directive describes how to map the work to each node. In this example, each node stores the calculated values in its local array $x$, which corresponds to a section of the virtual array *t*. More directives can be used, including the following: a reduction operation having the same meaning as that in OpenMP, or a "shadow" feature to declare the range of synchronized parts in the array data. "Shadow" is used to synchronize the nearest neighboring elements in a one-dimensional array, but even entire array elements can be declared as the synchronization target, which causes all-to-all communication when the elements are synchronized (this feature is called "full-shadow"). The programmer is responsible for taking care of the effect caused by shadow synchronization.

## 21.12.2 XcalableMP-dev (XMP-dev) Programming Model

XMP-dev is an XMP language extension designed to exploit thread-parallel execution on accelerators within the XMP framework. XMP-dev directives carry out typical data and work-sharing operations between the host and the device, such as the declaration of data in the device memory and data transport operations. As explained in Section 21.12.1, XMP directives enable data/task parallelization between nodes in a distributed memory system, whereas XMP-dev directives enable data/task parallelization between one or more acceleration devices. When programs are written using XMP-dev, XMP directives describe the distribution of data among the nodes, and on each node, XMP-dev directives parallelize the execution of the program between the host and device(s). This means that XMP-dev not only can be used to parallelize code that runs only on one accelerator-enhanced node, but also it can be used to parallelize code between nodes on a parallel system.

Figure 21.11 shows a parallelized program using four nodes of an accelerator-enhanced cluster using XMP-dev. XMP-dev directives are indicated by the "device" keyword. The accelerator-specific code is executed only when these XMP-dev directives are used. Since XMP-dev is an extension of XMP, we can use XMP directives, as shown in lines 3–6 to declare the number of nodes and to distribute the data. When executing accelerator-specific

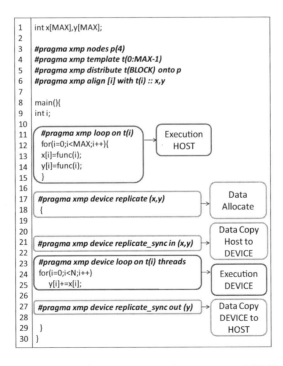

**FIGURE 21.11**: An example code segment of XMP-dev.

code, the directive "device replicate" declares what data will be distributed in the device's memory. The syntax is as follows:

```
#pragma xmp device replicate (list)
```

This pragma indicates that the device must allocate memory for the array in the `list`. This memory must first be allocated in the host memory, as shown in line 6 of Figure 21.10, because it is impossible to directly send data from another node to the device. The declared data are allocated only between lines 18 and 27, then are freed in line 29. By allocating memory only when needed and freeing it as soon as it is finished, we can efficiently use the limited memory of the device.

The "device replicate sync" directive is used to transport data between the host memory and the device memory. The syntax is as follows:

```
sync_clause ::= in (list) - out (list)
#pragma xmp device replicate_sync sync_clause
```

To use this directive, the data to be synchronized must be allocated in both the host memory and the device memory.

In this case, the data can be transported by using the "device replicate sync" directive. The keywords "in" and "out" declare whether the direction of data transport is "host to device" or "device to host," respectively. As stated in line 23, XMP-dev extends the "loop" directive in the XMP to describe the thread parallelism. The syntax is as follows:

```
#pragma xmp device loop on template
    loop-statement
```

When the directive is used, loop iteration is distributed among the threads by assigning iterations to the threads according to their index, and the XMP-dev compiler converts the serial code to code that can be executed on the accelerator. For example, loop iteration 1 (i.e., i=0) is assigned to thread number 1, and thread 1 executes one iteration of the loop.

### 21.12.3    HA-PACS and XcalableMP-dev

Currently, most GPU clusters are used by real applications with complicated programming styles such as the combination of MPI, OpenMP, and CUDA (or OpenCL), due to its hardware nature with distributed memory architecture and attached GPU devices in each node. It heavily reduces the productivity of application code development as well as requiring much cost of debugging and performance tuning. Since XcalableMP-dev combines the original XcalableMP's feature of easy programming on distributed memory system with GPU device offloading, the programmability and productivity of various fields of HPC coding will be greatly enhanced.

On HA-PACS, we have implemented XcalbaleMP-dev for CUDA [LTO⁺11] and OpenCL [NTL⁺12]. The real application coding by XcalableMP-dev has just been started, and we will apply this new programming method on various applications in CCS such as climate code, astrophysics, nuclear fusion, etc. Currently, the scalability with hundreds of nodes on HA-PACS is confirmed.

---

## Acknowledgments

The chapter author truly thanks all members of the Exascale Application Promotion Team and the Exascale System Development Team in the HA-PACS Project at the Center for Computational Sciences, University of Tsukuba.

# Part III

# Clouds and Grids in HPC

# Chapter 22

## Magellan: A Testbed to Explore Cloud Computing for Science

**Lavanya Ramakrishnan, Iwona Sakrejda, Shane Canon, Krishna Muriki, and Nicholas J. Wright**

*Lawrence Berkeley National Laboratory*

**Adam Scovel, Susan Coghlan, and Anping Liu**

*Argonne National Laboratory*

**Devarshi Ghoshal**

*Indiana University, Bloomington*

## 22.1    Overview

The Department of Energy's Magellan project was initiated in order to investigate the potential efficacy of cloud computing to address the computing needs of scientists funded by the DOE Office of Science. A significant part of the strategy to answering this question was the deployment of testbed systems at Argonne National Lab's Leadership Computing Facility (ALCF) and Lawrence Berkeley National Lab's NERSC Center. This chapter captures the aspects of this research-oriented testbed system. Many of the operational metrics that are discussed for other systems are not applicable since the testbed was not focused on providing production level services. We provide details about the purpose of the project and background information on cloud computing to help set the context. The Magellan project started in October 2009 and concluded in December 2011 and culminated in a final report [Mag] that provides a thorough description of the project, use cases, benchmarking, cost analysis, and a summary of key findings and recommendations. We encourage interested readers to review this report for further details.

Cloud computing has served the needs of enterprise web applications for the last few years. The term "cloud computing" has been used to refer to a number of different concepts (e.g., MapReduce, public clouds, private clouds, etc.), technologies (e.g., virtualization, Apache Hadoop), and service models (e.g., Infrastructure-as-a-Service [IaaS], Platform-as-a-Service [PaaS], Software-as-a-Service [SaaS]). Clouds have been shown to provide a number of key benefits including cost savings, rapid elasticity, ease of use, and reliability. Cloud computing has been particularly successful with customers lacking significant IT infrastructure or customers who have quickly outgrown their existing capacity.

The open-ended nature of scientific exploration and the increasing role of computing in performing science has resulted in a growing need for computing resources. There has been an increasing interest over the last few years in evaluating the use of cloud computing to address these demands. In addition, there are a number of key features of cloud environments that are attractive to some scientific applications. For example, a number of scientific applications have specific software requirements including OS version dependencies, compilers and libraries, and the users require the flexibility associated with custom software environments that virtualized environments can provide. An example of this is the Supernova Factory, which relies on large data volumes for the supernova search and has a code base which consists of a large number of custom modules [JMR+11]. The complexity of the pipeline necessitates having specific library and OS versions. Virtualized environments also promise to provide a *portable container* that will enable scientists to share an environment with collaborators. For example, the ATLAS experiment, a particle physics experiment at the Large Hadron Collider at CERN, is investigating the use of virtual machine images for distribution of all required software [CER]. Similarly, the MapReduce [GD04] model holds promise for data-intensive applications. Thus, cloud computing models promise to be an avenue to address new categories of scientific applications, including data-intensive science applications, on-demand/surge computing, and applications that require customized software environments. A number of groups in the scientific community have investigated and tracked how the cloud software and business model might impact the services offered to the scientific community. However, there is a limited understanding of how to operate and use clouds, how to port scientific workflows, and how to determine the cost/benefit trade-offs of clouds, etc., for scientific applications.

The goal of the Magellan project was to investigate how the cloud computing business model can be used to serve the needs of DOE Office of Science applications. Specifically, Magellan was charged with answering the following research questions:

- Are the open source cloud software stacks ready for DOE HPC science?

- Can DOE cyber security requirements be met within a cloud?

- Are the new cloud programming models useful for scientific computing?

- Can DOE HPC applications run efficiently in the cloud? What applications are suitable for clouds?

- How usable are cloud environments for scientific applications?

- When is it cost effective to run DOE HPC science in a cloud?

### 22.1.1 Timeline

Table 22.1 summarizes the timeline of key project activities. As the project began in late 2009, the focus was on gathering user requirements and conducting a user survey to understand potential applications and user needs. The core systems were deployed, tested and accepted in early 2010. Eucalyptus and Hadoop software stacks were deployed, and users were granted access to the resources shortly after the core systems were deployed. Other efforts in 2010 included early user access, benchmarking, and joint demos (MG-RAST and JGI) performed across the cloud testbed spanning both sites. A Eucalyptus 2.0 upgrade and OpenStack were provided to the users in early 2011. Further benchmarking to understand the impact of I/O and network interconnects was performed in spring and summer of 2011. The cloud portion of the Magellan project ended and a closeout user survey was performed in September 2011. Finally, support for Advanced Networking Initiative (ANI) research projects started in April 2011 and was completed in December 2011 with the end of the Magellan project.

## 22.2 System Overview

As part of the Magellan project, a dedicated, distributed testbed was deployed at Argonne 22.1 and NERSC 22.3. The two sites architected, procured, and deployed their testbed components separately, although the resources were chosen to complement each other. Deploying a testbed (versus acquiring services on existing commercial cloud systems) provided the flexibility necessary to address the Magellan research questions. Specifically our hardware and software were configured to cater to scientific application needs, which are different from the typical workloads that run on commercial cloud systems. For example, the ability to adjust aspects of the system software and hardware allowed the Magellan team to explore how these design points impact application performance and usability. In addition, the diverse user requirements for cloud computing, ranging from access to custom environments to the MapReduce programming model, led to a requirement for a dynamic and reconfigurable software stack. Users had access to customized virtual machines through OpenStack (at Argonne only) and Eucalyptus (at both sites), along with a Hadoop installation that allowed users to evaluate the MapReduce programming model and the Hadoop Distributed File System. Both OpenStack and Eucalyptus provide an application programming interface (API) that is compatible with the Amazon EC2 API, enabling users to port between commercial providers and the private cloud. Access to a traditional batch cluster environment was also used at NERSC to establish baseline performance and to collect data on workload

**TABLE 22.1**: Key Magellan project activities.

| Activity | Date |
| --- | --- |
| **Project start** | Sep 2009 |
| Requirements gathering and initial user survey | Nov 2009 - Feb 2010 |
| Core system deployed | Dec 2009 - Feb 2010 |
| Benchmarking of commercial cloud platforms | Mar - Apr 2010 |
| Early user access | Mar 2010 |
| Hadoop testing | Apr - Dec 2010 |
| Hadoop user access | May 2010 - Dec 2011 |
| Baseline benchmarking of existing private cloud platforms | May - June 2010 |
| Flash storage evaluation | June 2010 |
| Hardware as a service/bare metal access | Nov 2010 - Dec 2011 |
| Eucalyptus testing and evaluation | Dec 2009 - June 2010 |
| Joint science demo preparation and completion | Mar 2010 - June 2010 |
| OSG on Condor-G deployment | May 2010 |
| Nimbus deployment | June 2010 |
| GPFS-SNC evaluation | June 2010 - Dec 2010 |
| OpenStack testing | Dec 2010 - Mar 2011 |
| Eucalyptus 2.0 testing | Nov 2010 - Jan 2011 |
| Eucalyptus 2.0 deployed | Jan 2011 |
| Network interconnect and protocol benchmarking | Mar 2011 - Sep 2011 |
| User access OpenStack | Mar 2011 - |
| I/O benchmarking and forwarding work | Mar 2011 - Aug 2011 |
| GPU VOCL framework devel and benchmarking | Feb 2011 - Aug 2011 |
| ANI research projects | Apr 2011 - Dec 2011 |
| Closeout user survey | Sep 2011 |
| **Magellan cloud ends** | Sep 2011 |
| ANI 100G active | Oct 2011 |
| Virtualization overhead benchmarking | Sep 2011 - Nov 2011 |
| Magellan final report published | Dec 2011 |
| **Magellan ANI ends** | Dec 2011 |

characteristics for typical mid-range science applications that were considered suitable for cloud computing. The hardware and software deployed within the testbed are described in the following section.

## 22.3    Hardware Architecture

A key design criteria for the Magellan testbed was flexibility. For example, the testbed possessed commodity ethernet networks, as well as high-performance InfiniBand networks. The testbed also included novel or emerging hardware devices like flash storage and GPUs. In addition, Magellan was connected to the DOE-SC Advanced Networking Initiative (ANI), an effort to deploy a prototype 100 Gb national network.

IBM's iDataplex solution was chosen as the primary hardware platform at both Argonne and NERSC. The node configuration was similar at both sites, with each node typically having dual 2.66 GHz Intel Quad-core Nehalem processors and 24 GB or 48 GB of RAM. All nodes were configured with a Mellanox 40 Gb InfiniBand host-channel adapter (4x QDR). Management was done through a dedicated 1 Gb Ethernet network and power management was handled via IPMI. Nodes were also configured with a single 1 TB SATA drive.

**Argonne.** The Magellan testbed at Argonne includes computational, storage, and networking infrastructure (Figures 22.1 and 22.2). There is a total of 504 iDataplex nodes as described above. Beyond the core compute cloud, Argonne's Magellan has three additional types of hardware that one might expect to see within a typical HPC cluster: Active Storage servers, Big Memory servers, and GPU servers, all connected with QDR InfiniBand provided by two large, 648-port Mellanox switches.

There are 200 Active Storage servers, each with dual Intel Nehalem quad-core processors, 48 GB of memory, 8x500 GB SATA drives, 4x50 GB SSD, and a QDR InfiniBand adapter. The SSD was added to facilitate exploration of performance improvements for both multi-

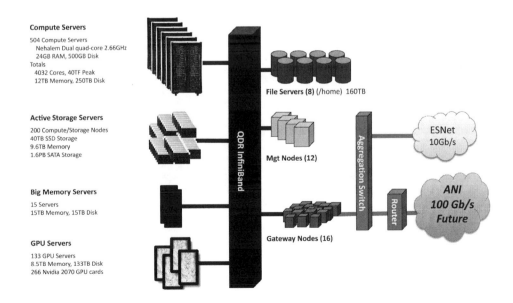

**FIGURE 22.1**: System architecture at Argonne.

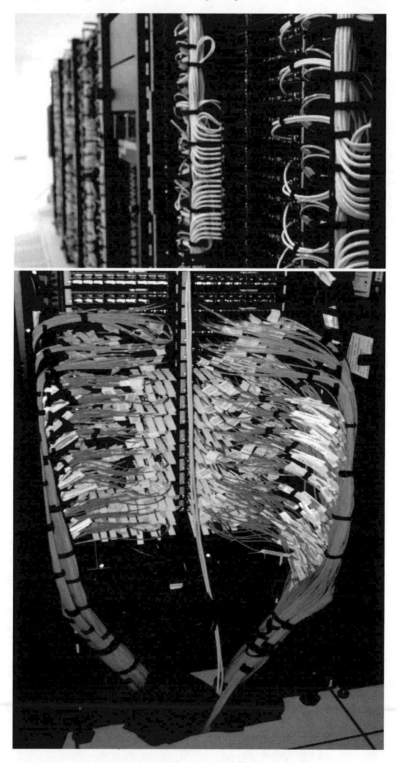

**FIGURE 22.2**: Photos of the Magellan system at Argonne. The top image shows the front of the compute cloud system as it is being installed. The bottom image shows the second IB rack after deployment of phase 2 hardware.

tiered storage architectures and Hadoop. These servers were also used to support the ANI research projects.

Accelerators and GPUs are becoming increasingly important in the HPC space. Virtualization of heterogeneous resources such as these is still a significant challenge. To support research in this area, Argonne's testbed was outfitted with 133 GPU servers, each with dual 6 GB NVIDIA Fermi GPU, dual 8-core AMD Opteron 2.0 GHz processors, 64 GB memory, 2x500 GB local disks, and a QDR InfiniBand adapter. Virtualization work on this hardware was outside of the scope of the Magellan project proper; see [JBD+, XBZ+] for details.

Several projects were interested in exploring the use of machines with large amounts of memory. To support them, 15 Big Memory servers were added to the Argonne testbed. Each Big Memory server was configured with 1 TB of memory, along with 4 Intel Nehalem quad-core processors, 2x500 GB local disks, and a QDR InfiniBand adapter. These were heavily used by the genome sequencing projects, allowing them to load their full databases into memory.

In total, the system has over 150 TF of peak floating point performance with 8,240 cores, 46 TB of memory, 1.4 PB of storage space, and a 100-gigabit (Gb) external network connection. A summary of the configuration for each node is shown in Table 22.2.

**TABLE 22.2**: Node configuration on the Argonne Magellan cluster. There are 852 nodes in the cluster.

| Feature | Description |
| --- | --- |
| Processor | Dual 2.66 GHz Intel Quad-core Nehalem (704 nodes), Quad Intel Nehalem Quad-core Nehalem (15 nodes), Dual 2 GHz 8-core AMD Opteron (133 GPU nodes) |
| GPUs | NVidia Fermi 2070 6 GB cards (133 nodes, 2 per node) |
| Memory | 24 GB (504 nodes), 48 GB (200 nodes), 64 GB (133 nodes), 1 TB (15 nodes) |
| Local Disk | 500 GB SATA (504 nodes), 8x500 GB SATA and 4x50 GB SSD (200 nodes), 2x500 GB SATA (148 nodes) |
| High Performance Network | 40 Gb InfiniBand (4X QDR) |
| Ethernet Network | On-board 1 Gb |
| Management | IPMI |

**NERSC.** The NERSC Magellan testbed also provided a combination of computing, storage, and networking resources (Figures 22.3 and 22.4). There are 720 iDataplex nodes as described earlier; 360 of them have local 1 TB drives. In addition, 20x400GB SSDs from Virident were acquired to explore the impact and performance of the SSD technology. The total system has over 60 TF of peak floating point performance. A summary of the configuration for each node is shown in Table 22.3.

The InfiniBand fabric was built using InfiniBand switches from Voltaire. Since the system is too large to fit within a single switch chassis, multiple switches are used, and they are connected together via 12x QDR links (120 Gb/s) configured as a fully connected mesh

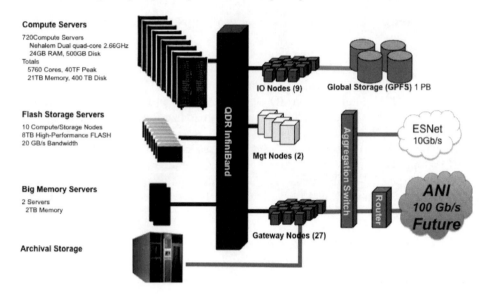

**FIGURE 22.3**: System architecture at NERSC.

**TABLE 22.3**: Node configuration on the NERSC Magellan cluster. There are 720 nodes in the cluster.

| Feature | Description |
| --- | --- |
| Processor | Dual 2.66 GHz Intel Quad-core Nehalem |
| Memory | 24 GB (48 GB in 160 nodes) |
| Local Disk | 1 TB SATA (in 360 nodes) |
| High Performance Network | 40 Gb InfiniBand (4X QDR) |
| Ethernet Network | On-board 1 Gb |
| Management | IPMI |

topology. This topology is less expensive than a traditional, full fat tree network yet still provides a relatively high bisection bandwidth.

In cooperation with vendors, a set of 66 nodes has been equipped in a dual port (IB, 10 GigE) cards and connected through a 10 GigE interface to compare and explore the RoCE protocol performance.

A high-performance scalable storage system was also deployed. The storage is configured to run IBM's high-performance parallel file system, GPFS. The storage hardware consists of four scalable storage units, each with 300 1 TB SATA drives. Each unit is capable of delivering over 5 GB/s of peak bandwidth. There is approximately 240 TB of RAID storage in each scalable unit. The total system provides almost 1 PB of total storage. The existing NERSC SAN was augmented to accommodate the additional storage. Nine Magellan I/O nodes are connected to the SAN and dedicated to providing GPFS services. The file system is mounted across the cluster and service nodes. These file systems are also shared across the center. The service nodes include the network nodes that were used for testing the Advanced Networking Initiative (ANI).

**FIGURE 22.4**: Photos of the Magellan system at NERSC. The top image shows the overhead cabling system which is suspended from the ceiling to seismically isolate the racks from each other. The lower image shows three racks of compute nodes. The seismic isolation platforms are visible below the racks.

## 22.4  System Software

Flexibility was a major objective in selecting the components of the software stack at the two sites. Table 22.4 summarizes the software stack at both sites. Since Magellan was to be used to explore a variety of cloud service models and programming models, it was critical that the software stack enable the system to be quickly reconfigured. Both sites used configuration tools often seen in the HPC computing world to provide flexible management of the software stacks. These tools allowed the sites to provision nodes in the cluster from traditional batch environments to Amazon EC2-like models to Hadoop-based MapReduce

**TABLE 22.4**: Software stack on Magellan.

| Layer | Argonne | NERSC |
|---|---|---|
| Hardware provisioning | bcfg and Heckle | xCAT |
| Operation system (Linux) version | Ubuntu | Scientific Linux |
| File system | GPFS | GPFS |
| Scheduler | - | MOAB |
| Virtualization software | Eucalyptus, OpenStack | Eucalyptus |
| Data-intensive tools | Hadoop | Hadoop |

clusters. With this, we were able to dynamically re-provision hardware between the different environments based on demand, energy consumption, utilization, as well as other factors.

Both sites deployed Hadoop as well. Hadoop has been attracting the attention of the scientific community for its power and simplicity as an analytical tool. From the user survey and discussions with users, Hadoop was cited as an area of high interest.

**Argonne.** The Argonne Magellan testbed uses the Argonne-developed tools bcfg2 [DL08, DBH06] and heckle to provide configuration management and advanced, bare-metal provisioning ("Hardware as a Service" or HaaS), respectively. Heckle allows users to dynamically provision different OS images across raw hardware quickly and easily, providing all the benefits of custom operating systems without the overheads and challenges of virtualizing specialized resources such as accelerators or high-performance networks.

Bcfg2 is a system management tool that provides facilities to build sophisticated configurations across large numbers of compute nodes. In the context of providing environments for HPC users on cloud resources, it fills the critical role of building customized per-user configurations in a flexible and inexpensive fashion. Heckle is a low-level node provisioning tool developed by Argonne as part of the Magellan project. It enables non-virtualized computational resources to be built on demand with user-provided configuration specifications. For example, users can request 10 nodes running a RedHat image; much as a cloud does, these nodes are built automatically with the user's image and the user receiving root access. Upon job completion, the nodes are deactivated, in preparation for the next user and associated software build. Both Bcfg2 and heckle are open-source, developed at Argonne, and form the basis for system management efforts on Magellan and elsewhere (used to manage several diverse testbed systems at Argonne, as well as used by many institutions around the world, from commercial companies such as LinkedIn to other national laboratories such as Oak Ridge National Laboratory). xCAT cluster management software [xCA] was used to provide access to the IPMI management interface to automatically power on and off nodes.

The core compute servers had numerous cloud software stacks installed in various stages of availability to the users during the project. These included Eucalyptus 1.6 and 2.0, OpenNebula, OpenStack and Nimbus. By the end of the project, these had converged to a large OpenStack public cloud, a small Nimbus cloud, and a small development OpenStack cloud. The public clouds were open to all users for science, development, and testing. Deploying many different cloud software stacks allowed Argonne to explore the state of open-source cloud software, and to evaluate status for usability, deployment, and support models. A portion of the Active Storage servers were configured as a persistent Hadoop cluster. A 100-node Hadoop cluster was provided to the users at Argonne. Although there was not heavy usage, it did allow the users to explore the Hadoop model for their applications. The remainder were configured as HaaS and were part of the raw provisioning pool, along with the GPU and Big Memory servers.

**NERSC.** Magellan at NERSC used a combination of xCAT and Adaptive Computing's Moab Adaptive Computing Suite to handle provisioning and resource management. The xCAT provisioning tool is an open source provisioning tool that is primarily maintained by IBM. xCAT supports a number of provisioning models and it can be controlled by the Moab scheduler to automate provisioning of resources based on demand. The Moab scheduler was used both to evaluate automatic provisioning as well as classic scheduling of traditional HPC workloads.

NERSC evaluated a number of software products associated with cloud computing. For example, NERSC deployed the Eucalyptus Cloud Software stack on portions of the Magellan testbed at NERSC. Both Eucalyptus 1.6 and 2.0 were tested. The size of the Eucalyptus testbed varied from 40 to 160 nodes and was used by a variety of science teams to explore cloud computing models. NERSC also evaluated the Hadoop Ecosystem. This included deployment of the Hadoop MapReduce framework and the Hadoop Distributed File System, as well as some of the associated tools (Pig and HBase). NERSC used the Hadoop version distributed by Cloudera for this testing. This version is heavily tested and includes a number of performance and bug fixes. NERSC tested Hadoop both with local SATA disk, SSD disk, and using a center-wide GPFS file system.

**Cybersecurity.** By necessity security was handled on a per-resource basis, and relied on established methods most applicable to the particular system in question. These methods can be generally categorized as user-access and network-level security.

*User Access.* Both Openstack and Eucalyptus rely on public-key encryption for virtual-cluster management and access. A public/private keypair and x509 certificate are generated for the user upon account creation, and is necessary for all interactions with the cluster API services. Missing, corrupted, or expired credentials are rejected outright, and considerable effort would be required to successfully forge or falsify them. Access to the virtual nodes themselves is enabled via injecting the user's public key into the nodes at the time of creation and launching a ssh server, which by default only accepts that key as valid authentication.

HaaS services varied greatly in the amount of security-awareness they provided. As such, it was necessary to place extra restrictions upon them. At Argonne, all access to HaaS infrastructure was secured behind a bastion host, which required the use of a cryptographic token for logon. Once logged in, access between the bastion host and individual nodes/services was secured using standard public-key authentication.

*Network Security.* Security was also implemented at the network level to ensure the safety of users' work. Individual users' privileges could be modified to allow or deny the opening of ports on a virtual node to the outside world, and could be further restricted with modification of the network gateway's configuration. Furthermore, at the time of a virtual node's instantiation, the only external access a user is given is via the aforementioned authenticated ssh channel.

Security between virtual networks was further strengthened by routing controls, which effectively isolated a user's virtual cluster from others. Along with the default authentication settings, this prevented users from accidentally or maliciously gaining access to other users' resources.

Unlike virtual services, HaaS resources were given no direct access to external networks. As previously mentioned, all inbound connectivity was mediated by a bastion host, and all outbound connectivity was routed through a gateway. This prevented users from making possibly harmful services accessible to the internet, while still allowing them to easily download data and install or upgrade necessary software packages. Standard security and intrusion-detection tools were installed on the gateway and bastion to log and notify administrators of any anomalous behavior.

## 22.5    Service Models

The term "cloud computing" covers a range of delivery and service models. The common characteristic of these service models is an emphasis on *pay-as-you-go* and elasticity, the ability to quickly expand and collapse the utilized service as demand requires. Thus new approaches to distributed computing and data analysis have also emerged in conjunction with the growth of cloud computing. These include models like MapReduce and scalable key-value stores like Big Table [CDG+06].

Cloud computing technologies and service models are attractive to scientific computing users due to the ability to get on-demand access to resources to replace or supplement existing systems, as well as the ability to control the software environment. Scientific computing users and resource providers servicing these users are considering the impact of these new models and technologies. In this section, we briefly describe the cloud service models and technologies to provide some foundation for the discussion.

Cloud offerings are typically categorized as Infrastructure as a Service (IaaS), Platform as a Service (PaaS), and Software as a Service (SaaS). Each of these models can play a role in scientific computing.

The distinction between the service models is based on the layer at which the service is abstracted to the end user (e.g., hardware, system software, etc.). The end user then has complete control over the software stack above the abstracted level. Thus, in IaaS, a virtual machine or hardware is provided to the end user and the user then controls the operating system and the entire software stack. We describe each of these service models and visit existing examples in the commercial cloud space to understand their characteristics.

### 22.5.1    Infrastructure as a Service

In the Infrastructure as a Service provisioning model, an organization outsources equipment including storage, hardware, servers, and networking components. The service provider owns the equipment and is responsible for housing, running, and maintaining it. In the commercial space, the client typically pays on a per-use basis for use of the equipment.

Amazon Web Services is the most widely used IaaS cloud computing platform today. Amazon provides a number of different levels of computational power for different pricing. The primary methods for data storage in Amazon EC2 are S3 and Elastic Block Storage (EBS). S3 is a highly scalable key-based storage system that transparently handles fault tolerance and data integrity. EBS provides a virtual storage device that can be associated with an elastic computing instance. S3 charges for space used per month, the volume of data transferred, and the number of metadata operations (in allotments of 1,000). EBS charges for data stored per month. For both S3 and EBS, there is no charge for data transferred to and from EC2 within a domain (e.g., the U.S. or Europe).

Eucalyptus, OpenStack, and Nimbus are open source software stacks that can be used to create a private cloud IaaS service. These software stacks provide an array of services that mimic many of the services provided by Amazon's EC2 including image management, persistent block storage, virtual machine control, etc. The interface for these services is often compatible with Amazon EC2 allowing the same set of tools and methods to be used.

We use Eucalyptus and OpenStack to set up a private cloud IaaS platform on Magellan hardware for detailed experimentation on providing cloud environments for scientific workloads. The IaaS model enables users to control their own software stack that is useful to scientists that might have complex software stacks.

IaaS is sometimes used to refer to provisioning of virtual machines specifically and "baremetal provisioning" is called Hardware as a Service (HaaS). The main distinction between this model and IaaS is that the user-provided operating system software stack is provisioned onto the raw hardware, allowing the users to provide their own custom hypervisor, or to avoid virtualization completely, along with the performance impact of virtualization of high-performance hardware such as InfiniBand. The other difference between HaaS and the other service models is that the user "leases" the entire resource; it is not shared with other users within a virtual space. With HaaS, the service provider owns the equipment and is responsible for housing, running, and maintaining it. HaaS provides many of the advantages of IaaS and enables greater levels of control on the hardware configuration.

### 22.5.2   Platform as a Service

Platform as a Service (PaaS) provides a computing platform as a service, supporting the complete life cycle of building and delivering applications. PaaS often includes facilities for application design, development, deployment and testing, and interfaces to manage security, scalability, storage, state, etc. Windows Azure, Hadoop, and Google App Engine are popular PaaS offerings in the commercial space.

Hadoop is an open-source software that provides capabilities to harness commodity clusters for distributed processing of large data sets through the MapReduce [DG04] model. The Hadoop streaming model allows one to create map-and-reduce jobs with any executable or script as the mapper and/or the reducer. This is the most suitable model for scientific applications that have years of code in place capturing complex scientific processes.

Hadoop provides a platform for managing loosely coupled data-intensive applications. Hadoop has been deployed on Magellan hardware to enable our users to experiment with the platform. PaaS provides users with the building blocks and semantics for handling scalability, fault tolerance, etc., in their applications.

### 22.5.3   Software as a Service

Software as a Service provides access to an end user for an application or software that has a specific function. Examples in the commercial space include services like SalesForce and Gmail. Science gateways or portals can also be viewed as providing a Software as a Service, since they typically allow remote users to perform analysis or browse data sets through a web interface. This model can be attractive since it allows the user to transfer the responsibility of installing, configuring, and maintaining an application and thus shields the end user from the complexity of the underlying software.

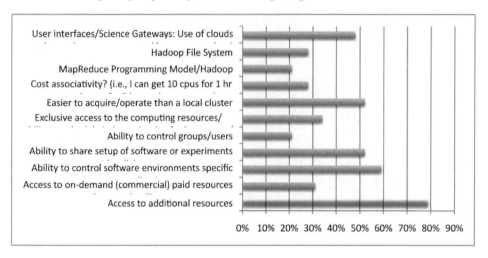

**FIGURE 22.5**: Features of cloud computing that are of interest to scientific users.

## 22.6    User Survey

We conducted a survey to understand the requirements and expectations of the user community. We requested NERSC users and other communities in DOE that were interested in cloud computing to detail their application characteristics and expectations from cloud computing. The survey was available through the NERSC Magellan website.[1] We asked our users to identify the features of cloud computing that were most attractive to them. Users were given several options and were allowed to select more than one category. Figure 22.5 shows the responses selected by our users. Access to additional resources was the most common motivation for most of our users and was selected by 79% of our respondents. A large number of users also wanted the ability to control software environments (59%) and share software or experiment setup with collaborators (52%), which is hard to do in today's supercomputing setup. Additionally, clouds were also attractive due to ease of operation compared to a local cluster (52%) and access to end users of science gateways (48%). A fraction of the users were interested in exploring the use of Hadoop and the MapReduce programming model and the Hadoop File System for their science problems.

## 22.7    Applications Characteristics

In this section we discuss application characteristics in cloud environments through discussion of select use cases from the Magellan project and our benchmarking efforts.

### 22.7.1    Use Cases

A diverse set of scientific applications have used the Magellan cloud testbed, resulting in significant scientific discoveries while helping to evaluate the use of cloud computing for

---

[1] http://magellan.nersc.gov

science. Early adopters of cloud computing have typically been scientific applications that are largely data parallel, since they are good candidates for cloud computing. These applications are primarily throughput-oriented (i.e., there is no tight coupling between tasks); the data requirements can be large but are well constrained; and some of these applications have complex software pipelines, and thus can benefit from customized environments. Cloud computing systems typically provide greater flexibility to customize the environment when compared with traditional supercomputers and shared clusters, so these applications are particularly well suited to clouds.

We outline select scientific case studies that have used Magellan successfully over the course of the project. Additional case studies are also available in the Magellan report [Mag]. The diversity of Magellan testbed setups enabled scientific users to explore a variety of cloud computing technologies and services, including bare-metal provisioning, virtual machines (VMs), and Hadoop. The Magellan staff worked closely with the users to reduce the learning curve associated with these new technologies. The case studies focus on the advantages of using cloud environments, and we identify gaps and challenges in current cloud solutions.

### 22.7.1.1   JGI Hardware Provisioning

Hardware as a Service (HaaS) offers one potential model for supporting the DOE's scientific computing needs. This model was explored early with Magellan when a facility issue at the Joint Genome Institute (JGI) led to their need for rapid access to additional resources. NERSC responded to this by allocating 120 nodes of Magellan to JGI.

Using ESnet's OSCARS [GRC+09] and Science Data Network, nine 1 Gb Layer 2 circuits were provisioned between NERSC's Oakland Scientific Facility (OSF) and the JGI Walnut Creek facility. In essence, the JGI internal network was extended 20 miles to the OSF. These two locations are adjacent on the ESnet Bay Area MAN (Metropolitan Area Network), and therefore there was ample bandwidth with relatively low latency. Dedicated switches at OSF were connected to the Layer 2 connection, and the allocated compute nodes were connected to this network. The InfiniBand network was disconnected on the allocated nodes to maintain isolation. OS provisioning was handled using JGI's existing management infrastructure, and the allocated nodes were booted over the Layer 2 network. As a result, the nodes had immediate access to all the critical data, databases, and account management services at JGI. This included accessing NFS file servers located in Walnut Creek. Within days, JGI users were running jobs on the allocated hardware. The hardware and network proved extremely stable. No changes were required on the part of the users—they simply submitted jobs to the existing Sun GridEngine scheduler as usual, and the jobs were transparently routed to the nodes in Magellan. This effort not only demonstrated the validity of hardware as a service, it enabled JGI to continue operations through a potential crisis with no impact on production sequencing operations.

While this demonstration was a success, the experience revealed several areas for improvement. Ultimately, true hardware as a service requires a nearly automated, on-demand ability to provision hardware and create the necessary network connections to remote resources. For example, the requirement to disconnect the InfiniBand network should be handled by software. This could potentially be addressed by disabling ports on the switch or in the subnet manager. Alternatively, virtualization could be used to create virtual machines that would aid in the separation of resources. Another improvement would be to automate the provisioning and configuration of the network. ESnet's OSCARS provides much of this capability, but it would need to be integrated with a resources manager like Moab or GridEngine. Eventually, one could envision a model where a system administrator at a DOE site would identify the need for more resources, and with a few simple commands could request resources from a cloud resource pool. The cloud scheduler would allocate the resources and communicate with OSCARS to provision the network link between the two distant sites. Finally, the nodes would be provisioned, either using a user-provided image or by directly booting from management services at the home site.

#### 22.7.1.2    E. coli

During the weekend of June 3–5, 2011, hundreds of scientists worldwide were involved in a spontaneous and decentralized effort to analyze two strains of *E. coli* implicated in an outbreak of food poisoning in Germany. Both strains had been sequenced only hours before and released over the internet. An Argonne and Virginia Tech team worked throughout the night and through the weekend to annotate the genomes and to compare them to known *E. coli* strains. During the roughly 48-hour period, many *E. coli* strains were annotated using Argonne's RAST annotation system, which used the Magellan testbed at ALCF to expand its compute capacity. Around the world, scientists were submitting additional *E. coli* genomes to the RAST servers to be annotated as word got out that DNA sequences were available. Additional backend computing instances were made available by the ALCF Magellan staff to keep up with demand for increased annotation. Such on-demand changes to handle the load and provide the fast turnaround were made possible by the Magellan cloud tools. This project was unique in that it utilized both bare-metal provisioning to leverage native hardware performance (provided by the Argonne bcfg2 and Heckle tools), as well as ALCF's OpenStack cloud for populating the databases.

Once the genomes were annotated, a comprehensive genome content analysis was done that required building molecular phylogenies (evolutionary trees) for each of the proteins in these new strains. These data sets enabled a detailed comparison to the nearly 200 strains of *E. coli* that are in the public databases. This comparative analysis was quickly published on the internet and made available to the community. Overall, work that normally would have required many months was completed in less than three days by leveraging the on-demand computing capability of the Magellan cloud. This effort demonstrated the potential value in using cloud computing resources to quickly expand the capacity of computational servers to respond to urgent increases in demand.

#### 22.7.1.3    STAR

STAR is a nuclear physics experiment that studies fundamental properties of nuclear matter from the data collected at Brookhaven National Laboratory's Relativistic Heavy Ion Collider. Previously, STAR has demonstrated the use of cloud resources both on Amazon and at other local sites [FGL10, LWGH10]. STAR used Magellan resources to process near-real-time data from Brookhaven for the 2011 run data. The need for on-demand access to resources to process real-time data with a complex software stack makes it useful to consider clouds as a platform for this application.

The STAR pipeline transferred the input files from Brookhaven to a NERSC scratch directory. The files were then transferred using *scp* to the VMs; and after the processing was done, the output files were moved back to the NERSC scratch directory. The output files were finally moved to Brookhaven, where the produced files were catalogued and stored in mass storage. STAR calibration database snapshots were generated every two hours. Those snapshots were used to update database information in each of the running VMs once per day. Update times were randomized between VMs to optimize the snapshot availability.

The STAR software stack was initially deployed on NERSC/Magellan. After two months of successful running, the software stack was expanded to a coherent cluster of over 100 VMs from three resource pools including NERSC Eucalyptus (up to 60 eight-core VMs), ALCF Nimbus cloud (up to 60 eight-core VMs), and ALCF OpenStack cloud (up to 30 eight-core VMs).

In summary, over a period of four months, about 18,000 files were processed, 70 TB of input data was moved to NERSC from Brookhaven, and about 40 TB of output data was moved back to Brookhaven. The number of simultaneous jobs over the period of time varied between 160 and 750. A total of about 25K CPU days or 70 CPU years was used for the processing.

The STAR data processing is a good example of applications that can leverage a cloud computing testbed such as Magellan. The software can be easily packaged as a virtual machine image, and the jobs within the STAR analysis also require little communication, thus having minimal impact from virtualization overheads. Using cloud resources enabled the data processing to proceed during the five months of experiments and to finish at nearly the same time.

There were a number of lessons learned. The goal was to build a VM image that mirrored the STAR reconstruction and analysis workflow from an existing system at NERSC. Building such an image from scratch required extensive system administration skills and took weeks of effort. Additionally, several days' effort was required when the image was ported to the ALCF Nimbus and OpenStack clouds. The image creator needs to be careful not to compromise the security of the VMs by leaving personal information like passwords or usernames in the images. Additionally, the image must be as complete as possible while limiting its size, since it resides in memory. Using cloud resources was not a turnkey operation and required significant design and development efforts. The team took advantage of on-demand resources with custom scripts to automate and prioritize the workflow.

### 22.7.1.4 Genome Sequencing of Soil Samples

Genome sequencing of soil samples from the Rothamsted Research Center in the UK, one of the oldest soil research centers with a controlled environment, off limits to farming and any other disturbances by humans, and reaching back 350 years, was performed jointly across both the ALCF and NERSC Magellan resources. The project's goal was to understand the impact of long-term plant influence (rhizosphere) on microbial community composition and function. For the joint Magellan demonstration, the project selected two distinct fields with two soil types (grassland and bare-fallow) and looked at the differences in microbial populations associated with different land management practices.

The project uses Argonne's MG-RAST metagenomics analysis software to perform the sequencing. Metagenomics uses shotgun sequencing methods to gather a random sampling of short sequences of DNA from community members in the source environment. MG-RAST provides a series of tools for analyzing the community structure and the proteins present in an environment. It also provides unique statistical tools including novel sequence quality assessment and sample comparison tools.

The joint demonstration utilized the testbeds at both sites and explored potential failover techniques within the cloud. The primary sequencing was done over a week using 150 nodes in ALCF's Magellan. Machines on ALCF's Magellan were intentionally failed to trigger automatic movement of the work onto replacement machines on the NERSC Magellan, allowing the computation to continue with only a slight interruption. The same base virtual machine image was used on both sets of resources. However, because of the difference in the cloud software stacks, this was not a simple port and required some changes to the image. All eight cores on each cloud node and about 40% of the available memory were used with each instance. The demonstration was a single run within the Deep Soil project and represents only 1/30th of the work to be performed.

Using the Magellan cloud, the project was able to dynamically utilize resources as appropriate, while continuing to work on algorithmic improvements. This demonstration showed the feasibility of running a workflow across both the cloud sites, using one site as a failover resource. The project had many challenges similar to STAR discussed above in terms of image management and application design and development.

### 22.7.2    Benchmark and Workload Analysis

We have performed a number of benchmarking experiments to understand the performance of applications in virtualized cloud environments as compared with traditional HPC systems. To understand which applications might work well in cloud environments, we conducted an exhaustive benchmarking study and workload analysis. Our results are discussed in greater detail elsewhere [Mag, JRM+10, RCM+11]; here we describe the key benchmarks.

We use standard benchmarks such as SPEC CPU, HPC-Challenge (HPCC) [DL05], and application benchmarks to understand how communication protocols impact performance and how they compare with the performance in virtualized environments. This approach enables us to determine the performance impact of the different protocols separate from the overhead from virtualization.

**SPEC CPU.** SPEC-CPU2006 is an intensive benchmarking suite made available by the Standard Performance Evaluation Corporation [SPE]. It is designed to stress the CPU, memory, and compiler of a given system for the purpose of acquiring general performance numbers. A total of 29 benchmarks were run in two passes on both the virtual machine and on raw hardware; the first pass used integer operations and the second pass used floating point operations. Only the time-to-solution is reported below.

At first glance, the results in Figure 22.6 seem to show greater performance for the virtualized machine; the most notable exception being MCF. This particular benchmark is noted as having been modified for increased memory cache performance. Two other benchmarks that show better performance on the raw hardware are MILC and CactusADM; these are also known as particularly memory-cache friendly applications. This leads us to believe that KVM hides the performance penalty associated with cache misses. As such, CPU cycles spent idle while an application replenishes its L2 cache are only added to the total runtime on hardware. Further investigation of the impact of the memory cache was out of the scope of this project. Other studies have shown the effects of memory performance in VMs [IHI11]

**HPCC.** In a previous study [RCM+12], we have used the High Performance Computing Challenge (HPCC) benchmark suite [DL05] to understand the communication characteristics of the different fabrics and protocols. Specifically, we used the two measures of latency and bandwidth from the three measures of network measurements in the HPCC suite: ping-pong, random-ring, and natural-ring. Ping-pong measures the point-to-point bandwidth. In random-ring each task simultaneously sends to a randomly selected partner. In natural-ring each task sends messages to another partner in its natural order. Ping-pong, natural-ring, and random-ring, in that order represent an increase in network contention. This allows us to understand the behavior of the interconnect under increasing load as well as if particular interconnects cope worse under load than others.

We ran the HPCC benchmark to understand the performance impact of the fabrics (InfiniBand, 10G) and protocols (InfiniBand, TCP, virtualization) between HPC and cloud resources. We measured the following on Magellan testbed: InfiniBand, TCP over Infini-Band, TCP over 10 G Ethernet, TCP over Ethernet with Virtualization, and TCP over 1 G Ethernet. Additionally, we also ran the tests on the Amazon Cluster Compute instance types, the specialized HPC offering from Amazon which uses 10 G Ethernet.

For ping-pong latency, InfiniBand shows the lowest latency and shows only a marginal increase with increased concurrency. The primary increase in latency occurs when switching to TCP over IB and the other configurations add only a small increase. The Amazon Cluster

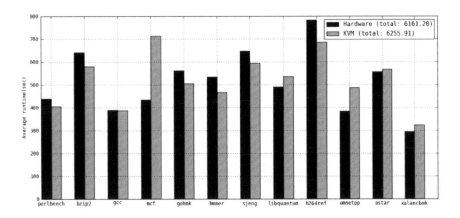

(a) Integer

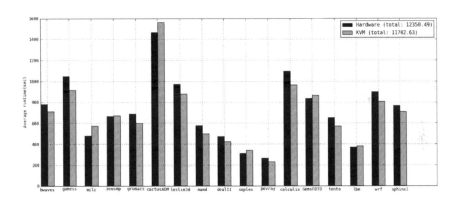

(b) Floating point

**FIGURE 22.6**: SPEC CPU benchmark results.

Compute and 10G - TCPoEth VM show a similar trend to their bare metal equivalent (10 G - TCPoEth) but have about a five times' increase in latency which is likely due to virtualization overhead. The random-ring latency shows a significant increase in latency for virtualized systems compared to its bare metal equivalent. Thus, increase in network contention seems to impact the virtualized environments significantly.

The ping-pong bandwidth demonstrates that the change in fabric (from IB to Ethernet) is minimal at lower concurrency but increases at higher concurrencies. Additionally, the Ethernet connection lacks the capability to handle large amounts of network connection, as demonstrated in the random-ring test. In general, performance of all interconnects decrease with contention and latency is affected more than the bandwidth.

**PARATEC and MILC performance.** For our application scaling performance study, we used two codes from the NERSC benchmark suite, PARATEC and MILC [RCM+12].

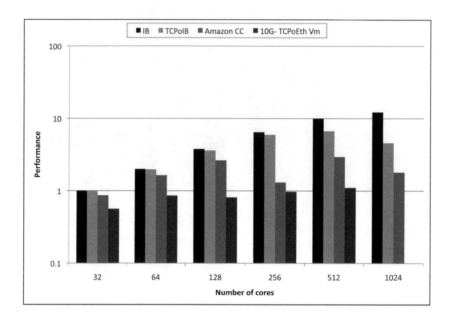

(a) PARATEC

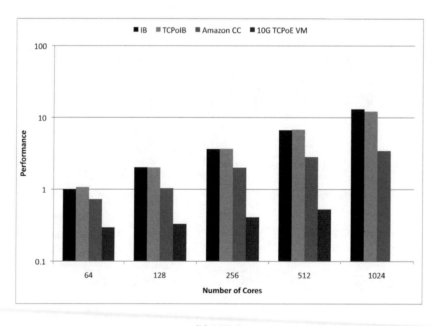

(b) MILC

**FIGURE 22.7**: Performance of a) PARATEC and b) MILC plotted on a log-log scale as a function of core count using several different interconnect technologies and/or protocols.

These two applications have differing communication characteristics, and therefore place different demands upon the network. [JRM+10].

MILC is a lattice gauge computation that is used to study Quantum ChromoDynamics (QCD). The problem size for this evaluation was $64 \times 32 \times 32 \times 72$ global lattice with 2 quark flavors, four trajectories, and 15 steps per trajectory, resulting in over 35,000 CG iterations per run.

PARAllel Total Energy Code (PARATEC) performs ab initio Density Functional Theory quantum-mechanical total energy calculations. The input set used here contains 686 silicon atoms in a diamond lattice configuration and runs for 20 conjugate gradient iterations.

Figure 22.7 shows the performance of PARATEC and MILC relative to the IB performance at the lowest core count. Specifically, we show the results for InfiniBand, TCP over InfiniBand, Amazon CC, and 10 G TCP over Ethernet virtual machine.

PARATEC is fastest with InfiniBand at all core counts. At higher core counts (512 and 1,024) the switch from IB to TCP affects the performance presumably since a larger number of smaller messages are being sent, which increases the TCP overhead. The 10 G TCPoEth VM displays the worst performance due to the overhead of virtualization. We also observed that the 10 G TCP over Ethernet VM did not track the trend of the 10 G TCP over Ethernet line (not shown in figure). In fact, as the concurrency increases, the virtualization overhead seems to increase. Amazon CC shows comparable performance to the 10 G TCP over Ethernet until 256 cores. We have limited insight into Amazon's network configuration but suspect the performance decrease at higher concurrency is due to virtualization overheads at higher core counts similar to the 10 G VMs on Magellan.

Figure 22.7(b) shows InfiniBand is also the fastest at all core counts for the MILC benchmark. At 1,024 cores, this application is still scaling well as compared to PARATEC. TCPoIB shows very similar performance to IB. The 10 G TCPoEth VM shows a performance that is almost $9\times$ worse than IB at 256 cores. Amazon CC shows a comparable performance to the 10 G TCP over Ethernet in this case presumably because the application is still scaling well.

The performance difference between interconnnects is lowest at low concurrency due to lower amounts of communication. As the application communicates more at higher concurrency, we see that the differences between the interconnect performances increase. This matches the trends in HPCC detailed above.

Scientific applications run at the highest concurrency that they can scale at in order to minimize the wall-clock time. A better interconnect can significantly affect the productivity gains for a scientist using a computing resource. The basic performance trends are similar to HPCC and at greater congestion at higher core counts the interconnect performance decreases considerably.

## 22.8 Storage, Visualization, and Analytics

Cloud computing technologies have largely evolved to process and store large data volumes of web and log data. Our earlier results have shown that the communication-intensive applications do poorly in virtualized cloud environments. However, there is limited understanding of the I/O performance in virtualized cloud environments. We perfomed a series of benchmarks to understand the I/O performance of scientific applications in these environments. We summarize the virtual machine I/O results in this section. More detailed results are available in [GCR11].

Hadoop has been used for processing large volumes of data. A key component of Hadoop is the Hadoop Distributed File System (HDFS) [SKRC10]. HDFS is a highly scalable, fault-tolerant file system modeled after the Google File System. The data locality features of HDFS are used by the Hadoop scheduler to schedule the I/O intensive *map* computations closer to the data. HDFS fundamentally differs from parallel file systems due to the underlying storage model. We outline the differences of HDFS with parallel file systems that are typically used in HPC systems for storage and discuss our benchmarking efforts.

### 22.8.1    Virtual Machine I/O

I/O performance is critical to understand for scientific applications especially for data-intensive applications. Scientific applications interface extensively with the storage model for reading input data, storing output data, for paging data when data may not fit in system memory, and for checkpointing. Many scientific applications running on HPC systems use parallel file systems such as Lustre or GPFS. These parallel file systems can stripe data across a large number of servers to provide scalability. Thus, it is important to understand the I/O performance users can expect in virtualized environments.

In previous work, we have studied the comparison of I/O performance on a range of storage options available in cloud environments [GCR11]. Each virtual machine comes with a local disk that is available for users to read and write their data. In addition, users can optionally mount a block store volume on the local disk. Our tests evaluated virtual environments both on Amazon as well as on the NERSC Magellan testbed. The performance in these virtual machines is between 20 and 100 MB/s and is significantly lower than what is achievable on NERSC scratch file systems (>2,500 MB/s). Amazon showed better I/O performance than our local VMs which is largely due to differences in hardware and software configurations.

The local disk on the instance performs better than the block store volumes on the VMs at NERSC. Amazon small instances show better local disk performance compared to the block store volumes and this could be attributed to the sharing of the network bandwidth across instances. On the other hand, block store volumes on extra-large instances show marginally better performance possibly due to higher network bandwidth associated with these types. Amazon's HPC offering cluster compute instances shows the best performance for EBS volumes and this is likely due to the 10 Gigabit Ethernet fabric they are connected to.

Read operations show similar trends. There is a fair amount of variability in the VM performance. I/O in a virtual machine is handled through a virtual machine monitor (VMM) or a privileged call for every I/O operation which is the cause of the degraded performance.

### 22.8.2    Hadoop Distributed File System

Table 22.5 shows a comparison of HDFS with parallel file systems such as GPFS and Lustre. HDFS fundamentally differs from parallel file systems due to the underlying storage model. HDFS relies on local storage on each node while parallel file systems are typically served from a set of dedicated I/O servers. Most parallel file systems use the POSIX interface that enables applications to be portable across different file systems on various HPC systems. HDFS on the other hand has its own interface requiring applications to be rewritten to leverage HDFS features. FUSE [FUS] provides a POSIX interface on top of HDFS but with a performance penalty.

TeraSort is a standard map/reduce application for Hadoop that was used in the terabyte sort competition. TeraGen generates the data, and TeraSort then samples the input data and uses map/reduce to sort the data in total order. HDFS and GPFS have been designed

**TABLE 22.5**: Comparison of HDFS with parallel file systems (GPFS and Lustre).

|  | HDFS | GPFS and Lustre |
|---|---|---|
| Storage Location | Compute Node | Servers |
| Access Model | Custom (except with Fuse) | POSIX |
| Typical Replication | 3 | 1 |
| Typical Stripe Size | 64 MB | 1 MB |
| Concurrent Writes | No | Yes |
| Performance Scales with | No. of Compute Nodes | No. of Servers |
| Scale of Largest Systems | O(10k) Nodes | O(100) Servers |
| User/Kernel Space | User | Kernel |

for largely different usage scenarios and it is difficult to do a quantitative performance comparison of the two systems. Each of these file systems has its own strengths for certain workloads. Our evaluation shows that the performance of GPFS shows a slight decrease in performance as the number of concurrent maps is increased. On the other hand, HDFS's performance significantly improves as the number of maps increases as HDFS is able to leverage the additional bandwidth available from disks in every compute node [FGCR12].

## 22.9 Facilities

### 22.9.1 The NERSC Magellan Facility

The Magellan system at NERSC was installed at the Oakland Scientific Facility in downtown Oakland, CA. NERSC first moved into the facility in 2000 and the facility houses all major NERSC systems. The facility underwent extensive seismic retrofitting prior to NERSC occupying the facility. The facility has 9 MW of electrical capacity but this can be expanded up to 12 MW of power with the installation of additional switch gear. During the installation of Magellan, the center was upgraded to provide additional electrical and cooling capacity. The facility has a 3 foot raised floor capable of supporting 250 lbs per sq ft.

The Magellan system was optimized to require minimal floor space and require as little additional cooling infrastructure as possible. This was one reason for the selection of the IBM iDataplex product line which is compact and energy efficient. In addition, NERSC installed water cooled doors. This allowed the rows to be arranged in a configuration where the exhaust air from one row was directed into the input side of the adjacent row, versus the typical hot aisle, cold aisle configuration. The water cooled doors operate with enough efficiency that the exhaust air temperature is actually cooler than the input temperature, even under peak load. The last row of compute node racks exhausts chilled air into racks containing standard server racks without water cooled doors as well as disk racks. The exhaust from these racks exhaust into an air handling unit. The Magellan system is physically combined with another system, Carver, which was purchased at the same time under a common contract. The combined systems are composed of fourteen iDataplex racks, nine of which were for Magellan and five of which were for Carver. In addition, there were five standard 19" 42U racks that housed login nodes, IO servers, and interconnect switches. The combined system used only 465 sq ft.

Another unique aspect of the mechanical system for NERSC's Magellan was the use of return water as input to the cooling distribution units (CDUs). The CDUs distribute the chilled water to the rear-door heat exchangers through a series of manifolds. At NERSC, the return water from the adjacent Franklin system was still sufficiently cool that it could be used as input water for the Magellan cooling infrastructure. This novel design allows NERSC to operate more efficiently since a higher $\Delta T$ can be attained between the chilled and return water.

The Oakland Scientific Facility is located in a seismically active region. All NERSC systems are installed with some manner of seismic protection. The Magellan system was installed on seismic isolation platforms, ISO-Base, manufactured by WorkSafe Technologies. This isolation system allows the computer system to remain stationary while the ground moves underneath during a seismic event. The system is capable of up to 7.7" of lateral movement. The cable trays between rows are suspended from the ceiling so that they are decoupled from compute racks. This allows the rows to move independently. The cable trays and seismic isolation system can be seen in Figure 22.4.

## 22.9.2    The ALCF Magellan Facility

Magellan at the Argonne Leadership Computing Facility (ALCF) was installed in the 25,000 sq ft datacenter in the Theory and Computing Sciences building at Argonne National Laboratory. This two-year-old datacenter has a raised floor sitting 4 feet above the concrete floor, which sits on compacted earth. The mechanical rooms holding the supporting conventional facility infrastructure (power, UPS, AHUs, etc.) are located to either side of the datacenter. The TCS has 20 MW of electrical capability in a redundant configuration (40 MW in a non-redundant configuration). The Magellan hardware installed into the TCS datacenter was able to utilize existing power and cooling infrastructure. This allowed the project to perform the facility upgrades (UPS, PDUs, air-cooling) during the first year of the project without delaying the installation of the core compute cloud. These upgrades included the installation of a 1,300-ton chiller and cooling tower at the Argonne Chilled Water Plant (CWP). Overall, the Magellan equipment provided no major challenges for the existing facility infrastructure.

Magellan's compute, active storage, gpus, big memory systems, and infrastructure support encompassed less than 1,000 SF in the south half of the datacenter. This included the 100 Gbit ANI switches, as well as the InfiniBand network. With the exception of the core compute cloud, which were IBM iDataPlex, the Magellan hardware was in standard 19" 42U racks. The iDataPlex racks are in what are basically 19" racks but turned 90 degrees. None of the racks was dense enough to require additional floor support.

The air cooling in the TCS is very efficient and air flow and pressure under the floor were more than adequate to cool all racks, including the GPUs (which had two NVIDIA Fermi adapters in each 1U server) and the dense iDataPlex racks. No special cooling mechanisms were required. The power for the equipment was configured to utilize the receptacles standardized for the TCS datacenter, and the power requirements were not exceptional.

To minimize the energy usage associated with producing chilled liquid to support the air handling units (AHUs), a water side economizer design is used for all ALCF cooling systems installed at the CWP. This maximizes free cooling capabilities when weather conditions are favorable. The installed oversized cooling towers increase the capacity of chilled water that could be produced via free cooling operation. Multiple blended modes were also designed into the CWP control sequences, allowing for partial free cooling and centrifugal chiller cooling operation simultaneously during high demand load scenarios. The 1,300-ton chillers currently installed at the CWP are high efficiency chillers with 0.571 KW/ton performance at max load conditions. During days in which a 100% of the CWP capacity can be produced through free cooling modes, the chillers can be bypassed resulting in 17,820 KW-hr saved per day. During the winter season, when temperatures allow for optimal free cooling (December through March) the CWP can potentially avoid using 2,174,040 KW-hr by not operating the chillers.

## 22.10   Summary

Cloud computing has gained traction in the last few years in serving the needs of commercial applications, especially web applications. The goal of the Magellan project funded through the U.S. Department of Energy (DOE) Office of Advanced Scientific Computing Research (ASCR) was to investigate the role of cloud computing for scientific workloads. The Magellan project adopted an *application-driven* approach to evaluate what performance and reliability applications can expect in cloud environments, the stability of current private cloud software, which user support models are best suited to cloud solutions, any security implications in these environments, the use of the MapReduce programming model and usability of these environments, as well as cost efficiency of the cloud business model. In addition to answering computer science research questions, Magellan resources played a key role in producing important science results for a diverse set of projects including MG-RAST (a metagenomics analysis server), the Joint Genome Institute, the STAR experiment at the Relativistic Heavy Ion Collider, and the Laser Interferometer Gravitational Wave Observatory (LIGO).

The Magellan final report [Mag] details the work that was performed during the project, along with the findings and recommendations of the project. There were many diverse findings, the key ones are discussed below.

### 22.10.1   Cloud Environments

HPC cluster software environments have been around for many years and are stable, scalable, and capable of being tuned to provide exceptionally high performance. The open-source virtualized cloud software stacks are much younger and, as a result, they are not as stable, scalable, or high-performance. These software stacks would greatly benefit from additional development, hardening, testing, and customization to support standard HPC policies and scientific workload needs. Beyond the lack of maturity of the open-source cloud software stacks, these environments present some unique security challenges. User-controlled images, dynamic networks, and the transient nature of virtual machines expose additional security risks compared to traditional DOE Center usage models. Constant monitoring and capturing critical system events and logs, coupled with running an intrusion detection system, can mitigate some, but not all, of these risks. However, there is a need for new approaches in order to fully support production use of virtualized cloud software stacks.

For users of these virtualized cloud environments, the support that they have come to expect from the HPC cluster resource providers — management of the complex software stacks, support for code optimizations to leverage the hardware benefits, etc. — now falls on the user. The cloud model provides them the flexibility of configuring their own software stacks but this is often complex and tedious and requires some level of system administration expertise. To efficiently use cloud software stacks, additional training is required, and a new support model that addresses specific user support needs, including providing base images, guiding users through complex tasks, and maintenance of the images, will be needed.

### 22.10.2    Applications

Applications with minimal communication and I/O are able to achieve similar performance in cloud environments as HPC environments. The performance impact for HPC applications comes from the absence of high bandwidth, low latency interconnects in virtualized environments. Thus a majority of current DOE HPC applications even in midrange concurrencies is unlikely to run efficiently in today's cloud environments. Similarly, I/O intensive applications take a substantial hit when run inside virtual environments.

Cloud programming models such as MapReduce and the resulting ecosystem show promise for addressing the needs of many data-intensive and high-throughput scientific applications. However, current tools have gaps for scientific applications. The MapReduce model emphasizes the data locality and fault tolerance that are important in large systems. Thus there is a need for tools that provide MapReduce implementations which are tuned for scientific applications.

Current cloud tools do not provide an out-of-box solution to address application needs. There is significant design and programming required to manage the data and workflows in these environments. Virtual machine environments require users to configure and create their software images with all necessary packages. Scientific groups will also need to maintain these images with security patches and application updates. There exist a number of performance, reliability, and portability challenges with cloud images that users must consider carefully. There are limited user-side tools available today to manage cloud environments.

### 22.10.3    Cost Model

One way clouds can achieve cost efficiency is though consolidation of resources. This typically leads to higher utilization, improved operational efficiency, and lower acquisition cost through increased purchasing power. If one looks across the scientific computing landscape within DOE there is a variety of models for how scientists access computing resources. These cover the full range of consolidation and utilization scales. At one end of the spectrum is the small group or departmental cluster. These systems are often under-utilized and represent the best opportunity to achieve better efficiency. Many of the DOE National Laboratories have already taken efforts to consolidate these resources into institutional clusters operating under a variety of business models (institutionally funded, buy-in/condo, etc.). In many ways, these systems act as private clouds tuned for scientific applications and effectively achieve many of the benefits of cloud computing. DOE HPC centers provide the next level of consolidation, since these facilities serve users from many institutions and scientific domains. This level of consolidation is one reason why many of the DOE HPC centers operate at high levels of utilization.

Cost-saving benefits from cloud computing depends on a number of factors and will need to be analyzed carefully for each scenario. This was noted in NIST's draft document on Cloud Computing, "Cloud Computing Synopsis and Recommendations" [NIS], which stated, *"Whether or not cloud computing reduces overall costs for an organization depends on a careful analysis of all the costs of operation, compliance, and security, including costs to migrate to and, if necessary, migrate from a cloud."*

## 22.10.4 Conclusion

Clouds have certain features that are attractive for scientific groups needing support for on-demand access to resources, sudden surges in resource needs, customized environments, periodic predictable resource needs (e.g., monthly processing of genome data, nightly processing of telescope data), or unpredictable events such as computing for disaster recovery. Cloud services essentially provide a differentiated service model that can cater to these diverse needs, allowing users to get a virtual private cluster with a certain guaranteed level of service. Clouds are also attractive to high-throughput and data-intensive workloads that do not fit in current-day scheduling and allocation policies at supercomputing centers. Before switching to clouds, a facility should consider whether the scientific needs could be met by adopting and integrating features of cloud computing into their operations in order to support more diverse workloads and further enable scientific discovery. This includes mechanisms to support more customized environments, but also methods of providing more on-demand access to cycles. This could be achieved by: a) maintaining idle hardware at additional costs to satisfy potential future requests, b) sharing cores/nodes typically at a performance cost to the user, and c) utilizing different scheduling policies such as preemption. Providing these capabilities would address many of the motivations that lead scientists to consider cloud computing while still preserving the benefits of typical HPC systems which are already optimized for scientific applications.

Cloud computing is essentially a business model that emphasizes on-demand access to resources and cost-savings through consolidation of resources. Overall, whether cloud computing is suitable for a certain application, science group, or community depends on a number of factors. As NIST's document said,

> *Inherently, the move to cloud computing is a business decision in which the business case should consider the relevant factors some of which include readiness of existing applications for cloud deployment, transition costs and life-cycle costs, maturity of service orientation in existing infrastructure, and other factors including security and privacy requirements.*

# Chapter 23

## FutureGrid: A Reconfigurable Testbed for Cloud, HPC, and Grid Computing

**Geoffrey C. Fox, Gregor von Laszewski, and Javier Diaz**

*Pervasive Technology Institute, Indiana University*

**Kate Keahey**

*Argonne National Laboratory*

**Jose Fortes and Renato Figueiredo**

*University of Florida*

**Shava Smallen**

*San Diego Supercomputer Center*

**Warren Smith**

*Texas Advanced Computing Center*

**Andrew Grimshaw**

*University of Virginia*

## 23.1   Overview

The FutureGrid project [vLFW+10] mission is to enable experimental work that advances

- innovation and scientific understanding of distributed computing and parallel computing paradigms,

- the engineering science of middleware that enables these paradigms,

- the use and drivers of these paradigms by important applications, and

- the education of a new generation of students and workforce on the use of these paradigms and their applications.

The implementation of the mission includes

- distributed flexible hardware with supported use,

- identified Infrastructure as a Service (IaaS) and Platform as a Service (PaaS) core software with supported use,

- a growing list of software from FutureGrid partners and users, and

- educational outreach.

Thereby the FutureGrid project provides a capability that makes it possible for researchers to tackle complex research challenges in computer and computational science related to the use and technology of high-performance computing (HPC) systems, grids [FK99], and clouds [AFG+09, KH11]. Topics range from programming models, scheduling, virtualization, middleware, storage systems, interface design and cybersecurity, to the optimization of grid-enabled and cloud-enabled computational schemes for researchers in astronomy, chemistry, biology, engineering, atmospheric science, and epidemiology.

### 23.1.1   Sponsor/Program Background

FutureGrid [wwwb] is sponsored by the National Science Foundation under Grant No. 0910812 [nsf09] to Indiana University for "FutureGrid: An Experimental, High-Performance Grid Test-bed." FutureGrid forms part of NSF's national high-performance cyberinfrastructure XSEDE [xse12]. It increases the capability of the XSEDE to support innovative computer science research requiring access to lower levels of the grid software stack and the networking software stack and to virtualization and workflow orchestration tools as well as new programming models such as MapReduce [DG08]. As it supports interactive use, it is well suited for testing and supporting distributed system and scientific computing classes. Education and broader outreach activities include the dissemination of curricular materials on the use of FutureGrid, prepackaged FutureGrid virtual machines (appliances) configured for particular course modules, and educational modules based on virtual appliance networks and social networking technologies [SBC+03, BFLK11].

Partners in the FutureGrid project include U. Chicago, U. Florida, San Diego Supercomputer Center - UC San Diego, U. Southern California, U. Texas at Austin, U. Tennessee at Knoxville, U. Virginia, T-U. Dresden, and Grid5000 [imp12b]. These cover hardware, software, and benchmarking.

### 23.1.2 Historical Aspects of Clouds - Grids - HPC

One of the unique aspects of FutureGrid is that it is targeted not only toward the use of high-performance computing but also toward the integration of clouds and grids. The concepts from these areas are strongly interconnected and can be put in a historical context as shown in Figure 23.1.

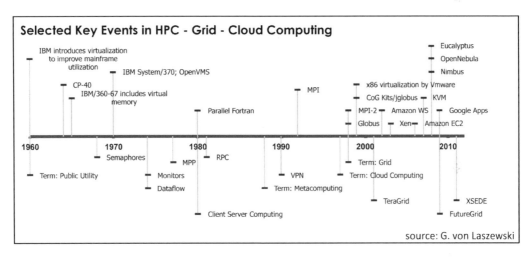

**FIGURE 23.1**: Selected key events in HPC, grid, and cloud computing.

## 23.2 Hardware Resources

FutureGrid (FG) is a national-scale grid and cloud testbed facility that includes a number of computational resources at distributed locations (see Table 23.1). The FutureGrid network is unique and can lend itself to a multitude of experiments specifically for evaluating middleware technologies and experiment management services [vLFW+10]. This network can be dedicated to conduct experiments in isolation, using a network impairment device for introducing a variety of predetermined network conditions. Figure 23.2 depicts the network infrastructure; Table 23.1 lists computational resources; Table 23.2 the storage resources. All network links within FutureGrid are dedicated (10 GbE lines for all but to Florida, which is 1 GbE), except the link to TACC. The significant number of distinct systems within FutureGrid provides a heterogeneous distributed architecture and are connected by high-bandwidth network links supporting distributed system research. One important feature to note is that some systems can be dynamically provisioned; e.g., these systems can be reconfigured when needed by special software that is part of FutureGrid with proper access control by users and administrators. A Spirent H10 XGEM Network Impairment emulator [imp12c] is colocated with the core router [jun12], a central resource to introduce network latency, jitter, loss, and errors to network traffic within FutureGrid.

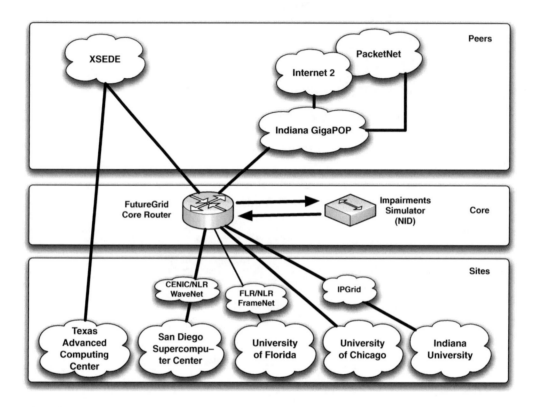

**FIGURE 23.2**: Network infrastructure of FutureGrid.

## 23.3   Software Services

In order for FG to operate we have to conduct a number of activities related to developing, deploying, and supporting the software for FG.

The goal set by FG is to provide a "an experimental Grid, Cloud, and HPC testbed." This goal naturally has a direct impact on our software design, architecture, and deployment. Hence, we revisit some of the elementary requirements influenced by the user community, various access models and services, and the desire to be able to conduct a variety of reproducible experiments. These requirements include the following:

**Support a Diverse User Community.** As part of our initial investigations, we have identified a number of different user communities that will benefit from a testbed such as FG. Naturally, the desire to support these communities governs our software design and the access to FG in general. We support the following communities:

**TABLE 23.1**: Current compute resources of FutureGrid as of April 2012.

| Name | System Type | Nodes | CPUs | Cores | TFLOPS | RAM GB | Site |
|------|-------------|-------|------|-------|--------|--------|------|
| india | IBM iDataplex | 128 | 256 | 1,024 | 11 | 3,072 | IU |
| hotel | IBM iDataplex | 84 | 168 | 672 | 7 | 2,016 | UC |
| sierra | IBM iDataplex | 84 | 168 | 672 | 7 | 2,688 | SDSC |
| foxtrot | IBM iDataplex | 32 | 64 | 256 | 3 | 768 | UF |
| alamo | Dell PowerEdge | 96 | 192 | 768 | 8 | 1,152 | TACC |
| xray | Cray XT5m | 1 | 168 | 672 | 6 | 1,344 | IU |
| bravo | HP Proliant | 16 | 32 | 128 | 1.7 | 3,072 | IU |
| delta | GPU Cluster | 16 | 32 | 192 | TBD | 3,072 | IU |
| | | | | 14,336* | | | |
| **Total** | | **457** | **1,080** | **4,384** | **>43.7** | **17,184** | |
| | | | | **14,336*** | | | |

*GPUS

**TABLE 23.2**: Storage resources of FutureGrid as of April 2012.

| System Type | Capacity (TB) | File System | Site |
|-------------|---------------|-------------|------|
| Xanadu 360 | 180 | NFS | IU |
| DDN 6620 | 120 | GPFS | UC |
| Sunfire x4170 | 96 | ZFS | SDSC |
| Dell MD3000 | 30 | NFS | TACC |
| IBM dx360 M3 | 24 | NFS | UF |

- *Application developers* that investigate the use of software and services provided by FG;

- *Middleware developers* that investigate the development of middleware and services for cloud and grid computing;

- *System administrators* that investigate technologies that they wish to deploy into their own infrastructure;

- *Educators* that like to expose their students to software and services to cloud and grid computing technologies as offered on the FG; and

- *Application users* that like to test out services developed by application and middleware developers.

To support this diverse community we have identified a number of key requirements we will be focusing on as part of FutureGrid.

**Support a Shifting Technology Base.** One of the observations that motivated FG is the rapidly developing technologies in the cloud and grid that may have profound impact on how we develop the next generation of scientific applications keeping these new developments in mind. The introduction of virtualization [AA06, CB09, cC05], Infrastructure as a Service (IaaS), and Platform as a Service (PaaS) paradigms

[LKN+09, KH11] calls for the ability to have access to software tools and services that allow a comparison of these paradigms with traditional HPC methodologies.

**Support a Diverse Set of Interface Methods.** Based on this technology shift and the interest posed by the various user communities to have easy interfaces to a testbed, we need to develop, as part of our software activities, appropriate interface tools and services. The interfaces include command line tools, APIs, libraries, and services. In addition, many users would like access to these new technologies through portals or GUIs.

**Support a Diverse Set of Access Methods.** While in previous decades the focus has been to provide convenient libraries, tools, and Web services we currently see an expansion into infrastructure and platform as services. Thus, a new generation of tools and services is provided as abstractions to a higher level of services, potentially replacing the traditional OS. Thus, not only will we offer access to Infrastructure as a Service (IaaS) framework, but we will also invest in providing PaaS endpoints, thereby allowing access to a new kind of abstraction.

**Support a Diverse Set of Access Services.** Due to the rapid development of new tools, services, and frameworks within the grid and cloud communities, it is important to facilitate a multitude of such environments. This support includes access to IaaS frameworks such as Nimbus [wwwc], Eucalyptus [wwwf], OpenNebula [wwwg], and OpenStack [wwwh]; PaaS frameworks such as Hadoop [wwwa]; and additional services and tools such as Unicore [OR02] and Genesis II [imp12a] that are provided and supported by the FG team members. Hence, users will have the ability to investigate a number of different frameworks as part of their activities on FG.

**Support Traditional Services.** We provide a number of additional services that users are accustomed to. This includes high-performance computing services [Com12], but also access to backup and storage. Naturally, we provide services for user support as part of a portal with access to information including a ticket system.

**Support Persistent Services and Endpoints.** One of the potential assets of FG is the ability to expose a number of students and practitioners to the new frameworks offered. However, the entry to set up such systems may have to be low in order to interest others in using such technologies. Hence, it is important to offer a number of persistent services and endpoints of such frameworks. Furthermore, we must make it easy for the teachers and administrators of FG to manage membership and access rights to such endpoints. In addition, we are interested in providing a number of "standard" images for educational purposes that can be used for teaching about particular aspects.

**Support Raining/Dynamic Provisioning.** As we are interested not only in offering a single, preinstalled OS or IaaS framework, we must provide additional functionality to reassign service nodes to a particular framework. To support this implicit move of resources to different services, we need to offer dynamic provisioning within FG not only within an IaaS framework, such as Nimbus, Eucalyptus, or OpenStack, but also any OS we choose. Furthermore this concept can be expanded to provision additional platforms and services. Hence, we use the term "raining" instead of just dynamic provisioning to indicate that we strive to dynamically provision not only on the OS level but also on the service and platform level [vLFW+10]. This combination will allow us to provide efficient assignment of resources to services governed by user needs. Thus, if there is no demand for running Eucalyptus staged images, the resources devoted to the Eucalyptus cloud can be de-registered and assigned to a different service. An additional aspect of our "rain" tool that we are developing is to specify the mapping onto specific resources, allowing us to compare services on the same hardware.

**Support a Viral User Contribution Model.** User contributions are possible at several levels. First is the development of shared images that are instantiated as part of an IaaS framework. Second is the development of middleware, either in the IaaS or PaaS models, that can be rained onto FG. Third is the creation of workflows that utilize a combination of the services offered as part of sophisticated experiment workflows, which we will explain in more detail later. Fourth is the contribution of educational material.

One of the important features to recognize is that FG distinguishes itself from current available systems. This includes traditional compute centers such as XSEDE [xse12], but also well known IaaS offerings, such as Amazon [Amaa].

In contrast to Amazon, we provide alternatives to the IaaS framework, but the biggest benefit stems from two unique features of FG. In FG we intend to allow the mapping of specific resources as part of the service instantiation. Thus, we can measure more realistically performance impacts of the middleware and the services developed by the FG testbed user. Furthermore, we allow authorized users a much greater level of access to resources by allowing the creation of images that not only can be placed in a virtual machine (VM) but also can be run on the "bare" hardware.

A big distinction between XSEDE and FG is that FG provides a more variable software stack and services. Traditionally, supercomputing centers that are part of XSEDE focus on large-scale, high-performance computing applications while providing a well-defined software stack. Access is based on job management and traditional parallel and distributed computing concepts. Virtual machine staging on XSEDE is not yet deemed to be a major part of its mission. FG is more flexible in providing software stacks to be dynamically adapted by the users.

## 23.3.1   Architecture Overview

To support our requirements, we have devised a flexible software architecture enabling us to gradually introduce and expand components in support of our mission. We distinguish the following components:

**Fabric:** The fabric layer contains the hardware resources, including the FG computational resources, storage servers, and network infrastructure including the network impairment device.

**Development and Support Fabric/Resources:** Additional resources are set aside that are helping us with the development and support of operational services. These include servers for portals, ticket systems, task management systems, code repositories, a machine to host an LDAP [KV04] server, and other services. It is important to recognize that such services should not be hosted on the "cluster" resources that constitute the main FG fabric as an outage of the cluster would affect important operational services.

**Operations Services:** In order to effectively communicate and conduct the development effort, the following elementary services have been provided: a website, a development wiki, a task management system to coordinate the software development tasks, and a ticket system. In addition, we need to provide security and accounting services to deal with authentication, authorization, and auditing.

**Base Software and Services:** The FG base services contain a number of services we rely on when developing software in support of the FG mission. These include software that is very close to the FG fabric and includes tools such as Moab [Com12], xCAT [wwwj], and also the base OS. This category of services will enable us to build experiment management systems utilizing dynamic provisioning.

**Management Services:** The management services are centered on FG experiments and the overall system integration, including information services and raining/dynamic provisioning (see Section 23.3.3), software stacks, and environments on the fabric.

**Access Services:** FG user services contain a variety of services. They include IaaS, PaaS, SaaS, and classical libraries that provide a service as an infrastructure to the users such as accessing MPI [SOHL+98] and others (see Section 23.3.2).

**User-Contributed Services (as part of additional services):** The architecture image does not explicitly distinguish user contributed services. It is important to note that user contributions take place on many different access levels. This is supported by our architecture by allowing the creation, distribution, reuse, and instantiation of user-contributed software as part of services or experiments within FG. Thus, we expect that the FG user-contributed services will grow over time while enhancing areas that we have not explicitly targeted ourselves. Instead, we provide mechanisms for community users to integrate their contributions into FG offered services. The only difference to these services may be the level of support offered in contrast to other FG services.

Together these components build our layered architecture view as depicted in Figure 23.3.

## 23.3.2    Access Services

Next we will be focusing our attention on the access services. As part of the access services, we distinguish the following areas:

- PaaS (Platform as a Service): Delivery of a computing platform and solution stack;

- IaaS (Infrastructure as a Service): Delivery a compute infrastructure as a service;

- Grid: Delivery of services to support the creation of virtual organizations contributing resources;

- HPCC (High-Performance Computing Cluster): Delivery of traditional high-performance computing cluster environment; and

- User and Support Services: Delivery of services to enable user support.

### 23.3.2.1    Access Service Demand

The question arises, which services should we offer in FutureGrid? To answer this question, we have identified user demand within the community as part of our project application process within FutureGrid. At registration time for a project, the project owners are presented with a number of choices of technologies that are most useful for their project or they desire to have access to. Project owners were able to choose multiple items. We obtained the following results while analyzing the requests from project owners: (a) Nimbus: (53.2%), (b) Eucalyptus: (50.8%), (c) Hadoop: (37.3%), (d) High Performance Computing Environment:

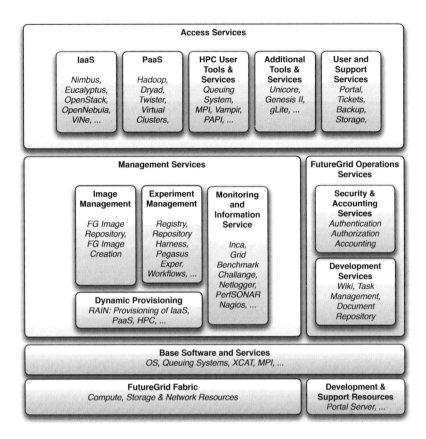

**FIGURE 23.3**: FutureGrid software architecture.

(35.7%), (e) MapReduce: (33.3%), (f) Common TeraGrid Software Stack: (27%), (g) Genesis II: (16.7%), (h) Twister: (15.9%), (i) OpenStack: (12.7%), (j) OpenNebula: (11.1%), (k) Unicore 6: (10.3%), and (l) gLite: (9.5%)

Please note that the data was collected only for each project owner and does not contain information gathered by members of projects or other FutureGrid users. We observed over time only slight changes in the requests for these services. However, most recently we have seen significantly increased demand for OpenStack. As part of this monitoring activity, we intend to be flexible in what we offer on FutureGrid and work with the community to strive toward fulfilling services needs that fall within our project goals. We realize that it may be biased as we gather the information from our current set of users, and therefore we are also monitoring the community actively (see Figure 23.4). This helps us attract new users and adapt our strategies to community needs [vLDWF12].

### 23.3.2.2 Infrastructure as a Service

In contrast to the traditional offering of supercomputer centers, FutureGrid provides a variety of Infrastructure as a Service (IaaS) frameworks on its resources. IaaS allows us to abstract the physical hardware and offers users instead access to virtual machines that are then mapped onto the hardware. Currently, one of the special features of FutureGrid is to provide not only one IaaS framework, but several of them.

The reason why FG provides multiple IaaS frameworks is based on the fact that any of

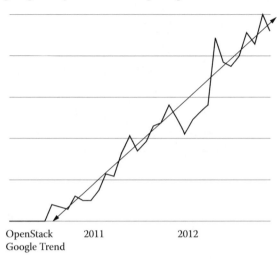

OpenStack    2011        2012
Google Trend

**FIGURE 23.4**: Google trends shows popularity of OpenStack to be significantly rising.

the IaaS frameworks are under heavy development. Features are added, and performance changes based on versions and deployment strategies. Thus it is important to offer a variety of IaaS frameworks to assist the users evaluating and identifying the IaaS and deployment strategies best suited for their applications. While on the surface client tools seem to offer similar capabilities, the difference may be in how such frameworks are implemented and how they perform and scale as part of an application integration. The current IaaS frameworks that are offered on FutureGrid include Nimbus [wwwc], Eucalyptus [wwwf], OpenStack [wwwh] and ViNe [TF06]. Some of our own projects also use OpenNebula [wwwg], but we have not yet made it publicly available.

*Nimbus.* The Nimbus project [wwwc] consists of an IaaS (Nimbus Infrasrtucture) and a PaaS component (Nimbus Platform).

*Nimbus Infrastructure* provides both compute and storage cloud compatiblility with Amazon Web Service's Elastic Compute Cloud (EC2) [Amaa] and Simple Storage Service (S3) [Amab], respectively. Nimbus targets features of interest to the scientific community, such as support for proxy credentials, enhanced scheduling options, and fast deployment of large virtual clusters. These features make it easy for scientific projects to experiment with FutureGrid Nimbus installations. Further, both Nimbus compute (Workspace Service [KFF+05]) and storage (Cumulus [BFLK10]) cloud components are provided as a high-quality, highly configurable, and extensible open-source implementations that allow students and scientists to modify them in order to experiment with new capabilities, as has been done in [MKF11, RTM+10]. The FutureGrid Nimbus deployment contains four independent clouds on Hotel, Sierra, Foxtrot and Alamo, allowing research in the development of heterogeneous cloud environments.

*Nimbus Platform* [KF08, BFLK11] is an integrated set of tools that allow users to provision resources across multiple infrastructure clouds, create virtual clusters across those clouds, and scale to demand. Coordinated deployment of complex resource configurations across multiple clouds is accomplished with Nimbus cloud [BFLK11], which allows users to develop a launchplan for such complex deployment once and then execute it many times. The Nimbus context broker [BFLK11] coordinates secure creation of "one click" virtual clusters, potentially distributed over multiple clouds. These services allow users to combine resources provisioned from Nimbus, OpenStack, and Amazon Web Services clouds and are designed to be extended to support other IaaS providers. We are in the process of developing multicloud autoscaling services that will further facilitate access to FutureGrid cloud resources.

*Eucalyptus.* Eucalyptus [wwwf] is a popular IaaS framework that has been commercialized since this project started. Our current deployment contains two independent services on India and Sierra allowing research in the development of heterogeneous cloud environments. Performance comparisons of Eucalyptus 2 to OpenStack and Eucalyptus 3 have showed that it is no longer competitive. Hence we have recently updated from Eucalyptus 2 to Eucalyptus 3. The ability to conduct such performance experiments on the same resources to gather this information is a significant strength of FutureGrid. Our results were presented at the Eucalyptus users group meeting in 2012 and were positively received not only by the community but also by the Eucalyptus team, as it gave insight in how our user community uses the various IaaS frameworks and compared them with each other.

*OpenStack.* Most recently OpenStack [wwwh] has been introduced to the community. It is driven by the community and has received significant community backing not only by the academic but also by the industrial community. The quality of the code base is rapidly improving. By now OpenStack has released a quite stable set of components that can be used to build significantly large clouds. The recent OpenStack user's community meeting was attended by 1,000 users. This in addition to the rising trend (see Figure 23.4) emphasizes that FutureGrid must support OpenStack on its resources.

*ViNe: User-Level Virtual Networks.* ViNe [TF06] is a project developed at University of Florida that implements routing and other communication mechanisms needed to deploy a user-level virtual network. ViNe is particularly appealing for cloud computing because it allows the establishment of wide-area virtual networks supporting symmetric communication among public and private network resources (even when they are behind firewalls), does not require changes to either the physical network or the OS of machines, and has low virtualization overheads. ViNe can provide communication among FutureGrid and external resources (including those with private IP addresses) without the need to reconfigure the (FutureGrid) physical network infrastructure.

In the first phase of FG, ViNe efforts focused on deploying and demonstrating overlay network capabilities. In the largest experiment, ViNe connected a virtual cluster (launched through Nimbus) across 3 FG (sierra, foxtrot, and hotel) and 3 Grid'5000 (Rennes, Lille, and Sophia) sites [imp12b]. The virtual cluster consisted of 750 VMs (1,500 cores), and executed BLAST on Hadoop (CloudBLAST) with speedup of up to 870X [MTF09].

In the second phase, ViNe efforts focused on adding management capabilities to the existing code. The goal is to make it easy for FG users to configure and operate ViNe software, without the needed overlay networks expertise.

In the third phase, building on the management capabilities implemented previously, high-level management services (e.g., end-to-end QoS, overlay network performance self-optimization, recovery in the presence of faults) will be developed.

### 23.3.2.3 Platform as a Service

In addition to the IaaS, FutureGrid offers the ability to provide Platform as a Service to the users. Platforms typically include a well-defined solution stack such as a customized operating system, a programming language execution environment, and databases, as well as platforms related to data analysis, such as map/reduce, grid computing, and even high-performance computing. Once committed to a platform, users rely on the platform to be deployed and develop their applications against such a platform. As each of these platforms could be differently installed and managed, it is sometimes beneficial to be able to install them in a different fashion. Thus, although we have provided a number of default implementations, users are typically able to assemble their own platforms to increase performance while targeting available resources for specific application performance characteristics.

*MapReduce.* Within FutureGrid we provide a number of ways for users to access MapReduce [DG08]. First we allow users to use the Hadoop-based map/reduce platform [wwwa] hosted on bare metal. However we also allow users to stage their own personalized versions of Hadoop so modifications and research can take place as part of improvements to the Hadoop code base. In addition we provide Hadoop as part of our dynamic provisioning service in order to simplify performance experimentations.

Hadoop is a very popular PaaS that provides users with the map/reduce framework. In addition to installing Hadoop on systems, FutureGrid has deployed myHadoop [KTB11], a set of scripts developed by SDSC that makes it easy to submit Hadoop jobs through the FutureGrid batch queue systems. Hadoop is also easy to customize and allows users to make their own copy and adjust default Hadoop settings or to specify an alternative Hadoop implementation. This is important, as some users may want to experiment with modified versions of Hadoop.

*High-Performance Computing Services.* To emphasize high-level platforms for high-performance computing and their special role, we have added a separate category for them in our architecture, as depicted in Figure 23.3. As we are part of XSEDE, some of our users need to test out software that will later be deployed in XSEDE. Hence providing regular HPC services such as access to a queuing system and being able to run MPI programs is possible. In addition to such bare-metal services, we have also developed examples of how such queuing systems can be set up via a single command-line tool in a cloud environment on, for example, OpenStack. This is important for future activities where users may experiment with queueing strategies and federated datacenters while simulating an XSEDE-like infrastructure in the cloud.

*Grid Services.* FutureGrid also offers a number of grid services, including access to Unicore and Genesis II. Not surprisingly, the demand for Globus was relatively low, as they have been available for some time on XSEDE and the users of such services seem to utilize the far larger XSEDE resources. Most of the demand for Globus stems from the workflow community, who try to also integrate FutureGrid into their workflows while relying on grid services, as well as the interoperability research community, who investigate tools to increase interoperability within grid environments.

More interesting for our community is the Globus Provision tool [glo12] for deploying fully configured Globus environments within cloud environments. It is designed to be simple to use and will allow users to deploy common Globus services, such as GridFTP and GRAM, in just minutes. Globus Provision will also take care of generating user accounts and certificates and setting up auxiliary services. Globus Provision can deploy these services in any combination needed. For example, one could deploy a single GridFTP server, a Condor pool [con] with ten worker nodes and a GRAM server, or 30 GridFTP servers to teach a tutorial where each student needs his own GridFTP server to play around with. Once these services are deployed, the user can dynamically add and remove software, hosts, and user accounts. We have made the current version of Globus provisioning available on FutureGrid but have not yet received much feedback about its functionality and usage.

*Symmetric Multiprocessing.* Symmetric multiprocessing (SMP) has been a fundamental driver in HPC, furthering the availability of parallel processing architectures to commodity multicore technology. While this multicore age has continued Moore's law, the growth rate of cores has been lackluster at best. Cache-coherent Non-Uniform Memory Access (ccNUMA) architectures, specifically based on the newest x86 processors, have the ability to turn a commodity cluster into a single, large-scale supercomputer. These ccNUMA machines provide large-scale multiprocessing and relative ease of use for data- and compute-intensive scientific applications, but the costs associated with such supercomputers make them prohibitively expensive for the vast majority of potential users.

Recently, virtualization has allowed for the ability to abstract hardware in order to create a virtualized SMP machine using commodity hardware. One such implementation, vSMP by ScaleMP Inc., provides such an experience [sca12]. However, as it is a virtualized access to SMP, it is important to measure performance impact on applications. A deployment within FutureGrid allows such analysis. Experiments conducted on FutureGrid using HPCC benchmarks show only a 4-6% drop in efficiency when compared with native cluster performance.

*PAPI and Vampir.* To support the development of performance-based experimentation on FutureGrid, we have deployed a number of tools for the user. These include PAPI and Vampir [vam12].

PAPI is an acronym for Performance Application Programming Interface [pap12]. The PAPI project is being developed at the University of Tennessee's Innovative Computing Laboratory in their Computer Science Department. This project was created to design, standardize, and implement a portable and efficient API (application programming interface) to access the hardware performance counters found on most modern microprocessors. PAPI is at this time enhanced to be able to work also on virtual machines.

Vampir provides a manageable framework for analysis, which enables developers to quickly display program behavior at any level of detail. Detailed performance data obtained from a parallel program execution can be analyzed with a collection of different performance views. Intuitive navigation and zooming are the key features of the tool, which help to quickly identify inefficient or faulty parts of a program code. Vampir implements optimized event analysis algorithms and customizable displays, which enable a fast and interactive rendering of very complex performance monitoring data.

### 23.3.3    Management Services

#### 23.3.3.1    Dynamic Image Provisioning with RAIN

Cloud computing has become an important driver for delivering Infrastructure as a Service to users with on-demand requests for customized environments and sophisticated software stacks. As we support a number of different IaaS frameworks, we have to consider the following issues:

1. Resources need to be managed within each IaaS.

2. Resources have to be assigned to each IaaS.

3. Sharing of resources and reallocating them are an integral part of FutureGrid services.

Within the FutureGrid project, we are devising a framework that allows this level of customization for administrators and users. The FutureGrid architecture, depicted in Figure 23.3, shows the two components, namely, *Image Management* and *Dynamic provisioning*, that are tightly interwoven to allow users to dynamically provision images on bare-metal and virtualized infrastructures.

Image management is a key component in any modern compute infrastructure, regardless if used for virtualized or nonvirtualized resources. We distinguish a number of important processes that are integral parts of the life-cycle management of images. They include (a) image creation and customization, (b) sharing the images via a repository, (c) registering the image into the infrastructure, and (d) image instantiation (see Figure 23.5). The problem of targeting not one, but multiple infrastructures amplifies the need for tools supporting these processes. Without them, only the most experienced users will be able to manage them under great investment of time.

Our design targets an end-to-end workflow to support users in creating abstract image management across different infrastructures easily [DvLWF12, DYvL+11]. To summarize the idea behind our design, we prefer users to be able to specify a list of requirements such as an OS, an architecture, software, and libraries in order to generate a personalized abstract image. This image is generic enough that through manipulations it can be adapted for several IaaS or HPC infrastructures with little effort by the users. It will support the management of images for Nimbus [wwwc], Eucalyptus [wwwf], OpenStack [wwwh], and bare-metal HPC infrastructures as they are either already deployed in FG or going to be deployed as in the case of OpenNebula [wwwg].

By supporting this image management workflow, our framework eases the use of IaaS and HPC frameworks and infrastructures for performance experiments based on abstract image management and uniform image registration. Consequently, users can build their own customized environments very easily. The complex processes of the underlying infrastructures are managed by our sophisticated software tools and services. Besides being able to manage images for IaaS frameworks, we allow the registration and deployment of images onto bare metal by the user. This level of functionality is typically not offered in an HPC infrastructure. However, our approach provides users with the ability to create their own environments, changing the paradigm of administrator-controlled dynamic provisioning to user-controlled dynamic provisioning. Thus, users obtain access to a testbed with the ability to manage state-of-the-art software stacks that would otherwise not be supported in typical compute centers. Security is also considered by vetting images before they are registered in an infrastructure.

The capabilities provided by our image management framework are advantageous for supporting repeatable performance experiments across a variety of infrastructures. To support a modular design, we have devised a component for each process. These include an image generation component to create images following user requirements; an image repository component to store, catalog, and share images; and an image registration component for preparing, uploading, and registering images into specific infrastructures such as HPC or different clouds.

As we can see in Figure 23.5, the architecture includes a convenient separation between client and server components for allowing users easily interact with the hosted services that manage our processes. Our design allows users access to the various processes via a python API, a REST service [Fie00], and a convenient command-line shell, as well as a portal interface. The image management server has the task to generate, store, and register the images with the infrastructure. The image management server also interfaces with external services, such as configuration management services to simplify the configuration steps, authentication, and authorization, and a service to verify the validity of an image including security checks.

One important feature in our design is how we are not simply storing an image but rather focusing on the way an image is created through abstract templating. Thus, it is possible at any time to regenerate an image based on the template describing the software stack and services for a given image. This enables us also to optimize the storage needs for users to manage many images. Instead of storing each image individually, we could just store the template or a pedigree of templates used to generate the images.

In order to aid storage reduction, our design includes data to assist in measuring usage and performance. This data can be used to purge rarely used images, which can be recreated on-demand by leveraging the use of templating. Moreover, the use of abstract image templating will allow us to automatically generate images for a variety of hypervisors and hardware platforms on demand. Autonomous services could be added to reduce the time

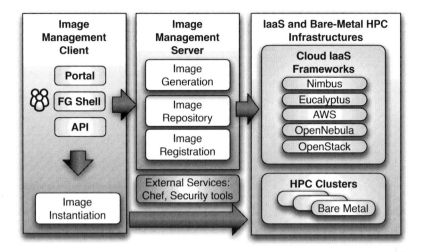

**FIGURE 23.5**: Architecture of RAIN to conduct image provisioning on IaaS and baremetal.

needed to create images or deploy them in advance. Reusing images among groups of users and the introduction of a cache as part of the image generation will reduce the memory footprint or avoid the generation altogether if an image with the same properties is already available.

*Image Generation.* Image generation provides the first step in our image management process allowing users to create images according to their specifications. As already mentioned, the benefit of our image generation tools and services is that we are not targeting just a single infrastructure type but a range of them.

The process is depicted in Figure 23.6. Users initiate the process by specifying their requirements. These requirements can include the selection of the OS type, version, architecture, software, services, and more. First, the image generation tool searches the image repository to identify a base image to be cloned if there is no good candidate, the base image is created from scratch. Once we have a base image, the image generation tool installs the software required by the user. This software must be in the official OS repositories or in the FG software repository. The latter contains software developed by the FG team or other approved software. The installation procedure can be aided by Chef [CHEa], a configuration management tool, to ensure that the software is installed and configured properly. After updating, the image, it is stored in the image repository and becomes available for registration in one of the supported infrastructures. Our tool is general to deal with installation particularities of different operating systems and architectures.

As noted, we can create images either from scratch or by cloning already created base images we locate in our repository to create an image from scratch, a single user identifies all specifications and requirements. This image is created using the tools to bootstrap images provided by the different operating systems, such as yum for CentOS and deboostrap for Ubuntu. To deal with different operating systems and architectures, we use cloud technologies. Consequently, an image is created with all user specified packages inside a VM instantiated on-demand. Therefore, multiple users can create multiple images for different operating systems concurrently; obviously, this approach provides us with great flexibility, architecture independence, and high scalability.

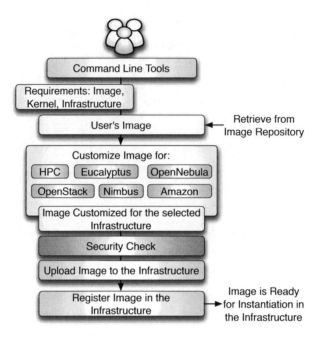

**FIGURE 23.6**: Image registration.

We can speed the process of generating an image by not starting from scratch but by using an image already stored in the repository. We have tagged such candidate images in the repository as base images. Consequently, modifications include installation or update of the packages that the user requires. Our design can utilize either VMs or a physical machine to chroot into the image to conduct this step.

Advanced features of our design include the automatic upgrade or update of images stored in the repository. The old image can be deleted after the user verifies the validity of the new image.

*Image Repository.* The image repository [DvLW+11] catalogs and stores images in a unified repository. It offers a common interface for distinguishing image types for different IaaS frameworks and bare-metal images. This allows us to include a diverse set of images contributed not only by the FG development team but also by the user community that generates such images and wishes to share them. The images are augmented with information about the software stack installed on them, including versions, libraries, and available services. This information is maintained in the catalog and can be searched by users and/or other FG services. Users looking for a specific image can discover available images fitting their needs using the catalog interface. In addition, users can upload customized images, share them among other users, and dynamically provision them. Through these mechanisms we expect our image repository to grow through community-contributed images.

Metadata included in the repository includes information about properties of the images, the access permission by users, and the usage. Access permissions allow the image owner to determine who can access this image from the repository. The simplest types of sharing include private to owner, shared with the public, or shared with a set of people defined by a group/project. Usage information includes how many times an image was accessed and by whom.

*Image Registration.* Once the image has been created and stored into the repository, we need to register it in the targeted infrastructure before we can instantiate it. User requirements are simply the image, the targeted infrastructure, and the kernel. The kernel is an optional requirement that allows advanced users to select the most appropriate kernel for their experiments. This tool provides a list of available kernels organized by infrastructure. Nevertheless, users may request support for other kernels like one customized by them. Registering an image also includes the process of adapting it for the infrastructure. Often we find differences between images, requiring us to provide further customizations, security check, the upload of the image to the infrastructure repository, and registering it. Customizations include the configuration of network IP, DNS, filesystem table, and kernel modules. Additional configuration is performed depending on the targeted deployed infrastructure.

In the HPC infrastructure the images are converted to network-bootable images to be provisioned on bare-metal machines. Here, the customization process configures the image so it can be integrated into the pool of deployable images accessible by the scheduler. In our case this is MOAB. Hence, if such an image is specified as part of the job description, the scheduler will conduct the provisioning of the image for us. These images are stateless, and the system is restored by reverting to a default OS once the running job requiring a customized image is completed.

Images targeted for cloud infrastructures need to be converted into VM disks. These images also need some additional configuration to enable VM's contextualization in the selected cloud. Our plan is to support the main IaaS clouds, namely, Eucalyptus, Nimbus, OpenStack, OpenNebula, and Amazon Web Service. As our tool is extensible, however, we can also support other cloud frameworks.

Of importance is a security check for images that are to be registered in the infrastructures. A separate process identifies approved images, which are allowed to be instantiated in FutureGrid. Approval can be achieved either by review or the invocation of tools minimizing and identifying security risks at runtime. Users may need to modify an image to install additional software not available during the image generation process or to configure additional services. Modified images need to go through some additional tests before they can be registered in the infrastructure. To perform these security tests, we plan to create a high-level platform for instantiating the images in a controlled environment such as a VM with limited network access. Hence, we can perform some tests to verify the integrity of the image and detect vulnerabilities and possible malicious software

If the image passes all the tests, it is tagged as approved. To provide authentication and authorization, images may interface with the FG account management. The process of registering an image needs to be done only once per infrastructure. Therefore, after registering an image in a particular infrastructure, that image can be used anytime to instantiate as many VMs or in the case of HPC as many physical machines as available to meet the users requirements.

*Dynamic Provisioning with RAIN.* Because the variety of services and limited resources accessible in FG, it is necessary to enable a mechanism to provision needed services onto available resources and suspend or shut down services that are not utilized. This includes the assignment of resources to different IaaS and PaaS frameworks. We need to develop a convenient abstraction that allows us to hide the many underlying tools and services to accomplish this task. We observed the following needs from the FutureGrid user community:

1. In contrast to grid frameworks such as Globus, we are not only interested in interfacing to the job management system or file transfer.

2. In contrast to IaaS environments, we are not just interested in provisioning an image as part of the virtualized environment. Instead, we would like to be able to "provision" the entire IaaS framework.

3. In contrast to environments based on a single operating system, we would like to man-

age the deployment on multiple base OS including the choice of which virtualization technology is used.

4. In contrast to just focusing on virtualized environments, we would also like to enable an environment allowing performance comparisons between the virtualized and the nonvirtualized versions of applications, e.g., comparing HPC vs. IaaS frameworks. Hence, it is important to recognize that this comprehensive view of "raining" an environment is a significant contribution of FG and allows comparative studies that are otherwise not easily possible.

We have developed, as a first step to addressing this challenge, a sophisticated image management toolkit that allows us to not only provision virtual machines but also provision directly onto bare-metal [DvLWF12]. Thus, we use the term *raining* to indicate that we can place an arbitrary software stack onto a resource. The toolkit to do so is called *RAIN*.

RAIN will make it possible to compare the benefits of IaaS and PaaS performance issues, as well as evaluating which applications can benefit from such environments and how they must be efficiently configured. As part of this process, we allow the generation of abstract images and universal image registration with the various infrastructures including Nimbus, Eucalyptus, OpenNebula, and OpenStack, as well as bare metal via the HPC services. It is one of the unique features of FutureGrid to provide an essential component to make comparisons between the different infrastructures more easily possible [vLDWF12]. Our toolkit RAIN also is tasked with simplifying the creation and deployment of customized environments. Internally RAIN may use a multitude of tools and components suitable to conduct the task indicated by the command-line tool. These may include MOAB, xCAT, TakTuk [tak12], and even IaaS frameworks where appropriate. It is important to recognize that, in order to allow repeatable experiments, the rain command will have to interact with a multitude of services. In the future, RAIN will allow specifically the recording of the resources participating in an experiment. Eventually, the experiment will be able to be shared with other users and replicated.

In summary, RAIN is a pivotal process in making the FG deployment unique and applicable to any set of scientific researchers requiring rapid deployment of IaaS, PaaS, and HPC environments (see Figure 23.7). We envision that RAIN will offer the following main features:

- Compare different infrastructures.

- Create customized environments on demand.

- Move resources from one infrastructure to another by changing the image they are running plus doing needed changes in the framework.

- Ease the system administrator burden for creating deployable images.

- Allow access to repeatable experiments.

Examples of "raining" are the deployment of a Hadoop cluster to run an experiment, the instantiation of a set of VMs with an specific OS, and the deployment of a virtual cluster based on SLURM [wwwi]. We envision that commands such as

```
fg-rain --hadoop -x india -m 10 -j jobscript.sh
fg-rain -os ubuntu11.04 -s sierra -m 25 -I
fg-rain --cluster slurm -x sierra -m 34
```

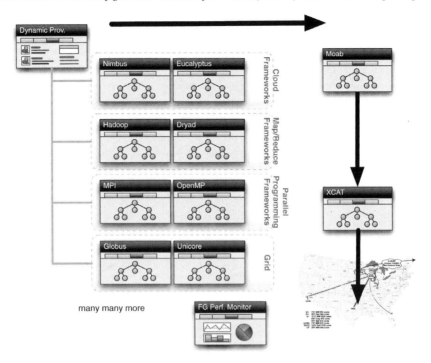

**FIGURE 23.7**: The concept of raining allows to dynamically provision images on baremetal, but also in virtualized environments. This allows performance experiments between virtualized and nonvirtualized infrastructures.

will be transparent enough for users to achieve provisioning on both bare metal and virtualized infrastructures (cloud). It is obvious that such a command will be extremely powerful and provide an important mechanism for abstracting the many different tools and services that are needed to accomplish the task. In this way, users don't need to be aware of the underlying details of each infrastructure. Hence, the command rain will provide the high-level interface to the FG fabric, which is essential to create deployment workflows in a simple fashion.

### 23.3.3.2   Monitoring, Information, and Performance Services

A critical component of FutureGrid is the ability to monitor the expected behavior of its systems and services. This is especially important because of the experimental nature of the FutureGrid mission. Monitoring activities in FutureGrid include testing the functionality and performance of FutureGrid services using Inca, collecting usage data with Netlogger, cluster monitoring with Ganglia, and network monitoring with perfSONAR and SNAPP. Administrators and users can then easily access the monitoring data generated by each tool through the user portal. Programmatic access to the monitoring data is also available through each of the tools, and work is ongoing to integrate the monitoring data into a common messaging system using AMQP for easier access. Each monitoring tool is described further in the subsections below. We also provide performance tools, PAPI and Vampir, for he image generation process for both virtual and bare-metal images.

*Inca.* Inca [SEHO07] is a monitoring framework designed to detect cyberinfrastructure problems by executing periodic, automated, user-level monitoring of CI software and services. Inca currently executes over 200 tests for FutureGrid's cloud, grid, HPC, and internal services: Eucalyptus, Ganglia, GCC, Genesis II, Globus GRAM, Globus GridFTP, HostCert/CRL, HPCC, IMPI, Inca, InfiniBand (Sierra), JIRA, LDAP, Modules, MongoDB, myHadoop, Openstack, NetLogger, Nimbus, OpenMPI, PAPI, perfSONAR, PGCC, the FG Portal, SSH, Torque/MOAB, Unicore, VampirTrace, Wiki, and XCAT. It also collects performance measurements for each of the cloud tools and HPCC performance data from the HPC partitions.

*Netlogger.* Netlogger [TJC$^+$98] is a tool for debugging and analyzing the performance of complex distributed applications. It is currently being leveraged to collect privileged usage data (number of deployed VMs and number of unique users) using small probes that execute with administrator credentials every hour for each of the cloud tools: Eucalyptus, Nimbus, and OpenStack.

*Ganglia.* Ganglia [MCC04] is a cluster monitoring tool used to monitor each of the FutureGrid clusters. It collects CPU, memory, disk, and network usage statistics for each cluster node. The monitoring data is then aggregated and published at a centralized Ganglia server.

*perfSONAR.* perfSONAR [HBB$^+$05] is an infrastructure for network performance monitoring. FutureGrid has deployed the perfSONAR-BUOY infrastructure to perform a full mesh of BWCTL measurements (regularly scheduled Iperf measurements). Currently, we have a basic setup of 60-second 1 G TCP measurements that are run every two hours.

*SNAPP.* SNAPP [SNA07] is a network statistical data collection and visualization tool that is used to collect high-performance, high-resolution SNMP data from the FutureGrid network.

### 23.3.4    Experiment and Project Management

Users obtain access to FutureGrid by submitting projects describing the nature and merit of their activity. Currently most projects tax FutureGrid not in number of resources requested but in the nature and support of requested software, and these issues are used in evaluation. We do not approve projects such as production science that are more suitable for other XSEDE sites. There are currently no restrictions on nationality or type (academic, government, industry) of users. We require, however, that the use of Future-Grid be documented and results be shared with the community. The FutureGrid portal https://portal.futuregrid.org/ [wwwb] has an open list of all projects, their results, papers on development, and reports on progress.

FutureGrid allows both federated and nonfederated experiments. Because of the variety of technologies that are supported, not all of them integrate well yet into a completely federated environment. We base our federated infrastructure on LDAP where possible, while using public keys. Surprisingly, it has been relatively easy so far to provide an IdP (Identity Provider) based on a simple verification process that included a Google search of academic publications, participation in source code development of established projects, or lookup on university Web sites. We also identified that we have users that are not and probably never will be part of the U.S. campus bridging IdP based on InCommon. An OpenID can be used to be associated with the portal account, effectively providing SSO with services such as Googledocs. This is especially important as we believe that in order to support the long tail of science we need to interface with such tools as they provide via Google Scholar, and collaborative document preparation popular in the education community.

Once a project is approved, users can conduct experiments. A result of such experiments can be a template that can be used to reproduce such an experiment or even an image that others can use by reusing the software stack promoted by this image.

We are in the process of developing a number of tools that together provide a sophisticated experiment management environment while leveraging lessons learned from our earlier experiences [vLYH+09, vL06]. This is done as part of a targeted software architecture that we make public as part of our activities. This architecture reuses a number of tools including Nimbus, OpenStack, OpenNebula, Eucalyptus, Globus, Unicore, Genesis II, and Pegasus [CD11, VDRB11]. For dynamic provisioning on bare metal and VMs we are using the term *rain* and developed the fg-rain prototype, which not only places the OS on the resources (virtualized and nonvirtualized) but also assembles the OS and the software stack as part of an image generation process [vLFW+10, DvLW+11, DvLWF12].

### 23.3.4.1   Interactive Experiment Management

The design philosophy of this set of tools is a Unix-style one where a user can use a set of independent tools together (via the command line or a script) to accomplish a complex goal.

Interactive experiment management is currently an ongoing research activity within FutureGrid. Various approaches to this exist within FutureGrid. One of these approaches is to create an experiment harness with existing and new tools such as TakTuk and the FutureGrid Host List Manager. These tools are used in conjunction with other tools such as Torque and Nimbus provisioning commands and even the Unix script command. TakTuk is a cluster fork or parallel shell type tool developed as part of the Grid 5000 project. The TakTuk user interface is a command line program that allows a user to easily and efficiently execute commands on sets of remote computer systems and transmit the output of these commands back to the TakTuk program. TACC developed the Host List Manager — a set of command-line programs that discovers what FutureGrid resources have been provisioned to a user (via Torque and Nimbus), organizes resources into groups (based on the tag(s) that the user assigns to each resource), and generates host list files for use by TakTuk or similar parallel shell tools.

A FutureGrid user can therefore use Torque and Nimbus commands to provision resources, use the Host List Manager to organize those resources into groups, execute commands on the resources via TakTuk, and record their entire session via a Unix script program.

TakTuk and the Host List Manager have been deployed on the Alamo, Hotel, India, and Sierra FutureGrid clusters and are available in production mode to FutureGrid users. The deployment includes the software itself and modules for including the software in a user's environment.

### 23.3.4.2   Workflow-Based Experiment Management

Scientific workflows have been popular within the grid community to coordinate the execution of large-scale workflows utilizing resources from a variety of grids. It is obvious that part of this strategy can be reused within the cloud environment. This strategy is followed by the Pegasus project provides to FutureGrid the promise to allow workflow and based experiment management to the FutureGrid community.

### 23.3.4.3   DevOps-Based Experiment Management

In addition to the experiment management strategies listed above, we support experiment management with tools that recently have become synonymous with DevOps. Here templates, scripts, or recipes are used to formulate in a templated fashion deployment descriptions to coordinate the creation of an experiment environment that includes resources as part of the compute fabric, the operating system and/or virtualization environments, and the instantiation of high-level platforms as part of the overall deployed experimental services. Such a mechanism is possible while leveraging tools such as Puppet or chef, as well as integrating them as part of our RAIN toolkit. The goal is to create small test deployments that with little effort can be rained onto larger resource fabrics when desired. It also allows the total reconfiguration of the environment while proposing the model of "nothing installed on the machine." Hence such an experiment management framework could also be used to bootstrap the previous two management frameworks that are positioned at a higher level and require certain software to be readily available.

#### 23.3.4.4    Rain-Based Experiment Management

One of the key components and services of FutureGrid is to dynamically provision operating systems, IaaS, and PaaS frameworks onto different resources, as well as the dynamic allocation based on user demand. Thus, it will be possible to create and recreate environments and experiment resources based on predefined specifications. This will help in setting up suitable experiment frameworks that allow comparison of features across infrastructures, platforms, operating systems, and other high-level tools. Hence it builds an elementary basic unit that can be used in workflow-based, interactive, and DevOps-based experiments — without doubt one of the most sophisticated services planned and offered in FutureGrid. To facilitate ease of use we take the ideas presented in [vLYH+09] and expose the functionality through a convenient command shell while also working toward integration into a portal.

### 23.3.5    Operations Services

*Authentication and Authorization.* We have devised our authentication strategy on LDAP and enabled the management of users through the portal. Our account policy is based on rules that all users must (a) have a portal account, (b) be in an approved project, and (c) have an ssh key uploaded. Accounts for Eucalyptus must currently be separately applied for, as the version of Eucalyptus we have access to is not yet integrated with LDAP. The LDAP servers are distributed, and Nimbus is already integrated with our LDAP server.

LDAP provided an excellent mechanism for our security needs. All clouds (Nimbus, Eucalyptus, OpenStack, OpenNebula) we consider for deployment currently or will support LDAP. We consulted with security experts that gave the recommendation to use LDAP. Originally we wanted to interface also with InCommon, for account vetting, but found that vetting accounts so far was not that much work and that the attributes provided by InCommon at this time do not allow us to eliminate our account vetting activities, as confirmed by experts from the InCommon community.

*Cloud Accounting.* An important part of FG is to be able to present accounting information for our deployed cloud environments. This has been surprisingly more challenging than we originally anticipated. First, the cloud framework support for accounting is minimal or nonexistent. In addition, we are investigating mechanisms not only to parse and monitor Eucalyptus logs, but also to confirm that we can integrate that information into a system such as Gold. However, the developers of Gold have recently discontinued support for it and recommend instead a commercial solution. We will reevaluate our strategy because it was based on Gold.

*HPC Accounting.* Accounting on HPC systems is important in order to identify how the systems were used. Although integration with the XSEDE central repository would be possible, we identified, together with the University of Buffalo, several challenges. First, the metrics we are interested in, such as VM monitoring and utilization, are not in the database and require significant modification. Second, because of the reconfigurable nature of FutureGrid, the number of nodes associated with the HPC services is not static and does not fit the current analysis and recoding model. Third, the type of jobs we ran is not as typical and CPU bound. For example, we find many users testing scientific workflows instead of conducting large-scale number crunching on our resources.

*Intelligent Resource Adaptations.* Once we have accounting information we will start an effort to utilize the accounting information to integrate it into a dynamic provisioning mechanism as part of RAIN. For example, if we detect that users do not want to use HPC resources or Eucalyptus resources, the machines hosting the compute nodes for these services can be assigned to, for example, Nimbus if Nimbus reports to us that more resources are needed. This strategy will lead to a metascheduler for cloud and HPC resources.

### 23.3.6    Development Services

Because of the size of the project, it is important to provide a good infrastructure in support of our collaborative efforts. This includes the deployment of a task management system, a wiki, and a continuous integration environment.

### 23.3.7    Portal

FutureGrid presents a sophisticated portal based on Drupal that not only integrates with several of our services but also provides the ability to foster a community. Of special importance is the integration of several workflows that make the review and the approval process of projects very simple.

## 23.4    Service Deployment

In Table 23.3 we list elementary services that have been deployed on various resources in FG.

## 23.5    Applications Using FutureGrid

More than 220 projects and 920 users are registered in FutureGrid. These projects cover a wide range from application to technology and from research to education. Recent projects have focused on integration testing for XSEDE, image management and dynamic provisioning on bare metal [DvLWF12], and scalability tests for cloud provisioning [vLDWF12]. These projects are groundbreaking as they introduce a testbed environment for XSEDE and also allow users facing dynamic provisioning something that is not normally offered by other resources. The scalability experiment showed certain limitations with standard cloud setups for use cases typical for scientific applications.

Additionally, we list in Table 23.4 a number of projects that have been undertaken on FutureGrid to provide an overview of the wide variety of projects. Each project must report its success and findings on the FutureGrid Web site [wwwb]. Currently, our portal is quite streamlined for the entire workflow related to user account creation, project creation, and reporting. In addition application user forums can be established for the projects if the project lead wishes. Thus, projects can be created in just a very short time period. In the

**TABLE 23.3**: Deployed services.

| | India | Sierra | Hotel | Foxtrot | Alamo | Xray | Bravo | Echo |
|---|---|---|---|---|---|---|---|---|
| myHadoop | (d) | (d) | | | (d) | | | |
| Nimbus | (d) | (d) | (d) | (d) | | | | |
| Eucalyptus | (d) | (d) | | | | | | |
| ViNe | (i) | (d) | (i) | (d) | (i) | | | |
| Genesis II | (d) | (d) | | | (d) | (d) | | |
| Unicore | (d) | (d) | | | | (d) | | |
| MPI | (d) | (d) | (d) | (d) | (d) | (d) | (d) | |
| OpenMP | | | | | (d) | | | |
| ScaleMP | (d) | | | | | | | |
| Ganglia | (d) | | (d) | | | | | |
| Pegasus | (i) | (i) | (i) | (i) | (i) | | | |
| Inca | (d) | (d) | (d) | (d) | (d) | (d) | | |
| Portal | (i) | (i) | (i) | (i) | (i) | (i) | | |
| PAPI | | | | | (d) | | | |
| Vampir | (d) | | | | | | (a) | |
| Vampir Trace | (d) | | | | | | (d) | |
| RAIN | (d) | | | | | | | |

Legend:
(d) deployed; (a) can be made available upon request; (i) information available in the portal

next sections we will present some selected projects. To see all of the projects conducted on FutureGrid, we recommend that the reader visit the FutureGrid portal.

### 23.5.1    Privacy Preserving Gene Read Mapping Using Hybrid Clouds

An example project investigating security aspects of hybrid clouds is found at [Cheb]. In this project the researchers study the possibility of doing read mapping using a hybrid cloud, in order to utilize public computing resources while preserving data privacy. The topic of this research is very timely in that it addresses requirements about privacy in bioinformatics as more and more data are generated. The team conducting this research also intends to increase the data processing speed in the area of bioinformatics and replace current read mapping tools. A typical experiment on FutureGrid will run for about two to three days.

One of the most important analyses of human DNA sequences is read mapping, which aligns a large number of short DNA sequences (called reads) produced by sequencers to a reference the human genome. The analysis involves intensive computation (calculating edit distances over millions upon billions of sequences) and therefore needs to be outsourced to low-cost commercial clouds. This asks for scalable privacy-preserving techniques to protect the sensitive information sequencing reads contain. Such a demand cannot be met by a existing techniques, which are either too heavyweight to sustain data-intensive computations or vulnerable to reidentification attacks. Our research, however, shows that simple solutions can be found by leveraging the special features of the mapping task, which cares only about small edit distances, and those of the cloud platform, which is designed to perform a large amount of simple, parallelizable computation. We implemented and evaluated such new techniques on hybrid cloud platforms built on FutureGrid. In our experiments, we utilized

**TABLE 23.4**: Selected FutureGrid projects.

| Project | Institution | Details |
|---|---|---|
| *Educational Projects* | | |
| System Programming and Cloud Computing | Fresno State | Teaches system programming and cloud computing in different computing environments |
| REU: Cloud Computing | University of Arkansas | Offers hands-on experience with FutureGrid tools and technologies |
| Workshop: A Cloud View on Computing | Indiana University | Boot camp on MapReduce for faculty and graduate students from underserved ADMI institutions |
| Topics on Systems: Distributed Systems | Indiana University | Covers core computer science distributed system curricula (for 60 students) |
| *Interoperability Projects* | | |
| SAGA | Rutgers | Explores use of FutureGrid components for extensive portability and interoperability testing of Simple API for grid and scale-up and scale-out experiments |
| *Applications* | | |
| Metagenomics Clustering | North Texas | Analyzes metagenomic data from samples collected from patients |
| Genome Assembly | Indiana School of Informatics | De novo assembly of genomes and metagenomes from next-generation sequencing data |
| Physics: Higgs Boson | Virginia | Matrix element calculations representing production and decay mechanisms for Higgs and background processes |
| Business Intelligence on MapReduce | Cal State LA | L.A. market basket and customer analysis designed to execute MapReduce on Hadoop platform |
| Computer Science Data Transfer Throughput | Buffalo | End-to-end optimization of data transfer throughput over wide-area, high-speed networks |
| Elastic Computing | Colorado | Tools and technologies to create elastic computing environments using IaaS clouds that adjust to changes in demand automatically and transparently |
| The VIEW Project | Wayne State | Investigates Nimbus and Eucalyptus as cloud platforms for elastic workflow scheduling and resource provisioning |
| *Technology Project* | | |
| ScaleMP for Gene Assembly | Indiana University | Pervasive Technology Institute (PTI) and biology investigates distributed shared memory over 16 nodes for SOAPdenovo assembly of *Daphnia* genomes |
| XSEDE | Virginia | Uses FutureGrid resources as a testbed for XSEDE software development |
| Cross Campus Grid | Virginia | Works on bridging infrastructure across different university campuses |

specially designed techniques based on the classic "seed-and-extend" method to achieve secure and scalable read mapping. The high-level design of our techniques is illustrated in Figure 23.8.

Here, the public cloud on FutureGrid delegated the computation over encrypted read data sets, while the private cloud directly works on the data. Our idea is to let the private cloud undertake a small amount of the workload to reduce the complexity of the computation that needs to be conducted.

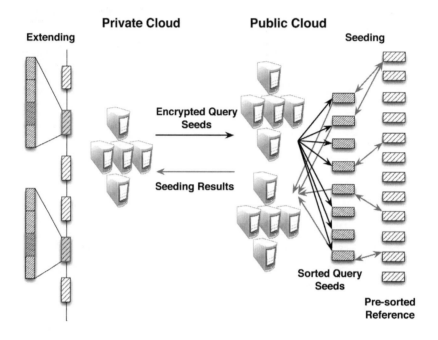

**FIGURE 23.8**: Using a public and private cloud for read mapping.

The researchers reported that their solution method is performed on the encrypted data, while still having the public cloud shoulder the major portion of a mapping task. They constructed a hybrid environment over FutureGrid while using the following two modes: First was a virtual mode in which 20 nodes of FutureGrid were used as the public cloud and 1 node was configured as a private cloud. Second was a real mode, in which nodes on FutureGrid were used as the public cloud and the computing system within the School of Informatics and Computing as the private cloud.

Our experiments demonstrate that our techniques are both secure and scalable. We successfully mapped 10 million real human microbiome reads to the largest human chromosome over this hybrid cloud. The public cloud took about 15 minutes to conduct the seeding, and the private cloud spent about 20 minutes on the extension.

## 23.5.2    SAGA on FutureGrid

An example of an interoperability project is the Simple API for Grid Applications (SAGA) [sag12, fg4]. It is based on an OGF standard [wwwe], and defines a high-level, application-driven API for developing first-principle distributed applications and distributed application frameworks and tools. SAGA provides API implementations in C++ and Python, which interface to a variety of middleware backends, as well as higher-level application frameworks, such as Master-Worker, MapReduce, AllPairs, and BigJob [sag]. For all those components, we use FutureGrid and the different software environments available on FG for extensive portability and interoperability testing, but also for scale-up and scale-out experiments. These activities allow us to harden the SAGA components described above and support computer science and science experiments based on SAGA. FG has provided a persistent, production-grade experimental infrastructure with the ability to perform controlled experiments, without violating production policies and disrupting production infrastructure priorities. These attributes, coupled with FutureGrid's technical support, have resulted in the following specific advances in a short period: (1) use of FG for standards-based development and interoperability tests; (2) use of FG for analyzing and comparing programming models and runtime tools for computation and data-intensive science; (3) development of tools and frameworks; (4) cloud interoperability experiments; and (5) data-intensive applications using MapReduce. SAGA will continue to use FG as a resource for SAGA development for testing of other SAGA-based components, to widen the set of middleware used for testing, to enhance the scope and scale of our scalability testing, and to test and harden our deployment and packaging procedures.

More details about SAGA on FutureGrid can be found on the portal [fg4].

## 23.6    Optimizing MapReduce

MapReduce has been introduced by the information retrieval community and has quickly demonstrated its usefulness, scalability, and applicability. Its adoption of a data-centered approach yields higher throughput for data-intensive applications.

One FutureGrid project centers on the investigation and improvement of MapReduce. As part of the project the team identifies the inefficiency of various aspects of MapReduce, such as data locality, task granularity, resource utilization, and fault tolerance, and proposes algorithms to mitigate the performance issues. Extensive evaluation is presented to demonstrate the effectiveness of their proposed algorithms and approaches. Observing the inability of MapReduce to utilize cross-domain grid resources motivated a proposal to extend MapReduce by introducing a Hierarchical MapReduce framework. The framework was tested on bioinformatics data visualization pipelines containing both single-pass and iterative MapReduce jobs; a workflow management system Hybrid MapReduce (HyMR) was developed and built upon Hadoop and Twister. A detailed performance evaluation of Hadoop and some storage systems provides useful insights to both framework and application developers. The work resulted in several papers and a Ph.D. thesis [Guo12].

## 23.7    Sensor Cloud

The Pervasive Technology Institute, Anabas, Inc., and Ball Aerospace have successfully collaborated to complete a cloud-based message passing middleware, referred to as the Sensor Cloud [FKH+12], to provide a research testbed for sensor-centric/Internet of Things application development.

The objective of the Sensor Cloud project was to provide a general-purpose messaging system for sensor data. For our purposes a sensor is defined as anything producing a time-ordered data stream. Examples of sensors include physical devices like web cams, robots, or a Kinect motion sensing input device. However, sensors can also be Twitter tweets, the results from some computational service, even a PowerPoint presentation; anything that produces a time-dependent data series can be a sensor.

The components of the Sensor Cloud are the Sensor Grid Server for message routing, a sensor grid building and management tool called the Grid Builder, and a robust API for developing new sensors and client applications. The Grid Builder has an intuitive interface for setting sensor policies as well as easy deployment and management of sensors across global networks. The key design objective of the Sensor Grid API is to create a simple integration interface for any third-party application client or sensor to the Sensor Grid Server. This objective is accomplished by implementing the publish/subscribe design pattern that allows for loosely coupled, reliable, scalable communication between distributed applications or systems.

The Sensor Cloud was developed and tested using the FutureGrid's Open Stack Infrastructure as a Service (IaaS) cloud. The FutureGrid provided a scalable geographically distributed environment in which to measure the Sensor Cloud system performance.

### 23.7.1    FutureGrid as a Testbed for XSEDE

In 2008, the NSF announced a competition for the follow-on to the TeraGrid project, known as eXtreme Digital (XD). In 2009, two proposal teams, one led by NCSA and the other by SDSC, were selected to prepare full proposals. In July 2010, the proposals were delivered; and in late 2010, the NCSA-led team was awarded the project, albeit with the instruction to incorporate the best ideas and personnel from the SDSC proposal.

The NCSA-led team proposed XSEDE, the eXtreme Science and Engineering Discovery Environment. The XSEDE architecture is a three-layer, federated, system-of-systems architecture. It includes the use of standard web services interfaces and protocols that define interactions between different components, tools, and organizations. Many different science communities will use XSEDE, whether at a national supercomputing center or through its delivery of campus bridging among research groups around the U.S. XSEDE will be, upon completion, one of the critical components of the national cyberinfrastructure.

The XSEDE web services architecture is based on a number of interchangeable components that implement standard interfaces. These include: (1) RNS 1.1 [MGT10], for Unix-directory-like namespace (e.g., /home/sally/work); (2) OGSA-ByteIO [Mor05] for POSIX filelike operations (create, read, update, delete); (3) OGSA Basic Execution (OGSA-BES) [GNPM08] for executing and managing jobs (create_activity, get_status, delete); and (4) WS Trust Secure Token Services (STS) [OAS07] for identity federation. The architectural goals have clearly specified standard interfaces that anybody can implement, and use best-of-breed components.

The initial realization of the XSEDE web services architecture uses interoperable implementation from two different software stacks: UNICORE 6 [Sne03] and Genesis II [Imp12a]. Together, UNICORE 6 and Genesis II provide a rich set of capabilities in the areas of data, computation, and identity management. These capabilities are grouped into two configuration items (CIs): Execution Management Services (EMS) and the Global Federated File System (GFFS).

The Execution Management Services CI is concerned with specifying, executing, and more generally managing jobs in the XSEDE grid. EMS capabilities include the following:

1. The ability to specify both single jobs and parameter space jobs in JSDL. Specified jobs may be sequential jobs or parallel (MPI) jobs.

2. The ability to manage jobs through their lifetime, i.e., from specification and submis-

sion to a compute resource to status checking and management during execution, as well as final cleanup.

3. A grid-queue (metascheduler) that matches jobs to a defined, configurable set of execution services and load balances between them.

4. The ability to specify either a single compute resource as a target, e.g., a particular queue on Ranger, or to specify a global metascheduler/queue as the target and have the metascheduler select the execution endpoint.

5. The ability to add compute resources (e.g., queues on specific machines such as Ranger, Alamo, Kraken, or local campus queues such as Centurion at UVA) into the XSEDE namespace and subsequently target jobs at them.

6. The ability to create metaschedulers/queues and configure them to use (schedule on) different compute resources.

7. A command-line interface to interact with grid compute resources.

8. A graphical user interface to interact with and manage the backend grid compute resources. This includes tools to: create and execute job descriptions, manage grid queues, and manage access to resources.

9. A set of Java classes (and associated APIs) to interact with and manage the backend grid resources.

The Global Federated File System presents a file-system-like view of diverse resources types located at service providers, campuses, research labs, and other institutions. Resources (e.g., files, directories, job submission queues) are mapped into a single global path-based namespace. Resources can be accessed by their path name in a location-, replication-, migration-, and failure-transparent manner. Resources can be accessed via command-line tools (a grid shell), a graphical user interface, or via the user's local file system and a FUSE mount.

The GFFS provides a number of capabilities. These capabilities include the following:

1. A single, secure, shared global namespace for a diversity of resource types. For example, a single namespace can include files, directories, execution services, execution queues, secure token services, and executing jobs.

2. A three-level naming scheme consisting of location-independent, human-readable names (paths) that map globally unique resources identities that in turn can be mapped (bound) to one or more resource instances. Collectively, the three layers provide an easy-to-use name space that transparently handles heterogeneous configurations for location, failure, replication, migration, and implementation.

3. The ability to securely map (share) Service Provider (SP), local, lab, and campus data into the shared global namespace.

4. The ability to securely map (share) SP, local, lab, and campus compute resources into the global namespace.

5. The ability to securely map (share) SP, local, lab, and campus identity resources into the global namespace.

6. The ability to transparently access from both campuses and national supercomputing centers to the global shared namespace, via either the file system (e.g., FUSE) or command-line tools and libraries. Such access includes the ability to perform create, read, update, and delete operations on files, directories, and other resource types.

7. A command-line interface to interact with backend grid resources. In particular, this allows interaction with Open Grid Forum RNS, ByteIO, WS-Naming, and BES services, as well as WC3 WS-Trust Secure Token Services.

8. A graphical user interface to interact with and manage the backend grid resources.

9. A set of Java classes (and associated APIs) to interact with and manage the backend grid resources.

10. The ability to integrate with existing, legacy, XSEDE Kerberos, and MyProxy [BYBS03] authentication mechanisms.

Before the capabilities of the CIs can be delivered to end users, they must be tested in as realistic an environment as possible. The testing needs to reflect both production workloads and extreme conditions including those that might crash production machines. What is therefore needed is an infrastructure that closely mimics the intended execution environment. This environment would be (1) a collection of geographically separated parallel processing systems of various types connected by high-speed networks; (2) connected to the national network backplane; and (3) able to be used for testing without negatively impacting the production workloads at the national centers. FutureGrid fits these requirements perfectly.

In December 2011, the XSEDE-testgrid (XTG) was brought up on FutureGrid and University of Virginia resources as part of the first integrated test plan for execution management services (EMS) and the Global Federated File System (GFFS). The root of the RNS namespace was set up at Virginia and UNICORE 6 servers brought up on X-Ray at Indiana (the Cray that is a small version of Kraken) and Sierra at SDSC. Genesis II servers were brought up at Virginia and TACC. Genesis II clients were brought up at Indiana, Virginia, TACC, and PSC on Blacklight.

Over the next two months, the tests described in the EMS and GFFS test plans were then executed by the XSEDE software development and integration (SD&I) team. These tests led to the discovery of several minor problems as well as a number of desired feature enhancements. Minor bugs and integration issues were resolved, and the increment 1.0 of EMS and GFFS was completed; and, in March 2012, they were turned over to the XSEDE operations team for learning and testing purposes.

XSEDE testing activities on FutureGrid bifurcated in April 2012. The XSEDE operations team began doing its own experimentation and testing on FutureGrid resources, and SD&I continued to use the XTG as a test infrastructure, in particular working with the XSEDE campus bridging team on the campus bridging pilot project. By the end of May 2012, operations had completed its EMS testing and was ready to start GFFS testing. In late June 2012, SD&I began testing the second release increment of the EMS and GFFS CIs.

As part of the campus bridging pilot project, data resources at three universities were incorporated into the XSEDE test grid in June 2012: Indiana University, Louisiana Tech, and LSU. These resources will be used to perform typical campus bridging test cases and to capture issues that arise with real users. To support job execution on a wider set of resources than are configured in the XTG, the compute resources in the Cross Campus Grid (XCG) were linked into the XTG.

The XCG is a Genesis II-based grid run by the University of Virginia with resources on FutureGrid and at the University of Virginia. The XCG has been in production use for over three years, during which time it has executed over 1.3 million jobs for a number of applications in areas such as economics, materials science, systems engineering, biology, and physics. Many of the XCG jobs have run on FutureGrid resources via the XCG.

FutureGrid has been an invaluable resource for XSEDE in testing the new generation of standards-based software described in the XSEDE proposal. Without FutureGrid, the XSEDE SD&I team would have been forced to use significantly smaller test machines at the centers and to execute its tests alongside production applications on the network and local parallel file systems. Instead, thanks to FutureGrid, the XSEDE team has been able to take advantage of a risk-free testing environment, collaborative systems administrators, and the similarity between the FutureGrid resources and its own. Given its ideal qualifications, we expect XSEDE to continue to use FutureGrid as a test environment.

## 23.8  Educational Outreach

The hardware resources and middleware of FutureGrid enable the creation of user-defined, dynamically provisioned environments and support a "viral" user contribution model. Education and outreach in FutureGrid leverage its underlying technology to deliver a system that enables advanced cyberlearning (learning and teaching enhanced or enabled by cyberinfrastructure) and to lead initiatives to broaden participation by lowering barriers to entry to the use of complex cyberinfrastructures.

In the context of education and outreach, FutureGrid technologies can aggregate and deliver user-provided educational materials including the executable software environment, middleware, and applications where repeatable hands-on experiments can be conducted. Thus, at the core of FutureGrid's educational mission is the ability to create consistent, controlled, and repeatable educational environments in areas of computer and computational science related to parallel, large-scale, or distributed computing and networking, as well as the availability, repeatability, and open sharing of electronic educational materials. FutureGrid has deployed a distributed platform where educators and students can create and access such customized environments for hands-on education and outreach activities on cloud, HPC, and grid computing environments.

Key components of the FutureGrid cyberlearning infrastructure are plug-and-play virtual appliances and virtual networks, which are used to support hands-on educational modules that run on self-contained virtual clusters. The target audience here is prospective modal users; hence the focus is on usability and low barrier to entry. There are three central principles in this approach: (1) allowing users and groups of users to create and manage their own groups through a Web-based portal, (2) automatically mapping these user relationships to network connections among computer resources using self-configuring Virtual Private Network (VPN) technologies; and (3) packaging these environments in self-contained, self-configuring virtual appliances that make it possible to effectively bring together a comprehensive suite of software and middleware tailored to target activities (e.g., to study parallel processing in the context of Condor, MPI, or Hadoop) while hiding the system's underlying complexity from its end users.

In terms of design and implementation, educational virtual clusters on FutureGrid can be created by end users and leverage a preconfigured grid appliance [WF11] image, which encapsulates software environments commonly used. These appliances are deployed on FutureGrid using IaaS middleware (Nimbus, Eucalyptus, or Openstack). Once appliances are deployed, a group virtual private network (GroupVPN DecentralVPN) is self-configured to provide a seamless IP-layer connectivity among members of a group and support unmodified middleware and applications. Within appliances, Condor is used as the core underlying scheduler to dispatch tasks. In our system, these tasks could be jobs students schedule directly with Condor, as well as tasks, which are used to bootstrap MPI, Hadoop, or Twister pools on demand. The GroupVPN virtual network and the Condor middleware are both self-configured by using a peer-to-peer distributed hash table as an information system to publish and query information about available job scheduler(s) and assign virtual IP addresses. Users create on-demand MPI, Hadoop, and Twister virtual clusters by submitting Condor jobs, which are "wrappers" for dispatching and configuring the respective run-time systems. MPI tasks are submitted together with the job that creates an MPI ring, while Hadoop and Twister tasks are submitted to the virtual cluster using standard tools. The entire system can be seamlessly deployed on a managed IaaS infrastructure, but it is also easily installable on end-user resources; the same virtual appliance image is used in both environments. On a managed cloud infrastructure, IaaS middleware is used to deploy appliances, while in desktop/user environments, appliances are deployed with the native user interface of a virtual machine monitor. The appliance has been tested on widely used open-source and commercial desktop and server virtualization technologies; the same image can be instantiated on VMware, KVM, and VirtualBox on x86-based Windows, MacOS, and Linux systems.

FutureGrid has been used successfully in hands-on activities in semester classes at universities, week-long workshops, and summer schools, as well as in short tutorials at conferences. Such educational and outreach activities have included the following:

- "A Cloudy View on Computing": A hands-on workshop for faculty from historically black colleges and universities conducted in June 2011 at Elizabeth City State University. The emphasis of the work was on MapReduce concepts and hands-on exercises using two different MapReduce platforms. Lectures focused on specific case studies of MapReduce, and the workshop concluded with a programming exercise (PageRank or All-Pairs problem) to ensure faculty members have a substantial knowledge of MapReduce concepts and the Twister/Hadoop API. The workshop highlighted two specific educational MapReduce virtual appliances: Hadoop and Twister.

- Computer science courses: FutureGrid was used in courses including distributed systems and cloud computing for data-intensive sciences at Indiana University, cloud computing courses at the University of Florida and at the University of Piemonte Orientale in Italy, and scientific computing at Louisiana State University. FutureGrid was used to build prototype systems and allow students to acquire in-depth understanding of essential issues in practice, such as scalability, performance, availability, security, energy-efficiency, and workload balancing. Students took advantage of FutureGrid's dynamic provisioning infrastructure to switch between bare metal and virtual machine environments.

- Hands-on tutorials: The tutorial "Using and Building Infrastructure Clouds for Science" was given at the SuperComputing11 conference The tutorial had around 75 attendees, who were able to get accounts on FutureGrid and interact with the infrastructure with hands-on activities that included the deployment of their own virtual machines on the infrastructure. In addition to synchronous tutorials, the FutureGrid portal hosts several self-learning tutorials that guide its users through the core steps needed to configure, instantiate, and access dynamically provisioned educational environments.

## 23.9   Operational Lessons

We have already learned several unexpected lessons that we summarize next. *Technology Breakdown*. One highlight is the division of usage with the over 100 FutureGrid projects: 47% computer science, 27% technology evaluation, 18% life science applications, 13% other applications, 8% education, and a small but important 3% interoperability (some projects covered multiple categories, and so the total is greater than 100%) [vLDWF12].

Education is actually more important and successful than the fraction indicates as a single class project implies 20-50 users of FutureGrid. Our usage profile is very different from other U.S. national infrastructures. We also found that the diverse needs of users require significant user support but that many users did not need huge numbers of nodes. Thus we changed plans and targeted more funds at user support and less on hardware expansion. The ability to request both bare metal and virtualized nodes was important in many projects. This was perhaps not unexpected but it is different from traditional environments with fixed software stacks. Further cloud technologies are rapidly changing on a 3-6 month cycle and in fact maturing, but these require a substantial effort from both software and systems groups to track, deploy, and support. These groups must collaborate closely; and, for example, automating of processes documented by the systems team through software development is helpful in providing a scalable service.

*Interoperability Experiments.* We have seen an interest by the community in interoperability experiments x1and infrastructure and have thus deployed endpoints for Unicore and Genesis II. In addition, collaborations are taking place with the Grid5000 [imp12b], the SAGA project [sag12], and the OCCI project [wwwd] in the Open Grid Forum (OGF) [wwwe].

## Acknowledgments

We thank the following people for their contributions to this chapter: Fugang Wang, Shava Smallen, Ryan Hartman, Koji Tanaka, Sharif Islam, David Hancock, Tom Johnson, John Bresnahan, Piotr Luszczek, Terry Moore, Mauricio Tsugawa, Thomas William, Andrew Younge, and the rest of the FutureGrid team. This work was supported in part by the U.S. Department of Energy under Contract DE-AC02-06CH11357.

# Chapter 24

## LLGrid: Supercomputer for Sensor Processing

Jeremy Kepner, William Arcand, Nadya Bliss, David Bestor, Chansup Byun,
Matthew Hubbell, Peter Michaleas, Julie Mullen, Andrew Prout, Albert
Reuther, Antonio Rosa, and Charles Yee

*MIT Lincoln Laboratory*

## 24.1   Overview

MIT Lincoln Laboratory is a federally funded research and development center that applies advanced technology to problems of national interest. Research and development activities focus on long-term technology development as well as rapid system prototyping and demonstration. A key part of this mission is to develop and deploy advanced sensor systems. Developing the algorithms for these systems requires interactive access to large-scale computing and data storage. Deploying these systems requires that the computing and storage capabilities are transportable and energy efficient. The LLGrid system of supercomputers allows hundreds of researchers simultaneous interactive access to large amounts of processing and storage for development and testing of their sensor processing algorithms. The requirements of the LLGrid user base are as diverse as the sensors they are developing: sonar, radar, infrared, optical, hyperspectral, video, bio, and cyber. However, there are two common elements: delivering large amounts of data interactively to many processors and high level user interfaces that require minimal user training. The LLGrid software stack pro-

This work is sponsored by the Department of the Air Force under Air Force Contract FA8721-05-C-0002. Opinions, interpretations, conclusions, and recommendations are those of the author and are not necessarily endorsed by the United States Government.

vides these capabilities on dozens of LLGrid computing clusters across Lincoln Laboratory. LLGrid systems range from very small (a few nodes) to very large (40+ racks).

### 24.1.1    Program Background

Sensor prototyping at Lincoln spans a wide range of sensor modalities: sonar, radar, infrared, optical, hyperspectral, video, and cyber. The goal is to demonstrate sensor systems that push the limits of size, resolution, and bandwidth. These requirements have been a part of Lincoln Laboratory since before its inception and can be traced back to the first radar processing systems developed at the MIT Radiation Laboratory during World War II [Sv48]. At the start of the Cold War MIT Lincoln Laboratory was established to develop anti-aircraft defenses. Interactive, high performance digital computing systems were at the core of this effort and led to such groundbreaking systems as Whirlwind, TX-0 (Transistor eXperiment zero), and TX-2 [Mck99]. Whirlwind was the first magnetic core memory system. The TX-0 design was spun out of Lincoln Laboratory and formed the basis of Digital Equipment Corporation (now a part of Hewlett-Packard). TX-0 was one of the first computer systems equipped with a graphical user interface (GUI) and among its many accomplishments were the interactive first video games.

Today, development of sensor systems at Lincoln requires access to parallel computing and parallel data storage by hundreds of users. In addition, the timeframe for sensor algorithm development is often very short (weeks to months). Algorithm developers need to work interactively in high level languages (e.g., MATLAB, Java, and Python). These requirements have led to the LLGrid family of supercomputers (TX-$\alpha$, TX-$\beta$, TX-2500, TX-3D, TX-DoD, TX-X, TX-Green, etc). The LLGrid parallel high level language work and interactive scheduler have been described extensively in the literature (see [Kep09, BIBO06, BlKe06] and references therein). In addition, the LLGrid architecture has had a significant impact outside of Lincoln Laboratory and has influenced the design and deployment of a range of systems such at the Mathworks Parallel Computing Toolbox and the Microsoft .NET framework.

As the amounts of data produced by sensors increases, sensor algorithms are increasingly being deployed in an energy constrained environment. Demonstrating the algorithms on energy efficient hardware reduces deployment risks. TX-Green is the first LLGrid system that will be an interactive supercomputer in a transportable and energy efficient infrastructure. In addition, TX-Green is the pathfinder for the 20 Megawatt Massachusetts Green High Performance Computing Center (MGHPCC.org) located next to the hydroelectric power station in Holyoke, MA.

The DoD High Performance Computing Modernization Program (HPCMP) has been the primary sponsor of many of the largest LLGrid systems via its Distributed High Performance Investments (DHPI) portfolio. The goal of DHPI is to address needs that lie outside of those normally met by the HPCMP supercomputing centers. These needs typically include novel hardware (in this case energy efficient supercomputing) and workloads (in this case interactive supercomputing via high level programming environments).

## 24.2    Applications and Workloads

The dominant use of LLGrid systems is for interactive processing of sensor data. This work typically occurs within the context of prototyping a new sensor system that consists of three components: sensors, algorithms, and computing. Likewise, the development of these systems typically occurs in three steps:

1. Collect initial sensor data

2. Develop algorithms

3. Port algorithms to an embedded real-time system

LLGrid primarily services users in steps 2 and 3 of this process. Sensor algorithm development is a highly interactive and iterative process that takes the algorithm analyst from a rudimentary understanding of the data to a complete characterization of all its signals, noise, and clutter. The iterative process consists of changing the algorithm code, running the code, and observing the results of the code. The goal of LLGrid is to allow the user to quickly complete these iterations on large data sets. A unique feature of LLGrid is that it is also a deployable system. Thus, if a user's code runs on LLGrid then it will also run on a similarly configured deployed system.

The above process requires LLGrid to be highly interactive. As such, all processors are devoted to interactive usage and users jobs run immediately. LLGrid systems are sized so that during normal loads, there are always some processors available to the users. Larger fractions of the system are available to the user upon requests that can usually be satisfied inside a few minutes. The median job on LLGrid is <30 seconds and is a result of users debugging their code. The mean job on LLGrid is >30 minutes and is a result of jobs that run for hours after the code is working properly.

## 24.2.1 Application Characteristics

The details of sensor processing algorithm development differ for each sensor. However, there are some common computational elements, such as:

- Data upload

- File format conversion

- Metadata harvesting

- Registration

- Clutter detection

- Clutter removal

- Background characterization

- Background normalization

- Target detection

- Target parameter estimate

- Target track estimation

- Track fusion

LLGrid users are first and foremost scientists and engineers. The LLGrid system has been optimized to help the users get through the above steps with as little effort as possible. For nearly all the steps, the focus is the LLGrid central file system. The inputs and output of nearly every stage of sensor processing development flow through the LLGrid central file system [WOrS+09].

## Data Upload

A typical data set will consist of a finite duration of data collected from a prototype sensor system. The volume of data is typically constrained to what can be held on several commodity storage devices. The data are typically in files with formats that are unique to the sensor. The size and number of files can range from many small files to a few large files. The first step is to transfer the data from the storage devices into the LLGrid central file system either via network or by directly connecting the storage devices into LLGrid. The data transfer time can range from hours to days. To make this process simple for the users, they can mount the LLGrid central file system to their desktop and simply copy files via "drag and drop."

## Conversion and Metadata Harvesting

The next step in the process is for the analyst to write a program that converts all the data from a custom file format to a more generally usable format. In addition, the file metadata (e.g., collection time, collection location, sensor parameters, etc.) will often be harvested and stored in a database. At this point the analyst is now in a position to start developing their signal processing algorithms.

## Registration

Sensors that are pointed toward the ground must be registered with respect to a global coordinate position. This can be as simple as reading the coordinate info from the metadata or as hard as comparing the image with a large collection of other images to determine the precise location of the image. In the former case, the computational power is minimal, while in the latter case a large amount of parallel computing power is required to compare many images. Often, a large part of the algorithm development effort can be expended during the highly iterative process of changing an algorithm and determining if the registration has improved. Typically high level languages are used during this algorithm development process. As the registration improves, the user will increase the number of images they test their algorithm on until eventually they are registering all of the images.

## Clutter

Many sensor systems have defects that cause them to produce spuriously high or low signals. Likewise, certain environmental conditions can cause similar sensor responses. Regardless of their source, these signals are clutter and need to be removed in order to see targets of interest. The process for detecting, characterizing and removing clutter is very similar to that for registration, although it is usually less computationally intensive. A highly iterative process of changing an algorithm and determining its effects on cluster is used. Typically these algorithms are implemented in high level languages.

## Background

The process of detecting targets typically consists of modeling the data as a combination of random background noise and non-random targets. Characterizing the background requires sampling some of the data to compute means, variances, and other statistical measures. These statistical measures are then applied to all the data to normalize or subtract off the background signal from the measurements. The algorithms for analyzing the background signal can range from fairly simple to very complex. The process of developing and testing background removal algorithms is similar to registration and clutter removal.

## Targets

After removing clutter and background noise, in theory, all that is left are the targets of interest. Target detection algorithms typically try to establish a noise varying threshold for determining that a target is present. In addition, after a detection has been made, the target parameters (e.g., location, size, and shape) are often estimated via additional algorithms. The ultimate goal of the entire registration, clutter removal, background subtraction, and detection process is to maximize the probability of detection ($P_D$) and minimize the probability of false alarm ($P_{FA}$). Developing these algorithms is similar to the processes mentioned in the previous steps. However, while the data read in is large (i.e., all the data that has come through the previous steps), ideally, the data written out is small. In addition, while the previous steps were data independent (i.e., the amount of processing does not depend upon the actual measured values), the amount of processing for targets is highly variable and depends upon the number and distribution of targets. In all the previous steps, all the data is read in and written out to a file system. In detection, it is common to write out target information to a database.

## Tracks

The increasing use of persistent sensors that cover large areas for long times can result in many detections. Detection measurements are aggregated into tracks that combine a whole series of related measurements. These tracks represent data over space and time and can contain a variety of metadata associated with these tracks. Track construction and analysis is an active area of research, but the approach to developing these algorithms is very similar to those for target detection, with the exception that input detections will usually come from a database. In addition, the mathematics of track analysis is often "sparse" or based on graphs [KeGi11] instead of dense and based on traditional signal processing techniques. As a result, the computational efficiency of these "post-detection" or "back-end" algorithms are often significantly lower than the "pre-detection" or "front-end" algorithms.

## Repeat

Development of large collections of track data has now spawned a whole new area often referred to as Signal Processing on Graphs (SPG)[MBW10]. In SPG, the techniques of registration, clutter removal, background subtraction, detection, and tracking are then reapplied to these large collections of relatively unstructured data to mine tracks of interest buried in collections of track data. This work is driving the development of an entirely new set of tools and mathematics to deal with the sparse signal processing of databases [KeGi11, Kep12, KAB+12].

### 24.2.2 Benchmarking

Benchmarking plays two important roles in LLGrid. The first is acceptance testing of the hardware to verify that the vendor has provided what was specified. The second is to optimize the software tools in the LLGrid software stack.

### Acceptance Testing

LLGrid is a fleet of dozens of clusters, made of mostly commodity components. Even the largest of these clusters is too small to justify the effort to develop a custom procurement and acceptance test. Furthermore, competitive pressures mean that the vendors can only devote a fixed amount of time to satisfying an acceptance test.

The LLGrid goal for acceptance testing is to verify that the hardware components delivered by the vendor are as specified. The HPC Challenge [LDK06] benchmark suite (see www.hpcchallenge.org) is one solution to this problem. HPC Challenge tests the four key components of an HPC system: processor, memory, network bandwidth, and network latency. HPC Challenge is an open benchmark freely available with publicly posted results. In addition, HPC Challenge is required by many large supercomputing procurements so vendors are familiar with it and often have in-house expertise in optimizing and running HPC Challenge.

The process LLGrid follows for using HPC Challenge in acceptance testing is as follows. After a vendor has been selected the peak HPC Challenge performance for the system is estimated by picking the closest equivalent system in the public HPC Challenge results and extrapolating to the precise size of the system being acquired. The HPC Challenge benchmarks are typically "contest" level benchmarks that are achieved with a significant amount of system tuning that may be specific to the benchmarks (e.g., specific network buffer sizes and memory swap sizes). For acquisition purposes, the performance on the system as it will be configured for use is more important, and the target performance is set at half the peak estimated performance. These targets provide for a good balance between customer verification and vendor time spent acceptance testing.

While HPC Challenge is good for measuring the peak performance of the system, there is also a need to do endurance testing to verify the reliability of the system. For endurance testing LLGrid again uses HPC Challenge and follows the DoD HPCMP acceptance testing procedures that are also well known to many supercomputing vendors. The HPCMP procedures indicate that endurance testing is to be conducted for 14 days while keeping the system at least 50% loaded. This is easily done with a simple set of scripts that continuously run HPC Challenge over a wide range of sizes. In addition, at the end of these tests there is a wealth of data that can be submitted to the HPC Challenge Web site for the benefit of the community.

### Optimization

LLGrid optimization is primarily focused on the LLGrid specific software stack after the hardware has been accepted. The most important of these is the optimization of the LLGrid central file system. The file system performance is measured using the IO Zone benchmark (see www.iozone.org).

Most LLGrid users use high level programming environments such as Java, Python, and MATLAB. Parallel MATLAB performance is optimized using the pMATLAB implementation of HPC Challenge [Kep09], which is a part of the pMATLAB package.

Increasingly, graph and database operations have become more important to LLGrid users. The Graph500 [BMG+06] benchmark (see www.graph500.org) is used for measuring the performance of both sparse matrix (i.e., graph) operations and database performance [BAB+12].

---

## 24.3  System Overview

LLGrid is designed for rapid prototyping of sensor processing algorithms. The LLGrid architecture meets this design goal by using:

- Commodity processing nodes that run standard software without recompilation

- Open source system software that allows the system to be tuned for its mission

- Application specific interfaces for rapidly prototyping sensor algorithms

## 24.4 Hardware Architecture

LLGrid compute hardware can be thought of as a commodity cluster with a few key distinguishing features. LLGrid compute nodes have high memory per core because high level programming environments are memory intensive. LLGrid compute nodes have a large amount of local RAID storage that can support various distributed file system and distributed database technologies.

The vast majority of LLGrid network traffic flows through its central file system [KeBA+11]. The LLGrid central storage array is not a commodity system and is usually the fastest system that can be purchased that runs an open source parallel file system. In addition, the network topology is designed around the file system. A single core switch is used so all nodes have equal access to the file system. Historically, the support for file IO has been broadest for the Ethernet fabrics and this is what LLGrid systems use.

## 24.5 System Software

LLGrid compute nodes need to run the same software that LLGrid users run on their desktops. The system software on LLGrid compute nodes is similar to a desktop Linux configuration with kernel extensions to support the parallel file system and additional security. The system software is updated monthly to keep up with the rapid pace of software packages in the Linux community. Many of the packages that LLGrid users run are large. To reduce pressure on the central file system these packages are installed on the compute nodes. Multiple versions of these packages are installed so that the compute node can exactly match the version of the software the users are running on their desktops. To support these large system images the LLGrid team has written a high performance system imager that it optimized to these particular requirements.

The central file system is mounted on every compute node, every login node, and every user's desktop system. All LLGrid software tools are made available to the users via the LLGrid central file system and most users run jobs on LLGrid directly from their desktop environment without logging into LLGrid. The central file system is an open source parallel file system (e.g., Lustre) that allows the LLGrid team to tune the performance via modifying the system parameters and by modifying the source code.

The interactive nature of LLGrid requires that jobs be launched immediately. All jobs run on LLGrid are executed and managed by open source schedulers (e.g., GridEngine). Using an open source scheduler allows the LLGrid team to tune the performance via modifying the scheduler parameters and by modifying the source code.

LLGrid system status information is collected in real-time on every node and every job run on LLgrid. This data is then fed into a set of high performance data analytics tools and databases. The data is analyzed and displayed in a 3D model of the LLGrid hardware that is accessible via a Massively Multiplayer On-line Role Playing Game (MMORPG) interface [HuKe12]. The interface provides instantaneous visual feedback on the health and status of all LLGrid resources. For example, nodes can change color, size, and position based on their state. The location of a node in the Game interface is identical to that in the real datacenter. The data analysis system continually compares all measured values (e.g., CPU load and free memory) with target values and sends out alerts whenever these are exceeded. These alerts have significantly improved the reliability of LLGrid as they identify transient behaviors in users' programs that can become unstable if they collide with other users. These program behaviors are almost always unintentional and the users are pleased to be made aware of these issues as it makes their programs run faster and more reliably.

More recently, the LLGrid stack has begun to incorporate the ability to launch Virtual Machines (VMs) and "Big Data" technologies (e.g., Hadoop). Interestingly, LLGrid users are most interested in the capability offered by these technologies, but not the specific technologies themselves (see next section).

## 24.6  Programming System

Distributed arrays (or Partitioned Global Address Spaces - PGAS) is the dominant programming model on LLGrid. Distributed arrays work naturally with matrices and linear algebra. Most LLGrid users have no prior experience in parallel computing. Distributed arrays allow these users to get up and running quickly. A typical LLGrid user can go from account setup to getting real speedup on their application in less than two hours.

Most LLGrid user programs follow the pattern of distributing an array across a large number of processors, performing calculations on the local part of the array, and then performing a collective operation on the entire array. This pattern is then looped over many times within the program. The distributed arrays programming model supports these programs very well. The distributed arrays programming model is independent of whether the user is running on distributed memory nodes, shared memory nodes, or a hybrid. Distributed arrays are also good for expert programmers because they support very complex data movements such as multi-dimensional transposes and nearest neighbor boundary conditions. Combining high level programming environments with distributed arrays consistently results in a high productivity parallel programming environment [FuHoKe06].

Message passing programming models are also supported by LLGrid. These are typically used via 3rd party software. LLGrid supports several flavors of open source MPI libraries so as to be compatible with these 3rd party packages.

Users do not need to write scheduler submission scripts to run a job on LLGrid. The appropriate scheduler scripts are automatically constructed when the user launches a parallel job in a high level environment. Some users do write scheduler submission scripts to execute programs that consist of running the same program on a list of inputs. These programs fall within the map/reduce parallel programming model. As the map/reduce parallel model grew in popularity, the LLGrid team implemented a simple LLGridMapReduce command line program that automatically generates and submits the appropriate scheduler scripts for such a job. Users enjoy the simplicity of map/reduce, but most outgrow it quickly [StKe12]. Map/reduce is a good entry point into parallel programming, but it is entirely encompassed by the distributed arrays model, which is more scalable and can handle more complex programs.

The increasing need to apply signal processing techniques to unstructured data (e.g., text, cyber record, DNA sequences) has led to the need to support databases for these applications. The LLGrid team has developed the Dynamic Distributed Dimensional Data Model (D4M) library to provide such an interface. D4M allows users to interact with unstructured data via strings and graphs. Data in a parallel program or in a database are both represented using an "associative" array which is a large sparse matrix that uses strings for the rows, columns, and values. The primary advantage of D4M is that it allows complicated algorithms to be written more quickly than using standard approaches [KAB$^+$12].

## 24.7 Computing Facilities

LLGrid is spread across a range of facilities that range from small rooms to the 300 rack MGHPCC. Increasingly, the energy cost and environmental impact of supercomputing have become important. To mitigate this, LLGrid has led in the development of datacenter capabilities in Holyoke, MA, next to the 50 megawatt hydroelectric station. At this site the electrical costs are approximately half what is paid at LLGrid's other sites and 90% of the electricity used emits no $CO_2$.

Costs are further reduced by using container based computing infrastructure that "breathes" in response to the computing load and the external environment. Using this approach it should be possible to avoid cooling for 90% of the year. Using direct expansion cooling eliminates the need for any water infrastructure. Finally, using a high speed digital power transfer switch eliminates the cost and infrastructure incurred by a backup generator.

# Bibliography

[100]        1000 genomes: A deep catalog of human genetic variation. http://www.1000genomes.org/.

[75485]      ANSI/IEEE Standard 754-1985. Standard for binary floating point arithmetic. Technical report, Institute of Electrical and Electronics Engineers, 1985.

[80p08]      80 PLUS, 2008.

[AA06]       Keith Adams and Ole Agesen. A comparison of software and hardware techniques for x86 virtualization. In *Proc. of the 12th Intl Conf. on Architectural Support for Programming Languages and Operating System*, 2006.

[AAD⁺]       E. Agullo, C. Augonnet, J. Dongarra, H. Ltaief, R. Namyst, S. Thibault, and S. Tomov. A hybridization methodology for high-performance linear algebra software for GPUs. In *GPU Computing Gems, Jade Edition*, 2:473–484, 2011.

[ABE⁺08]     Sadaf Alam, Richard Barrett, Markus Eisenbach, Mark Fahey, Rebecca Hartman-Baker, Jeffrey Kuehn, Stephen Poole, Ramanan Sankaran, and Patrick Worley. The Cray XT4 Quad-core: A first look. In *Proceedings of the 2008 CUG Conference*, Helsinki, Finland, 2008.

[ABF⁺10]     L. Adhianto, S. Banerjee, M. Fagan, M. Krentel, G. Marin, J. Mellor-Crummey, and N. R. Tallent. HPCToolkit: Tools for performance analysis of optimized parallel programs. *Concurrency and Computation: Practice and Experience*, 22(6):685–701, April 2010.

[AC00]       Wanda Andreoni and Alessandro Curioni. New advances in chemistry and material science with cpmd and parallel computing. *Parallel Computing*, 26:819–842, 2000.

[ADD⁺09]     E. Agullo, J. Demmel, J. Dongarra, B. Hadri, J. Kurzak, J. Langou, H. Ltaief, P. Luszczek, and S. Tomov. Numerical linear algebra on emerging architectures: The PLASMA and MAGMA projects. In *Journal of Physics: Conference Series*, volume 180, page 012037. IOP Publishing, 2009.

[AFG⁺09]     Michael Armbrust, Armando Fox, Rean Griffith, Anthony D. Joseph, Randy Katz, Andy Konwinski, Gunho Lee, David Patterson, Ariel Rabkin, Ion Stoica, and Matei Zaharia. Above the clouds: A Berkeley view of cloud computing. Technical report, University of California at Berkeley, February 2009.

[Ahm08]      M. Ahmed. Google Search Finds Seafaring Solution. In *The Times*, September 15, 2008.

[AKB+07]    Sadaf Alam, Jeff Kuehn, Richard Barrett, Jeff Larkin, Mark Fahey, Ramanan Sankaran, and Patrick Worley. Cray XT4: An early evaluation for petascale scientific simulation. In *SC'07: Proceedings of the 2007 ACM/IEEE Conference on Supercomputing*, pages 1–12, New York, NY, 2007. ACM.

[AKHB10]    Phil Andrews, Patricia Kovatch, Victor Hazlewood, and Troy Baer. Scheduling a 100,000 core supercomputer for maximum utilization and capability. In *ICPPW'10: Proceedings of the 2010 39th International Conference on Parallel Processing*, pages 421–427, Washington, DC, 2010. IEEE Computer Society.

[ALC]       ALCC:        ASCR        Leadership        Computing        Challenge. http://science.energy.gov/ascr/facilities/alcc/.

[All]       Allinea. Allinea ddt - the debugging tool for parallel computing. http://www.allinea.com/products/ddt/.

[Amaa]      Amazon. Elastic Compute Cloud.

[Amab]      Amazon. Simple Storage Services.

[Ama09]     S. Amarasinghe, D. Campbell, W. Carlson, A. Chien, W. Dally, E. Elnohazy, M. Hall, R. Harrison, W. Harrod, K. Hill, and A. Snavely ExaScale software study: Software challenges in Extreme scale systems. Technical report, DARPA IPTO, Air Force Research Labs, 2009.

[AMD]       AMD. Six-core AMD Opteron processor. http://www.amd.com.

[AMD12]     AMD, Inc. *AMD Opteron 6200 Series Processors Linux Tuning Guide*, 2012. http://developer.amd.com.

[ARK10]     R. Alverson, D. Roweth, and L. Kaplan. The Gemini system interconnect. In *High Performance Interconnects (HOTI), 2010 IEEE 18th Annual Symposium on*, pages 83–87. IEEE, Aug. 2010.

[ASM+08]    G. Alvarez, M.S. Summers, D.E. Maxwell, M. Eisenbach, J.S. Meredith, J.M. Larkin, J. Levesque, T.A. Maier, P.R.C. Kent, E.F. D'Azevedo, and T. C. Schulthess. New algorithm to enable 400+ tflop/s sustained performance in simulations of disorder effects in high-t c superconductors. In *2008 ACM/IEEE Conference on Supercomputing Conference on High Performance Networking and Computing*. IEEE Press Piscataway, NJ, USA, 2008.

[ASS09]     Yuichiro Ajima, Shinji Sumimoto, and Toshiyuki Shimizu. Tofu: A 6D mesh/-torus interconnect for exascale computers. *IEEE Computer*, 42(11):36–40, 2009.

[ATNW10]    C. Augonnet, S. Thibault, R. Namyst, and P. Wacrenier. StarPU: A unified platform for task scheduling on heterogeneous multicore architectures. *Concurrency Computat. Pract. Exper.*, 2010. (to appear).

[Att09]     N. Attig. Computational physics with PetaFlops computers. *Computer Physics Communications*, 180(4):555–558, 2009.

[B+04]      P. A. Boyle et al. Hardware and software status of QCDOC. *Nucl. Phys. Proc. Suppl.*, 129:838–843, 2004.

[BAB+08]   K. J. Bowers, B. J. Albright, B. Bergen, L. Yin, K. J. Barker, and D. J. Kerbyson. 0.374 pflop/s trillion-particle kinetic modeling of laser plasma interaction on roadrunner. In *Proceedings of the 2008 ACM/IEEE Conference on Supercomputing*, SC '08, pages 63:1–63:11, Piscataway, NJ, USA, 2008. IEEE Press.

[BAB+12]   C. Byun, W. Arcand, D. Bestor, B. Bergeron, M. Hubbell, J. Kepner, A. McCabe, P. Michaleas, J. Mullen, D. O'Gwynn, A. Prout, A. Reuther, A. Rosa, and C. Yee, "Driving Big Data With Big Compute," IEEE HPEC, Sep 10-12, 2012, Waltham, MA.

[Bae10]    Troy Baer. Quality of service for scheduling on Cray XT systems. In *Proceedings of the 2010 CUG Conference* [The10].

[Bak77]    H. Baker. The incremental garbage collection of processes. *Proceedings of the Symposium on Artificial Intelligence Programming Languages, SIGPLAN Notices*, 12, 1977.

[BBC+08]   Keren Bergman, Shekhar Borkar, Dan Campbell, William Carlson, William Dally, Monty Denneau, Paul Franzon, William Harrod, Kerry Hill, Jon Hiller, Sherman Karp, Stephen Keckler, Dean Klein, Robert Lucas, Mark Richards, Al Scarpelli, Steven Scott, Allan Snavely, Thomas Sterling, R Stanley Williams, Katherine Yelick, and Peter Kogge. Exascale Computing Study: Technology Challenges in Acheiving Exascale Systems. 2008.

[BBC12]    A. Wang, B.R. de Supinski, B.L. Bihari, M. Wong, and W. Chen. A case for including transactions in openmp ii: Hardware transactional memory. B.M. Chapman et al. (eds.), IWOMP 2012, (LNCS 7312):44–58, 2012.

[BBD+12]   G. Bosilca, A. Bouteiller, A. Danalis, T. Herault, P. Lemarinier, and J. Dongarra. DAGuE: A generic distributed DAG Engine for high performance computing. *Parallel Computing*, 38:27–51, 2012.

[BBK+08]   E. Bohm, A. Bhatele, L. V. Kalé, M. E. Tuckerman, J. A. Gunnels, and G. J. Martyna. Fine-grained parallelization on the Car-Parrinello *ab initio* molecular dynamics method on the IBM Blue Gene/L supercomputer. *IBM Journal of Research and Development*, 52(1/2):159, January/March 2008.

[BBSG11]   M. Butler, L. Barnes, D.D. Sarma, and B. Gelinas. Bulldozer: An approach to multithreaded compute performance. *Micro, IEEE*, 31(2):6–15, 2011.

[BCC+97]   L.S. Blackford, J. Choi, A. Cleary, E. d'Azevedo, J. Demmel, I. Dhillon, J. Dongarra, S. Hammarling, G. Henry, A. Petitet, K. Stanley, D. Walker, and R.C. Whaley. *ScaLAPACK Users' Guide*. Society for Industrial Mathematics, 1997.

[BDF+03]   Paul Barham, Boris Dragovic, Keir Fraser, Steven Hand, Tim Harris, Alex Ho, Rolf Neugebauer, Ian Pratt, and Andrew Warfield. Xen and the art of virtualization. In *Proceedings of the 19th ACM Symposium on Operating Systems Principles(SOSP)*, Bolton Landing, USA, 2003.

[BDH+07]   Tanmoy Bhattacharya, Marcus Daniels, David Heckerman, Brian Foley, Nicole Frahm, Carl Kadie, Jonathan Carlson, Karina Yusim, Ben McMahon, Brian Gaschen, Simon Mallal, James I. Mullins, David C. Nickle, Joshua Herbeck, Christine Rousseau, Gerald H. Learn, Toshiyuki Miura, Christian

Brander, Bruce Walker, and Bette Korber. Founder effects in the assessment of hiv polymorphisms and hla allele associations. *Science* (Washington DC), 315(5818):1583–1586, 2007.

[BdJK⁺06] E. J. Bylaska, W. A. de Jong, K. Kowalski, T. P. Straatsma, M. Valievand D. Wang, E. Apr, T. L. Windusand S. Hirata, M. T. Hackler, Y. Zhao, P.-D. Fan, R. J. Harrison, M. Dupuis, D. M. A. Smith, J. Nieplocha, V. Tipparaju, M. Krishnan, A. A. Auer, M. Nooijen, E. Brown, G. Cisnerosand, G. I. Fann, H. Frchtl, J. Garza, K. Hirao, R. Kendall, J. A. Nichols, K. Tsemekhman, K. Wolinski, J. Anchell, D. Bernholdt, P. Borowski, T. Clark, D. Clerc, H. Dachsel, M. Deegan, K. Dyall, D, Elwood, E. Glendening, M. Gutowski, A. Hess, J. Jaffe, B. Johnson, J. Ju, R. Kobayashi, R. Kutteh, Z. Lin, R. Littlefield, X. Longand B. Meng, T. Nakajima, S. Ni, L. Pollack, M. Rosing, G. Sandrone, M. Stave, H. Taylorand G. Thomas, J. van Lenthe, A. Wong, and Z. Zhang. Nwchem, a computational chemistry package for parallel computers, version 5.0, Pacific Northwest National Laboratory, Richland, WA, USA, 2006.

[Bec06] P. Beckman, K. Iskra, K. Yoshii, and S. Coghlan, The influence of operating systems on the performance of collective operations at extreme scale. In *IEEE Conference on Cluster Computing*, 2006.

[bes] Prace-Best Practice Guides. http://www.prace-project.eu/Best-Practice-Guides.

[BFLK10] J. Bresnahan, T. Freeman, D. LaBissoniere, and K. Keahey. Cumulus: Open source storage cloud for science. In *SC2010*, 2010.

[BFLK11] J. Bresnahan, T. Freeman, D. LaBissoniere, and K. Keahey. Managing appliance launches in infrastructure clouds. In *TeraGrid 2011*, 2011.

[bgc] Blue Gene Consortium. http://www.bgconsortium.org/.

[BGG⁺09] D. Buntinas, B. Goglin, D. Goodell, G. Mercier, and S. Moreaud. Cache-efficient, intranode, large-message mpi communication with mpich2-nemesis. In *Parallel Processing, 2009. ICPP'09. International Conference on*, pages 462–469. IEEE, 2009.

[BGKM⁺11] Leonardo Bautista-Gomez, Dimitri Komatitsch, Naoya Maruyama, Seiji Tsuboi, Franck Cappello, and Satoshi Matsuoka. FTI: High performance Fault Tolerance Interface for hybrid systems. In *Proceedings of the 2011 ACM/IEEE International Conference for High Performance Computing, Networking, Storage and Analysis*, Seattle, WA, USA, 2011.

[bgp] IBM Blue Gene Solution. http://domino.research.ibm.com/comm/research_projects.nsf/pages/bluegene.index.html.

[bgwa] Jülich Blue Gene/P Extreme Scaling Workshop 2009. http://www2.fz-juelich.de/jsc/bg-ws09.

[bgwb] Jülich Blue Gene/P Extreme Scaling Workshop 2010. http://www2.fz-juelich.de/jsc/bg-ws10.

[bgwc] Jülich Blue Gene/P Extreme Scaling Workshop 2011. http://www2.fz-juelich.de/jsc/bg-ws11.

[BHH⁺09]   Troy Baer, Victor Hazlewood, Junseong Heo, Rick Mohr, and John Walsh. Large Lustre file system experiences at NICS. In *Proceedings of the 2009 CUG Conference* [The09].

[BHP⁺05]   Ron Brightwell, Trammell Hudson, Kevin Pedretti, Rolf Riesen, and Keith Underwood. Implementation and performance of Portals 3.3 on the Cray XT3 cluster. In *2005 IEEE International Conference on Cluster Computing*, pages 1–10, 2005.

[BHS⁺95]   D. Bailey, T. Harris, W. Saphir, R. Van der Wijngaart, A. Woo, and M. Yarrow. The NAS Parallel Benchmarks 2.0. Technical Report NAS-95-020, NASA Ames Research Center, Moffett Field, CA, 1995.

[BIBO06]   N. Bliss, R. Bond, H. Kim, A. Reuther and J. Kepner, "Interactive Grid Computing at Lincoln Laboratory," *Lincoln Laboratory Journal*, 2006, Vol 16, no 1.

[Bih12]   B.L. Bihari. Transactional memory for unstructured mesh simulations. *Journal of Scientific Computing 2012*, 2012. DOI10.1007/510915-012-9643-2.

[BK11]   Jeff Brooks and Gerry Kirschner. Cray XT3 and Cray XT series of supercomputers. In David Padua, editor, *Encyclopedia of Parallel Computing*. Springer, 2011.

[BKMN09]   Holger Brunst, Dieter Kranzlmuler, Matthias S. Muller, and Wolfgang E. Nagel. Tools for scalable parallel program analysis; vampir ng, marmot, and dewiz. *Int. J. Comput. Sci. Eng.*, 4(3):149–161, July 2009.

[BlKe06]   N. Bliss and J. Kepner, "pMATLAB Parallel MATLAB Library," *International Journal of High Performance Computing Applications: Special Issue on High Level Programming Languages and Models*, J. Kepner and H. Zima (editors), Winter 2006 (November).

[BL09]   G. Grospellier and B. Lelandais. The arcane development framework. In POOSC '09, Article 4, 2009.

[BMG⁺06]   D. Bader, K. Madduri, J. Gilbert, V. Shah, J. Kepner, T. Meuse, and A. Krishnamurthy, "Designing Scalable Synthetic Compact Applications for Benchmarking High Productivity Computing Systems," *CT Watch*, Volume 2, Number 4A, November, 2006.

[BMH⁺10a]   Steve W. Bruenn, Anthony Mezzacappa, William R. Hix, John M. Blondin, P. Marronetti, O. E. Bronson Messer, Charlotte J. Dirk, and Shin Yoshida. 2D and 3D Core-Collapse Supernovae Simulation Results Obtained with the CHIMERA Code. *arXiv:1002.4914 [astro-ph.SR]*, 2010.

[BMH⁺10b]   Steve W. Bruenn, Anthony Mezzacappa, William R. Hix, John M. Blondin, P. Marronetti, O. E. Bronson Messer, Charlotte J. Dirk, and Shin Yoshida. Mechanisms of Core-Collapse Supernovae & Simulation Results from the CHIMERA Code. *arXiv:1002.4909 [astro-ph.SR]*, 2010.

[BMSea09]   M. Bernaschi, S. Melchionna, S. Succi, et al., *Comp. Phys. Comm.*, 180, 1495, 2009.

[BOA08]   ARCHITECTURE BOARD. Openmp version 3.0. In *http://www.openmp. org*, 2008.

[BOS+09]      Julian Borrill, Leonid Oliker, John Shalf, Hongzhang Shan, and Andrew Usel-
              ton. Hpc global file system performance analysis using a scientic-application
              derived benchmark. In *Parallel Computing*, volume 35, pages 358–373, June
              2009.

[BOS+10]      DH Barouch, KL O'Brien, NL Simmons, SL King,P Abbink,LF Maxfield, YH
              Sun, A La Porte, AM Riggs, DM Lynch,SL Clark, K Backus, JR Perry, MS
              Seaman, A Carville,KG Mansfield, JJ Szinger, W Fischer, M Muldoon, and
              B Korber.Mosaic HIV-1 vaccines expand the breadth and depth of cellular
              immune responses in rhesus monkeys. Nature Medicine, 16(5):319-323, 2010.

[BPU05]       Ron Brightwell, Kevin Pedretti, and Keith Underwood. Initial performance
              evaluation of the Cray SeaStar interconnect. In *HOTI'05: Proceedings of the
              13th Symposium on High Performance Interconnects*, pages 51–57, Washing-
              ton, DC, 2005. IEEE Computer Society.

[BPUH06]      R. Brightwell, K. T. Pedretti, K. D. Underwood, and T. Hudson. Seastar
              interconnect: Balanced bandwidth for scalable performance. *IEEE Micro*,
              26(3):41–57, May 2006.

[BR10]        M. Bruggencate and D. Roweth. Dmapp api for one-sided program models
              on baker systems. In *Cray User Group Meeting*, 2010.

[BSWL98]      R. L. Berger, C. H. Still, E. A. Williams, and A. B. Langdon. On the domi-
              nant and subdominant behavior of stimulated raman and brillouin scattering
              driven by nonuniform laser beams. *Phys. Plasmas*, 5:4337–4356, 1998.

[BWBJ11]      J.D. Brown, S. Woodward, B.M. Bass, and C.L. Johnson. IBM power edge
              of network processor: A wire-speed system on a chip. *Micro, IEEE*, 31(2):76
              –85, Mar-Apr 2011. http://dx.doi.org/10.1109/MM.2011.3.

[BWM+12]      A. S. Bland, J. C. Wells, O. E. Messer, O. R. Hernandez, and J. H. Rogers.
              Titan: Early experience with the Cray xk6 at Oak Ridge National Laboratory.
              In *Cray User Group Meeting*, 2012.

[BYBS03]      J. Basney, W. Yurcik, R. Bonilla, and A. Slagell. The credential wallet: A
              classification of credential repositories highlighting myproxy. In *31st Research
              Conference on Communication, Information and Internet Policy (TPRC
              2003)*, 2003.

[BZ02]        P.J. Braam and R. Zahir. Lustre: A scalable high-performance file system.
              *Cluster File Systems, Inc.* 2002.

[CA12]        N. Chaderjian and J. Ahmad. Detached eddy simulation of the UH-60 ro-
              tor wake using adaptive mesh refinement. In *Proceedings of the American
              Helicopter Society 68th Annual Forum*, 2012.

[Cal]         Jamie Callan. The clueweb09 dataset. http://lemurproject.org/clueweb09.php.

[CB09]        N.M. Mosharaf Kabir Chowdhurya and Raouf Boutaba. A survey of network
              virtualization. In *Computer Networks*, 54(5): 862-876, 2010.

[CB11]        N. Chaderjian and P. G. Buning. High resolution Navier-Stokes simulation of
              rotor wakes. In *Proceedings of the American Helicopter Society 67th Annual
              Forum*, 2011.

[cbe]       Cachebench home page. http://icl.cs.utk.edu/projects/llcbench/cachebench. html.

[cC05]      Susanta Nanda and Tzi Chiueh. A Survey on Virtualization Technologies. Technical report TR179, Department of Computer Science, State University of New York, 2005.

[CCD+05]    D. A. Case, T. E. Cheatham, T. Darden, H. Gohlke, R. Luo, K. M. Merz, A. Onufriev, C. Simmerling, B. Wang, and R. J. Woods. The Amber biomolecular simulation programs. *J. Comput. Chem*, 26, 1668-1688, 2005.

[CCN03]     Existing and Potential Energy Demands for Los Alamos National Laboratory, Compiled by Concerned Citizens for Nuclear Safety, September 2003.

[CD11]      Weiwei Chen and Ewa Deelman. Partitioning and scheduling workflows across multiple sites with storage constraints. In *9th International Conference on Parallel Processing and Applied Mathmatics*, Torun, Poland, Sept 2011.

[CDC+]      D.A. Case, T.A. Darden, T.E. Cheatham, III, C.L. Simmerling, J. Wang, R.E. Duke, R. Luo, R.C. Walker, W. Zhang, K.M. Merz, B. Roberts, S. Hayik, A. Roitberg, G. Seabra, J. Swails, A.W. Gtz, I. Kolossvry, K.F.Wong, F. Paesani, J. Vanicek, R.M.Wolf, J. Liu, X. Wu, S.R. Brozell, T. Steinbrecher, H. Gohlke, Q. Cai, X. Ye, J. Wang, M.-J. Hsieh, G. Cui, D.R. Roe, D.H. Mathews, M.G. Seetin, R. Salomon-Ferrer, C. Sagui, V. Babin, T. Luchko, S. Gusarov, A. Kovalenko, and P.A. Kollman. AMBER 12 Reference Manual. http://ambermd.org/doc12/Amber12.pdf.

[CDC+12]    D.A. Case, T.A. Darden, T.E. Cheatham, III, C.L. Simmerling, J. Wang, R.E. Duke, R. Luo, R.C. Walker, W. Zhang, K.M. Merz, B. Roberts, S. Hayik, A. Roitberg, G. Seabra, J. Swails, A.W. Gtz, I. Kolossvry, K.F.Wong, F. Paesani, J. Vanicek, R.M.Wolf, J. Liu, X. Wu, S.R. Brozell, T. Steinbrecher, H. Gohlke, Q. Cai, X. Ye, J. Wang, M.-J. Hsieh, G. Cui, D.R. Roe, D.H. Mathews, M.G. Seetin, R. Salomon-Ferrer, C. Sagui, V. Babin, T. Luchko, S. Gusarov, A. Kovalenko, and P.A. Kollman. AMBER 12, 2012. University of California, San Francisco.

[CDG+06]    Fay Chang, Jeffrey Dean, Sanjay Ghemawat, Wilson C. Hsieh, Deborah A. Wallach, Mike Burrows, Tushar Chandra, Andrew Fikes, and Robert E. Gruber. BigTable: A distributed storage system for structured data. In *OSDI '06: Proceedings of the 7th USENIX Symposium on Operating Systems Design and Implementation*, pages 15–15, Berkeley, CA, USA, 2006. USENIX Association.

[CDK+01]    Rohit Chandra, Leonardo Dagum, Dave Kohr, Dror Maydan, Jeff McDonald, and Ramesh Menon. *Parallel Programming in OpenMP*. Morgan Kaufmann Publishers, 2001.

[CEH+11]    D. Chen, N.A. Eisley, P. Heidelberger, R.M. Senger, Y. Sugawara, S. Kumar, V. Salapura, D.L. Satterfield, B. Steinmacher-Burow, and J.J. Parker. The IBM Blue Gene/Q interconnection network and message unit. In *High Performance Computing, Networking, Storage and Analysis (SC), 2011 International Conference for*, pages 1 –10, Nov 2011. http://dx.doi.org/10.1145/2063384.2063419.

[CEH+12]   D. Chen, N.A. Eisley, P. Heidelberger, R.M. Senger, Y. Sugawara, S. Kumar, V. Salapura, D. Satterfield, B. Steinmacher-Burow, and J. Parker. The IBM Blue Gene/Q interconnection fabric. *IEEE Micro*, 32(1):32–43, Jan-Feb 2012. http://dx.doi.org/10.1109/MM.2011.96.

[Cen]       Center for Analysis and Prediction of Storms, University of Oklahoma. The ARPS System. http://www.caps.ou.edu/ARPS/.

[CER]       Cern Virtual Machines. http://rbuilder.cern.ch/project/cernvm/releases.

[CER12]     CERN.  The Large Hadron Collider, 2012. http://public.web.cern.ch/public/en/lhc/lhc-en.html.

[cfe]       Configuration Management for Agile System Administrators. http://www.cfengine.org.

[CH11]      Ron C. Chiang and H. Howie Huang. Tracon: Interference-aware scheduling for data-intensive applications in virtualized environments. In *Proceedings of 2011 International Conference for High Performance Computing, Networking, Storage and Analysis*, SC, Seattle, WA, 2011.

[CHEa]      CompreHensive collaborativE Framework (Chef).

[Cheb]      Yangyi Chen.  Privacy preserving gene read mapping using hybrid cloud. FutureGrid Project.

[CHT+13]    P. Coteus, S. Hall, T. Takken, R. Rand, S. Tian, G. Kopcsay, R. Bickford, A. Lanzetta, F. Giordano, C. Marroquin, M. Jeanson, and R. Vossberg. Packaging the Blue Gene/Q Supercomputer. *IBM Journal of Research and Development*, 57(1/2), Jan 2013.

[CJKS10]    Mike A. Clark, Balint Joo, Anthony D. Kennedy, and Paulo J. Silva. Better HMC integrators for dynamical simulations. *PoS*, LATTICE2010:323, 2010.

[cli08]     ClimateSavers, 2008.

[Cola]      Chimera Collaboration. http://astrodev.phys.utk.edu/chimera/doku.php/.

[Colb]      MIMD Lattice Computation Collaboration.  MILC.  http://www.physics.indiana.edu/~sg/milc.html.

[Com12]     Adaptive Computing. MOAB Cluster Suit Webpage. Webpage, Last access Feb. 2012.

[con]       Condor: High Throughput Computing.

[Cor08]     NVIDIA Corporation. NVIDIA CUDA compute unified device architecture programming guide version 2.0. NVIDIA Corporation, California, 2008.

[cp2]       Cp2k. http://www.cp2k.org/.

[CPA+10]    Hank Childs, David Pugmire, Sean Ahern, Brad Whitlock, Mark Howison, Prabhat, Gunther Weber, and E. Wes Bethel. Extreme scaling of production visualization software on diverse architectures. *Computer Graphics and Applications*, 30(3):22–31, May/June 2010. special issue on ultrascale visualization.

[cra]        Cray xe6 mpp system. http://www.cray.com/Products/XE/CrayXE6System. aspx.

[Cra09a]     Cray, Inc. Cray XT system overview, S-2423-22. http://docs.cray.com, 2009.

[Cra09b]     Cray, Inc. Managing Lustre on a Cray XT System, S-0010-22. http://docs. cray.com, 2009.

[Cra11a]     Cray, Inc. Cray Application Developer's Environment User's Guide, S-2396-60. http://docs.cray.com, 2011.

[Cra11b]     Cray, Inc. Managing System Software for Cray XE and XT systems, S-2393-3103. http://docs.cray.com, 2011.

[Cra11c]     Cray, Inc. Using Cray Performance Analysis Tools, S–2376–53, December 2011. http://cray.docs.com.

[Cra12a]     Cray, Inc. Cray Application Developer's Environment User's Guide, S-2396-610, May 2012. http://cray.docs.com.

[Cra12b]     Cray, Inc. Introduction to Cray Data Virtualization Service, S0005-4003, March 2012. http://cray.docs.com.

[Cra12c]     Cray, Inc. Managing System Software for Cray XE and Cray XK Systems, S-2393-4003, March 2012. http://cray.docs.com.

[Cra12d]     Cray, Inc. Workload Management and Application Placement for the Cray Linux Environment, S–2496–4003, March 2012. http://cray.docs.com.

[CS79]       P.A. Cundall and O.D.L. Strack. A discrete numerical model for granular assemblies. *Geotechnique*, 29(1):47–65, 1979.

[CTM11]      Ivana Cerovečki, Lynne D. Talley, and Matthew R. Mazloff. A comparison of Southern Ocean air-sea buoyancy flux from an ocean state estimate with five other products. *Journal of Climate*, 24:6283–6306, 2011.

[CUD]        Cuda c best practices guide, may 2011. http://www.nvidia.com.

[Cup81]      J.J.M. Cuppen. A divide and conquer method for the symmetric tridiagonal eigenproblem. *Numer. Math*, 36:177–195, 1981.

[CV12]       Justus A. Calvin and Edward F. Valeev. TiledArray: An expressive block-sparse parallel tensor algebra in c++, 2012.

[CW11]       Charles F. Cornwell and Charles R. Welch. Very–high–strength (60–gpa) carbon nanotube fiber design based on molecular dynamics simulations. *J. Chem. Phys.*, 134(20):204708, 2011.

[Dau03]      W. Daughton. Electromagnetic properties of the lower-hybrid drift instability in a thin current sheet. *Physics of Plasmas*, 10(8):3103–3119, Aug 2003.

[DBH06]      Narayan Desai, Rick Bradshaw, and Joey Hagedorn. System management methodologies with Bcfg2. *;login : Magazine*, 31(1):11–18, February 2006.

[DCJWJH07]   Larry P. Davis, Roy L. Campbell, Jr., William A. Ward, Jr., and Cray J. Henry. High–performance computing acquisitions based on the factors that matter. *Computing in Science and Engineering*, 9(6):35–44, November 2007.

[DDN]          Data direct networks. ddn s2a9900. http://www.ddn.com/9900. Technical
               report.

[DDR+08]       S. Dorfman, W. Daughton, V. Roytershteyn, H. Ji, Y. Ren, and M. Yamada.
               Two-dimensional fully kinetic simulations of driven magnetic reconnection
               with boundary conditions relevant to the Magnetic Reconnection Experi-
               ment. *Physics of Plasmas*, 15(10), Oct 2008.

[ddt]          Allinea ddt debugger. http://www.allinea.com/products/ddt/.

[deia]         DEISA - Benchmarking & Benchmark Suite.

[deib]         DEISA: Distributed European Infrastructure for Supercomputing Applica-
               tions. http://www.deisa.eu/. Funding from the EU's Seventh Framework
               Programme (FP7/2007-2013) under grant agreement no. RI-222919.

[Den07a]       P. Deniel. Ganesha, a multiusage with large cache nfsv4 server. In *Proceedings
               of the 2007 Linux Symposium*, 2007.

[Den07b]       P. Deniel. Ganesha, a multiusage with large cache nfsv4 server. In *WiP topic
               at Usenix FAST2007*, 2007.

[Den09]        P. Deniel. Nfsv4 proxy in user space on massive clustered architecture, issue
               and perspective. In *WiP Topic and Poster at Usenix FAST2009*, 2009.

[DFF+08]       S. Dürr, Z. Fodor, J. Frison, C. Hoelbling, R. Hoffmann, S.D. Katz, S. Krieg,
               T. Kurth, L. Lellouch, T. Lippert, K.K. Szabo, and G. Vulvert. Ab initio
               determination of light hadron masses. *Science*, 322:1224, 2008.

[DFH+09]       S. Dürr, Z. Fodor, C. Hoelbling, R. Hoffmann, S.D. Katz, et al. Scaling study
               of dynamical smeared-link clover fermions. *Phys. Rev.*, D79:014501, 2009.

[DG04]         Jeffrey Dean and Sanjay Ghemawat. MapReduce: Simplified data processing
               on large clusters. In *OSDI '04*, pages 137–150, 2004.

[DG08]         J. Dean and S. Ghemawat. MapReduce: Simplified data processing on large
               clusters. *Commun. ACM*, 51(1):107–113, 2008.

[DGH+08]       Jack Dongarra, Robert Graybill, William Harrod, Robert Lucas, Ewing Lusk,
               Piotr Luszczek, Janice McMahon, Allan Snavely, Jeffrey Vetter, Katherine
               Yelick, Sadaf R. Alam, Roy Campbell, Laura Carrington, Tzu-Yi Chen, Omid
               Khalili, Jeremy S. Meredith, and Mustafa Tikir. *DARPA's HPCS Program:
               History, Models, Tools, Languages*, Volume 72, pages 1–100. Elsevier, 2008.

[DHAS09]       Ignacio Laguna, Gregory L. Lee, Ben Liblit, Barton P. Miller, Dong H. Ahn,
               Bronis R. de Supinski, and Martin Schulz. Scalable temporal order analysis
               for large scale debugging. In *Proceedings of Supercomputing 2009*, Portland,
               Oregon, November 2009.

[DKYC10]       G. Diamos, A. Kerr, S. Yalamanchili, and N. Clark. Ocelot: A dynamic
               optimization framework for bulk-synchronous applications in heterogeneous
               systems. In *Proceedings of the 19th International Conference on Parallel
               Architectures and Compilation Techniques*, PACT '10, pages 353–364, New
               York, NY, USA, 2010. ACM.

[DL05]     Jack Dongarra and Piotr Luszczek. Introduction to the HPC Challenge benchmark suite. Technical Report UT-CS-05-544, University of Tennessee, 2005.

[DL08]     Narayan Desai and Cory Lueninghoener. *Configuration Management with Bcfg2*. Usenix Association, Berkeley, CA, 2008.

[DLP03]    Jack J. Dongarra, Piotr Luszczek, and Antoine Petitet. The LINPACK benchmark: Past, present, and future. *Concurrency and Computation: Practice and Experience*, 15:1–18, 2003.

[DLSC⁺]    John Dennis, Rich Loft, Amik St-Cyr, Steve Thomas, Henry Tufo, and Theron Voran. High-Order Methods Modeling Environment (HOMME). http://www.homme.ucar.edu/.

[DMM⁺10]   A. Danalis, G. Marin, C. McCurdy, J. S. Meredith, P. C. Roth, K. Spafford, V. Tipparaju, and J. S. Vetter. The scalable heterogeneous computing (SHOC) benchmark suite. In *Proceedings of the 3rd Workshop on General-Purpose Computation on Graphics Processing Units*, GPGPU '10, pages 63–74, New York, NY, USA, 2010. ACM.

[DRA⁺09]   W. Daughton, V. Roytershteyn, B. J. Albright, H. Karimabadi, L. Yin, and Kevin J. Bowers. Influence of Coulomb collisions on the structure of reconnection layers. *Physics of Plasmas*, 16(7), Jul 2009.

[DRK⁺11]   W. Daughton, V. Roytershteyn, H. Karimabadi, L. Yin, B. J. Albright, B. Bergen, and K. J. owers. Role of electron physics in the development of turbulent magnetic reconnection in collisionless plasmas. *Nature Physics*, 7:539–542, 2011.

[DRKM⁺09]  Nicole A. Doria-Rose, Rachel M. Klein, Maura M. Manion, Sijy ODell, Adhuna Phogat, Bimal Chakrabarti, Claire W. Hallahan, Stephen A. Migueles, Jens Wrammert, Rafi Ahmed, Martha Nason, Richard T. Wyatt, John R. Mascola, and Mark Connors. Frequency and phenotype of human immunodeficiency virus envelope-specific b cells from patients with broadly crossneutralizing antibodies. *Journal of Virology*, 83(1):188–199, 2009.

[DS00]     Jack Dongarra and Francis Sullivan. Guest editors' introduction: The top 10 algorithms. *Journal Comput. Sci. Eng.*, 2(1):22–23, January/February 2000.

[DSK06]    William Daughton, Jack Scudder, and Homa Karimabadi. Fully kinetic simulations of undriven magnetic reconnection with open boundary conditions. *Physics of Plasmas*, 13(7), Jul 2006.

[DSK11]    R. Dominguez, D. Schaa, and D. Kaeli. Caracal: Dynamic translation of runtime environments for GPUs. In *Proceedings of the 4th Workshop on General-Purpose Computation on Graphics Processing Units*, Newport Beach, CA, USA, March 2011. ACM.

[DvLW⁺11]  Javier Diaz, Gregor von Laszewski, Fugang Wang, Andrew J. Younge, and Geoffrey C. Fox. FutureGrid image repository: A generic catalog and storage system for heterogeneous virtual machine images. In *Third IEEE International Conference on Cloud Computing Technology and Science (CloudCom2011)*, pages 560–564, Athens, Greece, Dec. 2011.

[DvLWF12]   Javier Diaz, Gregor von Laszewski, Fugang Wang, and Geoffrey C. Fox. Abstract image management and universal image registration for cloud and HPC infrastructures. In *IEEE Cloud 2012*, Honolulu, 2012.

[DYvL+11]   Javier Diaz, Andrew J. Younge, Gregor von Laszewski, Fugang Wang, and Geoffrey C. Fox. Grappling cloud infrastructure services with a generic image repository. In *Proceedings of Cloud Computing and Its Applications (CCA 2011)*, March 2011.

[ea98]   D. Chen et al. Gordon Bell Prize 1998: QCD in the QCDSP supercomputer, 1998. http://phys.columbia.edu/~cqft/gordonbell.htm.

[ea06]   P. Vranas et al. Gordon Bell Prize 2006: The Blue Gene/L Supercomputer and Quantum Chromodynamics, 2006. http://awards.acm.org/homepage.cfm?awd=160.

[EGH+06]   D. Ellsworth, B. Green, C. Henze, P. Moran, and T. Sandstrom. Concurrent visualization in a production supercomputing environment. *IEEE Transactions on Visualization and Computer Graphics*, 12(5):997–1004, 2006.

[EKLM11]   E. Epelbaum, H. Krebs, D. Lee, and Ulf-G. Meißner. Ab initio calculation of the Hoyle state. *Phys. Rev. Lett.*, 106:192501, 2011.

[EM]   J. Presper Eckert and John W. Mauchly. *Electronic Numerical Integrator and Computer, Pat. No. 3,120,606.* United States Patent Office. Filed June 26, 1947. Patented Feb. 4, 1964.

[EM08]   Toshio Endo and Satoshi Matsuoka. Massive supercomputing coping with heterogeneity of modern accelerators. In *22nd IEEE International Parallel & Distributed Processing Symposium (IPDPS 2008)*, pages 1–10, Miami, FL, April 2008.

[Ene08]   Energy Star, 2008.

[ENMM10]   Toshio Endo, Akira Nukada, Satoshi Matsuoka, and Naoya Matsuoka. Linpack evaluation on a supercomputer with heterogeneous accelerators. In *24th IEEE International Parallel & Distributed Processing Symposium (IPDPS 2010)*, pages 1–8, April 2010.

[Enz]   The Enzo project. Website. http://enzo-project.org/.

[ERM+10]   J. Enkovaara, C. Rostgaard, J. J. Mortensen, J. Chen, M. Dułak, L. Ferrighi, J. Gavnholt, C. Glinsvad, V. Haikola, H. A. Hansen, H. H. Kristoffersen, M. Kuisma, A. H. Larsen, L. Lehtovaara, M. Ljungberg, O. Lopez-Acevedo, P. G. Moses, J. Ojanen, T. Olsen, V. Petzold, N. A. Romero, J. Stausholm-Möller, M. Strange, G. A. Tritsaris, M. Vanin, M. Walter, B. Hammer, H. Häkkinen, G. K. H. Madsen, R. M. Nieminen, J. K. Nørskov, M. Puska, T. T. Rantala, J. Schiøtz, K. S. Thygesen, and K. W. Jacobsen. Electronic structure calculations with GPAW: A real-space implementation of the projector augmented-wave method. *J. Phys.: Condens. Matter*, 22:253202, 2010.

[ESJ]   TSUBAME ESJ — [GSIC] Tokyo Institute of Technology — Global Scientific Information and Computing Center. http://www.gsic.titech.ac.jp/en/TSUBAME_ESJ.

[ESJ10a]     TSUBAME e-Science Journal (ESJ). http://www.gsic.titech.ac.jp/sites/ default/files/TSUBAME_ESJ_01en.pdf, Volume 1 2010.

[ESJ10b]     TSUBAME e-Science Journal (ESJ). http://www.gsic.titech.ac.jp/sites/ default/files/TSUBAME_ESJ_02en.pdf, Volume 2 2010.

[ESJ11a]     TSUBAME e-Science Journal (ESJ). http://www.gsic.titech.ac.jp/sites/ default/files/TSUBAME_ESJ_03en.pdf, Volume 3 2011.

[ESJ11b]     TSUBAME e-Science Journal (ESJ). http://www.gsic.titech.ac.jp/sites/ default/files/TSUBAME_ESJ_04en.pdf, Volume 4 2011.

[ESJ12]      TSUBAME e-Science Journal (ESJ). http://www.gsic.titech.ac.jp/sites/ default/files/TSUBAME_ESJ_05en.pdf, Volume 5 2012.

[EZH+05]     Daniel J. Eisenstein, Idit Zehavi, David W. Hogg, Roman Scoccimarro, Michael R. Blanton, Robert C. Nichol, Ryan Scranton, Hee-Jong Seo, Max Tegmark, Zheng Zheng, Scott F. Anderson, Jim Annis, Neta Bahcall, Jon Brinkmann, Scott Burles, Francisco J. Castander, Andrew Connolly, Istvan Csabai, Mamoru Doi, Masataka Fukugita, Joshua A. Frieman, Karl Glazebrook, James E. Gunn, John S. Hendry, Gregory Hennessy, Zeljko Ivezi, Stephen Kent, Gillian R. Knapp, Huan Lin, Yeong-Shang Loh, Robert H. Lupton, Bruce Margon, Timothy A. McKay, Avery Meiksin, Jeffery A. Munn, Adrian Pope, Michael W. Richmond, David Schlegel, Donald P. Schneider, Kazuhiro Shimasaku, Christopher Stoughton, Michael A. Strauss, Mark SubbaRao, Alexander S. Szalay, Istvn Szapudi, Douglas L. Tucker, Brian Yanny, and Donald G. York. Detection of the baryon acoustic peak in the large-scale correlation function of sdss luminous red galaxies. *The Astrophysical Journal*, 633(2):560, 2005.

[Fah11]      Mark Fahey. SWTools. http://www.olcf.ornl.gov/center-projects/swtools, 2011.

[fARa]       University Corporation for Atmospheric Research. CESM Models: CCSM4.0. http://www.cesm.ucar.edu/models/ccsm4.0/.

[fARb]       University Corporation for Atmospheric Research. CESM Models: CESM1.0. http://www.cesm.ucar.edu/models/cesm1.0/.

[fARc]       University Corporation for Atmospheric Research. The Weather Research and Forecasting Model. http://www.wrf-model.org/index.php.

[FBB08]      Kurt B. Ferreira, Patrick Bridges, and Ron Brightwell. Characterizing application sensitivity to os interference using kernel-level noise injection. In *Proceedings of the 2008 ACM/IEEE Conference on Supercomputing*, SC '08, pages 19:1–19:12, Piscataway, NJ, USA, 2008. IEEE Press.

[FDMC11]     Yu Feng, Tiziana Di Matteo, Rupert Croft et al., Massiveblack: A large-scale simulation of the early universe, *ApJS* 2011.

[Fen03]      W. Feng. Making a case for efficient supercomputing. *ACM Queue*, 1(7):54–64, October 2003.

[Fen05]      W. Feng. The evolution of power-aware, high-performance clusters: From the datacenter to the desktop. In *IEEE International Parallel & Distributed Processing Symposium (IPDPS) Workshop on High-Performance, Power-Aware Computing*, April 2005. Keynote Talk.

[Fen06]    W. Feng. Global climate warming? Yes ... in the machine room. In *Clusters and Computational Grids for Scientific Computing*, September 2006.

[fft]    Fftw. http://www.fftw.org/.

[fg4]    SAGA Simple API for Grid Application, FutureGrid Project. FutureGrid Project.

[fGC]    Computational Infrastructure for Geodynamics (CIG). SPECFEM3D. http://www.geodynamics.org/cig/software/specfem3d.

[FGCR12]    Zacharia Fadika, Madhusudhan Govindaraju, Richard Shane Canon, and Lavanya Ramakrishnan. Evaluating hadoop for data-intensive scientific operations. In *IEEE Cloud 2012: 5th International Conference on Cloud Computing*, 2012.

[FGL10]    Michael Fenn, Sebastien Goasguen, and Jerome Lauret. Contextualization in practice: The Clemson experience. In *ACAT Proceedings*, 2010.

[FGML73]    H. Fritzsch, Murray Gell-Mann, and H. Leutwyler. Advantages of the color octet gluon picture. *Phys.Lett.*, B47:365–368, 1973.

[FH04]    W. Feng and C. Hsu. Green destiny and its evolving parts. In *International Supercomputing Conference*, June 2004. Innovative Supercomputer Architecture Award.

[Fie00]    Roy Thomas Fielding. *Architectural Styles and the Design of Network-based Software Architectures*. PhD thesis, University of California, Irvine, 2000.

[FJH10]    Mark Fahey, Nick Jones, and Bilel Hadri. The automatic library tracking database. In *Proceedings of the 2010 CUG Conference* [The10].

[FK99]    I. Foster and C. Kesselman. Globus: A toolkit-based grid architecture. *The Grid: Blueprint for a New Computing Infrastructure*, (pp. 259–278). Morgan Kaufmann, 1999.

[FKE+12a]    N. Farooqui, A. Kerr, G. Eiesenhauer, K. Schwan, and S. Yalamanchili. Lynx: A dynamic instrumentation system for data parallel applications on GPU architectures. In *Proceedings of the IEEE International Symposium on Performance Analysis of Systems and Software*. IEEE, March 2012.

[FKE+12b]    Naila Farooqui, Andrew Kerr, Greg Eisenhauer, Karsten Schwan, and Sudhakar Yalamanchili. Lynx: A dynamic instrumentation system for data-parallel applications on gpgpu architectures. In *ISPASS*, New Brunswick, NJ, USA, 2012.

[FKH+12]    Geoffrey C. Fox, Supun Kamburugamuve, and Ryan Hartman, Architecture and Measured Characteristics of a Cloud Based Internet of Things. API Workshop 13-IoT Internet of Things, Machine to Machine and Smart Services Applications (IoT 2012) at The 2012 International Conference on Collaboration Technologies and Systems (CTS 2012), Denver, May 21–25, 2012.

[For94]    Message Passing Interface Forum. MPI: A message-passing interface standard. *The International Journal of Supercomputer Applications and High Performance Computing*, 8, 1994.

[For95]     Message Passing Interface Forum. MPI: A message-passing interface Standard (version 1.1), 1995. Available at: http://www.mpi-forum.org/.

[For97]     Message Passing Interface Forum. MPI-2: Extensions to the Message-Passing Interface, 18 July 1997. Available at http://www.mpi-forum.org/docs/mpi-20.ps.

[FPH+09]    G. I. Fann, J. Pei, R. J. Harrison, J. Jia, J. Hill, M. Ou, W. Nazarewicz, W. A. Shelton, and N. Schunck. Fast multiresolution methods for density functional theory in nuclear physics. *Journal of Physics: Conference Series*, 180(1):012080, 2009. http://stacks.iop.org/1742-6596/180/i=1/a=012080.

[FPT+07]    Will Fischer, Simon Perkins, James Theiler, Tanmoy Bhattacharya, Karina Yusim, Robert Funkhouser, Carla Kuiken, Barton Haynes, Norman L. Letvin, Bruce D. Walker, Beatrice H. Hahn, and Bette T. Korber. Polyvalent vaccines for optimal coverage of potential t-cell epitopes in global hiv-1 variants. *Nature Medicine*, 13:100–106, January 2007.

[Fri]       W. Frings. LinkTest: Parallel MPI PingPong Test. http://www2.fz-juelich.de/jsc/linktest/.

[Fri76]     D. Friedman. *CONS Should Not Evaluate Its Arguments*. Edinburgh University Press, Edinburgh, 1976.

[FSM+10]    W. Frings, A. Schnurpfeil, S. Meier, F. Janetzko, and L. Arnold. A flexible, application- and platform-independent environment for benchmarking. In B. Chapman, F Desprez, G.R. Joubert, A. Lichnewsky, F. Peters, and T. Priol, editors, *Parallel Computing: From Multicores and GPU's to Petascale*, volume 19, Amsterdam, 2010. IOS Press.

[FTR+12]    F. Fressin, G. Torres, J. F. Rowe, D. Charbonneau, L. A. Rogers, S. Ballard, N. M. Batalha, W. J. Borucki, S. T. Bryson, L. A. Buchhave, D. R. Ciardi, J.-M. Désert, C. D. Dressing, D. C. Fabrycky, E. B. Ford, T. N. Gautier III, C. E. Henze, M. J. Holman, A. Howard, S. B. Howell, J. M. Jenkins, D. G. Koch, D. W. Latham, J. J. Lissauer, G. W. Marcy, S. N. Quinn, D. Ragozzine, D. D. Sasselov, S. Seager, T. Barclay, F. Mullally, S. E. Seader, M. Still, J. D. Twicken, S. E. Thompson, and K. Uddin. Two Earth-sized planets orbiting Kepler-20. *Nature*, 482(7384):195199, February 2012.

[Fur11]     Thomas R. Furlani, Matthew D. Jones, Steven M. Gallo, Andrew E. Bruno, Charng-Da Lu, Amin Ghadersohi, Ryan J. Gentner, Abani K. Patra, Robert L. DeLeon, Gregor von Laszewski, Lizhe Wang, and Ann Zimmerman. Performance metrics and auditing framework for high performance computer systems. In *Proceedings of the 2011 TeraGrid Conference: Extreme Digital Discovery*, TG '11, Salt Lake City, UT, 2011.

[FuHoKe06]  A. Funk, V. Basili, L. Hochstein, and J. Kepner, "Analysis of Parallel Software Development Using the Relative Development Time Productivity Metric," *CT Watch*, Volume 2, Number 4A, November 2006.

[FUS]       Fuse: File system in userspace. http://fuse.sourceforge.net.

[FWW02]     W. Feng, M. Warren, and E. Weigle. The bladed Beowulf: A cost-effective alternative to traditional Beowulfs. In *Proc. of the IEEE Int'l Conf. on Cluster Computing*, September 2002.

[fzj]          Forschungszentrum Jülich - Homepage.

[GAC09]        L. Grinberg, T. Anor, and E. Cheever. *Phil. Trans. Royal Soc. A*, 367 1896 2371, 2009.

[GBC+05]       A. Gara, M. A. Blumrich, D. Chen, G. L.-T. Chiu, P. Coteus, M. E. Giampapa, R. A. Haring, P. Heidelberger, D. Hoenicke, G. V. Kopcsay, T. A. Liebsch, M. Ohmacht, B. D. Steinmacher-Burow, T. Takken, and P. Vranas. Overview of the Blue Gene/L system architecture. *IBM Journal of Research and Development*, 49(2.3):195–212, Mar 2005. http://dx.doi.org/10.1147/rd.492.0195.

[GBD+11]       S Gnanakaran, T Bhattacharya, M Daniels, BF Keele, PT Hraber, AS Lapedes, T Shen, B Gaschen, M Krishnamoorthy, H Li, JM Decker, JF Salazar-Gonzalez, S Wang, C Jiang, F Gao, R Swanstrom, JA Anderson, L-H Ping, MS Cohen, M Markowitz, PA Goepfert, MS Saag, JJ Eron, CB Hicks, WA Blattner, GD Tomaras, M Asmal, NL Letvin, PB Gilbert, AC DeCamp, CA Magaret, WR Schief, Y-E Ban, M Zhang, KA Soderberg, JG Sodroski, BF Haynes, GM Shaw, BH Hahn, and B Korber. Recurrent signature patterns in HIV-1 B clade envelope glycoproteins associated with either early or chronic infections, PLoS Pathogens, 7(9):e1002209+, September 2011.

[GCfS]         Gauss Centre for Supercomputing. inSiDE: Innovatives Supercomputing in Deutschland. http://inside.hlrs.de/.

[GCR11]        Devarshi Ghoshal, Richard Shane Canon, and Lavanya Ramakrishnan. I/O performance of virtualized cloud environments. In *The Second International Workshop on Data Intensive Computing in the Clouds (DataCloud-SC11)*, 2011.

[gcs]          Gauss Centre for Supercomputing. http:/www.gauss-centre.eu/.

[GCZ+11]       X. Gao, X. Cao, W. Zhao, A. Zhang, and Z. Mo. Performance study of complex application programs on tens of thousands cores. *Journal of Software*, 22(2):157–162, 2011.

[GD04]         S. Ghemawat and J. Dean. Mapreduce: Simplified data processing on large clusters. In *Proceedings of the 6th Symposium on Operating System Design and Implementation (OSDI04), San Francisco, CA, USA*, 2004.

[GDH+09]       T.C. Germann, G. Dimonte, J.E. Hammerberg, Kadua K., J. Quenneville, and M.B. Zellner. Large-scale molecular dynamics simulations of particulate ejection and Richtmyer-Meshkov instability development in shocked copper. In *DYMAT 2009 - 9th International Conference on the Mechanical and Physical Behaviour of Materials under Dynamic Loading*, DYMAT 2009, pages 1499–1505. ISI Proceedings, 2009.

[GDS+05]       F. Gygi, E. W. Draeger, B. R. De Supinski, R. K. Yates, F. Franchetti, S. Kral, J. Lorenz, C. W. Ueberhuber, J. A. Gunnels, and J. C. Sexton. Large-scale first-principles molecular dynamics simulations on the Blue Gene/L platform using the Qbox code. In *Proceedings of Supercomputing 2005*, page 24, 2005. Conference on High Performance Networking and Computing, Gordon Bell Prize finalist.

[GDS+06]    F. Gygi, E. W. Draeger, M. Schulz, B. R. de Supinski, J. A. Gunnels, V. Austel, J. C. Sexton, F. Franchetti, S. Kral, C. W. Ueberhuber, and J. Lorenz. Large-scale electronic structure calculations of high-Z metals on the Blue-Gene/L platform. *In Proceedings of Supercomputing 2006*, 2006. International Conference on High Performance Computing, Network, Storage, and Analysis. 2006 Gordon Bell Prize winner (Peak Performance).

[gem]       The gemini network. White paper, Cray Inc.

[Gen]       Genome 10k: Unveiling animal diversity. http://www.genome10k.org/.

[GGS+09]    Vishakha Gupta, Ada Gavrilovska, Karsten Schwan, Harshvardhan Kharche, Niraj Tolia, Vanish Talwar, and Parthasarathy Ranganathan. GViM: GPU-accelerated Virtual Machines. In *Proceedings of the 3rd ACM Workshop on System-level Virtualization for High Performance Computing (HPCVirt)*, Nuremberg, Germany, 2009.

[GHY+]      Manfred G. Grabherr, Brian J. Haas, Moran Yassour, Joshua Z. Levin, Dawn A. Thompson, Ido Amit, Xian Adiconis, Lin Fan, Raktima Raychowdhury, Qiandong Zeng, Zehua Chen, Evan Mauceli, Nir Hacohen, Andreas Gnirke, Nicholas Rhind, Federica di Palma, Bruce W. Birren, Chad Nusbaum, Kerstin Lindblad-Toh, Nir Friedman, and Aviv Regev. Full-length transcriptome assembly from rna-seq data without a reference genome. *Nature Biotechnology*, 29(7):644–652.

[Gil94]     Peter M. W. Gill. Molecular integrals over Gaussian basis functions. *Advances in Quantum Chemistry*, 25:141–205, 1994. http://www.sciencedirect.com/science/article/pii/S0065327608600192.

[GKS09]     Timothy C. Germann, Kai Kadau, and Sriram Swaminarayan. 369 tflop/s molecular dynamics simulations on the petaflop hybrid supercomputer roadrunner. *Concurrency and Computation: Practice and Experience*, 21(17):2143–2159, 2009.

[GL96]      W. Ge and J. Li. Pseudo-particle approach to hydrodynamics of gas/solid two-phase flow. In *Proceedings of the 5th International Conference on Circulating Fluidized Bed*, Science Press, Beijing, pages 260–265, 1996.

[GL09]      Dorian Gahm and Mark Laatsch. Meeting the demands of computer cooling with superior efficiency. http://www.cray.com/Assets/PDF/products/xt/whitepaper\_ecophlex, 2009.

[glo12]     Globus Provision, 2012.

[GMP+11]    Sante Gnerre, Iain MacCallum, Dariusz Przybylski, Filipe J. Ribeiro, Joshua N. Burton, Bruce J. Walker, Ted Sharpe, Giles Hall, Terrance P. Shea, Aaron M. Sykes, Sean Berlin, Daniel Aird, Maura Costello, Riza Daza, Louise Williams, Robert Nicol, Andreas Gnirke, Chad Nusbaum, Eric S. Lander, and David B. Jaffe. High-quality draft assemblies of mammalian genomes for massively parallel sequence data. *Proceedings of the National Academy of Sciences USA*, 108(4):1513–1518, 2011.

[GNPM08]    A. Grimshaw, S. Newhouse, D. Pulsipher, and M. Morgan. Gfd108: Ogsa basic execution service. Web, 2008.

[GNU11]      GNU. Gcc: Gnu compiler collection. In *http://gcc.gnu.org*, 2011.

[Gon08]      M. Torrent, F. Jollet, F. Bottin, G. Zérah, X. Gonze. Abinit. In *Comput. Mat. Science,* 42, 337, 2008.

[Gor06]      S. Gorman. NSA risking electrical overload. In *The Baltimore Sun,* August 2006.

[gpf]        Gpfs file system. http://www-03.ibm.com/systems/software/gpfs/.

[GPW04]      David   J.   Gross,   H.   David   Politzer,   and   Frank   Wilczek. Press   Release:   The   2004   Nobel   Prize   in   Physics,   2004. http://www.nobelprize.org/nobel_prizes/physics/laureates/2004/press.html.

[GRA11]      The Graph 500 List. http://www.graph500.org, 2011.

[GRC+07]     J.N. Glosli, D.F. Richards, K.J. Caspersen, R.E. Rudd, J.A. Gunnels, and F.H. Streitz. Extending stability beyond CPU millennium: A micron-scale atomistic simulation of Kelvin-Helmholtz instability. *Supercomputing 2007, Proc. 2007 ACM/IEEE Conference,* pages 1–11 10–16, 2007.

[GRC+09]     Chin P. Guok, David W. Robertson, Evangelos Chaniotakis, Mary R. Thompson, William Johnston, and Brian Tierney. A user driven dynamic circuit network implementation. *DANMS08,* 2009.

[gre]        The Green500 list. Website. Available online at http://www.green500.org/lists/2011/06/top/list.php.

[gre08]      Green Data Centres, 2008.

[GRE11]      The Green 500 List. http://www.green500.org, 2010, 2012.

[groa]       Gromacs. http://www.gromacs.org/.

[Grob]       The HDF Group. The HDF5 Group. http://www.hdfgroup.org.

[GS06]       Rahul Garg and Yogish Sabharwal. Software routing and aggregation of messages to optimize the performance of the HPCC Random access benchmark. In *Proceedings of SC06,* Tampa, FL, November 11-17 2006.

[gsi]        GSI-Openssh. http://globus.org/toolkit/docs/4.2/4.2.1/security/openssh/.

[GST+11]     Vishakha Gupta, Karsten Schwan, Niraj Tolia, Vanish Talwar, and Parthasarathy Ranganathan. Pegasus: Coordinated scheduling for virtualized accelerator-based systems. In *Proceedings of the 2011 USENIX Conference on USENIX Annual Technical Conference (USENIX ATC),* Portland, OR, USA, 2011.

[GTA11]      M. J. Gillian, M. D. Towler, and D. Alfé. Petascale computing opens new vistas for quantum Monte Carlo. *Psi-K Newsletter,* 103:32, 2011.

[GTY+02]     Brian Gaschen, Jesse Taylor, Karina Yusim, Brian Foley, Feng Gao, Dorothy Lang, Vladimir Novitsky, Barton Haynes, Beatrice H. Hahn, Tanmoy Bhattacharya, and Bette Korber. Diversity considerations in hiv-1 vaccine selection. *Science,* 296(5577):2354–2360, 2002.

[Guo12]     Zhenhua Guo. *High Performance Integration of Data Parallel File Systems and Computing: Optimizing MapReduce.* PhD thesis, Indiana University, June 2012.

[GWW+10]    M. Geimer, F. Wolf, B. J. N. Wylie, E. Ábrahám, D. Becker, and B. Mohr. The Scalasca performance toolset architecture. *Concurrency and Computation: Practice and Experience*, 22(6):702–719, April 2010.

[GWY+11]    W. Ge, W. Wang, N. Yang, J. Li, M. Kwauk, F. Chen, J. Chen, X. Fang, L. Guo, X. He, et al. Meso-scale oriented simulation towards virtual process engineering (VPE)—the EMMS paradigm. *Chemical Engineering Science*, 66(19):4426–4458, 2011.

[GXX+13]    W. Ge, J. Xu, Q. Xiong, X. Wang, F. Chen, L. Wang, C. Hou, M. Xu, J. Li. Multi-scale continuum-particle simulation on CPU-GPU hybrid supercomputer (2013). In: D.A. Yuen, L. Wang, L. Johnsson, X. Chi, W. Ge, Y. Shi (eds.), *GPU Solutions to Multi-Scale Problems in Science and Engineering.* Springer. pp. 143-162.

[Gyg08]     F. Gygi. Architecture of Qbox: A scalable first-principles molecular dynamics code. *IBM Journal of Research and Development*, 52(1/2):137, 2008.

[HACC12]    Habib, S., Morozov, V., Finkel, H., Pope, A., Heitmann, K., Kumaran, K., Peterka, T., Insley, J., Daniel, D., Fasel, P., Frontiere, and N., Lukić, Z. The universe at extreme scale: multi-petaflop sky simulation on the BG/Q. *Proceedings of the International Conference on High Performance Computing, Networking, Storage and Analysis*, SC'12, pages 1-11, Los Alamitos, CA, USA, 2012, IEEE Computer Society Press.

[had12]     Hadron polarizibility, 2012. http://samurai.phys.gwu.edu/wiki/index.php/ Hadron_polarizability.

[HB10]      J. Hoberock and N. Bell. Thrust: A parallel template library, 2010. http: //www.meganewtons.com/.

[HBB+05]    Andreas Hanemann, Jeff W. Boote, Ericl. Boyd, Jerome Dur, Loukik Kudarimoti, Roman Aapacz, D. Martin Swany, Szymon Trocha, and Jason Zurawski. PerfSONAR: A service oriented architecture for multi-domain network monitoring. In *Proceedings of the Third International Conference on Service Oriented Computing (ICSOC 2005). ACM Sigsoft and Sigweb*, 2005.

[HBH+05]    M. A. Heroux, R. A. Bartlett, V. E. Howle, R. J. Hoekstra, J. J. Hu, T. G. Kolda, R. B. Lehoucq, K. R. Long, R. P. Pawlowski, E. T. Phipps, A. G. Salinger, H. K. Thornquist, R. S. Tuminaro, J. M. Willenbring, A. Williams, and K. S. Stanley. An overview of the trilinos project. *ACM Trans. Math. Softw.*, 31(3):397–423, September 2005.

[HBM+10]    T. Hanawa, T. Boku, S. Miura, M. Sato, and K. Arimoto. Pearl: Power-aware, dependable, and high-performance communication link using pci express. *Proc. of IEEE/ACM Int. Conf. on Green Computing and Communitations 2011 (GreenCom2010)*, pp. 284–291, 2010.

[HC05]      J. Hutter and A. Curioni. Car-Parrinello molecular dynamics on massively parallel computers. *ChemPhysChem*, 6:1788, 2005.

[hdf]         Parallel hdf5. http://www.hdfgroup.org/HDF5/PHDF5/.

[He,10a]      J. He, J. Bennett, and A. Snavely. DASH-IO: An Empirical Study of Flash-based IO for HPC. TeraGrid, Pittsburgh, PA., July 2010.

[He,10b]      J. He, A. Jagatheesan, S. Gupta, J. Bennett, and A. Snavely. DASH: A Recipe for a Flash-based Data Intensive Supercomputer. Supercomputing, New Orleans, LA, November 2010.

[HFJ10]       Bilel Hadri, Mark Fahey, and Nick Jones. Identifying software usage at HPC centers with the automatic library tracking database. In *Proceedings of the 2010 TeraGrid Conference*, TG '10, pages 8:1–8:8, New York, NY, USA, 2010. ACM.

[HFRR12]      Bilel Hadri, Mark Fahey, Timothy Robinson, and William Renaud. Software usage on Cray systems across three centers (NICS, ORNL and CSCS). In Cray User Group Meeting, *Proceedings of the 2012 CUG Conference*, Stuttgart, Germany, 2012.

[HFY$^+$04]   Robert J. Harrison, George I. Fann, Takeshi Yanai, Zhengting Gan, and Gregory Beylkin. Multiresolution quantum chemistry: Basic theory and initial applications. *The Journal of Chemical Physics*, 121(23):11587–11598, 2004. http://link.aip.org/link/?JCP/121/11587/1.

[hHcFA05]     Chung hsing Hsu, Wu chun Feng, and Jeremy S. Archuleta. Towards efficient supercomputing: A quest for the right metric. In *1st IEEE Workshop on High-Performance, Power-Aware Computing (in conjunction with the 19th International Parallel & Distributed Processing Symposium*, Denver, CO, April 2005.

[HJM$^+$10]   R. Hood, H. Jin, P. Mehrotra, J. Chang, J. Djomehri, S. Gavali, D. Jespersen, K. Taylor, and R. Biswas. Performance impact of resource contention in multicore systems. In *Proceedings of the IEEE International Parallel and Distributed Processing Symposium (IPDPS10)*, 2010.

[HJS96]       B. Hendrickson, E. Jessup, and C. Smith. A parallel eigensolver for dense symmetric matrices. Technical report, Sandia National Labs, Albuquerque, NM, 1996.

[HK92]        P. J. Hoogerbrugge and J. Koelman. Simulating microscopic hydrodynamic phenomena with dissipative particle dynamics. *Europhysics Letters*, 19(3):155–160, 1992.

[HM93]        M. Herlihy and J. E. B. Moss. Transactional memory: Architectural support for lock-free data structures. *SIGARCH Comput. Archit. News*, 51(2):289–300, 1993.

[HMCH07]      Chris Hill, Dimitris Menemenlis, Bob Ciotti, and Chris Henze. Investigating solution convergence in a global ocean model using a 2,048-processor cluster of distributed shared memory machines. *Scientific Programming*, 15:107–115, 2007.

[HOF$^+$12]   R.A. Haring, M. Ohmacht, T.W. Fox, M.K. Gschwind, D.L. Satterfield, K. Sugavanam, P.W. Coteus, P. Heidelberger, M.A. Blumrich, R.W. Wisniewski, A. Gara, G.L-T. Chiu, P.A. Boyle, N.H. Christ, and C. Kim. The

IBM Blue Gene/Q compute chip. *IEEE Micro*, 32(2):48–60, Mar-Apr 2012. http://dx.doi.org/10.1109/MM.2011.108.

[hon12] 2012. http://users.ece.gatech.edu/~bhong/publications.html.

[HSE+11] Matthias Hess, Alexander Sczyrba, Rob Egan, Tae-Wan Kim, Harshal Chokhawala, Gary Schroth, Shujun Luo, Douglas S. Clark, Feng Chen, Tao Zhang, Roderick I. Mackie, Len A. Pennacchio, Susannah G. Tringe, Axel Visel, Tanja Woyke, Zhong Wang, and Edward M. Rubin. Metagenomic discovery of biomass-degrading genes and genomes from cow rumen. *Science*, 331:463–467, 2011.

[HSL10] T. Hoefler, T. Schneider, and A. Lumsdaine. Characterizing the influence of system noise on large-scale applications by simulation. In *International Conference for High Performance Computing, Networking, Storage and Analysis (SC'10)*, November 2010.

[Ht11] R. Haring and the IBM Blue Gene Team. The Blue Gene/Q Compute Chip. In *Hot Chips 23: A Symposium on High Performance Chips*, Palo Alto, CA, 2011. http://www.hotchips.org/wp-content/uploads/hc_archives/hc23/HC23.18.1-manycore/HC23.18.121.BlueGene-IBM_BQC_HC23_20110818.pdf.

[HTD11] M. Horton, S. Tomov, and J. Dongarra. A class of hybrid LAPACK algorithms for multicore and GPU architectures. In *Proceedings of the 2011 Symposium on Application Accelerators in High-Performance Computing*, SAAHPC '11, pages 150–158, Washington, DC, USA, 2011. IEEE Computer Society.

[HTT09] Tony Hey, Stewart Tansley, and Kristin Tolle, editors. *The Fourth Paradigm: Data-Intensive Scientific Discovery*. Microsoft Research, Redmond, WA, 2009.

[HuKe12] M. Hubbell and J. Kepner, "Large Scale Network Situational Awareness Via 3D Gaming Technology," IEEE HPEC, Sep 10-12, 2012, Waltham, MA.

[HW11] Victor Hazlewood and Matthew Woitaszek. Securing science gateways. In *Proceedings of the 2011 TeraGrid Conference: Extreme Digital Discovery*, TG '11, pages 37:1–37:8, New York, NY, USA, 2011. ACM.

[HXW+12a] C. Hou, J. Xu, P. Wang, W. Huang, X. Wang, W. Ge, X. He, L. Guo, J. Li (2012) Petascale molecular dynamics simulation of crystalline silicon on Tianhe-1A. *Int. J. High Perform. Comput. Appl.* DOI:10.1177/1094342012456047

[HXW+12b] C. Hou, J. Xu, P. Wang, W. Huang, X. Wang (2012) Efficient GPU-accelerated molecular dynamics simulation of solid covalent crystals. *Computer Physics Communications*. DOI: 10.1016/j.cpc.2013.01.001.

[I5k] i5k insect and other arthropod genome sequence initative. http://arthropodgenomes.org/wiki/i5K.

[IAP] http://www.iapcm.ac.cn/jasmin.

[ias] Institute for Advanced Simulation, Forschungszentrum Jülich. http://www.fz-juelich.de/ias/EN.

[ICS11]      International Conference on Supercomputing.   http://ics-conference.org/, 2011.

[IFB+11]     S. S. Iyer, G. Freeman, C. Brodsky, A. I. Chou, D. Corliss, S. H. Jain, N. Lustig, V. McGahay, S. Narasimha, J. Norum, K. A. Nummy, P. Parries, S. Sankaran, C. D. Sheraw, P. R. Varanasi, G. Wang, M. E. Weybright, X. Yu, E. Crabbe, and P. Agnello. 45-nm silicon-on-insulator CMOS technology integrating embedded DRAM for high-performance server and ASIC applications. *IBM Journal of Research and Development*, 55(3):5:1–5:14, May-Jun 2011. http://dx.doi.org/10.1147/JRD.2011.2108112.

[IHI11]      K.Z. Ibrahim, S. Hofmeyr, and C. Iancu. Characterizing the performance of parallel applications on multi-socket virtual machines. In *Cluster, Cloud and Grid Computing (CCGrid), 2011 11th IEEE/ACM International Symposium on*, pages 1 –12, May 2011.

[imb]        Intel   mpi   benchmarks.       http://software.intel.com/en-us/articles/intel-mpi-benchmarks/.

[imp12a]     Genesis II. Standards-Based Grid Computing, 2012.

[imp12b]     Grid'5000, 2012.

[imp12c]     The Network Impairments device is Spirent XGEM, 2012.

[INCa]       "DOE   leadership   computing   INCITE   program,"   http://www.doeleadershipcomputing.org/incite-program. Technical report.

[INCb]       INCITE:   Impact   on   Theory   and   Experiment. http://www.doeleadershipcomputing.org.

[Inn]        Innovative Computing Laboratory, University of Tennessee Knoxville. PAPI - Performance Application Programming Interface. http://icl.cs.utk.edu/papi/.

[JAB+10]     C. Johnson, D.H. Allen, J. Brown, S. Vanderwiel, R. Hoover, H. Achilles, C.-Y. Cher, G.A. May, H. Franke, J. Xenidis, and C. Basso.   A wire-speed power$^{TM}$ processor: 2.3GHz 45nm SOI with 16 cores and 64 threads.   In *Solid-State Circuits Conference Digest of Technical Papers (ISSCC), 2010 IEEE International*, pages 104–105, Feb 2010. http://dx.doi.org/10.1109/ISSCC.2010.5434075.

[JBD+]       John Jenkins, Pavan Balaji, James Dinan, Nagiza F. Samatova, and Rajeev Thakur. Enabling fast, non-contiguous GPU data movement in hybrid MPI+GPU environments. *In submission.*

[JG03]       M. Jette and M. Grondona. Slurm: Simple Linux utility for resource management. In *ClusterWorld Conference and Expo. UCRL-MA-147996*, 2003.

[JJM+11]     H. Jin, D. Jespersen, P. Mehrotra, R. Biswas, L. Huang, and B. Chapman. High performance computing using MPI and OpenMP on multi-core parallel systems. *Parallel Computing*, 37:562–575, 2011.

[JL06]       J. Gimenez and J. Labarta. *Parallel Processing for Scientific Computing*, chapter 2: Performance analysis: From art to science. SIAM, 2006.

[JMR⁺11] Keith R. Jackson, Krishna Muriki, Lavanya Ramakrishnan, Karl J. Runge, and Rollin C. Thomas. Performance and cost analysis of the supernova factory on the amazon aws cloud. *Scientific Programming*, 19(2-3):107–119, 2011.

[JNL⁺07] Curtis L. Janssen, Ida B. Nielsen, Matthew L. Leininger, Edward F. Valeev, Joseph P. Kenny, and Edward T. Seidl. The Massively Parallel Quantum Chemistry program (MPQC), 2007. http://www.mpqc.org.

[Joh95] John D. McCalpin. Memory bandwidth and machine balance in current high performance computers. *IEEE Computer Society Technical Committee on Computer Architecture (TCCA) Newsletter*, December 1995.

[Joh02] George Johnson. At Los Alamos, Two Visions of Supercomputing. *The New York Times*, June 25, 2002.

[Jou05] H. Jourdren. Hera: A hydronamic AMR platform for multi-physics simulation. In *Adaptive Mesh Refinement — Theory and Application, Lecture notes in Computational Science and Engineering*, volume 41, 2005, pp. 283-294.

[Jou10] K. Pouget, M. Pérache, P. Carribault, and H. Jourdren. User level db : A debugging api for user-level thread libraries. In *Workshop on Multithreaded Architectures and Applications (MTAAP'2010) in conjunction with IPDPS 2010*, 2010.

[JRM⁺10] Keith Jackson, Lavanya Ramakrishnan, Krishna Muriki, Shane Canon, Shreyas Cholia, John Shalf, Harvey Wasserman, and Nicholas Wright. Performance analysis of high performance computing applications on the Amazon web services cloud. In *2nd IEEE International Conference on Cloud Computing Technology and Science*, 2010.

[JS12] Wayne Joubert and Shiquan Su. An analysis of computational workloads for the ORNL Jaguar system. In *Proceedings of the 26th International Conference on Supercomputing*, San Servolo Island, Venice, Italy, 25-29 June 2012.

[jsc] Jülich Supercomputing Centre. http://www.fz-juelich.de/ias/jsc/EN.

[jug] FZJ-JSC IBM Blue Gene/P - JUGENE home page. http://www.fz-juelich.de/ias/jsc/EN/Expertise/Supercomputers/JUGENE/JUGENE_node.html.

[jun12] The FG Router/Switch is a Juniper EX8208, 2012.

[jur] Jülich Research on Petaflop Architictures. http://www.fz-juelich.de/juropa/.

[Kah97] William Kahan. The baleful effect of computer benchmarks upon applied mathematics, physics and chemistry. The John von Neumann Lecture at the 45th Annual Meeting of SIAM, Stanford University, 1997.

[KAB⁺12] J. Kepner, W. Arcand, W. Bergeron, N. Bliss, R. Bond, C. Byun, G. Condon, K. Gregson, M. Hubbell, J. Kurz, A. McCabe, P. Michaleas, A. Prout, A. Reuther, A. Rosa, and C. Yee, "Dynamic Distributed Dimensional Data Model (D4M) Database and Computation System," ICASSP (International Conference on Accoustics, Speech, and Signal Processing), March 25-30, 2012, Kyoto, Japan.

[KB05]      S. Kelly and R. Brightwell. Software architecture of the lightweight kernel, catamount. In *Cray User Group Meeting*, 2005.

[KBB+08]    P. Kogge, K. Bergman, S. Borkar, D. Campbell, W. Carson, W. Dally, M. Denneau, P. Franzon, W. Harrod, K. Hill, et al. Exascale computing study: Technology challenges in achieving exascale systems. 2008.

[KBC+05]    D. H. Kalantar, J. F. Belak, G. W. Collins, J. D. Colvin, H. M. Davies, J. H. Eggert, T. C. Germann, J. Hawreliak, B. L. Holian, K. Kadau, P. S. Lomdahl, H. E. Lorenzana, M. A. Meyers, K. Rosolankova, M. S. Schneider, J. Sheppard, J. S. Stölken, and J. S. Wark. Direct observation of the $\alpha$-$\epsilon$ transition in shock-compressed iron via nanosecond x-ray diffraction. *Phys. Rev. Lett.*, 95:075502, Aug 2005.

[KBD+08]    Andreas Knüpfer, Holger Brunst, Jens Doleschal, Matthias Jurenz, Matthias Lieber, Holger Mickler, Matthias S. Müller, and Wolfgang E. Nagel. The Vampir performance analysis tool-set. In M. Resch, Rainer Keller, Valentin Himmler, Bettina Krammer, and Alexander Schulz, editors, *Tools for High Performance Computing*, pages 139–155. Springer Verlag, July 2008.

[KC]        Patricia Kovatch and Lonnie Crosby. Acceptance test results. Presented during NSF visits in July 2008, Feb 2009, and Nov 2009.

[KDJ+09]    E. Komatsu, J. Dunkley, N. Jarosik, L. Page, M. R. Nolta, C. L. Bennett, B. Gold, D. Larson, G. Hinshaw, A. Kogut, E. Wollack, M. Limon, D. N. Spergel, M. Halpern, R. S. Hill, J. L. Weiland, S. S. Meyer, G. S. Tucker, and Wright E. L. Five-year Wilkinson microwave anisotropy probe observations: Cosmological interpretation. *Astrophysical Journal, Supplement Series*, 180(2): 330–376, 2009.

[KEB12]     Patricia Kovatch, Matthew Ezell, and Ryan Braby. The Malthusian Catastrophe Is Upon Us! Are the Largest HPC Machines Ever Up? In Michael Alexander, Pasqua DAmbra, Adam Belloum, George Bosilca, Mario Cannataro, Marco Danelutto, Beniamino Di Martino, Michael Gerndt, Emmanuel Jeannot, Raymond Namyst, Jean Roman, Stephen Scott, Jesper Traff, Geoffroy Valle, and Josef Weidendorfer, editors, *Euro-Par 2011: Parallel Processing Workshops*, volume 7156 of *Lecture Notes in Computer Science*, pages 211–220. Springer Berlin / Heidelberg, 2012. 10.1007/978-3-642-29740-3_25.

[KeBA+11]   J. Kepner, C. Byun, W. Arcand, W. Bergeron, M. Hubbell, A. McCabe, P. Michaleas, and A. Reuther,"Persistent Surveillance Supercomputing using the LLGrid Filesystem," HPCMP Users Group Meeting, June 21-23, 2011, Portland, OR.

[KeGi11]    J. Kepner and J. Gilbert, "Graph Algorithms in the Language of Linear Algebra," SIAM Press, 2011.

[Kep09]     J. Kepner, "Parallel MATLAB for Multicore and Multinode System," SIAM Press, 2009.

[Kep12]     J. Kepner, "Spreadsheets, Big Tables, and the Algebra of Associative Arrays," MAA & AMS Joint Mathematics Meeting, Jan 4-7, 2012, Boston, MA.

[Kep04]     Jeremy Kepner. HPC productivity: An overarching view. *International Journal of High Performance Computing Applications*, 18(4), November 2004.

[KF08]      K. Keahey and T. Freeman. Contextualization: Providing one-click virtual clusters. In *eScience 2008*, Indianapolis, IN, 2008.

[KFF⁺05]    K. Keahey, I. Foster, T. Freeman, and X. Zhan. Virtual workspaces: Achieving quality of service and quality of life in the grid. *Scientific Programming*, 13: 265-275, 2005.

[KGLH02]    K. Kadau, T.C. Germann, P.S. Lomdahl, and B.L. Holian. Microscopic view of structural phase transitions induced by shock waves. *Science*, 296(5573):1681–1684, 2002.

[KGS⁺11]    Y. Kim, R. Gunasekaran, G.M. Shipman, D.A. Dillow, Z. Zhang, and B.W. Settlemyer. Workload characterization of a leadership class storage. In *5th Petascale Data Storage Workshop Supercomputing10 (PDSW10)*, 2011.

[KH11]      Geoffrey C. Fox, Kai Hwang, and Jack Dongarra. *Distributed and Cloud Computing: From Parallel Processing to the Internet of Things*. Morgan Kaufmann Publishers, 2011.

[KHG⁺11]    C. Kiris, J. Housman, M. Gusman, D. Schauerhamer, K. Deere, A. Elmiligui, K. Abdol-Hamid, E. Parlette, M. Andrews, and J. Blevins. Best practices for aero-database CFD simulations of Ares V ascent. In *Proceedings of the 49th AIAA Aerospace Sciences Meeting*, January 2011.

[KHZ⁺08]    S. Kumar, C. Huang, G. Zheng, E. Bohm, A. Bhatele, J. C. Phillips, H. Yu, and L. V. Kalé. Scalable molecular dynamics with namd on the IBM Blue Gene/L system. *IBM J. Res. Dev.*, 52(1/2):177–188, January 2008.

[Kiz98]     T. Kizuka. Atomic process of point contact in gold studied by time-resolved high-resolution transmission electron microscopy. *Physical Review Letters*, 81(20):4448–51, 1998.

[KLKA06]    Michael Karo, Richard Lagerstrom, Marlys Kohnke, and Carl Abling. Application level placement scheduler. In Cray User Group Meeting, *Proceedings of the 2006 CUG Conference*, Lugano, Switzerland, 2006.

[KMMB12]    Shinpei Kato, Michael McThrow, Carlos Maltzahn, and Scott Brandt. Gdev: first-class GPU resource management in the operating system. In *Proceedings of the USENIX Annual Technical Conference*, Boston, USA, 2012.

[KMT⁺00]    B. Korber, M. Muldoon, J. Theiler, F. Gao, R. Gupta, A. Lapedes, B. H. Hahn, S. Wolinsky, and T. Bhattacharya. Timing the ancestor of the hiv-1 pandemic strains. *Science*, 288(5472):1789–1796, 2000.

[Kob93]     R. Kobayashi. Modeling and numerical simulations of dendritic crystal growth. In *Physica D, Nonlinear Phenomena*, volume 63, pages 410–423, 1993.

[Kog08]     P. Kogge, K. Bergman, S. Borkar, D. Campbell, W. Carlson, W. Dally, M. Denneau, P. Franzon, A. Snavely, W. Harrod, and K. Hill. Exascale computing study: Technology Challenges in achieving exascale systems. Technical report, DARPA IPTO, Air Force Research Labs, 2008.

[Kov]       Patricia Kovatch. Acceptance test overview. Presented during NSF visits in July 2008, Feb 2009, and Nov 2009.

[KR78]      Brian W. Kernighan and Dennis M. Ritchie. *The C Programming Language*. Prentice-Hall, Upper Saddle River, New Jersey, 1978.

[Kra08]     William T.C. Kramer. *PERCU: A Holistic Method for Evaluating High Performance Computing Systems*. PhD thesis, EECS Department, University of California, Berkeley, November 2008.

[KTB11]     Sriram Krishnan, Mahidhar Tatineni, and Chaitanya Baru. myHadoop - Hadoop-on-Demand on traditional HPC resources. Technical report, 2011.

[KV04]      Vassiliki Koutsonikola and Athena Vakali. LDAP: Framework, practices, and trends. In *IEEE Internet Computing*, 8(5): 66-72, 2004.

[LA04]      C. Lattner and V. Adve. LLVM: A compilation framework for lifelong program analysis & transformation. In *Proceedings of the 2004 International Symposium on Code Generation and Optimization (CGO'04)*, Palo Alto, CA, Mar 2004.

[Laba]      Lawrence Livermore National Laboratory. Advanced simulation and computing: ASC purple. https://asc.llnl.gov/computing\_resources/purple/index.html.

[Labb]      Lawrence Livermore National Laboratory. Advanced Simulation and Computing: BlueGene/L. https://asc.llnl.gov/computing\_resources/bluegenel/.

[Labc]      Princeton Plasma Physics Laboratory. Gyrokinetic Toroidal Code (GTC). http://w3.pppl.gov/theory/proj\_gksim.html.

[Lak09]     G. Lakner. IBM System Blue Gene Solution: Blue Gene/P System Administration. *IBM Redpaper Publication*, 2009.

[lap]       LAPACK. Linear algebra package. http://www.netlib.org/lapack/.

[Lar08]     J. Larkin. A micro-benchmark evaluation of catamount and Cray Linux. environment (cle). performance. In *Cray User Group Meeting*, 2008.

[LD07]      Piotr Luszczek and Jack Dongarra. High performance development for high end computing with Python Language Wrapper (PLW). *International Journal of High Perfomance Computing Applications*, 21(2), Summer 2007.

[LDK06]     P. Luszczek, J. Dongarra, and J. Kepner, "Design and Implementation of the HPC Challenge Benchmark Suite," *CT Watch*, Vol. 2, Number 4A, November 2006.

[leg12]     Legion, 2012. http://developer.download.nvidia.com/GTC/PDF/GTC2012/Posters/P0535\_Legion\_GTC\_2012.pdf.

[LfCA]      San Diego Laboratory for Computational Astrophysics, University of California. Enzo - LCA portal. http://lca.ucsd.edu/portal/software/enzo.

[LGK09]     J. Li, W. Ge, and M. Kwauk. Meso-scale phenomena from compromise– a common challenge, not only for chemical engineering. *arXiv preprint arXiv:0912.5407*, 2009.

[LGW+13]   J. Li, W. Ge, W. Wang, N. Yang, X. Liu, L. Wang, X. He, X. Wang, J. Wang, and M. Kwauk. *From Multiscale Modeling to Meso-Science*. Springer, 2013.

[LGT09]   Sheng-Nian Luo, Timothy C. Germann, and Davis L. Tonks. Spall damage of copper under supported and decaying shock loading. *Journal of Applied Physics*, 106(12):123518, 2009.

[LHAP06]   Jiuxing Liu, Wei Huang, Bulent Abali, and Dhabaleswar K. Panda. High performance VMM-bypass I/O in virtual machines. In *Proceedings of the Annual Conference on USENIX '06 Annual Technical Conference*, ATEC '06, Berkeley, CA, USA, 2006. USENIX Association.

[LKN+09]   Alexander Lenk, Markus Klems, Jens Nimis, Stefan Tai, and Thomas Sandholm. What's inside the cloud? An architectural map of the cloud landscape. In *IEEE Cloud '09*, 2009.

[LLL+06]   Julie Langou, Julien Langou, Piotr Luszczek, Jakub Kurzak, Alfredo Buttari, and Jack Dongarra. Exploiting the performance of 32 bit floating point arithmetic in obtaining 64 bit accuracy. In *Proceedings of SC06*, Tampa, Florida, Nomveber 11-17 2006. See http://icl.cs.utk.edu/iter-ref.

[LM04]   D. Livescu and C. K. Madnia. Small scale structure of homogeneous turbulent shear flow. *Physics of Fluids*, 16(8):2864–2876, 2004.

[LM94]   J. Li and M. Kwauk. *Particle-Fluid Two-Phase Flow: the Energy-Minimization Multi-Scale Method*. Metallurgical Industry Press, 1994.

[Lou12]   G. Geneste, M. Torrent. F. Bottin and P. Loubeyre. Strong isotope effect for the structure of phase ii in dense solid hydrogen. *Submitted to Phys. Rev. Lett.*, 109, 155303 (2012).

[LR07]   D. Livescu and J. R. Ristorcelli. Buoyancy-driven variable-density turbulence. *Journal of Fluid Mechanics*, 591:43–71, 2007.

[LR08]   D. Livescu and J. R. Ristorcelli. Variable-density mixing in buoyancy-driven turbulence. *Journal of Fluid Mechanics*, 605:145–180, 2008.

[LRG+09]   D. Livescu, J. R. Ristorcelli, R. A. Gore, S. H. Dean, W. H. Cabot, and A. W. Cook. High-reynolds number Rayleigh-Taylor turbulence. *Journal of Turbulence*, 10(13):1–32, 2009.

[LRN10]   Michael J. Levine, Ralph Z. Roskies, and Nicholas A. Nystrom, *Blacklight: A Very Large Shared Memory System for Science and Engineering*, NSF Award 1041726, 2010.

[LS12]   J. Bontaz-Carion and L. Soulard. Experimental and numerical study of the tantalum single crystal spallation. *European Physical Journal B*, Sept. 2012.

[LTK88]   J. Li, Y. Tung, and M. Kwauk. *Multi-Scale Modeling and Method of Energy Minimization in Particle-Fluid Two-Phase Flow, in Circulating Fluidized Bed Technology II*. Pergamon Press, 1988.

[LTO+11]   J. Lee, M. T. Tran, T. Odajima, T. Boku, and M. Sato. An extension of xcalablemp pgas language for multi-node gpu clusters. *Proc. of HeteroPar 2011 (in EuroPar 2011)*, 2011.

[LUS]            http://wiki.lustre.org.

[LWGH10]         Jerome Lauret, Matthew Walker, Sebastien Goasguen, and Levente Hajdu.
                 From Grid to cloud, the STAR experience. *SciDAC 2010 Proceedings*, 2010.

[LZK05]          W.W. Liang, M. Zhou, and F.J. Ke. Shape memory effect in CU nanowires.
                 *Nano Letters*, 5(10):2039–2043, 2005.

[LZKS09]         J. Lofstead, F. Zheng, S. Klasky, and K. Schwan. Adaptable, metadata rich
                 IO methods for portable high performance IO. In *IPDPS 2009. IEEE Inter-
                 national Symposium on Parallel & Distributed Processing*, pages 1–10. IEEE,
                 2009.

[LZR$^+$10]       Ruiqiang Li, Hongmei Zhu Zhu, Jue Ruan, Wubin Qian, Xiaodong Fang,
                 Zhongbin Shi, Yingrui Li, Shengting Li, Gao Shan Shan, Karsten Kristiansen,
                 Songgang Li, Huanming Yang, Jun Wang, and Jian Wang. *De novo* assembly
                 of human genomes with massively parallel short read sequencing. *Genome
                 Research*, 20(2):265–272, 2010.

[M. 10]          M. Laurenzano, M. Tikir, L. Carrington, and A. Snavely. PEBIL: Efficient
                 Static Binary Instrumentation for Linux. Proceedings of the International
                 Symposium for Performance Analysis of Systems and Software (ISPASS),
                 White Plains, NY, March 2010.

[MAA$^+$05]       J. E. Moreira, G. Almasi, C. Archer, R. Bellofatto, P. Bergner, J. R. Brun-
                 heroto, M. Brutman, J. G. Castanos, P. G. Crumley, M. Gupta, T. In-
                 glett, D. Lieber, D. Limpert, P. McCarthy, M. Megerian, M. Mendell,
                 M. Mundy, D. Reed, R. K. Sahoo, A. Sanomiya, R. Shok, B. Smith, and
                 G. G. Stewart. Blue Gene/L programming and operating environment. *IBM
                 Journal of Research and Development*, 49(2/3):367 –376, Mar/May 2005.
                 http://dx.doi.org/10.1147/rd.492.0367.

[Mag]            Magellan   final   report.      http://science.energy.gov/~/media/ascr/pdf/
                 program-documents/docs/Magellan_Final_Report.pdf.

[mag12]          MAGMA version 1.2, 2012. http://icl.cs.utk.edu/magma.

[MAK$^+$11]       T. Matsunaga, J. Akola, S. Kohara, T. Honma, K. Kobayashi, E. Ikenaga,
                 R. O. Jones, N. Yamada, M. Takata, and R. Kojima. From local structure to
                 nanosecond recrystallization dynamics in aginsbte phase-change materials.
                 *Nature Mater.*, 10:129, 2011.

[MAM$^+$09]       J. S. Meredith, G. Alvarez, T. A. Maier, T. C. Schulthess, and J. S. Vetter.
                 Accuracy and performance of graphics processors: A quantum Monte Carlo
                 application case study. *Parallel Computing*, 35(3):151–163, 2009.

[MBea10]         S. Melchionna, M. Bernaschi, and S. Succi et al. *Comp. Phys. Comm.*, 181,
                 462, 2010.

[MBMdS10]        A. Moody, G. Bronevetsky, K. Mohror, and B. de Supinski. Detailed mod-
                 eling, design, and evaluation of a scalable multi-level checkpointing system.
                 *SuperComputing 2010 Proceedings*, 2010.

[MBR$^+$09]       E. I. Moses, R. N. Boyd, B. A. Remington, C. J. Keane, and R. Al-Ayat.
                 The national ignition facility: Ushering in a new age for high energy density
                 science. *Phys. Plasmas*, 16(041006):1–13, 2009.

[MBW10]     B. Miller, N. Bliss, and P. Wolfe, "Toward signal processing theory for graphs and non-Euclidean data," in *Proceedings of the IEEE International Conference on Acoustics, Speech, and Signal Processing*, 2010.

[Mck99]     J. McKenzie, "TX-0 Computer History," MIT RLE Technical Report No. 627, June, 1999.

[MCC04]     Matthew L. Massie, Brent N. Chun, and David E. Culler. The ganglia distributed monitoring system: Design, implementation, and experience. *Journal of Parallel Computing*, 30: 817-840, April 2004.

[MCF⁺02]     D.S. Montgomery, J.A. Cobble, J.C. Fernandez, R.J. Focia, R.P. Johnson, N. Renard-LeGalloudec, H.A. Rose, and D.A. Russell. Recent Trident single hot spot experiments: Evidence for kinetic effects, and observation of Langmuir decay instability cascade. *Physics of Plasmas*, 9(5, Part 2):2311–2320, May 2002. 43rd Annual Meeting of the Division of Plasma Physics of the American-Physical-Society, Long Beach, CA, Oct 29-Nov 2, 2001.

[Mei08]     J. Meichi. Building the data center of the future. In *NCSA Newsletters*, November 2008.

[Mei09]     Avery A. Meiksin. The physics of the intergalactic medium. *Rev. Mod. Phys.*, 81:1405–1469, Oct 2009.

[MFKN03]     J. Makino, T. Fukushige, M. Koga, and K. Namura. Grape-6: Massively-parallel special-purpose computer for astrophysical particle simulations. *Astronomical Society of Japan*, 55(6):1163–1187, 2003.

[MGAK03]     W. R. Mark, R. S. Glanville, K. Akeley, and M. J. Kilgard. Cg: A system for programming graphics hardware in a c-like language. In *ACM SIGGRAPH 2003 Papers*, San Diego, CA, 2003. ACM. 882362 896-907.

[MGT10]     M. Morgan, A.S. Grimshaw, and O. Tatebe. Rns specification. Web, 2010.

[MGV⁺11]     Alexander Merritt, Vishakha Gupta, Abhishek Verma, Ada Gavrilovska, and Karsten Schwan. Shadowfax: Scaling in heterogeneous cluster systems via GPGPU assemblies. In *Proceedings of the 5th International Workshop on Virtualization Technologies in Distributed Computing*, June 2011.

[MH06]     J. Markoff and S. Hansell. Hiding in plain sight, Google seeks more power. In *The New York Times*, June 14, 2006.

[Mic08]     Sun Microsystems. Lustre networking: High-performance features and flexible support for a wide array of networks. *DARPA*, white paper. Sun Microsystems. 2008.

[MKF11]     P. Marshall, K. Keahey, and T. Freeman. Improving utilization of infrastructure clouds. In *CCGrid 2011*, 2011.

[MM98]     P. Moin and K. Mahesh. Direct numerical simulation: A tool in turbulence research. *Annual Review of Fluid Mechanics*, 30:539–578, 1998.

[MNSM11]     Naoya Maruyama, Tatsuo Nomura, Kento Sato, and Satoshi Matsuoka. Physis: An implicitly parallel programming model for stencil computations on large-scale gpu-accelerated supercomputers. In *Proceedings of 2011 International Conference for High Performance Computing, Networking, Storage and Analysis*, SC '11, pages 11:1–11:12, New York, NY, USA, 2011. ACM.

[Mon92]     J.J. Monaghan. Smoothed particle hydrodynamics. *Annual Review of Astronomy and Astrophysics*, 30:543–574, 1992.

[Moo65]     Gordon E. Moore. Cramming more components onto integrated circuits. *Electronics*, 38(8), April 19, 1965.

[Mor05]     M. Morgan. Byteio specification. Web, October 2005.

[MP08]      R. Namyst, M. Pérache, and H. Jourdren. Mpc: A unified parallel runtime for clusters of numa machines. In *Euro-Par 2008*, 2008.

[MP09]      H. Jourdren, M. Pérache, and P. Carribault. An mpi implementation reducing the overall memory consumption. In *EuroMPI 2009*, 2009.

[MPI12]     Open MPI, 2012. http://www.open-mpi.org/.

[MRSV11]    J. S. Meredith, P. C. Roth, K. L. Spafford, and J. S. Vetter. Performance implications of nonuniform device topologies in scalable heterogeneous architectures. *IEEE Micro*, 31(5):66–75, 2011.

[MS12]      J. Gyllenhaal, M. Schulz, A. Wang, W. Karl, M. Schindewolf, and B.L. Bihari. What scientific applications can benefit from hardware transactional memory? *Lawrence Livermore National Laboratory Technical Report*, (LLNL-TR-560131), 2012.

[MSDS06]    Hans W. Meuer, Erich Strohmaier, Jack J. Dongarra, and Horst D. Simon. *TOP500 Supercomputer Sites*, 28th edition, November 2006. (The report can be downloaded from http://www.netlib.org/benchmark/top500.html).

[MSK+]      Allen Malony, Sameer Shende, Rick Kufrin, Shirley Moore, and Nick Nystrom. The point of performance – performance productivity from open, integrated tools. http://nic.uoregon.edu/mediawiki-point/images/4/40/POINT.pdf.

[MSK12]     V. Minden, B. F. Smith, and M. G. Knepley. Preliminary implementation of PETSc using GPUs. In *Proceedings of the 2010 Workshop of GPU Solutions to Multiscale Problems in Science and Engineering*, 2012.

[MTES94]    J. Makino, M. Taiji, T. Ebisuzaki, and D. Sugimoto. Grape-4: A one-tflops special-purpose computer for astrophysical n-body problem. *Proc. of Supercomputing'94*, pages 429–438, 1994.

[MTF09]     Andrea Matsunaga, Mauricio Tsugawa, and Jose Fortes. Cloudblast: Combining mapreduce and virtualization on distributed resources for bioinformatics applications. In *4th IEEE Intl Conference on eScience*, 2009.

[MYLK09a]   J. Mohd-Yusof, D. Livescu, and T. Kelley. In *Proceedings of SIAM Conference on Computational Science and Engineering*, 2009.

[MYLK09b]   J. Mohd-Yusof, D. Livescu, and T. Kelley. Adapting the CFDNS compressible Navier-Stokes solver to the roadrunner hybrid supercomputer. *Parallel Computational Fluid Dynamics Recent Advances and Future Directions*, pages 95–, 2009.

[MZ88]      G.R. McNamara and G. Zanetti. Use of the Boltzmann equation to simulate lattice-gas automata. *Physical Review Letters*, 61(20):2332–2335, 1988.

[MZC+10]  Zeyao Mo, Aiqing Zhang, Xiaolin Cao, Qingkai Liu, Xiaowen Xu, Hengbin An, Wenbing Pei, and Shaoping Zhu. Jasmin: A parallel software infrastructure for scientific computing. *Front. Comput. Sci. China*, 4(4):480–488, 2010.

[NB07]  J. Nickolls and I. Buck. NVIDIA CUDA software and GPU parallel computing architecture. In *Microprocessor Forum*, 2007.

[ND10]  J. Nickolls and W.J. Dally. The GPU computing era. *Micro, IEEE*, 30(2):56–69, 2010.

[Nea04]  The loblolly pine genome project: A prospectus to guide planning and funding of a USDA Forest Service led effort to develop an integrated genomics research program in loblolly pine. 2004.

[NHL94]  Jaroslaw Nieplocha, Robert J. Harrison, and Richard J. Littlefield. Global arrays: a portable "shared-memory" programming model for distributed memory computers. In *Supercomputing '94: Proceedings of the 1994 ACM/IEEE Conference on Supercomputing*, pages 340–349, New York, NY, USA, 1994. ACM.

[nic]  John von Neumann Institute for Computing. http://www2.fz-juelich.de/nic/.

[Nie]  E. Nielsen. FUN3D: Fully unstructured Navier-Stokes. Website. http://fun3d.larc.nasa.gov/.

[NIS]  Nist draft cloud computing synopsis and recommendations. http://csrc.nist.gov/publications/drafts/800-146/Draft-NIST-SP800-146.pdf.

[NJ00]  Ida M. B. Nielsen and Curtis L. Janssen. Multi-threading: A new dimension to massively parallel scientific computation. *Computer Physics Communications*, 128:238–244, June 2000.

[NLBS10]  M. Nakao, J. Lee, T. Boku, and M. Sato. Xcalablemp implementation and performance on nas parallel benchmarks. *Proc. PGAS10*, 2010.

[NPT+06]  J. Nieplocha, B. Palmer, V. Tipparaju, M. Krishnan, H. Trease, and E. Apra. Advances, applications and performance of the global arrays shared memory programming toolkit. *Int. J. High Perform. Comput. Appl.*, 20(2):203–231, May 2006.

[nr09]  IBM news room. Obama honors IBM's Blue Gene supercomputer with National Medal of Technology and Innovation, 2009. http://www-03.ibm.com/press/us/en/pressrelease/28423.wss.

[NSA08]  NSA Electrical Power Upgrade, January 2008.

[NSF05]  NSF. High performance computing system acquisition: Towards a petascale computing environment for science and engineering. http://www.nsf.gov/pubs/2005/nsf05625/nsf05625.htm, 2005.

[NSF06]  NSF Blue Ribbon Panel. Revolutionizing science and engineering through cyberinfrastructure. Technical report, NSF, 2006.

[NSF07]  NSF. National science board approves funds for petascale computing systems. http://www.nsf.gov/news/news\_summ.jsp?cntn\_id=109850, 2007.

[nsf09]      Futuregrid: An experimental, high-performance grid test-bed. Web Page, 2009. October 1, 2009 - September 30, 2013 (Estimated).

[NTB06]      R. H. Nichols, R. W. Tramel, and P. G. Buning. Solver and turbulence model upgrades to OVERFLOW 2 for unsteady and high-speed applications. In *Proceedings of the 25th AIAA Applied Aerodynamics Conference*, volume AIAA-2006-2824, June 2006.

[NTL+12]     T. Nomizu, D. Takahashi, J. Lee, T. Boku, and M. Sato. Implementation of xcalablemp device acceleration extention with opencl. *Proc. of PLC2012 (in IPDPS 2012)*, 2012.

[NVI]        NVIDIA m2090: http://www.nvidia.com/docs/IO/43395/Tesla-M2090-Board-Specification.pdf. Technical report.

[NVI09a]     NVIDIA. NVIDIA's Next Generation CUDA Compute Architecture: Fermi. Technical report, 2009.

[NVI09b]     NVIDIA Corp. NVIDIA's Next Generation CUDA Compute Architecture: Fermi. http://tinyurl.com/nvidia-fermi-whitepaper, 2009.

[Nvi11]      NVIDIA. NVIDIA CUDA Programming Guide v4.0, 2011.

[NVI11a]     NVIDIA. *NVIDIA Compute Visual Profiler*. NVIDIA Corporation, Santa Clara, CA, 4.0 edition, May 2011.

[NVI11b]     NVIDIA. *NVIDIA CUDA Tools SDK CUPTI*. NVIDIA Corporation, Santa Clara, CA, 1.0 edition, February 2011.

[NVI12a]     NVIDIA Corporation. CUDA Toolkit 4.2 CUBLAS Library, February 2012. http://developer.download.nvidia.com/compute/DevZone/docs/html/CUDALibraries/doc/CUBLAS\_Library.pdf.

[NVI12b]     NVIDIA Corporation. CUDA Toolkit 4.2 CUFFT Library, March 2012. http://developer.download.nvidia.com/compute/DevZone/docs/html/CUDALibraries/doc/CUFFT\_Library.pdf.

[NVI12c]     NVIDIA Corporation. CUDA Toolkit 4.2 CUSPARSE Library, February 2012. http://developer.download.nvidia.com/compute/DevZone/docs/html/CUDALibraries/doc/CUSPARSE\_Library.pdf.

[OAS07]      OASIS. Ws-trust. Web, March 2007.

[OBB+04]     Brian W. O'Shea, Greg Bryan, James Bordner, Michael L. Norman, Tom Abel, et al. Introducing Enzo, an AMR cosmology application. *IEEE Comput.Sci.Eng.*, 2004.

[OC98]       E. S. Oran, C. K. Oh, and B. Z. Cybyk. Direct simulation Monte Carlo: Recent advances and applications. *Annual Review of Fluid Mechanics*, 30:403–441, 1998.

[Oe11]       S. Otani et al. An 80gb/s dependable communication soc with pci express i/f and 8 cpus. *Proc. of ISSCC2011*, pages CD–ROM, 2011.

[OLG+05a]    J. D. Owens, D. Luebke, N. Govindaraju, M. Harris, J. Krger, A. E. Lefohn, and T. J. Purcell. A survey of general-purpose computation on graphics hardware. In *Eurographics 2005, State of the Art Reports*, pages 21–51, 2005.

[OLG+05b]   John D. Owens, David Luebke, Naga Govindaraju, Mark Harris, Jens Krger, Aaron E. Lefohn, and Timothy J. Purcell. A survey of general-purpose computation on graphics hardware. In *Eurographics 2005, State of the Art Reports*, pages 21–51, 2005.

[Opea]   Openacc, http://www.openacc-standard.org. Technical report.

[Opeb]   OpenFabrics Alliance. Website. http://www.openfabrics.org/.

[Opec]   OpenMP: Simple, portable, scalable SMP programming. http://www.openmp.org/.

[OR02]   Klaus-Dieter Oertel and Mathilde Romberg. The UNICORE Grid System, Tutorial 3, August 2002.

[Ora]   Oracle. Lustre. http://wiki.lustre.org.

[ORN07]   ASCR Computing News Roundup, October 2007.

[oT08]   University of Tennessee. Acceptance test plan, August 2008.

[Ot11]   M. Ohmacht and the IBM Blue Gene Team. Hardware support for transactional memory and thread-level speculation in the IBM Blue Gene/Q system. In *PACT 2011 Workshop on Wild and Sane Ideas in Speculation and Transactions*, Galveston, TX, 2011. http://wands.cse.lehigh.edu/IBM_BQC_PACT2011.ppt.

[otUoC]   The Regents of the University of California. IOR. https://github.com/chaos/ior.

[OWG+13]   M. Ohmacht, A.K.T Wang, T.M. Gooding, B.J. Nathanson, I.I. Nair, G. Janssen, and B.D. Steinmacher-Burow. The Blue Gene/Q memory subsystem with speculative execution and transactional memory support. *IBM Journal of Research and Development*, 57(1/2), Jan 2013.

[pap12]   PAPI, 2012.

[par]   ParMETIS - Parallel Graph Partitioning and Fill-reducing Matrix Ordering. Website. Available online at http://glaros.dtc.umn.edu/gkhome/metis/parmetis/overview.

[PBV+06]   Steve J. Plimpton, R. Brightwell, Courtney Vaughan, K. Underwood, and M. Davis. A simple synchronous distributed-memory algorithm for the HPCC RandomAccess benchmark. In *Proceedings of Cluster 2006 – IEEE International Conference on Cluster Computing*, September 2006.

[PBW+05]   James C. Phillips, Rosemary Braun, Wei Wang, James Gumbart, Emad Tajkhorshid, Elizabeth Villa, Christophe Chipot, Robert D. Skeel, Laxmikant Kale, and Klaus Schulten. Scalable molecular dynamics with NAMD. *Journal of Computational Chemistry*, 26:1781–1802, 2005.

[PC06]   C. Pierleoni and D. M. Ceperley. The coupled electron-ion Monte Carlo method. *Lecture Notes in Physics*, 703:641, 2006.

[PC10]   H. Jourdren, P. Carribault, and M. Pérache. Enabling low-overhead hybrid mpi/openmp parallelism with mpc. In *International Workshop on OpenMP IWOMP'2010*, 2010.

[PC11]        H. Jourdren, P. Carribault, and M. Pérache. Thread-local storage extension
              to support thread-based mpi/openmp applications. In *International Work-
              shop on OpenMP (IWOMP'2011)*, 2011.

[PCI10]       PCI-SIG. *PCI Express Base Specification, Rev. 3.0*, November 2010.

[PD11]        A. Cedeyn and P. Deniel. Give your machine a second life, turn it into a nfs
              server using nfsganesha. In *Flash Talk at the 2011 Linux Symposium*, 2011.

[pet]         Technical report.

[PHL+10]      Adrian Pope, Salman Habib, Zarija Lukic, David Daniel, Patricia Fasel, Ne-
              hal Desai, and Katrin Heitmann. The accelerated universe. *Computing in
              Science and Engineering*, 12:17–25, 2010.

[PKP03]       Fabrizio Petrini, Darren J. Kerbyson, and Scott Pakin. The case of the miss-
              ing supercomputer performance: Achieving optimal performance on the 8,192
              processors of ASCI Q. In *Proceedings of the ACM/IEEE SC2003 Conference
              on High Performance Networking and Computing*, page 55. ACM, November
              2003.

[PL10]        Mark R. Petersen and Daniel Livescu. Forcing for statistically stationary
              compressible isotropic turbulence. *Physics of Fluids*, 22(11):116101, 2010.

[Pli95]       Steve J. Plimpton. Fast parallel algorithms for short-range molecular dy-
              namics. *J. Comp. Phys*, 117:1–19, 1995. http://lammps.sandia.gov.

[PMGH+95]     J.I. Pascual, J. Mendez, J. Gomez-Herrero, A.M. Baro, N. Garcia, U. Land-
              man, W.D. Luedtke, E.N. Bogachek, and H.P. Cheng. Properties of metallic
              nanowires: From conductance quantization to localization. Technical Report
              5205, United States, 1995. Contract no.: FG05-86ER45234.

[PMH+10]      J. Poulson, B. Marker, J.R. Hammond, N.A. Romero, and R. van de Geijn.
              Elemental: A new framework for distributed memory dense matrix compu-
              tations. *ACM Transactions on Mathematical Software (TOMS). submitted*,
              2010. Available online at http://users.ices.utexas.edu/\textasciitildepoulson/
              publications/Elemental.pdf.

[pne]         Parallel netcdf: A high performance api for netcdf file access. http://trac.
              mcs.anl.gov/projects/parallel-netcdf.

[Pow]         Emerson Network Power.    http://www.emersonnetworkpower.com/en-US/
              Pages/Default.aspx.

[PPF]         M. J. Pandya, P. Parikh, and N. T. Frink. USM3Dns user's online manual.
              Website. http://aaac.larc.nasa.gov/tsab/usm3d/usm3d_52_man.html.

[PPL]         University of Illinois Urbana-Champaign Parallel Programming Laboratory.
              Parallel Languages/Paradigms: Charm ++ - Parallel Objects. http://charm.
              cs.uiuc.edu/research/charm/.

[praa]        Prace - Report on the Application Benchmarking Results of Prototype Sys-
              tems. http://www.prace-ri.eu/IMG/pdf/D5-4-extended.pdf.

[prab]        PRACE: Partnership for Advanced Computing in Europe. http://www.
              prace-project.eu/. Funding from the EU's Seventh Framework Programme
              (FP7/2007-2013) under grant agreements no. RI-261557 and no. RI-283493.

[PWDC]    A. Petitet, R.C. Whaley, J. Dongarra, and A. Cleary. HPL - a portable implementation of the high-performance linpack benchmark for distributed-memory computers. http://www.netlib.org/benchmark/hpl/.

[PWDC00]   Antoine Petitet, R. Clint Whaley, Jack J. Dongarra, and Andy Cleary. A Portable Implementation of the High-Performance Linpack Benchmark for Distributed-Memory Computers. Innovative Computing Laboratory, Available at http://icl.cs.utk.edu/hpl/ and http://www.netlib.org/hpl/, September 2000.

[PWDC08]   A. Petitet, R. C. Whaley, J. Dongarra, and A. Cleary. HPL - A Portable Implementation of the High-Performance Linpack Benchmark for Distributed-Memory Computers. http://www.netlib.org/benchmark/hpl, 2008.

[QLR⁺10]   Junjie Qin, Ruiqiang Li, Jeroen Raes, Manimozhiyan Arumugam, Kristoffer Solvsten Burgdorf, Chaysavanh Manichanh, Trine Nielsen, Nicolas Pons, Florence Levenez, Takuji Yamada, Daniel R. Mende, Junhua Li, Junming Xu, Shaochuan Li, Dongfang Li, Jianjun Cao, Bo Wang, Huiqing Liang, Huisong Zheng, Yinlong Xie, Julien Tap, Patricia Lepage, Marcelo Bertalan, Jean-Michel Batto, Torben Hansen, Denis Le Paslier, Allan Linneberg, H. Bjørn Nielsen, Eric Pelletier, Pierre Renault, Thomas Sicheritz-Ponten, Keith Turner, Hongmei Zhu, Chang Yu, Shengting Li, Min Jian, Yan Zhou, Yingrui Li, Xiuqing Zhang, Songgang Li, Nan Qin, Huanming Yang, Jian Wang, Søren Brunak, Joel Doré, Francisco Guarner, Karsten Kristiansen, Oluf Pedersen, Julian Parkhill, Jean Weissenbach, MetaHIT Consortium, Peer Bork, S. Dusko Ehrlich, and Jun Wang. A human gut microbial gene catalogue established by metagenomic sequencing. *Nature*, 464:59–65, 2010.

[qmc12]    QMCPACK, 2012. http://qmcpack.cmscc.org/.

[qua]     Quantum espresso. http://www.quantum-espresso.org/.

[QVZJ02]   A. Quarteroni, A. Veneziani, and P. Zunino, Mathematical and numerical modelling of solute dynamics in blood flow and arterial walls, *SIAM J. Num. Analysis*, 39, 1488, 2002.

[RB]      W. Rapin and B. Borucki. Characterization of Kepler's planetary candidates within the habitable zone. Poster displayed at Summer 2011 Higher Education Poster Symposium at NASA Ames Research Center. http://kepler.nasa.gov/multimedia/artwork/?ImageID=165.

[RC86]     D. C. Rapaport and E. Clementi. Eddy formation in obstructed fluid flow: A molecular dynamics study. *Physical Review Letters*, 57:695–698, 1986.

[RCM⁺11]   Lavanya Ramakrishnan, Richard Shane Canon, Krishna Muriki, Iwona Sakrejda, and Nicholas J. Wright. Evaluating interconnect and virtualization performance for high performance computing. In *Proceedings of 2nd International Workshop on Performance Modeling, Benchmarking and Simulation of High Performance Computing Systems (PMBS11)*, 2011.

[RCM⁺12]   Lavanya Ramakrishnan, Richard Shane Canon, Krishna Muriki, Iwona Sakrejda, and Nicholas J. Wright. Evaluating interconnect and virtualization performance for high performance computing. In *ACM Performance Evaluation Review, 40(20)*, 2012.

[Resa]        Cluster Resources. Adaptive Computing - MOAB HPC suite. http://www. adaptivecomputing.com/products/moab-hpc-suite-basic.php.

[Resb]        Cluster Resources. Adaptive Computing - TORQUE resource manager. http: //www.adaptivecomputing.com/products/torque.php.

[RHH12]       Matthew G. Reuter, Judith C. Hill, and Robert J. Harrison. Solving PDEs in irregular geometries with multiresolution methods I: Embedded Dirichlet boundary conditions. *Computer Physics Communications*, 183(1):1 – 7, 2012.

[Rie]         M. Rienecker. The GEOS-5 system. Website. http://gmao.gsfc.nasa.gov/ systems/geos5/.

[RKGS08]      Adit Ranadive, Mukil Kesavan, Ada Gavrilovska, and Karsten Schwan. Performance implications of virtualizing multicore cluster machines. In *Proceedings of the 2nd Workshop on System-level Virtualization for High Performance Computing*, HPCVirt '08, pages 1–8, New York, NY, USA, 2008. ACM.

[RLV+10]      A. Rahimian, I. Lashuk, S. Veerapaneni, A. Chandramowlishwaran, D. Malhotra, L. Moon, R. Sampath, A. Shringarpure, J. Vetter, R. Vuduc, D. Zorin, and G. Biros. Petascale direct numerical simulation of blood flow on 200k cores and heterogeneous architectures (Gordon Bell Award winner). In *2010 ACM/IEEE International Conference for High Performance Computing, Networking, Storage and Analysis (SC10)*, pages 1–11, New Orleans, LA, 2010. IEEE Computer Society, IEEE Computer Society.

[Rob10]       Robert J. Harrison, et al. Multiresolution ADaptive NumErical Scientific Simulation (MADNESS), 2010. http://code.google.com/p/m-a-d-n-e-s-s/.

[Rog]         Rogue Wave Software. TotalView. http://www.roguewave.com/products/ totalview.aspx.

[RSH+11]      G. Renker, N. Stringfellow, K. Howard, S. R. Alam, and S. Trofinoff. Deploying slurm on xt, xe, and future Cray systems. In *Cray User Group Meeting*, 2011.

[RTM+10]      P. Riteau, M. Tsugawa, A. Matsunaga, J. Fortes, T. Freeman, D. LaBissoniere, and K. Keahey. Sky computing on futuregrid and grid'5000. In *TeraGrid 2010*, 2010.

[RTMvL12]     Matthias Rupp, Alexandre Tkatchenko, Klaus-Robert Müller, and O. Anatole von Lilienfeld. Fast and accurate modeling of molecular atomization energies with machine learning. *Phys. Rev. Lett.*, 108:058301, 2012.

[RWH08]       B. Rockel, A. Will, and A. Hense. The regional climate model cosmo-clm (cclm). In *Meteorologische Zeitschrift*, volume 17, 2008.

[RYJ+08]      Yang Ren, Masaaki Yamada, Hantao Ji, Seth Dorfman, Stefan P. Gerhardt, and Russel Kulsrud. Experimental study of the Hall effect and electron diffusion region during magnetic reconnection in a laboratory plasma. *Physics of Plasmas*, 15(8), Aug 2008.

[S. 06]       S. Shende and A. D. Malony. The TAU Parallel Performance System. *International Journal of High Performance Computing Applications*, 20, 2006.

[SA10] Takashi Shimokawabe and Takayuki Aoki. Multi-gpu computing for next generation weather forecasting. In *The TSUBAME E-Science Journal*, volume 2, pages 11–15, GSIC Center, Tokyo Institute of Technology, November 2010.

[sag] SAGA BigJob.

[sag12] Saga Project, 2012.

[SAKD06] S. Scott, D. Abts, J. Kim, and W.J. Dally. The blackwidow high-radix clos network. In *Proceedings of the International Symposium on Computer Architecture (ISCA)* 34(2):16–28, 2006.

[SAM+10] Takashi Shimokawabe, Takayuki Aoki, Chiashi Muroi, Junichi Ishida, Kohei Kawano, Toshio Endo, Akira Nukada, Naoya Maruyama, and Satoshi Matsuoka. An 80-fold speedup, 15.0 tflops full gpu acceleration of non-hydrostatic weather model asuca production code. In *Proceedings of the 2010 ACM/IEEE International Conference for High Performance Computing, Networking, Storage and Analysis*, SC '10, pages 1–11, Washington, DC, USA, 2010. IEEE Computer Society.

[SB05] R. Schmidt and D. Beaty. ASHRAE committee formed to establish thermal guidelines for datacom facilities. *Electronics Cooling Magazine*, February 2005.

[SBC+03] Constantine P. Sapuntzakis, David Brumley, Ramesh Chandra, Nickolai Zeldovich, Jim Chow, Monica S. Lam, and Mendel Rosenblum. Virtual appliances for deploying and maintaining software. In *LISA*, pages 181–194. USENIX, 2003.

[SC11] The International Conference for High Performance Computing, Networking, Storage, and Analysis. http://supercomputing.org/, 2011.

[Sca] Scalapack scalable linear algebra package. http://www.netlib.org/scalapack/.

[sca12] ScaleMP, 2012.

[SDD+07] D. E. Shaw, M. M. Deneroff, R. O. Dror, J. S. Kuskin, R. H. Larson, J. K. Salmon, C. Young, B. Batson, K. J. Bowers, and J. C. Chao. Anton, a special-purpose machine for molecular dynamics simulation. In *34th Annual International Conference on Computer Architecture*, pages 1–12, 2007.

[SDOW09] G. Shipman, D. Dillow, S. Oral, and F. Wang. The spider center wide file system: From concept to reality. In *Proceedings, Cray User Group (CUG) Conference, Atlanta, GA*, 2009.

[SEHO07] Shava Smallen, Kate Ericson, Jim Hayes, and Catherine Olschanowsky. User-level grid monitoring with Inca 2. In *Proceedings of the 2007 Workshop on Grid Monitoring*, GMW '07, pages 29–38, New York, 2007. ACM.

[seq12] Sequoia, 2012. http://sequoia.stanford.edu/.

[SGS10] J. E. Stone, D. Gohara, and G. Shi. Opencl: A parallel programming standard for heterogeneous computing systems. *Computing in Science and Engineering*, 12(3):66–73, 2010.

[SH98]        I. Schoinas and M.D. Hill. Address translation mechanisms in network inter-
              faces. In *High-Performance Computer Architecture, 1998. Proceedings, 1998
              Fourth International Symposium on*, pages 219–230. IEEE, 1998.

[she12]       The SHEA group, 2012. http://www.chem.ucsb.edu/~sheagroup.

[SHG09]       Nadathur Satish, Mark Harris, and Michael Garland. Designing efficient
              sorting algorithms for manycore GPUs. In *Proceedings of the International
              Parallel and Distributed Processing Symposium (IPDPS 2009)*, Los Alamitos,
              CA, USA, 2009. IEEE Computer Society.

[ShHcF06]     Sushant Sharma, Chung hsing Hsu, and Wu chun Feng. Making a Case for a
              Green500 List. In *2nd IEEE Workshop on High-Performance, Power-Aware
              Computing (in conjunction with the 20th International Parallel*, Rhodes,
              Greece, April 2006.

[Sil09]       Silicon Graphics International. SGI Unveils Altix UV, the World's Fastest
              Supercomputer. http://www.sgi.com/company_info/newsroom/press_releases/
              2009/november/altix_uv.html, 2009.

[Sin05]       Abe Singer. Tempting Fate. *;login: the USENIX magazine*, 30(1), 2005.

[SJ08]        Jay Shendure and Hanlee Ji. Next-generation dna sequencing. *Nature
              Biotechnology*, 26(10):1135–1145, 2008.

[SJH+11]      S. Saini, H. Jin, R. Hood, D. Barker, P. Mehrotra, and R. Biswas. The
              impact of hyper-threading on processor resource utilization in production
              applications. In *Proceedings of the IEEE International Conference on High
              Performance Computing (HiPC11)*, 2011.

[SKM+08]      Sampa Santra, Bette T. Korber, Mark Muldoon, Dan H. Barouch, Gary J.
              Nabel, Feng Gao, Beatrice H. Hahn, Barton F. Haynes, and Norman L.
              Letvin. A centralized gene-based hiv-1 vaccine elicits broad cross-clade cel-
              lular immune responses in rhesus monkeys. *Proceedings of the National
              Academy of Sciences of the United States of America*, 105(30):10489–10494,
              2008.

[SKRC10]      K. Shvachko, Hairong Kuang, S. Radia, and R. Chansler. The hadoop dis-
              tributed file system. In *Mass Storage Systems and Technologies (MSST),
              2010 IEEE 26th Symposium on*, pages 1–10, May 2010.

[SM06a]       S. Shende and A.D Malony. The TAU parallel performance system. *Interna-
              tional Journal of High Performance Computing Applications*, 20(2):287–311,
              2006.

[SM06b]       S. S. Shende and A. D. Malony. The TAU parallel performance system. *Inter-
              national Journal of High Performance Computing Applications*, 20(2):287–
              331, 2006.

[SMM07]       Sameer Shende, Allen D. Malony, and Alan Morris. Workload character-
              ization using the tau performance system. In *Proceedings of the 8th In-
              ternational Conference on Applied Parallel Computing: State of the Art in
              Scientific Computing*, PARA'06, pages 289–296, Berlin, Heidelberg, 2007.
              Springer-Verlag.

[SMRS12]    Michael P. Schodlok, Dimitris Menemenlis, Eric Rignot, and Michael Studinger. Sensitivity of the ice shelf/ocean system to the sub-ice-shelf cavity shape measured by NASA IceBridge in Pine Island Glacier, West Antarctica. *Annals of Glaciology*, 53:156–162, 2012.

[SNA07]     SNAPP - SNMP Network Analysis and Presentation Package. http://snapp.sourceforge.net/, 2007.

[Sne03]     David Snelling. *Unicore and the Open Grid Services Architecture*, pages 701–712. John Wiley & Sons, Ltd, 2003.

[SOHL+98]   Marc Snir, Steve Otto, Steven Huss-Lederman, David Walker, and Jack Dongarra. *MPI-The Complete Reference, Volume 1: The MPI Core*. MIT Press, Cambridge, MA, 2nd. (revised) edition, 1998.

[SPE]       Spec website. https://portal.futuregrid.org/.

[spe08]     Standard Performance Evaluation Corporation, SPECPower, 2008.

[Spr]       Volker Springel. GADGET-2: A code for consmological simulations of sturcute formation. http://www.mpa-garching.mpg.de/gadget/.

[STBdf]     Jack Dongarra, Stanimire Tomov, and Marc Baboulin. Towards dense linear algebra for hybrid GPU accelerated manycore systems. *Linear Algebra Working Note 210*, 2008 (see http://www.netlib.org/lapack/lawnspdf/lawn210.pdf).

[STD12]     F. Song, S. Tomov, and J. Dongarra. Enabling and scaling matrix computations on heterogeneous multi-core and multi-GPU systems. *26th ACM International Conference on Supercomputing (ICS 2012)*, June 2012.

[StKe12]    M. Stonebraker and J. Kepner, "Possible Hadoop Trajectories," Association for Computing Machinery Blog, May 2, 2012.

[Sv48]      A. Svoboda, "Computing Mechanisms and Linkages," volume 27 of MIT Radiation Laboratory Series. McGraw-Hill, New York, 1948.

[SWE09]     David Schlegel, Martin White, and Daniel Eisenstein. The baryon oscillation spectroscopic survey: Precision measurements of the absolute cosmic distance scale. February 2009.

[tak12]     TakTuk, 2012.

[TDB10]     S. Tomov, J. Dongarra, and M. Baboulin. Towards dense linear algebra for hybrid GPU accelerated manycore systems. *Parallel Comput.*, 36(5-6):232–240, 2010.

[Tea08]     IBM Blue Gene Team. Overview of the IBM Blue Gene/P project. *IBM Journal of Research and Development*, 52(1.2):199–220, Jan 2008. http://dx.doi.org/10.1147/rd.521.0199.

[Tea13]     IBM Blue Gene Team. Design of the IBM Blue Gene/Q compute chip. *IBM Journal of Research and Development*, 57(1/2), Jan 2013.

[TF06]      Mauricio Tsugawa and Jose A. B. Fortes. A virtual network (vine) architecture for grid computing. In *20th Intl. Parallel and Distributed Processing Symposium (IPDPS)*, 2006.

[TFT05]     Tomohiro Takaki, Toshimichi Fukuoka, and Yoshihiro Tomita. Phase-field simulation during directional solidification of a binary alloy using adaptive finite element method. *J. Crystal Growth*, 283:263–278, 2005.

[TGW+04]    D. Tang, W. Ge, X. Wang, J. Ma, L. Guo, and J. Li. Parallelizing of macro-scale pseudo-particle modeling for particle-fluid systems. *Science in China Series B: Chemistry*, 47(5):434–442, 2004.

[Tha]       Arnold Tharrington. Test harness. National Center for Computational Sciences, Scientific Computing Group, Oak Ridge National Laboratory, Oak Ridge, TN.

[Thea]      The Locally-Self-Consistent Multiple-Scattering (LSMS) Code. http://www.ccs.ornl.gov/mri/repository/LSMS/index.html.

[Theb]      Theoretical and Computational Biophysics Group, NIH Resource for Macromolecular Modeling & Bioinformatics, University of Illinois at Urbana-Champaign. NAMD - Scalable Molecular Dynamics. http://www.ks.uiuc.edu/Research/namd/.

[The09]     The Cray User Group, Inc. Proceedings of the 2009 CUG Conference. In *Proceedings of the 2009 CUG Conference*, Atlanta, GA, 2009.

[The10]     The Cray User Group, Inc. Proceedings of the 2010 CUG Conference. In *Proceedings of the 2010 CUG Conference*, Edinburgh, Scotland, 2010.

[TJC+98]    Brian Tierney, William Johnston, Brian Cowley, Gary Hoo, Chris Brooks, and Dan Gunter. The netlogger methodology for high performance distributed systems performance analysis. In *Proc. 7th IEEE Symp. on High Performance Distributed Computing*, pages 260–267, 1998.

[TK06]      Nadya Travinin and Jeremy Kepner. pMATLAB parallel MATLAB library. *International Journal of High Perfomance Computing Applications*, 2006. Submitted to Special Issue on High Productivity Languages and Models.

[TND10]     S. Tomov, R. Nath, and J. Dongarra. Accelerating the reduction to upper Hessenberg, tridiagonal, and bidiagonal forms through hybrid GPU-based computing. *Parallel Computing*, 36(12):645–654, December 2010.

[TNLD10]    S. Tomov, R. Nath, H. Ltaief, and J. Dongarra. Dense linear algebra solvers for multicore with GPU accelerators. In *IPDPS Workshops*, 2010.

[TOPa]      Hans Meuer, Eric Strohmaier, Jack Dongarro, and Horst Simon, TOP500 Supercomputer sites, http://www.top500.org.

[Topb]      TOP500 – November 2008. Website. http://www.top500.org/lists/2008/11.

[TOP11]     The Top 500 List. http://www.top500.org, 2011.

[tri]       The trillinos project. http://trilinos.sandia.gov/.

[Tro09]     Troy Baer, Victor Hazlewood, Junseong Heo, Rick Mohr, John Walsh. Large Lustre File System Experiences at NICS. Cray User Group, Atlanta, GA., May 2009.

[tTP06]     K.H.W.J. ten Tusscher and A.V. Panfilov. Alternans and spiral breakup in a human ventricular tissue model. *American Journal of Physiology Heart and Circulatory Physiology, Heart and Circulatory Physiology*, 291(3):1088–1100, 2006.

[uni]       unidata. netCDF. http://www.unidata.ucar.edu/software/netcdf/docs/.

[UTa]       CCS U. Tsukuba. Center for computational sciences. http://www.ccs.tsukuba.ac.jp/.

[UTb]       CCS U. Tsukuba. Ha-pacs project. http://www.ccs.tsukuba.ac.jp/CCS/eng/research-activities/projects/ha-pacs/.

[Vï0]       C. Vömel. ScaLAPACK's MRRR algorithm. *ACM Transactions on Mathematical Software (TOMS)*, 37(1):1–35, 2010.

[vam12]     Vampir, 2012.

[Van06]     A. Vance. Microsoft's Data Center Offensive Sounds Offensive. In *The Register*, June 2006.

[VBO11]     A. Vishnu, M. Bruggencate, and R. Olson. Evaluating the potential of Cray Gemini interconnect for pgas models. In *International Symposium on High-Performance Interconnects (HotI)*, 2011.

[VDRB11]    J.-S. Vöckler, E. Deelman, M. Rynge, and G.B. Berriman. Experiences using cloud computing for a scientific workflow application. In *Workshop on Scientific Cloud Computing (ScienceCloud)*, June 2011.

[VF96]      Edward F. Valeev and Justin T. Fermann. The Massively Parallel Quantum Chemistry program (MPQC), 1996. https://sourceforge.net/projects/libint/.

[VGD+11]    J. S. Vetter, R. Glassbrook, J. Dongarra, K. Schwan, B. Loftis, S. McNally, J. Meredith, J. Rogers, P. Roth, K. Spafford, and S. Yalamanchili. Keeneland: Bringing heterogeneous GPU computing to the computational science community. *IEEE Computing in Science and Engineering*, 13(5):90–95, 2011.

[VJ04]      Edward F. Valeev and Curtis L. Janssen. Second-order Møller–Plesset theory with linear R12 terms (MP2-R12) revisited: Auxiliary basis set method and massively parallel implementation. *The Journal of Chemical Physics*, 121(3):1214–1227, 2004. http://link.aip.org/link/?JCP/121/1214/1.

[vL06]      Gregor von Laszewski. Java CoG kit workflow concepts. *Journal of Grid Computing*, 3(3-4):239–258, January 2006.

[vLDWF12]   Gregor von Laszewski, Javier Diaz, Fugang Wang, and Geoffrey C. Fox. Comparison of multiple cloud frameworks. In *IEEE Cloud 2012*, Honolulu, HI, 2012.

[vLFW+10]   Gregor von Laszewski, Geoffrey C. Fox, Fugang Wang, Andrew J Younge, Archit Kulshrestha, Gregory G. Pike, Warren Smith, Jens Voeckler, Renato J. Figueiredo, Jose Fortes, Kate Keahey, and Ewa Delman. Design of the future-grid experiment management framework. In *Proceedings of Gateway Computing Environments 2010 (GCE2010) at SC10*, New Orleans, LA, 2010. IEEE.

[vLYH+09]    Gregor von Laszewski, Andrew Younge, Xi He, Kumar Mahinthakumar, and Lizhe Wang. Experiment and workflow management using cyberaide shell. In *4th International Workshop on Workflow Systems in e-Science (WSES 09) in conjunction with 9th IEEE International Symposium on Cluster Computing and the Grid*, pages 568–573, Shanghai, China, May 2009. IEEE.

[Vot98]      A.F. Voter. Parallel replica method for dynamics of infrequent events. *Physical Review B (Condensed Matter)*, 57(22):R13985–8, 1998.

[VRB+11]     C. Vaughan, M. Rajan, R. Barrett, D. Doerfler, and K. Pedretti. Investigating the impact of the cielo Cray xe6 architecture on scientific application codes. In *Proceedings of the 2011 IEEE International Symposium on Parallel and Distributed Processing Workshops and PhD Forum*, IPDPSW '11, pages 1831–1837, Washington, DC, USA, 2011. IEEE Computer Society.

[VSE01]      D.A. Vorp, D.A. Steinman, and C.R. Ethier. Computational modeling of arterial biomechanics, *Comput. Sci. Eng.* p. 51, 2001.

[Wal07b]     Dave Wallace. Compute Node Linux: Overview, progress to date & roadmap. In Cray User Group Meeting, *Proceedings of the 2007 CUG Conference*, Seattle, WA, 2007.

[WBK09]      Patrick Worley, Richard Barrett, and Jeffrey Kuehn. Early evaluation of the Cray XT5. In *Proceedings of the 2009 CUG Conference* [The09].

[WF11]       David Wolinsky and Renato Figueiredo. Experiences with self-organizing, decentralized grids using the grid appliance. In *Proceedings of the 20th International ACM Symposium on High-Performance Parallel and Distributed Computing (HPDC-2011)*, San Jose, CA, June 2011. ACM.

[WFK+11]     G.R. Watson, W. Frings, C. Knobloch, C. Karbach, and A.L. Rossi. Scalable control and monitoring of supercomputer applications using an integrated tool framework. In *Parallel Processing Workshops (ICPPW), 2011 40th International Conference on*, pages 457 –466, Sept. 2011.

[WGF10]      John Wooley, Adam Godzik, and Iddo Friedberg. A primer on metagenomics. *PLoS Computational Biology*, 6(2):e1000667, 2010.

[WGS09]      Z. Wang, M. Gerstein, and M. Snyder. Rna-seq: A revolutionary tool for transcriptomics. *Nature Reviews Genetics*, 10(1):57–63, 2009.

[WHPF09]     Carl Wunsch, Patrick Heimbach, Rui M. Ponte, and Ichiro Fukumori. The global general circulation of the ocean estimated by the ECCO-consortium. *Oceanography*, 22:88–103, 2009.

[Wil00]      Frank Wilczek. What QCD tells us about nature – and why we should listen. *Nucl. Phys. A*, 663:3–20, 2000.

[WOS+09]     F. Wang, S. Oral, G. Shipman, O. Drokin, T. Wang, and I. Huang. Understanding Lustre filesystem internals. Technical report, ORNL/TM-2009/117, Oak Ridge National Lab., National Center for Computational Sciences, 2009.

[WOrS+09]    F. Wang, S. Oral, G. Shipman, O. Drokin, T. Wang, and I. Huang, "Understanding Lustre Filesystem Internals," Oak Ridge National Lab technical report ORNL/TM-2009/117, April, 2009.

[WPC⁺10]   Martin White, Adrian Pope, Jordan Carlson, Katrin Heitmann, Salman Habib, Patricia Fasel, David Daniel, and Zarija Lukic. Particle mesh simulations of the lyα forest and the signature of baryon acoustic oscillations in the intergalactic medium. *Astrophysical Journal*, 713(1):383–393, 2010.

[wu]       NVIDIA GeForce GTX 680 whitepaper: http://www.geforce.com/Active/en_US/en_US/pdf/GeForce-GTX-680-Whitepaper-FINAL.pdf.

[WWF02]    M. Warren, E. Weigle, and W. Feng. High-density computing: A 240-processor beowulf in one cubic meter. In *Proc. of ACM/IEEE SC2002*, November 2002.

[wwwa]     Apache Hadoop! Webpage.

[wwwb]     FutureGrid Portal. Webpage.

[wwwc]     Nimbus Project.

[wwwd]     Open Cloud Computing Interface (OCCI). Webpage.

[wwwe]     Open Grid Forum. Webpage.

[wwwf]     Open Source Eucalyptus. Webpage.

[wwwg]     OpenNebula. Webpage.

[wwwh]     OpenStack. Webpage.

[wwwi]     Simple Linux Utility for Resource Management (SLURM). Webpage.

[wwwj]     xCAT Extreme Cloud Administration Toolkit. Webpage.

[WYD⁺11]   F. Wang, C.Q. Yang, Y.F. Du, J. Chen, H.Z. Yi, and W.X. Xu. Optimizing Linpack benchmark on gpu-accelerated petascale supercomputer. *Journal of Computer Science and Technology*, 26(5):854–865, 2011.

[XBZ⁺]     Shucai Xiao, Pavan Balaji, Qian Zhu, Rajeev Thakur, Susan Coghlan, Heshan Lin, Gaojin Wen, Jue Hong, and Wu chun Feng. Transparent virtualization of graphics processing units. *In submission*.

[xCA]      From Clusters To Clouds: xCAT 2 Is Out Of The Bag. http://www.linux-mag.com/id/7230/.

[XLW⁺11]   M. Xie, Y. Lu, K. Wang, L. Liu, H. Cao, and X. Yang. Tianhe-1a interconnect and message-passing services. *IEEE Micro*, pages 8–20, 2011.

[XLZ⁺12]   Qingang Xiong, Bo Li, Guofeng Zhou, Xiaojian Fang, Ji Xu, Junwu Wang, Xianfeng He, Xiaowei Wang, Limin Wang, Wei Ge, and Jinghai Li. Large-scale DNS of gas-solid flows on Mole-8.5. *Chemical Engineering Science*, 71(0):442–430, 2012.

[XQF⁺11]   J. Xu, H. Qi, X. Fang, L. Lu, W. Ge, X. Wang, M. Xu, F. Chen, X. He, and J. Li. Quasi-real-time simulation of rotating drum using discrete element method with parallel GPU computing. *Particuology*, 9(4):446–450, 2011.

[xse12]    XSEDE - Extreme Science and Engeneering Environment, 2012.

[XWH+11]    J. Xu, X.W. Wang, X.F. He, Y. Ren, W. Ge, and J.H. Li. Application of the Mole-8.5 supercomputer: Probing the whole influenza virion at the atomic level. *Chinese Science Bulletin*, 56(20):2114–2118, 2011.

[YAB+07]    L. Yin, B. J. Albright, K. J. Bowers, W. Daughton, and H. A. Rose. Saturation of backward stimulated scattering of a laser beam in the kinetic regime. *Phys. Rev. Lett.*, 99:265004, Dec 2007.

[YAR+09]    L. Yin, B. J. Albright, H. A. Rose, K. J. Bowers, B. Bergen, D. S. Montgomery, J. L. Kline, and J. C. Fernandez. Onset and saturation of backward stimulated Raman scattering of laser in trapping regime in three spatial dimensions. *Physics of Plasmas*, 16(11), Nov 2009.

[YDK+08]    L. Yin, W. Daughton, H. Karimabadi, B. J. Albright, Kevin J. Bowers, and J. Margulies. Three-dimensional dynamics of collisionless magnetic reconnection in large-scale pair plasmas. *Phys. Rev. Lett.*, 101:125001, Sep 2008.

[YFG+04]    Takeshi Yanai, George I. Fann, Zhenting Gan, Robert J. Harrison, and Gregory Beylkin. Multiresolution quantum chemistry in multiwavelet bases: Hartree–Fock exchange. *The Journal of Chemical Physics*, 121(14):6680–6688, 2004. http://link.aip.org/link/?JCP/121/6680/1.

[YKD11]    A. YarKhan, J. Kurzak, and J. Dongarra. QUARK users' guide: QUeueing And Runtime for Kernels. *University of Tennessee Innovative Computing Laboratory Technical Report ICL-UT-11-02*, 2011.

[YLL+11]    X.J. Yang, X.K. Liao, K. Lu, Q.F. Hu, J.Q. Song, and J.S. Su. The tianhe-1a supercomputer: Its hardware and software. *Journal of Computer Science and Technology*, 26(3):344–351, 2011.

[YTD12]    I. Yamazaki, S. Tomov, and J. Dongarra. One-sided dense matrix factorizations on a multicore with multiple GPU accelerators. The International Conference on Computational Science (ICCS), June 4, 2012.

[YVO08]    Weikuan Yu, Jeffrey S. Vetter, and H. Sarp Oral. Performance characterization and optimization of parallel i/o on the Cray xt. In *22nd IEEE International Parallel & Distributed Processing Symposium (IPDPS 2008)*, 2008.

[YWGL03]    N. Yang, W. Wang, W. Ge, and J. Li. CFD simulation of concurrent-up gas–solid flow in circulating fluidized beds with structure-dependent drag coefficient. *Chemical Engineering Journal*, 96(1):71–80, 2003.

[YYX+07]    X. Yang, X. Yan, Z. Xing, Y. Deng, J. Jiang, and Y. Zhang. A 64-bit stream processor architecture for scientific applications. In *ISCA2007*, volume 35, pages 210–219. ACM, 2007.

[ZB08]    Daniel R. Zerbino and Ewan Birney. Velvet: Algorithms for *de novo* short read assembly using de bruijn graphs. *Genome Research*, 18:821–829, 2008.

[ZOK+12]    K. Zhang, D. O'Donnell, J. Kazil, P. Stier, S. Kinne, U. Lohmann, S. Ferrachat, B. Croft, J. Quaas, H. Wan, S. Rast, and J. Feichter. The global aerosol-climate model echam-ham, version 2: sensitivity to improvements in process representations. *Atmospheric Chemistry and Physics Discussions*, 12(3):7545–7615, 2012.

[ZY12]     Hao Zhang and Haihang You. Comprehensive workload analysis and modeling of a petascale supercomputer. In *16th Workshop on Job Scheduling Strategies for Parallel Processing*, Shanghai, China, May 2012.

# *Index*

Printed and bound by CPI Group (UK) Ltd, Croydon, CR0 4YY

25/10/2024

01779408-0004